www.wadsworth.com

wadsworth.com is the World Wide Web site for Wadsworth and is your direct source to dozens of online resources.

At *wadsworth.com* you can find out about supplements, demonstration software, and student resources. You can also send e-mail to many of our authors and preview new publications and exciting new technologies.

wadsworth.com
Changing the way the world learns®

SECOND EDITION

READINGS IN CHRISTIANITY

Robert E. Van Voorst

Western Theological Seminary

WADSWORTH

™

THOMSON LEARNING

Australia • Canada • Mexico • Singapore • Spain • United Kingdom • United States

Philosophy Editor: Peter Adams
Assistant Editor: Kara Kindstrom
Editorial Assistant: Mark Andrews
Marketing Manager: Dave Garrison
Print Buyer: Tandra Jorgensen
Permissions Editor: Joohee Lee
Compositor: G&S Typesetters, Inc.
Text and Cover Printer: Webcom Ltd.

Production Service: Matrix Productions
Copy Editor: Vicki Nelson
Cover Designer: Sandra Drooker
Cover: Upper left, Celtic Christian cross. Upper right, restoration of fifth century church pavement at Shavey Zion (courtesy of Hendrickson Publishers, Inc.). Lower right, handcraft cross from Mexico. Lower left, Byzantine reliquary cross of Justin, St. Peter's (Scala/Art Resource, NY).

Printed in Canada

3 4 5 6 7 04 03 02

Library of Congress Cataloging-in-Publication Data
Readings in Christianity / [compiled by] Robert E. Van Voorst.—
  2nd ed.
    p.   cm.
  Includes bibliographical references and index.
  ISBN 0-534-54662-5
  1. Christianity.   I. Van Voorst, Robert E.

BR53 .R39 2000
270—dc21
                                   00-042860

For more information about our products, contact us:
Thomson Learning Academic Resource Center
1-800-423-0563
http://www.wadsworth.com

Wadsworth/Thomson Learning
10 Davis Drive
Belmont, CA 94002-3098
USA

International Headquarters
Thomson Learning
290 Harbor Drive, 2nd Floor
Stamford, CT 06902-7477
USA

**UK/Europe/Middle East/
South Africa**
Thomson Learning
Berkshire House
168-173 High Holborn
London WC1V 7AA
United Kingdom

Asia
Thomson Learning
60 Albert Street, #15-01
Albert Complex
Singapore 189969

Canada
Nelson/Thomson Learning
1120 Birchmount Road
Toronto, Ontario M1K 5G4
Canada

To
I. John Hesselink, Western Theological Seminary
Donald W. Shriver, Jr., Union Theological Seminary (NY)
Gordon J. Van Wylen, Hope College
Dennis N. Voskuil, Western Theological Seminary

In appreciation for excellent presidential leadership
in the schools in which I have been privileged to study

Contents

CHAPTER FOUR

Christianity in Byzantine, Medieval, and Renaissance Times (500–1500)   **110**

CHAPTER FIVE
Reform in Western Christianity (1500–1600)   **157**

CHAPTER SIX

Early Modern Christianity (1600–1900)   213

CHAPTER SEVEN

Christianity in Modern Times (1900–PRESENT)   260

Preface

This book is designed to facilitate the encounter of the general reader and especially the student of Christianity with the primary written sources of Christianity. Its pages contain the most notable and instructive primary sources from the entire sweep of Christian history. The collection began with my efforts to collect readings for my students and organize them in a way helpful for teaching and learning. It presents primary readings and sets them in the context of their times, taking into account recent scholarship on Christianity. Although designed to stand alone as a primary text, this reader is easily adaptable to a range of primary textbooks and most of the current methods of teaching the Christian tradition and therefore can be used effectively as a supplementary text.

No one knows more acutely how selective any anthology in Christianity must be than one who has gone over so many of its writings. I have included here many important readings, but many more I must unhappily leave out. My main criterion for selection is to give students access to the most important writings from the past, ones that their textbooks and professors are likely to speak about. Moreover, I have tried to anthologize in a way that does some justice to the emphasis of contemporary scholarship on such issues as the role of women, diversity within the faith, the multicultural and universal nature of Christianity, and the like.

Readings in Christianity is organized as follows: The first chapter examines the study of Christianity by way of primary sources. Chapter 1 also introduces the reader to the art of reading sources with practical suggestions and other aids.

Each subsequent chapter presents important primary sources from different periods of Christian history and is organized as follows: three or four vignettes about the period draw the reader's interest and imagination. Then an Introduction sets the context of the readings by explaining the names of the period, giving a historical sketch of the period, and discussing the literary genres of the primary sources. The first grouping of readings concerns the historical events of the period and the people who shaped them. The second grouping covers the institutional life of the period, including church organization and worship. The third grouping deals with teachings of the period, including views of the nature and work of Jesus Christ, salvation, the sacraments, and so on. The fourth grouping focuses on ethics, both personal and social; topics such as war and peace, social justice, and the roles of women will be anthologized as fully as possible here. The last grouping focuses on relations of the Christianity of the period to its rivals inside and outside the Christian movement. Each chapter has full pedagogical aids, including an introduction to each reading, full annotations to explain difficult items in the readings (placed at the bottom of the page for easy access), questions for study and discussion, a glossary, and suggestions for further reading in the primary sources.

The translations used here have been selected for their accuracy and readability. I have happily received permission to reprint many of the finest translations. Where it has not been possible to get permission, or where recent English translations are incomplete or too technical for undergraduate students, I have relied on older translations that have proven their worth over time and are now in the public domain. I have edited these slightly to update their vocabulary, spelling, and occasionally syntax, but I have endeavored to let the "voice" of both text and translator come through. In about two dozen cases, I have made my own fresh translations from the best critical editions.

This second edition incorporates the following changes:

❖   Chapter 1 incorporates the latest discussion of historical study and adds a new section relating the study of Christianity's primary sources to the World Wide Web.

❖   A dedicated Internet site is available to assist students in their encounter with Christianity on the World Wide Web in conjunction with this book.

❖   Many vignettes that open each chapter have been updated and new ones added to keep them fully contemporary.

❖   New readings emphasize popular religion, the role of women, the Renaissance, and the developing world.

❖   The style of more than thirty readings has been edited to make them more accessible for today's students.

❖   Several pro-and-con readings have been added to spark critical thinking and discussion.

❖   Glossaries have been expanded.

❖   All scholarship is updated throughout.

I am very grateful for the favorable reception this book has received. I trust that this revision will continue stimulating its readers to explore the rich and fascinating world of Christianity more deeply.

Acknowledgments

Many people have kindly helped in the writing of this book. The faculty, staff, and administration of Western Theological Seminary have been wonderful colleagues and have encouraged me in the revision of this book. My capable secretary Marilyn Essink has assisted with the typing of the additions to the second edition. The staff of Lycoming College's Snowden Library and Western Seminary's Beardslee Library helped me in the large task of gathering materials. The librarians at the Bodleian Library, Oxford, where I spent a sabbatical in 1997, were unfailingly kind and helpful. Not least in importance, students in several courses at Lycoming College and Western Theological Seminary have used this book in whole or part, and contributed much to its revision.

The editorial staff at Wadsworth have been fine partners in developing this book. The many people whose names are listed on the copyright page have done outstanding work for me, but I owe a special word of thanks to religion editor Peter Adams for his steady support and remarkable resourcefulness.

Scholars at other institutions offered detailed, insightful critiques at several points along the way. I thank Dan Brown, California State University at Fullerton; Elton Bruins, Hope College; Richard DeMaris, Valparaiso University; Jeffrey Donnelly, Temple University; A. Joseph Everson, California Lutheran University; I. John Hesselink, Jr., Western Theological Seminary; Ann Matter, University of Pennsylvania; Alister McGrath, University of Oxford, England; Emmett McLaughlin, Villanova University; James North, Cincinnati Bible College and Seminary; Richard Penaskovic, Auburn University; Monica Saltarelli, Niagra University; Herbert Smith, McPherson College; Susan Wood, St. Johns University. For his contribution of an original essay to the second edition, I thank Jurgen Hendricks, University of Stellenbosch, South Africa. Though all these colleagues made this a much better book than it would have been, any errors that remain are mine alone. I would be most grateful if those of you who use it would send me your comments and suggestions for improving it. You can reach my by my postal address (101 E. 13th Street, Holland MI 49423-3622) or my e-mail address (bob.vanvoorst@westernsem.org).

Finally, I owe a debt of gratitude to my wife, Mary, and our two sons, Richard and Nicholas, for their love and support. Rich and Nick have been a constant source of joy. Mary has inspired me by her devotion to the Christian faith and her interest in its past, and she has made the wise words of Thomas Aquinas come true for me: "The best of friendships is between husband and wife."

CHAPTER ONE

The Study of Christianity Through Primary Sources

❖ In a remote village in New Guinea, North American and European missionaries trained in linguistics work to decipher a tribal language, commit it to writing, and educate the tribespeople to read it. The purpose of their work is to translate the New Testament into the tribal language for use in training new believers in the faith and as a tool for converting other members of the tribe. Despite arguments by others that it is eroding the tribe's native culture, this translation work and many others like it around the world continue.

❖ In 1994, *Chant* becomes an international popular music sensation. A Latin-language compact disc recording of medieval Gregorian sung prayers based on early Christian texts, it featured the singing Benedictine monks of Santo Domingo de Silos in northern Spain. Six million copies of *Chant* were sold worldwide, and it went as high as number three on the American pop music charts, where it lodged next to hits by Snoop Doggy Dog and Nine Inch Nails. In 1995, a follow-up CD was released, *The Soul of Chant*. As often happens in the music industry, the success of a "new" style spawned a wave of similar recordings. Medieval Christian music, including the songs of Julian of Norwich, gained a sudden popularity that has not subsided at the turn of the millennium.

❖ In Augsburg, Germany, officials of the Lutheran World Federation and the Vatican headquarters of the Roman Catholic Church meet on October 31, 1999. They have come to sign an agreement on faith and salvation that states that divine forgiveness and salvation come only through faith in God and that good human works flow from salvation. This formal agreement is the first between Catholics and Protestants in nearly five hundred years on a leading cause of the split between them at the time of the Reformation. While many other doctrinal issues divide Western Christianity, the agreement raises hopes that they too can be addressed.

❖ At the 1995 World Population Conference in Beijing, Alberto Fujimori, the president of Peru, makes a strong attack on Roman Catholic teaching forbidding artificial birth control, as stated in the 1968 papal document *On Human Life*. Fujimori argues that the policy makes it almost impossible for many nations to control rapid growth in population and that this growth threatens world peace and stability. What makes this attack so striking is that Fujimori is himself a devout Roman Catholic from a predominantly Catholic nation. His position, though unpopular with some, is still the official policy of Peru.

The influence of Christian writings is felt throughout the world in ways both extraordinary and commonplace. Not all use of these writings is as dramatic or controversial as that depicted in these sketches. They do indicate, though, that the writings of Christianity have a continuing profound impact on its life and the cultures of the world. This book invites you to study Christianity by way of primary sources from its past and present. You will listen to the voices of the past to hear their own meaning. Then you will relate the past to the present, the second necessary step in understanding Christianity.

This chapter begins by discussing the issues and methods in the study of Christianity, especially through its primary sources. The second section explains the nature and variety of the primary sources assembled here. The third section discusses the use of the World Wide Web in understanding Christianity through its primary sources on the Internet. The fourth section outlines the plan of this book, and the fifth makes some suggestions on how you can read these primary sources more profitably.

THE STUDY OF CHRISTIANITY

The academic study of Christianity, like the study of any other religion, is a complex activity. Religious study takes Christianity on its own terms and generally does not reduce it to a conglomeration of other disciplines. Nevertheless, religious studies as an academic discipline does not have a particular methodology that distinguishes it from other disciplines. The field of religion is multidisciplinary in nature and includes the study of primary sources. It draws on most of the humanities, especially history, literature, philosophy, and most of the social sciences, especially psychology, sociology, and anthropology. It uses many different methods from various disciplines. For example, from history religious study borrows archaeology and many methods for the study of texts; from philosophy it borrows methods of analyzing language and ethics; from sociology it borrows methods of survey, field study, and sociological theory.

The combination of so many disciplines and subjects makes religion a rich and complicated discipline, and the writings of Christianity are just as rich. The words of an advertising poster from a leading American religious publishing house express this richness: "Books about religion are also about love, sex, politics, AIDS, war, peace, justice, ecology, philosophy, addiction, recovery, ethics, race, gender, dissent, technology, old age, New Age, faith, heavy metal, morality, beauty, God, psychology, money, dogma, freedom, history, death and life."[1]

This anthology adopts an organization that is in part historical. Students are usually introduced to the Christian tradition by means of *narrative history,* a coherent interpretive account (usually chronologically ordered) of what people have done and said in the past. This narrative history school can be broken down into three other main types. *Political-social history* presents what people have done in national and international affairs, usually at a high level, as most important. This type of history is probably the one with which most undergraduates are familiar. *Economic history* focuses on how the desire to accumulate wealth affects the course of past events within and be-

---

[1] Copyright, 1990, Abingdon Press. Used by permission.

tween nations. With the strongly economic orientation of national life in early modern and modern times, this method of studying the past has become important, although it has not yet strongly influenced the writing of Christian history. *Intellectual history* views the development of higher thought and intellectual culture in both the arts and sciences as most important in the past. This book will draw on all these types of narrative history, but especially the first and the last.

Because some confusion surrounds the term *history,* we must pause to define it here. Often used to denote both the past and the study of the past, we will use it here in the latter sense. **History** is the scholarly study of the past, whether that past is remote (e.g., the beginnings of human society) or recent (e.g., the fall of communism in eastern Europe and the old Soviet Union).[2] The related word **historiography** denotes the principles, theory, traditions, and philosophy of historical study. This book will emphasize history, but historiographic issues will emerge at times as well.

Trends in the world of scholarship in the past thirty years (not just in religion, but in the arts and humanities as a whole), some of them controversial, have increased the complexity of studying Christianity. As new methods and perspectives have arisen, the traditional boundaries between these older ways of studying the past have become blurred. **Feminism** insists on seeing religion from the perspective of female-male equality. Thus it is concerned with recovering the lost voices of women past and present and discovering the life of these "people without a past." It brings "herstory" to history.[3] Feminism has also made the *construction of gender*—how societies shape normative notions of proper male and female roles—a topic of study. Religion scholars generally agree that feminism will continue to be an important trend in religious studies for a significant length of time.

Multiculturalism (or the closely related **pluralism**) argues for identifying and appreciating the contributions of the many different racial and ethnic groups that are a part of Christianity, especially in the United States.[4] Recent emphasis on global perspectives has led to a concern for the international and intercultural diversity of Christianity, including the ways in which Christianity relates to other religions. **Social history** (also called **popular history**) is the study of the everyday life of common people.

---

[2] Norman F. Cantor and Richard I. Schneider, in their generally excellent book, *How to Study History* (Arlington Heights, IL: Harlan Davidson, 1967), give their own definition as "what the historian does," arguing that this is "the only universally acceptable definition" of the term (p. 19). But this lowest-common-denominator type of definition is singularly unilluminating—just what does the historian do?

[3] Several recent publications have punned on the word "history"; e.g., B. MacHaffie, *Her Story: Women in Christian Tradition* (Minneapolis: Fortress, 1986); J. Sochen, *Herstory: A Record of the American Woman's Past* (Sherman Oaks, CA: Alfred, 1981); and Jon Klanchen, "History, Herstory, Theirstory, Ourstory," in David Perkins, ed., *Theoretical Issues in Literary History* (Cambridge: Harvard, 1995). These writers do not imply, however, that the original meaning of "history" is male oriented; it is not related to our English word *his* but comes rather from the Greek *historia,* "information," "narrative."

[4] Ray L. Hart remarks, "The growing public recognition of and respect for religious pluralism in American life, and a like recognition of global variety through enhanced media of communication worldwide, are said to be the two principal factors that account for the most dramatic changes in the study of religion in American higher education in the past two decades; they have set in motion trends and defined issues that will develop such study into the foreseeable future." Hart, "Religious and Theological Studies in American Higher Education: A Pilot Study," *Journal of the American Academy of Religion* 59, no. 4 (1992): 766–67.

It has supplemented and sometimes displaced the more traditional study that focuses on social elites and grand narratives. "A strongly populist inspiration is at work . . . reflecting the view that 'real' history [of Christianity] concerns itself with the outlook of ordinary people and not with the doctrines and theories of church leaders, canonists, and theologians."[5] In addition to the study of popular history by academics, nonacademics such as genealogists recently have sparked a remarkable growth of interest in popular history.[6] Dissatisfaction with traditional narrative history focusing on elites is leading to new experiments in writing about Christianity. For example, in a recent book on American religion edited by Thomas Tweed each chapter is framed within a different perspective, and in another fascinating book Colleen McDannell studies the material culture of American Christianity—such things as gravestones, portraits of Jesus, t-shirts and backyard statues of the Virgin Mary—for clues to the history of Christianity.[7]

Another recent trend is **psychohistory,** which attempts to use the insights and methods of depth psychology to study the lives of influential individuals in the past. Erik Erikson's *Young Man Luther: A Study in Psychoanalysis and History* is a prominent example.[8] Psychohistory has been a controversial perspective that some critics charge with reducing religion to mere patterns of behavior significant only for their psychological content. When psychohistorical methods are used to study obviously psychological phenomena in Christian writings, such as in a recent book analyzing the visions of the medieval mystic Mechthild of Magdeburg from the perspective of contemporary psychological theories,[9] this way of reading history seems more appropriate to most scholars. **Ecumenism** is the movement to build better relations among the various Christian churches. Although not itself an academic method, ecumenism has had an impact on scholarly research into Christianity.[10] The Christian tradition is typically studied by scholars today from a nondenominational, nonconfessional viewpoint.[11] For example, where in years past Protestant historians would view the late

---

[5] F. L. Cheyette and M. L. Colish, "Medieval Europe," in M. B. Norton, ed., *The American Historical Association's Guide to Historical Literature,* 3d ed. (New York/Oxford: Oxford University Press, 1995), 622.

[6] See Karen J. Winkler, "Who Owns History?" in *The Chronicle of Higher Education* 41, no. 19 (January 20, 1995): A10–11, 18.

[7] See Thomas A. Tweed, ed., *Retelling U.S. Religious History* (Berkeley: University of California Press, 1996); this book fights the urge to construct a master narrative of American religious history. See also Colleen McDannell, *Material Christianity: Religion and Popular Culture in America* (New Haven: Yale University Press, 1996).

[8] New York: Norton, 1958. Fawn Brodie, in her psychohistorical work, *Thomas Jefferson: An Intimate History* (New York: Norton, 1974), 16, says of this method, "The idea that a man's inner life affects every aspect of his intellectual life and also his decision-making should need no defense today. To illuminate this relationship, however, requires certain biographical techniques that make some historians uncomfortable. One must look for feeling as well as fact, for nuance and metaphor as well as idea and action."

[9] Ulrike Wiethaus, *Ecstatic Transformations: Transpersonal Psychology in the Work of Mechthild of Magdeburg* (Syracuse, NY: Syracuse University Press, 1996).

[10] This emphasis on commonalities (ecumenism) along with a newer emphasis on diversity (pluralism) has produced some tensions in both the practice and scholarly study of religion.

[11] Cheyette and Colish point to "the increasing shift of research . . . out of the hands of divinity professors charged with representing a particular brand of Christianity and into the hands of historians and professors of religious studies, who typically regard the writing of proselytizing church history as an abuse of their pro-

Middle Ages negatively and emphasize the discontinuities between it and the Reformation, today Protestant historians are more inclined to see continuities between currents in the Middle Ages and the Reformation.

Finally, the broad intellectual trend often labeled **postmodernism** has recently impacted the study of Christianity. Postmodernism, as its name implies, turns away from the overarching commitment to rationality and scientific approach characteristic of modern study (i.e., from the Enlightenment through the twentieth century). It is often vaguely used and impossible to define, but it has several components: a commitment to pluralism (it is "antitotalizing"); a commitment to relativism (it is "antifoundational"); and a commitment to showing the arbitrariness of language and moral systems (it is "demystifying"). Postmodernism has its opponents, but it remains a strong current in academia. In sum, all these new perspectives make the study of Christianity, including the reading of its sources, richer and more complicated.

The study of Christianity is challenging as well because Christianity itself is a complex, diverse religious tradition. Widely spread throughout the world, it is growing rapidly in the southern hemisphere. This wide distribution entails a strong variety of national and cultural expressions of the faith. Christianity has usually (but not always) affirmed some adaptability of the faith to all human cultures.[12] For example, Greek-speaking Eastern Orthodoxy did not insist that the Slavic language groups it converted use Greek in their services and religious writings, while the Roman church made just such a stipulation about the use of Latin from the early Middle Ages until the twentieth century. Such adaptability leads to more internal variety than in those religions that seek uniformity of key cultural aspects among all believers. Also, Christianity is divided into different branches and denominations, and even in single churches (the Roman Catholic Church, for example) a great deal of internal variety is visible. Finally, Christianity has a long and rich tradition that serves as a living foundation for the unities and diversities of its expression in the modern world.

The historical approach to Christianity has some weaknesses that you must keep in mind. For one, many people devalue the past by naively assuming that earlier times were less "enlightened" than our own and that whatever is more recent is better. Second, others just as naively assume the opposite, thinking that the earlier times were the best. A third weakness is that ordinary Christians generally do not use history to understand their faith and its practices. The past is not a primary avenue of perception for them. For example, when they go to church for divine worship, most Christians are not concerned about the historical origins of the rite or the style of architecture and art in the church building. Therefore, we are using a method of study that runs counter to how most Christians think of and live out their faith. This is not necessarily bad or unworkable, but we must recognize this limitation as we use history to study

---

fessional duties" ("Medieval Europe," 621). As importantly as that shift, "divinity professors" themselves have become more ecumenically oriented as their schools have become more ecumenical and as they have become as influenced by their wider scholarly profession as by their denominations.

[12] "[A]s its influence has spread, Christianity has not demanded that cultures should fall into line with its precepts; from the outset, Christianity has taken root in cultures, and set in motion a rich and dynamic process of interaction between the ideas and values of the gospel, and those already present in the culture." Alister McGrath, *The Christian Theology Reader* (Oxford, UK: Blackwell, 1995), xvi.

Christianity. A final weakness is that the literary remains of the past, especially before the nineteenth century, are largely silent about the roles of women, people from subcultures, and "common people." The voices we do hear from these groups come from patriarchal and nondemocratic times, and they have been filtered through a predominantly patriarchal tradition. So readers must beware of presuming that they are hearing voices equivalent to modern voices from these groups.[13]

Given these weaknesses of the historical approach, what strengths does it offer? First, we in the Western academic world often take a historical approach to study. Students and teachers are accustomed to studying the genesis and development of large contemporary institutions. We do not feel we know something about them unless we know about their past. As G. K. Chesterton once wrote, "History is a hill from which alone [people] see . . . the age in which they are living."[14] All the elements of contemporary Christianity, whether of belief or practice, are rooted in its past and often go beyond its own past into ancient Judaism. Thus, most textbooks on Christianity adopt an approach and organization that are largely historical,[15] and this book is no exception. Second, by the study of change in the past we learn how Christianity became the way it is today. To understand the unity of present Christianity (how it is all "Christianity") and its variety (how Christianity has significant internal differences), you must understand its past. Third, to make any intelligent predictions about the life of Christianity in the future, especially how it may continue to change, you must be able to trace out trends from the past, draw them through the present, and project them into the future.

Beside this general historical approach to Christianity, this book also takes a *topical* approach. (We will discuss this approach more fully later in this chapter under "The Plan of this Book," but a brief statement is in order here.) In addition to dividing Christianity into five main periods, this book will discuss in each period several topics: *events* that helped to shape Christianity; the *institution* of Christianity, especially its structure of office and worship; the *teachings* of the tradition; its *ethics;* and finally its *relations* with other institutions and systems of thought. These are not the categories of any formal method of studying religion, but they help to bring out some order within each period and will help you to trace various themes or topics through time.

THE NATURE AND VARIETY OF THE READINGS

The Christian tradition is present with us in many forms, both verbal and nonverbal. Tangible expressions include art, architecture, music, fine literature, formal theological works, church documents of all sorts, letters and journals, all of which can be studied to discern the meaning of Christianity's past and present. In this book, we will deal with written, often documentary evidence, with a special focus on primary literary

---

[13] One must not automatically identify the authentic voices of all women in the past with the concerns of the voices of modern feminists; some congruence may be present but should not be assumed.

[14] G. K. Chesterton, "On St. George Revivified," in his *All I Survey* (1933).

[15] An exception would be textbooks that deal with Christianity from a strictly phenomenological method, but these are comparatively rare, especially at the introductory level.

sources. "Literary sources" is a widely conceived category here; it encompasses musical lyrics, poetry, and inscriptions as well as both formal and personal documents.

Some definitions are in order here. A **primary source** is a work that was written about a subject at a time contemporary with the period being studied, forming the raw material of study. (An example would be Eusebius' writings about his contemporary, the emperor Constantine.) Primary sources stand close to the event, but they should not for that reason alone be considered purely "factual." They typically contain opinions, value judgments, and other evaluations that come from a definite perspective on their subject, whether that perspective is implicit or explicit. Primary sources are highly interpretive despite their contemporaneity. Therefore, primary sources must be read carefully and analytically. The reader should keep in mind a further distinction within primary sources, between those that give first-person accounts and those that give third-person accounts. For example, in the New Testament the apostle Paul's authentic writings are a first-person account of his activities and beliefs, while the *Acts of the Apostles* gives a third-person account of Paul by another person. A **secondary source** is a work written about a subject after its time, often containing explications and critiques of earlier, primary sources. (An example would be a twentieth-century work on Constantine.) These two types of sources, primary and secondary, encompass all the literary evidence that those studying Christianity will need.

The study of Christian history is divided into two segments, which we call *church history* and *history of theology*.[16] Textbooks and readers in Christianity often deal with either one or the other. In terms of the divisions within narrative history presented earlier, church history is a type of political-social history focusing on the institution of the church and history of theology is the church's intellectual history. However, life and thought go together in both the past and the present, and no clear line can be drawn between them. For example, a historical document such as Luther's *Ninety-Five Theses* is rich in theology, and a theological document such as Sallie McFague's *The World as God's Body* is fully engaged with history and like all thought has a "social location." Because life affects thought and thought influences life, this book of readings will pay attention to both.

Several disadvantages can be listed for approaching Christianity by reading primary literary sources.[17] First, primary sources offer *uneven coverage* of the past and sometimes the present. We do not have sufficient literary remains from early and medieval Europe or from premodern Christianity in most of Africa and Asia. Writing was comparatively sparse in these times and places, and much of what was written has simply

---

[16] Scholars differ on their precise definition of such terms as *history of doctrine, history of Christian thought,* or *history of dogma.* For example, the recent book by J. E. Bradley and R. A. Muller, *Church History: An Introduction to Research, Reference Works, and Methods* (Grand Rapids, MI: Eerdmans, 1995), argues that *church history* encompasses the whole of the Christian past, *history of theology* refers to the history of church doctrine, *history of dogma* to the history of the three particular doctrinal themes that have received official definition from the ancient church (Trinity, christology, grace), and *history of Christian thought* is the whole range of Christian conceptualizing. Most scholars would disagree with this restrictive definition of *history of dogma.*

[17] Some material in this and the following two sections is taken from Robert Van Voorst, *Anthology of World Scriptures,* 3d ed. (Belmont, CA: Wadsworth, 1999). Copyright © 2000, Wadsworth Publishing Company. Used by permission.

disappeared. For ancient and medieval times until about 1300 C.E., comparatively little was written and less survived the ravages of time. Around the year 1300, however, governments and churches began to use written records more extensively, and a significant increase in literacy meant that written materials were more widely circulated. Another reason for uneven coverage is that some parts of Christianity were (and are) not given to literary expression, and therefore only a few primary sources relating to them were written. Edwin Gaustad has illustrated this phenomenon as follows: "One might, in all fairness, search for the [written] response to an angry Anglican attack upon illiterate [American] frontier religion, but fail to find any such 'other side.'"[18] In some times and places, writing was forbidden to certain Christian groups. For example, most African-American slaves were forbidden to learn how to read and write, and so the vibrant form of Christianity that flourished among them has comparatively little primary literary source material.[19]

A second disadvantage is that most of us must *read many of these primary sources in translation*. For serious historians working at a high academic level, this is unacceptable; all research must be done in the original languages of the primary sources. For our purposes here, we must often rely on standard translations of the texts. For our level of work, that of reading primary sources at the beginning or intermediate stage in the study of Christianity, this is not such a hindrance.

A third disadvantage is a natural consequence of reading writings from the past, whether the near or far past: we *lack the full context* for interpreting the surviving sources. With the passing of time, much of the artifacts that enable us to understand the past have disappeared. For some eras and areas, especially from long ago, this is a more significant disadvantage than for later times (the nineteenth and twentieth centuries in Europe and North America, for example), for which we have ample sources.

Finally, the primary sources themselves *reflect biases* that must be taken into account when reading them. For example, women's voices have long been silenced in most of Christianity. What voices that do come from ancient, medieval, and sometimes modern periods are filtered through a traditionally patriarchal faith and culture. As mentioned earlier, early African-American voices and those of other subcultures have been suppressed as well.

The many advantages to using primary sources to understand Christianity more than compensate for these disadvantages. First, of all the remains of the past, literary sources *express their meaning most directly and unambiguously to us*. Compare, for example, the difficulty of interpreting a work of art or music to interpreting a text; both need interpretation, to be sure, but the text usually speaks more directly. Second, primary literary sources are *widespread*. Although they are not uniform and universal in Christianity, certainly not as much as we would like, most times and places have left some literary legacy. Third, primary sources are often *comprehensive*. They treat a wide variety of topics; usually matters considered important are written down and preserved

---

[18] Edwin S. Gaustad, *A Documentary History of Religion in America*, 2d ed. (Grand Rapids, MI: Eerdmans, 1993), xvi.

[19] This also complicates the interpretation of the reliability of the few slave narratives that do survive from the eighteenth century.

over time. Fourth, primary sources, especially official documents, are *authoritative.* Scripture, the primary source material for the beginnings of Christianity, is formally authoritative. Many other primary texts also have the force of authority: church constitutions and law, definitive statements of doctrine, and the like.

Finally, primary documents are *open to analysis.* They seem to invite reading, reflection, and reaction; often they are interesting, sometimes even exciting, to read. They are especially necessary for those seeking a firsthand knowledge of the Christian tradition. To quote the words of Hugh Kerr, "Direct acquaintance with the formative documents is much to be preferred to, and also much more interesting than, secondhand commentary. The development of independent judgment, the ability to make critical evaluations, the satisfying feel of handling authentic ideas—such vital learning processes require firsthand knowledge of the sources."[20] In conclusion, all these advantages make primary sources a rich avenue into the study of Christianity.

PRIMARY SOURCES OF CHRISTIANITY AND THE WORLD WIDE WEB

The last five years have seen an explosive growth in the World Wide Web, the linked computer system on the Internet. Much information about religious faith and practice can be found on the Web; it seems to be one of the Web's leading topics of discussion and inquiry. As a part of this interest in religion, many sites on the Web feature the primary sources of Christianity, from scriptures to current writings. Several positive features of this new opportunity to encounter primary sources on Christianity can be adduced. The access is almost always free, and the content is often very up to date. The number of writings on the Web is growing rapidly and may someday encompass most, or even all, Christian sources. The Internet is an appealing way for most young computer-oriented students (but not always their professors!) to encounter primary sources. It presents different ways of studying and learning—for example, the ability to search a text electronically. Finally, but not least, when students encounter a Christian site sponsored by the followers of a specific part of Christianity, they encounter that part a bit more "from within," as those Christians themselves understand it.

The drawbacks of studying the primary sources of Christianity on the Web are also significant. Some sites are not well constructed; they may have poor layout, little eye appeal, out-of-date links, or they may suffer from other technical deficiencies. While Internet coverage of Asian and African sources is growing, it is still largely incomplete. For many sources, the translations used are usually older, public-domain works that are out of date and left unedited for the current reader. When Christian groups post their writings for missionary and/or public relations purposes, the "spin" put on these documents may not agree with the current academic consensus on that religion. Most significantly, these electronic publications are subject to little or no scholarly control,

---

[20] Hugh T. Kerr, *Readings in Christian Thought* (Nashville: Abingdon, 1966), 5.

such as peer review before publication, so their quality varies greatly. The contents of some sites are excellent, some average, and some poor.

The result of this mixed situation is that many students need help in using and especially in analyzing critically these Web-based sites. The few books on this topic are of some value, especially Patrick Durusau's *High Places in Cyberspace*,[21] with its updates available online at http://scholar.cc.emory.edu/scripts/highplaces.html. For readers of this book, I have designed a special website to further their use of the Web in religious studies. This site has links to short, helpful essays on using the Internet in an academically appropriate way. It also features links to sites that my students and I have found useful in the study of Christianity. This listing cannot pretend to be comprehensive, but it does offer a starting place to surf and learn. Its address is: http://religion.wadsworth.com.

THE PLAN OF THIS BOOK

This book contains primary sources in the following order of chapters: the Bible, ancient Christianity after the New Testament period, medieval Christianity, the Reformation of Christianity, Christianity from Reform to modernity, and Christianity in modern times. We begin with the Bible because it witnesses to the foundation of the Christian tradition. The Bible, both the Old Testament (as Christians call it) and the New Testament, is the primary source of Christianity in its formative stages. Ancient Christianity extends from about 100 to 500 C.E., building on the foundation of the biblical stage; this period forms a common tradition for all subsequent Christianity. In medieval times (ca. 500–1500) the faith divides into Eastern and Western (European) expressions. In the era of Reform (ca. 1500–1650), the unity of the Western church is lost as Christianity splits into Protestant and Roman Catholic branches even as both branches seek the reform of doctrine and practice. The period that leads from Reform to early modern times (1650–1900) sees both the retrenchment and spread of Christianity. The final chapter treats modern Christianity (1900 to the present) in all of its diversity. These divisions are of course somewhat artificial, and scholars sometimes disagree over them; events do not often move in ways amenable to periodization.[22] However, some periodization must be used to organize the mass of material, and these periods are generally similar to the kinds that historians of Christianity most often employ.

Each chapter is structured as follows. An introduction briefly outlines the name(s) and main events of the period, especially to remind you of the context of the readings. This introduction also deals briefly with the main **genres** (types of literature) of the primary sources from the period under study. The first grouping of readings deals with important religious events in the period. These events deal with both individual people and wider institutions, with both ordinary and extraordinary occurrences. Second are passages covering the life of the institutional church, its organization, worship, and other features. Christianity as a religion is wider than the church, and many people have been attracted to Christianity but "put off" by the institutional church; nevertheless,

---

[21] Patrick Durusau, *High Places in Cyberspace*, 2d ed. (Atlanta: Scholars, 1998).

[22] At the beginning of each chapter of readings, the dating of each period will be discussed.

the church has always been the main cultural bearer of the Christian tradition.[23] Third is the teaching of Christianity on various subjects: on God, humanity, salvation, and so on. The body of Christian teaching is always growing and changing as it adapts itself to the life and circumstances of each succeeding age. Fourth, the ethics of the Christian tradition has its own grouping, although ethics is actually a branch of teaching. Personal morality is prominent, and social morality will also be extensively treated: war and peace, the status of women, justice in society, and so on. Finally are passages about the relationships of Christianity to its rivals inside and outside the Christian movement: diverse movements in the church (which the church sometimes calls *heresy*); other religions, especially Judaism; the civil government.

Of course, these categories usually overlap and cannot be neatly separated. The predominant rationale for this organization is *pedagogical*. It is meant to further your learning, especially as you are being introduced to the Christian religious tradition. North American readers are familiar with the groupings used here, and both teachers and students of religion will recognize them as a standard paradigm for research, teaching, and learning in religion.

SUGGESTIONS FOR READING PROFITABLY

Those who are reading extensive primary sources in religion for the first time often feel they are entering a strange new world. Some readings come from the distant past and speak about events and ideas seemingly far removed from contemporary life. Other readings come from today, but for a variety of reasons they may not strike a chord with the reader. So when you encounter some of the primary readings gathered here, you may be puzzled at first, but the process of wrestling as directly as possible with the readings is nonetheless a profitable one.

Each reader must ultimately find an individually suitable method for reading primary sources profitably. But the following suggestions drawn from my experience and the experience of others may be helpful.

1. *Use your knowledge of Christianity to set these readings in a fuller context.* Try to relate them as fully as possible to life. For example, when you are reading about ritual, visualize how the ritual is carried out. Or when you are reading about an event, imagine yourself to be a film director staging and filming it.

2. *Read the introductions to each chapter before you turn to the passages.* They will provide an important background for understanding the passages.

3. *Next, take a few moments to skim a selection before you read.* Having a general idea of "the lay of the land" will help you when you begin to read in detail.

4. *If you find that you are not grasping the content and meaning of the readings, you should take a more active approach to reading.* For example, form a hypothesis or ask a question on the basis of the caption and introduction to a selection before reading the

---

[23] Parareligious organizations like Alcoholics Anonymous and Habitat for Humanity are examples of other institutions which mediate Christianity to the world. While the work of such organizations has great social and spiritual importance, we cannot do justice to parareligious organizations here.

selection itself; then read to correct the hypothesis or answer the question. Testing a hypothesis or answering a question, no matter how tentative, helps you to read more actively and alertly.

5. *Mark the text as you read.* Research on reading shows that readers who mark the text, underlining or highlighting about three or four items per page, understand and remember more than readers who do not mark their text. Marking the text helps to make it your own.

6. *Pay attention to literary genre.* The form and content of any literary passage will reflect its genre. Read with a feeling for the differences between poetry, narrative, law, ritual, official pronouncement, and other terms. Genre also affects the tone and "liveliness" of a document. The pale, ponderous language of official church pronouncements, for example, does not begin to suggest the passionate debate that preceded them.

7. *Make a personal glossary of unfamiliar terms and names as you go along.* You can do this quite easily by circling them in the text and writing their meaning in the bottom margin. (Use circles or other type of marking that will distinguish them from other marked material.) Then you can go back later to make a short note of their meaning, also in the margin. The unfamiliarity and difficulty of so many words, both technical terms and personal names, is a large obstacle for many students of religion. With a little extra effort, you can reduce this difficulty.

8. *Read each selection repeatedly until you are familiar with it and can give a brief summary of its main points after you have read it.* Identify any problems you have in understanding it. View these problems as opportunities to achieve greater understanding, rather than as roadblocks to it.

9. *Put yourself, as well as you can, inside the minds and lives of those who originally wrote and used the selections.* What could they mean to you if you were among those who first encountered them? What could they mean to you today if they still affected you? By using your knowledge and imagination, you can participate to a degree in the fuller meaning of these texts. Then you can listen to the past in a way that lets it make its own meaning heard.

10. *Reflect on your own biases, pro and/or con, as you read.* Resist the temptation to impose your own value judgments on people and events, especially before you understand them on their own terms. Your value judgments are not necessarily wrong, but don't let them get in the way of understanding. As you read these selections, you will certainly encounter positions with which you strongly disagree. Think about your biases and try to deal with them.

11. *Don't assume that every reading here should be relevant to issues you may consider important.* Some speak of practices and attitudes very unfamiliar to modern North American students of Christianity. Use these readings to broaden your understanding of Christianity and its various forms, whether or not you see a relevance. As Ronald Wells has remarked, "While history is usable in understanding ourselves, if we approach history mainly to find a 'usable past' . . . then we have not really studied history." [24]

---

[24] R. W. Wells, *History through the Eyes of Faith* (San Francisco: HarperCollins, 1989), 2–3.

12.   *If you wish to explore the readings more fully, begin by reading them in their fuller, unexcerpted texts.* Next, you can study various other books and commentaries about them, many of which will be found in the Suggested Readings section of each chapter.

GLOSSARY

ecumenism the movement, largely begun in the twentieth century, that works toward greater Christian unity among churches and denominations. In scholarship, ecumenism stresses the common theological background of the churches.

feminism the movement that teaches and promotes equality between the sexes. In religious study, it seeks to give a full voice to women from the past and present.

genre a type of literary form, such as poetry, proverb, narrative, law, and so on.

historiography the principles, theory, and philosophy of history; the scholarly study of historical scholarship.

history the scholarly study of the past; distinguished here from the past itself.

multiculturalism the belief that nations are composed of at least several different cultures, all of which should be affirmed and cultivated for the good of the whole. Closely related to **pluralism.**

pluralism the affirmation of the distinct values of different groups within a nation or culture.

popular history (see **social history**)

postmodernism a recent broad movement that rejects the objective rationality of modern times to emphasize pluralism, subjectivity, and the social origin of values.

primary source a work that was written about a subject at a time basically contemporary with the period being studied; the "raw material" of the study of the past and the present.

psychohistory the study of the past, especially individuals in the past, by psychological theory.

secondary source a work written about a subject after its time; contains explications and critiques of primary sources.

social history the study of the everyday life of common people; also called **popular history.**

QUESTIONS FOR STUDY AND DISCUSSION

1.   Give your reflections on this quote from Marcel Proust's *Remembrance of Things Past:* "The past is not only not dead; it isn't even past."

2.   How can the different understandings of history outlined in this chapter shape your reading of Christian writings?

3.   What type of narrative history (political-social, economic, or intellectual) seems most interesting or important to you? Why?

4.   What are the commonalities in the new ways of reading history (feminism, popular history, and postmodernism)?

5.   State in your own words the difference between primary and secondary sources, and give an example of each.

6.   What other advantages and disadvantages of using the Internet in the study of Christianity occur to you, besides the ones given here?

7.   Which of the suggestions for reading profitably seem most helpful to you? Why?

SUGGESTIONS FOR FURTHER READING

H. Bettenson, *Documents of the Christian Church,* 3d ed. Oxford: Oxford University Press, 1996. A standard collection of more or less official documents from the second century to about 1960, with some special attention to the English church.

E. Gaustad, *A Documentary History of Religion in America,* 2d ed.; 2 vols. Grand Rapids, MI: Eerdmans, 1993. A fascinating, relatively up-to-date collection of official and unofficial documents from the entire sweep of religion (including several non-Christian religions) in the United States.

H. Kerr, *Readings in Christian Thought,* 2d ed. Nashville: Abingdon, 1990. An excellent selection of primary sources in theology from the beginning of the second century through the middle of the twentieth.

B. MacHaffie, *Readings in Her Story: Women in Christian Tradition.* Minneapolis: Fortress, 1992. A fine collection of primary texts by and/or about women from the Bible and church history, with an emphasis on the American church.

C. Manschreck, *A History of Christianity: Readings in the History of the Church from the Reformation to the Present.* Englewood Cliffs, NJ: Prentice-Hall, 1962. An excellent collection of readings both historical and theological. The companion volume to Petry (following); both are now out of print but can be found in most academic libraries.

A. E. McGrath, *The Christian Theology Reader.* Oxford, UK: Blackwell, 1995. A collection of 280 texts in the history of theology, many quite brief, with full pedagogical aids. The best collection available for the student beginning a study of Christian thought.

R. J. Plantinga, ed., *Christianity and Plurality: Classic and Contemporary Readings.* Oxford: Blackwell, 1999. Primary readings, from scripture through the end of the twentieth century, on how Christianity relates to other religions.

R. Petry, *A History of Christianity: Readings in the History of the Early and Medieval Church.* Englewood Cliffs, NJ: Prentice-Hall, 1962. Readings from the second century to the fifteenth.

J. F. White, *Documents of Christian Worship: Descriptive and Interpretive Sources.* Louisville: Westminster/John Knox, 1992. A survey of key historical documents relating to many different types of Christian worship.

CHAPTER TWO

Biblical Foundations

❖ In Laramie, Wyoming, local police keep a close eye on demonstrators outside the funeral of Matthew Sheppard, a young gay man brutally killed for his sexual orientation. Some demonstrators carry signs with words from the Bible: "You shall not lie with men as with women; it is an abomination," and other verses. Inside the Episcopal Church, words from scripture are also prominent, promoting tolerance and nonviolence.

❖ In Chicago, the Council of Bishops of the Evangelical Lutheran Church in America deals with a challenge to the traditional names of God used in baptism—"Father, Son and Holy Spirit," words taken from the Gospel of *Matthew*. Attacking these names as sexist, some congregations of that church have substituted the words "Creator, Redeemer, and Sanctifier." The bishops reject this move on biblical, theological, and ecumenical grounds, instructing churches to use the traditional names of God at baptism.

❖ In New York City, a Jewish group calling itself the "Committee for Truth and Justice" takes out a large, expensive advertisement on the op-ed page of the *New York Times*. This "Open Letter to Pope John Paul II," on the occasion of his visit to New York, urges the pope to "rightfully revise those chapters in the Four Gospels that tell of the trial of Jesus." This should be done, the committee claims, to eliminate all reference to Jewish participation in the death of Jesus. Such references are unhistorical and anti-Semitic, the advertisement argues, and still contribute to the suffering of the Jewish people.

INTRODUCTION

The Bible is our primary source for the foundation of Christianity. Its Old Testament, also called the Hebrew Bible/Scriptures, tells the story of Israel from its beginnings until about the fourth century B.C.E. The writings of the New Testament tell the story, and explain the significance, of Jesus Christ for the earliest Christians. They cover the period from about 27 to 120 C.E. Both the Old and New Testaments are influential in the continuing life of the Christian tradition. In this chapter we will sample the writings of the Bible and indicate their importance for their own time and for the continuing history of Christianity. But first, by way of introduction, we will consider the Bible's names, history, literary genres, and use.

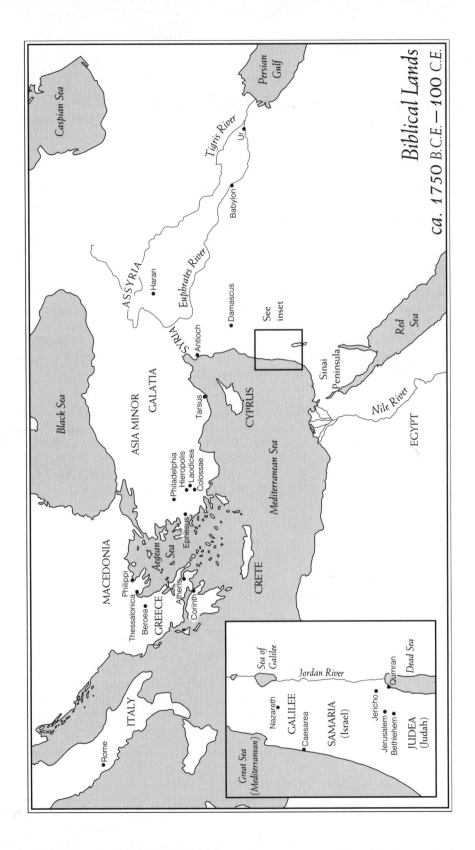

Biblical Lands
ca. 1750 B.C.E. – 100 C.E.

Names

The common name in Christianity for its scriptures is the Bible ("Book"), composed of both the Old Testament and the New Testament.[1] As in the Jewish Bible, **testament** or its synonym *covenant* refers to the relationship God has established with people. *New* signifies the early Christian belief that in Jesus God has acted in a new way for salvation. This is seen as a fulfillment of the promises made by God to the Jewish people. The term *new testament* or *new covenant* can be seen in II Corinthians 3:6–15, where the early Christian missionary Paul calls Christian believers members of the new covenant while the books of Moses (the Jewish Bible) are the old covenant. This term looks back to Jeremiah 31:31, in which God promises, "I will make a new covenant with the house of Israel and the house of Judah." *New covenant* was also used in the early Christian celebration of the ritual of Holy Communion, as its earliest recorded form attests: "In the same way [Jesus] took the cup also, after supper, saying, "This cup is the new covenant in my blood" (I Corinthians 11:25).

In sum, *new covenant* or *new testament* was a common term in early Christianity, and it did not take long to be formally attached to the body of Christian scripture. The advantage of New Testament as the title of the Christian scriptures is that it suggests the complexity of the early Christian attitude to its relationship with Judaism and the Jewish Bible. This relationship has both continuity with Judaism, as expressed by *covenant,* and discontinuity, as expressed by the qualifier *new*. A disadvantage is that it leads to an all-too-easy misunderstanding of the role of the Jewish Bible in Christianity—that it is "old," outmoded, and completely replaced by the New Testament. Christianity has had continual problems in understanding the role of the Old Testament in the church. In recent years there has been a growing tendency to counter this disadvantage by labeling the twenty-seven books of the New Testament the *Christian Scriptures.* But this title is even more misleading than New Testament because it strongly implies that the Jewish Bible is not a part of the Christian scriptures. On the whole, then, it seems best to use the term *New Testament.* Despite its disadvantages, it is the commonly accepted label within the Christian church and in the academic community and will be used here.

Historical Sketch

In this section, we will consider the story of how the books of the Bible were formed. In the course of this sketch, the general course of events narrated in the Bible will also be outlined.

The books of the Old Testament had a long history of formation in oral tradition, initial reduction to writing, editorial polishing, and formal adoption as scripture. Because this process of development is shrouded in the mists of antiquity, scholarly judgments will vary, but the following summary has some consensus. The writing probably began about 1100 B.C.E., after the Israelites entered Palestine, when the oldest

---

[1] Parts of this chapter are taken from R. Van Voorst, *Anthology of World Scriptures,* 3d ed. (Belmont, CA: Wadsworth, 1999). Copyright © Wadsworth Publishing Company, 2000. Used by permission.

sections of poetry and historical narratives were written (e.g., the Songs of Moses and Miriam in Exodus 15; the Song of Deborah in Judges 5). Under Solomon, the story of his father David began to be written (II Samuel 9–I Kings 2). The Yahwistic source of the **Torah** (Genesis through Deuteronomy), so called because it uses the divine name "Yahweh," which told of creation and the patriarchs as a prelude to the formation of Israel, was written in southern Israel. The Elohistic source of the Torah, so called because it uses the divine name "Elohim," was written in northern Israel from a northern religious and political perspective. The eighth century B.C.E. saw a flowering of literary effort in which the disciples of the prophets Amos, Hosea, Isaiah, and Micah began to write down their words. When the North fell in 721 B.C.E., the Yahwistic and Elohistic sources were combined into the "Old Epic" narrative to give us much of Genesis. In 621, the finding of a law scroll probably containing the substance of Deuteronomy 12–26 gave an impetus for writing of the rest of this book.

The exile of the Jews in Babylon (587–520) after the conquest of the Southern Kingdom was a fruitful period of literary activity. Jeremiah, Ezekiel, and Second Isaiah (chapters 40–55) were largely written by their disciples. The Deuteronomic history (Deuteronomy, Joshua, Judges, I–II Samuel, and I–II Kings) probably was completed at the end of the Exile. Priestly sections of the Torah were completed and many of the Psalms were written down at this time.

After the Exile, Jewish scriptural activity centered on Jerusalem and its Temple. More prophetic books were completed: Third Isaiah (Isaiah 56–66), Malachi, and Joel were written, and Haggai edited to its final form. By the year 400 B.C.E. the Torah probably reached its present form as it was finished and edited by the Jerusalem priests, becoming the first and primary section of Jewish scripture. Genesis through Deuteronomy was labeled Torah, and Moses was said to be its author. Around 350 B.C.E. the historical work of the Chronicler, I–II Chronicles and Ezra-Nehemiah, was completed. The later wisdom books, Job and Ecclesiastes, were compiled. Two short stories, Ruth and Esther, appeared. By 200, the Prophetic section with its eight books was complete. The final stratum of the Jewish scripture was the apocalyptic type: Isaiah 24–27, Ezekiel 38, and especially the book of Daniel, the last book to be written, in 160 B.C.E. The Writings section was basically collected by about 100 B.C.E., but the status of some books in it (especially Esther and the Song of Songs) was debated later.

The full and formal **canonization** (making an official list of books regarded as scriptural) of the entire Old Testament as we now have it—the Torah, Prophets, and Writings—took place at the end of the first century C.E. No one disagreed on the books of the Torah and the Prophets—this had been settled for several centuries. The Jewish council at Jamnia (ca. 90 C.E.) seems to have ruled on the writings as we have them, but it took some years for this ruling to be widely accepted. The main criterion for canonicity was the recognition that God was revealed in these books and spoke to people in them. Canonization did not *create* the scripturality of a book. Rather, it was the official and formal recognition of a longstanding reception and use of these books as holy and scriptural by the religious community itself. Once it was given, canonization then helped reinforce the holiness and authority of these books. The same basic process of canonization would be used to form the New Testament.

At first glance, it would seem that the New Testament was written perhaps only one or two generations after the death and resurrection of Jesus and the birth of the church.

Yet modern biblical scholarship has discovered that its writing was not completed until perhaps ninety years after Jesus' death. (The process of forming the New Testament canon was even longer; this will be treated in the introduction to Chapter 3.) The pace of writing was retarded by three main factors. First, the early church, which began as a group within Judaism, already had a complete body of scripture—the Jewish Bible. At first it found this scripture sufficient for its life, especially when it could interpret and use the Jewish Bible in its own way to bolster its claim that Jesus was the Messiah, the promised deliverer of Israel. Second, the early Christians quite comfortably used the words and deeds of Jesus in primarily oral form. They did not remember Jesus as a writer, and there was no urgency to write down his words. Third, many early Christians believed that the end of the world was near, and with this expectation the lengthy process of writing, copying (by hand), and distributing books was not to be expected.

How, then, did the process of writing what was to become the *New Testament* begin? The genuine Pauline **letters** (which some call by the more formal name **epistles**) came first. Paul wrote letters to keep in contact with the churches he founded on his missionary travels. He used them to instruct and exhort his churches, and as a substitute for his own personal presence. These letters gained more importance after Paul's death (probably in the mid-60s), and after his death his co-workers continued to write letters in his name to perpetuate and adapt his teachings for a new generation. Of course, at this stage there was probably no thought by Paul and his followers that these letters would become a part of a new body of Christian scripture. Letters and other types of literature then followed from other writers in the period of 70–120 C.E.

Second, the **Gospels** began to be written down around 70 C.E. This word is derived from the Anglo-Saxon *god-spell,* or "good news." The Greek word (all the New Testament was written in Greek, the common language of the Mediterranean world) is *euangelion,* "good news," from which we get *evangelical.* The structure of a gospel narrative seems to have been invented by Mark: Jesus' ministry in Galilee, his journey to Jerusalem, teaching in Jerusalem, arrest, trial, death and resurrection. This structure is followed by the other two gospels, Matthew and Luke, that (the vast majority of scholars conclude) use Mark as a source. John does not use Mark as a source, so it differs from this basic outline. These two parts of the New Testament, commonly called "the gospel and the apostle," were the basic building blocks of the canon.

Literary Genres of the Primary Sources

When reduced to their most basic form, the genres of the Old Testament literature may be summarized as follows. The first book of the Torah, *Genesis,* is a narrative both mythic and historical of how God created the world good, but humanity fell into sin and rebellion. After the growth of the human race through many generations, Abraham responded to God's call by migrating from Mesopotamia to Palestine. In *Exodus,* Moses arose to lead the Hebrews by God's power from Egypt into the Sinai Peninsula between Egypt and Palestine, where the people received the law of God, which Exodus relates to some length. *Leviticus* contains God's instruction for worship and ritual purity, and *Numbers* relates how they wandered in the wilderness until they were ready to enter the Promised Land. In *Deuteronomy,* the people receive the law a second time as Moses warns them against serving other gods. These five books are together known as the *Torah*, "teaching, instruction," and are the most important books of the Old Testament scriptures.

The next section of the Bible, the *Prophets*, is subdivided into two parts, Former and Latter Prophets. *Former* and *Latter* refer to their position in the canon, not to the time of their composition. The Former Prophets include *Joshua, Judges, Samuel*, and *Kings*. These books narrate the history of Israel from the conquest of Canaan (Palestine) to the Babylonian victory over the Southern Kingdom of Judah and the Exile in Babylon.

The Latter Prophets begin with *Isaiah*, a composite book that contains the word of God to Isaiah in the eighth century and the messages of *Second Isaiah* and *Third Isaiah* in the sixth century. *Jeremiah* is the message of the mournful prophet who saw the destruction of Jerusalem by the Babylonians. *Ezekiel* prophesied hope among the Jewish exiles in Babylon. The next book among the Prophets is *The Twelve*, called in English "The Minor Prophets" because of the relatively small size of their books, not for the importance of their message. Formerly they were written on one scroll. The Twelve are: Hosea, Joel, Amos, Obadiah, Jonah, Micah, Nahum, Habakkuk, Zephaniah, Haggai, Zechariah, and Malachi. The careers of these prophets run from the 700s to the 500s B.C.E. Their books are usually in poetic format. Although all the prophetic books bear the names of men, we know that women were also among the Israelite prophets.

The third section of the Jewish Bible is the Writings. As this name suggests, the Writings are a miscellaneous collection of several types of literature. It begins with the *Psalms*, song-prayers for Temple use. *Proverbs* and *Job* are books that deal with wisdom, the former a collection of wise sayings attributed to Solomon and the latter a drama about the perennial question, "If God is good, why do good people suffer?" *Ruth* tells the beautiful story of how a non-Israelite woman became a part of the people of God and the ancestor of King David. The *Song of Songs* is a collection of poetry that celebrates love between a man and a woman, traditionally interpreted by Jews (and later by Christians) as symbolic of the relationship of God and God's people. *Ecclesiastes* offers a reduced expectation of what wisdom and life have to offer. *Lamentations*, traditionally ascribed to the prophet Jeremiah, mourns the destruction of Jerusalem by the Babylonians. *Esther* is a dramatic story of how a Jewish woman delivers her people from destruction by a Persian king. *Daniel* contains visions of the end of time. *Ezra-Nehemiah* records the return of the Jewish exiles from Babylon at the end of the sixth century B.C.E., the reconstruction of Jerusalem, and the reconstitution of Judaism. Finally, I–II Chronicles tell much the same story as I–II Kings (in the Former Prophets), but from the perspective of the Jerusalem priesthood. (The Jewish scriptures are summarized in Table 2.1.)

The Jewish people did not stop writing religious literature during the period between the testaments. They penned wisdom books, historical books, and apocalypses, often putting them under the name of some more ancient prophet or writer. These books were influential in the rise of the New Testament, especially the relatively few that found their way into the **Septuagint,** the Greek translation of the Hebrew Bible made in the second century B.C.E. (See Table 2.2 for a list of these books.)

We turn now to a sketch of the New Testament's genres. The first four books are the *Gospels*, "good news" of the story of Jesus. Matthew tells the story of Jesus the Savior as the promised Messiah of Israel, going from his conception by the Holy Spirit in the Virgin Mary through his appearances after his resurrection from the dead. Mark tells the story of Jesus from baptism through the resurrection, presenting Jesus as the

Table 2.1

The Books of the Hebrew Bible

Division	English Name	Hebrew Name	Chapters
Torah ("Teaching, Law")	Genesis	*Bereshith* ("in the beginning")	50
	Exodus	*Shemoth* ("names")	40
	Leviticus	*Wayiqra* ("and he called")	27
	Numbers	*Bemidbar* ("in the wilderness")	36
	Deuteronomy	*Debarim* ("words")	34
Nevi'im ("Prophets")	Joshua	*Yehoshua*	24
	Judges	*Shofetim* ("judges")	21
	I, II Samuel	*Shemuel*	31, 24
	I, II Kings	*Melakim* ("kings")	22, 25
	Isaiah	*Yeshayahu*	66
	Jeremiah	*Yirmeyahu*	52
	Ezekiel	*Yehezgel*	48
	The Twelve:		
	Hosea	*Hoshea*	14
	Joel	*Yoel*	3
	Amos	*Amos*	9
	Obadiah	*Obadyahu*	1
	Jonah	*Yonah*	4
	Micah	*Micah*	7
	Nahum	*Nahum*	3
	Habakkuk	*Habaqquq*	3
	Zephaniah	*Zephanyah*	3
	Haggai	*Haggai*	2
	Zechariah	*Zekaryahu*	14
	Malachi	*Malaki*	4
Kethuvim ("Writings")	Psalms	*Tehillim* ("Praises")	150
	Job	*Iyyob*	31
	Proverbs	*Mishle* ("Proverbs of")	42
	Ruth	*Ruth*	4
	Song of Songs	*Shir Hashirim* ("Song of Songs")	8
	Ecclesiastes	*Koheleth* ("Preacher")	12
	Lamentations	*Ekah* ("How")	5
	Esther	*Ester*	10
	Daniel	*Daniel*	12
	Ezra-Nehemiah	*Ezra-Nehemyah*	10, 13
	I, II Chronicles	*Dibre Hayamin* ("words of")	29, 36

Savior of the Gentiles (non-Jews). Luke also presents Jesus as the savior of the Gentiles, and has a secondary theme of God's concern for the poor, women, outcasts, etc. These three gospels are known as **synoptic** ("seen in one view") because of their parallel structure and content. John is the story of Jesus as the eternal, divine Son of God who came to earth to show God's glory in his life, death, and resurrection from the dead. The Gospels are followed up by the *Acts of the Apostles,* the only book of the New Testament devoted to a historical account of the early church, telling of the beginning of the church and its growth through its first approximately thirty-five years.

Table 2.2

The Books of the Greek Version of the Jewish Bible

Genesis	Proverbs
Exodus	Ecclesiastes
Leviticus	*Wisdom of Solomon
Numbers	*Wisdom of Sirach
Deuteronomy	*Psalms of Solomon
Joshua	Isaiah
Judges	Jeremiah
Ruth	Lamentations
I Kings (I Samuel)	*Baruch
II Kings (II Samuel)	*Letter of Jeremiah
III Kings (I Kings)	Ezekiel
IV Kings (II Kings)	Daniel
I Chronicles	*Susanna
II Chronicles	*Bel and the Snake
*I Esdras	Hosea
II Esdras (Ezra-Nehemiah)	Joel
*Tobit	Amos
*Judith	Obadiah
Esther	Jonah
*I Maccabees	Micah
*II Maccabees	Nahum
*III Maccabees	Habakkuk
*IV Maccabees	Zephaniah
Job	Haggai
Psalms	Zechariah
*Odes	Malachi

* These apocryphal, or deutero-canonical, books are not included in the canon of the Hebrew scriptures or in the Bibles of most Protestant churches. They are included in the Bibles of the Eastern Orthodox and Roman Catholic churches, but the Catholic canon excludes I Esdras, III and IV Maccabees, Odes, and Psalms of Solomon. Some Bibles used by Orthodox Christians omit IV Maccabees, Odes, and Psalms of Solomon.

The rest of the New Testament is largely composed of the *Letters* (or Epistles) of instruction and correction written by church leaders to various churches. Some scholars dispute the names on these letters, arguing that they are **pseudonymous,** written by someone other than the given author, usually one of his followers or co-workers after his death. Letters thought to be genuinely written by the stated person are called **authentic.** This section begins with the letters of the missionary-apostle *Paul,* which are arranged in the canon mostly by length, from the longest to the shortest, and are named according to their destination. *Romans* presents Paul's understanding of Christian teaching in a rather systematic way to a church that he did not establish, but was soon to visit. In *I Corinthians* Paul discusses various issues related to Christian doctrine, morality and worship. In *II Corinthians,* Paul's main concern is to keep this gentile-Christian church from straying to Jewish Christianity. *Galatians* has much this same theme—Christians from non-Jewish backgrounds need not be Jewish as well as Christian. *Ephesians,* probably written by a fellow worker of Paul's after his death, presents

Jesus Christ as the cosmic savior who unifies races and nations. *Philippians,* a genuine Pauline letter, urges Christians to find joy in Christ. *Colossians,* probably written under Paul's name by a co-worker, seeks like Ephesians to correct error by presenting Jesus Christ as the all-sufficient savior of the universe, not just of the church. *I Thessalonians* answers questions about what happens when the Lord Jesus returns in glory to judge the world at the end of time. *II Thessalonians,* probably pseudonymously written after the death of Paul, instructs Christians about how to wait for Jesus' return. The next three letters, *I* and *II Timothy* and *Titus,* are called the Pastoral Letters because they are instructions under Paul's name about pastoral offices and church life at the end of the first century. Finally, *Philemon* is Paul's attempt to reconcile a Christian slave-owner to his runaway Christian slave, a slave now seeking to return to that master.

The next section of the New Testament is known as the General or Catholic letters. Like the Pauline letters, these also are seemingly arranged by length. It begins with *Hebrews,* an anonymous letter written to encourage Christians not to turn to Judaism. The book of *James* exhorts its audience to live wise, righteous, and socially responsible lives. *I Peter* offers guidelines on Christian behavior, especially to those undergoing persecution. *II Peter* urges its readers to stay true to traditional Christian teaching and reject false forms of the faith. The three *Letters of John* combat false teachers while promoting love and hospitality among Christians. *Jude* is very similar in content and purpose to *II Peter,* defending the faith against falsehoods. Finally, *Revelation,* an **apocalyptic** document, offers visions of the future triumph of God at the end of the world, delivering believers from persecution by establishing the kingdom of heaven on earth. The order, authors (those probably pseudonymous noted as disputed), dates, genres, and size (in number of chapters) of the New Testament literature are charted in Table 2.3.

Uses

Because the Bible is by far the most influential literary source in Christianity, not just for its witness to the formation of Christianity but also for its continuing impact on the faith, we will trace briefly here the ways in which it is typically used. As in Judaism, the primary use of the Christian Bible has always been in the service of divine worship. The entire worship of the church is saturated with the Bible. One of the high points of the service in all Catholic and many Protestant churches is the reading of a selection from the Old Testament and two selections from the New, the last one always a gospel reading. This **lectionary** system arose in the early Greek church, probably as an inheritance from Judaism. It quickly passed into Western Catholic Christianity. In the twentieth century, especially in its last quarter, many Protestant and Roman Catholic churches in Europe and North America have adopted basically the same lectionary, with the result that on any given Sunday most American Christians hear the same scripture readings and sermons based more or less on them. (Independent-minded Protestants, such as fundamentalists and Pentecostalists, do not follow this system.)

The Bible itself occupies a privileged place in the physical arrangement of the typical Christian church. In churches of a "higher," more elaborate form of worship, it is often placed on a special ornate lectern. In more formal Roman Catholic Masses, the book of the Gospels is often brought before the altar, "incensed" and kissed by the

Table 2.3

The Books of the New Testament

Book	Traditional and/ or Given Author	Date (C.E.)	Genre	Size in Chapters
Matthew	Matthew (disputed)	80s	gospel	28
Mark	Mark (disputed)	70	gospel	16
Luke	Luke (disputed)	80s	gospel	24
John	John (disputed)	90	gospel	21
Acts of the Apostles	Luke (disputed)	80s	history	28
Romans	Paul	55	letter	16
I Corinthians	Paul	53	letter	16
II Corinthians	Paul	55	letter	13
Galatians	Paul	55	letter	6
Ephesians	Paul (disputed)	90	letter	6
Philippians	Paul	61	letter	4
Colossians	Paul (disputed)	80s	letter	4
I Thessalonians	Paul	51	letter	5
II Thessalonians	Paul (disputed)	80s	letter	3
I Timothy	Paul (disputed)	90s	letter	6
II Timothy	Paul (disputed)	90s	letter	4
Titus	Paul (disputed)	90s	letter	3
Philemon	Paul	50s	letter	1
Hebrews	Anonymous	80s	letter-sermon	13
James	James (disputed)	90	letter-sermon	5
I Peter	Peter (disputed)	80	letter	5
II Peter	Peter (disputed)	120	letter	3
I John	John "the Elder"	95	essay	5
II John	John "the Elder"	96	letter	1
III John	John "the Elder"	97	letter	1
Jude	Jude (disputed)	100	letter	1
Revelation	John "the Prophet"	90s	apocalypse	22

priest as a sign of its holiness before it is read. In both Catholic and Eastern Orthodox traditions, the scripture books are large and often richly bound and decorated with gold, jewels, and icons. But even in Protestant churches with less formal worship, the Bible is reverenced. In such churches a large Bible is often placed on the pulpit from which the minister conducts the entire service. In churches of the Baptist wing of Protestantism it is not unusual to see the preacher carrying a typically sized Bible in one hand and referring to it constantly during the sermon.

This formal use of the Bible is supplemented by many Christians with private de-votional reading. Since the times of the Reformation in the sixteenth century, the Protestant churches have promoted (with varying degrees of insistence) the right and duty of every Christian to read the Bible individually. This reading includes prayerful meditation on the meaning of the words and the implication of this meaning for the life of the reader. Our present-day verse divisions were first introduced in the Geneva Bible of 1560, to assist in more detailed study and reference. Reading is also often done aloud by families as a part of the main meal of the day. This private and familial use of scripture has formed a large part of Protestant spirituality. In the twentieth century, and especially since the reforms of the Second Vatican Council in the 1960s, Roman Catholics have also emphasized the importance of private devotional study of the Bible. Despite this emphasis on private use of scripture, most Christians throughout the world still come into contact with their Bible mostly during church services.

Alongside this religious use of the Bible is its academic study by means of the *historical-critical method*. This method, which arose in the last three hundred years, seeks to understand the various parts of the Bible in their original historical context and tries to determine what it meant to its original readers. It tends to disregard the teachings of the various churches about the content of Scripture. Because it approaches the Bible as it does any other book from the ancient world, this approach is strongly rejected by fundamentalists, both Protestant and Catholic alike. The historical-critical method is today accepted by most mainline Protestant churches throughout the world. Mainstream Catholics, and increasingly Eastern Orthodox believers, have learned to make use of the historical-critical approach to the Bible. In most Catholic and Orthodox seminaries, new clergy are trained in understanding and using the academic approach to the Bible in their pastoral ministry, and as time goes on this approach will probably become more fully accepted.

Because the Bible has exercised its influence over the Christian church and the wider world in its many translations and versions, we will sample three main English versions here. The readings from the Old Testament are taken from *TANAKH: The Holy Scriptures,* the most prominent Jewish translation into English.[2] Most readings from the New Testament are taken from the New Revised Standard Version of the Bible.[3] The Sermon on the Mount is given in the King James Version as an illustration of that important translation.

---

[2] *TANAKH: The Holy Scriptures* (Philadelphia: Jewish Publication Society, 1985). Copyright © 1985, by the Jewish Publication Society. Used by permission.

[3] *The New Revised Standard Version of the Bible* (New York: Oxford University Press, 1991). Copyright 1989 by Division of Christian Education of the National Council of the Churches of Christ in the USA. All rights reserved. Used by permission.

EVENTS

The Call of Abraham*

The history of the Jewish people and, in a sense, Christianity begins with Abraham, whose name was Abram at first. As a part of the covenant, God calls on him to journey to Canaan (ancient Palestine) and promises that his descendants will form a great nation, will inherit the land of Canaan,

and will become a source of blessing to the world. Early Christians saw this blessing as Jesus Christ, in whom the covenant with Abraham is extended to all peoples who believe.

Now the Lord said to Abram, "Go from your country and your kindred and your father's house to the land that I will show you. I will make of

---

* Genesis 12:1–7

you a great nation, and I will bless you, and make your name great, so that you will be a blessing. I will bless those who bless you, and the one who curses you I will curse; and in you all the families of the earth shall be blessed."

So Abram went, as the Lord had told him; and Lot went with him. Abram was seventy-five years old when he departed from Haran.[4] [5] Abram

---

[4] *Haran:* the city in northern Mesopotamia (modern-day Iraq) where Abraham lived.

took his wife Sarai and his brother's son Lot, and all the possessions that they had gathered, and the persons whom they had acquired in Haran; and they set forth to go to the land of Canaan. When they had come to the land of Canaan, Abram passed through the land to the place at Shechem, to the oak of Moreh. At that time the Canaanites were in the land. Then the Lord appeared to Abram, and said, "To your offspring I will give this land." So he built there an altar to the Lord, who had appeared to him.

Deliverance from Egypt*

The dramatic climax of the Exodus is the Israelites' escape through the sea and the destruction of the Egyptians who pursued them. The story of the deliverance from slavery and death in Egypt is the center of the Passover celebration in Judaism and from there passed into the Christian Eucharist. Christians have traditionally understood the death and resurrection of Jesus in terms of the Exodus, and its more overt political meanings are important in Liberation theology.

When the king of Egypt was told that the people [of Israel] had fled, Pharaoh and his courtiers had a change of heart about the people and said, "What is this we have done, releasing Israel from our service?" He ordered his chariot and took his men with him; he took six hundred of his picked chariots, and the rest of the chariots of Egypt, with officers in all of them. The Lord stiffened the heart of Pharaoh king of Egypt, and he gave chase to the Israelites. . . .

[10] As Pharaoh drew near, the Israelites caught sight of the Egyptians advancing upon them. Greatly frightened, the Israelites cried out to the Lord. And they said to Moses, "Was it for

want of graves in Egypt that you brought us to die in the wilderness? What have you done to us, taking us out of Egypt?" . . . But Moses said to the people, "Have no fear! Stand by, and witness the deliverance which the Lord will work for you today; for the Egyptians whom you see today you will never see again. The Lord will battle for you; you hold your peace!" . . .

[19] The angel of God, who had been going ahead of the Israelite army, now moved and followed behind them; and the pillar of cloud shifted from in front of them and stood up a place behind them, [20] and it came between the army of the Egyptians and the army of Israel. Thus there was the cloud with the darkness, and it cast a spell upon the night, so that the one could not come near the other all through the night.

Then Moses held out his arm over the sea and the Lord drove back the sea with a strong east wind all that night, and turned the sea into dry ground. The waters were split, and the Israelites went into the sea on dry ground, the waters forming a wall for them on their right and on their left. The Egyptians came in pursuit after them into the sea, all of Pharaoh's horses, chariots, and horsemen. At the morning watch, the Lord looked down upon the Egyptian army from a pillar of fire and cloud, and threw the Egyptian

---

* Exodus 14:5–8, 10–11, 13–26, 28, 31

army into panic. [25] He locked the wheels of their chariots so that they moved forward with difficulty. And the Egyptians said, "Let us flee from the Israelites, for the Lord is fighting for them against Egypt."

Then the Lord said to Moses, "Hold out your arm over the sea, that the waters may come back upon the Egyptians." . . . [28] The waters turned

back and covered the chariots and the horsemen—Pharaoh's entire army that followed them into the sea; not one of them remained. . . .

[31] And when Israel saw the wondrous power which the Lord had wielded against the Egyptians, the people feared the Lord; they had faith in the Lord and His servant Moses.

Ezra's Enforcement of Law Observance*

The return of the Jewish exiles from Babylon in the sixth century B.C.E. brought a new dedication to keep the Mosaic law. One way that this observance was enforced was in the divorce of Jewish men from their non-Jewish wives. (The Old Testament book of Ruth, perhaps written near this time, has a more liberal view of mixed marriages.) Marriage only within the faith became the rule in Jewish law, and then in Christian law and custom, until very recent times in the West. In other parts of world Christianity, it is usually still the rule.

After these things had been done, the officials approached me and said, "The people of Israel, the priests, and the Levites have not separated themselves from the peoples of the lands with their abominations. . . . They have taken some of their daughters as wives for themselves and for their sons. Thus the holy seed has mixed itself with the peoples of the lands, and in this faithlessness the officials and leaders have led the way." When I heard this, I tore my garment and my mantle, and pulled hair from my head and beard, and sat appalled.[5] Then all who trembled at the words of the God of Israel, because of the faithlessness of the returned exiles, gathered around me while I sat appalled until the evening sacrifice.

[5] At the evening sacrifice I got up from my fasting, with my garments and my mantle torn, and fell on my knees, spread out my hands to the Lord my God, and said, "O my God, I am too ashamed and embarrassed to lift my face to you, my God, for our iniquities have risen higher than our heads, and our guilt has mounted up to the heavens." . . .

[10:1] A very great assembly of men, women, and children gathered to [Ezra] out of Israel; the people also wept bitterly. Shecaniah son of Jehiel, of the descendants of Elam, addressed Ezra, saying, "We have broken faith with our God and have married foreign women from the peoples of the land, but even now there is hope for Israel in spite of this. So now let us make a covenant with our God to send away all these wives and their children, according to the counsel of my lord and of those who tremble at the commandment of our God; and let it be done according to the law." . . .

All the people sat in the open square before the house of God, trembling because of this matter and because of the heavy rain. [10] Then Ezra the priest stood up and said to them, "You have trespassed and married foreign women, and so increased the guilt of Israel. Now make confession to the Lord the God of your ancestors, and do his will; separate yourselves from the peoples of the land and from the foreign wives." Then all the assembly answered with a loud voice, "It is so; we must do as you have said."

---

* Ezra 9:1–6; 10:3–12

[5] *I tore my garment . . . and sat appalled:* all signs of mourning.

The Birth of Jesus the Messiah*

The gospels of Matthew and Luke present Jesus as conceived by the action of the Spirit of God in the Virgin Mary. This miraculous conception signifies the divine sonship of Jesus and would also be seen in early Christianity as conferring a special status on Mary. The passage also focuses on the name Jesus, which in the Aramaic language of Palestine means "he will save."

Now the birth of Jesus the Messiah took place in this way. When his mother Mary had been engaged to Joseph, but before they lived together, she was found to be with child from the Holy Spirit. Her husband Joseph, being a righteous man and unwilling to expose her to public disgrace, planned to dismiss her quietly. [20] But just when he had resolved to do this, an angel of the Lord appeared to him in a dream and said, "Joseph, son of David, do not be afraid to take Mary as your wife, for the child conceived in her is from the Holy Spirit. She will bear a son, and you are to name him Jesus, for he will save his people from their sins." All this took place to fulfill what had been spoken by the Lord through the prophet: "Look, the virgin shall conceive and bear a son, and they shall name him Emmanuel," which means, "God is with us." When Joseph awoke from sleep, he did as the angel of the Lord commanded him; he took her as his wife, [25] but had no marital relations with her until she had borne a son;[6] and he named him Jesus.

_____

* Matthew 1:18–25

_____

[6] *until she had borne a son:* Roman Catholics, who confess the lifelong virginity of Mary, do not interpret this verse to mean that Mary and Joseph did have sexual relations after Jesus' birth.

Jesus' Miracles**

In the Gospels, as in the Hebrew scriptures, miracles signify the incursion of God into human life. They are not seen as "violations of natural law," but as acts of divine power for salvation. This selection has two types of miracles characteristic of the ministry of Jesus: exorcism of demons, showing the power of Jesus over supernatural evil; and healing of the sick, showing Jesus' ultimate victory over physical evil and death so central to early Christianity. Miracles continued to be important in various periods of Christianity; both in the ancient church and more recently in parts of the Third World, belief in miracles has contributed to the growth of the church.

Then they arrived at the country of the Gerasenes, which is opposite Galilee. As he stepped out on land, a man of the city who had demons met him. For a long time he had worn no clothes, and he did not live in a house but in the tombs. When he saw Jesus, he fell down before him and shouted at the top of his voice, "What have you to do with me, Jesus, Son of the Most High God? I beg you, do not torment me"—for Jesus had commanded the unclean spirit to come out of the man. (For many times it had seized him; he was kept under guard and bound with chains and shackles, but he would break the bonds and be driven by the demon into the wilds.) [30] Jesus then asked him, "What is your name?" He said, "Legion"; for many demons had entered him. They begged him not to order them to go back into the abyss.[7]

Now there on the hillside a large herd of swine was feeding; and the demons begged Jesus to let

_____

** Luke 8:26–56

_____

[7] *abyss:* a section of hell in which demons are confined to await final destruction.

them enter these. So he gave them permission. Then the demons came out of the man and entered the swine, and the herd rushed down the steep bank into the lake and was drowned. When the swineherds saw what had happened, they ran off and told it in the city and in the country. [35] Then people came out to see what had happened, and when they came to Jesus, they found the man from whom the demons had gone sitting at the feet of Jesus, clothed and in his right mind. And they were afraid. Those who had seen it told them how the one who had been possessed by demons had been healed. Then all the people of the surrounding country of the Gerasenes asked Jesus to leave them; for they were seized with great fear. So he got into the boat and returned. The man from whom the demons had gone begged that he might be with him; but Jesus sent him away, saying, "Return to your home, and declare how much God has done for you." So he went away, proclaiming throughout the city how much Jesus had done for him.

[40] Now when Jesus returned, the crowd welcomed him, for they were all waiting for him. Just then there came a man named Jairus, a leader of the synagogue. He fell at Jesus' feet and begged him to come to his house, for he had an only daughter, about twelve years old, who was dying. As he went, the crowds pressed in on him. Now there was a woman who had been suffering from hemorrhages for twelve years; and though she had spent all she had on physicians, no one could cure her. She came up behind him and touched the fringe of his clothes, and immedi-

ately her hemorrhage stopped. [45] Then Jesus asked, "Who touched me?" When all denied it, Peter said, "Master, the crowds surround you and press in on you." But Jesus said, "Someone touched me; for I noticed that power had gone out from me." When the woman saw that she could not remain hidden, she came trembling; and falling down before him, she declared in the presence of all the people why she had touched him, and how she had been immediately healed. He said to her, "Daughter, your faith has made you well; go in peace."

While he was still speaking, someone came from the leader's house to say, "Your daughter is dead; do not trouble the teacher any longer." [50] When Jesus heard this, he replied, "Do not fear. Only believe, and she will be saved." When he came to the house, he did not allow anyone to enter with him, except Peter, John, and James, and the child's father and mother. They were all weeping and wailing for her; but he said, "Do not weep; for she is not dead but sleeping."[8] And they laughed at him, knowing that she was dead. But he took her by the hand and called out, "Child, get up!" [55] Her spirit returned, and she got up at once. Then he directed them to give her something to eat. Her parents were astounded; but he ordered them to tell no one what had happened.[9]

---

[8] *sleeping:* Jesus knows the girl is dead but soon to be brought to life, so her condition is like sleep from which one awakens.
[9] *tell no one what had happened:* probably connected with the "messianic secret."

The Arrest, Trial and Death of Jesus*

The sufferings of Jesus at the end of his life include betrayal by his disciple Judas, denial by Peter, a trial before the Jews on religious charges, a trial before the Roman governor Pontius Pilate on civil charges, and condemnation to be crucified. Throughout their narration of these sufferings,

Mark and the other gospels portray Jesus gently accepting his suffering as the will of God, and they implicitly portray his death as a sacrifice for the sin of the world.

Immediately, while he was still speaking, Judas, one of the twelve, arrived; and with him there was a crowd with swords and clubs, from the chief

---

* Mark 14:43–50, 53–65; 15:1–41

priests, the scribes, and the elders. Now the betrayer had given them a sign, saying, "The one I will kiss is the man; arrest him and lead him away under guard." [45] So when he came, he went up to him at once and said, "Rabbi!" and kissed him. Then they laid hands on him and arrested him. But one of those who stood near drew his sword and struck the slave of the high priest, cutting off his ear. Then Jesus said to them, "Have you come out with swords and clubs to arrest me as though I were a bandit? Day after day I was with you in the temple teaching, and you did not arrest me. But let the scriptures be fulfilled." [50] All of them deserted him and fled. . . .

[53] They took Jesus to the high priest; and all the chief priests, the elders, and the scribes were assembled. Peter had followed him at a distance, right into the courtyard of the high priest; and he was sitting with the guards, warming himself at the fire. [55] Now the chief priests and the whole council were looking for testimony against Jesus to put him to death; but they found none. For many gave false testimony against him, and their testimony did not agree. Some stood up and gave false testimony against him, saying, "We heard him say, 'I will destroy this temple that is made with hands, and in three days I will build another, not made with hands.'" But even on this point their testimony did not agree. [60] Then the high priest stood up before them and asked Jesus, "Have you no answer? What is it that they testify against you?" But he was silent and did not answer. Again the high priest asked him, "Are you the Messiah, the Son of the Blessed One?" Jesus said, "I am; and 'you will see the Son of Man seated at the right hand of the Power,' and 'coming with the clouds of heaven.'"[10] Then the high priest tore his clothes and said, "Why do we still need witnesses? You have heard his blasphemy! What is your decision?" All of them condemned him as deserving death. [65] Some be-

gan to spit on him, to blindfold him, and to strike him, saying to him, "Prophesy!" The guards also took him over and beat him.

[15:1] As soon as it was morning, the chief priests held a consultation with the elders and scribes and the whole council. They bound Jesus, led him away, and handed him over to Pilate. Pilate asked him, "Are you the King of the Jews?" He answered him, "You say so." Then the chief priests accused him of many things. Pilate asked him again, "Have you no answer? See how many charges they bring against you." [5] But Jesus made no further reply, so that Pilate was amazed.

Now at the festival he used to release a prisoner for them, anyone for whom they asked. Now a man called Barabbas was in prison with the rebels who had committed murder during the insurrection. So the crowd came and began to ask Pilate to do for them according to his custom. Then he answered them, "Do you want me to release for you the King of the Jews?" [10] For he realized that it was out of jealousy that the chief priests had handed him over. But the chief priests stirred up the crowd to have him release Barabbas for them instead. Pilate spoke to them again, "Then what do you wish me to do with the man you call the King of the Jews?" They shouted back, "Crucify him!" Pilate asked them, "Why, what evil has he done?" But they shouted all the more, "Crucify him!" [15] So Pilate, wishing to satisfy the crowd, released Barabbas for them; and after flogging Jesus, he handed him over to be crucified.

Then the soldiers led him into the courtyard of the palace (that is, the governor's headquarters); and they called together the whole cohort. And they clothed him in a purple cloak; and after twisting some thorns into a crown, they put it on him. And they began saluting him, "Hail, King of the Jews!" They struck his head with a reed, spat upon him, and knelt down in homage to him. [20] After mocking him, they stripped him of the purple cloak and put his own clothes on him. Then they led him out to crucify him.

---

[10] Quoted from Daniel 7:13 in the Hebrew scriptures, with an allusion to Psalm 110:1.

They compelled a passer-by, who was coming in from the country, to carry his cross; it was Simon of Cyrene, the father of Alexander and Rufus.[11] Then they brought Jesus to the place called Golgotha (which means the place of a skull). And they offered him wine mixed with myrrh; but he did not take it. And they crucified him, and divided his clothes among them, casting lots to decide what each should take. [25] It was nine o'clock in the morning when they crucified him. The inscription of the charge against him read, "The King of the Jews." And with him they crucified two bandits, one on his right and one on his left. Those who passed by derided him, shaking their heads and saying, "Aha! You who would destroy the temple and build it in three days, [30] save yourself, and come down from the cross!" In the same way the chief priests, along with the scribes, were also mocking him among themselves and saying, "He saved others; he cannot save himself. Let the Messiah, the King of Israel, come down from the cross now, so that we may see and believe." Those who were crucified with him also taunted him.

---

[11] *Simon, Rufus:* that these names are given probably indicates that these men were known to the first readers of Mark.

When it was noon, darkness came over the whole land until three in the afternoon. At three o'clock Jesus cried out with a loud voice, "Eloi, Eloi, lema sabachthani?" which means, "My God, my God, why have you forsaken me?" [35] When some of the bystanders heard it, they said, "Listen, he is calling for Elijah."[12] And someone ran, filled a sponge with sour wine, put it on a stick, and gave it to him to drink, saying, "Wait, let us see whether Elijah will come to take him down." Then Jesus gave a loud cry and breathed his last. And the curtain of the temple was torn in two, from top to bottom. Now when the centurion, who stood facing him, saw that in this way he breathed his last, he said, "Truly this man was God's Son!"

[40] There were also women looking on from a distance; among them were Mary Magdalene, and Mary the mother of James the younger and of Joses, and Salome. These used to follow him and provided for him when he was in Galilee; and there were many other women who had come up with him to Jerusalem.

---

[12] *Elijah:* a fairly widespread Jewish belief at this time was that Elijah, the ancient Israelite prophet, would return at the end of time; compare the contemporary Jewish practice of leaving an empty seat at the Passover meal for Elijah.

The Resurrection of Jesus*

After Joseph of Arimathea buried the body of Jesus, three women from among his followers came on Sunday morning to finish the tasks of the funeral. They become the first witnesses of Jesus' resurrection. In this passage, the "young man" is an angel, and his message is that God has raised Jesus from the dead. The resurrection of Jesus and the life it brings became the center of early Christian belief. In Luke-Acts, the resurrection is followed after forty days by the ascension of Jesus to heaven.

When the sabbath was over, Mary Magdalene, and Mary the mother of James, and Salome bought spices, so that they might go and anoint him. And very early on the first day of the week, when the sun had risen, they went to the tomb. They had been saying to one another, "Who will roll away the stone for us from the entrance to the tomb?"[13] When they looked up, they saw that the stone, which was very large, had already

---

[13] *roll away the stone:* a massive disk-shaped stone has been rolled over the entrance of the tomb.

been rolled back. [5] As they entered the tomb, they saw a young man, dressed in a white robe, sitting on the right side; and they were alarmed. But he said to them, "Do not be alarmed; you are looking for Jesus of Nazareth, who was crucified. He has been raised; he is not here. Look, there is the place they laid him. But go, tell his disciples and Peter that he is going ahead of you to Galilee; there you will see him, just as he told you." So they went out and fled from the tomb, for terror and amazement had seized them; and they said nothing to anyone, for they were afraid.

The Coming of the Holy Spirit*

In dealing with the "speaking in tongues" that occurs on Pentecost day, Acts works with two traditions: first, that the apostles are speaking an actual foreign language and second, that they speak in a language not human, but one interpreted by the listeners as their own. (Modern Pentecostalism, which practices "speaking in tongues," picks up on the second tradition.) Peter's speech on this occasion explains the meaning of the Holy Spirit's coming as the fulfillment of scripture and the divine plan, bringing the presence and power of God to all in the church regardless of gender or social standing.

When the day of Pentecost had come, they were all together in one place. And suddenly from heaven there came a sound like the rush of a violent wind, and it filled the entire house where they were sitting. Divided tongues, as of fire, appeared among them, and a tongue rested on each of them. All of them were filled with the Holy Spirit and began to speak in other languages, as the Spirit gave them ability.

[5] Now there were devout Jews from every nation under heaven living in Jerusalem. And at this sound the crowd gathered and was bewildered, because each one heard them speaking in the native language of each. Amazed and astonished, they asked, "Are not all these who are speaking Galileans? And how is it that we hear, each of us, in our own native language? Parthians, Medes, Elamites, and residents of Mesopotamia,

Judea and Cappadocia, Pontus and Asia, [10] Phrygia and Pamphylia, Egypt and the parts of Libya belonging to Cyrene and visitors from Rome, both Jews and proselytes,[14] Cretans and Arabs—in our own languages we hear them speaking about God's deeds of power." All were amazed and perplexed, saying to one another, "What does this mean?" But others sneered and said, "They are filled with new wine."

But Peter, standing with the eleven, raised his voice and addressed them, "Men of Judea and all who live in Jerusalem, let this be known to you, and listen to what I say. [15] Indeed, these are not drunk, as you suppose, for it is only nine o'clock in the morning. No, this is what was spoken through the prophet Joel: 'In the last days it will be, God declares, that I will pour out my Spirit upon all flesh, and your sons and your daughters shall prophesy, and your young men shall see visions, and your old men shall dream dreams. Even upon my slaves, both men and women, in those days I will pour out my Spirit; and they shall prophesy. And I will show portents in the heaven above and signs on the earth below, blood, fire, and smoky mist. [20] The sun shall be turned to darkness and the moon to blood, before the coming of the Lord's great and glorious day. Then everyone who calls on the name of the Lord shall be saved.'"

---

* Acts 2:1–21

[14] *Jews and proselytes:* born Jews and Gentiles converted to Judaism. All the nationalities listed in this "Table of Nations" are Jews now living in Jerusalem.

Persecution of the Apostles*

The early church met opposition from the same forces that acted to do away with Jesus. The apostles' calm and confident attitude to their persecutions is underscored here, and this attitude would remain important in the next few centuries as Roman persecution of the church grew stronger. In verse 29 a theme is sounded that echoes through the history of the church: when the laws of this world and the laws of God collide, "We must obey God rather than any human authority."

When [the Jewish high council] had brought [the apostles], they had them stand before the council. The high priest questioned them, saying, "We gave you strict orders not to teach in this name, yet here you have filled Jerusalem with your teaching and you are determined to bring this man's blood on us." But Peter and the apostles answered, "We must obey God rather than any human authority. [30] The God of our ancestors raised up Jesus, whom you had killed by hanging him on a tree. God exalted him at his right hand as Leader and Savior that he might give repentance to Israel and forgiveness of sins. We are witnesses to these things, and so is the Holy Spirit whom God has given to those who obey him." When they heard this, they were enraged and wanted to kill them. But a Pharisee in the council named Gamaliel, a teacher of the law, respected by all the people, stood up and ordered the men to be put outside for a short time. [35] Then he said to them . . . [38] "Keep away from these men and let them alone; because if this plan or this undertaking is of human origin, it will fail; but if it is of God, you will not be able to overthrow them—in that case you may even be found fighting against God!" They were convinced by him, [40] and when they had called in the apostles, they had them flogged. Then they ordered them not to speak in the name of Jesus, and let them go. As they left the council, they rejoiced that they were considered worthy to suffer dishonor for the sake of the name. And every day in the temple and at home they did not cease to teach and proclaim Jesus as the Messiah.

* Acts 5:27–35, 38–42

Two Views of the Council at Jerusalem*

Whether Gentile converts to Christianity should be required to be circumcised and keep at least some of the laws of Moses was a difficult issue in early Christianity. In the first selection, the author of Acts gives his version of a "council" at Jerusalem to deal with this matter. Paul and Peter argued no; some conservative Jewish Christians, converts from the Pharisees, said yes. James the kinsman of Jesus, the leader of the Jerusalem church at this time, gave the compromise ruling: no circumcision is required of Gentile converts, but certain minimal laws of purity would be imposed. The result of this decision was that Christianity began to separate from its roots in Judaism, becoming a different religion. In the second selection, Paul gives his own version of the account, which stresses his own independence and the validity of his version of Christianity.

Then certain individuals came down from Judea and were teaching the brothers, "Unless you are circumcised according to the custom of Moses, you cannot be saved." And after Paul and Barnabas had no small dissension and debate with them, Paul and Barnabas and some of the others were appointed to go up to Jerusalem to discuss this question with the apostles and the elders. So they were sent on their way by the church, and as they passed through both Phoenicia and

* Acts 15:1–21; Galatians 2:1–10

Samaria, they reported the conversion of the Gentiles, and brought great joy to all the believers. When they came to Jerusalem, they were welcomed by the church and the apostles and the elders, and they reported all that God had done with them. [5] But some believers who belonged to the sect of the Pharisees stood up and said, "It is necessary for them to be circumcised and ordered to keep the law of Moses."

The apostles and the elders met together to consider this matter. After there had been much debate, Peter stood up and said to them, "My brothers, you know that in the early days God made a choice among you, that I should be the one through whom the Gentiles would hear the message of the good news and become believers. And God, who knows the human heart, testified to them by giving them the Holy Spirit, just as he did to us; and in cleansing their hearts by faith he has made no distinction between them and us. [10] Now therefore why are you putting God to the test by placing on the neck of the disciples a yoke that neither our ancestors nor we have been able to bear? On the contrary, we believe that we will be saved through the grace of the Lord Jesus, just as they will."

The whole assembly kept silence, and listened to Barnabas and Paul as they told of all the signs and wonders that God had done through them among the Gentiles. After they finished speaking, James replied, "My brothers, listen to me. Simeon[15] has related how God first looked favorably on the Gentiles, to take from among them a people for his name. [15] This agrees with the words of the prophets, as it is written, 'After this I will return, and I will rebuild the dwelling of David, which has fallen; from its ruins I will rebuild it, and I will set it up, so that all other peoples may seek the Lord—even all the Gentiles over whom my name has been called. Thus says the Lord, who has been making these things known from long ago.' Therefore I have reached the decision that we should not trouble those Gentiles who are turning to God, [20] but we should write to them to abstain only from things polluted by idols and from fornication and from whatever has been strangled and from blood.[16] For in every city, for generations past, Moses has had those who proclaim him, for he has been read aloud every Sabbath in the synagogues."

[Galatians 2:1] Then after fourteen years I went up again to Jerusalem with Barnabas, taking Titus along with me. I went in response to a revelation. Then I laid before them (though only in a private meeting with the acknowledged leaders) the gospel that I proclaim among the Gentiles, in order to make sure that I was not running, or had not run, in vain. But even Titus, who was with me, was not compelled to be circumcised, though he was a Greek. But because of false believers secretly brought in, who slipped in to spy on the freedom we have in Christ Jesus, so that they might enslave us—[5] we did not submit to them even for a moment, so that the truth of the gospel might always remain with you. And from those who were supposed to be acknowledged leaders (what they actually were makes no difference to me; God shows no partiality)—those leaders contributed nothing to me. On the contrary, when they saw that I had been entrusted with the gospel for the uncircumcised, just as Peter had been entrusted with the gospel for the circumcised (for he who worked through Peter making him an apostle to the circumcised also worked through me in sending me to the Gentiles), and when James and Cephas[17] and John, who were acknowledged pillars, recognized the grace that had been given to me, they gave to Barnabas and me the right hand of fellowship, agreeing that we should go to the Gentiles and they to the circumcised. [10] They asked only one thing, that we remember the poor, which was actually what I was eager to do.

---

[15] *Simeon:* Peter.

[16] *from things polluted . . . and from blood:* foods offered to idols in sacrifice and meat not ritually butchered, respectively.
[17] *Cephas:* Peter's name in its Aramaic form.

INSTITUTION

The Twelve Apostles and Their Mission*

The apostles, twelve in number to suggest the twelve tribes of ancient Israel, are named and commissioned here. Both the situation of Jesus (the restriction of this mission to the Jews) and the later church (itinerant prophets and evangelists) are reflected. This type of mission was important in the early spread of Christianity through Palestine and Syria.

Then Jesus summoned his twelve disciples and gave them authority over unclean spirits, to cast them out, and to cure every disease and every sickness. These are the names of the twelve apostles: first, Simon, also known as Peter, and his brother Andrew; James son of Zebedee, and his brother John; Philip and Bartholomew; Thomas and Matthew the tax collector; James son of Alphaeus, and Thaddaeus; Simon the Cananaean, and Judas Iscariot, the one who betrayed him.

[5] These twelve Jesus sent out with the following instructions: "Go nowhere among the Gentiles, and enter no town of the Samaritans, but go rather to the lost sheep of the house of Israel. As you go, proclaim the good news, 'The kingdom of heaven has come near.' Cure the sick, raise the dead, cleanse the lepers, cast out demons. You received without payment; give without payment. Take no gold, or silver, or copper in your belts, [10] no bag for your journey, or two tunics, or sandals, or a staff; for laborers deserve their food. Whatever town or village you enter, find out who in it is worthy, and stay there until you leave. As you enter the house, greet it.[18] If the house is worthy, let your peace come upon it; but if it is not worthy, let your peace return to you. If anyone will not welcome you or listen to your words, shake off the dust from your feet as you leave that house or town.[19] [15] Truly I tell you, it will be more tolerable for the land of Sodom and Gomorrah[20] on the day of judgment than for that town.

---

* Matthew 10:1–15

[18] *greet it:* give the inhabitants of the house a blessing, such as, "Peace be to your house."

[19] *shake the dust from your feet:* an action symbolizing condemnation for rejecting the message.

[20] *Sodom and Gomorrah:* cities destroyed by God for their wickedness (Genesis 19:1–28).

Peter as the Rock**

Jesus here renames Simon as Peter, the rock on which the church is founded. In Greek, "Peter" (Petros) is similar to "rock" (petra). Jesus gives Peter "the keys of the kingdom of heaven." Catholicism sees this act as establishing the doctrine of the papacy, that the bishop of Rome is the successor of Peter and holds universal power over the church by these "keys."

Now when Jesus came into the district of Caesarea Philippi, he asked his disciples, "Who do people say that the Son of Man is?" And they said, "Some say John the Baptist, but others Elijah, and still others Jeremiah or one of the prophets." [15] He said to them, "But who do you say that I am?" Simon Peter answered, "You are the Messiah, the Son of the living God." And Jesus answered him, "Blessed are you, Simon son of Jonah! For flesh and blood has not revealed this to you, but my Father in heaven. And I tell

---

** Matthew 16:13–20

you, you are Peter, and on this rock I will build my church, and the gates of Hades will not prevail against it. I will give you the keys of the kingdom of heaven, and whatever you bind on earth will be bound in heaven, and whatever you loose on earth will be loosed in heaven." [20] Then he sternly ordered the disciples not to tell anyone that he was the Messiah.[21]

---

[21] *not to tell anyone that he was the Messiah:* the reason for this "messianic secret" has been debated for more than a century, with little consensus among scholars.

Early and Late Pauline Teaching on Church Leadership*

In the first reading, Paul greets the many people he knows in the Roman church. He mentions many people prominent in the leadership of his churches, among whom are several women. In the second reading, probably written by a follower of Paul in the 90s, we see the beginning of the threefold office in the church: bishop, presbyter (from which the word priest *comes), and deacon. This has been the most common pattern of church office among most Christians, even when these names are not used. We can infer their duties from the following lists of qualifications. Note that both bishops and deacons in the second reading are male.*

I commend to you our sister Phoebe, a deacon of the church at Cenchreae, so that you may welcome her in the Lord as is fitting for the saints, and help her in whatever she may require from you, for she has been a benefactor of many and of myself as well. Greet Prisca and Aquila,[22] who work with me in Christ Jesus, and who risked their necks for my life, to whom not only I give thanks, but also all the churches of the Gentiles. [5] Greet also the church in their house. Greet my beloved Epaenetus, who was the first convert in Asia[23] for Christ. Greet Mary, who has worked very hard among you. Greet Adronicus

and Junia, my relatives who were in prison with me; they are prominent among the apostles, and they were in Christ before I was.

[I Timothy 3:1–13] The saying is sure: whoever aspires to the office of bishop desires a noble task. Now a bishop must be above reproach, married only once, temperate, sensible, respectable, hospitable, an apt teacher, not a drunkard, not violent but gentle, not quarrelsome, and not a lover of money. He must manage his own household well, keeping his children submissive and respectful in every way—[5] for if someone does not know how to manage his own household, how can he take care of God's church? He must not be a recent convert, or he may be puffed up with conceit and fall into the condemnation of the devil. Moreover, he must be well thought of by outsiders, so that he may not fall into disgrace and the snare of the devil.

Deacons likewise must be serious, not double-tongued, not indulging in much wine, not greedy for money; they must hold fast to the mystery of the faith with a clear conscience. [10] And let them first be tested; then, if they prove themselves blameless, let them serve as deacons. Women likewise must be serious, not slanderers, but temperate, faithful in all things.[24] Let deacons be married only once, and let them manage their children and their households well; for those who serve well as deacons gain a good standing for themselves and great boldness in the faith that is in Christ Jesus.

---

* Romans 16:1–7; I Timothy 3:1–13

[22] *Prisca and Aquila:* a wife-and-husband apostolic team who were related to the Pauline mission. That the woman is mentioned first here is probably not because of polite custom, but rather an indication that Prisca was the leading member of the team.

[23] *Asia:* the Roman province of Asia, in modern western Turkey.

[24] *Women likewise . . . all things:* Scholars debate whether these women themselves are deacons or wives of deacons.

The Eucharist*

The Eucharist ("Thanksgiving") also goes by the names "The Lord's Supper" and "Holy Communion." The first passage relates its institution during Jesus' last Passover meal, when he identified the bread and wine of the Passover with his body and blood. These were soon to be shed on the cross for the establishing of a "new covenant" of forgiveness and life. In the second passage, Jesus makes this identification more fully in a way that has had a strong influence on how Christians view the Eucharist: his body and blood nourish one to eternal life.

On the first day of Unleavened Bread the disciples came to Jesus, saying, "Where do you want us to make the preparations for you to eat the Passover?" He said, "Go into the city to a certain man, and say to him, 'The Teacher says, My time is near; I will keep the Passover at your house with my disciples.'" So the disciples did as Jesus had directed them, and they prepared the Passover meal. . . .

While they were eating, Jesus took a loaf of bread,[25] and after blessing it he broke it, gave it to the disciples, and said, "Take, eat; this is my body." Then he took a cup, and after giving thanks he gave it to them, saying, "Drink from it, all of you; for this is my blood of the covenant, which is poured out for many for the forgiveness of sins. I tell you, I will never again drink of this fruit of the vine until that day when I drink it new with you in my Father's kingdom."

[John 6:35] Jesus said to them, "I am the bread of life. Whoever comes to me will never be hun-gry, and whoever believes in me will never be thirsty. But I said to you that you have seen me and yet do not believe. Everything that the Father gives me will come to me, and anyone who comes to me I will never drive away; for I have come down from heaven, not to do my own will, but the will of him who sent me. And this is the will of him who sent me, that I should lose nothing of all that he has given me, but raise it up on the last day. [40] This is indeed the will of my Father, that all who see the Son and believe in him may have eternal life; and I will raise them up on the last day."

Then the Jews began to complain about him because he said, "I am the bread that came down from heaven." They were saying, "Is not this Jesus, the son of Joseph, whose father and mother we know? How can he now say, 'I have come down from heaven'?" Jesus answered them, "Do not complain among yourselves. No one can come to me unless drawn by the Father who sent me; and I will raise that person up on the last day. [45] It is written in the prophets, 'And they shall all be taught by God.' Everyone who has heard and learned from the Father comes to me. Not that anyone has seen the Father except the one who is from God; he has seen the Father. Very truly, I tell you, whoever believes has eternal life. I am the bread of life. Your ancestors ate the manna in the wilderness, and they died. [50] This is the bread that comes down from heaven, so that one may eat of it and not die. I am the living bread that came down from heaven. Whoever eats of this bread will live forever; and the bread that I will give for the life of the world is my flesh."

---

* Matthew 26:17–19, 26–29; John 6:35–51
[25] *a loaf of bread:* a piece of unleavened bread.

Baptism*

At the conclusion of Matthew, the triadic divine name—Father, Son, and Holy Spirit—is com-

---

* Matthew 28:16–20; Romans 6:1–11

manded to be used in the baptism of people from all the nations of the earth. In Romans 6, Paul explains that when Christians are baptized they die with Christ to sin and begin to live holy lives for God. Baptism becomes the foundation for the Christian vision of the moral life.

Now the eleven disciples went to Galilee, to the mountain to which Jesus had directed them. When they saw him, they worshiped him; but some doubted.[26] And Jesus came and said to them, "All authority in heaven and on earth has been given to me. Go therefore and make disciples of all nations, baptizing them in the name of the Father and of the Son and of the Holy Spirit, [20] and teaching them to obey everything that I have commanded you. And remember, I am with you always, to the end of the age."

[Romans 6:1] What then are we to say? Should we continue in sin in order that grace may abound? By no means! How can we who died to sin go on living in it? Do you not know that all of us who have been baptized into Christ Jesus were baptized into his death? Therefore we have been buried with him by baptism into death, so that, just as Christ was raised from the dead by the glory of the Father, so we too might walk in newness of life.

[5] For if we have been united with him in a death like his, we will certainly be united with him in a resurrection like his. We know that our old self was crucified with him so that the body of sin[27] might be destroyed, and we might no longer be enslaved to sin. For whoever has died is freed from sin. But if we have died with Christ, we believe that we will also live with him. We know that Christ, being raised from the dead, will never die again; death no longer has dominion over him. [10] The death he died, he died to sin, once for all; but the life he lives, he lives to God. So you also must consider yourselves dead to sin and alive to God in Christ Jesus.

---

[26] *some doubted:* some among the eleven disciples still doubted the reality of Jesus' resurrection.

[27] *the body of sin:* the sinful self, not the physical body.

Women in the Church*

Christianity's traditional attitude to women, which argues inconsistently for some degree of equality and subjection at the same time, has its roots in the New Testament. In the first passage, Jesus shows that women should participate with men in hearing his teaching, although this might conflict with traditional roles. In the second reading, Paul takes a much more restrictive attitude to the roles of women in the church. "Veiling" here probably refers to the length and style of a woman's hair. The third reading has been very influential in the Christian movement for equality. The last passage features the most patriarchal statement of the place of women in the church, and this passage has been very influential in the history of Christianity.

Now as they went on their way, he entered a certain village, where a woman named Martha welcomed him into her home. She had a sister named Mary, who sat at the Lord's feet and listened to what he was saying. [40] But Martha was distracted by her many tasks; so she came to him and asked, "Lord, do you not care that my sister has left me to do all the work by myself? Tell her then to help me." But the Lord answered her, "Martha, Martha, you are worried and distracted by many things; there is need of only one thing. Mary has chosen the better part, which will not be taken away from her."

[I Corinthians 11:2] I commend you because you remember me in everything and maintain the traditions just as I handed them on to you. But I want you to understand that Christ is the

---

* Luke 10:38–42; I Corinthians 11:2–16; Galatians 3:27–28; I Timothy 2:8–15

head of every man, and the husband is the head of his wife, and God is the head of Christ. Any man who prays or prophesies with something on his head disgraces his head, [5] but any woman who prays or prophesies with her head unveiled disgraces her head—it is one and the same thing as having her head shaved. For if a woman will not veil herself, then she should cut off her hair; but if it is disgraceful for a woman to have her hair cut off or to be shaved, she should wear a veil. For a man ought not to have his head veiled, since he is the image and reflection of God; but woman is the reflection of man. Indeed, man was not made from woman, but woman from man. Neither was man created for the sake of woman, but woman for the sake of man. [10] For this reason a woman ought to have a symbol of authority on her head, because of the angels. Nevertheless, in the Lord woman is not independent of man or man independent of woman. For just as woman came from man, so man comes through woman; but all things come from God. Judge for yourselves: is it proper for a woman to pray to God with her head unveiled? Does not nature itself teach you that if a man wears long hair, it is degrading to him, [15] but if a woman has long hair, it is her glory? For her hair is given to her for a covering. But if anyone is disposed to be contentious—we have no such custom, nor do the churches of God.

[Galatians 3:25–28] Now that faith has come, we are no longer subject to a disciplinarian,[28] for in Christ Jesus you are all children of God through faith. As many of you as were baptized into Christ have clothed yourselves with Christ. There is no longer Jew or Greek, there is no longer slave or free, there is no longer male and female; for all of you are one in Christ Jesus.

[I Timothy 2:8–15] I desire, then, that in every place the men should pray, lifting up holy hands without anger or argument; also that the women should dress themselves modestly and decently in suitable clothing, not with their hair braided, or with gold, pearls, or expensive clothes, [10] but with good works, as is proper for women who profess reverence for God. Let a woman learn in silence with full submission. I permit no woman to teach or to have authority over a man; she is to keep silent. For Adam was formed first, then Eve; and Adam was not deceived, but the woman was deceived and became a transgressor. [15] Yet she will be saved through childbearing, provided they continue in faith and love and holiness, with modesty.

---

[28] *disciplinarian:* the Law of Moses.

TEACHING

Creation and Revolt*

Two Genesis narratives tell of God's creation of the world: one from Priestly (P) traditions (1:1– 2:3), the other from Old Epic (J and E) traditions (2:4–25). They vary in content and style. In the first, God creates an orderly cosmos out of primeval chaos, with humankind as the capstone of creation.

In the second, the creation of humanity is the main topic. Note the different ways the two stories account for the creation of woman. Humanity falls into sin by rebelling against its Maker. God punishes the guilty in various ways, but the chief punishment for humanity is to be driven out of the garden-paradise. This account of creation and fall was the most important and fought-over biblical

---

* Genesis 1:26–2:9; 2:15–3:24

passage in argument in the ancient church between orthodox Christians and Gnostic Christians, and in modern times it looms large in debates over evolution and creation.

Then God said, "Let us make humankind in our[29] image, according to our likeness; and let them have dominion over the fish of the sea, and over the birds of the air, and over the cattle, and over all the wild animals of the earth, and over every creeping thing that creeps upon the earth." So God created humankind in his image, in the image of God he created them; male and female he created them. God blessed them, and said to them, "Be fruitful and multiply, and fill the earth and subdue it; and have dominion over the fish of the sea and over the birds of the air and over every living thing that moves upon the earth." God said, "See, I have given you every plant yielding seed that is upon the face of all the earth, and every tree with seed in its fruit; you shall have them for food. [30] And to every beast of the earth, and to every bird of the air, and to everything that creeps on the earth, everything that has the breath of life, I have given every green plant for food." And it was so. God saw everything that he had made, and indeed, it was very good. And there was evening and there was morning, the sixth day.

[2:1] Thus the heavens and the earth were finished, and all their multitude. And on the seventh day God finished the work that he had done, and he rested on the seventh day from all the work that he had done. So God blessed the seventh day and hallowed it, because on it God rested from all the work that he had done[30] in creation. These are the generations of the heavens and the earth when they were created.

In the day that the Lord God made the earth and the heavens, [5] when no plant of the field was yet in the earth and no herb of the field had yet sprung up—for the Lord God had not caused it to rain upon the earth, and there was no one to till the ground; but a stream would rise from the earth, and water the whole face of the ground—then the Lord God formed man from the dust of the ground, and breathed into his nostrils the breath of life; and the man became a living being. And the Lord God planted a garden in Eden, in the east; and there he put the man whom he had formed. Out of the ground the Lord God made to grow every tree that is pleasant to the sight and good for food, the tree of life also in the midst of the garden, and the tree of the knowledge of good and evil. . . .

[15] The Lord God took the man and put him in the garden of Eden to till it and keep it. And the Lord God commanded the man, "You may freely eat of every tree of the garden; but of the tree of the knowledge of good and evil you shall not eat, for in the day that you eat of it you shall die."

Then the Lord God said, "It is not good that the man should be alone; I will make him a helper as his partner." So out of the ground the Lord God formed every animal of the field and every bird of the air, and brought them to the man to see what he would call them; and whatever the man called every living creature, that was its name. [20] The man gave names to all cattle, and to the birds of the air, and to every animal of the field; but for the man there was not found a helper as his partner. So the Lord God caused a deep sleep to fall upon the man, and he slept; then he took one of his ribs and closed up its place with flesh. And the rib that the Lord God had taken from the man he made into a woman and brought her to the man. Then the man said, "This at last is bone of my bones and flesh of my flesh; this one shall be called Woman, for out of Man this one was taken." Therefore a man leaves his father and his mother and clings to his wife, and they become one flesh. [25] And the man and his wife were both naked, and were not ashamed.

[3:1] Now the serpent was more crafty than any other wild animal that the Lord God had

---

[29] *us, our:* God and the beings of the heavenly court. There is probably no idea of the plurality of God here.

[30] *God blessed the seventh day . . . done:* an allusion to the law of rest and renewal on the seventh day, the sabbath.

made. He said to the woman, "Did God say, 'You shall not eat from any tree in the garden'?" The woman said to the serpent, "We may eat of the fruit of the trees in the garden; but God said, 'You shall not eat of the fruit of the tree that is in the middle of the garden, nor shall you touch it, or you shall die.'" But the serpent said to the woman, "You will not die; [5] for God knows that when you eat of it your eyes will be opened, and you will be like God, knowing good and evil." So when the woman saw that the tree was good for food, and that it was a delight to the eyes, and that the tree was to be desired to make one wise, she took of its fruit and ate; and she also gave some to her husband, who was with her, and he ate. Then the eyes of both were opened, and they knew that they were naked; and they sewed fig leaves together and made loincloths for themselves.

They heard the sound of the Lord God walking in the garden at the time of the evening breeze, and the man and his wife hid themselves from the presence of the Lord God among the trees of the garden. But the Lord God called to the man, and said to him, "Where are you?" [10] He said, "I heard the sound of you in the garden, and I was afraid, because I was naked; and I hid myself." He said, "Who told you that you were naked? Have you eaten from the tree of which I commanded you not to eat?" The man said, "The woman whom you gave to be with me, she gave me fruit from the tree, and I ate." Then the Lord God said to the woman, "What is this that you have done?" The woman said, "The serpent tricked me, and I ate." The Lord God said to the serpent, "Because you have done this, cursed are

you among all animals and among all wild creatures; upon your belly you shall go, and dust you shall eat all the days of your life. [15] I will put enmity between you and the woman, and between your offspring and hers; he will strike your head, and you will strike his heel."

To the woman he said, "I will greatly increase your pangs in childbearing: in pain you shall bring forth children, yet your desire shall be for your husband, and he shall rule over you."

And to the man he said, "Because you have listened to the voice of your wife, and have eaten of the tree about which I commanded you, 'You shall not eat of it,' cursed is the ground because of you; in toil you shall eat of it all the days of your life; thorns and thistles it shall bring forth for you; and you shall eat the plants of the field. By the sweat of your face you shall eat bread until you return to the ground, for out of it you were taken; you are dust, and to dust you shall return." . . .

[20] The man named his wife Eve, because she was the mother of all living. And the Lord God made garments of skins for the man and for his wife, and clothed them.

Then the Lord God said, "See, the man has become like one of us, knowing good and evil; and now, he might reach out his hand and take also from the tree of life, and eat, and live forever"—therefore the Lord God sent him forth from the garden of Eden, to till the ground from which he was taken. He drove out the man; and at the east of the garden of Eden he placed the cherubim, and a sword flaming and turning to guard the way to the tree of life.

The Oneness of God*

In Judaism, this passage is known as the Shema, "Hear," and is a statement of the oneness of God and the duty of obeying God alone in all of life.

---

* Deuteronomy 6:4–9

This and other Old Testament affirmations of monotheism became very important in the early church as Christianity struggled to articulate its doctrine of the Trinity while still maintaining a foundation of the oneness of God.

Hear, O Israel: The Lord is our God, the Lord alone. [5] You shall love the Lord your God with all your heart, and with all your soul, and with all your might. Keep these words that I am commanding you today in your heart. Recite them to your children and talk about them when you are at home and when you are away, when you lie down and when you rise. Bind them as a sign on your hand, fix them as an emblem on your forehead, and write them on the doorposts of your house and on your gates.

The Parables of Jesus*

The parables were Jesus' distinctive form of teaching. Parables are stories that compare an experience in everyday life with some aspect of religious life, especially life in the Kingdom of God. The first passage is a collection of parables made by Mark or in the oral tradition that reached him. Many scholars view the interpretation of the parable of the sower in the third paragraph as not from Jesus, but from the early church. In the second passage, Jesus uses a story of a Good Samaritan to illustrate his ideal of love for the stranger who is really a "neighbor."

Again he began to teach beside the sea. Such a very large crowd gathered around him that he got into a boat on the sea and sat there, while the whole crowd was beside the sea on the land. He began to teach them many things in parables, and in his teaching he said to them: "Listen! A sower went out to sow. And as he sowed, some seed fell on the path, and the birds came and ate it up. [5] Other seed fell on rocky ground, where it did not have much soil, and it sprang up quickly, since it had no depth of soil. And when the sun rose, it was scorched; and since it had no root, it withered away. Other seed fell among thorns, and the thorns grew up and choked it, and it yielded no grain. Other seed fell into good soil and brought forth grain, growing up and increasing and yielding thirty and sixty and a hundred-fold." And he said, "Let anyone with ears to hear listen!"

[10] When he was alone, those who were around him along with the twelve asked him about the parables. And he said to them, "To you has been given the secret of the kingdom of God, but for those outside, everything comes in parables; in order that 'they may indeed look, but not perceive, and may indeed listen, but not understand; so that they may not turn again and be forgiven.'"

And he said to them, "Do you not understand this parable? Then how will you understand all the parables? The sower sows the word. [15] These are the ones on the path where the word is sown: when they hear, Satan immediately comes and takes away the word that is sown in them. And these are the ones sown on rocky ground: when they hear the word, they immediately receive it with joy. But they have no root, and endure only for a while; then, when trouble or persecution arises on account of the word, immediately they fall away. And others are those sown among the thorns: these are the ones who hear the word, but the cares of the world, and the lure of wealth, and the desire for other things come in and choke the word, and it yields nothing. [20] And these are the ones sown on the good soil: they hear the word and accept it and bear fruit, thirty and sixty and a hundred-fold."

He said to them, "Is a lamp brought in to be put under the bushel basket, or under the bed, and not on the lampstand? For there is nothing hidden, except to be disclosed; nor is anything secret, except to come to light. Let anyone with ears to hear listen!" And he said to them, "Pay attention to what you hear; the measure you give will be the measure you get, and still more will be given you. [25] For to those who have, more will be given; and from those who have nothing, even what they have will be taken away."

* Mark 4:1–34; Luke 10:29–37

He also said, "The kingdom of God is as if someone would scatter seed on the ground, and would sleep and rise night and day, and the seed would sprout and grow, he does not know how. The earth produces of itself, first the stalk, then the head, then the full grain in the head. But when the grain is ripe, at once he goes in with his sickle, because the harvest has come."

[30] He also said, "With what can we compare the kingdom of God, or what parable will we use for it? It is like a mustard seed, which, when sown upon the ground, is the smallest of all the seeds on earth; yet when it is sown it grows up and becomes the greatest of all shrubs, and puts forth large branches, so that the birds of the air can make nests in its shade."

With many such parables he spoke the word to them, as they were able to hear it; he did not speak to them except in parables,[31] but he explained everything in private to his disciples.

---

[31] *except in parables:* that is, that Jesus' teaching was characteristically illustrated by parables, not that the parable was his only form of teaching.

[Luke 10:29–37] But wanting to justify himself, [the lawyer] asked Jesus, "And who is my neighbor?" [30] Jesus replied, "A man was going down from Jerusalem to Jericho, and fell into the hands of robbers, who stripped him, beat him and went away, leaving him half dead. Now by chance a priest was going down that road; and when he saw him, he passed by on the other side. So likewise a Levite, when he came to the place and saw him, passed by on the other side. But a Samaritan while traveling came near him; and when he saw him, he was moved with pity. He went to him and bandaged his wounds, having poured oil and wine on them. Then he put him on his own animal, brought him to an inn, and took care of him. [35] The next day he took out two denarii, gave them to the innkeeper, and said, 'Take care of him; and when I come back, I will repay you whatever more you spend.' Which of these three, do you think, was a neighbor to the man who fell into the hands of the robbers?" He said, "The one who showed him mercy." Jesus said to him, "Go and do likewise."

The Word Became Human*

This hymn to Christ as the divine Word made human is perhaps the New Testament's most exalted view of the savior. Largely on the strength of John's gospel in the early church, with help from some other writers (especially Paul), the early church came to see the divine nature of Jesus as the divine Son from all eternity. This main theme alternates with a secondary theme, that John the Baptist is not the messiah.

In the beginning was the Word, and the Word was with God, and the Word was God. He was in the beginning with God. All things came into

---

* John 1:1–18

being through him, and without him not one thing came into being. What has come into being in him was life, and the life was the light of all people. [5] The light shines in the darkness, and the darkness did not overcome it.

There was a man sent from God, whose name was John. He came as a witness to testify to the light, so that all might believe through him. He himself was not the light, but he came to testify to the light. The true light, which enlightens everyone, was coming into the world. [10] He was in the world, and the world came into being through him; yet the world did not know him. He came to what was his own, and his own people did not accept him. But to all who received him, who believed in his name, he gave power to become children of God, who were born, not of blood or of the will of the flesh or of the will of man, but of God.

And the Word became flesh and lived among us, and we have seen his glory, the glory as of a father's only son, full of grace and truth. [15] (John testified to him and cried out, "This was he of whom I said, 'He who comes after me ranks ahead of me because he was before me.'") From his fullness we have all received, grace upon grace. The law indeed was given through Moses; grace and truth came through Jesus Christ. No one has ever seen God. It is God the only Son, who is close to the Father's heart, who has made him known.

Attack on Gnosis*

*Already in the first century the movement called **Gnosticism,** which taught salvation by secret knowledge (Greek gnosis), was threatening the Christian movement. Some Gnostics within the church argued that Jesus was not fully human or "has come in the flesh." This passage places a premium on discerning between truth and error. The "spirits" are supernatural powers, both good and evil, that accompany the two main confessions about Jesus Christ delineated here.*

Beloved, do not believe every spirit, but test the spirits to see whether they are from God; for many false prophets have gone out into the world. By this you know the Spirit of God: every spirit that confesses that Jesus Christ has come in the flesh is from God, and every spirit that does not confess Jesus is not from God. And this is the spirit of the antichrist, of which you have heard that it is coming; and now it is already in the world. Little children, you are from God, and have conquered them; for the one who is in you is greater than the one who is in the world. [5] They are from the world; therefore what they say is from the world, and the world listens to them. We are from God. Whoever knows God listens to us, and whoever is not from God does not listen to us. From this we know the spirit of truth and the spirit of error.

---

* I John 4:1–6

Results of Justification**

Justification *is God's act of making believers righteous through faith in the crucified and resurrected Jesus. In this justification, believers are reconciled to God. Protestant churches have used this and similar passages to support their leading doctrines of justification by faith alone rather than through human obedience to religious law.*

Therefore, since we are justified by faith, we have peace with God through our Lord Jesus Christ, through whom we have obtained access to this grace in which we stand; and we boast in our hope of sharing the glory of God. And not only that, but we also boast in our sufferings, knowing that suffering produces endurance, and endurance produces character, and character produces hope, [5] and hope does not disappoint us, because God's love has been poured into our hearts through the Holy Spirit that has been given to us. For while we were still weak, at the right time Christ died for the ungodly. Indeed, rarely will anyone die for a righteous person—though perhaps for a good person someone

---

** Romans 5:1–11

might actually dare to die. But God proves his love for us in that while we still were sinners Christ died for us. Much more surely then, now that we have been justified by his blood, will we be saved through him from the wrath of God. [10] For if while we were enemies, we were reconciled to God through the death of his Son, much more surely, having been reconciled, will we be saved by his life.[32] But more than that, we even boast in God through our Lord Jesus Christ, through whom we have now received reconciliation.

---

[32] *his life:* Jesus' eternal life after his resurrection.

The End of Time*

Many New Testament teachings about the end of time are taken from Judaism and adapted to Christianity. In the first passage, Matthew relates the teaching of Jesus about his role as judge at the final judgment. In the second, Revelation presents in striking apocalyptic style dreams and visions about the end.

[Jesus said:] "When the Son of Man comes in his glory, and all the angels with him, then he will sit on the throne of his glory. All the nations will be gathered before him, and he will separate people one from another as a shepherd separates the sheep from the goats, and he will put the sheep at his right hand and the goats at the left. Then the king will say to those at his right hand, 'Come, you that are blessed by my Father, inherit the kingdom prepared for you from the foundation of the world; [35] for I was hungry and you gave me food, I was thirsty and you gave me something to drink, I was a stranger and you welcomed me, I was naked and you gave me clothing, I was sick and you took care of me, I was in prison and you visited me.'

"Then the righteous will answer him, 'Lord, when was it that we saw you hungry and gave you food, or thirsty and gave you something to drink? And when was it that we saw you a stranger and welcomed you, or naked and gave you clothing? And when was it that we saw you sick or in prison and visited you?' [40] And the king will answer them, 'Truly I tell you, just as you did it to one of the least of these who are members of my family, you did it to me.' Then he will say to those at his left hand, 'You that are accursed, depart from me into the eternal fire prepared for the devil and his angels; for I was hungry and you gave me no food, I was thirsty and you gave me nothing to drink, I was a stranger and you did not welcome me, naked and you did not give me clothing, sick and in prison and you did not visit me.' Then they also will answer, 'Lord, when was it that we saw you hungry or thirsty or a stranger or naked or sick or in prison, and did not take care of you?' [45] Then he will answer them, 'Truly I tell you, just as you did not do it to one of the least of these, you did not do it to me.' And these will go away into eternal punishment, but the righteous into eternal life."

[Revelation 20:1] Then I saw an angel coming down from heaven, holding in his hand the key to the bottomless pit and a great chain. He seized the dragon, that ancient serpent, who is the Devil and Satan, and bound him for a thousand years, and threw him into the pit, and locked and sealed it over him, so that he would deceive the nations no more, until the thousand years were ended. After that he must be let out for a little while. Then I saw thrones, and those seated on them were given authority to judge. I also saw the souls of those who had been beheaded for their testimony to Jesus and for the word of God. They had not worshiped the beast or its image

---

* Matthew 25:31–46; Revelation 20:1–21:4

and had not received its mark on their foreheads or their hands. They came to life and reigned with Christ a thousand years. [5] (The rest of the dead did not come to life until the thousand years were ended.) This is the first resurrection. Blessed and holy are those who share in the first resurrection. Over these the second death has no power, but they will be priests of God and of Christ, and they will reign with him a thousand years.

When the thousand years are ended, Satan will be released from his prison and will come out to deceive the nations at the four corners of the earth, Gog and Magog,[33] in order to gather them for battle; they are as numerous as the sands of the sea. They marched up over the breadth of the earth and surrounded the camp of the saints and the beloved city. And fire came down from heaven and consumed them. [10] And the devil who had deceived them was thrown into the lake of fire and sulfur, where the beast and the false prophet were, and they will be tormented day and night forever and ever.

Then I saw a great white throne and the one who sat on it; the earth and the heaven fled from his presence; and no place was found for them. And I saw the dead, great and small, standing before the throne, and books were opened. Also another book was opened, the book of life. And the dead were judged according to their works, as recorded in the books. And the sea gave up the dead that were in it, Death and Hades[34] gave up the dead that were in them, and all were judged according to what they had done. Then Death and Hades were thrown into the lake of fire. This is the second death, the lake of fire; [15] and anyone whose name was not found written in the book of life was thrown into the lake of fire.

[21:1] Then I saw a new heaven and a new earth; for the first heaven and the first earth had passed away, and the sea was no more. And I saw the holy city, the new Jerusalem, coming down out of heaven from God, prepared as a bride adorned for her husband. And I heard a loud voice from the throne saying, "See, the home of God is among mortals. He will dwell with them as their God; they will be his peoples, and God himself will be with them; he will wipe every tear from their eyes. Death will be no more; mourning and crying and pain will be no more, for the first things have passed away."

---

[33] *Gog and Magog:* nations allied with Satan to oppose the coming God's kingdom. In Ezekiel 38–39, these are probably code words for the nation of Babylon, which in the book of *Revelation* is code in turn for Rome.

[34] *Death and Hades* (Hell) are personified in this passage.

ETHICS

The Ten Commandments*

The Ten Commandments (also called the Decalogue) lead off the series of laws given by God to Israel at Mount Sinai after the Exodus from Egypt. The first group of commandments, up through false swearing, deals with humanity's duty to God; the last group deals with person-to-person obligations. Of all ancient laws (Jewish or Greco-Roman) that have influenced the moral structure of Christianity, the Ten Commandments are the most influential.

---

* Exodus 20:1–19

Then God spoke all these words: I am the Lord your God, who brought you out of the land of Egypt, out of the house of slavery; you shall have no other gods before me.

You shall not make for yourself an idol, whether in the form of anything that is in heaven above, or that is on the earth beneath, or that is in the water under the earth. [5] You shall not bow down to them or worship them; for I the Lord your God am a jealous God, punishing children for the iniquity of parents, to the third and the fourth generation of those who reject me, but showing steadfast love to the thousandth generation of those who love me and keep my commandments.

You shall not make wrongful use of the name of the Lord your God, for the Lord will not acquit anyone who misuses his name.

Remember the Sabbath day, and keep it holy. Six days you shall labor and do all your work. [10] But the seventh day is a Sabbath to the Lord your God; you shall not do any work—you, your son or your daughter, your male or female slave, your livestock, or the alien resident in your towns. For in six days the Lord made heaven and earth, the sea, and all that is in them, but rested the sev-

enth day; therefore the Lord blessed the Sabbath day and consecrated it.

Honor your father and your mother, so that your days may be long in the land that the Lord your God is giving you.

You shall not murder.

You shall not commit adultery.

[15] You shall not steal.

You shall not bear false witness against your neighbor.

You shall not covet your neighbor's house; you shall not covet your neighbor's wife, or male or female slave, or ox, or donkey, or anything that belongs to your neighbor.

The Sermon on the Mount*

The Sermon on the Mount is the Gospels' longest collection of the moral teachings of Jesus. It is largely a collection by the gospel writer, probably drawing on an early collection of Jesus' sayings called by modern scholars the Quelle *("source") and also on special material found only in Matthew. The sermon contains his understanding of Jesus' teaching on what it is to follow Jesus. The themes are many and varied: blessings on obedience, the law of Moses, the practice of piety, use of possessions, and following Jesus' words. The wording is taken (with a few slight editorial changes) from the King James Version (1611), the literary qualities of which the New Revised Standard Version has tried to retain.*

And seeing the multitudes, he went up into a mountain; and when he was set, his disciples came unto him. And he opened his mouth and taught them, saying, "Blessed are the poor in spirit, for theirs is the kingdom of heaven. Blessed are they that mourn, for they shall be comforted. Blessed are the meek,[35] for they shall inherit the earth. Blessed are they who hunger and thirst af-

ter righteousness, for they shall be filled. Blessed are the merciful, for they shall obtain mercy. Blessed are the pure in heart, for they shall see God. Blessed are the peacemakers, for they shall be called the children of God. Blessed are they who are persecuted for righteousness' sake, for theirs is the kingdom of heaven. Blessed are you, when men shall revile you, and persecute you, and shall say all manner of evil against you falsely, for my sake. Rejoice, and be exceeding glad; for great is your reward in heaven; for so persecuted they the prophets which were before you.

"You are the salt of the earth; but if the salt has lost its savor, wherewith shall it be salted? It is thenceforth good for nothing, but to be cast out and to be trodden under foot by men. You are the light of the world. A city that is set on a hill cannot be hid. Neither do men light a candle, and put it under a bushel, but on a candlestick; and it giveth light unto all that are in the house. Let your light so shine before men, that they may see your good works, and glorify your Father which is in heaven.

"Think not that I am come to destroy the law, or the prophets; I am not come to destroy, but to fulfill. For verily I say unto you, till heaven

---

* Matthew 5–7

[35] *meek*: humble.

and earth pass, one jot or one tittle [36] shall in no wise pass from the law, till all be fulfilled. Whosoever therefore shall break one of these least commandments, and shall teach men so, he shall be called the least in the kingdom of heaven; but whosoever shall do and teach them, the same shall be called great in the kingdom of heaven. For I say to you, that except your righteousness shall exceed the scribes and Pharisees, you shall in no case enter in the kingdom of heaven.

"You have heard that it was said by them of old time, thou shalt not kill; and whosoever shall kill shall be in danger of the judgment. But I say to you, that whosoever is angry with his brother without cause shall be in danger of the judgment; and whosoever shall say to his brother, Raca, shall be in danger of the council; but whosoever shall say, thou fool, shall be in danger of hell fire. Therefore if thou bringest thy gift to the altar, and there rememberest that thy brother hath aught against thee; leave there thy gift before the altar, and go thy way; first be reconciled to thy brother, and then come and offer thy gift. Agree with thine adversary quickly, while thou art in the way with him; lest at any time the adversary deliver thee to the judge, and the judge deliver thee to the officer, and thou be cast in prison. Verily I say unto thee, thou shalt by no means come out, till thou has paid the uttermost farthing.

"You have hear that it was said by them of old time, thou shalt not commit adultery. But I say unto you, that whosoever looketh on a woman to lust after her hath committed adultery with her already in his heart. If thy right eye offend thee, pluck it out, and cast it from thee; for it is profitable for thee that one of thy members should perish, and not that thy whole body should be cast into hell. And if thy right hand offend thee, cut it off, and cast it from thee; for it is profitable for thee that one of thy members should perish, and not that thy whole body should be cast into hell.

"It hath been said, whoever shall put away his wife, let him give her a writing of divorcement;

but I say unto you, that whoever shall put away his wife, save for the cause of fornication, causeth her to commit adultery; and whosoever shall marry her that is divorced committeth adultery.

"Again, you have heard that it hath been said by them of old time, thou shalt not forswear thyself, [37] but shalt perform unto the Lord thine oaths. But I say unto you, Swear not at all; neither by heaven, for it is God's throne; nor by the earth, for it is his footstool; neither by Jerusalem, for it is the city of the great King. Neither shalt thou swear by thy head, because thou canst not make one hair white or black. But let your communication be Yea, yea, Nay, nay; whatsoever is more than these cometh of evil.

"You have heard that it hath been said, an eye for an eye, and a tooth for a tooth. But I say unto you, resist not evil. Whosoever shall smite thee on thy right cheek, turn to him the other also. And if any man will sue thee at the law, and take away thy coat, let him have thy cloak also. And whoever shall compel thee to go a mile, go with him twain. Give to him that asketh thee, and from him that would borrow of thee turn not thou away.

"You have heard that it hath been said, thou shalt love thy neighbor, and hate thine enemy. But I say unto you, love your enemies, bless them that curse you, do good to them that hate you, and pray for them which spitefully use you, and persecute you. Then you may be children of your Father who is in heaven; for he maketh his sun to rise upon the evil and the good, and sendeth rain on the just and on the unjust. For if you love them which love you, what reward have you? Do not even the publicans [38] the same? And if you salute only your brethren, what more are you doing than others? Do not even the Gentiles do the same? Be perfect, therefore, even as your Father in heaven is perfect. [39]

[6:1] "Take heed that you do not your alms before men, to be seen by them; otherwise you

---

[36] *Jot . . . tittle:* the smallest markings in written Hebrew.

[37] *forswear thyself:* swear falsely.

[38] *publicans:* tax collectors.

[39] *perfect:* not sinless, but mature and complete.

have no reward from your Father which is in heaven. Therefore when you doest alms, do not sound a trumpet before thee, as the hypocrites [40] do in the synagogues and in the streets, that they have glory from men. Verily I say to you, they have their reward. But when thou doest alms, do not let thy left hand know what right hand is doing, so that thy alms may in secret; and thy Father who seeth in secret shall reward thee openly.

[5] "And when thou prayest, be not like the hypocrites; for they love to pray standing in the synagogues and at the street corners, that they may be seen by men. Verily I say unto you, they have their reward. But whenever thou prayest, go into thy closet and shut the door and pray to thy Father who is in secret; and thy Father who sees in secret shall reward thee openly.

"But when you pray, use not vain repetitions as the heathen do; for they think that they shall be heard for their many words. Be not ye like unto them, for your Father knoweth what things ye have need of, before ye ask him. After this manner pray: [41]

Our Father which art in heaven,
hallowed be thy name.
[10] Thy kingdom come.
Thy will be done in earth as it is in heaven.
Give us this day our daily bread.
And forgive us our debts,
    as we forgive our debtors.
And lead us not into temptation,
    but deliver us from evil.
For thine is the kingdom, and the power, and
    the glory, for ever. Amen.

For if you forgive men their trespasses, your heavenly Father shall also forgive you; [15] but if you do not forgive men, neither will your Father forgive your trespasses.

"Moreover when you fast, be not, like the hypocrites, of a dismal countenance; for they disfigure their faces so they may appear unto men to fast. Verily I say unto you, they have their reward. But thou, when thou fastest, anoint thine head and wash thy face, that thy fasting may not to men, but to thy Father which is in secret; and thy Father who sees in secret shall reward thee openly.

"Lay not up for yourselves treasures on earth, where moth and rust doth corrupt, where thieves break through and steal; [20] but lay up for yourselves treasures in heaven, where neither moth nor rust doth corrupt, and where thieves do not break through nor steal. For where your treasure is, there shall your heart be also.

"The eye is the light of the body. [42] If therefore thine eye be single, [43] thy whole body shall be full of light. But if thine eye be evil, thy whole body shall be full of darkness. If therefore the light that is in thee be darkness, how great is that darkness!

"No man can serve two masters; for either he will hate the one and love the other, or else he will hold to the one and despise the other. You cannot serve God and mammon. [44]

[25] "Therefore I say unto you, take no thought [45] for thy life, what you shall eat or what you shall drink; nor for your body, what you shall put on. Is not life more than meat, and the body than raiment? Behold the fowls of the air; they sow not, neither do they reap, nor gather into barns; yet your heavenly Father feedeth them. Are you not much better than they? Which of you by worrying can add one cubit to his stature? And why take you thought about clothing? Consider the lilies of the field, how they grow; they toil not, neither do they spin: yet I say unto you, that even Solomon in all his glory was not arrayed like one of these. [30] Therefore, if God so

---

[40] *hypocrites:* not those who are evil on the inside and yet act righteously, but those who are basically good yet have moral faults that mar their goodness.

[41] *pray this way:* Jesus gives this prayer as a model; prayer should be full yet brief. That some English-speaking Christians say "debts" and others "trespasses" comes from different English versions of the Bible.

[42] *eye:* probably the heart as the seat of emotions and thought; perhaps the conscience.

[43] *single:* healthy.

[44] *Mammon:* wealth.

[45] *take no thought:* do not worry.

clothe the grass of the field, which today is, and tomorrow is cast into the oven, shall he not much more clothe you, O you of little faith? Therefore take no thought, saying, 'What shall we eat?' or 'What shall we drink?' or 'Wherewithal shall we be clothed?' For after all these things the Gentiles seek; and thy heavenly Father knoweth that you have need of all these things. But seek you first the kingdom of God and his righteousness, and all these things shall be added unto you. Take no thought about the morrow, for the morrow shall take thought for the things of itself. Sufficient unto the day is the evil thereof.

[7:1] "Judge not, that you be not judged. For with the judgment you make you shall be judged, and the measure you mete, it shall be meted to you again. Why beholdest thou the mote[46] in thy neighbor's eye, but considerest not the beam in thine own eye? Or how wilt thou say to thy brother, 'Let me pull out the mote from thine eye,' and behold, a beam is in thine own eye? [5] Thou hypocrite, first cast out the beam from thine own eye, and then thou shalt see clearly to take the mote out of thy brother's eye.

"Give not what is holy unto the dogs; neither cast your pearls before swine, lest they trample them under foot and turn and rend you.

"Ask, and it shall be given you; seek, and you shall find; knock, and it shall be opened for you. For everyone who asketh receiveth, and he that seeketh findeth, and him that knocketh, it shall be opened. Or what man is there among you, whom if his son ask for bread, will he give him a stone? [10] Or if he asks for a fish, will he give a him a serpent? If you then, being evil, know how to give good gifts unto your children, how much more shall thy Father in heaven give good things to them that ask him!

"Therefore all things whatsoever you would that men should do to you, do you even so to them; for this is the law and the prophets.[47]

"Enter in at the strait gate; for wide is the gate, and broad is the way, that leadeth to destruction, and there are many who go in thereat. Because strait is the gate, and narrow is the way, that leadeth unto life, and few there be who find it.

[15] "Beware of false prophets, which come to you in sheep's clothing but inwardly are ravening wolves. You shall know them by their fruits. Do men gather grapes from thorns, or figs from thistles? Even so every good tree bringeth forth good fruit; but a corrupt tree bringeth forth evil fruit. A good tree bring forth evil fruit, neither can a corrupt tree bring forth good fruit. Every tree that does not bring forth good fruit is cut down and cast into the fire. [20] Thus you by their fruits you shall know them.

"Not everyone that saith to me, Lord, Lord, shall enter the kingdom of heaven; but he that doeth the will of my Father in heaven. Many will say to me on that day, Lord, Lord, have we not prophesied in thy name, and cast out devils in thy name, and done many deeds of power in thy name? Then I will declare to them, I never knew you; depart from me, you that work iniquity.

"Therefore whosoever heareth these sayings of mine and doeth them will be like a wise man who built his house upon a rock. [25] The rain descended, the floods came, and the winds blew and beat upon that house; and it did not fall, because it had been founded upon a rock. And every one who heareth these sayings of mine and doeth them not shall be like a foolish man who built his house on sand. The rain descended, and the floods came, and the winds blew and beat upon that house, and it fell; and great was its fall!"

And it came to pass, when Jesus had ended these sayings, the people were astonished at his doctrine; for he taught them as one having authority, and not as the scribes.[48]

---

[46] *mote:* speck.

[47] This is the "Golden Rule." Expressed in its positive form, it is the essence of self-giving love.

[48] *not as their scribes:* Jewish scribes taught on the authority of other scribal experts; Jesus teaches on his own authority.

Love*

This "Hymn to Love," perhaps written by Paul or adapted by him for use in this letter, extols love as the greatest spiritual gift. It has three sections in these three paragraphs: first, it contrasts love with other spiritual gifts; second, it describes love; third, it extols the persistence of love.

If I speak in the tongues of mortals and of angels, but do not have love, I am a noisy gong or a clanging cymbal. And if I have prophetic powers, and understand all mysteries and all knowledge, and if I have all faith, so as to remove mountains, but do not have love, I am nothing. If I give away all my possessions, and if I hand over my body so that I may boast, but do not have love, I gain nothing.

Love is patient; love is kind; love is not envious or boastful or arrogant [5] or rude. It does not insist on its own way; it is not irritable or resentful; it does not rejoice in wrongdoing, but rejoices in the truth. It bears all things, believes all things, hopes all things, endures all things.

Love never ends. But as for prophecies, they will come to an end; as for tongues, they will cease; as for knowledge, it will come to an end. For we know only in part, and we prophesy only in part; [10] but when the complete comes, the partial will come to an end. When I was a child, I spoke like a child, I thought like a child, I reasoned like a child; when I became an adult, I put an end to childish ways. For now we see in a mirror, dimly, but then we will see face to face. Now I know only in part; then I will know fully, even as I have been fully known. And now faith, hope, and love abide, these three; and the greatest of these is love.

* I Corinthians 13:1–13

Ethics in the Christian Household*

This discussion of ethics in the Christian household contains instructions for wives, husbands, children, parents, slaves and masters. It presupposes the legitimacy of the household structure of the times but seeks to transform it with the Christian ethic. Christians unquestioningly accepted the legitimacy of this moral structure until quite recent times, when first slavery was done away with, and now the submission of women is under attack in many parts of the world.

Be subject to one another out of reverence for Christ. Wives, be subject to your husbands as you are to the Lord. For the husband is the head of the wife just as Christ is the head of the church, the body of which he is the Savior. Just as the church is subject to Christ, so also wives ought to be, in everything, to their husbands. [25] Husbands, love your wives, just as Christ loved the church and gave himself up for her, in order to make her holy by cleansing her with the washing of water by the word, so as to present the church to himself in splendor, without a spot or wrinkle or anything of the kind—yes, so that she may be holy and without blemish. In the same way, husbands should love their wives as they do their own bodies. He who loves his wife loves himself. For no one ever hates his own body, but he nourishes and tenderly cares for it, just as Christ does for the church, [30] because we are members of his body. For this reason a man will leave his father and mother and be joined to his wife, and the two will become one flesh. This is a great mystery, and I am applying it to Christ and the church. Each of you, however, should love his wife as himself, and a wife should respect her husband.

* Ephesians 5:21–6:9

[6:1] Children, obey your parents in the Lord, for this is right. "Honor your father and mother"—this is the first commandment with a promise: "so that it may be well with you and you may live long on the earth." And, fathers, do not provoke your children to anger, but bring them up in the discipline and instruction of the Lord.

[5] Slaves, obey your earthly masters with fear and trembling, in singleness of heart, as you obey Christ; not only while being watched, and in order to please them, but as slaves of Christ, doing the will of God from the heart. Render service with enthusiasm, as to the Lord and not to men and women, knowing that whatever good we do, we will receive the same again from the Lord, whether we are slaves or free. And, masters, do the same to them. Stop threatening them, for you know that both of you have the same Master in heaven, and with him there is no partiality.

RELATIONS

Christians and Gentile Life*

In Romans, Paul argues that both Gentile and Jew (i.e., all people) are under God's judgment. Paul's view of Gentile life was largely inherited from the Jewish view of Gentiles. Gentiles have turned away from God's self-revelation in nature, and from this denial of the one, holy God all sorts of evils have come. In the second passage, Paul argues that Christians should keep themselves separate from the worship of other gods but that meat offered in sacrifice to these gods and later sold in temple markets or restaurants may be eaten, if it can be done in good conscience and in love toward other Christians. This is a rather liberal attitude toward "idol meat"; in subsequent centuries, when the contest between Christianity and the Roman Empire became intense, Christians were forbidden to consume it. In the third passage, the author of Luke-Acts presents Paul as an early Christian philosopher as he argues with other Greek philosophers about the one God. Later Christian apologists of both ancient and modern times would also use the reason, knowledge, and poetry of their times to explain Christianity to its "cultured despisers."

For the wrath of God is revealed from heaven against all ungodliness and wickedness of those who by their wickedness suppress the truth. For what can be known about God is plain to them, because God has shown it to them. [20] Ever since the creation of the world his eternal power and divine nature, invisible though they are, have been understood and seen through the things he has made. So they are without excuse; for though they knew God, they did not honor him as God or give thanks to him, but they became futile in their thinking, and their senseless minds were darkened. Claiming to be wise, they became fools; and they exchanged the glory of the immortal God for images resembling a mortal human being or birds or four-footed animals or reptiles.

Therefore God gave them up in the lusts of their hearts to impurity, to the degrading of their bodies among themselves, [25] because they exchanged the truth about God for a lie and worshiped and served the creature rather than the Creator, who is blessed forever! Amen. For this reason God gave them up to degrading passions. Their women exchanged natural intercourse for unnatural, and in the same way also the men, giving up natural intercourse with women, were consumed with passion for one another. Men committed shameless acts with men and received in their own persons the due penalty for their error.

And since they did not see fit to acknowledge God, God gave them up to a debased mind and

---

* Romans 1:18–32; I Corinthians 8; Acts 17:22–28

to things that should not be done. They were filled with every kind of wickedness, evil covetousness, malice. Full of envy, murder, strife, deceit, craftiness, they are gossips, [30] slanderers, God-haters, insolent, haughty, boastful, inventors of evil, rebellious toward parents, foolish, faithless, heartless, ruthless. They know God's decree, that those who practice such things deserve to die—yet they do not only do them but even applaud others who practice them.

[I Corinthians 8:4] As to the eating of food offered to idols, we know that "no idol in the world really exists," and that "there is no God but one." [5] Indeed, even though there may be so-called gods in heaven or on earth—as in fact there are many gods and many lords—yet for us there is one God, the Father, from whom are all things and for whom we exist, and one Lord, Jesus Christ, through whom are all things and through whom we exist.

It is not everyone, however, who has this knowledge. Since some have become so accustomed to idols until now, they still think of the food they eat as food offered to an idol; and their conscience, being weak, is defiled. "Food will not bring us close to God." We are no worse off if we do not eat, and no better off if we do. But take care that this liberty of yours does not somehow become a stumbling block to the weak. [10] For if others see you, who possess knowledge, eating in the temple of an idol, might they not, since their conscience is weak, be encouraged to the point of eating food sacrificed to idols? So by your knowledge those weak believers for whom Christ died are destroyed. But when you thus sin against members of your family, and wound

their conscience when it is weak, you sin against Christ. Therefore, if food is a cause of their falling, I will never eat meat, so that I may not cause one of them to fall.

[Acts 17:22–28] Then Paul stood in front of the Areopagus and said, "Athenians, I see how extremely religious you are in every way. For as I went through the city and looked carefully at the objects of your worship, I found among them an altar with the inscription, 'To an unknown god.' What therefore you worship as unknown, this I proclaim to you. The God who made the world and everything in it, he who is Lord of heaven and earth, does not live in shrines made by human hands, [25] nor is he served by human hands, as though he needed anything, since he himself gives to all mortals life and breath and all things. From one ancestor he made all nations to inhabit the whole earth, and he allotted the times of their existence and the boundaries of the places where they would live, so that they would search for God and perhaps grope for him and find him—though indeed he is not far from each one of us. For 'In him we live and move and have our being'; as even some of your poets have said, 'For we too are his offspring.' Since we are God's offspring, we ought not to think that the deity is like gold, or silver, or stone, an image formed by the art and imagination of human beings. While God has overlooked the times of human ignorance, now he commands all people everywhere to repent, because he has fixed a day on which he will have the world judged in righteousness by a man whom he has appointed, and of this he has given assurance to all by raising him from the dead."

Paul on Judaism*

In this selection, Paul argues that Jews, like Gentiles, are in need of salvation through faith in Jesus Christ. At the same time, they have a special standing in God's plan for humanity, and God's covenant with the Jews continues. This twofold attitude calls for a balance in Christian relations with Judaism that the church has found difficult to maintain.

* Romans 2:17–3:4

But if you call yourself a Jew and rely on the law and boast of your relations to God and know his will and determine what is best because you are instructed in the law, and if you are sure that you are a guide to the blind, a light to those who are in darkness, [20] a corrector of the foolish, a teacher of children, having in the law the embodiment of knowledge and truth, you, then, that teach others, will you not teach yourself? While you preach against stealing, do you steal? You that forbid adultery, do you commit adultery? You that abhor idols, do you rob temples? You that boast in the law, do you dishonor God by breaking the law? For, as it is written, "The name of God is blasphemed among the Gentiles because of you."

[25] Circumcision indeed is of value if you obey the law; but if you break the law, your circumcision has become uncircumcision. So, if those who are uncircumcised keep the requirements of the law, will not their uncircumcision be regarded as circumcision? Then those who are physically uncircumcised but keep the law will condemn you that have the written code and circumcision but break the law. For a person is not a Jew who is one outwardly, nor is true circumcision something external and physical. Rather, a person is a Jew who is one inwardly, and real circumcision is a matter of the heart—it is spiritual and not literal. Such a person receives praise not from others but from God.

[3:1] Then what advantage has the Jew? Or what is the value of circumcision? Much, in every way. For in the first place the Jews were entrusted with the oracles of God. What if some were unfaithful? Will their unfaithfulness nullify the faithfulness of God? By no means! Although everyone is a liar, let God be proved true, as it is written, "So that you may be justified in your words, and prevail in your judging."[49]

---

[49] Psalm 51:4.

Two Attitudes toward Government*

Romans 13 is the most important treatment in the New Testament of the relationship between the believer and the government, and the most influential through the history of the church. It couples specific and positive instructions about being subject to governing authorities with more general instructions about social ethics. The second reading, from Revelation, is the flip side of the first. The city of Rome is depicted symbolically as a "great whore," and the scarlet beast she rides is the Roman Empire. This selection concludes with a funeral song sung over the fallen Rome. This approach encourages quiet opposition to idolatrous and persecuting government, longing for its downfall at the coming of God's kingdom.

Let every person be subject to the governing authorities; for there is no authority except from God, and those authorities that exist have been instituted by God. Therefore whoever resists authority resists what God has appointed, and those who resist will incur judgment. For rulers are not a terror to good conduct, but to bad. Do you wish to have no fear of the authority? Then do what is good, and you will receive its approval; for it is God's servant for your good. But if you do what is wrong, you should be afraid, for the authority does not bear the sword in vain! It is the servant of God to execute wrath on the wrongdoer. [5] Therefore one must be subject, not only because of wrath but also because of conscience. For the same reason you also pay taxes, for the authorities are God's servants, busy with this very thing. Pay to all what is due them— taxes to whom taxes are due, revenue to whom revenue is due, respect to whom respect is due, honor to whom honor is due.

Owe no one anything, except to love one another; for the one who loves another has fulfilled the law. The commandments, "You shall

---

* Romans 13:1–10; Revelation 17:1–8; 18:1–5

not commit adultery; You shall not murder; You shall not steal; You shall not covet"; and any other commandment, are summed up in this word, "Love your neighbor as yourself." [10] Love does no wrong to a neighbor; therefore, love is the fulfilling of the law.

[Revelation 17:1] Then one of the seven angels who had the seven bowls came and said to me, "Come. I will show you the judgment of the great whore who is seated on many waters, with whom the kings of the earth have committed fornication, and with the wine of whose fornication the inhabitants of the earth have become drunk." So he carried me away in the spirit into a wilderness, and I saw a woman sitting on a scarlet beast that was full of blasphemous names, and it had seven heads and ten horns. The woman was clothed in purple and scarlet, and adorned with gold and jewels and pearls, holding in her hand a golden cup full of abominations and the impurities of her fornication; [5] and on her forehead was written a name, a mystery: "Babylon the great,[50] mother of whores and of earth's abomination." And I saw that the woman was drunk with the blood of the saints and the blood of the witnesses to Jesus.

---

[50] *Babylon the great:* a code name for Rome, taken from the name of a great oppressing city-empire in the Jewish Bible.

When I saw her, I was greatly amazed. But the angel said to me, "Why are you so amazed? I will tell you the mystery of the woman, and of the beast with seven heads and ten horns that carries her. The beast that you saw was, and is not, and is about to ascend from the bottomless pit and go to destruction. And the inhabitants of the earth, whose names have not been written in the book of life from the foundation of the world, will be amazed when they see the beast, because it was and is not and is to come. . . .

[18:1] After this I saw another angel coming down from heaven, having great authority; and the earth was made bright with his splendor. He called out with a mighty voice, "Fallen, fallen is Babylon the great! It has become a dwelling place of demons, a haunt of every foul and hateful bird, a haunt of every foul and hateful beast. For all the nations have drunk of the wine of the wrath of her fornication, and the kings of the earth have committed fornication with her, and the merchants of the earth have grown rich from the power of her luxury."

Then I heard another voice from heaven saying, "Come out of her, my people, so that you do not take part in her sins, and so that you do not share in her plagues; [5] for her sins are heaped high as heaven, and God has remembered her iniquities."

ADDITIONAL BIBLE READINGS

For reasons of space, many important readings in the Bible could not be included here. Readers may want to supplement each category with the following.

In **Events:** The Call of Moses (Exodus 3:1–20); The Covenant with Israel (Exodus 19: 1–8); The Bitter Experience of Exile (Psalms 137); The Beginning of Jesus' Ministry (Mark 1:1–2:12); Jesus Argues with his Opponents (Luke 11:37–54).

In **Institution:** The Establishment of Circumcision (Genesis 17:9–27); The Establishment of Passover (Exodus 12); The Observance of the Sabbath (Exodus 31:12–17); Kosher and Nonkosher Foods (Leviticus 16); The Ordination of Priests (Exodus 29:1–37); The Call to be a Prophet (Isaiah 6:1–13); Matthew's Church Order (Matthew 18:1–22); Divine Worship in Corinth (I Corinthians 14:26–33).

In **Teaching:** God as the Divine Shepherd (Psalms 23); Divine Majesty and Human Dignity (Psalms 8); Prayer for Divine Deliverance (Psalms 5); A Light to the Nations (Isaiah 42:1–7); The Messianic King (Isaiah 11:1–9); The Final Judgment of the World (Daniel 7:1–14); Jesus Forgives a Sinful Woman (Luke 7:36–50); Nicodemus Visits Jesus (John 3:1–21); A Hymn to Christ (Philippians 2:1–11); The Resurrection of Christ and the Believer (I Corinthians 15).

In **Ethics:** Laws on Slaves, Violence, and Property (Exodus 21–22); Equal Justice for All (Exodus 23:1–9); Sexual Love (Song of Solomon/Songs 1:1–2:17); What God Requires (Amos 4:1–13); Two Views of Wisdom (Proverbs 1:1–33, Ecclesiastes 1:1–9); The Virtuous Wife (Proverbs 31:10–31); Paul's Directions Concerning Marriage (I Corinthians 7)

In **Relations:** Holy War (Deuteronomy 20:1–20); Christianity and Judaism (Romans 9–11).

GLOSSARY

apocalyptic theology, and the writings based on it, that emphasizes the imminent end of the world and the coming of God's kingdom.

authentic writings commonly accepted by most modern biblical scholars as actually written by the persons whose names they bear.

canonization the process of recognizing certain books as scriptural.

covenant see **testament.**

epistles see **letters.**

Gnosticism a movement both within and outside Christianity that taught eternal salvation by means of esoteric self-knowledge.

gospel at first, the oral message of "good news" about salvation in Jesus; then, the name given to the books that tell the story of the life, death, and resurrection of Jesus.

lectionary an official list of scripture readings for divine worship.

letters writings of instruction addressed to churches, so called because they share many or all the features of the common Greco-Roman letter; also called **epistles,** which indicate letters more formal in style and content.

pseudonymous writings not commonly accepted by most modern biblical scholars as authentic.

Septuagint the translation of the Hebrew Bible into Greek by Greek-speaking Jews in the third and second centuries B.C.E.; the main Bible of earliest Christianity.

synoptic gospel books that can be "seen in one view" ("synopsis") because of their parallel structure and content: Matthew, Mark, and Luke.

testament also called **covenant,** the relationship God established with his people. Christians saw a "New Covenant" established in Jesus, leading them to call their new scriptures the New Testament.

Torah "teaching, law"; more specifically, the first five books of the Hebrew Bible.

QUESTIONS FOR STUDY AND DISCUSSION

1.   What has it meant for relations between Jews and Christians that they share a large part of the Bible? How has this fact both improved and complicated their relations?

2.   What basic teachings and religious patterns of the Hebrew Bible have continued into Christianity without substantial change?

3.   Comment on the following provocative statement: "Christianity is one of Judaism's gifts to the world."

4.   In what ways do the four Gospels center on the suffering, death, and resurrection of Jesus?

5.   Summarize in your own words the main points of the teaching of Jesus. How does the teaching of Jesus relate to the life, death, and resurrection of Jesus as portrayed in the Gospels?

6.   In what ways do the acts and teaching of Jesus, the Acts of the Apostles, and the letters of Paul show Christianity to be a "missionary religion"?

7.   What degree of continuity and discontinuity can be discerned in these readings between the teaching of Jesus and the teaching of Paul?

8.   Why is Jesus so harsh toward hypocrisy in the Sermon on the Mount? In what ways could hypocrisy have been a problem within early Christianity?

9.   In what ways does the New Testament better the condition of women, and in what ways does it not? Discuss both the first century and today.

10.   How does the New Testament promote love as the chief virtue in the Christian life?

SUGGESTIONS FOR FURTHER READING

B. M. Metzger and R. E. Murphy, eds., *The New Oxford Annotated Bible*. New York: Oxford University Press, 1991. The New Revised Standard Version of the Bible in an edition with excellent introductions and notes.

V. R. Gold et al., eds., *The New Testament and Psalms: A New Inclusive Translation* (New York: Oxford University Press, 1995). Similar to the New Revised Standard version in style but avoiding language seen by some to be noninclusive of women, persons with disabilities, persons of color, enslaved persons, and Jews.

M. J. Suggs et al., eds., *The Oxford Study Bible: Revised English Bible with the Apocrypha*. New York: Oxford University Press, 1992. A British translation known for its literary beauty, with full introductions and notes.

The Orthodox Study Bible. New York: Nelson, 1993. With annotations from early church fathers, a lectionary, reproductions of icons, and other orthodox-oriented features. Unfortunately, it uses the text of the New King James Version, not critically accepted as a good translation from the best manuscripts.

D. Senior et al., eds., *The Catholic Study Bible*. New York: Oxford University Press, 1990. An excellent study Bible for both Catholics and others who wish to know more about the contemporary Catholic understanding of the Bible. It contains the text of the New American Bible, which is similar to that of the Revised Standard Version.

CHAPTER THREE

Ancient Christianity (100–500)

❖ In Beijing, China, many Chinese Christians expect a crackdown on secret, unregistered churches and persecution of their members. The communist government of China views these organizations as treasonous and subversive and is alarmed by their growth. They are especially suspicious of the Roman Catholic Church, remembering that Pope John Paul II had a key role in the toppling of communist governments in eastern Europe. These Christians mirror in their own experience the investigation and persecution of ancient Christians in the times of the Roman empire.

❖ In the United States, theologians representing several Protestant denominations meet to discuss the Nicene Creed, particularly the *filioque* clause, which states that the personal being of the Son of God proceeds from the Father *and the Son* (Latin *filioque*). This clause was not a part of the original text of the creed but was added in Western, Roman Catholic Christianity. Under urging from the Eastern Orthodox Churches, the theologians agree that this clause should be taken out of the Western form of the Nicene Creed. They participate in an argument over this clause that is more than a thousand years old and the chief theological reason that the Eastern and Western churches separated.

❖ In Jerusalem, Roman Catholic nuns from India worship in the Church of the Holy Sepulchre, which covers the traditional site of Jesus' crucifixion and tomb. The pilgrims are amazed and a bit bewildered by the many rites of the place, Eastern and Roman Catholic, and with photography forbidden they wonder how they will describe it to Christian friends back home. Their experience in this church is reminiscent of that of the ancient Spanish pilgrim nun Egeria, who wrote a full report of the wonders of this place in the fifth century.

INTRODUCTION

The period that extends from roughly the second century C.E. to the end of the fifth century is, after the first century, the most important era in the formation of Christianity. In this period, Christianity grew to be a major religion in the Roman Empire, spread beyond its borders, survived persecution and triumphed over its opponents, defined itself against several rival forms of Christianity, and developed the organization that was to mark it through today. All later Christianity throughout the world is based to a significant degree on the teaching, organization and life of this ancient period. As Henry Chadwick has remarked, "[M]ost of the main issues then faced by the church . . .

have remained virtually permanent questions in Christian history—questions which receive an answer but are then reiterated in a modified shape in every age."[1]

Names

Scholars of Christianity have given two different names to this period. Most refer to it simply as Early or Ancient Christianity.[2] This name is accurate in that this period is indeed, in a general sense, early and ancient compared to later times, but otherwise it is misleading. *Early* and *ancient* imply that this is the original stage of Christianity, completely ignoring the first-century period in which Christianity arose. The reason for the ubiquity of this label is largely an academic one. Early in the history of European scholarship (in the late medieval universities), a division was made between New Testament study and Church History, with the latter field beginning where the former left off, around 100 C.E. This division still continues today in the academic curriculum and in scholarly writing, with some modification.[3] The student of Christianity must understand, however, that church history actually begins with the birth of Christianity in the first century.

The other main term for the study of this period is **patristics.** This term refers to the "Fathers" (Latin *patres*) of the church, the leading bishop-theologian-writers who had a profound influence on Christianity in this period. In the West, the "Fathers" included in this period extend from the **Apostolic Fathers** at the beginning of the second century (so called because they supposedly knew and continued the direct tradition of the apostles of Christ)[4] to the Fathers of the fifth century. The Eastern Orthodox branch of Christianity also recognizes some theologians from the Middle Ages as Fathers of the Church. *Patristic* as a label for this period has recently fallen into disuse. Its strongly male orientation tends to exclude the lives of women, and its orientation to the highest levels of church leadership and power tends to exclude the contribution of ordinary people.

Which of these two terms is preferable, if we must choose between them? This book will opt for the more accurate and inclusive *Ancient Christianity.* The reader should remember, however, that ancient Christianity *continues* from about 100–500. While this period is indeed ancient, it is the continuation of an even more ancient century in the life of Christianity.

---

[1] Henry Chadwick, *The Early Church* (London: Penguin, 1968), 285.

[2] Compare, for example, the titles of these books by four of the twentieth century's leading scholars of Christianity, all of which deal almost exclusively with the 100–400 C.E. period: *Orthodoxy and Heresy in Earliest Christianity,* by Walter Bauer (Philadelphia: Fortress, 1971; German original, 1934); *The Early Church,* by Henry Chadwick (London: Penguin, 1967); *Early Christian Doctrines,* by J. N. D. Kelly (New York: Harper & Row, 1958); and *The Body and Society: Men, Women, and Sexual Renunciation in Early Christianity,* by Peter Brown (New York: Columbia University Press, 1988).

[3] One such modification is the tendency among some scholars to speak of the New Testament period as "Primitive Christianity," but this name carries its own rather obvious problems.

[4] Some writers still use the older term "sub-Apostolic Age/Fathers" to refer to this time and its leading writers.

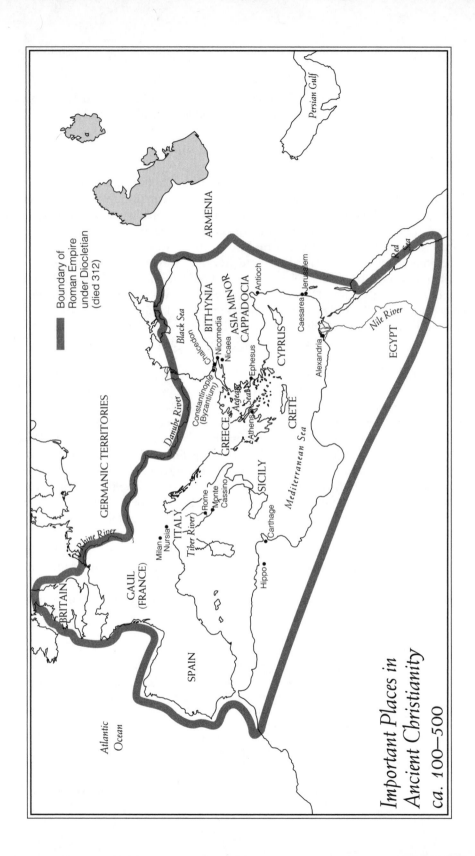

Important Places in Ancient Christianity ca. 100—500

Boundary of Roman Empire under Diocletian (died 312)

Persian Gulf

Red Sea

Nile River

ARMENIA

Black Sea

BITHYNIA

Chalcedon

Nicomedia

Nicaea

ASIA MINOR

CAPPADOCIA

Antioch

Caesarea

Jerusalem

Ephesus

CYPRUS

Alexandria

EGYPT

Constantinople (Byzantium)

Aegean Sea

Athens

GREECE

CRETE

Mediterranean Sea

GERMANIC TERRITORIES

Danube River

SICILY

Rome

Monte Cassino

ITALY

Tiber River

Milan

Nursia

Carthage

Hippo

Rhine River

BRITAIN

GAUL (FRANCE)

SPAIN

Atlantic Ocean

Historical Sketch

At the end of the first century, Christianity had established itself in every major city, and many secondary cities, in the eastern half of the Roman Empire. The apostle Paul and other missionaries had founded many churches, but other churches, most prominently that at Rome itself, seem to have grown from the bottom up without any formal mission effort.

These churches, based in houses, were not very large, and Christians were probably not a majority in any town or city, but they were strategically placed. They also experienced rapid growth, the reasons for which were many and varied. To begin with, Christians were generally assertive about spreading what they called the Good News. The message and experience of ancient Christianity offered things that many people in the ancient world were seeking: the promise of eternal life, meaning and happiness in this world, a higher religious (if not always socioeconomic) standing for women and slaves, and a loving social support network. These were centered around the Good News of Jesus Christ as experienced in the church.

As Christianity spread among Gentiles, it outgrew its early status as a Jewish sect. Much of this development had already taken place in the first century, and the second and third centuries were to finish this process. The separation between Judaism and Christianity was perhaps inevitable. The earliest church taught that Jesus had been put to death by the Roman government after a conspiracy of some Jewish religious leaders; some Jewish leaders occasionally persecuted Jews who converted to Christianity; and by the end of the first century the Jewish religious establishment began to decree that Jews confessing Jesus to be the messiah were to be excommunicated from the synagogue. Conversion of Gentiles was much more rapid than conversion of Jews, and as time went by the church became predominantly Gentile in membership and orientation.

By about 150, the church's change from Jewish to Gentile was becoming obvious to Roman authorities. Christians lost their status as practitioners of an officially permitted religion, which they had enjoyed as long as Christianity was taken as a Jewish sect. As Christians began to outnumber Jews in some cities, Christian pressure on Jews began, only to increase in 313 when Christianity became officially permitted. Thus a bitter legacy of Christian **anti-Semitism** (prejudice against the Jewish people) and **anti-Judaism** (prejudice against the Jewish religion) was formed, one that was to haunt the relationship of Jews and Christians through our own time.[5] Judaism and Christianity are sister faiths, but as in most "family fights" the ongoing conflict (mostly onesided, with the much larger Christianity dominating Judaism) has been intense and sad.

As Christianity grew, it also challenged the Roman Empire. During New Testament times, this challenge was muted. For example, Jesus was presented as a man dying innocent of all crime, and the author of the Acts of the Apostles wrote repeatedly that Christians were no lawbreakers or threats to Roman rule. But at the end of the first century, with the outbreak of sporadic but intense imperial persecutions, the New Tes-

---

[5] Some scholars argue that no distinction should be made between these two terms. Scholars debate the presence of anti-Semitism and anti-Judaism in the New Testament; the current consensus is that these two biases do begin in New Testament times.

tament Book of Revelation attacked Rome as the "great whore" corrupting the whole earth and predicted its fall.

In the second century, Christianity took upon itself the religious duty of spiritually and socially (never militarily) challenging the legitimacy of the empire and the Roman religious system with which it was allied. This stand led to a Roman reaction of even more persecutions and martyrdoms, sporadic but often fierce. Romans also countered Christianity in an informal, popular way by spreading rumors about Christian superstition, cannibalism, sexual improprieties, and the like. Some intellectuals, chief among them Celsus, also took it upon themselves to attack the beliefs of Christians. The church's writers responded to these in books called *apologies,* to be considered later.

The teaching and organization of the church was also challenged from within by **heresy,** opposition to the teaching of mainstream Christianity that often resulted in an alternative church. Heresy arose in the second century, especially in the form of Gnosticism. Gnosticism was a diverse movement itself, but most Gnostics believed that this material world is evil and hostile to the good. However, a few people here possess a divine spark that makes them "spiritual" beings. By turning inward from this material world to discover one's own spiritual essence, these few humans could ascend to the divine source from which they originally came. The way to this knowledge (*gnosis*) for most Gnostics was through moral and physical self-control and withdrawal from this physical world. But some Gnostics taught and practiced the opposite view— that the spiritual person rises beyond good and evil—and they practiced their faith in orgiastic rituals. Since Gnosticism did not have room for a good Creator of this evil world or a human Savior to lead people from it, the mainstream church regarded it as a heresy that cut at the roots of the faith.

Mainstream Christianity gradually defined itself against Gnosticism and other movements, leading to the rise of formal **orthodoxy,** "right belief" and practice. Heretical churches can be studied as alternative forms of Christianity. Indeed, they viewed themselves as the true form of Christianity, and some were more conservative (e.g., the various Jewish-Christian churches) and morally rigorous (e.g., the Marcionite church and Donatist churches) than the orthodox church.[6] The most able opponent of heresy was Irenaeus, the second-century bishop of Lyon. Irenaeus defined heresy as a departure from the scriptures and the rule of faith, and he urged other bishops to identify heresy and combat it. This method of dealing with heresy worked well at first, especially against Gnosticism. But the church later found it necessary to call councils to adjudicate charges of heresy. Some regional councils were called in the third century, but it was not until the reign of Constantine that a full ecumenical council was held. Ecumenical councils derived their authority from both imperial patronage and general acceptance by the church. For example, the Councils of Nicea (325) and Constantinople (381) condemned Arianism as a heresy and formulated the official teaching of the Trinity. The councils of Ephesus (431) and Chalcedon (451) condemned Nestorianism

---

[6] "Differences among Christians help us understand a great deal about how they experienced their faith. Heresies and heretics can tell us almost as much about the nature of Christian experience as do orthodoxy and saints. . . . [H]eretics were not always wrong doctrinally; sometimes they were simply the losers in political or institutional controversies." Paul R. Spickard and Kevin M. Cragg, *God's Peoples: A Social History of Christians* (Grand Rapids, MI: Baker, 1994), 10.

and Monophysitism, respectively, as heresies, and in so doing formulated the official teaching of the human and divine natures in Christ.

The emperor Constantine's acceptance of Christianity in 312 ushered in a new era in the faith, one that many historians view as lasting until the twentieth century. This era featured the close association of church and state. By moving his capital to Constantinople in northern Asia Minor, Constantine created a new civilization that attempted to preserve the best of ancient Greece and Rome and yet transform it through the Christian faith. The Eastern Orthodox branch of Christianity, and the cultures it has shaped, is the continuation of this effort. Constantine began the short (one-century) process by which Christianity went from being persecuted to favored and promoted. Not only did Constantine and most of his successors promote the church, but they took a leading interest in preserving the institutional and doctrinal unity of the church. For the rest of the ancient period of Christianity, "Constantinianism" prevailed in the East and West, the mainstream church consolidated its doctrine and organization against heresy, and Christianity spread beyond the borders of the Roman Empire.

We will illustrate this historical sketch by discussing one of the main issues in the ancient period that has continuing crucial importance for all periods of Christianity, the story of how the New Testament canon was formed. As is often remarked, the New Testament is the only thing that all Christians have in common. Church structure, ways of worship, creeds, moral patterns, and other aspects of Christianity show a rich variety. The New Testament, however, is held in common by all and therefore has had a crucial role in preserving the unity of the Christian tradition.

Beginning in the second century C.E., Christians began forming a **canon,** an official list of books considered to be a part of the New Testament, by sorting out true Christian writings from ones they considered false and heretical. The details of this process are hazy, but the main features seem clear. First, a canonical writing had to have a claim to apostolic authorship or authority. It had to be seen as either being written by an apostle (e.g., the Gospels of Matthew and John, the Letters of Peter and Paul) or by someone under apostolic authority (e.g., the Gospels of Mark and Luke). It had to give the appearance of going back to the first two Christian generations. Second, the content of the writings was weighed. In the fight with heresy during the second century, doctrinal content was important because writings the church deemed heretical also claimed to be written by the apostles, and the only way to tell them from false teaching was to compare the content of their teaching to books held to be genuinely apostolic in content.

The third main factor in the process of canonization was the actual scripture usage of prominent Christian churches. Among the Gospels, for example, Antioch promoted the Gospel of Matthew, the province of Asia Minor (modern western Turkey) used the Gospels of John and Luke, and Rome used Mark. The support of these large and influential centers of early Christianity was crucial in the formation of the canon. The final factor was the competing canons of groups that the mainstream church considered heretical. Marcion, an early Christian leader who came to Rome about 145 C.E., argued that the God revealed by Jesus was not the creator God revealed in the Jewish Bible. As a result, Marcion totally rejected the Jewish Bible as canonical and made a special canon of Christian books out of the Gospel of Luke only and ten Pauline letters, rejecting everything else. This selection probably spurred the early church to begin to draw up its own formal lists insisting on a wider canon: the four Gospels, all the Pauline letters that looked genuinely apostolic in content, and other letters from the apostles to their churches.

Thus, a consensus grew during the third and fourth century around the main books of the emerging canon of the New Testament. Seven books remained in doubt during this time, accepted by some churches but not by all: Hebrews, James, II and III John, Jude, II Peter, and Revelation. But as the widely scattered churches grew closer together in the third and fourth centuries, they began accepting these disputed books from each other. Official actions of leading bishops and councils sealed the twenty-seven-book canon, especially the Easter letter of Athanasius in 367 and the Synod of Carthage in 397.

Literary Genres of the Primary Sources

Christians in this period used several types of writing to express and explain their faith. Some carried on the genres of the New Testament: epistles, gospels, histories, and so on. A knowledge of the typical structure and content of the genres will help you to understand these important primary sources.

Epistles in the early part of this period, like those of the New Testament, are letters usually addressed to a specific audience and dealing with a particular issue or issues, usually to correct a doctrinal, moral, or organizational problem. The original audience found these letters so important that they were copied and circulated to other churches. Many of the early Apostolic Fathers relied heavily on epistles for almost all their writing. Some of these letters were so highly respected that they appear in a few second- and third-century lists of the New Testament canon. Over time the epistolary genre was used less, but even in the fourth century a few major church leaders like Ambrose of Milan used it quite extensively.

Gospels also continue the first-century genre. Two features of new gospels in this period should be noted. First, many gospels that arose in the mainstream church are popular in orientation. They are filled with often-legendary stories about the childhood of Jesus and his ministry, death, and resurrection. Second, gospels that arose in the Gnostic Christian church are most often concerned to relate the secret (Gnostic) teachings of the risen Jesus, teachings that (by comparison with the canonical Gospels at least) are difficult to understand. They usually do not narrate his birth, ministry, or death.

Sermons (also called **homilies**) arose from the Christian service of divine worship. The sermonic literature that survives extends from the second century (e.g., Melito of Sardis) through the fourth (e.g., John Chrysostom, the most famous preacher of the ancient church, whose sermon style and content had a great influence through the entire course of Eastern Orthodoxy). *Catechetical lectures,* which are related to the sermon, instructed new converts in the essentials of the faith, especially in preparation for baptism.

Apologies are defenses of the Christian faith and church. (*Apology* here does not carry the connotation of "excuse.") They are directed against the opponents of Christianity and seek to establish the truth and reasonableness of Christianity in the face of opposition and persecution. Two main types of apologies can be found in the second and third centuries, those against the Jews and those against followers of Greco-Roman religions. Apologies against the Jews tended to use appeals to the Jewish scriptures to argue that Jesus is the Messiah/Christ. Apologies against the followers of Greco-Roman religions tended to use arguments from reason (philosophy) and history to show that Christianity is the one true religion. Many of these apologies were addressed to the Roman emperor, but recent scholarship has tended to view them as missionary writings; they seem to have had much more influence on the church than on Rome. When Christianity began to be the official religion of the Empire in the fourth century, a new type of apology arose whose purpose was to show that Christianity is the true successor of Greco-Roman religion and philosophy.

Histories in this period are closely related in purpose to apologies. They are designed to show the truth of Christianity by demonstrating its growth despite internal trouble and external persecution. Eusebius, bishop of Caesarea, was the first major historian of the church. He had a strong interest in demonstrating the truth of Christianity by showing its fulfillment of Scripture. Eusebius' work and the writings of other church historians of this period contain much material copied wholesale from earlier documents that otherwise would have been lost to us. Despite their argumentative nature, these histories are valuable sources for our knowledge of ancient Christianity.

Martyrologies, stories of martyrs, come in two forms. The "Passions" (from the Latin *passio,* "suffering") are accounts of the last days and death of the martyr, as in *The Passion of Perpetua and Felicity.* The "Acts" are accounts of the martyr's trials before the Roman authorities. Both forms of martyrologies were written to encourage Christians facing persecution to be faithful and brave. The words of Perpetua to the other Christians to be martyred shortly after her were directed to all Christians of her time: "Remain strong in your faith, and love one another. Do not let our excruciating sufferings become a stumbling block for you."

The **rule of faith** is a short summary of the basic points of Christian teaching. It has its roots in the summaries of the basic Christian message that are found in several New Testament books, especially the Acts of the Apostles. The rule of faith soon evolved into an interpretation of the message of scripture and was used in the fight against heresy, especially in the second century. In contrast with the creeds, the various forms of the rule of faith have no fixed, definite wording, although their organization and general content tend to be the same.

Creeds arose as doctrinal controversy and church politics became more complex and Christians needed a fixed definition of orthodoxy and heresy. Derived from the Latin *credo,* "I believe," a creed is a formal, short, official statement of the main points of Christian belief. They were (and are) most often used in divine worship. Creed-like statements can be found in the New Testament ("Jesus is Lord," for example), but creeds themselves originated in the baptismal ceremony, especially that used in Rome. They have a trinitarian structure and are cumulative in content: the Apostles' Creed leads to the Nicene Creed of 325, which leads in turn to the fuller Niceno-Constantinopolitan Creed of 381. The ecumenical creeds were accepted by the entire church as authoritative and continue to be so today. (Some fundamentalist Protestant groups have rejected the formal authority of these creeds, saying "No creed but the Bible," but their doctrines are as much shaped by the creeds as those of any other type of church.) Other regional creeds arose as well, such as the Athanasian Creed in sixth-century France.

EVENTS

The Martyrdom of Peter and Paul Recollected*

Clement, the bishop of Rome from about 88 to 97 C.E., wrote in 96 to the Christian church in Corinth, Greece. The unity of that church was threatened by jealousy and rivalries, and younger members had deposed the older leadership. Clement attempts to correct these problems and relates information about the deaths of Peter and Paul. He uses these two apostles as examples of lives worthy of imitation, particularly in the area of surviving in the face of rivalry. This letter to the Corinthians also testifies to the rising power and influence of the bishop of Rome, who takes it upon himself to correct the problems of distant churches.[7]

Let us take [as examples] the noble examples of our own generation. By reason of rivalry and envy the greatest and most righteous pillars (of the Church) were persecuted, and battled to the death. Let us set before our eyes the noble apostles. Peter, by reason of wicked jealousy, not only once or twice but frequently endured suffering. Bearing his witness,[8] he went to the glorious place which he merited. By reason of rivalry and contention Paul showed how to win the prize for patient endurance. Seven times he was in chains; he was exiled, received a stoning, became a herald (of the gospel) in East and West, and won the noble renown which his faith merited. He taught righteousness to the whole world, and reaching the limits of the West he bore his witness before rulers. And so, released from this world, he was taken up into the holy place and became the greatest example of patient endurance.

---

* Clement, *First Epistle to the Corinthians* 5
[7] Taken, with editing, from Kirsopp Lake, *The Apostolic Fathers*, vol. 1 (Cambridge, MA: Harvard University Press, 1912), 15.

[8] *bearing his witness:* carries the implication of dying for the faith.

Roman Investigation of Christians**

Pliny the Younger (ca. 61–113), a prominent Roman writer and public official, authored ten books of letters, the last of which contains letters written to the Emperor Trajan and Trajan's replies. In two of these letters dating from about 112, Pliny discusses his investigation of Christians while he was the Roman governor of Bithynia, a Roman province in modern northern Turkey. The charges against Christians may have originated in personal, factional, or religious rivalries. Trajan replies that Christians were guilty merely because they were Christians but were not to be hunted down or prosecuted on the basis of anonymous accusations. This policy formed the basic guidance for most imperial actions toward Christianity for the next two centuries, except at the times of the great persecutions. In the course of this letter, Pliny gives the earliest description by an outsider of Christian worship.[9]

I have never taken part in the trials of Christians. Therefore I do not know for what crime or to what extent it is customary to punish or investigate them. I am unsure if any difference is made for age, or whether there should be a difference made in treating the weaker or the stronger. Is

---

** Pliny, *Letters* 10.96, 97

[9] Translated by the author.

pardon granted in case of repentance, or does he who has always been a Christian gain nothing by ceasing to be one? Is the name itself punished without proof of [other] crimes, or are the crimes inseparably connected with the name punished?

Meanwhile I have followed this procedure in the case of those who have been brought before me as Christians. I asked them whether they were Christians, and if they said yes, I asked a second and a third time and with threats of punishment. I questioned those who confessed; I ordered those who were obstinate to be executed. For I am sure that, whatever it was they confessed, their stubbornness and unshakable obstinacy certainly ought to be punished. There were others of similar fanaticism who were Roman citizens, and I have written them up for sending to the City [of Rome].

Soon the crime spread, as is usual when attention is called to it, and more cases arose. An anonymous accusation containing many names was circulated. Those on this list who denied that they were or had been Christians ought, I thought, to be released. They did those things which, they say, those who are really Christians cannot be compelled to do: they repeated after me a prayer to the gods and made supplication with incense and wine to your image, which I had ordered to be brought for the purpose together with the statues of the gods. Besides these things, they said derogatory things about Christ. Others, accused by an informer, said that they were Christians but denied it to me; in fact they had been but had ceased to be, some many years ago, some even twenty years before. They all worshipped your image and the statues of the gods, and spoke derogatory things about Christ. They continued to maintain that this was the amount of their fault or error, that on a fixed day they were accustomed to come together before daylight and to sing by turns a hymn to Christ as a god. They bound themselves by oath, not for some crime but that they would not commit robbery, theft, or adultery, that they would not betray a trust nor deny a deposit when called upon. After this they adjourned to come together again

to partake of food, of an ordinary and harmless kind, however. Even this they had ceased to do after the publication of my edict which according to your command had forbidden associations. Hence I believed it even more necessary to examine two female slaves, who were called deaconesses, in order to find out what is true, and to do it by torture. I found nothing but a vicious, extravagant superstition.

Therefore I have postponed the examination and hurry to consult you. It seemed to me that the subject would justify consultation, especially because of the number of those in peril. Many of all ages, of every rank, and even of both sexes are and will be called into danger. The infection of this superstition has not only spread to the cities but even to the villages and country districts.[10] It seems possible to halt it and bring about a reform. The temples, which had been almost deserted, have begun to be frequented again. The sacred rites, which had been neglected for a long time, have begun to be restored, and food for victims,[11] for which until now there was scarcely a buyer, is sold. From this one may readily judge that a number of people can be reclaimed if repentance is permitted.

[Trajan's reply:] You have followed the correct procedure, my dear Pliny, in conducting the cases of those who were accused before you as Christians. No general rule can be laid down as a set procedure. They ought not to be sought out, but if they are brought before you and convicted they ought to be punished.[12] However, he who denies that he is a Christian, and proves this by making supplication to our gods, shall secure pardon however much he may have been under suspicion in the past. But pay no attention to anonymous charges, for they are a bad precedent and are not worthy of our age.

---

[10] *even to the villages and country districts:* at the end of the first century, Christianity was largely a religion of city dwellers; Pliny finds its growth in the more religiously conservative countryside remarkable.

[11] *victims:* animals to be sacrificed.

[12] *ought to be punished:* by death.

Martyrdom of a Young Christian Woman*

Like other numerous stories of martyrs, The Passion of Perpetua and Felicitas *was written to encourage other Christians to witness bravely to the point of death. The story of her martyrdom in Carthage, North Africa, in 203 is based on a journal kept by Perpetua in prison. Despite its Montanist leanings, which (in the mainstream church's view) overemphasized the presence and power of the Holy Spirit, this book became so popular among ancient Christians that two hundred years later St. Augustine had to warn them not to look upon it as equal to the scriptures. Note that the narration switches between first-person (Perpetua's journal) and third-person voices.*[13]

What we have heard and seen, brothers and dear ones, we declare to you, so that those of you who were eyewitnesses of these deeds may be reminded of the glory of the Lord. Those of you now learning of it through this narration may commune with the holy martyrs and, through them, with the Lord Jesus Christ to whom be glory and honor forever. Amen.

[1.1] The young catechumens[14] Revocatus, Felicitas (both slaves), Saturninus and Secundulus were arrested. Among them was also Vibia Perpetua, a young married woman of good family and upbringing. She had a father, mother, two brothers (one was a catechumen like herself), and an infant son whom she was nursing. She was about twenty years old. The following account of her martyrdom is her own, a record in her own words.

While I was still with the police authorities, she says, my father out of love for me tried to dissuade me from my resolution. "Father," I said, "do you see here, for example, this as a pitcher or as something else?" "I see it," he said. "Can it be

named anything else than what it really is?", I asked, and he said, "No." "So I also cannot be called anything else than what I am, a Christian." Enraged by my words, my father came at me as if to tear out my eyes. He only annoyed me, but he left, overpowered by his devilish arguments. For a few days my father stayed away. I thanked the Lord and felt relieved because of my father's absence. At this time we were baptized and the Spirit instructed me not to pray for anything while I was being baptized except endurance of physical suffering.[15]

A few days later we were imprisoned. I was terrified because never before had I experienced such darkness. What a terrible day! We were crowded together, the soldiers treated us roughly, and the heat was unbearable. My condition was aggravated by my anxiety for my baby. Then Tertius and Pomponius, those kind deacons who were taking care of our needs, paid for us to be moved for a few hours to a better part of the prison where we might refresh ourselves. Leaving the dungeon we all went about our own business. I nursed my child, who was already weak from hunger. In my anxiety for the baby I spoke to my mother about him, and tried to console my brother, and asked that they care for my son. I suffered terribly because I sensed their agony on my account. These were the trials I had to endure for many days. Then I was granted the privilege of having my son remain with me in prison. Relieved of my anxiety and concern for the infant, I immediately regained my strength. Suddenly the prison became my palace, and I loved being there rather than any other place. . . . [There follows a vision in which Perpetua realizes that she is to be martyred.] . . .

[2.2] Hilarian, the governor who assumed power after the death of the proconsul Minucius Timinianus, said, "Have pity on your father's grey head; have pity on your infant son; offer sacrifice for the emperor's welfare." But I answered,

---

* *Passion of Perpetua and Felicitas,* Preface, 1.1–2, 2.2, 6.1–4
[13] Taken, with editing, from Alexander Robertson and James Donaldson, eds., *The Ante-Nicene Fathers,* vol. 3 (New York: Scribners, 1905), 699–701, 704–705.

[14] *catechumen:* one undergoing instruction in the faith as a preparation for baptism.

[15] *physical suffering:* of martyrdom.

"I will not." Hilarion asked, "Are you a Christian?" And I answered, "I am a Christian." . . . Then the sentence was passed; all of us were condemned to the beasts. We were overjoyed as we went back to the prison cell. Since I was still nursing my child who was ordinarily in the cell with me, I quickly sent the deacon Pomponius to my father's house to ask for the baby, but my father refused to hand him over. Then God saw to it that my child no longer needed my nursing, nor were my breasts inflamed. After that I was no longer tortured by anxiety about my child or by pain in my breasts. . . .

[6.1] The day of their victory dawned, and with joyful countenances they marched from the prison to the arena as though on their way to heaven. If there was any trembling it was from joy, not fear. Perpetua followed with quick step as a true spouse of Christ, the dear one of God, her brightly flashing eyes quelling the gaze of the crowd. Felicitas too, joyful because she had safely survived child-birth and was now able to participate in the contest with the wild animals, passed from one shedding of blood to another; from midwife to gladiator, about to be purified after child-birth by a second baptism. As they were led through the gate they were ordered to put on different clothes; the men, those of the priests of Saturn, the women, those of the priestesses of Ceres. But that noble woman stubbornly resisted even to the end. She said, "We have come this far voluntarily in order to protect our rights, and we have pledged our lives not to do anything like this. We made this agreement with you." Injustice bowed to justice and the guard conceded that they could enter the arena just as they were. Perpetua was singing victory psalms. . . . Revocatus, Saturninus and Saturus were warning the spectators, and as they came within sight of Hilarion they informed him by nods and gestures; "You judge us; God will judge you."[16] This so infuriated the crowds that they demanded the whipping of these men by the gladiators as they passed by their line. But they rejoiced that they had obtained yet another share in the Lord's suffering.

He who said, "Ask and you shall receive,"[17] gave to these petitioners the particular death that each one chose. . . . For the young women the devil had readied a mad cow, an animal not usually used at these games, but selected so that the women's sex would be matched with that of the animal. After being stripped and enmeshed in nets, the women were led into the arena. How horrified the people were as they saw that one was a young girl and the other, her breasts dripping with milk, had just recently given birth to a child. Consequently both were recalled and dressed in loosely fitting gowns.

Perpetua was tossed first [by the cow] and fell on her back. She sat up and covered her thighs with her tunic which had been torn down one side, being more concerned with her sense of modesty than with her pain. Finding her hairclip which had fallen out, she pinned back her loose hair, thinking it improper for a martyr to suffer with dishevelled hair; it might seem that she was mourning in her hour of triumph. Then she stood up. Noticing that Felicitas was badly bruised, she went to her, reached out her hands and helped her to her feet. As they stood there the brutality of the crowds seemed to be appeased and they were sent to the Sanavivarian Gate.[18] There Perpetua was taken care of by a certain catechumen, Rusticus, who stayed near her. She seemed to be waking from a deep sleep (so completely had she been entranced and imbued with the Spirit). She began to look around her and to everyone's astonishment asked, "When will we be led out to that cow?" She would not believe that it had already happened until she saw the various markings of the tossing on her body and clothing. She then called for her brother and said to him and the catechumen, "Remain strong in your faith, and love one another. Do

---

[16] *they informed him . . . God condemns you:* usually done by four gestures in immediate succession: first to the condemning crowd, next to oneself, then to the sky (God), and finally to the crowd.

[17] *ask and you shall receive:* the words of Jesus as recorded in the Gospels.

[18] *Sanavivarian Gate:* i.e., at the edge of the arena.

not let our sufferings become a stumbling block for you." . . .

The others, without making any movement or sound, were killed by the sword. But Perpetua, to feel some of the pain, groaned as she was first stabbed between the ribs, and then took the young gladiator's trembling hand [and] guided his sword to her throat. Perhaps so great a woman, feared as she was by the unclean spirit, could not have been slain unless she herself had willed it.

The Great Persecutions*

Lactantius was a Christian apologist from North Africa. In 314–315 he wrote The Deaths of the Persecutors, *in which he argues that the imperial persecutors of the church, from Nero in the first century to his own time, met an evil death in which God punished them. This passage narrates the beginning of the great persecution under Emperor Diocletian and his co-ruler ("Caesar") Galerius, which took place in the eastern half of the empire in 302–303. All churches were to be destroyed, all clergy arrested and compelled on pain of death to sacrifice to the old gods.[19]*

The mother of Galerius, a woman exceedingly superstitious, was devoted to the gods of the mountains. She made sacrifices almost every day, and she feasted her servants on the meat offered to idols. The Christians of her family would not partake of those entertainments; while she feasted with the Gentiles,[20] they continued in fasting and prayer. On this account she conceived ill-will against the Christians, and by feminine complaints instigated her son, no less superstitious than herself, to destroy them. So, during the whole winter, Diocletian and Galerius held councils together, at which no one else helped. It was the universal opinion that their conferences dealt with the most momentous affairs of the empire. . . . A few civil magistrates and a few military commanders were admitted to give their counsel; and the question was put to them according to priority of rank. Some, through personal ill-will toward the Christians, thought they ought to be destroyed, as enemies of the gods and adversaries of the established religious ceremonies. Others thought differently, but having understood the will of Galerius, they agreed with his opinion either from a fear of displeasing him or from a desire of gratifying him. Yet not even then could they prevail upon Diocletian to assent. He decided above all to consult his gods, and he dispatched a soothsayer to ask Apollo at Miletus. Apollo's answer was such as might be expected from an enemy of the divine religion. So Diocletian was drawn over from his purpose. . . . A fit and auspicious day was sought out for the accomplishment of this undertaking. The festival of the god Terminus celebrated on the seventh of March, was chosen, instead of all others, to terminate, so to speak, the Christian religion. . . .

When that day dawned . . . suddenly, while it was yet hardly light, the prefect, with chief commanders, tribunes, and officers of the treasury, came to the church in Nicomedia, and the gates having been forced open, they searched everywhere for an image of the Divinity. The books of the Holy Scriptures were found, and they were committed to the flames; the utensils and furniture of the church were looted. Looting, confusion, and tumult were everywhere. . . . Then the Pretorian Guards came in battle array, with axes and other iron instruments. Having been let loose everywhere, in a few hours they leveled that very lofty building to the ground.

---

* Lactantius, *The Deaths of the Persecutors* 11–13
[19] Taken, with editing, from Alexander Roberts and James Donaldson, *The Ante-Nicene Fathers,* vol. 7 (New York: Scribners, 1905), 305–06.
[20] *Gentiles:* here the old Jewish term for non-Jews is applied by Christians to non-Christians.

On the next day an edict was published, depriving the Christians of all honors and dignities. It also ordered that . . . they should be subject to torture, and that every lawsuit filed against them should be accepted. They were barred from being plaintiffs in questions of wrongdoing, adultery or theft, and finally, that they should have no freedom or the right to vote.

The Victory and Conversion of Constantine*

Eusebius, bishop of Caesarea in the early fourth century, was the first and greatest historian of the ancient church. He took a special interest in Constantine and saw the new standing of the church under Constantine as a confirmation of divine providence. Here the conversion of Constantine is a military matter, not primarily a spiritual one. Eusebius' overall aim is to present Constantine as a Christian, but the careful reader of this passage can see that Eusebius has skillfully (and probably accurately) blended Constantine's worship of the Unconquered Sun with his growing faith in the Son of God.[21]

Constantine was convinced that he needed more powerful aid than his military forces could provide him, because of the wicked and magical enchantments which were so diligently practiced by the tyrant [Maxentius]; so he sought Divine assistance. He thought the possession of arms and a large army of secondary importance, believing that the cooperating power of a God was invincible and could not be shaken. He considered, therefore, on what God he might rely for protection and assistance. While engaged in this inquiry, the thought occurred to him that of the many emperors who had preceded him, those who had rested their hopes in a multitude of gods and served them with sacrifices and offerings had been deceived by flattering predictions and oracles which promised them all prosperity. They all met with an unhappy end, and not one of their gods had warned them of the impending wrath of heaven. But only one[22] had pursued an entirely different course, had condemned error and honored the Supreme God during his whole life, and had found him to be the Savior and Protector of his empire and the Giver of every good thing.

He also weighed the fact that they who had trusted in many gods had also fallen by many forms of death, leaving behind them neither family nor offspring, stock, name, or memorial. But the God of his father had given to him, on the other hand, manifestations of his power and very many divine signs. He also considered that those who had already taken arms against the tyrant, and had marched to the battlefield under the protection of a multitude of gods, had met with a dishonorable end. He judged it to be folly to join in the idle worship of those who were no gods, and to err from the truth after such convincing evidence. Therefore, he felt it necessary to honor his father's God alone.

Accordingly he called on God with earnest prayer and supplications to reveal himself to him in his present difficulties. While he was praying fervently, a most marvelous sign appeared to him from heaven, the account of which it might have been hard to believe had it been related by any other person. But since the victorious emperor himself long afterwards declared it to the writer of this history, when he was honored with his acquaintance and society, and confirmed his statement by an oath, who could hesitate to accredit the relation, especially since later testimony has established its truth? He said that about noon, when the day was already beginning to decline,

* Eusebius, *Life of Constantine*
[21] Taken, with editing, from Philip Schaff and Henry Wace, *Nicene and Post-Nicene Fathers*, vol. 1, 2d series (New York: Christian Literature Company, 1890), 489–91.

[22] *only one:* Constantius, Constantine's father, who was devoted to the monotheistic religion of the Unconquered Sun.

he saw with his own eyes a cross of light in the heavens, above the sun, and bearing the inscription, CONQUER BY THIS. He was struck with amazement, and his whole army also, which followed him on this expedition and witnessed the miracle.

He said, moreover, that he wondered what the meaning of this apparition could be. And while he continued to ponder and reason on its meaning, night suddenly came on. Then in his sleep the Christ of God appeared to him with the same sign which he had seen in the heavens. He commanded him to make a likeness of that sign which he had seen in the heavens, and to use it as a safeguard in all engagements with his enemies.

At dawn he arose and communicated the marvel to his friends. Calling together the workers in gold and precious stones, he sat in the middle of them, and described to them the figure of the sign he had seen, ordering them to represent it in gold and precious stones. And this representation I myself have had an opportunity to see.

Now it was made in the following manner. A long spear, overlaid with gold, formed the figure of the cross by means of a transverse bar laid over it. On the top of the whole was fixed a wreath of gold and precious stones. Within this wreath was a symbol of the Savior's name, two letters indicating the name of Christ by means of its initial letters, the letter P [Rho] being intersected by X [Chi] in its center.[23] . . . The emperor constantly made use of this sign of salvation as a safeguard against every adverse and hostile power, and commanded that others similar to it should be carried at the head of all his armies.

---

[23] *the letter P . . . center:* this is the Chi-Rho christogram. When combined with a cross, it is known as the *labarum.*

The Edict of Toleration*

Soon after his victory over Maxentius, Constantine and his co-emperor Licinius issued a decree that gave religious freedom to adherents of all religions. Addressed to governors of provinces throughout the empire, this edict brought the persecutions to an end and boosted the growth of Christianity. Christianity was still in the minority, but it had effectively triumphed over its rivals and was soon to become the religion of the majority.[24]

We, Constantine Augustus and Licinius Augustus, had fortunately met near Mediolanum (Milan), and considered everything that pertained to the public welfare and security. We thought that, among other things which would be for the good of many, we should make those regulations pertaining to the reverence of the Divinity first. We should grant to the Christians and to all others full authority to observe the religion that each preferred. Thus any Divinity at all in the seat of the heavens may be propitious and kindly disposed to us and all who are placed under our rule. By this wholesome counsel and most upright provision we thought to arrange that no one should be denied the opportunity to give his heart to the observance of the Christian religion, or of that religion which he should think best for himself, so that the supreme Deity, to whose worship we freely yield our hearts, may show in all things His usual favor and benevolence. Therefore, you should know that it has pleased us to remove all conditions that were in the rescripts[25] formerly given to you officially concerning the Christians. Now any one of these who wished to

---

* Lactantius, *The Death of the Persecutors* 48
[24] Taken, with editing, from Alexander Roberts and James Donaldson, *The Ante-Nicene Fathers,* vol. 7 (New York: Scribners, 1905), 320.

[25] *rescripts:* imperial orders, usually in response to written questions from lesser officials to the emperor.

observe the Christian religion may do so freely and openly, without any disturbance or molestation. We commend these things most fully to your care that you may know that we have given Christians free and unrestricted opportunity of religious worship. When you see that we have granted them this, you will know that we have also conceded to other religions the right of open and free worship for the sake of the peace of our times. All peoples may have the free opportunity to worship as they please. This regulation is made that we may not seem to detract anything from any dignity or any religion.

Moreover, in the case of the Christians especially, we esteemed it best to order that if anyone has bought from our treasury or from anyone else those places where they were previously accustomed to assemble, concerning which a certain decree had been made and a letter sent to you officially, the same shall be restored to the Christians without payment or any claim of recompense and without any kind of fraud or deception. . . . All this property ought to be delivered at once to the community of the Christians. These Christians have possessed not only those places in which they were accustomed to assemble, but also other property, namely the churches, belonging to them as a corporation and not as individuals. All these things that we have included under the above law you will order to be restored, without any hesitation or controversy at all, to these Christians.

Theodosius' Prohibition of Worship of the Roman Gods*

In 392, Emperor Theodosius, a strong defender of the orthodox church and the place of Christianity, outlawed the practice of the old Roman religion. This decree is one of a series of laws prohibiting paganism. These laws dealt a strong blow to the old religion but did not bring it to an end, despite the occasionally strong measures taken for their enforcement.[26]

From now on no one of any race or rank, whether placed in office or discharged with honor, powerful by birth or humble in condition and fortune, shall anywhere or in any city sacrifice an innocent [animal] victim to a senseless image. He shall not venerate with fire the household deity by a more private offering, as it were the spirit of the house or the Penates,[27] and burn lights, place incense, or hang up garlands. If any one undertakes by way of sacrifice to slay a victim or to consult the smoking entrails, let him as guilty of treason receive the appropriate sentence. He shall be convicted by a lawful indictment, although he may not have sought anything against the safety of the princes or concerning their welfare. It is a crime of this nature to wish to repeal the laws, to spy into unlawful things, to reveal secrets, to attempt forbidden things, to seek the end of another's welfare, or to promise the hope of another's ruin.[28]

If any one by placing incense venerates either images made by mortal labor, or those which are enduring, or if any one from now on ridiculously venerates what he has represented, either by a tree encircled with garlands or an altar of cut turfs, though the advantage of such service is small, the injury to religion is complete. He is guilty of sacrilege, and shall be punished by the loss of that house or possession in which he worshipped according to the heathen superstition. All places that smoke with incense, if they are

---

* *Theodosian Code* 16:10, 12

[26] Taken, with editing, from J. C. Ayer, *A Source Book for Ancient Church History* (New York: Scribners, 1913), 346–48.

[27] *Penates:* Roman deities of the household and family.

---

[28] *repeal the laws . . . ruin:* these things could be sought by way of sacrifice to pagan gods.

proved to belong to those who burn the incense, shall be confiscated. If anyone should venture this sort of sacrifice in temples or public sanctuaries or buildings and fields belonging to another, and if it appears that he did these acts without the knowledge of the owner, let him be compelled to pay a fine of twenty-five pounds of gold. Let the same penalty apply to those who connive at this crime as well as those who sacrifice.

INSTITUTION

Papal Primacy Derived from Petrine Primacy*

Pope Leo I, called "Leo the Great," bishop of Rome from about 440 to 461, was a staunch promoter of papal power. This passage is the classic early statement on the origin and nature of papal power. Leo uses an interpretation of several New Testament passages to claim that the bishop of Rome is the successor of Peter. This argument was influential on emperor Valentinus III, who in 445 decreed that the bishop of Rome is head of the entire church.[29]

It is profitable and worthy to raise the mind's eye to the contemplation of the glory of the most blessed apostle Peter, and to celebrate this day[30] in honor of him. He was watered with so many large streams from the very fountain of all graces that he received many special privileges of his own, while no privilege has passed to others except through him. . . .

"You are Peter, and on this rock I will build my Church, and the gates of hell shall not prevail against it."[31] On this strength, he says, I will build an eternal temple, and the loftiness of my Church, reaching to heaven, shall rise upon the firmness of this faith. . . . "I will give you the keys of the kingdom of heaven; whatever you bind on earth shall be bound in heaven, and whatever you loose on earth shall be loosed in heaven."[32] The right of this power did indeed pass on to the other apostles, and the order of this decree passed on to all the leaders of the Church. But this power that was imparted to all was first entrusted to one person. Therefore this power is granted to Peter separately, because all the rulers of the Church are invested with the figure of Peter. Peter's privilege remains wherever judgment is passed from him. . . .

Again as his passion came near, which was to shake the firmness of the disciples, the Lord says, "Simon, behold Satan has desired to have you that he may sift you as wheat. But I have prayed for you that you faith may not fail, and when you have returned, strengthen your brothers, that you may not enter temptation."[33] The danger from the temptation was common to all apostles, and they all needed the help of divine protection, since the devil wanted to harass and shatter them all. Yet the Lord takes special care of Peter, because the state of the others would be more certain if the mind of their leader were not overcome. So then in Peter the strength of all is fortified, and the help of divine grace is given so that the stability that Christ gave to Peter is conveyed through Peter to the apostles.

Beloved, since we see such protection divinely granted to us, we justly rejoice in the merits and dignity of our leader [Peter]. We render thanks to the eternal King, our Redeemer, the Lord

---

* Pope Leo I, *Sermons* 4.2–4

[29] Taken, with editing, from T. W. Allies, *The See of Peter* (London, 1850).

[30] *this day:* the anniversary day of Pope Leo, as mentioned at the end of this selection.

[31] *On this rock . . . it:* a quotation of Jesus in Matthew 16:18.

---

[32] Matthew 16:19.

[33] Luke 22:31–32.

Jesus Christ, for having given so great a power to him whom he made chief of the whole Church. If anything, even in our time, is rightly done and rightly ordered, we must ascribe it to Peter's working and his guidance, to whom Christ said, "And when you have returned, strengthen your brethren." The Lord after his resurrection, in answer to the triple profession of eternal love, said three times to Peter, with mystical intent, "Feed my sheep."[34] Beyond a doubt, the pious shep-

herd does this even now, and fulfills the charge of his Lord. He confirms us with his exhortations, and does not cease to pray for us, so that we may not be overcome by temptation. If, as we must believe, he extends this care of his piety to all God's people everywhere, how much more will he condescend to grant his help to us his children. . . . Therefore, let us ascribe to him this anniversary day of us his servant, and this festival, by whose patronage we have been thought worthy to share his seat itself.

---

[34] John 21:15–19.

The Scripture Canon in Formation*

Marcion was one of the most influential Christian leaders of the second century. His rival church spread throughout the Roman Empire until it was absorbed by the Gnostic and Manichean movements. Marcion rejected the religion of the Old Testament as true for Christians. He accepted only the Gospel of Luke and ten letters of Paul as authoritative and scriptural, editing out of them all traces of the God of the Old Testament. His was probably the first Christian canon, and it impelled other Christians to justify a larger New Testament canon and the continuing significance of the Old Testament. None of Marcion's writings have survived; the first selection is Irenaeus' quite hostile description of it.[35]

The second selection, the Muratorian Canon, was written in Rome perhaps around 200. Its name comes from its eighteenth-century discoverer, L. A. Muratori. Originally in Greek, it was translated into such crude Latin that some of the text is difficult to interpret, and this translation into English preserves much of the barbarousness of the

Latin. The beginning (which probably spoke about the Gospel of Matthew) and the ending are lost. This text is important for its indication of the motives and process of canonization.[36]

Marcion of Pontus succeeded [Cerdon, an early Gnostic], and developed his school, advancing the most daring blasphemy against the God of the law and the prophets. He declared him to be the author of evil, a lover of war, inconsistent in judging, and inconsistent in himself. Jesus was derived from that Father who is above the God that made the world. . . . He abolished the prophets and the law, and all the works of that God who made the world, whom also he calls "Ruler of the World." Beside all this, Marcion mutilates the Gospel according to Luke, removing all that is written about the birth of the Lord, and setting aside a great deal of his teachings in which the Lord is recorded as clearly confessing that the Maker of this universe is his Father. He likewise persuaded his disciples that he himself was more worthy of belief than those apostles who have handed down the gospel to us; he gave his

---

* Irenaeus, *Against Heresies* 1.27.2; *Muratorian Canon*
[35] Taken, with editing, from Alexander Roberts and James Donaldson, *The Ante-Nicene Fathers,* vol. 1 (New York: Scribners, 1905), 352.

[36] E. S. Buchanon, "The Codex Muratorianus," *Journal of Theological Studies* 8 (1907): 540–43.

disciples only a fragment of the Gospel. In a similar manner he also dismembered the epistles of Paul, removing all that is said by the apostle about that God who made the world. . . . He also removed those passages from the prophetic writings[37] which the apostle quotes to teach us that the prophets announced beforehand the coming of the Lord.

[The Muratorian Canon] The third Gospel book is that according to Luke. This physician Luke after Christ's ascension, since Paul had taken him with him as a legal expert, composed it in his own name according to (his) thinking. Yet he himself did not see the Lord in the flesh; and therefore, as he was able to ascertain it, he begins to tell the story from the birth of John. The fourth of the Gospels [is] that of John of the Decapolis, one of the disciples. When his fellow-disciples and bishops urged him, he said: Fast with me from today for three days, and what will be revealed to each one let us relate to one another. In the same night it was revealed to Andrew, one of the apostles, that, while all were to go over (it), John in his own name should write everything down. And therefore, though various rudiments are taught in the several Gospel books, yet that matters nothing for the faith of believers, since by the one and guiding Spirit everything is declared in all. . . .

Luke, writing to the "most excellent Theophilus," summarizes the several things that in his own presence have come to pass, as also by the omission of the suffering of Peter he makes quite clear, and equally by [the omission] of the journey of Paul, who from the city [Rome] proceeded to Spain.

The letters of Paul themselves make clear to those who wish to know it which were written by him, from what place and for what reason. First of all to the Corinthians [to whom he forbids] the heresy of schism, then to the Galatians [to whom he forbids] circumcision, and then to the Romans, he explains that Christ is the rule of the Scriptures and moreover their principle, he has written at considerable length. We must deal with these serially, since the blessed apostle Paul himself, following the rule of his predecessor John, writes by name only to seven churches in the following order: to the Corinthians the first [epistle], to the Ephesians the second, to the Philippians the third, to the Colossians the fourth, to the Galatians the fifth, to the Thessalonians the sixth, to the Romans the seventh. Although he wrote to the Corinthians and to the Thessalonians once more for their reproof, it is yet clearly recognizable that over the whole earth one church is spread. For John also in the Revelation writes indeed to seven churches, yet speaks to all. But to Philemon one, and to Titus one, and to Timothy two, [letters written] out of goodwill and love, are yet held sacred to the glory of the catholic Church for the ordering of ecclesiastical discipline. There is current also [an epistle] to the Laodiceans, another to the Alexandrians, forged in Paul's name for the sect of Marcion, and several others, which cannot be received in the catholic Church, as it is not fitting that honey should be mixed with gall.

The letter of Jude and two under the name of John are accepted as sound in the catholic Church, and the Wisdom written by friends of Solomon[38] in his honour. Also of the revelations we accept only those of John and Peter, which some of our people do not want to have read in the Church. But Hermas wrote the Shepherd quite lately in our time in the city of Rome, when on the throne of the church of the city of Rome the bishop Pius, his brother, was seated. And therefore it ought indeed to be read, but it cannot be read publicly in the Church to the people either among the prophets, whose number is settled, or among the apostles to the end of time.

---

[37] *prophetic writings:* from the Old Testament.

[38] *Wisdom . . . of Solomon:* a book of the deuterocanonical Old Testament.

Offices of the Church in the Second Century *

Polycarp, bishop of Smyrna (Asia Minor) and one of the Apostolic Fathers, was martyred ca. 156. In his letter to the church in Philippi, Greece, he lays down these rules for church offices and for unofficial groups (e.g., young men and women) within the church. These rules are very similar to the church order in the Pastoral Epistles (I and II Timothy, Titus) of the New Testament, and this entire selection is richly illustrated with quotations from, and allusions to, the New Testament.[39]

Let us first of all teach ourselves to walk in the commandment of the Lord. Then we must teach our wives in the faith delivered to them, and in love and purity, to cherish their own husbands in all fidelity, to love all others equally in all chastity, and to educate their children in the fear of God. The widows should be discreet in their faith pledged to the Lord, praying unceasingly on behalf of all, refraining from all slander, gossip, false witness, love of money, in fact, from evil of any kind. They should know that they are God's altar, that everything is examined for blemishes, and nothing escapes him whether of thoughts or sentiments, or any of "the secrets of the heart."[40] Knowing that "God is not mocked,"[41] we ought to live worthily of his commandment and glory.

[5.1] Likewise the deacons should be blameless before his righteousness, as servants of God and Christ and not of men. They should not be slanderers, or double-tongued, not lovers of money, temperate in all matters, compassionate, careful, living according to the truth of the Lord, who became a servant of all. If we are pleasing in the present age, we shall also obtain from him the age to come, because he promised to raise us from the dead. And if we bear our citizenship worthy of him, "we shall also reign with him"[42]— provided, of course, that we have faith.

Similarly also the younger ones must be blameless in all things, especially taking thought of purity and bridling themselves from all evil. It is a fine thing to cut oneself off from the lusts that are in the world. "Every passion of the flesh wages war against the Spirit," and "neither fornicators nor male prostitutes nor homosexuals will inherit the Kingdom of God,"[43] nor those who do perverse things. Therefore it is necessary to refrain from all these things, and be obedient to the presbyters and deacons as unto God and Christ. The young women must live with a blameless and pure conscience.

The presbyters must be compassionate, merciful to all, turning back those who have gone astray, looking after the sick, and not neglecting the widow or orphan or one that is poor. He must be "always taking thought for what is honorable in the sight of God and of men,"[44] refraining from all anger, partiality, unjust judgment, keeping far from all love of money, not hastily believing evil of anyone, nor being severe in judgment, knowing that we all owe the debt of sin. If we pray the Lord to forgive us, we ourselves ought also to forgive. We are all before the eyes of the Lord our God, and "everyone shall stand before the judgment seat of Christ and give an account of himself."[45] So then let us "serve him with fear and all reverence," as he himself has commanded,[46] and also the apostles who preached the gospel to us and the prophets who foretold the coming of the Lord.

---

* Polycarp, *Letter to the Philippians* 4.2–6.3
[39] Taken, with editing, from Kirsopp Lake, *The Apostolic Fathers*, vol. 1 (Cambridge, MA: Harvard University Press, 1912), 289–90.
[40] I Corinthians 14:25.
[41] Galatians 6:7.
[42] II Timothy 2:12.
[43] The first quotation is from I Peter 2:11, the second from I Corinthians 6:9–10.
[44] Proverbs 3:4.
[45] Romans 14:10.
[46] Psalms 2:11; Hebrews 12:28.

The Deaconess*

The Didascalia Apostolorum *("Teaching of the Apostles") is a manual of church government from third-century Syria. In the New Testament, women deacons seem to have ministered to both men and women. Here the deaconesses assist the bishop in his ministry to women. They are to assist in the baptism of women and be official visitors to Christian women living in non-Christian households.*[47]

Therefore, bishop, appoint righteous workers as helpers who may co-operate with you for salvation. Of those that please you out of all the people, choose and appoint men as deacons for the performance of the most things that are required, but appoint women for the ministry to women. For there are houses where you cannot send a deacon to the women, on account of the heathen, but may send a deaconess.

Also in many other matters the office of a deaconess is required. In the first place, when women go down into the water, those who go down into the water ought . . . to be anointed by a deaconess with the oil of anointing. Where there is no woman at hand, and especially no deaconess, he who baptizes must anoint her who is being baptized. But where there is a woman, and especially a deaconess, it is not fitting that women should be seen by men. . . . Afterwards—whether you yourself baptize, or you command the deacons or presbyters to baptize—let a woman deacon, as we have already said, anoint the women. But let a man pronounce over them the invocation of the divine Names in the water.

When she who is being baptized has come up from the water, let the deaconess receive her and teach and instruct her how the seal of baptism ought to be (kept) unbroken in purity and holiness. For this cause we say that the ministry of a woman deacon is especially necessary and important. For our Lord and Savior also was ministered unto by women ministers, Mary Magdalene, and Mary the daughter of James and mother of Jose, and the mother of the sons of Zebedee, with other women besides. You also need the ministry of a deaconess for other things. A deaconess is required to go into the houses of the heathen where there are believing women, to visit those who are sick, to minister to their needs, and to bathe those who have begun to recover from sickness.

---

* *Teaching of the Apostles* 3.15–17

[47] Taken, with editing, from Alexander Roberts and James Donaldson, eds., *The Ante-Nicene Fathers*, vol. 7 (New York: Scribners, 1905), 431.

An Ancient Christian Service**

As a part of his defense of Christianity, Justin briefly describes a Christian service from the middle of the second century. It begins with one who has just been baptized being escorted to the service.[48]

After thus washing[49] the one who has been convinced and signified his assent, we lead him to those who are called brethren, where they are assembled. The memoirs of the apostles or the writings of the apostles are read, as long as time permits; then, when the reader has ceased, the president verbally instructs and exhorts us to imi-

---

** Justin, *Apology* 65–66

[48] Taken, with editing, from Alexander Roberts and James Donaldson, *The Ante-Nicene Fathers*, vol. 1 (New York: Scribners, 1905), 185. A composite translation from chapters 65–66.

---

[49] *washing:* baptizing.

tate these good things. Then we rise together and pray. We pray that we may be made worthy, having learned the truth, to be found good citizens and keepers of what is commanded, so that we may be saved with eternal salvation. On finishing the prayers we greet each other with a kiss. Then bread and a cup of water and mixed wine[50] are brought to the president of the brethren. Taking

them, he sends up praise and glory to the Father of the universe through the name of the Son and the Holy Spirit, and offers thanksgiving at some length that we have been deemed worthy to receive these things from him. When he has finished the prayers and the thanksgiving, the whole congregation present assents, saying, "Amen." ("Amen" in the Hebrew language means "So be it.") When the president has given thanks and the whole congregation has assented, those whom we call deacons give a portion of the consecrated bread and wine to all those present, and they take it to the absent.

---

[50] *a cup of water and mixed wine:* wine and water are combined in the communion cup, as was also the common practice in the Roman world for ordinary daily use of wine.

Baptism in the Second and Third Centuries*

The Teaching of the Twelve Apostles, *more commonly known by its shorter Greek name* Didache *("Teaching"), is an early second-century church order from Syria and the first of several church order books to come. Its description of baptism is the oldest we have after the New Testament; note the almost extreme simplicity of baptism here.*[51] *Hippolytus' church order comes from the early third century and reflects the much more developed ceremonies of the church in Rome, which Hippolytus urged on other churches.*[52]

The procedure for baptizing is this. After completing all the preliminaries, baptize in running water,[53] "In the Name of the Father, and of the Son, and of the Holy Spirit." If no running water is available, baptize in ordinary water. This

should be cold water, if possible; otherwise warm. If neither is practicable, then pour water three times on the head, "In the name of the Father, and of the Son, and of the Holy Spirit." Both baptizer and baptized ought to fast before the baptism, as well as any others who can do so. The candidate himself should be told to keep a fast for a day or two beforehand.

[*Apostolic Tradition*] At the hour when the cock crows they shall first pray over the water. . . . The candidates shall put off their clothes. They shall baptize the little children first. If they can answer for themselves, let them answer. But if they cannot, let their parents answer or someone from their family. Next they shall baptize the grown men and last the women, who shall have loosed their hair and laid aside their gold ornaments. Let no one go down to the water having any alien object with them.

At the time determined for baptizing, the bishop shall give thanks over the oil and put it into a vessel; it is called the Oil of Thanksgiving. He shall take other oil and exorcise over it, and it is called the Oil of Exorcism.[54] Let a

---

* *The Teaching of the Twelve Apostles* [*Didache*] 7; Hippolytus, *Apostolic Tradition* 3.21.1–3.22.6

[51] Taken, with editing, from Kirsopp Lake, *The Apostolic Fathers,* vol. 1 (Cambridge, MA: Harvard University Press, 1912), 319–21.

[52] Taken from B. S. Easton, *The Apostolic Tradition of Hippolytus* (Cambridge: Cambridge University Press, 1924), 33–41. Used by permission.

[53] *running water:* literally, "living water." This reflects the Jewish practice of ritual bathing in natural, flowing water.

[54] *Exorcism:* driving out of evil spirits.

deacon carry the Oil of Exorcism and stand on the left hand of the presbyter. Another deacon shall take the Oil of Thanksgiving and stand on the right hand.

When the presbyter takes hold of each one of those who are to be baptized, let him bid him renounce, saying, "I renounce you, Satan, and all your service and all your works." When he has said this let him anoint him with the Oil of Exorcism, saying: "Let all evil spirits depart far from you." In this way he shall hand him over to the presbyter who stands by the water to baptize.

A deacon shall descend with him in this way. When the one who is baptized has descended into the water, he who baptizes him shall lay a hand on him and say: "Do you believe in God the Father Almighty?" He who is being baptized shall say, "I believe." Let him immediately baptize him, once, having his hand laid upon his head.

After this let him say: "Do you believe in Christ Jesus the Son of God, who was born of the Holy Spirit and the Virgin Mary, who was crucified in the days of Pontius Pilate, and died, and rose the third day living from the dead, and ascended into the heavens, and sat down at the right hand of the Father, and will come to judge the living and the dead?" And when he says "I believe," let him baptize him the second time.

Again let him say, "Do you believe in the Holy Spirit in the Holy Church, and the resurrection of the flesh?" He who is being baptized shall say, "I believe." And so let him baptize him a third time.

Afterwards when he comes up he shall be anointed by the presbyter with the Oil of Thanksgiving, saying, "I anoint you with holy oil in the name of Jesus Christ." After they have dried themselves, they shall put on their clothes.

Then the bishop shall lay his hand upon them invoking and saying, "Lord God, you did count these worthy of deserving the forgiveness of sins by the bath of regeneration; make them worthy to be filled with your Holy Spirit and send upon them your grace, that they may serve you according to your will; for to you is the glory, to the Father and to the Son with the Holy Spirit in the holy church, both now and ever, world without end."

After this, pouring the consecrated oil and laying his hand on his head, he shall say: "I anoint you with holy oil in God the Father Almighty, and Christ Jesus and the Holy Spirit." And sealing him on the forehead he shall give him the kiss and say, "The Lord be with you." He who has been sealed shall say, "And with your spirit." So he shall do to each one. Then they shall pray henceforth together with all the people.

The Eucharist*

Hippolytus wrote in part to formalize the rites and put an end to the widespread improvisation in the Eucharist suggested in the previous readings. This order for the Eucharist is fairly typical, but the blessing of other foods appended at the end is unique. Hippolytus is careful to distinguish the blessing and eating of these foods from the main Eucharistic offering. This form of the Eucharist became influential in both the Eastern and Western churches.[55]

Then the deacons shall bring the offering to [the bishop], and he, laying his hand upon it, shall say with all the presbyters as the thanksgiving: The Lord be with you.

---

* Hippolytus, *Apostolic Tradition* 43

[55] Taken, with editing, from B. J. Kidd, *Documents Illustrative of the History of the Church,* vol. 1 (New York: Macmillan, 1920), 171–72.

And all shall say: And with your spirit.
[Bishop:] Lift up your hearts!
[People:] We lift them up unto the Lord.
[Bishop:] Let us give thanks to the Lord.
[People:] It is proper and right.
And then he shall proceed immediately:

We give you thanks, O God, through your beloved Servant[56] Jesus Christ, whom at the end of time you sent to us as a Savior and Redeemer and the Messenger of your counsel. He is your Word, inseparable from you, through whom you made all things and in whom you are well pleased. You sent him from heaven into the womb of the Virgin, and who, dwelling within her, was made flesh, and was manifested as your Son, being born of [the] Holy Spirit and the Virgin. He, fulfilling your will, and winning for himself a holy people, spread out his hands when he came to suffer, that by his death he might set free those who believe on you. Before he was betrayed to his willing death, that he might bring death to naught, and break the bonds of the devil, and tread hell under foot, and give light to the righteous, and set up a boundary post, and manifest his resurrection, taking bread and giving thanks to you, he said: Take, eat; this is my body, which is broken for you. And likewise also the cup, saying: This is my blood, which is shed for you. As often as you perform this, you perform my memorial.

Having in memory, therefore, his death and resurrection, we offer to you the bread and the cup, yielding you thanks, because you have counted us worthy to stand before you and to minister to you.

And we pray that you would send your Holy Spirit upon the offerings of your holy church; that you, gathering them into one, would grant to all your saints who partake to be filled with [the] Holy Spirit, that their faith may be confirmed in truth, that we may praise and glorify you; through your Servant Jesus Christ, through whom be to you glory and honor, with [the] Holy Spirit in the holy church, both now and always and world without end. Amen.

If anyone offers oil, he shall give thanks as at the offering of the bread and wine, though not with the same words but in the same general manner, saying: Sanctify this oil, O God, with which you anointed kings, priests and prophets; grant health to them who use it and partake of it, so that it may bestow comfort on all who taste it and health on all who use it.

Likewise, if anyone offers cheese and olives, let him say thus: Sanctify this milk that has been united into one mass, and unite us to your love. Let your loving kindness ever rest upon this fruit of the olive, which is a type[57] of your bounty, which you caused to flow from the tree unto life for them who hope in you.

But at every blessing shall be said: Glory be to you, with [the] Holy Spirit in the holy church, both now and always and world without end.

---

[56]*Servant:* the Greek word can also be translated "Child/Son."

---

[57] *type:* symbol.

A Pilgrim Nun Worships in Eastern-Rite Jerusalem*

Egeria, an early fifth-century nun from Spain (whose name is also known as Aetheria, Etheria, and Echeria), wrote an account of her pilgrimage to Egypt, Palestine, and Asia Minor for her religious community. In Jerusalem, she visited the leading churches and monasteries. One of the earliest extant firsthand accounts of pilgrimage that we have, Egeria and Her Travels furnishes a wealth of detail on the activities at the holy sites and is a rich source for our knowledge of early worship in the Eastern branch of Christianity. In this selection,

---

* Egeria and Her Travels, 24–25

Egeria describes first the daily services in the Church of the Resurrection (Anastasis), then the main Sunday service.[58]

Loving sisters, I am sure it will interest you to know about the daily services they have in the holy places, and I must tell you about them. All the doors of the Anastasis are opened before cockcrow each day, and the *monazontes* and *parthenae*,[59] as they call them here, come in, and also some laymen and -women, at least those who are willing to wake at such an early hour. From then until daybreak they join in singing the refrains to the hymns, psalms, and antiphons.[60] There is a prayer between each of the hymns, since there are two or three presbyters and deacons each day by rotation, who are there with the *monazontes* and say the prayers between all the hymns and antiphons.

As soon as dawn comes, they start the Morning Hymns, and the bishop with his clergy comes and joins them. He goes straight into the cave,[61] and inside the screen he first says the Prayer for All (mentioning any names he wishes) and blesses the catechumens, and then another prayer and blesses the faithful. Then he comes outside the screen, and everyone comes up to kiss his hand. He blesses them one by one and goes out, and by the time the dismissal takes place it is already day.

Again at midday everyone comes into the Anastasis and says psalms and antiphons until a message is sent to the bishop. Again he enters, and, without taking his seat, goes straight inside the screen in the Anastasis (which is to say into the cave where he went in the early morning), and again, after a prayer, he blesses the faithful and comes outside the screen, and again they come to kiss his hand.

At three o'clock they do once more what they did at midday, but at four o'clock they have *Lychnicon*, as they call it, or in our language, Lucernare.[62] All the people congregate once more in the Anastasis, and the lamps and candles are all lit, which makes it very bright. The fire is brought not from outside, but from the cave—inside the screen—where a lamp is always burning night and day. For some time they have the Lucernare psalms and antiphons; then they send for the bishop, who enters and sits in the chief seat. The presbyters also come and sit in their places, and the hymns and antiphons go on. [5] Then, when they have finished singing everything which is appointed, the bishop rises and goes in front of the screen (i.e., the cave). One of the deacons makes the normal commemoration of individuals, and each time he mentions a name a large group of boys responds *Kyrie eleison* (in our language, "Lord, have mercy"). Their voices are very loud. As soon as the deacon has done his part, the bishop says a prayer and prays the Prayer for All. Up to this point the faithful and the catechumens are praying together, but now the deacon calls every catechumen to stand where he is and bow his head, and the bishop says the blessing over the catechumens from his place. There is another prayer, after which the deacon calls for all the faithful to bow their heads, and the bishop says the blessing over the faithful from his place. Thus the dismissal takes place at the Anastasis, and they all come up one by one to kiss the bishop's hand. . . .

But on the seventh day, the Lord's Day, there gather in the courtyard before cockcrow all the people, as many as can get in, as if it was Easter. . . . Soon the first cock crows, and at that the bishop enters, and goes into the cave in the Anastasis. The doors are all opened, and all the people come into the Anastasis, which is already ablaze with lamps. When they are inside, a psalm is said by one of the presbyters, with everyone responding, and it is followed by a prayer; then a psalm is said by one of the deacons, and another

---

[58] Translated by the author from *S. Silviae Peregrinatio* (*Corpus Scriptorum Ecclesiasticorum Latinorum,* vol. 39; Vienna: Teubner, 1900), pp. 73–74.

[59] *monazontes:* monks (literally, "those who live alone"); *parthenai:* nuns (literally, "virgins").

[60] *antiphons:* a responsive chanting of a series of verses.

[61] *the cave:* in which was the tomb of Jesus.

[62] *Lychnicon, Lucernare:* lighting of the evening lamps.

prayer; then a third psalm is said by one of the clergy, a third prayer, and the Commemoration of All.[63] [10] After these three psalms and prayers they take censers into the cave of the Anastasis, so that the whole Anastasis basilica is filled with the smell. Then the bishop, standing inside the screen, takes the Gospel book and goes to the door, where he himself reads the account of the Lord's resurrection. At the beginning of the reading the whole assembly groans and laments at all that the Lord underwent for us, and the way they weep would move even the hardest heart to tears. When the Gospel is finished, the bishop comes out, and is taken with singing to the Cross, and they all go with him. They have one psalm

there and a prayer, then he blesses the people, and that is the dismissal. As the bishop goes out, everyone comes to kiss his hand. . . .

[25.1] At daybreak the people assemble in the Great Church built by Constantine on Golgotha Behind the Cross. It is the Lord's Day, and they do what is everywhere the custom on the Lord's Day. But you should note that here it is usual for any presbyter who has taken his seat to preach, if he so wishes, and when they have finished there is a sermon from the bishop. The object of having this preaching every Sunday is to make sure that the people will continually be learning about the Bible and the love of God. Because of all the preaching it is a long time before the dismissal, which takes place not before ten or even eleven o'clock.

---

[63] *Commemoration of All:* i.e., all the faithful departed.

The Beginnings of Monasticism*

These two selections portray two important aspects of early monasticism: monastic poverty as a way of following Christ and monasticism as a replacement for martyrdom. Although Anthony was not (as is often said) the first monk or the founder of monasticism, he had a profound influence on its early development in both the East and West, and Athanasius' Life of Saint Anthony became a model for later writings about saints.[64]

Going according to custom into the Lord's House, he communed with himself and reflected as he walked how the apostles left all and followed the savior, how they in the Acts sold their possessions and brought them and laid them at the apostles' feet for distribution to the needy, and how great a hope was laid up for them in heaven. Pondering on these things he entered the church, and it happened the gospel was be-

ing read, and he heard the Lord saying to the rich man, "If you would be perfect, go and sell what you have and give to the poor; and come follow me and you shall have treasure in heaven." Anthony went out immediately from the church and gave the possessions of his forefathers to the villagers—they were three hundred acres, productive and very fair—that they should no longer be a burden upon himself and his sister. And all the rest that was moveable he sold, and having got together much money he gave it to the poor, reserving a little, however, for his sister's sake. . . .

But the devil, who hates and envies what is good, could not endure to see such a resolution in a youth. . . . First of all he tried to lead him away from the discipline, whispering to him the remembrance of his wealth, care for his sister, claims of kindred, love of money, the various pleasures of the table and the other relaxations of life, and at last the difficulty of virtue and the labor of it. . . . The devil, unhappy soul, one night even took upon him the shape of a woman and imitated all her acts simply to beguile Anthony.

---

* Athanasius, *Life of Saint Anthony* 2, 5, 9, 14, 47
[64] Taken, with editing, from Philip Schaff and Henry Wace, *Nicene and Post-Nicene Fathers,* vol. 4 (2d series; New York: Scribners, 1900), 196–209.

But he, his mind filled with Christ and the nobility inspired by him, and considering the spirituality of the soul, quenched the coal of the other's deceit. . . . In the night the demons made such a din that the whole of that place seemed to be shaken by an earthquake, and the demons as if breaking the four walls of the dwelling seemed to enter through them, coming in the likeness of beasts and creeping things. And the place was suddenly filled with the forms of lions, bears, leopards, bulls, serpents, asps, scorpions, and wolves . . . altogether the noises of the apparitions, with their angry raging, were dreadful. . . .

And so for nearly twenty years he continued training himself in solitude, never going out, and seldom seen by anyone. After this, many were eager and wishful to imitate his discipline, and his acquaintances came and began to cast down and wrench off the door by force. Then Anthony, as if from a shrine, came forth initiated in the mysteries and filled with the Spirit of God. For the first time he was seen outside the fort by those who came to see him. And they, when they saw him, wondered at the sight, for he had the same habit of body as before, and was neither fat, like a man without exercise, nor lean from fasting and striving with the demons, but he was just the same as they had known him before his withdrawal. And again his soul was free from blemish, for it was neither contracted as if by grief nor relaxed by pleasure, nor possessed by laughter or dejection, for he was not troubled when he beheld the crowd, nor overjoyed at being saluted by so many. By him the Lord healed the bodily ailments of many present, and cleansed others from evil spirits. And he gave grace to Anthony in speaking. . . . He persuaded many to embrace the solitary life. Thus it happened in the end that cells arose even in the mountains, and the desert was colonized by monks, who came forth from their own people, and enrolled themselves for the citizenship in heaven. . . .

Anthony was a daily martyr to his conscience, and contended in the conflicts of faith. And his discipline was much severer [than a martyr's], for he was always fasting, and he had a garment of hair on the inside, while the outside was skin, which he kept until his end.[65] He neither bathed his body with water to free himself from filth nor did he ever wash his feet, nor even endure so much as to put them into water, unless compelled by necessity. Nor did any one even see him unclothed, nor his body naked at all, except after his death, when he was buried.

---

[65] This "hair shirt" would of course make its wearer very uncomfortable.

The Earliest Surviving Hymn*

The earliest church used the Psalms of the Old Testament as its hymns, especially those that were interpreted christologically. We have original Christian hymns in the New Testament that go back to the foundation of Christianity, but no music. This Greek-language hymn, the earliest to survive with its music, is from third-century Egypt; it was printed on the back of a papyrus corn account.

Because there are holes in the papyrus, the translation given below is only a close approximation.[66]

Let not the prince[67] be silent,
Nor the bright stars stop [making music].
You sources of rushing waters,

---

[66] Translated by the author from B. P. Grenfell and A. S. Hunt, *The Oxyrhynchus Papyri*, part 15 (London: Egypt Exploration Society, 1922), 21–23.

[67] *the prince:* perhaps the sun.

---

* *Oxyrhynchus Papyri* 15.1786

Let all sing hymns through the Father, Son and Holy Spirit.
Let all powers cry out loud: Amen, Amen.

[Sing praise to the] eternal Sovereign,
To the only giver of all good things.
Amen, Amen.

TEACHING

The Rule of Faith*

This rule of faith, like others, has a striking similarity to current baptismal confessions and the later Apostles' Creed, but most historians argue that no simple line of development connects them. Tertullian, although considered heretical by the orthodox church for going off into Montanism, wrote influential denunciations of other heresies as he defended the rule of faith.[68]

There is only one God, who is none other than the Creator of the world, who produced everything from nothing through his Word, sent forth before all things. This Word is called his Son, and in the Name of God was seen in different ways by the patriarchs, was always heard in the prophets and finally was brought down by the Spirit and power of God the Father into the Virgin Mary, was made flesh in her womb, was born of her and lived as Jesus Christ. He proclaimed a new law and a new promise of the kingdom of heaven, worked miracles, was crucified, on the third day rose again, was caught up into heaven and sat down at the right hand of the Father. He sent in his place the power of the Holy Spirit to guide believers. He will come with glory to take the saints up into the fruition of the life eternal and the heavenly promises and to sentence the wicked to everlasting fire, after the resurrection of both good and evil with the restoration of their bodies.

This Rule, as it will be proved, was taught by Christ. It permits no disputes among us, except those which heresies introduce and which make heretics.

---

* Tertullian, *Prescription against Heretics* 13

[68] Taken, with editing, from Alexander Roberts and James Donaldson, *The Ante-Nicene Fathers,* vol. 3 (New York: Scribners, 1905), 249.

Gnostic Christianity and Orthodox Christianity in Conflict**

The Gospel of Truth, *from the Nag Hammadi Codex, was known to Irenaeus. Some historians argue that the early Christian Gnostic Valentinus was the author of this gospel; at the least it reflects Valentinianism. It begins with a discussion of the* pleroma *("fullness"), which many Gnostics believed to be the supreme God who includes the emanations involved in creation and salvation.*[69]

The second selection is from the leading Christian opponent of Christian Gnosticism, Irenaeus, bishop of Lyon. First he gives a defense of orthodox

---

** *Gospel of Truth* 34–41; Irenaeus, *Against Heresies,* Preface 1.1–2, 7.1–5

[69] From J. M. Robinson, ed., *The Nag Hammadi Library in English* (New York: Harper & Row, 1977), 45–49. Copyright © 1977 by E. J. Brill, Leiden, The Netherlands. Reprinted by permission of HarperCollins Publishers, Inc.

Christianity against Valentinianism, then a succinct description of its main teaching.[70]

This is the word of the gospel of the discovery of the pleroma, for those who await the salvation which is coming from on high. While their hope which they are waiting for is waiting—they whose image is light with no shadow in it—then at that time the pleroma is about to come. The deficiency of matter has not arisen through the limitlessness of the Father, who is about to bring the time of the deficiency, although no one could say that the incorruptible one will come in this way. But the depth of the Father was multiplied and the thought of error did not exist with him. It is a thing that falls, it is a thing that easily stands upright again in the discovery of him who has come to him whom he shall bring back. For the bringing back is called repentance.

For this reason incorruptibility breathed forth; it pursued the one who had sinned in order that he might rest. For forgiveness is what remains for the light in the deficiency, the word of the pleroma. . . .

That is why Christ was spoken of in their midst, so that those who were disturbed might receive a bringing back, and he might anoint them with the ointment. The ointment is the mercy of the Father who will have mercy on them. But those whom he has anointed are the ones who have become perfect. For full jars are the ones that are usually anointed. But when the anointing of one jar is dissolved, it is emptied, and the reason for there being a deficiency is the thing through which its ointment goes. For at that time a breath draws it, one by the power of the one with it. But from him who has no deficiency no seal is removed, nor is anything emptied. But what he lacks the perfect Father fills again. He is good. He knows his plantings because it is he who planted them in his paradise. Now his paradise is his place of rest. . . .

When therefore it pleased him that his name which is uttered should be his Son, and he gave the name to him, that is, him who came forth from the depth, he spoke about his secret things, knowing that the Father is a being without evil. For that very reason he brought him forth in order to speak about the place and his resting-place from which he had come forth, and to glorify the pleroma, the greatness of his name and the gentleness of the Father. About the place each one came from he will speak, and to the region where he received his essential being he will hasten to return again, and to be taken from that place—the place where he stood—receiving a taste from that place and receiving nourishment, receiving growth. And his own resting-place is his pleroma.

Therefore all the emanations of the Father are pleromas, and the root of all his emanations is in the one who made them all grow up in himself. He assigned them their destinies. Each one of them is apparent in order that through their own thought. . . . For the place to which they send their thought, that place is their root, which takes them up in all the heights to the Father. They possess his head which is rest for them and they hold on close to him, as though to say that they have participated in his face by means of kisses. But they do not appear in this way, for they did not surpass themselves nor lack the glory of the Father nor think of him as small nor that he is harsh nor that he is wrathful, but a being without evil, imperturbable, gentle, knowing all spaces before they have come into existence, and having no need to be instructed.

This is the manner of those who possess something from above of the immeasurable greatness, as they stretch out after the one alone and the perfect one, the one who is there for them. And they do not go down to Hades nor have they envy nor groaning nor death within them, but they rest in him who is at rest, not striving nor being involved in the search for truth. But they themselves are the truth; and the Father is within them and they are in the Father, being perfect, being undivided in the truly good one, being in no way deficient in anything, but they are set at

---

[70] Taken, with editing, from Alexander Roberts and James Donaldson, *The Ante-Nicene Fathers*, vol. 1 (New York: Scribners, 1905), 315–16, 325–26.

rest, refreshed in the Spirit. And they will heed their root. They will be concerned with those things in which he will find his root and not suffer loss to his soul. This is the place of the blessed; this is their place.

[Irenaeus, *Against Heresies*] Certain men have set the truth aside, and bring in lying words and vain genealogies, which, as the apostle says, "minister disputes rather than godly edifying which is in faith." By means of their craftily-constructed plausibilities, they draw away the minds of the inexperienced and take them captive. Therefore I have felt constrained, my dear friend, to compose the following treatise in order to expose and counteract their machinations. These men falsify the words of God, and prove themselves evil interpreters of the good word of revelation. They also overthrow the faith of many by drawing them away, under a pretense of [superior] knowledge,[71] from Him who founded and adorned the universe, as if they had something more excellent and sublime to reveal than that God who created the heaven and the earth and all things that are in them. By means of specious and plausible words, they cunningly allure the simple-minded to inquire into their system. But they nevertheless clumsily destroy them, while they initiate them into their blasphemous and impious opinions about the Demiurge.[72] These simple ones are unable, even in such a matter, to distinguish falsehood from truth.

Error is never set forth in its naked deformity, lest, being thus exposed, it should at once be detected. But it is craftily decked out in an attractive dress, so as, by its outward form, to make it appear to the inexperienced (ridiculous as the expression may seem) more true than the truth itself. . . . Therefore, some are to be carried off, even as sheep are by wolves, because they do not perceive the true character of these men. Outwardly they are covered with sheep's clothing

(against whom the Lord has enjoined us to be on our guard), and because their language resembles ours, while their sentiments are very different. Thus I have deemed it my duty (after reading some of the *Commentaries,* as they call them, of the disciples of Valentinus, and after making myself acquainted with their tenets through personal dealings with some of them) to unfold to you, my friend, these portentous and profound mysteries, which do not fall within the range of every intellect, because all have not sufficiently purged their brains. I do this in order that you, obtaining an acquaintance with these things, may in turn explain them to all those with whom you art connected. Exhort them to avoid such an abyss of madness and of blasphemy against Christ. . . .

[7.1] When all the seed shall have come to perfection, they state that then their mother Achamoth shall pass from the intermediate place, and enter in within the Pleroma, and shall receive as her spouse the Savior, who sprang from all the Aeons, that thus a conjunction may be formed between the Savior and Sophia, that is, Achamoth. These, then, are the bridegroom and bride, while the nuptial chamber is the full extent of the Pleroma. The spiritual seed, again, being divested of their animal souls, and becoming intelligent spirits, shall in an irresistible and invisible manner enter in within the Pleroma, and be bestowed as brides on those angels who wait upon the Savior. The Demiurge himself will pass into the place of his mother Sophia; that is, the intermediate habitation. In this intermediate place, also, shall the souls of the righteous repose; but nothing of an animal nature shall find admittance to the Pleroma. When these things have taken place as described, then shall that fire which lies hidden in the world blaze forth and burn; and while destroying all matter, shall also be extinguished along with it, and have no further existence. They affirm that the Demiurge was acquainted with none of these things before the advent of the Savior.

There are also some who maintain that he also produced Christ as his own proper son, but of an

---

[71] *knowledge:* the Greek original is *gnosis,* from which *Gnostic* is derived.

[72] *Demiurge:* the evil aeon who made the world.

animal nature, and that mention was made of him by the prophets. This Christ passed through Mary just as water flows through a tube. A dove, that Savior who belonged to the Pleroma, descended upon him at the time of his baptism. In him there existed also that spiritual seed which proceeded from Achamoth. They hold, accordingly, that our Lord, while preserving the type of the first-begotten and primary tetrad, was compounded of these four substances—of the spiritual, in so far as He was from Achamoth; of the animal, as being from the Demiurge by a special dispensation; of the bodily, formed with unspeakable skill; and of the Savior, as respects that dove which descended upon Him. He also continued free from all suffering, since indeed it was not possible that He should suffer who was at once incomprehensible and invisible. And for this reason the Spirit of Christ, who had been placed within Him, was taken away when He was brought before Pilate. They maintain, further, that not even the seed which He had received from the mother [Achamoth] was subject to suffering. It, too, was impassible,[73] because it was spiritual, and invisible even to the Demiurge himself. It follows, then, according to them, that the animal Christ, and that which had been formed mysteriously by a special dispensation, underwent suffering, that the mother might exhibit through him a type of the Christ above, namely, of him who extended himself through Stauros,[74] and imparted to Achamoth shape, so far as substance was concerned. For they declare that all these transactions were counterparts of what took place above.

------

[73] *impassable:* not capable of suffering.

[74] *Stauros:* the Greek word for "cross."

Women and Gnosticism*

In this Christian-Gnostic book from the second century, Mary Magdalene encourages the disciples of Jesus to carry out the task of preaching he has given them, and she relates to them some of the teaching Jesus had given privately to her, including a vision of the ascending soul being questioned by the heavenly powers. This text shows that women often had a higher place in Gnostic Christianity than in orthodox Christianity, but even in Gnosticism their position was challenged.[75]

When the blessed one had said this he greeted them all, saying, "Peace be with you. Receive my peace to yourselves. Beware that no one lead you astray, saying, 'Lo here!' or 'Lo there!' For the Son of Man is within you. Follow after him!

Those who seek him will find him. Go then and preach the gospel of the kingdom. Do not lay down any rules beyond what I appointed for you, and do not give a law like the lawgiver[76] lest you be constrained by it." When he had said this, he departed.

But they were grieved. They wept greatly, saying, "How shall we go to the Gentiles and preach the gospel of the kingdom of the Son of Man? If they did not spare him, how will they spare us?"

Then Mary stood up, greeted them all, and said to her brethren, "Do not weep and do not grieve nor be irresolute, for his grace will be entirely with you and will protect you. But rather let us praise his greatness, for he has prepared us (and) made us into men."[77] When Mary said this,

------

* *Gospel of Mary 7:8–18*

[75] From J. M. Robinson, ed., *The Nag Hammadi Library in English* (New York: Harper & Row, 1977), 45–49. Copyright © 1977 By E. J. Brill, Leiden, the Netherlands. Reprinted by permission of HarperCollins Publishers, Inc.

[76] *lawgiver:* Moses.

[77] *made us into men:* the Gnostic Christian *Gospel of Thomas* ends with this same teaching of "making women male." Scholars disagree about its meaning.

she turned their hearts to the Good, and they began to discuss the words of the [Savior].

[10] Peter said to Mary, "Sister, we know that the Savior loved you more than the rest of women. Tell us the words of the Savior which you remember—which you know (but) we do not, nor have we heard them."

Mary answered and said, "What is hidden from you I will proclaim to you." And she began to speak to them these words: "I," she said, "I saw the Lord in a vision and I said to him, 'Lord, I saw you today in a vision.' He answered and said to me, 'Blessed are you, that you did not waver at the sight of me. For where the mind is, there is the treasure.' I said to him, 'Lord, now does he who sees the vision see through the soul or through the spirit?' The Savior answered and said, 'He does not see through the soul nor through the spirit, but the mind which [is] between the two—that is [what] sees the vision and it is. . . .'[78] [15] And desire said, 'I did not see you descending, but now I see you ascending. Why do you lie, since you belong to me?' The soul answered and said, 'I saw you. You did not see me nor recognize me. I served you as a gar-

---

[78] Pages 11–14 of the manuscript are missing at this point.

ment, and you did not know me.' When it had said this, it went away rejoicing greatly. . . ."

When Mary had said this, she fell silent, since it was to this point that the Savior had spoken with her. But Andrew answered and said to the brethren, "Say what you [wish to] say about what she has said. I at least do not believe that the Savior said this. For certainly these teachings are strange ideas." Peter answered and spoke concerning these same things. He questioned them about the Savior: "Did he really speak privately with a woman [and] not openly to us? Are we to turn about and all listen to her? Did he prefer her to us?"

Then Mary wept and said to Peter, "My brother Peter, what do you think? Do you think that I thought this up myself in my heart, or that I am lying about the Savior?" Levi answered and said to Peter, "Peter, you have always been hot-tempered. Now I see you contending against the woman like the adversaries. But if the Savior made her worthy, who are you indeed to reject her? Surely the Savior knows her very well. That is why he loved her more than us. Rather let us be ashamed and put on the perfect man, and separate as he commanded us and preach the gospel, not laying down any other rule or other law beyond what the Savior said."

The Threefold Interpretation of Scripture Explained and Illustrated*

Origen of Alexandria (ca. 185–284) held that just as a human is composed of body, soul, and spirit, the scriptures have these three senses. The "body" is its literal, historical and/or grammatical sense; the "soul" is its moral teaching and ability to build faith; the "spirit" is its heavenly or divine meaning, often found allegorically. The first reading is Origen's best explanation of this view,[79] and the second illustrates it with his interpretation of the parable of the Good Samaritan. This view of scripture and its interpretation was to predominate in the Western church until the Renaissance and Reformation and in the Eastern church until recent times.

One must portray the meaning of the sacred writings in a threefold way upon one's own soul, so that the simple person may be edified by what we may call the body of the scripture, the name given to the obvious interpretation. The person who has made some progress may be edified by its soul, as it were; and the one who is perfect

---

* Origen, *On First Principles* 4.2.4–4.3.5; *Homily on Luke* 2
[79] Taken from H. Butterworth, *Origen on First Principles* (London: SPCK, 1936), 272–78, 293–94, 295–97.

may be edified by the spiritual law, which has "a shadow of the good things to come."[80] For just as a person consists of body, soul, and spirit, so in the same way does the scripture, which has been prepared by God to be given for man's salvation. But since there are certain passages of scripture which, as we shall show in what follows, have no bodily [literal] sense at all, there are occasions when we must seek only for the soul and the spirit, so to speak, of the passage.

That it is possible to derive benefit from the first, and to this extent helpful meaning, is witnessed by the multitudes of sincere and simple believers. But if the usefulness of the law and the sequence and ease of the narrative were at first sight clearly discernible throughout, we should be unaware that there was anything beyond the obvious meaning for us to understand in the scriptures. Consequently the Word of God has arranged for certain stumbling-blocks, so to speak, and hindrances and impossibilities to be inserted in the law and the history, in order that we may not be completely drawn away by the sheer attractiveness of the language. . . .

Now what man of intelligence will believe that the first and the second and the third day, and the evening and the morning existed without the sun and the moon and stars? And that the first day, if we may so call it, was even without a heaven? And who is so silly as to believe that God, after the manner of a farmer, "planted a paradise eastward in Eden," and set in it a visible and touchable "tree of life," of such a sort that anyone who tasted its fruit with his bodily teeth would gain life; and again that one could partake of "good and evil" by chewing the fruit taken from the tree of that name? And when God is said to "walk in the paradise in the cool of the day" and Adam to hide himself behind a tree, I do not think anyone will doubt that these are figurative expressions which indicate certain mysteries through a semblance of history and not through actual events. . . .

When the passage as a connected whole is literally impossible, whereas the outstanding part of it is not impossible but even true, the reader must endeavor to grasp the entire meaning. The reader must connect by an intellectual process the account of what is literally impossible with the parts that are not impossible but are historically true. These are interpreted allegorically in common with the parts which, so far as the letter goes, did not happen at all. For our contention with regard to the whole of divine scripture is, that it all has a spiritual meaning, but not all a bodily [literal] meaning; for the bodily meaning is often proved to be an impossibility. Consequently the man who reads the divine books reverently, believing them to be divine writings, must exercise great care.

[*Homily on Luke*[81]] 'A man went down from Jerusalem to Jericho.' We see in this man Adam, man and his true destiny, the fall which followed disobedience. Jerusalem is paradise or the heavenly Jerusalem; Jericho is the world; the robbers represent the hostile powers, the demons of those false doctrines which came before Christ; the wounds are disobedience and sin; the theft of clothing symbolizes the stripping off of incorruptibility and immortality, along with all the virtues. The man left half-conscious represents the present state of our nature which has become semi-mortal (in fact the soul is immortal); the priest is the law; the Levite the Prophets; the Samaritan is the Christ who took flesh in Mary's womb; the beast of burden is the body of Christ; the wine is the word of his teaching; the oil is the word of goodwill and merciful compassion to men; the inn is the church; the innkeeper represents the apostles and their successors, the bishops and teachers of the church . . . the return of the Samaritan is the second coming of Christ.

---

[80] Hebrews 10:1.

[81] Translated by the author from Paul Koetschau, *Origines Werke*, vol. 4 (Leipzig: Hinrichs, 1913) 273. For a modern translation of the Good Samaritan story, see page 43.

The Ecumenical Creeds*

The creeds (from Latin credo, *"I believe,") grew out of baptismal questions. The Apostles' Creed puts an emphasis on the early Christian proclamation of Jesus Christ; it is widely used in the Western churches, but not in the Eastern. The Nicene Creed is given here in its early (325) and later (Niceno-Constantinopolitan, 381) versions; the differences should be closely compared. This creed is used in the baptismal rites of the Eastern church and the Eucharist of both the Eastern and Western churches.*[82] *The Chalcedonian Creed (451) emphasizes the doctrine of the one person of Jesus Christ in two natures (divine and human).*[83]

[Apostles' Creed] I believe in God the Father Almighty, Maker of heaven and earth;

And in Jesus Christ his only Son our Lord; Who was conceived by the Holy Spirit, born of the Virgin Mary; Suffered under Pontius Pilate, was crucified, died, and was buried; He descended into hell; The third day he rose again from the dead; He ascended into heaven, and sits on the right hand of God the Father Almighty; From there he shall come to judge the living and the dead.

I believe in the Holy Spirit; The holy Catholic Church; The communion of saints; The forgiveness of sins; The resurrection of the body, and the life everlasting.

[The Original Nicene Creed, with the additions of the Niceno-Constantinopolitan Creed in italics] We believe in one God the Father Almighty, Maker of *heaven and earth, and of* all things visible and invisible;

And in one Lord Jesus Christ, the Son of God, begotten from the Father *before all worlds,* God

from God, Light from Light, true God from true God; Begotten, not made; Being of one substance with the Father; By whom all things were made, things in heaven and things on earth; Who for us men and for our salvation came down *from heaven* and was incarnate by the Holy Spirit of the Virgin Mary, and was made man: He suffered *also for us under Pontius Pilate* and rose again on the third day *according to the Scriptures;* And ascended into heaven, *and sits on the right hand of the Father,* and will come to judge the living and the dead.

And *we believe* in the Holy Spirit, *the Lord and Giver of Life, Who proceeds from the Father [and the Son*[84] *]; Who with the Father and the Son is worshipped and glorified; Who spoke by the Prophets; And in one Catholic and Apostolic Church. We acknowledge one Baptism for the remission of sins; and we look for the resurrection of the dead and the life of the world to come.*

[Chalcedonian Creed] We, then, following the holy Fathers, all with one consent, teach men to confess one and the same Son, our Lord Jesus Christ, the same perfect in divinity and also perfect in humanity; truly God and truly man, of a reasonable soul and body; of the same substance[85] with the Father according to divinity, and of the same substance with us according to the humanity; in all things like unto us, without sin; begotten before all ages of the Father according to the divinity, and in these latter days, for us and for our salvation, born of the Virgin Mary, the Mother of God, according to the Manhood; one and the same Christ, Son, Lord,

---

* Apostles' Creed, original Nicene Creed, Niceno-Constantinopolitan Creed, Chalcedonian Creed

[82] Texts from *The Book of Common Prayer* (New York: Seabury, 1948).

[83] From Philip Schaff, *The Creeds of Christendom,* vol. 2 (New York: Harper, 1932), pp. 62–63.

[84] *and the Son:* this clause, known from its Latin word *filioque,* was added to the Western church's creed in 589 by the Third Council of Toledo. Although based on the theology of Augustine, this addition was strongly rejected on both theological and political grounds by the Eastern churches and became a continued point of difference between East and West.

[85] *the same substance:* Greek *homoousios;* the movement being condemned spoke of "a similar substance" (*homoiousios*).

Only-begotten, to be acknowledged in two natures, inconfusedly, unchangeably, indivisibly, inseparably; the distinction of natures being by no means taken away by the union, but rather the property of each nature being preserved, and concurring in one Person and one Subsistence, not parted or divided into two persons, but one and the same Son, and only-begotten, God the Word, the Lord Jesus Christ; as the prophets from the beginning have declared concerning him, and the Lord Jesus Christ himself has taught us, and the Creed of the holy Fathers has handed down to us.

These things, therefore, having been expressed by us with the greatest accuracy and attention, the holy Ecumenical Synod defines that no one shall be permitted to bring forward a different faith, nor to write, nor to put together, nor to excogitate, nor to teach it to others. But some dare either to put together another faith, or to bring forward or to teach or to deliver a different Creed to such as wish to be converted to the knowledge of the truth from the Gentiles,[86] the Jews, or any heresy whatever. If they are bishops or clerics let them be deposed, the bishops from the episcopate, and the clerics from the clergy; but if they are monks or laity, let them be anathematized.

---

[86] *Gentiles:* followers of Greco-Roman religion.

The Arian Controversy*

The Nicene controversy deals with the status of the Son of God—was he fully divine, eternal, and equal to God the Father, or was he the first created being? This question had been present in the church since the second century, but now in the fourth century it would become a burning issue. In the first reading from 320, Arius defends his teaching that Christ is not equal to God in being or eternity.[87] In the second reading from 325, Constantine summarizes the teaching of the Council of Nicea, which he called.[88] In the last reading from around 328, Athanasius, the chief theological opponent of Arius, defends his teaching and the creed of Nicea.[89] In modern times, the nature of Jesus Christ and his relation to God the Father is still an important issue among many Christians.

To his very dear lord the orthodox Eusebius, the faithful man of God, Arius, unjustly persecuted by Pope Alexander[90] on account of that all-conquering truth which you also defend as with a shield, sends greeting in the Lord.

As Ammonius, my father, was going to Nicomedia, I thought it right and my bounden duty to greet you by him, and also to make mention of that inborn love and kindly disposition which you bear towards the brethren for the sake of God and of his Christ. I want to tell you that the bishop makes great havoc of us and persecutes us severely, and is in full sail against us. He has driven us out of the city as atheists, because we do not concur in what he publicly preaches, namely, that 'God has always been, and the Son has always been; Father and Son exist together; the Son has his existence unbegotten along with God, ever being begotten, without having been begotten; God does not precede the Son by thought or by

---

* Letter of Arius to Eusebius of Nicomedia; Letter of Constantine to the Orthodox churches of Alexandria, Egypt; Athanasius, *Against the Arians* 3.4

[87] Taken, with editing, from Philip Schaff and Henry Wace, *Nicene and Post-Nicene Fathers,* vol. 3, 2d series (New York: Scribners, 1900), 41.

[88] Taken, with editing, from Philip Schaff and Henry Wace, *Nicene and Post-Nicene Fathers,* vol. 2, 2d series (New York: Scribners, 1900), 13–14.

[89] Taken, with editing, from Philip Schaff and Henry Wace, *Nicene and Post-Nicene Fathers,* vol. 4, 2d series (New York: Scribners, 1900), 395.

---

[90] *Pope Alexander:* the bishop of Alexandria.

any interval however small; God has always been, the Son has always been; the Son is from God himself'.

Eusebius, your brother in Caesarea, Theodotus, Paulinus, Athanasius, Gregory, Aëtius, and all the bishops of the East, have been made anathema because they say that God has existence without beginning prior to his Son: except Philogonius, Hellanicus, and Macarius, who are heretical fellows, and uncatechized. One of them says that the Son is an effusion, another that he is an emission, another that he is also unbegotten.

These are impieties to which we could not listen, even though the heretics should threaten us with a thousand deaths. But as for us, what do we say, and believe, and what have we taught, and what do we teach? That the Son is not unbegotten, nor in any way part of the unbegotten; nor from some lower essence (i.e., from matter); but that by his own (i.e., the Father's) will and counsel he has subsisted before time, and before ages as God full of grace and truth, only-begotten, unchangeable.

And [we teach] that he was not, before he was begotten, or created, or purposed, or established. For he was not unbegotten. We are persecuted because we say, 'the Son had a beginning, but God is without beginning'. This is really the cause of our persecution; and, likewise, because we say that he is from nothing. And this we say, because he is neither part of God, nor of any lower essence. For this are we persecuted; the rest you know. Farewell in the Lord. As a fellow-disciple of Lucian, and as a truly pious man, as your name implies, remember our afflictions.

[Letter of Constantine] To attain this goal [purity of teaching in the church and the rout of the Arians], by divine admonition I assembled most of the bishops at the city of Nicaea. I myself also, as one of you, rejoicing exceedingly in being your fellow-servant, undertook the investigation of the truth. Accordingly, all points which seemed to produce doubt or excuse for discord have been discussed and accurately examined. And may the Divine Majesty pardon the fearful enormity of the blasphemies which some were shamelessly uttering concerning our Savior, our life and hope, declaring and confessing that they believe things contrary to the divinely inspired Scriptures and to the holy faith.

More than three hundred bishops remarkable for their moderation and shrewdness were unanimous in their confirmation of one and the same faith, which is in accurate conformity to the truth expressed in the laws of God. Arius alone, beguiled by the subtlety of the devil, was discovered to be the sole disseminator of this mischief, with unhallowed purposes, first among you, and afterwards among others also. Let us therefore embrace that judgement which the Almighty has presented to us. . . . For that which has commended itself to the judgement of three hundred bishops cannot be other than the judgement of God; seeing that the Holy Spirit dwelling in the minds of persons of such character and dignity has effectually enlightened them respecting the Divine will. Wherefore let no one vacillate or linger, but let all with alacrity return to the undoubted path of truth. When I shall arrive among you, which will be as soon as possible, I will return due thanks to God with you, the inspector of all things, for having revealed the true faith, and restored to you the love for which you have prayed.

[Athanasius, *Against the Arians*] For [the Father and the Son] are one, not as one thing divided into two parts, and these nothing but one, nor as one thing twice named, so that the Same becomes at one time Father, at another His own Son, for this Sabellius holding was judged an heretic. But they are two, because the Father is Father and is not also Son, and the Son is Son and not also Father. But the nature is one; (for the offspring is not unlike its parent, for it is his image), and all that is the Father's is also the Son's. Therefore neither is the Son another God, for He was not procured from without, else were there many, if a godhead be procured foreign from the Father's. If the Son be other, as an Offspring, still He is the Same as God; and He and the Father are one in propriety and peculiarity of nature, and in the identity of the one Godhead, as has been said. For the radiance also is light, not second to the sun, nor a different light, nor from participation of it, but a whole and proper offspring of it. And such an offspring is necessar-

ily one light; and no one would say that they are two lights, but sun and radiance two, yet one the light from the sun enlightening in its radiance all things. So also the Godhead of the Son is the Father's; whence also it is indivisible. Thus there is one God and none other but He. So, since they are one, and the Godhead itself one, the same things are said of the Son which are said of the Father, except His being said to be Father.

Pelagius and Augustine on Free Will, Human Responsibility, and Divine Election*

Pelagius (ca. 350–425) was a British monk who founded a movement emphasizing the importance of free will, human responsibility, and good works in salvation. He attacked Augustine's emphasis on the bondage of the human will to sin and the necessity of divine grace for salvation. He was particularly upset at Augustine's prayer in his Confessions, *"Give what you command and command what you want."*[91] *Challenged by Pelagius, Augustine articulated more fully his ideas of predestination, original sin, and grace. In this second reading, he addresses these three doctrines.*[92] *The Council of Carthage (417) strongly condemned Pelagianism, but its decisions were not popular in much of the Western church and Augustine's teaching on grace were not widely accepted.*[93] *These difficult issues were to be taken up again in the Reformation, when Luther and Calvin asserted the strong Augustinian teaching. In modern times these issues are still alive.*

We rail at God, saying, "These commands are too difficult! We cannot keep them! We are only human, and our weak human nature gets in the way!" What blind madness is this! What obvious arrogance! By saying this, we accuse the God of all knowledge with a double ignorance: we make him ignorant of his own creation and his own commands. . . . May God forgive us! At the same time we ascribe unrighteousness to the Righteous One, and cruel sin to the Holy One. We do this by complaining that God has commanded us to do the impossible, and by imagining that God will condemn some people for not doing what they cannot do. This is blasphemy! It implies that God wants our condemnation, not our salvation. . . . God has not commanded anything impossible, for God is righteous; he will not condemn anyone for what they cannot keep, for God is holy.

[Augustine, *Admonition and Grace*] The Lord Himself not only shows us the evil we are to avoid and the good we are to do (which is all that the letter of the law can do), but also helps us to avoid evil and to do good—things that are impossible without the spirit of grace. If grace is lacking, the law is there simply to make culprits and to slay; for this reason, the Apostle said: "The letter kills, the spirit gives life."[94] He, therefore,

---

* Pelagius, *Letter to Demetrias;* Augustine, *Admonition and Grace* 1.2, 2.3–4, 7.13, 17; The Decrees of the Council of Carthage

[91] Translated by the author from Pelagius, *Letter to Demetrias* 16, in J.-P. Migné, *Patrologia Latina*, vol. 33 (Paris: Migné, 1889) cols. 1110 A–B.

[92] Taken, with editing, from Philip Schaff, *The Nicene and Post-Nicene Fathers,* vol. 4 (New York: Scribners, 1905), 264–65.

[93] Taken, with editing, from A. J. Ayer, *Source Book for Ancient Church History* (New York: Scribners, 1926), 464–65.

---

[94] II Corinthians 3:6.

who uses the law according to the law learns from it good and evil. Trusting not in his own strength, he has recourse to grace, which enables him to avoid evil and to do good. But when has a man recourse to grace, except when the steps of a man be directed by the Lord and he delights in His way? Therefore, even the desire for the help of grace is itself the beginning of grace; about it he said: "And I said: Now have I begun; this is a change due to the right hand of the Most High."[95]

It must, therefore, be admitted that we have a will free to do both evil and good. But in doing evil, one is free of justice and the slave of sin. On the other hand, in the matter of good no one is free unless he be freed by Him who said: "If the Son makes you free, you will be free indeed."[96] Not, however, as if one no longer needed the help of his liberator, once he has been freed from the domination of sin; rather, hearing from Him: "Without me you can do nothing,"[97] one must oneself say: "Be my helper, forsake me not."[98] . . .

This is the right understanding of the grace of God through Jesus Christ our Lord, by which alone men are freed from evil, and without which they do no good whatsoever, either in thought, or in will and love, or in action. Not only do men know by its showing what they are to do, but by its power they do with love what they know is to be done.

Accordingly, let no one deceive himself saying: "Why are we preached to, and given commands, in order to have us avoid evil and do good, if it is not we ourselves who do these things, but God who effects in us the will and the deed?" Let them rather grasp the fact that, if they are the sons of God, they are acted on by the Spirit of God in order that they may do what ought to be done. And when they have done it, let them give thanks to Him by whom they did it. They are acted on, in order that they may act, not in order that they

may have nothing to do. And to this end it is shown them what they ought to do, in order that, when they do it as it ought to be done—that is, with love and delight in justice—they may rejoice in the experience of the sweetness which the Lord gave, that their earth might bring forth its fruit. On the other hand, when they fail to act, either by doing nothing at all, or by not acting out of charity, let them pray to receive what they do not yet have. For what will they have, except what they shall receive? And what have they, except what they have received? . . .

As for those who by the bounty of divine grace are singled out of that original body of the lost, there is no doubt that the opportunity to hear the Gospel is arranged for them. When they hear, they believe, and persevere unto the end in the faith which worketh by charity; and, if ever they go off the track, they are chastised by admonitions; and some of them, even though they are not admonished by men, return to the path they had abandoned; and some, too, having received grace at various ages, are withdrawn from the dangers of this life by a swift death. All these things are done in them by Him who made them vessels of mercy, and who also chose them in His Son before the foundation of the world by a gracious choice. "And if out of grace, then not in virtue of works; otherwise grace is no longer grace."[99] For they are not so called, as not to be chosen; for which reason it is said, "Many are called, but few are chosen."[100] But, since they are called according to God's purpose, they are surely chosen by the choice which we have termed gracious. It is not made in view of their preceding merits, because their every merit is a grace.

[Decrees of the Council of Carthage] If any one says that Adam, the first man, was created mortal, so that, whether he sinned or not, he would have died from natural causes, and not as the wages of sin, let him be anathema.

---

[95] Psalm 76:11.
[96] John 8:36.
[97] John 15:5.
[98] Psalm 26:9.

---

[99] Romans 11:6.
[100] Matthew 20:16.

If any one says that newborn children need not be baptized, or that they are baptized for the remission of sins but that no original sin is derived from Adam to be washed away in the laver of regeneration, so that in their case the baptismal formula "for the remission of sins" is to be taken in a fictitious and not in its true sense, let him be anathema.

That there is in the Kingdom of Heaven, or in any other place, any middle place, where children who depart this life unbaptized live in bliss, let him be anathema.

That the grace of God, by which man is justified through Jesus Christ our Lord, avails only for the remission of sins already committed, and not for assistance to prevent the commission of sins, let him be anathema.

That this grace . . . only helps us to avoid sin in this way; that by it we are given by revelation an understanding of God's commands that we may learn what we ought to strive for and what we ought to avoid, but that it does not give us also the delight in doing, and the power to do, what we have recognized as being good, let him be anathema.

That the grace of justification is given to us that we may more easily perform by means of grace that which we are bidden to do by means of our free choice; as if we could fulfil those commands even without the gift of grace, though not so easily, let him be anathema.

Popular Christian Beliefs on Death and Eternal Life*

The catacombs (*artificial caverns used as burial places by Jews and then by Christians) are our primary source of Christian art from the second through fourth centuries. The inscriptions in the Roman catacombs are one of our main sources of knowledge of ancient popular Christianity. These inscriptions are testimony to the way ordinary Christians viewed life and death.*[101]

From the Cemetery of Priscilla (first to third century):
Stafilius, peace be with you in God. Hail and farewell.

Tertius my [our] brother, be of good courage; no one is immortal.

O Father of all, take into your keeping Irene, Zoe and Marcellus whom you made; to you be the glory in Christ.

From Cemetery of Callixtus (third and fourth centuries):
To dear Cyriacus, our sweetest son. May you live in the Holy Spirit.

Septimus Praetextatus Caecilianus, the servant of God, after a worthy life. I do not regret that I have served you thus and I give thanks unto your name. He gave up his soul to God, aged thirty-three years, six months.

Heraclitus, one who was dear to God, lived eight years plus thirteen days; he was ill twelve days. He expired before the eleventh of the kalends[102] of May, Pius and Pontianus, consuls.

Aurelius Xanthias, father, to a child so sweet, light and life.

In Chirst [sic] from Virginius. So nicely you lived with me as a freed wife, most innocent Cervonia Silvana.

---

* Roman catacomb inscriptions
[101] Taken from H. P. V. Nunn, *Christian Inscriptions* (London: SPCK, 1920).

---

[102] *kalends:* month.

Eat the refrigerium[103] with a holy spirit. Deposited on the Kalends of April. Tiberianus II and Dio, Consuls.

Here sleeps Artemidora. In peace.

---

[103] *refrigerium:* a meal in memory of a dead person.

[From an unknown source:]
I, Petronia, wife of a deacon, of modest appearance, here lay down my bones and place them in their resting place. Cease from weeping, my husband and sweet children, and believe that it is not right to mourn one that lives in God.

ETHICS

The Two Ways*

One of the main features of the Didache *is basic moral teaching about the Christian view of right and wrong. The teaching that there are two ways to live—the right way that leads to life and the wrong/evil way that leads to death—is an idea ancient in both Jewish religion and Greek philosophy. The numerous quotations in the first section are from Jesus' teaching in the Sermon on the Mount (Matthew 5–7).*[104]

There are two Ways, one of Life and one of Death, and there is a great difference between them.

The Way of Life is this: "First, you shall love the God who made you, secondly, your neighbor as yourself; and whatever you would not have done to yourself, do not do to another."

Now, the teaching of these words is this: "Bless those that curse you, and pray for your enemies, and fast for those that persecute you. For what credit is it to you if you love those that love you? Do not even the heathen do the same?" But, for your part, "Love those that hate you," and you will have no enemy. "Abstain from carnal" and bodily "lusts." "If any man smite you

on the right cheek, turn to him the other cheek also," and you will be perfect. "If any man forces you to go with him one mile, go with him two. If any man take your coat, give him your shirt also. If any man will take from you what is yours, do not refuse it"[105]—not even if you can. "Give to everyone that asks you, and do not refuse," for the Father's will is that we give to all from the gifts we have received. Blessed is he that gives according to the mandate; for he is innocent. Woe to him who receives! If any man receives alms under pressure of need he is innocent; but he who receives it without need shall be tried as to why he took it and for what, and being in prison he shall be examined as to his deeds, and "he shall not come out thence until he pay the last farthing."[106] But concerning this it was also said, "Let your alms sweat into your hands until you know to whom you are giving."[107] . . .

[5] But the Way of Death is this: First of all, it is wicked and full of cursing, murders, adulteries, lusts, fornications, thefts, idolatries, witchcrafts, charms, robberies, false witness, hypocrisies, a double heart, fraud, pride, malice, stubbornness, covetousness, foul speech, jealousy, impudence,

---

* *Didache* 1, 5–6

[104] Taken, with editing, from Kirsopp Lake, *The Apostolic Fathers,* vol. 1 (Cambridge, MA: Harvard University Press, 1912), 309–11, 317–19.

[105] These quotations are taken from the Jesus' Sermon on the Mount (Matthew 5–7).

[106] Matthew 5:26.

[107] *Let your alms . . . giving:* a quotation from an unknown apocryphal gospel.

haughtiness, boastfulness. [Those on the Way of Death are] persecutors of the good, haters of truth, lovers of lies, knowing not the reward of righteousness, not cleaving to the good nor to righteous judgment, spending wakeful nights not for good but for wickedness, having no meekness and patience, loving vanity, following after reward, unmerciful to the poor, not helping him who is oppressed with toil, without knowledge of him who made them, murderers of children, corrupters of God's creatures, turning away the needy, oppressing the distressed, advocates of the rich, unjust judges of the poor, altogether sinful. May you be delivered, my children, from all these.

See that no one make you to err from this Way of the teaching, for he teaches you without God. If you can bear the whole yoke of the Lord, you will be perfect; but if you cannot, then do what you can. And concerning food, bear what you can, but keep strictly from food offered to idols, for it is the worship of dead gods.

Christian Morality in Diverse Cultures*

The Epistle to Diognetus *is an anonymous Christian apology, probably from the second century. The most famous part of this work is its eloquent description of the moral behavior of Christians in the context of their cultures.*[108]

The distinction between Christians and other people is not in country or language or customs. They do not live together in cities or in some place of their own; they do not use a different form of speech; they do not follow an extraordinary manner of life. Their doctrine has not been discovered by the ingenuity or deep thought of inquisitive men, nor do they put forward a merely human teaching, as some people do. Although they live in Greek and barbarian cities alike, as each man's lot has been cast, and follow the customs of the country in clothing and food and other matters of daily living, at the same time they prove the remarkable and extraordinary constitution of their own commonwealth.

They live in their own countries, but only as aliens. They have a share in everything as citizens, and endure everything as foreigners. Every foreign land is their fatherland, and yet for them every fatherland is a foreign land. They marry, like everyone else, and they beget children, but they do not cast out their offspring.[109] They offer free hospitality, but they guard their purity. They are "in the flesh," but they do not live "according to the flesh." They busy themselves on earth, but their citizenship is in heaven. They obey the established laws, but in their own lives they surpass the laws. They love all men, and they are persecuted by all men. They are unknown, and still they are condemned; they are put to death, and yet they are brought to life. They are poor, and yet they make many rich; they are completely destitute, and yet they enjoy complete abundance. They are dishonored, and in their very dishonor are glorified; they are defamed, and are vindicated. They are insulted, and yet they bless; when they are affronted, they still pay due respect. When they do good, they are punished as evil-doers; undergoing punishment, they rejoice because they are brought to life. They are treated by the Jews as foreigners and enemies, and are hunted down by the Greeks[110]; and those who hate them cannot justify their hatred.

---

* *Epistle to Diognetus* 5

[108] Taken, with editing, from Kirsopp Lake, *The Apostolic Fathers,* vol. 2 (Cambridge, MA: Harvard University Press, 1912), 359–61.

---

[109] *cast out their offspring:* infanticide by abandonment.

[110] *Greeks:* peoples of all religions other than Jewish and Christian.

Two Views of War*

*In the first reading, Tertullian expresses the opposi-
tion that many ancient Christians had toward
the military. Note that some opposition is directed
against the Roman religious ceremonies in which
every soldier participated and some is based on opposition to violence.*[111] *In the second reading, Augustine's* City of God *explains the relationship
between the two realms ("cities") of heaven and
earth. Augustine argues that Christianity supports just rulers and legitimate governments in
their promotion of the welfare of society, and he
deals with the problem of war and under what
circumstances it could be justified. All subsequent
Western theories of just war are built on it.*[112]
*Christianity has lived through most of its history
with these two conflicting visions of the moral status of war.*

Is it right to make an occupation of the sword,
when the Lord proclaims that he who uses the
sword shall perish by the sword? Shall the son of
peace take part in the battle when it does not become him even to sue at law? Shall he apply the
chain, and the prison, and the torture, and punishment, when he is not even the avenger of
his own wrongs? Shall he keep guard before the
temples which he has renounced? Shall he take a
meal where the apostle has forbidden him?[113]
Shall he diligently protect by night those who in
the daytime he has put to flight by his exorcisms,
leaning and resting on the spear with which
Christ's side was pierced? Shall he carry a flag,
too, which is hostile to Christ? . . . Putting all my

strength to the main questions, I banish us from
military life.

[Augustine, *The City of God*] After the city comes
the world. This is the third stage of human society. First, we have the home; then the city;
finally, the world. And as with the perils of the
ocean, the bigger the community, the fuller it is
of misfortunes.

First is the lack of communication resulting
from language differences. Take two men who
meet and find that some common need calls on
them to remain together rather than to part company. Neither knows the language of the other.
As far as intercommunication goes, these two,
both men, are worse off than two speechless animals, even of different kinds. Their common human nature is of no social help, so long as the
language barrier makes it impossible for them to
tell each other what they are thinking about.
That is why a man is more at home with his dog
than with a foreigner.

The Roman Empire, in the interests of peaceful collaboration, imposes on nations it has conquered the unifying yoke of both law and language. . . . But how many great wars, how much
slaughter and bloodshed, have provided this
unity! Yet, when wars are ended, there are new
calamities brewing. To begin with, there never
has been, nor is there today, any absence of
hostile foreign powers to provoke war. What is
worse, the very development of the empire leads
to more terrible wars within. I refer to the civil
wars and social uprisings that involve even more
wretched anxieties for human beings, either
shaken by their actual impact, or living in fear of
their renewal. Massacres, frequent and sweeping,
and hardships too dire to endure are but a part
of the ravages of war. I am utterly unable to describe them as they are, and as they ought to be
described; and even if I should try to begin,
where could I end?

But, they say, a good ruler will wage wars only
if they are just. Surely, if he will only remember

---

* Tertullian, *On the Crown* 11; Augustine, *The City of God* 19.7
[111] Taken, with editing, from Alexander Roberts and James
Donaldson, *The Ante-Nicene Fathers*, vol. 3 (New York:
Scribners, 1905), 99–100.
[112] Taken, with editing, from Philip Schaff, *The Nicene and
Post-Nicene Fathers*, vol. 2 (1st series; New York: Scribners,
1905), 405.
[113] *take a meal . . . forbidden him:* the Apostle Paul forbids
participation in temple worship in I Corinthians, but he does
not actually forbid eating in a temple restaurant, as Tertullian
says here.

that he is a man, he will begin by bewailing the necessity he is under of waging even just wars. A good man would be under compulsion to wage no wars at all, if there were no such thing as a just war. A just war, moreover, is justified only by the injustice of an aggressor. That kind of injustice ought to be a source of grief to any good man, because it is human injustice. It would be deplorable in itself, apart from its being a source of conflict.

Augustine's Conversion*

Conversion has always been one of the centers of Christian experience, from Jesus' message of repentance and belief through today. Augustine's conversion—like those of the Apostle Paul, Martin Luther, John Wesley, and countless others—became the center of his religious experience and the basis of the new moral vision.[114]

When a profound reflection had drawn up out of the secret depths of my soul all my misery and had heaped it up before the sight of my heart, there arose a mighty storm accompanied by a mighty rain of tears. That I might give way fully to my tears and lamentations, I stole away from Alypius,[115] for it seemed to me that solitude was more appropriate for the business of weeping. . . . This was the way I felt at the time, and he realized it. I suppose I had said something before I started up and he noticed that my voice was choked. And so he stayed alone, where we had been sitting together, greatly astonished. I flung myself down under a fig tree and gave free course to my tears. The streams of my eyes gushed out an acceptable sacrifice to you. And, not indeed in these words, but to this effect, I cried to you: "How Long, O Lord? Will you be angry forever? Oh, remember not against us our former iniquities!"[116] For I felt that I was still enthralled by them. I sent up these sorrowful cries: "How long, how long? Tomorrow and tomorrow? Why not now? Why not this very hour make an end to my uncleanness?"

I was saying these things and weeping in the most bitter contrition of my heart, when suddenly I heard the voice of a boy or a girl—I know not which. It was coming from the neighboring house, chanting over and over again, "Pick it up and read; pick it up and read." Immediately I ceased weeping and began most earnestly to think whether it was usual for children in some kind of game to sing such a song, but I could not remember ever having heard it. So, damming the torrent of my tears, I got to my feet, for I could not but think that this was a divine command to open the Bible and read the first passage I should happen upon. For I had heard how Anthony, accidentally coming into church while the gospel was being read, received the admonition as if what was read had been addressed to him: "Go and sell what you have and give it to the poor, and you shall have treasure in heaven; and come and follow me."[117] By such an oracle he was immediately converted to you.

So I quickly returned to the bench where Alypius was sitting, for there I had put down the apostle's book when I had left there. I snatched it up, opened it, and in silence read the paragraph on which my eyes first fell: "Not in rioting and drunkenness, not in debauchery and wantonness, not in strife and envying, but put on the Lord Jesus Christ, and make no provision for the flesh, to fulfill its lusts."[118] I wanted to read no further, nor did I need to. Instantly, as the sentence ended, there was infused in my heart something like the light of full certainty, and all the gloom of doubt vanished away.

---

* *Confessions* 8.12.28–30
[114] Taken, with editing, from Philip Schaff, *Nicene and Post-Nicene Fathers*, vol. 1 (1st series; New York: Scribners, 1905), 127–28.
[115] *Alypius* was Augustine's friend.
[116] Psalm 6:3 and 79:8.

[117] Matthew 19:21.
[118] Romans 13:13.

RELATIONS

Opposing Attitudes toward Greek Philosophy*

The early church had two distinct attitudes to Greek philosophy: those who saw it as useful in presenting the faith and those who saw it as the enemy of faith. The former attitude is related in the first reading from Clement of Alexandria.[119] Tertullian's attitude in the second reading expresses a sharp and famous condemnation of using "Athens" (Greek learning, especially philosophy) to explain "Jerusalem" (Christianity).[120] By the end of the ancient period, Clement's attitude had largely won the field, and Christian theologians regularly used philosophy and other "secular" means of knowledge to understand and advance the faith. But Christianity has always had a vocal minority advocating Tertullian's position.

Philosophy was necessary to the Greeks for righteousness, until the coming of the Lord. Now it helps toward true religion as a preparatory training for those who arrive at faith by way of reasoning. "Your foot shall not stumble" if you attribute all good to Providence, whether it belongs to the Greeks or to us. For God is the source of all good things; of some primarily, as the Old and New Testaments; of others secondarily, as philosophy. It may indeed be that philosophy was given to the Greeks immediately and primarily until the Lord called the Greeks. For philosophy was a "schoolmaster" to bring the Greek mind to Christ, as the Law [of Moses] brought the Hebrews. Thus philosophy was a preparation, paving the way toward perfection in Christ.

[Tertullian, *Prescription against the Heretics*] These [heresies] are human and demonic doctrines, produced for itching ears by the worldly wisdom which the Lord called foolishness, choosing the foolish things of the world to put philosophy to shame. For philosophy is produced by worldly wisdom, with its rash interpretation of God's nature and purpose. Philosophy instigates heresies. . . . A plague on Aristotle, who taught [the heretics] dialectic, the art which destroys as much as it builds, which changes its opinions like a coat, forces its conjectures, is stubborn in argument, completely contradictory, and embarrassing to itself. It reconsiders every point to make sure it never finishes a discussion.

From philosophy come those fables and endless genealogies and fruitless questionings. . . . To hold us back from such things the Apostle testifies expressly in his letter to the Colossians that we should beware of philosophy. "Take heed lest any man circumvent you through philosophy or vain deceit, after the tradition of men," against the providence of the Holy Spirit.[121] He had been at Athens where he had come to grips with the human wisdom which attacks and perverts truth, being itself divided up into its own swarm of heresies by the variety of its mutually antagonistic sects. What has Jerusalem to do with Athens, the Church with the Academy, the Christian with the heretic? Our principles come from the Porch[122] of Solomon, who had himself taught that the Lord is to be sought in simplicity of heart.[123] Away with all attempts to produce a Stoic or a Platonic or a dialectic

---

* Clement of Alexandria, *Stromata* 1; Tertullian, *Prescription against the Heretics* 7
[119] Taken, with editing, from Alexander Roberts and James Donaldson, *The Ante-Nicene Fathers*, vol. 4 (New York: Scribners, 1905), 305.
[120] Taken, with editing, from Alexander Roberts and James Donaldson, *The Ante-Nicene Fathers*, vol. 3 (New York: Scribners, 1905), 246.

---

[121] The quotations in this paragraph are from I Tim. 1:4; II Tim. 2:17; Col. 2:8.
[122] *Porch:* the "Porch" (Greek *Stoa*) was the most famous building of the philosophers of Athens.
[123] Wisdom of Solomon 1:1.

Christianity! After Jesus Christ we have no need of speculation, after the Gospel no need of inquiry. When we come to believe, we have no desire to believe anything else; for we begin by believing that there is nothing else which we have to believe.

Popular Opposition to Christians *

We know a good deal about official and intellectual opposition to ancient Christianity; the Christian apologies deal with it extensively. However, very little evidence of popular opposition (and the Christian response to it) has survived. Perhaps the most famous example of this evidence is the graffito from the second or third century found on the Palatine Hill in Rome. It shows a youth raising his hand in worship toward a figure on a cross, a figure with a human body and an ass's head. The Greek inscription reads, "Alexamanos worships God." This crude caricature is based on the idea, found as well in cultured Roman writers such as Tacitus, that Christians (as did the Jews) worshipped a God who was an ass.[124]

---

* The Alexamenos graffito

[124] Sketch taken from R. Garrucci, *Storia dell'arte christiana nei primi otto secoli della chiesa* (Prato, 1881), as found in E. H. Swift, *Roman Sources of Christian Art* (New York: Columbia University Press, 1951), 161.

Christianity and Judaism*

The proper relationship of Christianity with its parent faith of Judaism has been a continuing challenge. In ancient times the superiority of Christianity to Judaism was assumed by all Christians, but with two forms. One form sought to convert Jews by dialogue and debate, as Justin argues with his Jewish counterpart Trypho.[125] *The other refused dialogue and aimed only for conversion or (more commonly) suppression. It often led to stark forms of anti-Semitism, as in this passage's imputation of responsibility for the death of Jesus to all Jews.*[126]

Trypho said, "You endeavor to prove an incredible and almost impossible thing, that God endured to be born and become man."

"If I undertook," I said, "to prove this by doctrines or arguments of man, you should not bear with me. But if I quote frequently Scriptures, and so many of them, referring to this point, and ask you to comprehend them, you are hard-hearted in the recognition of the mind and will of God. But if you wish to remain so, I would not be injured at all; and for ever retaining the same [opinions] which I had before I met with you, I shall leave you."

And Trypho said, "Look, my friend, you made yourself master of these [truths] with much labor and toil. And we accordingly must diligently scrutinize all that we meet with, in order to give our assent to those things which the Scriptures compel us [to believe]." . . .

I continued again: "In addition to the questions I have just now put to you, I wish to put more. By means of these questions I shall try to bring the discourse to a speedy conclusion."

And Trypho said, "Ask the questions."

Then I said, "Do you think that any other one is said to be worthy of worship and called Lord and God in the Scriptures, except the Maker of all, and Christ, who by so many Scriptures was proved to you to have become man?"

And Trypho replied, "How can we admit this, when we have instituted so great an inquiry as to whether there is any other than the Father alone?"

Then I again said, "I must ask you this also, that I may know whether or not you are of a different opinion from that which you admitted some time ago."

He replied, "It is not, sir."

Then again I said, "Since you certainly admit these things, and since Scripture says, 'Who shall declare His generation?',[127] ought you not now to suppose that He is not the seed of a human race?"

Trypho said, "How then does the Word say to David, that out of his loins God shall take to Himself a Son, and shall establish His kingdom, and shall set Him on the throne of His glory?"

I said, "Trypho, if the prophecy which Isaiah uttered, 'Behold, the virgin shall conceive,' is said not to the house of David, but to another house of the twelve tribes, perhaps the matter would have some difficulty. But since this prophecy refers to the house of David, Isaiah has explained how that which was spoken by God to David in mystery would take place. Perhaps you are not aware of this, my friend, that there were many sayings written obscurely, or parabolically, or mysteriously, and symbolical actions, which the prophets who lived after the persons who said or did them expounded."

[*Sermons against Judaizing Christians*]: Let us not only ask if many were filched away[128]; let us

---

* Justin, *Dialogue with Trypho* 68; John Chrysostom, *Sermons against Judaizing Christians* 8.5

[125] Taken, with editing, from Alexander Roberts and James Donaldson, *The Ante-Nicene Fathers*, vol. 1 (New York: Scribners, 1905), 232–33.

[126] From Paul Harkins, *Saint John Chrysostom: Sermons against Judaizing Christians* (Washington, DC: Catholic University of America Press, 1979), pp. 220–24. Used by permission.

[127] *Who . . . generation:* a quotation from Isaiah 53:8, a favorite text among some ancient church writers to defend the preexistence of Christ.

[128] *filched away:* from Christianity to Judaism.

ask how we may bring them back. Let us not exalt our enemies' side and destroy our own. Let us not show that they are strong and that our side is weak. Let us do quite the opposite. Rumor can often destroy a soul but, just as often, it can lift it up. . . .

If we hear something good [about our side], let us broadcast it to all; if we hear something bad or evil, let us keep that hidden among ourselves and do everything we can to get rid of the evil. Therefore, let us now go forth, let us get busy and search for the sinner, let us not shrink back even if we must go into his home. If you do not know him, if you have no connection with him, get busy and find some friend or relative of his, someone to whom he pays particular attention. Take this man with you and go into his home. Do not blush or feel ashamed. If you were going there to ask for money or to get some favor from him, you would have reason for feeling ashamed. If you hurry there to save the man, no one can find fault with your motive for entering his home. Sit down and talk with him. But start your conversation on other topics so that he does not suspect that the real purpose of your visit is to set him straight.

Say to him: "Tell me, do you approve of the Jews for crucifying Christ, for blaspheming him as they still do, and for calling him a lawbreaker?" If the man is a Christian, he will never put up with this; even if he be a Judaizer times without number, he will never bring himself to say: "I do approve." Rather, he will stop up his ears and say to you: "Heaven forbid! Be quiet, man." Next, after you find that he agrees with you, take up the matter again and say: "How is it that you attend their services, how is it you participate in the festival, how is it you join them in observing the fast?" Then accuse the Jews of being obsti-

nate. Tell him about their every transgression which I recounted to your loving assembly in the days just past. . . . Show him how the whole ritual of the Jews is useless and unavailing. . . .

[5] Furthermore, remind him of hell. Remind him of the test he will undergo before the Lord's dread tribunal of judgment. Remind him that we will give an accounting for all these things and that no small punishment awaits those who dare to do what he is doing. Remind him that Paul said: "You who are justified in the Law have fallen away from grace." Remind him of Paul's threat: "If you be circumcised, Christ will be of no advantage to you." Tell him that, as is the case with circumcision, so, too, the fasting of the Jews drives from heaven the man who observes the fast, even if he has ten thousand other good works to his credit. Tell him that we have the name of Christians because we believe in Christ and not because we run to those who are His foes.

Suppose he uses the cures which the Jews effect as his excuse. Suppose he says: "They promise to make me well, and so I go to them." Then you must reveal the tricks they use, their incantations, their amulets, their charms and spells. This is the only way in which they have a reputation for healing; they do not effect genuine cures. Heaven forbid they should! Let me go so far as to say that even if they really do cure you, it is better to die than to run to God's enemies and be cured that way. What use is it to have your body cured if you lose your soul? . . .

We are the ones God led to a greater life of virtue. He opened the door for us to rise again. He gave the command to us not to love our dwelling here on earth but to keep all our hopes aimed at the life to come.

Conflict between Christian Emperor and Church*

Constantine brought Christianity and the Emperor into a close relationship. As Eusebius wrote,

Christians thought that there was one God, one Church, and one Emperor, all working together for good. But this close relationship between church and state was to be difficult in both East and West.

---

* Ambrose, *Letters* 20.19, 22–28

Here Ambrose, the bishop of Milan, writes to the Christian emperor Theodosius I in 385 after a standoff in the cathedral of Milan. The emperor's soldiers had tried to take the church, and Ambrose refused; now he writes to the emperor to defend his actions and defuse trouble.

At length came the command, "Deliver up the Basilica"; I replied, "It is not lawful for us to deliver it up, nor for your Majesty to receive it. By no law can you violate the house of a private man, and do you think that the house of God may be taken away? It is asserted that all things are lawful to the Emperor, that all things are his. But do not burden your conscience with the thought that you have any right as Emperor over sacred things. Do not exalt yourself, but if you would reign the longer, be subject to God. It is written, 'Give to God what belongs to God, and to Caesar what belongs to Caesar.'[129] The palace is the Emperor's, the Churches are the Bishop's. To you is committed jurisdiction over public, not over sacred buildings." Again the Emperor is said to have issued his command, "I also ought to have one Basilica." I answered, "It is not lawful for you to have her. What have you to do with an adulteress who is not bound with Christ in lawful wedlock?"

Thus I spoke, wondering if the Emperor's mind could be softened by the zeal of the soldiers, by the entreaties of the nobles, by the prayers of the people. Meanwhile I was informed that a Secretary had come with the mandate. I retired a little, and he notified to me the mandate. "What has been your design," says he, "in acting against the Emperor's orders?" I replied, "What has been ordered I know not, nor am I aware what is alleged to have been wrongly done." He says, "Why have you sent presbyters to the Basilica? If you are a tyrant I would gladly know it, that I may know how to arm myself against you." I replied by saying that I had done nothing which assumed too much for the Church, but when I heard it was filled with soldiers, I only uttered

deeper groans, and though many urged me to proceed there, I replied, "I cannot give up the Basilica, yet I must not fight." That afterwards, when I was told that the Imperial hangings were removed, and that the people required me to go there, I had directed the presbyters to do so, but that I was unwilling to go myself, saying, "I trust in Christ that the Emperor himself will espouse our cause."

If this seems like domineering, I grant indeed that I have arms, but only in the name of Christ; I have the power of offering up my body. Why, I asked, did he delay to strike if he considered my power unlawful? By ancient right Priests have conferred sovereignty, never assumed it, and it is a common saying that Emperors have coveted the Priesthood more often than Priests sovereignty. Christ fled that He might not be made a king. We have a power of our own. The power of a Priest is his weakness; "When I am weak," it is said, "then am I strong." But let him against whom God has raised up no adversary beware lest he raise up a tyrant for himself. Maximus did not say that I domineered over Valentinian, though he complains that my embassage prevented his passing over into Italy. I added, that priests were never usurpers, but that they had often suffered from usurpers.

The whole of that day was passed in this affliction; meanwhile the boys tore the imperial hangings in derision. I could not return home, because the Church was surrounded by a guard of soldiers. We recited the Psalms with our brethren in the little Basilica belonging to the Church.

[25] On the following day, the book of Jonah was read in due course, after which, I began [a] discourse [on Jonah]. . . .

Immediate tidings are brought to me that the Emperor had commanded the soldiers to withdraw from the Church; and that the fine which had been imposed on the merchants on their condemnation should be restored. What joy then prevailed among the whole people, what applause, what congratulations! Now it was the day whereon the Lord delivered Himself up for us, the day whereon there is a relaxation of penance in the Church. The soldiers eagerly brought the

---

[129] Matthew 22:21.

tidings, running in to the altars, and giving the kiss, the emblem of peace. . . .

These are the past events, and would that they were terminated, but the excited words of the Emperor show that heavier trials are awaiting us. I am called a tyrant, and even more than tyrant. For when the nobles sought the Emperor to go to the Church, and said that they did so at the request of the soldiers, he replied, "You would deliver me up to chains, if Ambrose asked you." I leave you to judge what awaits us after these words; all shuddered at hearing them, but there are those about him who exasperate him.

Lastly Calligonus the Grand Chamberlain ventured to address himself especially to me. "Do you, while I live, despise Valentinian? I will have your head!" I replied, "May God grant you to fulfil your threat. I shall suffer as befits a Bishop, you will act as befits a eunuch." May God indeed turn them aside from the Church! May all their weapons be directed against me, and may they quench their thirst in my blood!

Christianity and the Fall of Rome*

In defending Christianity against the charge of toppling the Roman Empire by its neglect of traditional Roman religion, Augustine in his City of God *(ca. 413–427) developed a Christian view of history and eternity symbolized by the two terms,* City of God *and* City of Man. *In this selection, Augustine defends Christianity against the complaint that the fall of Rome was caused by the rise of Christianity.*[130]

I began in the previous Book to speak of the City of God, and it moved me to undertake, with God's help, this entire work. My first plan was to challenge the view of those who hold that the Christian religion is responsible for all the wars desolating this miserable world and, in particular, for the recent barbarian sack of the City of Rome. It is true that the Christian religion forbids pagans to honor demons with unspeakable sacrifices. But, as I pointed out, they should thank Christ for the boon that, out of regard for His Name and in disregard of the traditional customs of war, the barbarians gave them immunity in spacious Christian buildings. What is more, they treated both the genuine followers of Christ and many who through fear pretended to be followers with great concern. They refused to take measures against them which the laws of war permitted.

Then arose the question: Why did God, on the one hand, bestow His good things upon the impious and the thankless, while, on the other, the enemy's hard blows fell with equal weight upon the good and the wicked alike? In order to answer this all-embracing question as fully as the scope of my work demanded, I lingered on it for various reasons. First, many are disturbed in mind when they observe how, in the daily round of life, God's gifts and man's brutalities oftentimes fall indifferently and indiscriminately to the lot of both the good and the bad. Above all, I wanted to offer to those pure and holy women whose modesty had been outraged by the barbarian soldiers, but whose purity of soul had stood adamant, the consoling assurance that they have no reason to bewail their lives, since there is no personal guilt for them to bewail. Now, I propose to speak of the calamities that befell the city from the beginning of its history, both at home and in its provinces—all of which our calumniators would have attributed to the Christian religion, if at that time the Gospel teaching had been freely bearing witness against their false and deceiving gods.

[2.3] Bear in mind that, in recounting these things, I am still dealing with those ignorant dupes who gave birth and popular currency to

---

* Augustine, *City of God* 2.2–3
[130] Taken, with editing, from Philip Schaff, *Nicene and Post-Nicene Fathers,* vol. 2 (1st series; New York: Scribners, 1890), 23–24.

the saying: "If there is a drought, blame the Christians." As for those among them who have received a liberal education and appreciate the value of history, they can very easily inform themselves. In order to arouse popular hatred against us, they pretend ignorance and strive to instill into people's minds the common notion that the misfortunes which afflict the human race are due to the expansion of Christianity and to the eclipse of the pagan gods by the bright glory of its reputation and renown.

Let them, therefore, recall with me the calamities which so often and in so many ways set back the prosperity of Rome, and remember, too, that all this happened long before Christ came in the flesh, long before His Name shone before men with that glory which they vainly begrudge Him. In the face of those disasters, let them defend their gods if they can, remembering that they were worshiped precisely to prevent the evils recorded. Yet, if any of those evils befall them now, we Christians must bear the blame. Why, then, did the gods permit the misfortunes I shall mention to fall on their devotees before the promulgation of Christ's teaching provoked their wrath and prohibited their sacrifices?

Augustine on the Suppression of Heresy *

What steps should the church take, and to what length, in dealing with dissenting movements? Augustine wrestled with this issue for most of his career as a bishop, and his conclusions influenced how the Roman Catholic Church dealt with people it considered heretics. These three passages from his letters mark the progression of Augustine's thought. The first letter is from 392, the second from 408, and the third from 417.[131]

[Letter 23.7] I do not propose to compel men to embrace the communion of any party, but desire the truth to be made known to persons who, in their search for it, are free from disquieting fears. On our side there shall be no appeal to men's fear of the civil power; on your side let there be no intimidation by a mob of Circumcellions.[132] Let us attend to the real matter in debate, and let our arguments appeal to reason and to the authoritative teaching of the divine scriptures, dispassionately and calmly, so far as we are able. Let us ask, seek and knock, that we may receive and find, and that to us the door may be opened.

[Letter 93.16–17] You must not consider just the mere fact of the coercion, but the nature of that to which one is coerced, whether it be good or bad. Not that anyone can become good in spite of his own will, but that, through fear of suffering what he does not desire, he either renounces his hostile prejudices or is compelled to examine the truth of which he had been contentedly ignorant. Under the influence of this fear he repudiates the error he defended, or seeks the truth of which he formerly knew nothing, and now willingly holds what he formerly rejected. . . .

Originally my opinion was that no one should be coerced into the unity of Christ, that we must act only by words, fight only by arguments, and prevail by force of reason, lest we should have heretics pretending to be Catholics. But this opinion of mine was overcome not by the words of those who contested it, but by the conclusive evidence to which they could point.

[Letter 185.11–24] There is a persecution of unrighteousness, which the impious inflict upon the church of Christ; and there is a righteous persecution, which the church of Christ inflicts

---

* *Letters* 23.7, 93.16–17, 185.11–24

[131] Taken, with editing, from Philip Schaff, *Nicene and Post-Nicene Fathers*, vol. 1 (1st series; New York: Scribners, 1905), 242, 388, 551.

[132] *Circumcellions:* "circlers" who were socially oppressed members of a violent protest movement associated with the Donatists.

upon the impious. . . . Moreover she persecutes in the spirit of love, they in the spirit of wrath. . . . The power which the church has received by divine appointment in its due season, through the religious character and the faith of kings, is the instrument by which those who are found in the highways and hedges—that is, in heresies and schisms—are compelled to come in.

GLOSSARY

anti-Judaism prejudice against the Jewish religion.

anti-Semitism prejudice against the Jewish people. (Some argue that there can be no distinction between anti-Judaism and anti-Semitism.)

apology a document defending Christianity against its opponents.

Apostolic Fathers church leaders and writers of the early second century (such as Clement of Rome, Ignatius, and Polycarp) who supposedly knew the apostles and continued their direct tradition.

canon an official list of books considered to be Holy Scripture.

creed a short statement of the main points of Christian belief.

epistles writings of instruction addressed to churches, so called because they share many or all the features of the common Greco-Roman epistle; also called **letters.**

Eucharist "Giving Thanks," the part of the divine service that celebrates the Holy Communion of bread and wine.

gospels the name given to the books that tell the story of the ministry, death, and resurrection of Jesus; second- and third-century Gnostic gospels generally feature only teachings of the resurrected Christ.

heresy opposition to a formal teaching of orthodox Christianity; often used to connote organized opposition.

history a book-length narrative of the growth of the church, especially in the face of persecution and heresy.

martyrology story of the trial and/or death of Christians killed for their faith by the Romans.

orthodoxy right belief and practice, as contrasted with heresy.

patristics study of Christianity in the age of the "Fathers," from the close of the New Testament to about 500 C.E. in the West and 600 in the East.

rule of faith a summary of basic points of Christian teaching used to denote the interpretation of apostolic teaching that became the norm for the orthodox church.

sermon a speech given during the course of divine worship; also called a **homily.**

QUESTIONS FOR STUDY AND DISCUSSION

1. Discuss this statement by the contemporary British theologian John Hick, a leading philosopher of religion: "A Christian does not have to accept those philosophical and theological doctrines [about the nature of Christ] of the third and fourth centuries. . . . [W]e can base our Christianity on Jesus' teachings concerning the reality and love and claim of God, and upon the love ethic that has developed out of it" (from *Free Inquiry* [Fall 1985]).

2. Explain the statement, "The canon was recognized, not made." Do you agree? Why, or why not?

3.   Why were so many ancient Christians fearless in the face of martyrdom, or even eager for it?

4.   How did the self-understanding and essence of Christianity change with Constantine? In your opinion, was the "Constantinian revolution" good or bad for Christianity?

5.   What are some of the features of this period that contributed to the later split between Eastern and Western Christianity?

6.   How and why did Christian monasticism develop? How did this institution influence basic ideas of what being a Christian means?

7.   Discuss the state of women in the church during ancient times. How true, in your view, is this statement: "No period of Christianity has so silenced the voices of women as the ancient period."

8.   Discuss the differences and similarities between mainstream Christianity and Gnostic Christianity.

SUGGESTIONS FOR FURTHER READING

J. K. Elliott, *The Apocryphal Jesus: Legends of the Early Church.* Oxford: Oxford University Press, 1996. A good collection of stories relating to the gospels, the apostles and their ministries, and life after death.

B. D. Ehrman, *After the New Testament: A Reader in Early Christianity.* New York: Oxford University Press, 1999. A well-organized collection of primary sources on early Christianity.

D. J. Geanakoplos, *Byzantium: Church, Society, and Civilization Seen Through Contemporary Eyes.* Chicago: University of Chicago Press, 1984. A thorough anthology of the Eastern Roman Empire from Constantine forward, with excellent treatment of Byzantine Christianity.

J. Stevenson, *A New Eusebius: Documents Illustrating the History of the Church to A.D. 337,* rev. ed. by W. H. C. Frend. London: SPCK, 1987. More than three hundred selections, most of them less than one page, from second-century through fourth-century writers.

J. Stevenson, *Creeds, Councils and Controversies: Documents Illustrating the History of the Church, A.D. 337–461,* rev. ed. by W. H. C. Frend. London: SPCK, 1989. The companion volume to *A New Eusebius,* with especially full treatment of the doctrinal controversies of the fourth and fifth centuries.

R. Macmullen and E. N. Lane, *Paganism and Christianity, 100–425 C.E.* Minneapolis: Fortress, 1992. Sets the Christian religion in the context of other religions, especially traditional Greco-Roman and the newer mystery religions.

R. E. Van Voorst, *Jesus Outside the New Testament: An Introduction to the Ancient Evidence.* Grand Rapids, MI: Eerdmans, 2000. A collection and treatment of primary texts about Jesus from Judaism, Greco-Roman writers, and both pre– and post–New Testament Christian writings.

P. Wilson-Kastner et al., *A Lost Tradition: Women Writers of the Early Church.* Washington, DC: University Press of America, 1981. Translations and critical commentary on four early Christian women writers: Egeria, Perpetua, Proba and Eudokia.

CHAPTER FOUR

Christianity in Byzantine, Medieval, and Renaissance Times (500–1500)

❖ In New York, a college student and would-be candidate for the priesthood in the Russian Orthodox church visits his bishop to inquire about seminary training and expectations for ordination. He is somewhat startled by two of the three elements of the bishop's advice: grow a beard, finish college, and get married. As the student will soon learn, these expectations are a part of the ancient tradition for almost all Eastern Orthodox clergy.

❖ In Athens, Archbishop Kallinikos of the Greek Orthodox Church issues a response to Pope John Paul II, who has expressed a desire to visit Greece in pilgrimage in the year 2000. The pope is welcome as the head of the Vatican state, the archbishop rules. But he cannot make a religious visit as the head of the Catholic church until Rome "does penance" for all the indignities done to the Eastern churches when the two branches of Christianity formally split in the eleventh century.

❖ In Collegeville, Minnesota, St. John's University announces that it will acquire a true manuscript Bible, entirely handwritten by monks in Wales under the direction of Donald Jackson, a world-renowned calligrapher. The seven-volume, 1,150-page English Bible will cost $3 million and will be the only Bible to be entirely handwritten since the advent of the printing press at the end of the Middle Ages.

❖ On Mount Athos, an island off the coast of eastern Greece, a monk quietly recites the Jesus Prayer. Concentrating his thoughts and controlling his breath, he whispers many times, "Lord Jesus Christ, have mercy on me." He continues a tradition of meditation and prayer going back almost one thousand years.

INTRODUCTION

The period that extends from roughly 500 to 1500 C.E. is probably the least understood and appreciated era of Christianity. Yet during this period Christianity grew by missionary efforts to encompass all of Europe. Eastern Christianity reached its full flower in the Byzantine empire and passed on its faith to the Slavic nations to its north, especially Russia, before the Byzantine empire itself was conquered by Islam. Western

Roman Christianity preserved the tattered remnants of ancient civilization, especially by means of new monastic movements. These monastic orders and the founding of universities effected a shift in the center of theological activity of Western Christianity from the Mediterranean world of ancient times to northern Europe, especially Germany, France, and England. But Western Christianity was still largely ruled from Rome, and the ensuing struggle between northern and southern Europe over the nature of Christianity was to mark much of the later Middle Ages. As religious development continued, movements for reform of the Catholic Church grew stronger and set the stage for both Protestant and Catholic reform in the next period. At the end of the medieval period, the rebirth of classical learning and the heritage of ancient Christianity contributed to the ferment for change.

With this rise of activity, many issues were debated that are still important today. Some of these issues had already been encountered but not resolved in the ancient period of Christianity, such as the relationship of faith and reason as well as conflicts between church and state. Others were mostly new to this period: the systematization of doctrine, a full-fledged doctrine of the church, stagnation and corruption in the church, and the challenge of humanism.

Names

The term **Middle Ages** and its adjective *medieval* were coined in the fifteenth century by Renaissance thinkers. They devalued the long period between the ancient Roman world and their own time, which they viewed as a new historical period of rebirth (**Renaissance** is French for "rebirth," although this name did not come until later). By the 1700s, *Middle Ages* was in general use among historians; later it would become a household word. In 1860, the German historian Jakob Burckhardt portrayed the Middle Ages as lacking the individualism, a sense of discovery of the self and the world, and an appreciation for the heritage of ancient Greece and Rome that marks the Renaissance as the beginning of the modern world.[1] As a historical term, *medieval* is generally used objectively today to denote a period of time. But it still carries some of the stigma the Renaissance attached to it—to call something "medieval" is to label it outmoded. The term *Dark Ages*, found in older literature but not commonly used today, is even more obviously prejudicial. It denotes the period from roughly 500 to 1000, the first half of the Middle Ages, which was characterized by political and cultural instability. *Later* or *High Middle Ages* refers to the second half of this period.

But like all terms for large periods of history (*ancient, Renaissance, modern*), *Middle Ages* is imprecise. For example, some historians date the beginnings of this era to Alaric's sack of the city of Rome in 410, some from the year 500, others as late as the crowning of Charlemagne as Holy Roman Emperor in 800. Disagreement also exists about when the Middle Ages end. Historians generally hold that it ends with the Renaissance, but the Renaissance came to different areas at different times. Since most

---

[1] Jakob Burckhardt, *The Civilization of the Renaissance in Italy* (London: Penguin, 1990; first published in German, 1860).

Important Places at the
End of the Middle Ages

historians date the entire period from approximately 500 to 1500, we will use this dating here.

This term is suited to Western Christianity, but it is not appropriate for Eastern Christianity. This branch of the faith keeps the name *Byzantine Age* to define approximately the same period of time. The Byzantine Age lasts from 330, when Constantine established Constantinople in the East as the capital of the eastern half of the Roman Empire, until about 1453, when Constantinople fell to the Muslims. Because the ancient Eastern Roman Empire (Byzantium) never fell to the "barbarians" and never experienced a Renaissance on the order of Western Europe's, its reference points differ from those of the West.

Historical Sketch

The Eastern Roman empire (Byzantium), with its capital of Constantinople, lasted for more than a thousand years from its creation by Emperor Constantine in 330 to the Turkish Muslim conquest in 1453. The eastern emperors, especially Justinian, were deeply involved in the affairs of the church. Western historians have coined the term **Caesaropapism** for the emperor's leadership of both church and state. Eastern tradition itself prefers the term *symphonia*.

This power was curtailed as a result of the **iconoclast** movement of the eighth and ninth centuries. This movement was initiated by some emperors who wanted to end the veneration of images and physically remove them from the church. Leading monks and several empresses resisted the iconoclasts (literally, "icon breakers"), and the icons were restored. The controversy over images cemented their place as an essential (some would say *the* essential) element of the Eastern Orthodox identity. Image veneration represented a commitment to the reality of the full incarnation of the Son of God in the person of Jesus Christ. When the controversy ended, the power of the church to direct its own doctrine and worship was strengthened. The controversy also strengthened the tendency of Eastern Christianity to define itself in terms of worship and devotion rather than, as in Roman Catholicism, institution and doctrine.

Byzantine Christianity also sponsored missionary activity, especially to the north. Bulgaria, Russia, and Moravia were evangelized in the ninth century, Hungary in the tenth, and Poland in the tenth through twelfth. A unique feature of Orthodox missions was their commitment to preserving indigenous cultures. In the Catholic West, Latin was the language of the church and the Bible; in the Orthodox East, missionaries translated the Bible and the liturgy into the language of the peoples they encountered. This extensive missionary work and accommodation to indigenous languages created a strong Slavic Orthodoxy to the north even as Islam gradually ate away at the southern portions of the empire. Slavic Orthodoxy—especially the Moscow patriarchate, which styled itself as "the third Rome"—was to carry on the Christian heritage of Byzantium when the Eastern empire finally fell in 1453.

In the Latin West, the pope as bishop of Rome set the tone for the continuing development of Christianity. By the end of the ancient period of Christianity, the pope had already asserted his leadership over much of Christianity. When the Western Roman Empire fell in the fifth century, the pope came to represent the main embodiment of continuity with ancient Rome. Over time, the pope extended his power over many of the European states. Those new states, formed by the Teutonic tribes that settled in western Europe in the "Dark Ages," found the papacy an established force to be reckoned with. The Franks quickly allied themselves with Rome as early as the fifth century and became the leading nation in northern Europe during the Middle Ages. The German tribes, slower to give up their old religions, made a slower entry into political and cultural power. Southern England was also evangelized early, but Scandinavia was not until the tenth through the twelfth centuries. Gradually the influence of Rome spread across the entire western half of the European continent.

Medieval Christianity in the West expressed itself not only through pope, bishop, and priest, but also through monk and friar. Monasticism in Western Christianity was always stronger (at least in numbers) than in Byzantine Christianity, and monks became the bearers of civilization in the West. It was the monks who preserved the literary and some of the scientific heritage of Rome, which would have perished for lack of manuscript copying and study. Many of the earliest missionaries were monks; medieval reformers within the Catholic Church, such as Bernard of Clairvaux and Pope Gregory VII, were **friars** (members of the new monastic orders that arose in the twelfth century as opposed to monks in the older monastic orders). Most of the theologians who systematized and developed Christian doctrine in the high Middle Ages, such as Anselm and Aquinas, were monks. Moreover, the man who would begin a reform movement in the next period that split the Roman church, the Augustinian friar Martin Luther, would also be a monastic. The monastic movement also sought to purify itself continually with new monastic orders and more faithful practice of the monastic ideal. Some of the new movements preached the gospel to the people both in churches and outdoors. Through this reform the life of the whole Catholic Church was enriched and renewed.

At the end of the Middle Ages, life in Western Christianity began to be changed in the Renaissance. Greco-Roman classical ideals in art, architecture, philosophy, and literature were reborn first at high levels of society. These reborn ideals soon reached down to transform everyday life: food and dress, family life, and commerce. This rebirth of ancient culture also impacted the Christian faith. It called the church back *ad fontes,* "to its foundations" in the New Testament and the ancient church. Not trusting in tradition for tradition's sake, the Renaissance examined received institutions and teachings. It promoted a human-centered view of life, often a Christian humanism but sometimes not, in place of the medieval heaven-centered view. In Renaissance art, for example, realistically portrayed saints on earth and persons and scenes with no overt religious meanings replaced the saints in heaven.

The Renaissance began in Italy, especially the city-state of Florence, around 1400. Soon the glories of its thought and culture, especially art and architecture, spread through Italy and were embraced in large measure by the Catholic church. Then the Renaissance spread across the Alps, resulting in a "Northern Renaissance" which began to flourish around 1450. This stage tended to be more sedate, but it had an even more profound impact on Christianity than the Italian Renaissance. To anticipate the next chapter here, the Christian humanism of Erasmus of Rotterdam, the leading figure of the Northern Renaissance, prodded the church into self-examination and eventual reform, both Protestant and Catholic. Most mainline Protestant reformers—Luther, Calvin, Zwingli, and the rest—were "Renaissance men" steeped in the wide intellectual and spiritual values of the Renaissance. But not every aspect of the Renaissance would prove to be positive. For example, the Renaissance hastened the rise of the nation-state and nationalism, ending the medieval Catholic ideal of a Europe united by a common faith. Also, some strains of Renaissance humanism would lead in early modern times to the notion that life could be lived without any reference to God or received teachings of Christianity.

Finally, both Eastern and Western Christianity were forced in medieval, Renaissance, and Byzantine times to come to grips with the existence and rising power of Islam. From its beginning in 622, Islam spread rapidly in the Middle East, much more rapidly than Christianity had ever spread in its east or west. Soon almost all the Middle East and North Africa were Islamic, and much of the Christian population converted. Muslim forces took over the major church centers of ancient eastern Christianity, Jerusalem and Alexandria, Egypt, among them. Small Christian minorities lived somewhat peaceably under Islamic rule, protected by Islamic law. Islam continued to press on the Byzantine empire until 1453, when Constantinople itself became a Muslim city and its ancient cathedral built by Justinian, the Church of Holy Wisdom (Greek *Hagia Sophia*), became a mosque. The main confrontation of Western Christianity with Islam would take place in the Crusades (1095–1291), when Christian forces from all over Europe tried repeatedly to regain the holy places in Palestine from the Muslims, an effort that eventually failed.

Literary Genres of the Primary Sources

Christians of the period 500–1500, as in the ancient period, employed many different written genres to express and explain Christianity. First, histories in this time usually took the form of **chronicles,** a chronologically ordered narrative of events, usually continuous and detailed but lacking overall analysis or interpretation. Chronicles often arose from the needs of governments and church officials to keep running records of events in their purview. Other chronicles arose from letters reporting the activities of missionaries. Some more advanced histories, such as Bede's *Ecclesiastical History of England,* did take a more analytical approach. But while biblical and ancient Christian histories were apologetic, both types of medieval histories lost this overt purpose to the more sober, straightforward chronology.

Formal, legal pronouncements typically have their own genre. The **papal bull** (Latin, *bulla,* seal) is one type of such formal pronouncement. Bulls, papal letters, and other pronouncements, especially excommunications, feature lengthy, ponderous sentences and paragraphs designed to be weighty in tone. They are known by their Latin titles, drawn from the first words of the document; we will give English translation of these titles along with the Latin. When you read examples of such legal genres, look for the main point near the end. Some official pronouncements directed at what their author considers heresy have a good deal of **invective,** cleverly abusive insults. For example, the German king Henry IV called Pope Gregory VII "not Pope but a false monk" and urged him, "Descend, descend [from the papal throne], to be damned forever." The use of invective, an ancient Greek rhetorical device, continues through the Middle Ages into the Reformation. Though it sounds harsh to the modern ear, in much of the Western tradition it was the educated, proper way to talk about one's opponent.

A new type of genre in the Middle Ages is the **monastic rule.** These are formal, lengthy regulations for life in the monastery. Such life was rigidly controlled, and the rules sought to cover every aspect of the monk's life in order to achieve the goals of the order. We will sample the *Rule* of St. Benedict, one of the founders of Western monasticism in general and the founder of the Benedictines in particular. But the rules of other, later orders are similar and in fact are based on Benedict's.

Hymns continue to be an established genre in this period. Both rhythm and rhyme are a feature of medieval and Byzantine hymnody. Although this book must lack the important context of the music, the words of happier hymns such as the *Akathistos* hymn to the Virgin Mary and St. Francis' "Hymn to Brother Sun," as well as the sobering words of the "Day of Wrath" hymn, still stand on their own. Byzantine hymns were intended to evoke feeling for the sublime, heavenly realm, allowing worshippers to feel that they were already in heaven. This was a continuation of the intent of ancient Christian hymns. Western hymns, on the other hand, came during the Middle Ages to stress human religious emotions before God, such as suffering and joy. They retain this orientation even today in both Roman Catholic and Protestant Christianity.

Mysticism, the direct and often emotional vision of God, leads to writings that are challenging to read and interpret. Much of the deeper spirituality of the Middle Ages is expressed in mystical writings. Some mystical writings are highly symbolic and often lengthy; their style reflects the mystery of the visions they are based upon. Much of the medieval mystical literature is from women, especially cloistered women; mystical writing was perhaps the only serious form of religious literary expression open to them. Feminine images for God, present in some of the ancient writers such as Augustine, grew stronger in these writings, as for example when the nun Julian of Norwich refers jointly to the persons of the Trinity as "Mother." On the other hand, mysticism could be simple and straightforward, as the famous writing of Thomas à Kempis, *The Imitation of Christ.*

Finally, and importantly, the later Middle Ages sees the rise of academic theological writings. A **scholastic** (academic) style features close reasoning on the faith, emphasizing the rational understanding and presentation of Christian belief. Sometimes this takes the form of a dialogue between two partners, as in Anselm's *Why God Became Human.* This scholastic text, like most other scholastic writings, features extremely close, intricate reasoning that demands a great deal of attention from its readers to follow it. In the writings of Thomas Aquinas, the scholastic form reaches its height. Scholastic theology was written not for the common person or even the clergy, but (like most academic theology today) for other academic theologians. This fact explains much of its demanding character. Thomas's *Summa theologiae* (or *theologica;* "The Height of Theology," usually called only by its Latin title) consists entirely of questions, each beginning an article in which important answers are summarized and critiqued. At the end of each article Thomas gives his own position on the question and replies to objections. The full form of this Thomistic style is given in the reading entitled, "The Rise of Scholastic Theology"; other readings from Aquinas excerpt only the main statement of his own position. When you are reading scholastic theology, it is especially important to make sure that you follow the progression and content of the reasoning.

EVENTS

Benedict's Life and Miracles*

Pope Gregory I (540–604) had himself been a monk and wrote to extol the virtues of the most famous leader of monks in the West, Benedict. The second book of his Dialogues *is the earliest written treatment of Benedict. It relates in a sober fashion the events of Benedict's life and, in a way more characteristic of popular religion, his miracles. The miracle recounted here is known as the "Poisoned Loaf."*[2]

Some years ago there lived a man who was revered for the holiness of his life. Benedict was his name, and he was indeed blessed[3] with God's grace. During his boyhood he showed mature understanding, and strength of character far beyond his years kept his heart detached from every pleasure. Even while still living in the world, free to enjoy all it had to offer, he saw how empty it was and turned from it without regret.

He was born in Norcia of distinguished parents, who sent him to Rome for a liberal education. When he found many of the students there abandoning themselves to vice, he decided to withdraw from the world he had been preparing to enter. He was afraid that if he acquired any of its learning he would be drawn down with them to his eternal ruin. In his desire to please God alone, he turned his back on further studies, gave up home and inheritance and resolved to embrace the religious life. He took this step, fully aware of his ignorance; yet he was truly wise, uneducated though he may have been. . . .

The progress of the saint's work could not be stopped. His reputation for holiness kept on growing and with it the number of vocations to a more perfect state of life. This only infuriated Florentius[4] all the more. He still longed to enjoy the praise the saint was receiving, yet he was unwilling to lead a praiseworthy life himself. At length his soul became so blind with jealousy that he decided to poison a loaf of bread and send it to the servant of God as a sign of Christian fellowship. Though aware at once of the deadly poison it contained, Benedict thanked him for the gift.

At mealtime a raven used to come out of the nearby woods to receive food from the saint's hands. On this occasion he set the poisoned loaf in front of it and said, "In the name of our Lord Jesus Christ, take this bread and carry it to a place where no one will be able to find it." The raven started to caw and circled around the loaf of bread with open beak and flapping wings as if to indicate that it was willing to obey but found it impossible to do so. Several times the saint repeated the command. "Take the bread," he said, "and do not be afraid! Take it away from here and leave it where no one can find it." After hesitating for a long while, the raven finally took the loaf in its beak and flew away. About three hours later, when it had disposed of the bread, it returned and received its usual meal from the hands of the man of God.

---

* Pope Gregory I, *Dialogues on the Lives and Miracles of the Italian Fathers* 2, Preface

[2] Taken from O. J. Zimmerman and B. R. Avery, *Life and Miracles of St. Benedict* (Collegeville, MN: St. Johns Abbey Press, 1949), 1–2. Copyright 1949, St. John's Abbey Press. Used by permission of the Liturgical Press.

[3] *blessed:* "Benedict" comes from the Latin, "blessed."

---

[4] *Florentius:* a rival of Benedict.

Two Early Missions*

Augustine (called "of Canterbury" or "of St. Andrew" to distinguish him from Augustine of Hippo), the leader of a Roman monastery, was sent with about forty other monks by Gregory I to preach to the Anglo-Saxon peoples of Britain. Eventually King Ethelbert and many of his subjects were converted in 597. This selection from Bede's eighth-century history relates some of the difficulties Augustine encountered.[5]

In the second reading, John of Monte Corvino, Italy relates his work among the Mongols in China. John has to contend with Nestorian Christians in China just as earlier Roman missionaries had to deal with Arian Christianity among the German tribes.[6]

In the year of our Lord 582, Maurice, the fifty-fourth [ruler] from Augustus, ascended the throne [of the city of Rome] and reigned for twenty-one years. In the tenth year of his reign, Gregory, a man famous for learning and behavior, was promoted to the apostolic see of Rome, and presided over it for thirteen years, six months and ten days. In the fourteenth year of the same emperor, and about the one hundred and fiftieth after the coming of the English into Britain, he was moved by Divine inspiration and sent the servant of God, Augustine, to preach the word of God to the English nation. Several other monks who feared the Lord went with him. In obedience to the pope's commands, they began that work, but were, on their journey, seized with a sudden fear, and began to think of returning home, rather than go to a barbarous, fierce, and unbelieving nation, to whose very language they were strangers. They sent back Augustine, who had been appointed to be consecrated as a bishop

in case they were received by the English, that he might, by humble entreaty, obtain of the holy Gregory that they should not be compelled to undertake so dangerous, toilsome, and uncertain a journey. The pope, in reply, sent them an encouraging letter, persuading them to proceed in the work of the Divine word, and rely on the assistance of the Almighty. . . .

Augustine, thus strengthened by the confirmation of the blessed Father Gregory, returned to the work of the word of God, with the servants of Christ, and arrived in Britain. . . . They had, by order of the blessed Pope Gregory, taken interpreters from the nation of the Franks. They sent to Ethelbert, saying that they had come from Rome, and brought a joyful message, which assured to all that took advantage of it everlasting joys in heaven, and a kingdom that would never end, with the living and true God. When the king heard this, he ordered them to stay in that island where they had landed, and that they should be furnished with all necessary things, until he should consider what to do with them. For he had already heard of the Christian religion, having a Christian wife from the royal family of the Franks, called Bertha. He had received her from her parents, upon condition that she should be permitted to practice her religion with the Bishop Luidhard, who was sent with her to preserve her faith.

Some days after, the king came into the island, and sitting in the open air, ordered Augustine and his companions to be brought into his presence. For he had taken precautions that they should not come to him in any house, lest, according to an ancient superstition, if they practiced any magical arts, they might get the better of him. But they came furnished with Divine power, not with magical power, bearing a silver cross for their banner, and the image of our Lord and Savior painted on a board. Singing the litany, they offered up their prayers to the Lord for the eternal salvation both of themselves and of those to whom they were come. When he had sat

---

* Bede, *Ecclesiastical History of England* 1.23, 25; John of Monte Corvino, Letter from China

[5] From J. E. Giles, trans., *Bede's Ecclesiastical History of England* (London: Bohn, 1847), 34–35.

[6] Taken, with editing, from Henry Yule, *Cathay and the Way Thither* (London: Hakluyt Society, 1866), 197–99.

down, according to the king's commands, he preached to him and his attendants the word of life.

Then the king answered, "Your words and promises are very fair. But they are new to us, and of uncertain meaning, so I cannot approve of them and forsake that which I have so long followed with the whole English nation. But because you are come from afar into my kingdom, and desire to impart to us those things that you believe to be true and most beneficial, we will not molest you, but give you favorable reception. We will take care to supply you with your necessary sustenance. We do not forbid you to preach and gain as many as you can to your religion." Accordingly he permitted them to reside in the city of Canterbury,[7] which was the metropolis of all his dominions, and, according to his promise, besides allowing them sustenance, did not refuse them liberty to preach.

[Letter from China of John of Monte Corvino] I, Friar John of Monte Corvino, of the order of Minor Friars,[8] departed from Tauris, a city of the Persians, in the year of the Lord 1291, and proceeded to India. . . .

I proceeded on my further journey and made my way to Cathay, the realm of the Emperor of the Tartars who is called the Grand Khan. To him I presented the letter of our lord the Pope, and invited him to adopt the Catholic Faith of our Lord Jesus Christ, but he had grown too old in idolatry. However, he bestows many kindnesses upon the Christians, and these two years past I have been living with him. The Nestorians,[9] a certain body who profess to bear the Christian name, but who deviate sadly from the Christian

religion, have grown so powerful in those parts that they will not allow a Christian of another ritual to have ever so small a chapel, or to proclaim any doctrine different from their own. . . . The Nestorians, either directly or through others whom they bribed, have brought on me sharp persecutions. For they invented stories that I was not sent by our lord the Pope, but was a great spy and impostor. . . . Many a time I was dragged before the judgment seat with shameful treatment and threats of death. At last, by God's providence, the emperor, through the confessions of a certain individual, came to know my innocence and the malice of my adversaries. Then he banished them with their wives and children.

In this mission I lived alone and without any associate for eleven years. It is now going on two years since Friar Arnold, a German of the province of Cologne, joined me. I have built a church in the city of Khanbalik, in which the king has his chief residence. I completed this six years ago; and I have built a bell-tower to it, and put three bells in it. I have baptized there, as well as I can estimate, up to this time some 6,000 persons. If those charges against me of which I have spoken had not been made, I should have baptized more than 30,000. I am often still engaged in baptizing. Also I have gradually bought one hundred and fifty boys, the children of pagan parents, and of ages varying from seven to eleven, who had never learned any religion. I have baptized them, and I have taught them Greek and Latin after our custom. Also I have written out psalters for them, with thirty hymnbooks and two breviaries.[10] By help of these, eleven of the boys already know our service, and form a choir and take their weekly turn of duty as they do in convents, whether I am there or not. . . . I have the bells rung at all the canonical hours, and with my congregation of babies and infants I perform divine service. We do the chanting by ear because I have no service book with the notes.

---

[7] *Canterbury* thus became the first and foremost bishopric in England, and remains so today in the Anglican Church.

[8] *order of Minor Friars:* a branch of the Franciscans that followed the original rule of St. Francis.

[9] *Nestorians:* a church that refused to confess the Orthodox belief in the two natures (divine and human) in the one person of Jesus Christ. They call themselves the "Church of the East."

---

[10] *breviaries:* liturgical books containing the Daily Office of monastic services.

Pope Urban II Calls for a Crusade, and a Noble Dissent*

Urban II addressed the Council of Clermont in 1095, urging reforms in the church and society, especially an end to warfare between the European states. At the conclusion of his address, he called for a holy war to provide military relief to the Eastern (Byzantine) empire and then free the Holy Land from Muslim domination, a war that would become known as the Crusades. In the second reading, Roger Niger criticizes the third crusade in language applicable to all the crusades.[11]

O sons of God, you have promised more firmly than ever to keep the peace among yourselves and to preserve the rights of the church. But an important work remains for you to do. . . . Your brethren in the east are in urgent need of your help, and you must hasten to give them the aid that has often been promised them. As most of you have heard, the Turks and Arabs have attacked them and have conquered the territory of Romania[12] as far west as the shore of the Mediterranean and the Hellespont. They have occupied more and more of the lands of those Christians, and have overcome them in seven battles. They have killed and captured many, and have destroyed the churches and devastated the empire. If you permit them to continue with impunity, the faithful of God will be much more widely attacked by them. On this account I, or rather the Lord, beseech you as Christ's heralds to publish this everywhere and to persuade all people of whatever rank, foot-soldiers and knights, poor and rich, to carry aid promptly to those Christians and to destroy that vile race from the lands of our friends. I say this to those who are present; it is also meant for those who are absent. Moreover, Christ commands it.

All who die on the way, whether by land or by sea, or in battle against the pagans, shall have immediate remission of sins. I grant them this through the power of God with which I am invested. O what a disgrace if such a despised and base race, which worships demons, should conquer a people which has the faith of omnipotent God and is made glorious with the name of Christ! With what reproaches will the Lord overwhelm us if you do not aid those who, with us, profess the Christian religion! Let those who have been accustomed unjustly to wage private warfare against the faithful[13] now go against the infidels and end with victory this war which should have been begun long ago. Let those who have been robbers for a long time now become knights. Let those who have been fighting against their brothers and relatives now fight in a proper way against the barbarians. Let those who have been serving as mercenaries for small pay now obtain the eternal reward. Let those who have been wearing themselves out in both body and soul now work for a double honor.

[Roger Niger, *On a Military Matter*] Because of our own sins Palestine is given over to our enemies. The wrath of the Lord has descended upon us Christians because we were unwilling to be one finger behind Saladin[14] in riches. But what has happened there is less of a menace than the heresies of the Manichees and many other condemned sects which swarm in these times. Illiterates desert the church and the clergy. They deny the sacraments of the church, and affirm many other blasphemies with such boldness that they are ready to die for their assertion. . . . By good deeds they spread nefarious opinions. When such evil is done to the faith at home,

---

* *Acts of God through Francis* 1.382–84; Roger Niger, *On a Military Matter*
[11] From O. J. Thatcher and E. H. McNeal, *A Source Book for Medieval History* (New York: Scribners, 1905), 514–17.
[12] *Romania:* the Byzantine empire.

[13] *wage private war against the faithful:* Urban refers here to the evils of constant wars in Christian Europe, which he has condemned in the first part of his address.
[14] *Saladin:* leader of the Muslim empire controlling Palestine.

what hope is there that the occident can help the orient? What good will it be if Palestine is delivered from the Saracens if infidelity flourishes at home?

Besides, are the Saracens to be killed because God has given Palestine to them? Does not God say, "I desire not the death of a sinner?"[15] The Saracens are men of like nature with us. They may be repelled if they invade our territory . . .

---

[15] Ezekiel 33:11.

but the medicine should not exceed the disease. They are to be struck with the sword of the spirit so that they may come voluntarily to the faith, because God hates forced worship. The Lord Pope . . . has offered indulgences for the remission of all sins to those who go on [crusade] pilgrimages. I will not contest his competence, but God does not remit penalties until after sins have been repudiated. And what shall we say of the participation of so many priests, who are not permitted to pollute their sacred hands by bloodshed?

East and West Formally Separate*

Despite the good things said about Eastern Christians by Pope Urban II when he called for a crusade, tensions had been building between Eastern and Western Christianity since the seventh century. In the eleventh century, these tensions led to formal separation. The churches of Sicily were mostly Eastern Orthodox, and when Rome tried to assert rule over them, Patriarch of Constantinople Michael Cerularius closed the churches of the Latin rite in his territories and attacked the legitimacy of Roman Catholic Christianity. Pope Leo IX responded by sending Cardinal Humbert to Constantinople in 1054. In the first reading, Archbishop Humbert excommunicates Michael in a letter laid on the main altar of Hagia Sophia cathedral as the service was about to begin. In the second reading, Michael responds in kind, listing the errors of the Roman Catholics and excommunicating them. These mutual excommunications lasted until 1965, when Pope Paul VI and Patriarch Athenagoras revoked them in a mutual declaration of reconciliation.[16]

Humbert, by the grace of God cardinal-bishop of the Holy Roman Church; Peter, archbishop of Amalfi; Frederick, deacon and chancellor; to all sons of the Catholic church:

The holy Roman, first, and Apostolic See[17] has deigned to appoint us legates to this city. . . . Let the glorious emperors, the clergy, the Senate, and the people of this city of Constantinople, and the entire Catholic church, know that we have noted here a great good, on account of which we deeply rejoice in the Lord. But we have also perceived a very great evil, which makes us extremely sad.

With respect to the pillars of the empire and its wise and honored citizens, this city is most Christian and orthodox. However, Michael, falsely called patriarch, and his followers in folly, sow too many weeds of heresies in its midst.[18] For the Simoniacs sell God's gift; the Valesians castrate their guests and promote them not only to the priesthood but even to the episcopate. The Arians rebaptize people already baptized (especially Latins) in the name of the Holy Trinity. The Donatists affirm that, excepting for the Greek

---

*Humbert of Silva Candida, Letter Excommunicating Michael Cerularius; Michael Cerularius, Decree of Excommunication

[16] The first reading translated by the author from J.-P. Migné, *Patrologiae Graecae,* vol. 120 (Paris, Migne, 1890), cols. 836–44; the second and third are translated by the author from Cornelius Will, *Acta et Scripta* (Leipzig: Teubner, 1861), pp. 153–68.

[17] *See:* center of a bishop's area.

[18] *heresies . . . in its midst:* Humbert here begins to compare the practices of the Orthodox Church to ancient heresies condemned by both East and West.

church, Christ's church and the true sacrifice [of the Mass] and baptism have perished from the whole world. The Nicolaites permit and defend marriage for ministers of the holy altar. The Severians maintain that the law of Moses is accursed. The Pneumatomachians [enemies of the Holy Spirit] or Theoumachians [enemies of God] have deleted from the creed the procession of the Holy Spirit from the Son.[19] The Manichaeans declare, among other things, that anything fermented is alive. The Nazarenes . . . keep their beards and hair, and do not receive into communion those who cut their hair and shave their beards according to the custom of the Roman church.[20] Although admonished by our Lord Pope Leo regarding these errors and many other of his deeds, Michael himself has contemptuously disregarded these warnings. Moreover, he denied his presence and any oral communication to us, [Leo's] ambassadors, who are seeking faithfully to stamp out the cause of such great evils. He forbade [us the use of] churches to celebrate Mass in, just as earlier he had closed the Latin churches [in Constantinople]. Calling the Latins "Unleavened Ones,"[21] he hounds them everywhere in word and deed. Indeed, he cursed the Apostolic See by cursing its sons, and in opposition [to Rome] he signed himself "ecumenical patriarch."[22]

We cannot put up with this unheard of slander and insult to the first, holy, Apostolic See. Because they assault the Catholic faith in so many ways, we, by the authority of the undivided and Holy Trinity and that of the Apostolic See, whose embassy we constitute, and by the authority of all the orthodox fathers of the seven [ecumenical] councils and that of the entire Catholic church, whatever our most reverend lord the Pope has denounced in Michael and his followers, unless they repent, we declare to be anathematized. May Michael, false upstart patriarch . . . and all [his] followers in the previously stated errors and presumptions be anathematized, Maranatha,[23] with the Simoniacs, Valesians, Arians, Donatists, Nicolaites, Severians, Pneumatomachians, Manichaeans, and Nazarenes, and with all heretics, indeed with the devil and his angels, unless by some chance they repent. Amen. Amen. Amen.

[Michael's Decree] The decree in response to the bull of excommunication cast before the holy altar by the legates of Rome against the most Holy Patriarch Michael in the month of July of the 7th indiction [1054]:

When Michael, our most holy ruler and ecumenical patriarch was presiding, certain impious and disrespectful men (what else could a pious man call them?) came out of the darkness, because they were begotten of the West.[24] They came to this pious and God-protected city from which the springs of orthodoxy flow as if from on high, disseminating the teachings of piety to the ends of the world. To this city they came like a thunderbolt, or an earthquake, or a hailstorm, or to put it more directly, like wild wolves trying to defile the Orthodox belief by different dogmas. . . .

We do not wish to tamper with the sacred and holy creed . . . by the use of wrongful arguments and illegal reasoning and extreme boldness. Unlike them we do not wish to say that the Holy Spirit proceeds from the Father and the Son— What a devilish deceit!—but we say that the Holy Spirit proceeds from the Father. We declare that they do not follow the Scripture which says "Do not shave your beards."[25] Nor do they want to

---

[19] *deleted . . . from the Son:* Catholics argued that the phrase "and the Son" was originally present in the Nicene Creed.
[20] *cut . . . beards:* another point of contention between the Roman and Eastern churches was the Eastern requirement of a bearded clergy, and the Latin practice of being clean-shaven.
[21] *Unleavened Ones:* those who celebrate the Holy Communion with unleavened bread (wafers).
[22] *ecumenical patriarch:* bishop ("patriarch") of the whole Christian world.

[23] *Maranatha:* An Aramaic word meaning, "Our Lord, come."
[24] *the West:* where the sun sets, therefore a land of darkness.
[25] Possibly a reference to Leviticus 19:27.

fully understand that God the Creator in an appropriate way created woman, and he decreed that it was improper for men to be alone. . . . We continue to observe inviolate the ancient canons of the apostolic perfection and order, and wish to affirm that the marriage of ordained men should not be dissolved and they should not be deprived of having sexual relations with their wives, which from time to time is appropriate. So if anyone is found to be worthy of the office of deacon or subdeacon, he should not be kept from this office. He should be restored to his lawful wife in order that what God has himself ordained and blessed should not be dishonored by us, especially since the Gospel declares "Those whom God has joined together, let not man put asunder." [26] If someone then dares against the apostolic canons to remove anyone of the clergy who

is a presbyter, deacon, or subdeacon, depriving him of his lawful bond with his wife, let him be excommunicated. . . .

But they come against us and against the Orthodox church of God . . . arriving before the most pious emperor. They intrigued against the faithful and even "counterfeited" their arrival with the pretext that they came from Rome, and pretended that they were sent by the pope. . . . They even produced fraudulent letters which allegedly had been given them by him. This fraud was detected, among other things, also from the seals which were clearly tampered with. . . . The original of the impious document deposited on the altar of the Great Church by these irreligious and accursed men was not burned, but was placed in the depository in order that it be to the perpetual dishonor of those who have committed such blasphemies against us, and as permanent evidence of this condemnation.

---

[26] Matthew 19:6; Mark 10:9.

Popular Religious Responses to the Great Plague*

Jean le Bel, a priest in the cathedral of Liège, wrote his True Chronicles *on the events of 1326–61. Here he chronicles the main popular religious responses to the Black Death (1347–48): forms of extreme public penance, then anti-Semitism.*[27]

There was current at this time a common and general mortality, throughout the world, from a sickness which was called the plague. It took some on the left arm and others in the groin, and they died within three days. When it struck a street or a lodging, one caught it from another,

so few dared to help or visit the sick. They could not make their confessions, for it was almost impossible to find a priest who would hear them. No one dared to clothe or touch the sick.

People could not think what to make of this affliction or what remedy to offer for it, but many believed that this was a divine vengeance on the sins of the world. Therefore some began to do great penance in diverse ways by way of devotion. Among others, the people of Germany began to go through the country on the main roads in companies, carrying crucifixes, standards and great banners, and in processions. They went through the streets, two by two, singing loudly hymns to God and our Lady, rhymed and with music. Then they assembled together and stripped to their underclothes twice a day and beat themselves as hard as they could with knotted lashes embedded with needles. The blood flowed down from their shoulders on all sides, while all the time they were singing their songs.

---

* Jean le Bel, *True Chronicles,* for the years 1347–48
[27] From Jean Comby, *How to Read Church History,* vol. 1. Translated by John Bowden and Margaret Lydamore from the French *Pour lire L'Histoire de L'Eglise,* tome 1, published in 1984 by Les Editions du Cerf, 29 bd. Latour-Maubourg, Paris. Copyright John Bowden and Margaret Lydamore 1985. Used with permission of the Crossroad Publishing Company, New York, and SCM Press Ltd., London.

Then they threw themselves to the earth three times in devotion and went around among one another with great humility.

When people saw that this mortality and pestilence did not cease as a result of the penitence that they did, a rumor was heard that it came from the Jews. It said that the Jews had thrown poison into wells and fountains throughout the world to poison all Christians, to have lordship and control over all the world. Therefore every-one, great and small, was so aroused against them that they were all burned to death in the market places where flagellants[28] went, by the lords and judges of those places. They went to their deaths dancing and singing as joyfully as if they were going to a wedding. They did not want to become Christians nor would they allow their children to receive baptism.

[28] *flagellants:* those who whip themselves in penance.

Women and Witchcraft*

The Hammer against Witches *(Latin* Malleus Maleficarum*) was written in 1486 by two leading Dominican inquisitors. Incorporating many common popular ideas about witches, it nonetheless received a papal endorsement in its preface. Its purpose was to label witchcraft as real and threatening; earlier European Christian tradition from about 1300 back to Charlemagne (800) had forbidden thinking of witches as real. Its most striking feature is its virulent attack on women. The hunt for witches in the late Middle Ages saw perhaps the height of misogyny in European history. As this selection shows, this book restates many of the misogynist arguments current in its day.*[29]

In these times witchcraft is more often found in women than in men. If anyone is curious as to the reason, we may add this to what has already been said: since women are feebler both in mind and body, it is not surprising that they should come more under the spell of witchcraft. . . .

A woman is more carnal than a man, as is clear from her many carnal abominations. There was a defect in the formation of the first woman, since she was formed from a bent rib, that is, a rib of the breast, which is bent as it were in a contrary direction to a man. Through this defect she is an imperfect animal, so she always deceives. For Cato says that when a woman weeps she weaves snares . . . to deceive a man. This is shown by Samson's wife, who coaxed him to tell her the riddle he had propounded to the Philistines, and told them the answer, and so deceived him. And it is clear in the case of the first woman that she had little faith. . . . All this is indicated by the etymology of the word; for *femina* comes from *fe* and *minus,*[30] since she is always weaker to hold and preserve the faith. However, faith never failed in the Blessed Virgin, by nature and by grace, even at the time of Christ's Passion, when it failed in all men.[31] Therefore a woman is by her nature quicker to waver in faith, and consequently quicker to deny the faith, which is the root of witchcraft.

Now about her other mental quality, her natural will. When she hates someone whom she formerly loved, she seethes with anger and impatience in her whole soul, just as the tides of the sea are always heaving and boiling. . . . Seneca

---

* Heinrich Kramer and Jacobus Sprenger, *Hammer against Witches*

[29] Taken, with editing, from Heinrich Kramer [Latin, Institoris] and Jacobus Sprenger, *Malleus Maleficarum* (London: Pushkin Press, 1948), 44–47.

[30] *fe:* faith; *minus:* small.

[31] The authors note the exceptional faith of the Virgin Mary but look on it as "the exception that proves the rule" of feminine weakness.

says, "No might of flames or of swollen winds, no deadly weapon, is so much to be feared as the lust and hatred of a woman who has been divorced from the marriage bed." . . .

Through their second defect, excessive affections and passions, women search for, brood over, and inflict various vengeance on others, either by witchcraft or by some other means. . . . Women also have weak memories. It is a natural vice in them not to be disciplined, but to follow their own impulses without any sense of what is proper. . . .

[Women do not employ] the snare of hunters, but of devils. For men are caught not only through their own carnal desires, when they see and hear women. . . . When it is said that her heart is a net, it speaks of the inscrutable malice which reigns in them. Her hands are like bands

for binding. When women place their hands on a creature to bewitch it, they perform their plans with the help of the devil.

To conclude: All witchcraft comes from carnal lust, which is insatiable in women. See Proverbs 30, "There are three things that are never satisfied, yes, and a fourth thing which never says 'enough'; that is, the mouth of the womb." Therefore to satisfy their lusts [witches] even copulate with devils. More reasons could be brought forward, but it is sufficiently clear that it is no wonder that more women than men are infected with the heresy of witchcraft. Therefore, it is better called the heresy of witches than of wizards. Blessed be the Highest, who has so far preserved the male sex from so great a crime! Since he was willing to be born and to suffer for us, therefore he has granted to us men this privilege.

Historical Criticism Begins in the Italian Renaissance*

Lorenzo Valla (1407–1457) was a Renaissance humanist who turned his keen historical skills to debunking legends of earlier church history. His works and method had a strong influence on Erasmus and the Protestant Reformers. In this book, Valla takes on the legend that the Apostles' Creed was written by the Twelve Apostles.[32]

A few days ago a certain Brother Antonio Bentontio of the Friars Minor[33] came to Rome preaching, or better to say bellowing. I came upon him as he was teaching the creed to a group of boys, telling them that Peter had said, "I believe in God the Father almighty"; that Andrew had said, "Maker of heaven and earth"; and so on for the rest of the Apostles and through the creed. I challenged him and asked who had ever

heard that the creed was given by the Apostles article by article.

He answered, "The Doctors of the Church."

"Which ones?" I replied.

"The Doctors approved by the Church are Ambrose, Jerome, Augustine, and Gregory." He also said that Bonaventure said so and he is as great as any.

I told him that in matters of reason the testimony of later authority was as good as early authority, but when it comes to what actually happened in the past we can't pass over the testimony of people who lived in the past. . . .

Some time later a Dominican, reputed to be an Inquisitor, asked me pointedly whether I believed the creed was given by the Apostles. I told him that I thought it came from the Nicene Council. He replied that this was heresy and unless I recanted he would damn me.

"I believe what Mother Church believes," I replied.

"Revoke your statement!" he shouted.

---

* Lorenzo Valla, *Theological Calumnies*
[32] Translated by the author from *Calumnia theologica Laurentio Vallensi* (Strasburg, 1522).
[33] *Friars Minor:* a Franciscan.

"Show me why I should revoke it! . . . Are you trying to change my mouth or my mind? What good will it do if I confess with my mouth what I do not believe with my mind? I tell you, I believe what Mother Church believes even if she doesn't know anything about it."

INSTITUTION

The Organization of Monastic Communities*

Benedict borrowed freely from earlier monastic writers to produce his Rule. *Consisting of seventy-three chapters, it regulates the life of the monastery in some detail. This life featured worship (the Divine Office), study, and manual labor. Monks were not priests but laymen called to this special life of spiritual discipline.*[34]

[22] The monks shall sleep separately in individual beds, and the abbot shall assign them their beds according to their conduct. If possible all the monks shall sleep in the same dormitory, but if their number is too large to allow this, they are to be divided into tens or twenties and placed under the control of some of the older monks. A candle shall be kept burning in the dormitory all night until daybreak. The monks shall go to bed clothed and belted with belts and cords, but shall not have their knives at their sides, lest in their dreams they injure one of the sleepers. They should be always in readiness, rising immediately upon the signal and hastening to the service, but appearing there gravely and modestly. The beds of the younger brothers should not be placed together, but should be scattered among those of the older monks. When the brothers arise they should gently exhort one another to hasten to the service, so that the sleepy ones may have no excuse for coming late. . . .

[33] The sin of owning private property should be entirely eradicated from the monas-tery. No one shall presume to give or receive anything except by the order of the abbot. No one shall possess anything of his own, books, paper, pens, or anything else. Monks are not to own even their own bodies and wills to be used at their own desire, but are to look to the father [abbot] of the monastery for everything. So they shall have nothing that has not been given or allowed to them by the abbot. All things are to be held in common according to the command of the Scriptures, and no one shall consider anything as his own property.[35] If anyone has been found guilty of this most grievous sin, he shall be admonished for the first and second offense, and then if he does not mend his ways he shall be punished.

[38] There should always be reading during the common meal, but it shall not be left to chance, so that anyone may take up the book and read. On Sunday one of the brothers shall be appointed to read during the following week. . . . At the common meal, the strictest silence shall be kept, that no whispering or speaking may be heard except the voice of the reader. The brothers shall mutually wait upon one another by passing the food and drink, so that no one shall have to ask for anything. If this is necessary, it shall be done by a sign rather than by words, if possible. . . .

Idleness is the great enemy of the soul. Therefore the monks should always be occupied, either in manual labor or in holy reading. The

---

* *The Benedictine Rule* 22, 33, 38, 58
[34] Taken from O. J. Thatcher and E. H. McNeal, *Source Book for Medieval History* (New York: Scribners, 1905), 434–59.

[35] *All things . . . his own property:* see Acts of the Apostles 2:43–47, 4:32–35.

hours for these occupations should be arranged according to the seasons, as follows. From Easter to the first of October, the monks shall go to work at the first hour and labor until the fourth hour, and the time from the fourth to the sixth hour shall be spent in reading. After dinner, which comes at the sixth hour, they shall lie down and rest in silence; but anyone who wishes may read, if he does it so as not to disturb anyone else. Nones[36] shall be observed a little earlier, about the middle of the eighth hour, and the monks shall go back to work, laboring until vespers. But if the conditions of the locality or the needs of the monastery, such as may occur at harvest time, should make it necessary to labor longer hours, they shall not feel themselves ill-used, for true monks should live by the labor of their own hands, as did the apostles and the holy fathers. But the weakness of human nature must be taken into account in making these arrangements. . . .

[58] Entrance into the monastery should not be made too easy, for the apostle says: "Try the spirits, whether they are of God."[37] So when anyone applies at the monastery, asking to be accepted as a monk, he should first be proved by every test. He shall be made to wait outside four or five days, continually knocking at the door and begging to be admitted. Then he shall be taken in as a guest and allowed to stay in the guest chamber a few days. If he satisfies these preliminary tests, he shall then be made to serve a novitiate[38] of at least one year. During the novitiate he shall be placed under the charge of one of the older and wiser brothers, who shall examine him and prove, by every possible means, his sincerity, his zeal, his obedience, and his ability to endure shame. He shall be told in the plainest manner all the hardships and difficulties of the life which he has chosen. If he promises never to leave the monastery, the rule shall be read to him after the first two months of his novitiate, and again at the end of six more months, and finally, four months later, at the end of his year. Each time he shall be told that this is the guide which he must follow as a monk. The reader says to him at the end of the reading, "This is the law under which you have expressed a desire to live; if you are able to obey it, enter; if not, depart in peace." Thus he shall have been given every chance for mature deliberation and every opportunity to refuse the yoke of service. But if he still persists in asserting his eagerness to enter and his willingness to obey the rule and the commands of his superiors, he shall then be received into the congregation. He shall understand that from that day forth he shall never be permitted to draw back from the service or leave the monastery.[39]

---

[36] *Nones:* the ninth hour of the day, counting from sunrise; in medieval monastic practice it usually fell around 3 p.m.
[37] 1 John 4:1.

[38] *Novitiate:* probationary period as a novice.
[39] *never be permitted . . . to leave the monastery:* i.e., as a monk.

The Iconoclastic Controversy*

The controversy over the veneration of religious images (icons) in Eastern Christianity lasted from about 726 when emperor Leo III issued an edict against all uses of images, until 843 with Empress

Theodora's "restoration of orthodoxy." The **iconoclasts,** *who opposed (sometimes destroyed) images, pointed to the Second Commandment's prohibition of graven images, and they equated icon veneration with pagan worship. The* **iconodules** *held that icons were useful in teaching the faithful, were extensions of the incarnation itself, and as such were worthy of veneration. This controversy was*

---

* John of Damascus, *On Holy Images* 4.16; Decree of the Council of 754; Decree of the Seventh Ecumenical Council (787)

only about two-dimensional images; statues, even crucifixes, were always banned by all Orthodox churches as tending to idolatry. The first reading is the influential 730 work of the monk John of Damascus defending images.[40] The second reading is the decree of 754 condemning icons; and the third is a decree from 787 restoring them.[41] The arguments used here are similar to those that will be used in Protestant and Catholic arguments over images in Reformation times.

The invisible things of God since the creation of the world are made visible through images. We see images in creation which remind us faintly of God, as when, for instance, we speak of the holy and adorable Trinity, imaged by the sun, or light, or burning rays, or by a running fountain, or a full river, or by the mind, speech, or the spirit within us, or by a rose tree, or a sprouting flower, or a sweet fragrance.

Again, an image is expressive of something in the future, mystically shadowing forth what is to happen. For instance, the ark represents the image of Our Lady, Mother of God; so does the staff and the earthen jar. The serpent brings before us Him who vanquished on the cross the bite of the original serpent; the sea, water, and the cloud the grace of baptism. . . . We preserve in writing the images and the good deeds of the past. Therefore either take away images altogether and be out of harmony with God who made these regulations, or receive them with the language and in the manner which befits them.

Worship is the symbol of veneration and of honor. Let us understand that there are different degrees of worship. First is the true worship called *latreia*,[42] which we show to God, who alone by nature is worthy of worship. Then, for the sake of God who is worshipful by nature, we give honor [*douleia*] to his saints and servants. . . .

From ancient times, God was never depicted, for he is unbodied and unbounded. Now, however, when God is seen clothed in flesh, and conversing with men, I make an image of the God whom I see. I do not worship matter; I worship the God of matter, who became matter for my sake, and deigned to inhabit matter, who worked out my salvation through matter. I will not cease from venerating that matter which works my salvation. I venerate it, though not as God. How could God be born out of lifeless things? And if God's body is God by union, it is immutable. The nature of God remains the same as before, the flesh created in time is quickened by a logical and reasoning soul. I honor all matter besides, and venerate it. Through it, filled, as it were, with a divine power and grace, my salvation has come to me. Was not the thrice happy and thrice blessed wood of the Cross matter? Was not the sacred and holy mountain of Calvary matter? What of the life-giving rock, the Holy Sepulcher, the source of our resurrection: was it not matter? . . . And more important than all these things, is not the body and blood of our Lord[43] matter? Either do away with the veneration and worship due to all these things, or submit to the tradition of the Church in the veneration of images, honoring God and his friends, and following the grace of the Holy Spirit.

[The Council of 754] In order to save mankind thoroughly, God sent his own Son, who turned us away from error and the worshipping of idols, and taught us the worshipping of God in spirit and in truth. As messengers of his saving doctrine, he left us his Apostles and disciples, and these adorned the Church, his Bride, with his glorious doctrines. The holy Fathers and the six Ecumenical Councils have preserved this ornament of the Church inviolate. But [Satan] could not endure the sight of this adornment, and grad-

---

[40] Taken, with editing, from M. H. Allies, *St. John Damascene on Holy Images* (London: Burns and Oates, 1898), 10–17.

[41] The second reading and third readings are taken from Philip Schaff and Henry Wace, eds., *A Select Library of Nicene and Post-Nicene Fathers of the Christian Church*, vol. 14 (2d series; New York: Scribners, 1905), 543–44, 550.

[42] *latreia*, "worship" is usually distinguished from *douleia*, "veneration" to saints, icons, and the like.

[43] *body and blood of our Lord:* the Eucharist.

ually brought back idolatry under the appearance of Christianity. As Christ armed his Apostles against ancient idolatry with the power of the Holy Spirit, and sent them out into all the world, so has he awakened against the new idolatry his servants our faithful Emperors, and has endowed them with the same wisdom of the Holy Spirit. Impelled by the Holy Spirit, they could no longer be witnesses of the Church being laid waste by the deception of demons. They summoned the sanctified assembly of the God-beloved bishops, that they might institute at a synod a scriptural examination into the deceitful coloring of the pictures which draws down the spirit of man from the lofty adoration of God to the low and material adoration of the creature. . . .

Therefore we thought it right to show forth with all accuracy in our present definition the error of those who make and venerate these icons. It is the unanimous doctrine of all the holy Fathers and of the six Ecumenical Synods, that no one may imagine any kind of separation or mingling in opposition to the unsearchable, unspeakable, and incomprehensible union of the two natures in the one person. What avails, then, the folly of the painter, who from sinful love of gain depicts that which should not be depicted? With his polluted hands he tries to fashion that which should only be believed in the heart and confessed with the mouth. He makes an image and calls it Christ. The name Christ signifies God and Man. His image depicts God and man, and consequently he has in his foolish mind, in his representation of the created flesh, depicted the Godhead which cannot be represented. He has mingled what should not be mingled. . . .

Some say that we might be right in regard to the images of Christ, on account of the mysterious union of the two natures, but it is not right for us to forbid also the images of the altogether spotless and ever glorious Mother of God, of the prophets, apostles, and martyrs, who were men and did not consist of two natures. We reply first of all: If those [icons of Christ] fall away, there is no longer need of these. But we will also consider what may be said against these in particu-

lar. Christianity has rejected the whole of heathenism, and so not merely heathen sacrifices, but also the heathen worship of images. The Saints live on eternally with God, although they have died. If anyone thinks to call them back again to life by a dead art, discovered by the heathen, he makes himself guilty of blasphemy. Who dares attempt with heathen art to paint the Mother of God, who is exalted above all heavens and the Saints? Christians, who have the hope of the resurrection, are not permitted to imitate the customs of demon-worshippers, and to insult the Saints, who shine in so great glory, by common dead matter.

[Decree of the Seventh Ecumenical Council (787)] Following the royal pathway and the divinely inspired authority of our Holy Fathers and the traditions of the Catholic Church (for, as we all know, the Holy Spirit indwells her), we determine with all certitude and accuracy that just as the figure of the precious and life-giving Cross, so also the venerable and holy images, as well in painting and mosaic as of other fit materials, should be set forth in the holy churches of God, and on the sacred vessels and on the vestments and on hangings and in pictures both in houses and by the wayside, namely, the figure of our Lord God and Savior Jesus Christ, of our spotless Lady, the Mother of God, of the honorable Angels, of all Saints and of all pious people. The more frequently they are seen in artistic representation, the more readily we are lifted up to the memory of their prototypes, and to a longing after them. Due salutation and honorable reverence [*proskynesis*] should be given to them, not indeed that true worship of faith [*latreia*] which belongs only to the divine nature. But to these, as to the figure of the precious and life-giving Cross and to the Book of the Gospels and to other holy objects, incense and lights may be offered according to ancient pious custom. For the honor which is paid to the image passes on to that which the image represents, and he who reveres the image reveres in it the subject represented.

Mandatory Celibacy of Roman Catholic Clergy*

Celibacy (abstention from marriage and sexual intercourse) for all clergy came gradually into Western Christianity. It was required for monks from the earliest times of monasticism, and with the passage of time it was adopted for priests as well. In 1074, the reforming Pope Gregory VII issued this law in a series of decrees, attempting with some success to enforce celibacy.[44]

If there are any priests, deacons, or subdeacons who are married, by the power of omnipotent God and the authority of St. Peter we forbid them to enter a church until they repent and mend their ways. But if any remain with their wives, no one shall dare hear them [when they officiate in the church], because their benediction is turned into a curse, and their prayer into a sin. For the Lord says through the prophet, "I will curse your blessings."[45] Whoever refuses to obey this most beneficial command shall be guilty of the sin of idolatry.

* *Body of Canon Law* 81.15
[44] Taken, with editing, from O. J. Thatcher and E. H. McNeal, *Source Book for Medieval History* (New York: Scribners, 1905), 135.

[45] Malachi 2:2.

Devotion to the Virgin Mary**

Eastern Christianity surpassed Western Christianity for almost a thousand years in its devotion to the Virgin Mary. By the later Middle Ages/Byzantine period, she had become in both East and West the primary intercessor between humans and God. While theologians everywhere tended to be quite restrained in their treatment of Mary, popular preaching and devotion became ever stronger. The first reading illustrates popular devotion to the Virgin from Caesar of Heisterbach (1170–1240), whose Dialogues *mix details of life in the monastery with credulous popular tales of saints and sinners.*[46] *The second is perhaps the most famous hymn in Eastern Orthodoxy, the beautiful sixth-century song to the Virgin known as the "Akathistos Hymn."*[47] *The last reading features the prayers to the Virgin: the "Hail Mary" with its early-medieval first half drawn from Luke 1 and its fifteenth-century second half; and the "Angelus," prayed by pious Christians in the morning, at noon, and in the early evening, as signaled by church bells.*

Not many years ago, in a certain monastery of nuns, of which I do not know the name, there lived a virgin named Beatrix. She was beautiful in form, devout in mind, and most fervent in the service of the mother of God. As often as she could she secretly offered special prayers and supplications to the Virgin, and she took much delight in them. When she was made custodian of the oratory,[48] her devotion became even more devout.

A certain priest, seeing and lusting after her, began to tempt her. When she spurned his words of lust, he insisted the more strenuously, and the old serpent[49] enkindled her breast so strongly that she could not bear the flames of love. Coming to the altar of the Blessed Virgin, the patron-

** Caesar of Heisterbach, *Dialogues on Miracles* 7.34; *Akathistos* hymn; Hail Mary and Angelus Prayers
[46] Taken from *Translations and Reprints from the Original Sources of European History* (Philadelphia: University of Pennsylvania, 1894–1900), 2.4.2.
[47] From G. G. Meersseman, *The Akathistos Hymn* (Fribourg, 1958), 25–37.

[48] *oratory:* a chapel for prayer.
[49] *the old serpent:* Satan.

ess of the oratory, she said, "Mistress, I have served you as devoutly as I could. I resign your keys to you, for I cannot withstand the temptations of the flesh any longer." Then she placed the keys on the altar and secretly followed the priest.

When that wretched man had corrupted her, he abandoned her after a few days. Since she had no means of living and was ashamed to return to the convent, she became a prostitute. After she had continued in that vice publicly for fifteen years, she came one day in ordinary dress to the door of the monastery. She said to the doorkeeper, "Did you know Beatrix, formerly custodian of this oratory?" When the latter replied, "I know her very well. She is an honest and holy woman, and from infancy even to the present day she has remained in this monastery without fault." She heard the man's words, but did not understand them. When she wished to go away, the mother of mercy appeared in her well-known image and said to her, "During the fifteen years of your absence, I have performed your task. Now return to your place and do penance, for no one knows of your departure." In fact, the Mother of God had performed the duties of custodian in the appearance and dress of that woman. Beatrix entered at once and returned thanks as long as she lived, revealing through the confessional what had been done for her.

[The *Akathistos* Hymn]
To you, protectress, leader of my army, victory!
I, your city, from danger freed
this song of thanks inscribe to you, Mother of God.
Since you have an unconquerable power,
free me from all danger,
that I may sing to you:
Hail, mother undefiled!

A prince of angels
was sent from heaven
to greet the Mother of God,
and upon his unbodied word,

seeing You, O Lord, take body,
he stood in ecstasy
and cried to you [Mary] this greeting:

Hail, by whom gladness will be enkindled;
hail, by whom the curse will be quenched.
Hail, righting of the fallen Adam;
Hail, ransom of Eve's tears.

Hail, height unscaled by human reasonings;
hail, depth inscrutable even to angel's eyes.
Hail, for you are the king's seat;
hail, for you bear him, who bears all.
Hail, you star that makest the sun to shine;
Hail, you womb of God's incarnation.
Hail, you by whom all creation is renewed;
hail, you through whom the Creator became a baby.
Hail, mother undefiled.

The blessed virgin, knowing herself chaste,
said unto Gabriel resolutely:
"The contradiction in your statement
seems very hard to my soul.
You foretell me a childbirth
by seedless conception, and cry: Alleluia!"

The virgin, yearning to know
the unknowable knowledge, exclaimed to the servant:
"From my maiden womb how may a child be born?
Tell me."
He answered her reverently, crying out:

Hail! initiated into the unspeakable counsel;
hail! faith in what has to remain secret.
Hail! of Christ's wonders the beginning;
hail! of all beliefs about him the summary.
Hail! heavenly ladder by which God came down;
hail! bridge that carries the earth-born into heaven.

Hail! marvel much spoken of by the angels;
hail! wounding most lamentable for the demons.
Hail! who mysteriously gave birth to the light.
Hail! who the manner to none has taught.

Hail! who outsoars the learning of the wise;
hail! who enlightens the mind of the faithful.
Hail! mother undefiled.

The power from on high
overshadowed the undefiled maid, and she
    conceived;
it converted her fruitless womb
into a meadow sweet to all people,
who sought to reap salvation
by singing: Alleluia!

[Hail Mary] Hail Mary, full of grace! The Lord
    is with you. Blessed are you among women,
    and blessed is the fruit of your womb, Jesus.
    Holy Mary, Mother of God, pray for us sin-
    ners now and at the hour of our death.

[Angelus] The Angel of the Lord declared to
    Mary,
and she conceived by the Holy Spirit.
Hail Mary . . .

Behold the handmaid of the Lord.
Be it done unto me according to your word.
Hail Mary . . .

And the Word was made flesh,
and dwelt among us.
Hail Mary . . .

Pray for us, O holy Mother of God,
that we may be made worthy of the promises of
    Christ.
Let us pray.[50] Pour forth, we beg you, O Lord,
your grace into our hearts;
that we, to whom the Incarnation of Christ
    your Son
was made known by the message of an Angel,
may by his passion and cross
be brought to the glory of his Resurrection;
through the same Jesus Christ our Lord. Amen.

---

[50] *Let us pray:* the prayer to the Virgin ends, and a prayer to God begins.

The Jesus Prayer*

Symeon, called the "New Theologian," was an eleventh-century Byzantine monk and mystic. He was closely associated with the rise of the "Jesus Prayer," which involved quiet, special breathing and meditation techniques, and repetition of the words, "Lord Jesus Christ, have mercy on me." All this was thought to bring a vision of the same divine light that surrounded Christ at his transfiguration (Mark 9:2–8). The Jesus Prayer movement has lasted through today, where it is especially strong at the monastery on Mt. Athos, Greece, the center of Orthodox spirituality.[51]

Now we begin to speak of the third prayer. It is strange and hard to explain. . . . The mind should be in the heart. It should guard the heart while it prays, remaining always within, and offer pray-

ers to God from the depths of the heart. . . . One who does not pay attention and does not guard the mind cannot become pure in heart and cannot see God. . . .

You should observe two most important things. First, [have] freedom from all cares, not only evil and empty cares but even cares about good things. In other words, you should become dead to everything. Your conscience should be completely clear and accuse you in nothing. Second, you should have complete absence of passionate attachment, so that your thoughts incline to nothing in this world. Keep your attention within yourself (in your heart, not in your head). The mind will wrestle in this position, but it will find the place of the heart. This occurs as grace produces sweetness and warmth in prayer. From that moment, whenever a thought appears, the mind at once will dispel it before it has time to enter and become a thought or mental picture. The mind will destroy it by the Jesus Prayer, "Lord Jesus Christ, have mercy on me."

---

* Symeon the New Theologian, *Method of Holy Prayer and Attention*
[51] Translated by the author from Irénée Hausherr, ed., "Vie de Symeon le nouveau theologien," *Orientalia Christiana* 9 (1927), 158–59.

The Late Medieval View of Death*

This hymn from the funeral mass is considered one of the most beautiful and powerful hymns of the Western church. It testifies eloquently to the strong late-medieval concern with death. Dating from the thirteenth century, it is traditionally ascribed to Thomas of Celano, Italy. It has been set to music in requiem (funeral) masses by such noted composers as Mozart, Beethoven, and Berlioz.[52]

Day of wrath! O Day of mourning!
See fulfilled the prophet's warning,
Heaven and earth in ashes burning!

O what fear man's bosom rends,
When from heaven the Judge descends,
On whose sentence all depends!

Wondrous sound the trumpet flings,
Through earth's sepulchers it rings,
All before the throne it brings.

Death is struck, and nature quaking,
All creation is awaking,
To its Judge an answer making.

Lo, the book, exactly worded
Wherein all has been recorded;
Thence shall judgment be awarded.

When the Judge his seat attains,
And each hidden deed arraigns,
Nothing unavenged remains.

What shall I, frail man, be pleading,
Who for me be interceding,
When the just are mercy needing?

King of majesty tremendous,
Who does free salvation send us,
Fount of pity, then befriend us!

Think, kind Jesus, my salvation
Caused your wondrous incarnation;
Leave me not to reprobation!

Faint and weary you have sought me,
On the cross of suffering bought me;
Shall such grace have vainly brought me?

Righteous Judge! for sin's pollution
Grant your gift of absolution,
Ere that day of retribution!

Guilty, now I pour my moaning,
All my shame with anguish owning;
Spare, O God, your suppliant, groaning!

You the sinful woman saved,
You the dying thief forgave;
Now to me a hope vouchsafe!

Worthless are my prayers and sighing,
Yet, good Lord, in grace complying,
Rescue me from fires undying!

With your favored sheep, O place me!
Not among the goats abase me;
But to your right hand upraise me.

While the wicked are confounded,
Doomed to flames of woe unbounded,
Call me, with your saints surrounded.

Low I kneel, with heart's submission;
See, like ashes, my contrition;
Help me in my last condition!

Ah! that Day of tears and mourning!
From the dust of earth returning,
Man for judgment must prepare:
Spare, O God, in mercy spare!

Lord all pitying, Jesus blest,
Grant them your eternal rest!

---

* "Day of Wrath" hymn
[52] Taken from the translation by W. J. Irons (1848) as found in R. C. Petry, *A History of Christianity* (Englewood Cliffs, NJ: Prentice-Hall, 1962), 436–38.

TEACHING

The First Eucharistic Debate*

The first book devoted solely to the Eucharist was written around 844 by Radbertus of the monastery at Corbey, France. His emphasis on the real presence of Christ's flesh anticipates later medieval doctrines of transubstantiation, although Radbertus identified the eucharistic elements with the incarnate Jesus, not (as all later eucharistic Christian theology in the West would do) with the risen Jesus.[53] This provoked a strong response in a book by the same title from Ratramnus, a monk in the same abbey, who objected to Radbertus' realistic emphasis and argued that the bread and the wine were "figurative," or symbolic. (Ratramnus' position was condemned by the church in 1050.)[54] This debate prefigures struggles in the sixteenth century over the presence of Christ in the Eucharist.

Let no man be moved from this body and blood of Christ which in a mystery are true flesh and true blood since the Creator so willed it. . . . [It is] nothing different, of course, from what was born of Mary, suffered on the cross, and rose again from the tomb. . . .

Christ's sacraments in the church are Baptism and anointing, and the Lord's body and blood.[55] They are called sacraments because under their visible appearance the divine flesh is secretly consecrated through [divine] power, so that they are inwardly in truth what they are outwardly believed to be by the power of faith. . . .

[4] No one doubts that in truth the body and blood are created by the consecration of the mystery. We believe the divine words when the

Truth says: "For my flesh is truly food, and my blood is truly drink."[56] When his disciples did not rightly understand, he clearly identified what flesh he meant, and what blood: "He who eats my flesh and drinks my blood, abides in me and I in him." Therefore, if it is truly food, it is true flesh, and if it is truly drink, it is true blood. How else will what he says be true: "The bread which I shall give, my flesh, is for the life of the world," unless it be true flesh, and the "bread which came down from heaven," true bread? But because it is not right to devour Christ with the teeth, he willed in the mystery that this bread and wine be created truly his flesh and blood through consecration by the power of the Holy Spirit. By daily creating it, it is mystically sacrificed for the life of the world.

[Ratramnus, *Christ's Body and Blood*] Your majesty inquires whether that which in the church is received into the mouth of the faithful becomes the body and blood of Christ in a mystery or in truth.[57] . . .

If that mystery [of Holy Communion] is not performed in any figurative sense, then it is not rightly given the name of mystery. Since that cannot be called a mystery in which there is nothing hidden, nothing removed from the physical senses, nothing covered over with any veil. But that bread which through the ministry of the priest comes to be Christ's body exhibits one thing outwardly to human sense, and it proclaims another thing inwardly to the minds of the faithful. Outwardly it has the shape of bread which it had before, the color is exhibited, the flavor is received, but inwardly something far

---

* Paschasius Radbertus, *Christ's Body and Blood* 1, 3, 4; Ratramnus, *Christ's Body and Blood* 5–11, 49
[53] Translated by the author from J.-P. Migné, *Patrologiae Latina,* vol. 120 (Paris: Migne, 1867).
[54] Translated by the author from J.-P. Migné, *Patrologiae Latina,* vol. 121 (Paris: Migne, 1867).
[55] *Christ's sacraments . . . blood:* note that Radbertus at this early time enumerates only three sacraments.

[56] All scripture quotations in this paragraph are from John 6:50–55.
[57] *Your majesty . . . truth:* this book was commissioned by Charles the Bald, King of the Franks.

different, much more precious, much more excellent, becomes known. Something heavenly, something divine, that is, Christ's body, is revealed, which is not beheld, or received, or consumed by the fleshly senses but in the gaze of the believing soul.

[10] The wine also, which through priestly consecration becomes the sacrament of Christ's blood, shows, so far as the surface goes, one thing; inwardly it contains something else. What else is to be seen on the surface than the substance of wine? Taste it, and it has the flavor of wine; smell it, and it has the aroma of wine; look at it, and the wine color is visible. But if you think of it inwardly, it is now to the minds of believers not the liquid of Christ's blood, and when tasted, it has flavor; when looked at, it has appearance; and when smelled, it is proved to be

such. Since no one can deny that this is so, it is clear that the bread and wine are Christ's body and blood in a figurative sense. For as to outward appearance, the aspect of flesh is not recognized in that bread, nor in that wine is the liquid blood shown, when they are, after the mystical consecration, no longer called bread or wine, but Christ's body and blood.

[49] From all that has thus far been said it has been shown that Christ's body and blood which are received in the mouth of the faithful in the church are figures according to their visible appearance, but according to their invisible substance, that is, the power of the divine Word, truly exist as Christ's body and blood. Therefore, with the visible creation, they feed the body; with the power of a stronger substance, they feed and sanctify the souls of the faithful.

Scholastic Argument on Proving the Existence of God*

In his Proslogion *("Preface"), written in 1079, Anselm of Canterbury, England argues from the idea of God to the existence of God. If God is "a being than which no one greater can be thought," an idea that seems to proceed from the very idea of a God, then God must also exist in fact.*[58] *In the second selection, Anselm's contemporary, the Benedictine monk Gaunilo, strikes at Anselm's argument by reasoning that having an idea of something does not necessarily prove its existence. He takes the role of the "fool" that Anselm had used as a foil.*[59] *The last selection is from Thomas Aquinas'* Summa theologiae *(1265–1273). This encyclopedic work is not only the greatest product of medieval Christian thought, but has had a continuing strong influence on Roman Catholic theology. It presents five other ways to argue for the existence of God.*[60]

O Lord, since you give understanding to faith, give me to understand—as far as you know it to be good for me—that you do exist, as we believe, and that you are what we believe you to be. Now we believe that you are a being than which no one greater can be thought. Or could it be that there is no such being, since "The fool has said in his heart, 'There is no God'"?[61] But when this same fool hears what I am saying—"A being than which no one greater can be thought"—he understands what he hears. What he understands is in his understanding, even if he does not understand that it exists. For it is one thing for an object to be in the understanding, and another

* Anselm, *Preface* 2–3; Gaunilo, *Response to Anselm* 6; Aquinas, *Summa theologiae* 1a, Q. 2

[58] Translated by the author from F. S. Schmitt, *Sancti Anselmi Opera Omnia*, vol. 1 (Edinburgh: Nelson, 1946), 102–103.

[59] Translated by the author from F. S. Schmitt, *Sancti Anselmi Opera Omnia*, vol. 1 (Edinburgh: Nelson, 1946), 128.

[60] Taken, with editing, from Fathers of the English Dominican Province, *The Summa Theologica of St. Thomas Aquinas* (New York: Benziger, 1920), 13–14.

[61] Psalm 14:1.

thing to understand that it exists. For example, when a painter considers beforehand what he is going to paint, he has it in his understanding, but he does not suppose that what he has not yet painted already exists. But when he has painted it, he both has it in his understanding and understands that what he has now produced exists.

Therefore, even the fool must be convinced that a being than which no one greater can be thought exists at least in his understanding, since when he hears this he understands it, and whatever is understood is in the understanding. But clearly that than which a greater thing cannot be thought cannot exist in the understanding alone. For if it is actually in the understanding alone, it can be thought of as existing also in reality, and this is greater. Therefore, if that than which a greater thing cannot be thought is in the understanding alone, this same thing than which a greater cannot be thought is that than which a greater can be thought. But obviously this is impossible. Therefore, there certainly exists, both in the understanding and in reality, something than which a greater thing cannot be thought.

Certainly it exists so truly that it cannot be thought of as nonexistent. For something can be thought of as existing, which cannot be thought of as not existing, and this is greater than that which can be thought of as not existing. Thus, if that than which a greater thing cannot be thought can be thought of as not existing, this very thing than which a greater cannot be thought is not that than which a greater cannot be thought. But this is contradictory. Therefore, there truly is a being than which a greater cannot be thought—so truly that it cannot even be thought of as not existing.

And *you* are this thing, O Lord our God! You so truly exist, O Lord my God, that you cannot even be thought of as not existing. And this is right. For if some mind could think of something better than you, the creature would rise above the Creator and judge its Creator; but this is altogether absurd. Indeed, whatever exists can be thought of as not existing, except you alone. You alone of all beings have being in the truest

and highest sense, since no other being so truly exists as you do, and thus every other being has less being. Why, then, has "The fool said in his heart, 'There is no God'," when it is so obvious to the rational mind that, of all beings, you do exist supremely? Why indeed, unless he is a stupid fool?

[Gaunilo, *Response to Anselm*] To illustrate my argument [that the idea of something does not necessitate its actual existence], people say that somewhere in the ocean is an island which some have called the "Lost Island" because of the difficulty, and indeed the impossibility, of finding it. They say that it has all kinds of priceless riches and abundant delights . . . .

Now, if someone were to tell me about this island, I would easily understand what they said, because it is not difficult. But suppose that someone then told me, as if it were a direct result of this, "You cannot any more doubt that this island that is more excellent than any other land does in fact exist in reality, than you can doubt that it is in your mind. Since it is more excellent for it to exist in reality than just in your mind, therefore it must exist in reality." I say that if someone tried to convince me in this way that this island really exists beyond any doubt, I would think that they are joking with me. I would wonder which of us is a bigger fool: I myself, if I agreed with them, or they, if they thought that they had certainly proved the existence of this island.

[Aquinas, *Summa theologiae*] The existence of God can be proved in five ways. The first and most obvious is the argument from motion.[62] It is certain, and evident to our senses, that in the world some things are in motion. Now whatever is moved is moved by something else, for nothing can be moved except it is potentially that to-

---

[62] *motion:* another way to translate the Latin (*ex parte motus*) is by "change," and Thomas seems to be using both meanings in this section.

wards which it is moved, but that which moves it is actual. For motion is nothing else than the reduction of something from potentiality to actuality. But nothing can be reduced from potentiality to actuality, except by something actual. Thus that which is actually hot, as fire, makes wood, which is potentially hot, to be actually hot, and thus moves and changes it.

Now it is impossible for the same thing to be at once actual and potential in the same respect, but only in different respects. For what is actually hot cannot simultaneously be potentially hot; but it is simultaneously potentially cold. It is therefore impossible that in the same respect and in the same way a thing should be both mover and moved, i.e., that it should move itself. Therefore, whatever is moved must be moved by another. If that by which it is moved be itself moved, then this also must needs be moved by another, and that by another again. But this cannot go on infinitely, because then there would be no first mover. Consequently, there would be no other mover, because subsequent movers move only as they are moved by the first mover, as for example a walking stick moves only because it is moved by the hand. Therefore we must arrive at a First Mover, moved by no one else. Everyone understands this to be God.

The second way is from the nature of efficient cause. In the world of observable things we find there is an order of efficient causes. There is no case known (neither is it, indeed, possible) in which a thing is found to be the efficient cause of itself. Then it would be prior to itself, which is impossible. Now in efficient causes it is not possible to go back infinitely, because in all efficient causes following in order, the first is the cause of the intermediate cause and the intermediate is the cause of the ultimate cause, whether the intermediate cause is several or only one. Now to take away the cause is to take away the effect. Therefore, if there is no first cause among efficient causes, there will be no ultimate cause nor any intermediate cause. But if in efficient causes it is possible to go back infinitely, there will be no first efficient cause. So there would be no ulti-

mate effect or any intermediate efficient causes, all of which is plainly false. Therefore we must admit a first efficient cause, to which everyone gives the name of God.

The third way is taken from possibility and necessity [of existence], and runs like this. We find in nature things that are possible to be or not be, since they are born and die; thus it is possible for them to be or not to be. But it is impossible for them to exist always, for at some time things which pass in and out of existence do not exist. Therefore, if everything potentially does not exist, then at some time nothing would exist. Now if this were true, even now nothing would exist, because what does not exist begins to exist only through something already existing. Therefore, if at one time nothing was in existence, it would have been impossible for anything to have begun to exist. Thus even now nothing would exist, which is absurd. Therefore, not all beings are merely possible, but there must be something which necessarily exists. But every necessary thing either has its necessity caused by another, or not. Now it is impossible to back infinitely in necessary things which have their necessity caused by another, as has been already proved about efficient causes. Therefore we must admit the existence of some being having in itself its own necessity. This being does not receive existence from another, but rather causes it in others. Everyone calls this being God.

The fourth way is from the gradation found in things. Among beings there are some more and some less good, true, noble, etc. This "more" and "less" is found in different things according to how they measure up to the greatest quality. For example, a thing is said to grow hotter as it more and more resembles that which is hottest. So there is something which is truest, something best, something noblest, and, consequently, something which is most fully exists, for those things that are greatest in truth are greatest in being, as it is written in *Metaphysics* 2. Now the maximum in any genus is the cause of all things in that genus, as fire, which is the maximum of heat, is the cause of all hot things, as is said in the same book. Therefore there must also be something which is the cause of all being, goodness, and every other perfection. We call this something God.

The fifth way is taken from the governance of the world. We see that things which lack knowledge, such as natural bodies, act for a purpose. This is evident from their acting always, or nearly always, in the same way, to obtain the best result. They obviously achieve their purpose by design, not by chance. Now whatever lacks knowledge cannot be purposeful, unless it is directed by some being with knowledge and intelligence, as the arrow is directed by the archer. Therefore some intelligent being exists who directs natural things to their purpose. This being we call God.

The Relationship of Faith and Reason*

The relationship of faith and reason had been considered for more than a thousand years before Aquinas. He draws on Augustine and others to argue that reason expressed through philosophy can be of great assistance for faith, but cannot replace it. In this reading, "philosophy" and "the philosophical disciplines" refer to all human knowledge not revealed by God, not just to philosophy proper. (Even today, most academic doctorates in the sciences and humanities are the Ph.D., "Doctor of Philosophy.") This reading shows the full typical form of a section in Thomas's Summa theologiae: *(1) statement of the question; (2) statement of objections; (3) Thomas's answer to the question; (4) Thomas's reply to objections on the basis of his answer.*[63]

Beside philosophical learning, is any further learning required?

Objection 1. It seems that we have no need of any further learning beside philosophy. For one should not seek to know what is above reason: "Do not seek the things that are too high for you."[64] Whatever is not above reason is sufficiently considered in philosophy. Therefore any other learning beside philosophy is unnecessary.

Objection 2. Further, learning can be concerned only with being, for nothing can be known, except the true, which is concerned with being. But everything that exists is considered in the philosophical disciplines, even God Himself. So there is a part of philosophy called theology, or the divine science, as is clear from Aristotle. Therefore, beside philosophy, there is no need of any further learning.

On the contrary, it is written, "All Scripture inspired of God is profitable for teaching, for reproof, for correction, to instruct in justice."[65] Now Scripture, inspired by God, is not a part of the philosophical disciplines discovered by human reason. Therefore it is useful that beside the philosophical disciplines there should be another science, i.e., one inspired by God.

I answer that it was necessary for man's salvation that there should be a doctrine revealed by God, beside the philosophical disciplines investigated by human reason. First, man is directed to God for a purpose that surpasses the grasp of his reason: "The eye has not seen, O God, beside You, what things You have prepared for them that wait for You."[66] But the purpose must first be known by men who direct their intentions and actions to the purpose. Thus it was necessary for the salvation of humankind that certain truths which exceed human reason should be made known by divine revelation. Even those truths about God which human reason can investigate were necessarily taught to man by divine revelation. For the truth about God, as far as reason can know it, would only be known by a few, and moreover after a long time, and with many errors mixed in. But the whole of human salvation,

---

* Aquinas, *Summa theologiae* 1a.1.1
[63] Taken, with editing, from the Fathers of the English Dominican Province, *The "Summa Theologica" of St. Thomas Aquinas* (New York: Benziger, 1915), 1–2.
[64] Ecclesiasticus 3:22.

[65] II Timothy 3:16.
[66] Isaiah 64:4.

which is in God, depends upon the knowledge of this truth. Therefore, in order that salvation might be brought about more fitly and more certainly, divine truths must be taught by divine revelations. It was therefore necessary that, besides the philosophical disciplines investigated by reason, there should be a sacred doctrine by way of revelation.

Reply to Objection 1. Those things which are beyond human knowledge may not be sought for through human reason. Nevertheless, what is revealed by God must be accepted through faith. So the sacred text continues, "Many things are shown to you above the understanding of man." [67] In such things sacred doctrine consists.

Reply to Objection 2. Sciences are diversified according to the diverse nature of their knowable objects. For the astronomer and the physicist both prove the same conclusion, for example, that the earth is round. The astronomer proves it by means of mathematics (i.e., abstracting from matter), but the physicist by means of matter itself. Thus there is no reason why those things which are treated by the philosophical disciplines, so far as they can be known by the light of natural reason, may not also be treated by another science so far as they are known by the light of the divine revelation. The theology included in sacred doctrine differs in type from that theology which is part of philosophy.

---

[67] Ecclesiasticus 3:25.

Theories of the Atonement*

Anselm advanced a judicial or "forensic" theory of the atonement: only one who is both divine and human can "make satisfaction" (atone) for human sin.[68] His Why God Became Human *is written as a dialogue between the author and his interlocutor Boso. Peter Abelard criticized this idea, and in his* Commentary on Romans *(where he deals with Romans 3:21–26), he argues for the "moral influence" theory. It believes that human realization of the love of God (as shown in the death of Jesus) causes a love for God to arise, one that overcomes the power of sin and restores us to God.[69]*

Anselm: Tell me what you think still remains to be answered of the question you posed at the beginning, which forced so many other questions on us.

Boso: The heart of the question was this: Why did God become human, to save humans by his

death, when it seems that he could have done this in some other way? You have answered this by showing, by several necessary reasons, how it would not have been right for the restoration of human nature to be left undone, and how it could not have been done unless humankind paid what it owed to God for sin. But the debt was so great that although humankind alone owed it, only God could pay it, so that the person who paid it must be both human and God. Thus God had to take human nature into the unity of the divine, so that humankind who is its own nature ought to pay the debt was in a person who could pay. Then you showed that the person who also was God had to be born from a Virgin in the person of the Son of God, and how he could be taken from the sinful mass of humankind without sin. Also, you have proved most clearly that the life of this Man was so wonderful and valuable that it can suffice to pay what all humankind owes for its sins, and infinitely more. Now it remains to be shown how it is paid to God for the sins of humankind.

A.: There is no need to explain what a great gift the Son gave freely.

B.: That is very clear.

---

* Anselm, *Why God Became Human* 1.25; Abelard, *Exposition of the Epistle to the Romans* 3
[68] Translated by the author from F. S. Schmitt, *Sancti Anselmi Omnia Opera*, vol. 1 (Edinburgh: Nelson, 1946).
[69] Translated by the author from J.-P. Migné, *Patrologia Latina*, vol. 178 (Paris: Migné, 1867), col. 836.

A.: You will not think that he who gives such a great gift to God ought to go unrewarded.

B.: Not at all! I see how necessary it is for the Father to reward the Son. . . .

A.: He who rewards someone either gives what the other does not have or gives up something that he can expect of him. But before the Son did this great work, all that belonged to the Father belonged to him. What can be given to him as a reward, when he needs nothing and has nothing to be forgiven for? . . . It must be paid to someone else, since it cannot be paid to him. . . . To whom would it be more fitting for him to give the fruit of his death that to those for whose salvation (as true reasoning has taught us) he made himself human, and to whom by dying he gave an example of dying for justice's sake? They will imitate his death in vain if they do not share in his merit.

[Abelard, *Commentary on Romans*] We have been justified by the blood of Christ and reconciled to God as follows. Through this unique act of grace manifested to us, that God's Son has taken upon himself our human nature and continued in it while teaching us by word and example even unto death, God has more fully bound us to himself by love. Therefore our hearts should be kindled by such a gift of divine grace, and true love should not shrink from enduring anything for God.

We do not doubt that the ancient Fathers [before the birth of Christianity], waiting in faith for this same gift, were aroused to very great love of God in the same way as men of this covenant of grace, since it is written: "Those who went before and those who followed cried out, 'Hosanna to the Son of David,'" etc.[70] Yet everyone becomes more righteous—a greater lover of the Lord—after the Passion of Christ than before, since a realized gift inspires greater love than one which is only hoped for. Therefore, our redemption through Christ's suffering is that deeper love in us which not only frees us from slavery to sin, but also wins for us the true liberty of sons of God. Now we do everything out of love rather than fear. We love him who has shown us a grace that cannot be surpassed, as he himself says, "Greater love than this no man has, that a man lay down his life for his friends."[71] The Lord says elsewhere about this love, "I am come to throw fire on the earth, and what do I desire, but that it blaze forth?"[72] So does he bear witness that he came for the express purpose of spreading this true liberty of love among men.

---

[70] Mark 11:19.
[71] John 15:13.
[72] Luke 12:49.

Mystical Views of Christ*

Much of medieval religious literature came from monks and nuns engaged in contemplative life. Some of this literature was mystical, stressing a direct, emotional connection with God. Excerpted here are writings of three women mystics. Their writings, along with that of male mystics, provide an alternative to the more traditional and popular patterns. In the first selection, from 1141, Hildegard of Bingen, Germany, has visions of the Trinity as Divine Light.[73] In the second, from 1378,

---

* Hildegard of Bingen, *Visions* 2; Catherine of Siena, *Dialogue* 26–28; Julian of Norwich, *Revelations of Divine Love* 58

[73] Taken, with editing, from F. M. Steele, *The Life and Visions of St. Hildegarde* (London: Heath, Cranton and Ousely, 1914).

Catherine of Siena, Italy, relates her vision of Jesus as the divine Bridge.[74] In the third, from about 1373, Julian of Norwich, England, speaks about the love of God in terms of God's Motherhood.[75]

Then I saw a most splendid light, the whole of which burnt in a most beautiful, shining fire. In that light was the figure of a man of a sapphire color, and that most splendid light poured over the whole of that shining fire, and the shining fire over all that splendid light, and that most splendid light and shining fire over the whole figure of the man, appearing one light in one virtue and power. I heard that living Light saying to me: This is the meaning of the mysteries of God, that it may be discerned and understood discreetly what that fullness may be, which is without beginning and to which nothing is wanting, who by the most powerful strength planted all the rivers of the strong (places). For if the Lord is lacking in His own strength, what then would his work be?

[His work would be] certainly in vain, and so in a perfect work we see who its maker was. Therefore you gave this most splendid Light, which is without beginning and to whom nothing can be lacking. This means the Father, and in that figure of a man of a sapphire color, without any spot of the imperfection of envy and iniquity, is declared the Son, born of the Father, according to the Divinity before all time, but afterwards incarnate according to the humanity, in the world, in time. The whole of which burns in a most beautiful, shining fire, which fire without a touch of any dark mortality shows the Holy Spirit, by whom the same only-begotten Son of God was conceived according to the flesh, and born in time of the Virgin, and poured forth the light of true brightness upon the world.

But that splendid Light pours forth all that shining fire, and that shining fire all that splendid Light, and the splendid shining light of the fire, the whole of the figure of the man, making one Light existing in one strength and power. This is because the Father, who is the highest equity, but not without the Son nor the Holy Spirit, and the Holy Spirit who is the kindler of the hearts of the faithful, but not without the Father and the Son, and the Son who is the fullness of virtue, but not without the Father and the Holy Spirit, are inseparable in the majesty of the Divinity. The Father is not without the Son, neither the Son without the Father, nor the Father and the Son without the Holy Spirit, neither the Holy Spirit without them, and these three Persons exist one God in one whole divinity of majesty. The unity of the Divinity lives inseparable in the three Persons, because the Trinity is not able to be divided, but remains always inviolable without any without the word, nor the word without life. And where does the word remain? In the man. Whence does it go out? From the man. In what way? From the living man.

Thus the Son is in the Father, whom the Father for the salvation of men sitting in darkness, sent to earth, to be conceived in the Virgin by the Holy Spirit. The Son was only-begotten in his divinity, so he was only-begotten in virginity, and as he is the only Son of the Father, so he is the only Son of his mother, because as the Father begot him before all time, so his Virgin Mother bore him only in time, because she remained Virgin after his birth. . . .

Therefore, O man, embrace your God in the courage of your strength, before the Judge of your works shall come, when all things shall be manifested, lest anything hidden should be left, when those times come which in their duration shall not fail. . . He who sees with watchful eyes, and hears with attentive ears, offers an embrace to these mystic words of mine which emanate from me.

[Catherine of Siena, *Dialogue*] Then God eternal, to stir up even more that soul's love for the

---

[74] From Suzanne Noffke, *Catherine of Siena: The Dialogue* (Classics of Western Spirituality Series. New York: Paulist, 1980). Copyright © 1980, Paulist Press. Used by permission.
[75] From C. Jones, "The English Mystic: Julian of Norwich," in K. M. Wilson, *Medieval Women Writers* (Athens, GA: Georgia University Press, 1984), 286–87. Used by permission.

salvation of souls, responded to her: Before I show you what I want to show you, and what you asked to see, I want to describe the bridge for you. I have told you that it stretches from heaven to earth by reason of my having joined myself with your humanity, which I formed from the earth's clay.

This bridge, my only-begotten Son, has three stairs. Two of them he built on the wood of the most holy cross, and the third even as he tasted the great bitterness of the gall and vinegar they gave him to drink. You will recognize in these three stairs three spiritual stages.

The first stair is the feet, which symbolize the affections. For just as the feet carry the body, the affections carry the soul. My Son's nailed feet are a stair by which you can climb to his side, where you will see revealed his inmost heart. For when the soul has climbed up on the feet of affection and looked with her mind's eye into my Son's opened heart, she begins to feel the love of her own heart in his consummate and unspeakable love. (I say consummate because it is not for his own good that he loves you; you cannot do him any good, since he is one with me.) Then the soul, seeing how tremendously she is loved, is herself filled to overflowing with love. So, having climbed the second stair, she reaches the third. This is his mouth, where she finds peace from the terrible war she has had to wage because of her sins.

At the first stair, lifting the feet of her affections from the earth, she stripped herself of sin. At the second she dressed herself in love for virtue. And at the third she tasted peace. So the bridge has three stairs, and you can reach the last by climbing the first two. The last stair is so high that the flooding waters cannot strike it—for the venom of sin never touched my Son.

But though this bridge has been raised so high, it still is joined to the earth. Do you know when it was raised up? When my Son was lifted up on the wood of the most holy cross he did not cut off his divinity from the lowly earth of your humanity. So though he was raised so high he was not raised off the earth. In fact, his divinity is kneaded into the clay of your humanity like one bread. Nor could anyone walk on that bridge until my Son was raised up. This is why he said, "If I am lifted up high I will draw everything to myself."[76]

When my goodness saw that you could be drawn in no other way, I sent him to be lifted onto the wood of the cross. I made of that cross an anvil where this child of humankind could be hammered into an instrument to release humankind from death and restore it to the life of grace. In this way he drew everything to himself; for he proved his unspeakable love, and the human heart is always drawn by love. . . .

This bridge has walls of stone so that travelers will not be hindered when it rains . . . stones of true solid virtue. These stones were not, however, built into walls before my Son's passion. So no one could get to the final destination, even though they walked along the pathway of virtue. For heaven had not yet been unlocked with the key of my Son's blood, and the rain of justice kept anyone from crossing over.

But after these stones were hewn on the body of the Word, my gentle Son built them into walls, tempering the mortar with his own blood. His blood was mixed into the mortar of his divinity with the strong heat of burning love. By my power the stones of virtue were built into walls on no less a foundation than himself, for all virtue draws life from him, nor is there any virtue that has not been tested in him. So no one can have any life giving virtue but from him, that is, by following his example and his teaching. He perfected the virtues and planted them as living stones built into walls with his blood. So now all the faithful can walk without hindrance and with no cringing fear of the rain of divine justice, because they are sheltered by the mercy that came down from heaven through the incarnation of this Son of mine.

---

[76] John 12:32.

And how was heaven opened? With the key of his blood. So, you see, the bridge has walls and a roof of mercy. And the hostelry of holy Church is there to serve the bread of life and the blood, lest the journeying pilgrims, my creatures, grow weary and faint on the way. . . .

At the end of the bridge is the gate (which is, in fact, one with the bridge), which is the only way you can enter. This is why he said, "I am the Way and Truth and Life; whoever walks with me walks not in darkness but in light."[77] And in another place my Truth said that no one could come to me except through him, and such is the truth.

[Julian of Norwich, *Revelations of Divine Love*] Thus in our creation God almighty is our kindly Father, and God who is all wisdom is our kindly Mother, with the love and the goodness of the Holy Ghost—all of whom are one God and one Lord. . . .

I saw the working of the blessed Trinity in this vision and I saw and understood three properties: the property of fatherhood, motherhood,

---

[77] John 14:6

and lordship in one God. In our Almighty Father we have our protection and our bliss as regards the nature of our substance, which belongs to us from our Creation for eternity; and in the second person through understanding and wisdom we have our protection regarding our sensuality [physical nature] and our restoration and our salvation, for he is our Mother, Brother, and Savior. . . . I saw and understood that the noble strength of the Trinity is our Father, and the depth of wisdom of the Trinity is our Mother, and the great love of the Trinity is our Lord. Furthermore, I saw that the second person, who is our Mother, substantially the same beloved person, is now our Mother sensual, for we have a double nature from God's making, that is to say substantial [spiritual] and sensual [physical]. Our substance is the higher part which we have in our Father, Almighty God; and the second person of the Trinity is our Mother in the nature of our substantial making, in Whom we are grounded and rooted, and he is our Mother of mercy concerning our physical needs. And so, our Mother works in us in various ways. . . . In our Mother, Christ, we profit and grow, and in mercy he reforms and restores us.

The High Point of Renaissance Humanism*

The heart of the Renaissance was a high view of humanity and its place in the universe. Here one of the leading humanists of the Italian Renaissance, Pico della Mirandola, reflects with a type of Christian humanism on the elevated place that God has given to humans. Note the mixture of Christian and pagan-classical references.

The Supreme Father, God the Architect, having already used up all the forms in the creation of the world, wondered what special distinction was

---

* Pico della Mirandola, "Oration on the Dignity of Man"

left for him to confer upon man. He decided that man's singularity would consist in his freedom to participate in all the forms. Therefore God addressed Adam, "We have conferred upon you no single seat, no proper form, no peculiar function, so that you might choose what seat, form and function you prefer by your own choice. . . . I have set you in the middle of the world that you may better survey what is in the world. We have made you neither celestial or terrestrial, neither mortal nor immortal, in order that as a free and sovereign modeler and sculptor, so to speak, you may fashion yourself into the form you prefer. You are able to degenerate into the lower forms, which are the animals, and to regenerate your-self by your own will into the higher, which are divine."

O supreme liberality of God the Father, O supreme and admirable happiness of man! Let us then mount above all that is on the earth to the heavenly court which is closest to the emi-nent divinity. . . . We ascend first by the ladder of philosophy. She is able to allay the dissentions which vex, distress and lacerate the mind, yet al-ways reminding us of the dictum of Heraclitus that nature is born to strife. Therefore true quiet and solid peace are the reward and privilege of her mistress, theology. As the Master says when he sees us struggling, "Come to me all you that labor, come and I will refresh you. Come and I will give you the peace which the world can-not give."[78]

Let us with winged feet like terrestrial Mer-curies fly up to the embrace of the Most Blessed Mother to enjoy the peace we desire, the peace

---

[78] Matthew 11:28, John 14:27.

most holy, the union indissoluble, the friendship in which all souls not only agree in that one mind which is above every mind, but are also fused into one. Finally comes the vision through the light of theology. Who would not desire to be initiated into these rites? Who would not desire, while still on earth, to be a companion of the gods, inebriated with the nectar of eternity? . . . Who would not wish to be seized by the frenzy of Socrates, that sped by the oars of winged feet he might ascend rapidly from this evil world to the New Jerusalem? . . . Then Bacchus, the leader of the Muses, showing to us by his mys-teries the invisible things of God . . . will intoxi-cate us from the richness of the divine abode in which, if we are faithful like Moses, holy theol-ogy will animate us with a double fury. Then lifted to eminent height we shall measure from eternity all that was and is and is to be. . . . As seers of Phoebus we shall be winged lovers, rapt by an ineffable love, stung as by a barb; like flam-ing Seraphim we shall be beyond ourselves, full of God. We shall no longer be ourselves, but rather He who made us.

ETHICS

A Christian Mother's Instructions to Her Son*

Dhuoda, an educated laywoman of the ninth cen-tury, wrote a moral handbook for her elder son Wil-liam, from whom she was separated. Her short book is a remarkable glimpse into the spirituality of her time, and one of the few women's writings to emerge from the "Dark Ages." The Manual of William *is notable for its piety infused with parental love.[79]*

Here Begins the Manual of Dhuoda which she sent to her son, William.

I have noticed that most women in this world are able to live with and enjoy their children. However, seeing myself, Dhuoda, living far away from you, my dear son William,[80] I am filled with anxiety. With the desire to help you, I am send-ing you this little manual, which I have written, for your study and education. Thus I rejoice that, though I am absent in body, this little book will recall to your mind, as you read it, the things you must do for my sake.

---

* Dhuoda, *Manual of William*
[79] Translated by the author from J.-P. Migné, *Patrologia Latina*, vol. 106 (Paris: Migné, 1867), cols. 109–18.

[80] *far away from . . . William:* In 841 Dhuoda's husband, Bernhard of Semptimania, had sent William to King Charles the Bald.

What shall I say, fragile vessel that I am? I shall turn to others as a friend. If the heavens and the earth were spread through the air like a parchment, and if all the various parts of the sea were transformed into ink, and if all the inhabitants of the earth born into this world from the beginning of humankind up to now were writers, which is an impossible thing contrary to nature, they would not be able to comprehend (in writing) the greatness, the breadth, the height, the sublimity, the profundity of the Almighty. They would not be able to tell the divinity, wisdom, piety, and mercy of him who is called God. Since he is thus and so great that no one can comprehend his essence, I beg you to fear him and to love him with all your heart, all your mind, all your understanding, to bless him in all your ways and deeds and to sing, "God is good, for his mercy endures forever!" Believe him to be above, below, inside, and outside of you, for he is superior, inferior, interior, and exterior.

I also urge you, O my handsome and lovable son William, that amid the mundane cares of this world you not neglect the acquisition of many books, in which you may understand and learn something greater and better than is written here concerning God, your Creator, through the teaching of the most blessed doctors. . . .

What more can I say? Your admonisher, Dhuoda, is always with you, son, and if I be absent because of death, which must come, you will have this little book of moral teaching as a memorial. In it you will be able to see me as the reflection in a mirror, reading and praying to God in mind and body, and you will find fully set down the duties you must perform for me. Son, you will have teachers who will teach you other documents of greater utility, but not under the same conditions, not with a soul burning in their breast as I, your mother, have, O firstborn son. . . .

Son William, keep watch, ask of God and pray in a short, firm, and pure speech. . . . As the Fathers say, although God was the Supreme Creator of all, he was willing to take on the form of a slave. He raises the powerful in order to plunge them into the depths, and he exalts the humble, that they may rise to the heights. . . . If he, great as he is, acts thus toward lesser ones, how should we, small as we are, act toward those who are worse off? Those who are able ought to help them, and, according to the urgings and words of the Apostle Paul, bear one another's burdens.[81] . . .

Cherish and befriend those whom you wish to befriend you. Love, venerate, and honor all people, so that you may be worthy to receive of all reciprocal retribution and due honor. For example, a certain learned man, making a comparison with a dumb animal for our edification,[82] offered a great and clear sermon in a few words. He said in elucidating Psalm 41, "Harts have this custom. When several of them wish to cross a large river of swirling waters, one after the other they place their horned heads on the back of their companions and hold up each other's necks; thus, by taking a little rest, they can make a more rapid crossing. They have such intelligence and such wisdom in them that, when they perceive the first to be tiring, they change places one after the other, and they let the second be first, now upholding and comforting the others. Thus alternating one by one, they each have pass through them the compassion of brotherly love, always taking care that the head with the horns be shown and held up, lest they be submerged in the waters."

What meaning is hidden here is not hidden from the learned. Everything is immediately clear to their eyes. This changing of place shows the love which is to be kept by all in the human race, both to the great and to the small through brotherly love. The upholding of the heads and

---

[81] Galatians 6:2.

[82] *making a comparison . . . edification:* An examination of animal life to show the proper ways of Christian behavior was a common moral device in medieval writing and preaching. These examinations, collected into books called "bestiaries," were very popular and had an enormous influence on medieval art and literature.

the horns shows that the faithful in Christ must always keep their hearts and minds on Him. . . .

God has said: "1. He who walks without blemish, 2. who works justice, 3. who speaks the truth, 4. who does not use deceit in his tongue, 5. who does not evil to his neighbor, 6. who does not swear to his neighbor to deceive him, 7. who does not put his money to usury, 8. who does not reproach his neighbor, 9. who does not take bribes against the innocent, 10. who patiently tolerates injuries, 11. who is pure in heart and chaste in body, 12. who is innocent in hands, 13. who is able to transgress and yet does not transgresses, 14. who can do evil things and yet does not do them, 15. who reaches out his hand to the poor as often as he can," such a person will be perfect with the aid of God.

Read this little book frequently. Noble child, always be strong and brave in Christ! . . .

Reader, pray for Dhuoda, if you wish to have the merit of seeing Christ in eternal happiness.

Christians and the Natural World*

Saint Francis saw all created things as good and beautiful because God made them so. This poem, written in Italian, is wonderfully ambiguous; Francis seems to be both praising God for the creation and praising God through the creation. It remains one of the most important Christian affirmations of the goodness of creation.[83]

Most high, omnipotent, good Lord,
Praise, glory and honor and blessing all, are
   Yours.
To You alone do they belong, most High,
And there is no one fit to mention You.

Praise be to You, my Lord, with all Your
   creatures,
Especially to my worshipful brother sun,
Which lights up the day, and through him You
   brightness give;
And beautiful is he and radiant with splendor
   great;
Of You, most High, revelation gives.

Praised be my Lord, for sister moon and for
   the stars,

In heaven You have formed them clear, precious and fair.
Praised be my Lord for brother wind,
For air and clouds and fair and every kind of
   weather,
By which You give to Your creatures
   nourishment.
Praised be my Lord for sister water,
Which is greatly helpful, humble, precious
   and pure.

Praised be my Lord for brother fire,
By which You light up the dark.
Fair is he and gay and mighty and strong.

Praised be my Lord for our sister, mother
   earth,
Which sustains and keeps us,
And brings forth diverse fruits with grass and
   flowers bright.

Praised be my Lord for those who for Your love
   forgive
And weakness bear and tribulation.
Blessed are those who shall in peace endure,
For by You, most High, shall they be crowned.

Praised be my Lord for our sister, the bodily
   death,
From which no living man can flee.
Woe to them who die in mortal sin;

---

* Francis of Assisi, "The Song of Brother Sun"
[83] From Paschal Robinson, *The Writings of Saint Francis of Assisi* (Philadelphia: Dolfin, 1906), 152–53.

Blessed those who shall find themselves in
    Your most holy will,
For the second death shall do them no ill.

Praise and bless my Lord, and give him
    thanks,
And be subject to him with great humility.

Complaints about University Students*

Universities began as cathedral schools and grew into more independent centers of higher learning. But in the Middle Ages and early Renaissance they were always under the control of the church, with administration and faculty drawn from the ranks of the clergy. This reading about student vices sounds remarkably modern at points, but it comes from the early 1300s. Alvarus Pelagius was a Franciscan monk who wrote a rambling, cranky condemnation of all the perceived faults of his time. This selection from his work provides an insight into the popular practice of Christianity among university students.[84]

Sometimes they [university students] wish to be above their masters,[85] impugning their statements more with wrong-headedness than with reason. . . . Those wish to become masters who were not legitimate students. They attend classes but make no effort to learn anything. . . . They frequently learn what they would better ignore . . . such things as forbidden sciences, how to talk about love, and superstitions. On obscure points they depend upon their own judgment, passing over scripture and canonical science[86] of which they are ignorant. And so they become masters of error. For they are ashamed to ask of others what they themselves don't know, which is stupid pride. . . .

They defraud their masters of their due salaries, although they are able to pay.[87] Therefore they are legally bound to make restitution. . . .

They have among themselves evil and disgraceful societies, associating together for ill. While in residence they sometimes are guilty of vices, against which their masters ought to take action so far as they can. . . . They are disobedient to the masters and rectors of the universities and sometimes transgress the statutes which they have sworn to observe. Sometimes they contend against and resist the officials, for which they should be subjected to blows of rods. . . .

On feast days they don't go to church to hear divine service and sermons and above all the full Mass which all Christians are supposed to attend, but gad about town with their friends or attend lectures or write up their notes at home. Or, if they go to church, it is not for worship but to see the girls or swap stories. . . . If they are clergy with parishes, when they go off to universities, they do not leave good and sufficient vicars in their churches to care diligently for the souls of their parishioners. Or they hear lectures in fields forbidden to them, such as the law.

The expense money which they have from their parents or churches they spend in taverns, conviviality, games and other unnecessary things, and so they return home empty, without knowledge, conscience, or money. . . . They contract debts and sometimes withdraw from the university without paying them. So they are excommunicated but do not care; they may not be absolved.

---

* Alvarus Pelagius, *The Church's Complaint*
[84] From Lynn Thorndike, trans., *University Records and Life in the Middle Ages* (New York: Columbia University Press, 1944), 173–74. Copyright © 1944 Columbia University Press. Used by permission.
[85] *masters:* teachers.
[86] *canonical science:* the church's law codes.

---

[87] *They defraud . . . pay:* medieval university students paid their professors directly.

The Discipline of the Inner Life*

No book, with the exception of the Bible, has been translated into more languages than Thomas à Kempis's devotional classic, The Imitation of Christ. *An Augustinian friar from the Low Countries who died in 1471, Thomas speaks an almost timeless language of simple Christian mysticism.*[88]

"God's kingdom lies within you," the Lord says.[89] You must turn to him, the Lord, with all your heart, and leave this wretched world behind you, if your soul is to find rest. Learn to despise this world of outward things, and devote yourself to what lies within; there, within you, you will see the coming of God's kingdom. That's what "God's kingdom" means—peacefulness and rejoicing in the Holy Spirit, something denied to the irreligious. Christ is ready to come to you, with what kindness in his glance! But you must make room, deep in your heart, to entertain him as he deserves; it is for the inward eye, all the splendor and beauty of him; deep in your heart is where he likes to be. Where he finds a man whose thoughts go deep, he is a frequent visitor; such pleasant conversation, such welcome words of comfort, such deep rest, such intimate friendship, are almost past belief.

Up with you then, faithful soul, get your heart ready for the coming of this true Lover, or he will never consent to come and make his dwelling in you; that is his own way of putting it, "If a man has any love for me, he will be true to my word; and we will come to him, and make our abode with him."[90] You must make room for Christ, then, and shut the door upon all intruders.

If Christ is yours, then wealth is yours; he satisfies all your wants. He will look after you, manage all your affairs for you most dutifully; you will need no human support to rely on. Our human friends change so easily, fail us after such a short time. Christ abides for ever, and stands loyally, to the last, at our side.

A human friend, that shares our frail mortality, may do us good service and endear himself to us, but it is a mistake to repose much confidence in him. Why should we make such a tragedy of it if he takes the wrong side now and again, in opposition to us? Friends today, enemies tomorrow, and the other way around—it's always the same; men's hearts change like the breeze. Put all your trust in God; center in him all your fear and all your love; he will make himself responsible for you, and all will go well as he sees best.

This world is no native country of yours; go where you will, you are only a foreigner, only a visitor in it. Nothing will ever bring you rest, except being closely united to Jesus. Why stand gaping here? This is no place for you to settle down. Heaven is your destination, and you should look upon this earthly scene only as a transit camp. Transient, all created things, and you as much as the rest of them; cling to them, and you will get caught up in them, and be lost. All your thoughts must be at home with God, all your prayer make its way up to Christ continually.

Ah, you complain that it is above your reach, such high contemplation of heavenly things. Why then, let your mind come to rest in Christ's Passion, and find in his sacred wounds the home it longs for. . . . How little you will care for the contempt of your fellow men, how easily you will put up with their criticisms!

When Christ lived in the world, he too met with human contempt. His own intimate friends, at the hour of his greatest need, left him to face insult. Christ so ready to suffer and be despised, and have you complaints to make? Christ with enemies and slanderers all about him, and do you expect to find nothing but friendship and kindness? The crown is for endurance; where is it going to come from, if you never meet with

---

* Thomas à Kempis, *The Imitation of Christ* 2.1
[88] From Ronald Knox and Michael Oakley, trans., *The Imitation of Christ* (New York: Sheed & Ward, 1959), 60–63.
[89] Luke 17:21.
[90] John 14:23.

difficulties? If you want to have everything your own way, you are no friend of Christ's; you must hold out with him, and for love of him, before you can share his kingdom.

If you would ever really get inside the mind of Jesus, ever have a single taste of his burning love, considerations of your own loss or gain would mean nothing to you. You would be glad to have insults heaped on you—the love of Jesus fills us with self-contempt.

If you love Jesus, if you love the truth, if you really direct your gaze inward, and rid yourself of uncontrolled emotions, then you can turn to God at will, lifted out of yourself by an impulse of the spirit, and rest in him contentedly.

RELATIONS

Byzantine Views of Church and Empire*

Justinian, emperor in the East from 527 to 565, is known for his reform of the laws, especially his Codex *["Book"], which was influential in both eastern and western Europe. In this selection we see a view of church and state that is the culmination of developments since Constantine.*[91]

The church and the Empire are the two greatest blessings which God in his infinite mercy has bestowed on humanity. The church deals with divine matters, and the empire is set over and directs human matters. Both proceed from the same source and promote the life of humankind. Therefore nothing should be a greater concern to the emperors as the honor of the priests who constantly pray to God for their welfare. If the church is everywhere free of blame, and if the Empire, full of confidence in God, is administered fairly and justly, then general good will result, and all benefits will be bestowed upon the human race. Therefore we have the greatest concern for true teaching about God and the preservation of the church's honor. If these are maintained, they will result in the greatest advantages that can be conferred upon us by God. We will be confirmed in those things which we already enjoy, and we shall acquire whatever we do not yet have. . . . We think that this will happen if the sacred rules of the Church are obeyed. These are the rules which the righteous, praiseworthy, and venerable Apostles . . . handed down to us, and which the Holy Fathers have explained and preserved for us.

---

* Justinian, *The New Laws*, Title 6: *Sixth New Constitution*, Preface of the *First Collection*

[91] Translated by the author from R. Schoell, *Corpus Iuris Civilis*, vol. 3, *Novellae* (Berlin, 1912), 35–36.

A Christian Elf Charm**

As Christianity took over Britain, it adapted itself to pre-Christian popular Anglo-Saxon religion. A late tenth-century manuscript gives a Christian charm called the "Field Remedy Ritual" for warding off the evil power of elves. Note how Christian words and ritual actions are mixed with the Anglo-Saxon.[92]

** The Cotton Caligula Manuscript

[92] Taken from Karen Louise Jolly, *Popular Religion in Late Saxon England: Elf Charms in Context* (Chapel Hill: University of North Carolina Press, 1996), 6–8. Used by permission.

Here is the remedy, how you may better your land, if it will not grow well or if some harmful thing has been done to it by a sorcerer or by a poisoner.

Take then at night, before dawn, four sods from four sides of the land, and mark where they were before.

Then take oil and honey and yeast, and milk of each animal that is on the land, and a piece of each type of tree that grows on the land, except hard beams, and a piece of each herb known by name, except burdock only, and put then holy water thereon, and drip it three times on the base of the sods, and say then these words:

Crescite, grow, et multiplicamini, and multiply, et replete, and fill, terre, the earth. In nomine patris et filii et spiritus sancti sit benedicti. [In the name of the Father and the Son and the Holy Spirit, be blessed.] And the Pater Noster [the Our Father prayer] as often as the other.

And then carry the sods into church, and let a masspriest sing four masses over the sods, and let someone turn the green [sides] to the altar, and after that let someone bring the sods to where they were before, before the sun sets.

And have made for them four signs of Christ [crosses] of quickbeam and write on each end: Matthew and Mark, Luke, and John. Lay that sign of Christ in the bottom of the pit [where each sod had been cut out], saying then: crux Matheus, crux Marcus, crux Lucas, crux sanctus Johannes.

Take then the sods and set them down there on [the crosses], and say then nine times these words, Crescite [grow], and as often the Pater Noster, and turn then to the east, and bow nine times humbly, and speak then these words:

Eastwards I stand, for mercies I pray,
I pray the great domine [lord], the powerful
    lord,
I pray the holy guardian of heaven-kingdom,
earth I pray and sky
and the true sancta [holy] Mary
and heaven's might and high hall,
that I may this charm by the gift of the lord

open with [my] teeth through firm thought,
to call forth these plants for our worldly use,
to fill this land with firm belief,
to beautify this grassy turf, as the wiseman
    said
that he would have riches on earth who alms
gave with justice by the grace of the lord.

Then turn three times with the sun's course, stretch then out lengthwise and enumerate there the litanies and say then: Sanctus [holy], sanctus, sanctus to the end. Sing then Benedicite with outstretched arms and Magnificat and Pater noster three times, and commend it [the land] to Christ and Saint Mary and the holy cross for praise and for worship and for the benefit of the one who owns that land and all those who are serving under him. When all that is done, then let a man take unknown seed from beggars and give them twice as much as he took from them, and let him gather all his plough tools together; then let him bore a hole in the beam [of the plough, putting in] incense and fennel and hallowed soap and hallowed salt. Take then that seed, set it on the plough's body, say then:

Erce, Erce, Erce, earth's mother,
May the all-ruler grant you, the eternal lord,
fields growing and flourishing,
propagating and strengthening,
tall shafts, bright crops,
and broad barley crops,
and white wheat crops,
and all earth's crops.
May the eternal lord grant him,
and his holy ones, who are in heaven,
that his produce be guarded against any ene-
    mies whatsoever,
and that it be safe against any harm at all,
from poisons sown around the land.
Now I bid the Master, who shaped this world,
that there be no speaking-woman nor artful
    man
that can overturn these words thus spoken.

Then let a man drive forth the plough and cut the first furrow, and then say:

Whole may you be, earth, mother of men!
May you be growing in God's embrace,
with food filled for the needs of men.

Take then each kind of flour and have someone bake a loaf [the size of] a hand's palm and
knead it with milk and with holy water and lay it
under the first furrow. Say then:

Field full of food for mankind,
bright-blooming, you are blessed

in the holy name of the one who shaped heaven
and the earth on which we live;
the God, the one who made the ground, grant
     us the gift of growing,
that for us each grain might come to use.

Say then three times Crescite in nomine patris sit
benedicti [Grow in the name of the father, be
blessed]. [Say the] Amen and Pater Noster three
times.

Christianity and Islam in Conflict*

*Islam arose in the sixth century and soon posed a
threat to both Eastern and Western Christianity.
It recognized Jews and Christians as "People of the
Book" and tolerated them within its territory. But
as the first reading makes plain, Islam saw itself
as the successor and replacement of both Judaism
and Christianity.[93] In the second reading, Thomas
Aquinas attacks Islam as a perversion of biblical
religion.[94] Note how both writers complain that the
other religion misunderstands scripture.*

They say, "No one shall enter Paradise except for
Jews or Christians"; that is their faith. You[95]
must say, "Bring your proofs, if what you say is
true." . . . The Jews say, "Christians rest on nothing," and Christians say, "Jews rest on nothing."
Yet they both read the Book. God will judge between them on resurrection day. . . .

They say, "God has a Son." God be praised![96]
His are all things in the heavens and the earth,
and all things obey him.

Those who do not know (the Scriptures) say,
"Unless God speaks to us, or there comes a
sign [we will not believe]." Those before them
said the same thing about signs; their hearts are
all alike. We have given signs to a people, sure
signs. . . .

Jews will not be satisfied with you, or the
Christians, until you follow their creed. Say,
"God's guidance is *the* guidance. If you follow in
their way after God's knowledge has come to
you, God will not be your patron or your help."

Those to whom we have brought the Book[97]
and who read it as it should be read, believe in it;
those who do not believe in it will be lost.

[Aquinas, *Summa against the Pagans*] Some of
the Gentiles, such as the Mohammedans and the
pagans, do not agree with us in accepting the authority of any Scripture, by which they may be
convinced of their error. Thus, against the Jews
we are able to argue by means of the Old Testament, while against heretics we are able to argue by means of the New Testament. But the

---

*Quran 2:105–115; Aquinas, *Summa against the Pagans*
1.2.3; 1.6.4

[93] Taken, with editing, from E. H. Palmer, *The Qur'an* (Oxford: Clarendon Press, 1880), pp. 15–17. The verse numbers
followed are from Palmer's translation and may differ from
later translations.

[94] Taken from A. C. Pegis, *On the Truth of the Catholic Faith,
Summa Contra Gentiles*, Book One (Garden City, NY: Dou-
bleday, 1955), pp. 62, 73–74. Copyright © 1955 by Dou-
bleday Publishers. Used by permission.

[95] *You*: Muhammad.

---

[96] *God be praised!*: i.e., God forbid!

[97] *Book*: the Quran.

Mohammedans and the pagans accept neither the one nor the other. We must, therefore, have recourse to the natural reason, to which all men are forced to give their consent. However, it is true that in divine matters the natural reason has its failings. . . .

Mohammed seduced the people by promises of carnal pleasure to which the concupiscence[98] of the flesh goads us. His teaching also contained precepts that were in conformity with these promises, and he gave free rein to carnal pleasure. In all this, as is not unexpected, he was obeyed by carnal men. . . . The truths that he taught he mingled with many fables and with doctrines of the greatest falsity. He did not bring forth any signs produced in a supernatural way,

which alone fittingly gives witness to divine inspiration. . . . On the contrary, Mohammed said that he was sent in the power of his arms—which are signs not lacking even to robbers and tyrants. . . . Those who believed in him were brutal men and desert nomads, utterly ignorant of all divine teaching, through whose numbers Mohammed forced others to become his followers by the violence of his arms. Nor do divine pronouncements by preceding prophets offer him any witness. On the contrary, he perverts almost all the testimonies of the Old and New Testaments by making them into fabrications of his own, as can be seen by anyone who examines his law. It was, therefore, a shrewd decision on his part to forbid his followers to read the Old and New Testaments, lest these books convict him of falsity. It is thus clear that those who place any faith in his words believe foolishly.

---

[98] *concupiscence:* sinful desire.

The Peace of God and the Truce of God*

A major problem of early medieval times was near-constant warfare. The church tried to mitigate this violence by proclamations of the "Peace of God," which prohibited military attacks on sacred places and people, and the "Truce of God," which prohibited warfare on certain days of each week and during holy periods such as Holy Week, Lent, and Advent. Here are two local examples, the first from 989 and the second from 1063, of these laws.[99]

Following the example of my predecessors, I, Gunbald, archbishop of Bordeaux, called together the bishops of my diocese in a synod at Charroux . . . and we, assembled there in the name of God, made the following decrees:

Anathema[100] against those who break into churches. If anyone breaks into or robs a church, he shall be anathema unless he makes satisfaction. Anathema against those who rob the poor. If anyone robs a peasant or any other poor person of a sheep, ox, ass, cow, goat, or pig, he shall be anathema unless he makes satisfaction. Anathema against those who injure clergymen. If anyone attacks, seizes, or beats a priest, deacon, or any other clergyman, who is not bearing arms (shield, sword, coat of mail, or helmet), but is going along peacefully or staying in the house, the sacrilegious person shall be excommunicated and cut off from the church, unless he makes satisfaction, or unless the bishop discovers that the clergyman brought it upon himself by his own fault.

[Truce for the Bishopric of Terouanne] Drogo, bishop of Terouanne, and count Baldwin [of

---

* Declaration of the Synod Charroux; Declaration of Drogo, Bishop of Terouanne
[99] Taken, with editing, from O. J. Thatcher and E. H. McNeal, *Source Book for Mediaeval History* (New York: Scribners, 1905), 412, 417–18.

---

[100] *Anathema:* a religious curse, excluding one from salvation.

Hainault] have established this peace with the cooperation of the clergy and people of the land.

Dearest brothers in the Lord, these are the conditions which you must observe during the time of the peace which is commonly called the truce of God, and which begins with sunset on Wednesday and lasts until sunrise on Monday.

During those four days and five nights no man or woman shall assault, wound, or slay another, or attack, seize, or destroy a castle, town, or village, by craft or by violence.

If anyone violates this peace and disobeys these commands of ours, he shall be exiled for thirty years as a penance, and before he leaves the bishopric he shall make compensation for the injury which he committed. Otherwise he shall be excommunicated by the Lord God and excluded from all Christian fellowship.

All who associate with him in any way, who give him advice or aid, or hold converse with him, unless it be to advise him to do penance and to leave the bishopric, shall be under excommunication until they have made satisfaction.

If any violator of the peace shall fall sick and die before he completes his penance, no Christian shall visit him or move his body from the place where it lay, or receive any of his possessions.

In addition, brethren, you should observe the peace in regard to lands and animals and all things that can be possessed. If anyone takes from another an animal, a coin, or a garment, during the days of the truce, he shall be excommunicated unless he makes satisfaction. If he desires to make satisfaction for his crime he shall first restore the thing which he stole or its value in money, and shall do penance for seven years within the bishopric. If he should die before he makes satisfaction and completes his penance, his body shall not be buried or removed from the place where it lay, unless his family shall make satisfaction for him to the person whom he injured.

During the days of the peace, no one shall make a hostile expedition on horseback, except when summoned by the count. All who go with the count shall take for their support only as much as is necessary for themselves and their horses. All merchants and other men who pass through your territory from other lands shall have peace from you.

You shall also keep this peace every day of the week from the beginning of Advent to the octave of Epiphany and from the beginning of Lent to the octave of Easter, and from the feast of Rogations[101] to the octave of Pentecost. We command all priests on feast days and Sundays to pray for all who keep the peace, and to curse all who violate it or support its violators.

If anyone has been accused of violating the peace and denies the charge, he shall take communion and undergo the ordeal of hot iron. If he is found guilty, he shall do penance within the diocese for seven years.

---

[101] *Rogations:* the Monday before Ascension Day.

The Investiture Controversy*

*The **Investiture Controversy** was a struggle from 1075 to 1122 over the right to appoint bishops, abbots, and parish priests. This right had been exercised by kings and princes for centuries, but in 1075*

---

* Henry IV, Letter to Pope Gregory VII; Pope Gregory VII, Letter to Henry IV

it was claimed by Pope Gregory VII in an attempt to stamp out the buying and selling of church offices. This sparked a long and difficult struggle over control of the church, especially in England and Germany. In 1076, Henry IV of Germany attempted to dethrone Pope Gregory VII by playing the "divine right of kings" against the divine power of the pope, an effort that failed and ultimately resulted in more Roman power over the church in Germany. The first reading is from Henry's letter to the pope, and the second is the pope's sharp response.[102]

Henry, king not through usurpation but through the holy ordination of God, to Hildebrand,[103] at present not pope but false monk. You have merited such a greeting through your disturbances, for there is no rank in the church which you have omitted to make a partaker not of honor but of confusion, not of blessings but of curses. To mention few special cases out of many, not only have you not feared to lay hands upon the rulers of the holy church, the anointed of the Lord— the archbishops, namely, bishops and priests— but you have trampled them under foot like slaves ignorant of what their master is doing. You have won favor from the common herd by crushing them; you have looked upon all of them as knowing nothing, upon yourself alone as knowing all things. This knowledge, however, you have used not for edification but for destruction. . . . We have endured all this, being eager to guard the honor of the apostolic see. You, however, have understood our humility to be fear, and you have not, accordingly, shunned to rise up against the royal power conferred upon us by God, daring to threaten to divest us of it. As if we had received our kingdom from you! As if the kingdom and the empire were in your hand and not in God's!

Although our Lord Jesus Christ did call us to the kingdom, he did not call you to the priesthood. For you have ascended by the following steps. By wiles, which the profession of monk abhors, you have achieved money; by money, favor; by the sword, the throne of peace. From the throne of peace you have disturbed peace, because you have armed subjects against those in authority over them; because you, who were not called, have taught that our bishops called of God are to be despised; because you have usurped for laymen the ministry over their priests, allowing them to depose or condemn those whom they themselves had received as teachers from the hand of God through the laying on of hands of the bishops. On me also who, although unworthy to be among the anointed, have nevertheless been anointed to the kingdom, you have laid your hand. As the tradition of the holy Fathers teaches, declaring that I am not to be deposed for any crime unless, which God forbid, I should have strayed from the faith, I am subject to the judgment of God alone. For the wisdom of the holy fathers committed even Julian the Apostate not to themselves, but to God alone, to be judged and to be deposed. For the true pope himself, Peter, also exclaims: "Fear God, honor the king."[104] You do not fear God, but you dishonor in me his appointed one. St. Paul . . . says: "If anyone, either I or an angel from Heaven, should preach a gospel other than that which has been preached to you, he shall be damned."[105]

You, therefore, damned by this curse and by the judgment of all our bishops and by our own, descend and relinquish the apostolic chair which you have usurped. Let another ascend the throne of St. Peter, who shall not practice violence under the cloak of religion, but shall teach the sound doctrine of St. Peter. I, Henry, king by the grace of God, say unto you with all our bishops: Descend, descend, to be damned throughout the ages.

[Gregory, Letter to Henry] I had no thought of ascending your [Peter's] chair through force, and that I would rather have ended my life as a pilgrim than, by secular means, to have seized your chair for the sake of earthly glory. Therefore I believe it to be through your grace and not through my own deeds that it has pleased and does please

---

[102] Taken, with editing, from O. J. Thatcher and E. H. Mc-Neal, *Source Book for Mediaeval History* (New York, Scribners, 1905), pp. 151–152.
[103] *Hildebrand:* name of Gregory VII before he became Pope in 1073.

[104] I Peter 2:17.
[105] Galatians 1:9.

you that the Christian people, who have been especially committed to you, should obey me. And especially to me, as your representative and by your favor, has the power been granted by God of binding and loosing in heaven and on earth. On the strength of this belief, for the honor and security of your church, in the name of Almighty God, Father, Son and Holy Spirit, I withdraw, through your power and authority, from Henry the king, son of Henry the emperor, who has risen against your church with unheard of insolence, the rule over the whole kingdom of the Germans and over Italy. I absolve all Christians from the bonds of the oath which they have made or shall make to him; and I forbid any one to serve him as king.

He who strives to lessen the honor of your church should himself lose the honor which belongs to him. He has scorned to obey as a Christian, and has not returned to God, whom he had deserted. He deals with the excommunicated, practices many types of iniquities, spurns my commands which, as you bear witness, I issued to him for his own salvation, separates himself from your church, and strives to tear it. Therefore, I bind him in your place with the chain of the anathema. Leaning on you, I so bind him that the people may know and have proof that you are Peter, and on your rock the Son of the living God has built his church, and the gates of hell shall not prevail against it.

GLOSSARY

Byzantine Age the period in the East between about 330 and 1453 C.E.

Caesaropapism see *symphonia.*

celibacy abstention from marriage and all forms of sexual activity; required for all Roman Catholic clergy and for Eastern monks and bishops.

chronicle a chronologically ordered narrative of official events.

Dark Ages the period of time in the West between the fall of ancient Rome and about 1000 C.E.; roughly the first half of the Middle Ages.

friar a member of the new monastic orders that arose in the twelfth century.

iconoclasts those in the eighth- and ninth-century Eastern Orthodox church who opposed worship of images; the word literally means "icon breakers."

iconodules those in the Eastern church who held that the veneration (Greek *douleia*) of images was proper; this became the Orthodox position.

invective studied, often flowery insults sometimes used in religious arguments.

Investiture Controversy the struggle from about 1075 to 1122 between the pope and civil rulers for the right to appoint clergy, especially bishops.

Middle Ages the period of time in the West between the fall of ancient Rome and the Renaissance, roughly 500–1500 C.E.

monastic rule formal regulations for life in the monastery.

mysticism a form of religious experience and writing that emphasizes direct and often intuitive personal experience of God.

papal bull formal church pronouncements on faith and practice issued by the pope.

Renaissance the rebirth of ancient culture after the Middle Ages, effectively ending them.

Scholasticism a type of Christian theology that flourished in the Middle Ages, emphasizing the rational understanding and presentation of Christian belief; theologians who practiced this method are known as **scholastics.**

symphonia the close blending of church and empire in Byzantium; called **Caesaropapism** by Western historians.

QUESTIONS FOR STUDY AND DISCUSSION

1.   What are some of the reasons why many people today devalue the Middle Ages and its contribution to Christianity?

2.   In what ways did Christianity expand during this period?

3.   What are the reasons that the Orthodox and Catholic churches separated in the Middle Ages? Which are most important, and why?

4.   What contribution to Christianity did women mystics make in this period?

5.   How would you describe the piety of the Middle Ages, to judge from these readings? How can it be compared to the piety of ancient Christianity?

6.   What were, in your view, the positive and negative contributions of monasticism in the Middle Ages?

7.   What were the major issues in church-state relations at this time?

8.   How did Renaissance humanism arise from medieval Catholic thought? What are its major similarities and differences to the medieval mind?

SUGGESTIONS FOR FURTHER READING

D. J. Geanakoplos, *Byzantium: Church, Society, and Civilization Seen Through Contemporary Eyes.* Chicago: University of Chicago Press, 1984. This thorough anthology of Eastern Christianity has excellent treatment of the Byzantine period of Christianity.

E. A. Petroff, *Medieval Women's Visionary Literature.* New York: Oxford University Press, 1986. Twenty-nine selections from women's mystical/visionary literature from the third century to the fifteenth.

B. Tierney, *The Middle Ages,* vol. 1: *Sources of Medieval History.* New York: Knopf, 1970. A useful anthology covering all important aspects of medieval history, including Western Christianity.

K. M. Wilson, ed., *Medieval Women Writers.* Athens, GA: University of Georgia Press, 1984. Selections from the most important works of fifteen women writers, most on religious themes; excellent introductions accompany the translations.

CHAPTER FIVE

Reform in Western Christianity (1500–1600)

❖ In London, the Church of England takes up proposed legislation to liberalize its policy on the remarriage of divorced persons. The proposed policy would allow most divorced church members to remarry in the church. British politicians pay special attention because it would permit Charles, Prince of Wales and heir to the monarchy, to marry his long-time mistress, Camilla Parker-Bowles, with the church's blessing. Since Reformation times, British law forbids a person remarried outside the Church of England from holding the throne, but with a new policy in place a possible constitutional crisis would be avoided.

❖ In Lancaster County, Pennsylvania, a group of Old Order Amish has met in a home for worship. As their horses and buggies wait outside, they conduct a two-hour service of hymns, prayers, scripture readings, and sermon, all in their own "Pennsylvania Dutch" language, which is actually a Swiss dialect of German. No cleric conducts the service, for in Amish religious life the men are all equal. Their worship and lifestyle continues the same pattern of "coming out from the world and being separate" that their Anabaptist ancestors practiced at the dawn of the Reformation.

❖ In a small chapel in France, a dissenting group of Roman Catholics has met for worship. The Mass they celebrate is almost entirely in Latin, because this group (along with hundreds like it in Europe and North America) has rejected the form of the mass given in the twentieth-century Second Vatican Council. Rather, they believe that the form of the Mass given at the Council of Trent during the Catholic Reform is the only permissible form. Other features of this Mass are kept as well: old-style chants and hymns, women with their heads covered, and the priest saying most of the Mass facing the altar with his back to the congregation.

INTRODUCTION

The sixteenth century was an era of vast change in Western Christianity, change that would eventually shape Christianity throughout the world. The several movements for reform of church doctrine and practice in the late Middle Ages, and the growing forces of Christian humanism in the Renaissance, seemed to indicate that the time was right for widespread overhaul of Christianity. Martin Luther began this movement, and soon he and Rome had separated, with Luther forming an Evangelical (later called "Lutheran") church. The Anabaptist wing of reform arose almost simultaneously with the Lutheran movement. Then, in the "second generation," the Calvinist/Reformed

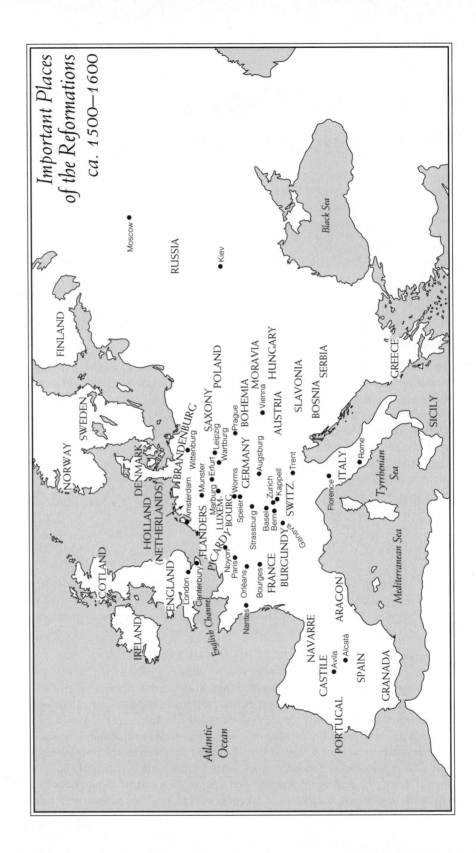

Important Places
of the Reformations
ca. 1500–1600

Atlantic
Ocean

IRELAND

SCOTLAND

ENGLAND
London
Canterbury

English Channel

Nantes

NORWAY

SWEDEN

FINLAND

DENMARK

HOLLAND
(NETHERLANDS)

FLANDERS
Amsterdam • Munster
BRANDENBURG
Wittenburg
Marburg • Erfurt
LUXEM- Worms Wartburg
PICARD- BOURG
Noyon • Speier
Paris Strassburg
Bourges Basel
FRANCE Bern Zurich
Geneva Kappell
BURGUNDY SWITZ.

Orléans

Leipzig SAXONY
GERMANY
Augsburg
Trent

POLAND

Prague BOHEMIA

MORAVIA

Vienna
AUSTRIA HUNGARY

SLAVONIA

BOSNIA SERBIA

Florence
ITALY

Rome •

Tyrrhenian
Sea

SICILY

Mediterranean Sea

NAVARRE

CASTILE

PORTUGAL

• Avila
Alcatá •
SPAIN

ARAGON

GRANADA

RUSSIA

Moscow •

Kiev •

Black Sea

GREECE

movement followed the Lutheran reform and became the most international wing of mainstream Protestantism. England also began a process of reform, directed by the monarch and resulting in an Anglican state church. After almost forty years of mostly ineffective responses, the Roman Catholic church finally dealt with the challenge of Protestantism, especially by instituting the reforms of the Council of Trent and with the activities of a zealous new religious order, the Society of Jesus (Jesuits). By the end of the century, Europe had been split between the Church of Rome and Protestantism in northern Europe, a Protestantism that was becoming increasingly aware of its political and religious pluralism. This split in Western Christianity was to prove more significant and harder to overcome than the old break between Rome and the Eastern Orthodox churches.

Names

The term **Reformation** is used in a variety of ways, and the student of Christianity must distinguish them carefully. The most basic sense of the term covers all the area of church reform in this period, both Protestant and Catholic. Because almost all Christian activity in Europe in the sixteenth century is related in some way to the Reformation, the whole period is often simply known as the **Reformation Era.** The **Protestant Reformation** covers all the Lutheran, Calvinist, Anglican, and Anabaptist activity but of course excludes the Catholic reform.

The Protestant Reformation is itself composed of two parts, usually called the Magisterial Reformation and the Radical Reformation. The **Magisterial Reformation** denotes the rise of the Lutheran, Calvinist, and Anglican churches; this is sometimes called the mainstream of the Reformation. It is called *magisterial* because in these churches the secular authorities (magistrates) had a role in the life of the church; church and state were closely tied. The **Radical Reformation** was concerned to separate the church from what it viewed as the godless state. *Radical* implies several things: going back to the "root" (Latin *radix*) of the New Testament; being against the magisterial Reformation; and propagating political and social teachings that were left of center, sometimes extremely so, for their time. (The Yale historian Roland Bainton called the Radicals "the left wing of the Reformation.") The Radical Reformers were initially called **Anabaptists,** "rebaptizers," because they insisted that only adults could be baptized; all Christians of the time, who had of course been baptized in the Catholic church as infants, needed to be rebaptized as adults.

The term **Protestant** derives from the official protest that many German princes and cities made against the decision of the imperial Diet of Speyer (1529), which decided to end toleration of Lutheranism in Germany. Although *Protestant* began as a term for Lutherans, it eventually became applied to other branches of the Reform as well, even to Anabaptists. (The term is also applied to Lutheran activity between 1517, the traditional date of the beginning of the Reformation, and 1529, which is obviously anachronistic.) In other words, *Protestant* became a generic word for "non-Roman Catholic Western Christians." Reformers (especially Lutherans) called themselves **Evangelicals,** following the gospel (*evangel*) of Christ. This term has persisted in Europe and America until today. For example, when several American Lutheran denominations merged into one church in the 1980s, they called their new church the "Evangelical Lutheran Church in America."

The term **Catholic Reformation** is used today to denote the correction and strengthening of the Roman church during this time, especially after the Council of Trent (1545). The Catholic Reformation corrected many abuses that Protestants (and contemporary humanists and medieval reformers before them) had complained about. It enforced higher standards for priests and bishops, clarified and reinforced key Catholic doctrines against the Protestant onslaught, and reformed monastic life. An older term for this activity, still used by some, is the **Counter-Reformation.** While much of the Catholic reform activity in the sixteenth century was indeed undertaken to counter the Protestant Reformation, the Catholic Reformation was much wider and deeper than that of a mere reaction to Protestantism. So the term *Counter-Reformation* has fallen somewhat into disuse as negative and misleading; *Catholic Reformation* is preferable, and will be used here. Some scholars, in order to avoid the confusion that sometimes results when both the Protestant and Catholic programs of change are called "Reformation," have taken to using the term **Catholic Reform.**

Historical Sketch

Movements for the reform of the life and doctrine of the church were prevalent in the later Middle Ages and became stronger in the Renaissance. Academic theologians, movements like the "Spiritual" Franciscans, and occasionally popes, led reforms that preserved the church in several crises and enabled it to adapt to changing times. This reform usually expressed itself *through* monasticism, the church hierarchy, and the other traditional structures of the Catholic church. It strengthened the life of the local churches and tended to reinforce the hierarchy of the church. Where occasionally reform did not express itself through and for the Catholic church, as for example in the cases of John Wycliffe (1329–1384) in England and John Hus (1373–1415) in Bohemia, it was declared heretical and stamped out by force.

With Martin Luther (1483–1546), however, a reform movement arose that soon turned *against* the traditional church. Luther was an Augustinian friar, a priest, and a professor of Bible studies at Wittenberg University in east central Germany. Like almost all would-be reformers before him, Luther initially saw himself as a loyal son of the Holy Mother Church, calling her back to her original purity. But he soon found himself so at odds with the Roman Catholic church that he moved to create an alternative church. Luther called for such thorough reforms that papacy, hierarchy, and monasticism would be done away with. He envisioned Germany, and probably other nations as well, having their own more indigenous forms of Christianity. He put no faith in the hierarchy to reform itself or in a new church council to right the perceived wrongs. Rather, Luther and his followers moved to put the Gospels, the essential religious message of Jesus Christ, at the center of Christianity. He stressed doctrines such as salvation by faith, not religious works; the central role of God's love/grace; and the sole authority of the Bible over the Church. When Luther's movement was protected and furthered by several German princes, it gained a foothold that would enable it to endure and spread to other parts of Germany. By the end of the sixteenth century, Evangelical reform had spread to much of Germany and all of Scandinavia.

The Radical (Anabaptist) Reformation arose during the 1520s in Zurich, Switzerland in connection with Huldreich Zwingli's magisterial reform there. Conrad Grebel (1498?–1526), one of the founders of the Swiss Brethren movement that soon became known as Anabaptism, and others insisted that Zwingli was inconsistent and half-hearted in his reforms. They argued for what they saw as pure "New Testament Christianity": baptism of adult believers only; separation of the church from the civil government; pacifism and refusal of military service; some common ownership of property; strict church discipline; and other practices. In the 1520s, the movement spread through Switzerland and later found a home in all Protestant lands, where Lutheranism and Calvinism had to contend with it. Eventually Anabaptists (and their successors, the Baptists) became the most widespread Protestant church, even spreading to lands like Russia where other Protestant churches could not penetrate.

Like the Anabaptist movement, the **Reformed Church** or **Calvinist** branch of Protestantism was born in the political world of the Swiss city-republics. (Here the term *reform* gets even more complex. In a sense, all Protestant churches were "reformed," but the churches born of the Calvinist branch of the Reformation called themselves in particular the Reformed Church, a name that has continued until today.) Zwingli began the Reformed movement in Zurich, but in the next three decades it shifted to Berne, Basel, and especially French-speaking Geneva. There the Frenchman John Calvin (1509–1564), who had studied at the University of Paris, reformed the city to Protestant ideals. He stressed (in addition to Luther's main ideas) such teachings as the sovereignty of God over all life, divine predestination to salvation, and human responsibility to live out one's Christian calling in everyday life. Like Luther, Calvin wrote prolifically, and soon his ideas for reform spread throughout Europe. Calvin was known not only as a biblical commentator, but as a systematizer of Protestant Christianity; his book, *The Institutes* [Foundations] *of the Christian Religion,* became the leading textbook of Protestantism. Calvinist churches were found by the end of the century not only in Switzerland, but also in France, the Low Countries, Germany, Hungary, and Scotland. Calvinism also had, of all the branches of the Reformation, the leading role in the rise of English Protestantism, both its Anglican (state) Church and the dissenting churches. From England Calvinism came to America via the Puritans and had a rich influence on the formation of the American religious and political character.

Reformation came to England by way of politics. Because King Henry VIII had earlier written against Luther, Pope Leo X gave him the title "Defender of the Faith." But soon Henry would oppose the pope over his right to divorce and remarry. In 1529 Henry began the process of forming an "Anglican [English] Church" under his control which was to become a middle way between Catholic and Protestant, especially in worship and organization. By the reign of his daughter Elizabeth I, the Anglican Church was firmly established in the land.

The Catholic Reformation was slow in coming. Late medieval movements and councils within the church had carried out some reforms. When independent movements, such as the Lollards in England or the followers of Jan Hus in Moravia, threatened more thorough reforms, the church violently subdued them. The church first tried to stamp out Lutheranism by condemning it, then by trying to turn the political leaders of the Holy Roman Empire against Luther. Protestants and many reform-minded Catholics hoped that Pope Leo X would be forced to call an ecumenical council to reform the church, but for political reasons the pope was reluctant to do so. When the initial measures did not prove effective, in 1545 Pope Paul III finally called a Council at Trent in northern Italy to strike back at Protestantism. Widespread reforms of church life resulted, and many of the more glaring abuses that humanists and reformers had complained about were removed. With the help of the Jesuit order, the reforms of Trent were carried out in nations and regions that were still predominantly Roman Catholic. Even there, the reforms of Trent were subject to national policy; for example, France rejected them as too conservative and intrusive, and Spain rejected them as too liberal. For areas that had already become mostly Protestant (half of Europe above the Alps), the reforms of Trent were "too little, too late." Other features of the Catholic Reformation included a revival of mysticism, especially in Spain, and a new focus on the system of Thomas Aquinas as a theological bulwark against Protestant thought. In all, the Roman church emerged severely chastened in numbers and political influence, but strengthened in spirit.

To conclude this historical sketch: the sixteenth century was an era of tumultuous change, unleashing an impulse for reform that was to continue in Western Christianity for centuries. In Protestantism, efforts at continual reform led to increasing fragmentation of the unity of the church, both for theological and national differences. In Roman Catholicism, the reforms of Trent would solidify the continuing structures and theology of the Catholic church, so much so that we can speak of "Tridentine (Trentian) Catholicism." In the era of Reformation, Christianity became much more diverse and invigorated; it also became fractured and divisive. Only the events of the twentieth century, a new era of reform in the Protestant and especially the Roman Catholic church, would begin to reverse the fragmentation of Christianity that began in the sixteenth century.

Literary Genres of the Primary Sources

The sixteenth century was a polemical age, and its writings reflect verbal warfare. Protestants attacked Roman Catholic Christianity, Roman Catholics attacked Protestantism, and then the various Protestant groups attacked each other. Many of the older literary genres in Christianity—history, hymns, liturgies, and systematic writings—were adapted for the new situation of the Reformation. A few new genres, especially the confession and catechism, were invented as well.

Polemical writings often took the form of **theses,** propositions for debate, usually academic debate. Luther's famous document that (seen in retrospect) began the Reformation, the *Ninety-Five Theses,* is such a list of propositions for debate. Sometimes the individual theses became longer and were called "articles of belief." Such articles, formed into lists, such as the *Twelve Articles of the Peasants,* often made up the manifestos of Protestant movements. In reading such lists, you will want not only to note the different points they relate, but also to relate these points to each other and analyze the view of Christianity they present.

Because the reform of Christianity was deeply connected to the politics and government of the time, religious edicts from kings and queens are an important primary source of our knowledge of the sixteenth century. German princes, the Holy Roman Emperor, the kings of France and England all find a voice in this chapter. These laws and decrees are cast in a usually formal legal format—complex, comprehensive, and verbose. Each law or decree is generally presented in one sentence. Here you must read for the main point of the law and relate it to its context in history.

Liturgical literature, especially the Mass, undergoes change in this period. All Reformers, even Anabaptists who tried to bypass completely the Roman liturgy, adapted the basic form of the Mass: gathering, confession, scripture, sermon, communion, and dismissal. Luther adapted it in his *German Mass,* and Pope Pius V, under the charge of Trent, revised the Latin Mass and imposed it on the whole Catholic Church. Protestants also wrote new hymns to express their vision of Christian doctrine and piety. Martin Luther was an accomplished musician with a high view of the role of music in worship; he wrote many hymns to express his theology and gave them popular tunes. Calvin was not a musician, but he brought to Geneva one of the best French poets of the day to metrify the psalms for use by the people in worship.

Some academic theological writings can also be found in the Reformation period, although the tumult of the times did not encourage the kind of leisurely, comparatively dispassionate theologizing that Scholastic writers in the high Middle Ages enjoyed. Most Protestant writings are not systemic, sustained treatments of Christian doctrine. Luther, whose treatises tend to deal with one subject at a time, produced almost none of this; the Anabaptists produced even less. (Some Protestants were too busy surviving hostility from Catholics and other Protestants to explain themselves systematically!) The only true systematic theologian of the major reformers is John Calvin, whose *Institutes of the Christian Religion* grew over several editions to be the most comprehensive and influential statement of Protestant Christianity to emerge from the sixteenth century.

Two new genres emerge in this period, the confession and the catechism. **Confessions** are lengthy, definitive formulations of doctrine. They grew out of the ancient creeds but were so lengthy and intricate that they were never recited in worship. The first true confession in the Christian tradition is the (Lutheran) Augsburg Confession of 1530. Other confessions, such as the Schleitheim Confession of the Anabaptists, followed in Protestantism, and in a sense the Roman Catholic *Profession of Tridentine Faith* is a confession as well.

Catechism comes from the Greek word "to teach." In the ancient and medieval church converts and youths were taught the faith by means of question-and-answer manuals. The Reformers also wrote documents setting out the basics of the faith by the responsive method and used them much more extensively than they had ever been used before. Luther used the term to describe his *Smaller Catechism* of 1529 and from him it carried on to all other Protestant documents of the sort. Luther's catechism explains the Ten Commandments, the Apostles' Creed, the Lord's Prayer, and the sacraments. The instruction of the common people in the basics of Christianity by means of the catechism was a hallmark of Protestantism in the Reformation. It worked so well that soon the Catholic Reformation imitated it. Peter Canisius' *Sum of Christian Doctrine* (1554) was the first to explain Catholic Christianity in catechism form, with

211 questions and answers. The catechism then became one of the major tools for the teaching of doctrine in Catholicism.

EVENTS

A Critique of the Church's Ills*

The Dutch scholar Erasmus was the leading Christian humanist at the dawn of the reform. He wished the church to be reformed from within, returning to the teachings of Christ. Both the Protestant and Catholic reforms eventually passed him by, but his writings have had enormous influence in his own time and through the ages. The Praise of Folly has gone through more than 600 editions since its first publication in 1509. A satirical work, it nevertheless powerfully criticizes a church Erasmus sees as badly in need of correction.[1]

The next I place among the regiment of fools are those who make a business of telling or inquiring after incredible stories of miracles and prodigies. Never doubting that a lie will choke them, they muster up a thousand strange stories of spirits, ghosts, apparitions, raisings of the devil, and similar bogeys of superstition. The farther they are from being probably true, the more greedily they are swallowed, and the more devoutly believed. These absurdities not only bring an empty pleasure and cheap entertainment, but they are a good business and produce a comfortable income for those priests and friars who profit by them.

Closely related to these are other people who attribute strange powers to the shrines and images of saints and martyrs. They would make their credulous proselytes believe that if they pay their devotion to St. Christopher in the morning, they shall be guarded and secured that day from all dangers and misfortunes. Soldiers, when they first take arms, come and mumble over such a set prayer before the picture of St. Barbara, thinking they shall return safe from all engagements. If someone prays to St. Erasmus[2] on particular holidays, with the ceremony of wax candles and other affectations, he shall in a short time be rewarded with a plentiful increase of wealth and riches. . . .

What shall I say about those who hawk and maintain the cheat of pardons and indulgences?[3] Do people rightly think that by these things each soul's residence in purgatory is computed, and assigned a longer or shorter stay, according to how many of these paltry pardons they buy? . . .

To list all [the saints] would be extremely tedious. There is a Catholic saint petitioned to on every occasion, especially the Virgin Mary, whose blind devotees think it is proper now to place before her Son. The content of these prayers and intercessions is no more than downright folly. . . .

Now if any serious wise man should stand up and unseasonably speak the truth, telling every one that a pious life is the only way of securing a happy death; that the best title to a pardon of our sins is purchased by a hearty abhorrence of our guilt and sincere resolutions of amendment; that the best devotion which can be paid to any saints is to imitate them in their exemplary life—if he

---

* Desiderius Erasmus, *The Praise of Folly*
[1] Taken, with editing, from Desiderius Erasmus, *The Praise of Folly* (London: Hamilton & Adams, 1887), 90–96, 143–49, 164–69.

[2] *Erasmus:* the saint after whom Desiderius Erasmus is named.
[3] *indulgences:* documents certifying the forgiveness of temporal punishment still owed to God after sin is forgiven.

should proceed in this way to inform them of their mistakes, there would be quite a different estimate put upon tears, vigils, Masses, fastings, and other severities. . . .

Now for some reflections upon cardinals and bishops, who in pomp and splendor have almost equaled if not outdone secular princes. . . . As to their flock, they either commend them to the care of Christ himself, or commit them to the guidance of some inferior vicars and curates. They do not even remember what their name of bishop entails, namely, labor, pains and diligence. Instead, by base simony[4] they are in a profane sense *Episcopi*, i.e., they are overseers of their own gain and income.[5] . . .

The popes of Rome pretend themselves Christ's vicars. But their status would be in a better condition if they would only imitate Christ's exemplary life, [if they would practice] a continuous course of preaching [and] and poverty, nakedness, hunger and a contempt of this world; if they only would consider the meaning of the word "pope," which signifies a father; or if they practiced their surname of "most holy." . . .

But all this supposes that [the popes] understand what circumstances they are placed in. By a wholesome neglect of thinking, they live as well as the heart can wish. Whatever toil and drudgery belongs to their office they assign to St. Peter or St. Paul, who have time enough to mind it. But anything of pleasure and grandeur they assume to themselves. . . . No people live more to their own ease and content. They think that they satisfy that Master they pretend to serve, our Lord and Savior, with their great state and magnificence, with the ceremonies of installments, with the titles of reverence and holiness, and with exercising their episcopal function only in blessing and cursing.

---

[4] *Simony*: the practice of buying church offices.
[5] *Episcopi . . . overseers*: the Latin word for bishop, *episcopus*, is based on a Greek word that means "overseer."

Sermon for the Sale of Indulgences*

Despite the criticism of indulgences by Erasmus and others, the practice grew. To raise funds for the rebuilding of St. Peter's Church in Rome, Pope Leo X organized the sale of indulgences in Germany, Poland and Scandinavia. One of the German supervisors was the Dominican monk John Tetzel, an experienced and effective seller of indulgences. Tetzel wrote and sent to every parish in his area instructions to priests on the sale of indulgences and included sample sermons on indulgences for their use. This short segment from the second of these sermons shows the emotional power that preachers used to sell indulgences.[6]

Do you not hear the voice of your parents and other deceased loved ones crying loudly and saying, "Have mercy, have mercy on me, especially you my friends, because the hand of the Lord has touched me! We are in strong punishment and torment, from which you are able to rescue us with only a little money, but yet you do not want to!" Open your ears, as the father says to his son and the mother says to her daughter, "Why do you punish me, and are not satisfied with my flesh?" It is as if they were saying, "We gave you birth, we fed you, we raised you, we left you our earthly goods, and yet you are cruel and hard to us. You are able to free us easily [by purchase of indulgences], but you let us lie in flames, and you delay the glory promised to us."

---

* John Tetzel, *Specimen Sermon 2*
[6] Translated from Latin by the author from B. J. Kidd, *Documents Illustrative of the Continental Reformation* (Oxford: Clarendon Press, 1911), 18.

Luther's Protest against Indulgences*

Luther proposed these theses, or points for debate, on October 31, 1517, traditionally regarded as the date of the Reformation's beginning. Luther also sent a copy of his theses, with a cover letter, to Prince Albert of Mainz. Unknown to Luther, and so not reflected in the theses, Albert was (by prior arrangement with the church) using half of the indulgence proceeds to repay the Fugger banking family money he had paid the pope to secure the archbishopric of Mainz. The theses, which drew in part on popular discontent with indulgences, were quickly published and widely circulated in Germany and beyond. They contain the basis for Luther's later view of Christianity: forgiveness comes from the free grace of God based on the death of Jesus; salvation is gained by faith, not by religious deeds; the gospel must rule the church.[7]

Out of love and zeal for truth and the desire to bring it to light, the following theses will be publicly discussed at Wittenberg under the chairmanship of the reverend father Martin Luther, Master of Arts and Sacred Theology and regularly appointed Lecturer on these subjects at that place. He requests that those who cannot be present to debate orally with us do so by letter.[8] In the name of Our Lord Jesus Christ; amen.

1. When our Lord and Master Jesus Christ said, "Repent,"[9] he wanted the entire life of believers to be one of repentance. 2. This word cannot be understood as referring to the sacrament of penance, that is, confession and satisfaction as administered by the clergy. 3. Yet it does not mean solely inner repentance; such inner repentance is worthless unless it produces various outward mortifications of the flesh. 4. The penalty of sin remains as long as the hatred of self, that is, true inner repentance, until our entrance into the kingdom of heaven.

5. The pope neither desires nor is able to remit any penalties except those imposed by his own authority or that of the canons. 6. The pope cannot remit any guilt except by declaring and showing that God has remitted it. . . .

27. Those who say, "As soon as the money clinks into the money chest, the soul flies out of purgatory" preach only human doctrines.[10] 28. It is certain that when money clinks in the money chest, greed and avarice can be increased. The church intercedes, but the result is in the hands of God alone. . . . 32. Those who believe that they can be certain of their salvation because they have indulgence letters will be eternally damned, together with their teachers. 33. Men must especially be on their guard against those who say that the pope's pardons are that priceless gift of God by which we are reconciled to him. . . .

35. They who teach that contrition is not necessary for those who intend to buy souls out of purgatory or buy confessional privileges preach unchristian doctrine. 36. Any truly repentant Christian has a right to full remission of penalty and guilt, even without indulgence letters. 37. Any true Christian, whether living or dead, participates in all the blessings of Christ and the church; and this is granted him by God, even without indulgence letters. . . .

40. A Christian who is truly contrite seeks to pay penalties for his sins. The bounty of indulgences, however, relaxes penalties and causes men to hate them; at least it furnishes occasion for hating them. . . . 55. It is certainly the pope's sentiment that if indulgences, which are a very insignificant thing, are celebrated with one bell, one procession, and one ceremony, then the gospel, which is the very greatest thing, should be

---

* Martin Luther, *Ninety-Five Theses*

[7] Translated by the author from *Kritische Gesamtausgabe der Werke Luthers*, vol. 1 (Weimar, 1804).

[8] No debate on the *Ninety-Five Theses* was in fact held, but they were widely spread by word of mouth and publication in the press.

[9] Matthew 4:17.

---

[10] *They preach . . . flies out of purgatory:* this thesis refers to the rhyme that indulgence sellers were said to use, "As soon as the coin into the coffer rings, the soul from purgatory springs."

preached with a hundred bells, a hundred processions, a hundred ceremonies. . . .

81. This unbridled preaching of indulgences makes it difficult even for learned men to rescue the reverence which is due the pope from slander, or from the shrewd questions of the laity. 82. For example: "Why does not the pope simply empty purgatory for the sake of holy love and the dire need of the souls that are there?". . . 86. Again, "Why does not the pope, whose wealth is greater than the wealth of the richest Crassus, build the Basilica of St. Peter with his own money rather than with the money of poor believers?" . . . 90. To repress these very sharp arguments of the laity by force alone, and not to resolve them by giving reasons, exposes the church and the pope to the ridicule of their enemy and makes Christians unhappy. . . .

92. Away then with all those prophets who say to the people of Christ, "Peace, peace," and there is no peace. 93. Away with all those prophets who say to the people of Christ, "Cross, cross," and there is no cross. 94. Christians should be exhorted to be diligent in following Christ their Head through penalties, death, and hell. 95. Thus they will be confident of entering into heaven through many tribulations rather than through the false security of peace.

Luther Defies Charges of Heresy*

Emperor Charles V was not persuaded by Luther's writings and was distressed by the controversy they aroused. In 1521, he summoned Luther to a trial at the Diet (assembly of nobles) meeting in Worms. Luther, facing a charge of heresy, dramatically and resolutely appealed to justification by faith and refused to recant. Johann Eck, with whom he had recently debated, interrogated him.[11]

Eck: "His Imperial Majesty has assigned this time to you, Martin Luther, to answer for the books which you yesterday openly acknowledged to be yours. . . . Now at last reply to the demand of his Majesty, whose clemency you have experienced in obtaining time to deliberate. Do you wish to defend all of your books or to retract part of them?"

Luther: "I beg your Most Sacred Majesty and your Lordships to consider that all my books are not of the same kind. In some I have treated piety, faith, and morals so simply and evangelically that my adversaries themselves are forced to confess that these books are useful, innocent, and worthy to be read by Christians. Even the bull,[12] though fierce and cruel, states that some things in my books are harmless, although it condemns them by a judgment simply monstrous. If I should undertake to recant these, would I alone not damn the truth which all, friends and enemies alike, confess?

"The second class of my works opposes the papacy for laying waste all Christendom, body and soul. No one can deny or dissemble this fact, since common complaints witness that the consciences of all believers are snared, harassed, and tormented by the laws of the Pope and the doctrines of men. Also, the goods of this famous German nation have been and are devoured in numerous and ignoble ways. Yet the Canon Law provides that the laws and doctrines of the Pope contrary to the Gospel and the Fathers are to be held erroneous and rejected. If, therefore, I should withdraw these books, I would add strength to tyranny and open windows and doors to their impiety. . . .

"In a third sort of books I have written against some private individuals who defend the Roman tyranny and tear down my pious doctrine. I confess I was more bitter than is proper for a

---

* Martin Luther, Speech before the Diet of Worms
[11] Taken, with editing, from C. D. Warner, *Library of the World's Best Literature* (New York: Warner, 1913), 9328–32.

---

[12] *bull:* official papal document condemning Luther's attack on indulgences.

minister of religion. For I do not pose as a saint, nor do I discuss my life but the doctrine of Christ. Yet neither is it right for me to recant what I have said in these books, for then tyranny and impiety would rage and reign against the people of God more violently than ever. . . .

"From this I think it is sufficiently clear that I have carefully considered and weighed the discords, perils, imitations, and dissension excited by my teaching, concerning which I was gravely and urgently admonished yesterday. To me the happiest part of the whole affair is that the Word of God is made the object of debate and dissent. . . . We must fear God. I do not say this as though your Lordships needed either my teaching or my admonition, but because I could not shirk the duty I owed Germany. With these words I commend myself to your Majesty and your Lordships, humbly begging that you will

not let my enemies make me hateful to you without cause."

Eck: "Luther, you have not answered the question. . . . I beg you to give a simple, unsophisticated answer without horns[13]: Will you recant or not?"

Luther: "Since your Majesty and your Lordships ask for a plain answer, I will give you one without either horns or teeth. Unless I am convicted by Scripture or by right reason (for I trust neither in popes nor in councils, since they have often erred and contradicted themselves), I am bound by the texts of the Bible, and my conscience is captive to the Word of God. I cannot and will not recant anything, since it is neither right nor safe to act against one's conscience. Here I stand; I can do nothing else. God help me. Amen."

---

[13] *without horns:* unqualified.

The Peasants' Revolt*

In 1525, peasants in southern and central Germany revolted violently. Unrest over their unjust treatment had been brewing for centuries, but now Luther's attacks on evils in the established order helped to ignite a war, and soon almost 300,000 peasants were under arms. Some of them were led by a priest turned radical reformer, Thomas Müntzer. The first reading shows Müntzer's sympathy with the peasants and his aggressive attitude to Luther.[14] The second is the Twelve Articles of the Peasants, a confession of their faith and appeal for justice.[15] Luther agreed with most of the articles, but when the peasants revolted violently to secure them, Luther turned against them and penned the

third reading, commanding that the revolt be put down at all costs.[16] The brutal massacres that resulted damaged the cause of the Protestant reform, as the peasants turned against Luther and Roman Catholics saw the war as a divine judgment against Protestantism.

That indulgent fellow, Father Pussyfoot,[17] comes along and says I want to stir up an insurrection. . . . He suppresses the most vital point[:] . . . the power of the sword as well as the key to release sins is in the hand of the whole community. . . . There is no greater abomination on earth than when no one is prepared to take up the cause of the needy.

The poor flatterer tries to use Christ to cover himself, adducing a counterfeit type of clemency, which is contrary to Paul's text in I Timothy 1. . . .

---

* Thomas Müntzer, *Vindication and Refutation; Twelve Articles of the Peasants;* Martin Luther, *Against the Murdering and Pillaging Peasants*

[14] From Peter Matheson, *The Collected Works of Thomas Müntzer* (Edinburgh: Clark, 1988), 334–35, 348. Used by permission.

[15] Taken, with editing, from *Translations and Reprints from the Original Sources of European History,* vol. 2, no. 6 (Philadelphia: University of Pennsylvania, 1905), 25–29.

---

[16] Taken, with editing, from Preserved Smith, *Life and Letters of Martin Luther* (New York: Houghton Mifflin, 1911).

[17] *Father Pussyfoot:* Luther, whom Müntzer thought was too half hearted in his reforms.

He suppresses here, however, the basic reason for all theft. . . . The evil brew from which all usury, theft and robbery springs is the assumption of our lords and princes that all creatures are their property. The fish in the water, the birds in the air, the plants on the face of the earth—it all has to belong to them! Isaiah 5.[18] To add insult to injury, they have God's commandment proclaimed to the poor: God has commanded that you should not steal. But it does them no good. For while they do violence to everyone, flay and fleece the poor farm worker, tradesman and everything that breathes, Micah 3, yet should any of the latter commit the pettiest crime, he must hang. And Doctor Liar[19] responds, Amen. The lords themselves make the poor man their enemy. If they refuse to do away with the causes of insurrection how can trouble be avoided in the long run? If saying that makes me an inciter to insurrection, so be it!

The insane folly of your boasting simply sends one to sleep. That you stood up at Worms before the Empire is to the credit of the German nobility, whose great mouths you smeared with honey, for they were quite sure that your preaching would present them with monasteries and foundations on the Bohemian pattern.[20] Now you promise these to the princes. . . . You and your followers resorted to crazy tricks and deceptions. You let yourself be captured at your own suggestion and then pretended it was against your will. Anyone who had not seen through your rascally behavior would swear that you are a pious Martin indeed.

Sleep softly, dear flesh! I would prefer to smell you roasting in your arrogance in a pot or in a cauldron by the fire, Jeremiah 1, smitten by God's wrath, and then stewing in your own juice. May the devil devour you! Ezekiel 23. Your flesh is like that of an ass; it would be a long time cooking and would turn out to be a tough dish indeed for your mealy-mouth friends.

[*Twelve Articles of the Peasants*] Many evil writings put forth of late take occasion, on account of the assembling of the peasants, to cast scorn upon the Gospel, saying: Is this the fruit of the new teaching,[21] that no one should obey but all should everywhere rise in revolt, and rush together to reform, or perhaps destroy entirely, the authorities, both ecclesiastical and lay? The articles below shall answer these godless and criminal faultfinders. They shall also serve to remove the reproach from the word of God and to give a Christian reason for the disobedience or even the revolt of the entire Peasantry. . . . In the second place, it is clear that the peasants demand that this Gospel be taught them as a guide in life, and they ought not to be called disobedient or disorderly. . . .

First, it is our humble petition and desire, as also our will and resolution, that in the future we should have power and authority so that each community should choose and appoint a pastor. We should have the right to depose him should he conduct himself improperly. The pastor thus chosen should teach us the Gospel pure and simple. . . .

Second, since the just tithe is established by the Old Testament and fulfilled in the New, we are ready and willing to pay the fair tithe of grain. . . . We desire that for the future our church provost, whomever the community may appoint, shall gather and receive this tithe. From this he shall give to the pastor, elected by the whole community, a decent and sufficient maintenance for him and his, according to the judgment of the whole community. What remains over shall be given to the poor of the place. . . .

Third, it has been the custom until now for men to hold us as their own property. This is pitiable, considering that Christ has delivered and redeemed us all, without exception, by the shedding of his precious blood, the lowly as well as the great. Accordingly, it is consistent with Scripture

---

[18] *Isaiah 5:* Müntzer's writings are studded with quick citations of the Bible in this fashion.

[19] *Dr. Liar:* Luther. The German word for liar, *Lügner,* is similar to "Luther."

[20] *for they were quite sure . . . pattern:* in the Hus movement of the previous century, the monasteries were secularized and taken over by the princes.

---

[21] *the new teaching:* Protestant reforms.

that we should be free and wish to be so . . . unless it should be shown us from the Gospel that we are serfs.

Fourth,[22] it has been the custom that no poor man should be allowed to touch venison or wild fowl, or fish in flowing water. This seems to us quite unseemly and unbrotherly, as well as selfish and not agreeable to the word of God. . . .

Fifth, we are aggrieved in the matter of wood-cutting, for the noble folk have appropriated all the woods to themselves alone. . . . It should be free to every member of the community to help himself to such firewood as he needs in his own home. . . .

Sixth, excessive services are demanded of us, which are increased from day to day. We ask that this matter be properly looked into, so that we shall not continue to be oppressed in this way. . . .

Seventh, we will no longer allow ourselves to be oppressed by our lords, but will let them demand only what is just and proper according to the word of the agreement between the lord and the peasant. . . .

Eighth, we are greatly burdened by holdings, which cannot support the rent exacted from them. The peasants suffer loss in this way and are ruined. We ask that the lords may appoint persons of honor to inspect these holdings, and fix a rent in accordance with justice. . . .

Tenth, we are aggrieved by the appropriation by individuals of meadows and fields, which at one time belonged to a community. These we will take again into our own hands. It may, however, happen that the land was rightfully purchased, but when the land has unfortunately been purchased in this way, some brotherly arrangement should be made according to circumstances.

Eleventh, we will entirely abolish the due called Todfall,[23] and will no longer endure it, nor allow widows and orphans to be thus shamefully robbed against God's will. . . .

Twelfth, it is our conclusion and final resolution, that if any one or more of the articles here set forth should not be in agreement with the word of God, as we think they are, such article we will willingly recede from, when it is proved really to be against the word of God by a clear explanation of the scripture. . . . Likewise, if more complaints should be discovered, which are based upon truth and the scriptures, and relate to offences against God and our neighbor, we have determined to reserve the right to present these also, and to exercise ourselves in all Christian teaching. For this we shall pray God, since He can grant these, and he alone. The peace of Christ abide with us all.

[Luther, *Against the Murdering and Pillaging Peasants*] In my former book[24] I dared not judge the peasants, since they asked to be instructed, and Christ says, "Judge not." But before I could look around they forget their request and take to violence. They rob, rage, and act like mad dogs, whereby one may see what they had in their false minds, and that their pretense to speak in the name of the gospel in the Twelve Articles was a simple lie. They do the devil's work, and especially that Satan of Mühlhausen[25] does nothing but rob, murder, and pour out blood. . . .

Therefore, my lords, free, save, help, and pity the poor people; stab, smite, and slay all you that can. If you die in battle you could never have a more blessed end, for you die obedient to God's Word in Romans 13, and in the service of love to free your neighbor from the hands of hell and the devil. I implore everyone who can to avoid the peasants as he would the devil himself. I pray God will enlighten them and turn their hearts. But if they do not turn, I wish them no happiness forevermore. . . . No one who considers how intolerable this rebellion is should think that this is too hard.

---

[22] Articles 4, 5, and 10 develop the Anabaptist views on common property.

[23] *Todfall:* the feudal tax paid to the lord by survivors upon the death of a male peasant.

[24] *my former book:* Luther's *Exhortation to Peace,* written earlier in 1525, which counsels both nobles and peasants to moderate their claims and reach a just compromise.

[25] *Satan of Mühlhausen:* Müntzer.

The Trial and Death of Michael Sattler*

Michael Sattler, the author of the Schleitheim Confession, *had been a priest in the Catholic Church before becoming a leading Anabaptist. He was tried for heresy in Austria and executed in 1527. This selection from an Anabaptist book of martyrs written in 1660 shows the main points of his belief and the tenacity with which he held them.*[26]

After many legal transactions on the day of his departure from this world, the articles against him being many . . . Michael Sattler . . . requested that they might once more be read to him and that he might again be heard upon them. . . . He undauntedly answered as follows: "In regard to the articles relating to me and my brethren and sisters, hear this brief answer:

"First, that we have acted contrary to the imperial mandate, we do not admit. For the same says that the Lutheran doctrine and delusion is not to be adhered to, but only the gospel and the Word kept. We have kept this. I am not aware that we have acted contrary to the gospel and the Word of God. I appeal to the words of Christ.

[Here follows Sattler's brief statement and defense of seven charges, about the real presence of Christ in Communion, infant baptism, extreme unction, Mary, oaths before authorities, marriage of clergy, and pacifism.][27] "In conclusion, ministers of God, I admonish you to consider the purpose for which God has appointed you, to punish the evil and to defend and protect the pious. Because we have not acted contrary to God and the gospel, you will find that neither I nor my brothers and sisters have offended in word or

deed against any authority. If you have neither heard nor read the Word of God, send for the most learned men and for the sacred books of the Bible in whatsoever language they may be and let them confer with us in the Word of God. If they prove to us with the Holy Scriptures that we err and are in the wrong, we will gladly desist and recant and also willingly suffer the sentence and punishment for that of which we have been accused. But if no error is proven to us, I hope to God that you will be converted and receive instruction."

Upon this speech the judges laughed and put their heads together, and the town clerk said: "Yes, you infamous, desperate rascal of a monk, should we dispute with you? The hangman will dispute with you, I assure you!" Michael responded, "God's will be done." . . .

Then the judges arose and went into another room where they remained for an hour and a half and determined on the sentence. In the meantime some of the soldiers in the room treated Michael Sattler most unmercifully, heaping reproach upon him. . . . When the judges returned to the room, the sentence was read. It was as follows: "In the case of the attorney of His Imperial Majesty vs. Michael Sattler, judgment is passed that Michael Sattler shall be delivered to the executioner, who shall lead him to the place of execution and cut out his tongue, then fasten him to a wagon and with red-hot tongs twice tear pieces from his body. After he has been brought outside the gate, he shall be torn five times more in the same manner . . ."

After this had been done in the manner prescribed, he was burned to ashes as a heretic. His fellow brothers were executed with the sword, and the sisters drowned. His wife, after being subjected to many pleas, admonitions and threats, under which she remained steadfast, was drowned a few days afterward. Done the 21st day of May, A.D. 1527.

---

* Thieleman van Braght, *Martyr's Mirror*
[26] From George H. Williams and Angel M. Mergal, eds. *Spiritual and Anabaptist Writers* (Philadelphia: Westminster, 1957). Copyright 1957, Westminster Press. Used by permission.
[27] Most of these items are discussed in the *Schleitheim Confession,* written by Sattler, which follows.

The King of England Becomes Head of the Anglican Church*

In 1532, Henry VIII required the clergy to submit to the national monarch. In 1534, Parliament passed an act making the monarch Supreme Head (later, under Elizabeth I, "Supreme Governor") of the Church of England. It gave the monarch the right to teach and enforce correct doctrine in the reform of the church. Henry argued that he was only reasserting the ancient rights of kings to guide the church in their realms.[28]

The king justly and rightfully is and ought to be the supreme head of the Church of England, and so is recognized by the clergy of this realm in their Convocations.[29] Yet nevertheless for corroboration and confirmation, and for increase of virtue in Christ's religion within this realm of England, and to repress and extirp all errors, heresies, and other enormities and abused heretofore used in the same; be it enacted by authority of this present Parliament, that the king our sovereign lord, his heirs and successors, kings of this realm, shall be taken, accepted, and reputed the only supreme head in earth of the Church of England called *Anglicana Ecclesia*.[30] He shall have and enjoy, annexed and united to the imperial crown of this realm, as well the title and style thereof, as all honors, dignities, preeminences, jurisdictions, privileges, authorities, immunities, profits, and commodities to the said dignity of supreme head of the same Church belonging and appertaining. Our said sovereign lord, his heirs and successors, kings of this realm, shall have full power and authority form time to time to visit, repress, redress, reform, order, correct, restrain, and amend all such errors, heresies, abuses, offences, contempts, and enormities, whatsoever they be, which by any manner spiritual authority or jurisdiction ought or may lawfully be reformed, repressed, ordered, redressed, corrected, restrained, or amended, most to the pleasure of Almighty God, the increase of virtue in Christ's religion, and for the conservation of the peace, unity, and tranquillity of this realm; any usage, custom, foreign law, foreign authority, prescription, or any other thing or things to the contrary notwithstanding.[31]

---

* English Parliament, *Supremacy Act*

[28] From Henry Gee and W. J. Hardy, *Documents Illustrative of English Church History* (London: Macmillan, 1896).

[29] *Convocations:* the meetings of clergy in Canterbury and York earlier in 1534, which recognized Henry as Supreme Head.

[30] *Anglicana Ecclesia:* the Anglican Church.

[31] *any usage . . . notwithstanding:* directly mainly at the Roman Catholic Church.

The Execution of Michael Servetus Contested**

Michael Servetus, a Spanish theologian and physician, wrote several books attacking orthodox Christian doctrine, both Catholic and Protestant. Condemned by the Inquisition in Vienne, he escaped to Geneva, where he was retried, convicted, and burned at the stake in 1553. John Calvin agreed with the verdict but vainly urged the more humane method of execution by beheading. Servetus' arrest and execution provoked a controversy over religious toleration. In the first reading, the Anabaptist David Joris appeals on Servetus' behalf; in the second, the Genevan court justifies its sentence.

Most noble, just, worthy, gracious, dear lords, now that I, your friend and brother in the Lord Jesus Christ, have heard what has happened to

---

** David Joris, Letter to Servetus's Judges; Court of Geneva, Verdict and Sentence for Michael Servetus

the good, worthy Servetus, how that he was delivered into your hands and power by no friendliness and love but through envy and hate, as will be made manifest in the days of judgment to those whose eyes are now blinded by cunning so that they cannot understand the ground of the truth. God give them to understand. The report has gone everywhere, and even to my ears, that the learned preachers or shepherds of souls have taken counsel and written to certain cities who have resolved to pass sentence to put him to death. This news has so stirred me that I can have no peace on behalf of our religion and the holy churches far and near, which stand fast in the love and unity of Christ, until I have raised my voice as a member of the body of Christ, until I have opened my heart humbly before your Highnesses and freed my conscience. I trust that the learned, perverted, carnal, and bloodthirsty may have no weight and make no impression on you, and if they should ingratiate themselves with you as did the scribes and Pharisees with Pilate in the case of our Lord Jesus, they will displease the King of kings and the teacher of all, Christ, who taught that no one should be crucified or put to death for his teaching.

He himself was rather crucified and put to death. Yes, not only that, but he has severely forbidden persecution. Will it not then be a great perversion, blindness, evil, and darkness to indulge in impudent disobedience through hate and envy? They must first themselves have been deranged before they could bring a life to death, damn a soul forever, and hasten it to hell. Is that a Christian procedure or a true spirit? I say eternally no, however plausible it may appear.

If the preachers are not of this mind and wish to avoid the sin against the Holy Spirit, let them be wary of seizing and killing men for their good intentions and belief according to their understanding, especially when these ministers stand so badly in other people's books that they dare not go out of their own city and land. Let them remember that they are called, sent, and anointed of God to save souls, to bring men to right and truth—that is, to make alive the dead, and

not to destroy, offend, and corrupt, let alone to take life. This belongs to him alone to whom it is given, who was crucified, who died, and who suffered. . . .

Noble, wise, and prudent lords, consider what would happen if free rein were given to our opponents to kill heretics. How many men would be left on earth if each had this power over the other, inasmuch as each considers the other a heretic? The Jews so regard the Christians, so do the Saracens and the Turks, and the Christians reciprocate. The papists and the Lutherans, the Zwinglians and the Anabaptists, the Calvinists and the Adiaphorists, mutually ban each other. Because of these differences of opinion should men hate and kill each other? "Whoso sheddeth man's blood, by man shall his blood be shed," as Scripture says. Let us, then, not take the sword, and if anyone is of an erroneous and evil mind and understanding let us pray for him and awaken him to love, peace, and unity. . . . And if the aforementioned Servetus is a heretic or a sectary before God . . . we should inflict on him no harm in any of his members, but admonish him in a friendly way and at most banish him from the city, if he will not give up his obstinacy and stop disturbing the peace by his teaching . . . that he may come to a better mind and no longer molest your territory. No one should go beyond this. . . .

The Lord himself will judge of soul and spirit and will separate the good from the bad. . . . He "maketh his sun to rise on the evil and the good" and wills that we should imitate him in his long-suffering, graciousness, and mercy. He instructed the servants, who wished to anticipate the harvest as the apostles wished to call down fire from heaven, to leave the tares with the wheat. At the harvest he will send his angels who have knowledge and understanding to separate the good from the bad, the lies from the truth, the pure from the impure, for God's judgments are true and eternal and cannot fail . . . but great insufficiency shall be found in men when the day of light and the spirit of perfection shall appear. . . .

Those who have an evil spirit should be instructed, not put to death in the time of their ignorance and blindness similar to Paul's. That no one should assume judgment, the Lord has given us a new commandment in love that we do unto others as we would that they should do unto us. So be merciful, kind, and good, doing as it has been done to your Honors, and as the Lord wishes. "Judge not that you be not condemned." Shed no blood and do no violence, my dear lords. Understand whose disciples you are, for nothing has the Lord punished more and forgiven less than the shedding of innocent blood and idolatry. Follow no one and believe in no one above God or Christ, who is Lord in spirit and truth. . . . Although I have withheld my name, you should not give this communication less consideration.

[Statement of the Genevan Court] Michael Servetus de Villeneufve of the Kingdom of Aragon in Spain some twenty-three or twenty-four years ago printed a book at Hagenau in Germany against the Holy Trinity containing many great blasphemies to the scandal of the said churches of Germany, which book he freely confesses to have printed in the teeth of the remonstrances made to him by the learned and evangelical doctors of Germany. Nevertheless he continued in his errors, and, in order the more to spread the venom of his heresy, he printed secretly a book in Vienne of Dauphiny full of the said heresies and horrible, execrable blasphemies against the Holy Trinity, against the Son of God, against the baptism of infants and the foundations of the Christian religion. He confesses that in this book he called believers in the Trinity Trinitarians and atheists. He calls this Trinity a diabolical monster with three heads. He blasphemes detestably against the Son of God, saying that Jesus Christ is not the Son of God from eternity. He calls infant baptism an invention of the devil and sorcery. His execrable blasphemies are scandalous against the majesty of God, the Son of God and the Holy Spirit. This entails the murder and ruin of many souls. Moreover he wrote a letter to one of our ministers in which, along with other numerous blasphemies, he declared our holy evan-

gelical religion to be without faith and without God and that in place of God we have a three-headed Cerberus. He confesses that because of this abominable book he was made a prisoner at Vienne and perfidiously escaped. He has been burned there in effigy together with five bales of his books. Nevertheless, having been in prison in our city, he persists maliciously in his detestable errors and calumniates true Christians and faithful followers of the immaculate Christian tradition.

Wherefore we Syndics, judges of criminal cases in this city, having witnessed the trial conducted before us at the instance of our lieutenant against you "Michael Servetus de Villeneufve" of the Kingdom of Aragon in Spain, and having seen your voluntary and repeated confessions and your books, judge that you, Servetus, have for a long time promulgated false and thoroughly heretical doctrine, despising all remonstrances and corrections and that you have with malicious and perverse obstinacy sown and divulged even in printed books opinions against God the Father, the Son and the Holy Spirit, in a word against the fundamentals of the Christian religion, and that you have tried to make a schism and trouble the church of God by which many souls may have been ruined and lost, a thing horrible, shocking, scandalous and infectious. You have had neither shame nor horror of setting yourself against the divine Majesty and the Holy Trinity, and so you have obstinately tried to infect the world with your stinking heretical poison. . . . For these and other reasons, desiring to purge the church of God of such infection and cut off the rotten member, having taken counsel with our citizens and having invoked the name of God and the Holy Scriptures before our eyes, speaking in the name of the Father, Son and Holy Spirit, we now in writing give final sentence and condemn you, Michael Servetus, to be bound and taken to Champel and there attached to a stake and burned with your books to ashes. And so you shall finish your days and give an example to others who would commit the like.

Elizabeth I Enforces the "Middle Way"*

Queen Elizabeth I defended the "middle way" of Anglicanism against Roman Catholics (especially Jesuits) on the one hand and Puritans and other nonconformists on the other. Here is her 1593 decree forbidding Puritan worship and enforcing all her subjects to attend the official services of the Church of England, known here as "common prayer." Elizabeth was largely effective in establishing this middle way.[32]

For the preventing and avoiding of such great inconveniences and perils as might happen and grow by the wicked and dangerous practices of seditious sectaries and disloyal persons; be it enacted by the Queen's most excellent majesty, and by the Lords spiritual and temporal, and the Commons, in this present Parliament assembled, and by the authority of the same, that if any person or persons above the age of sixteen years, who shall obstinately refuse to repair to some church, chapel, or usual place of common prayer, to hear divine service established by her majesty's laws and statutes, and shall forbear to do the same by the space of a month, without lawful cause, shall at any time after forty days next after the end of this session of Parliament, by printing, writing, or express words or speeches, advisedly and purposely practice or go about to move or persuade any of her majesty's subjects, or any other within her highness's realms or dominions, to deny, withstand, and impugn her majesty's power and authority in causes ecclesiastical, united and annexed to the imperial crown of this realm; or to that end or purpose shall advisedly and maliciously move or persuade any other person whatsoever to forbear or abstain from coming to church to hear divine service, or to receive Communion according to her majesty's laws and statutes aforesaid, or to come to or be present at any unlawful assemblies, conventicles, or meetings, under colour or pretence of any exercise of religion, contrary to her majesty's said laws and statutes; or if any person or persons which shall obstinately refuse to go to some church, chapel, or usual place of common prayer, and shall forbear by the space of a month to hear divine service, as is aforesaid, shall after the said forty days, either of him or themselves, or by the motion, persuasion, enticement, or allurement of any other, willingly join, or be present at, any such assemblies, conventicles, or meetings, under colour or pretence of any such exercise of religion, contrary to the laws and statutes of this realm, as is aforesaid; that then every such person so offending as aforesaid, and being thereof lawfully convicted, shall be committed to prison, there to remain without bail or mainprise,[33] until they shall conform and yield themselves to come to some church, chapel, or usual place of common prayer, and hear divine service, according to her majesty's laws and statutes aforesaid, and to make such open submission and declaration of their said conformity, as hereafter in this Act is declared and appointed.

---

* English Parliament, *Act against Puritans*
[32] Taken from Gee and Hardy, *Documents Illustrative of English Church History*.

[33] *mainprise:* legal assurance to a court that one will produce an accused person for trial at a specified date.

Religious Liberty in France**

The Edict of Nantes, *issued by King Henry IV in 1598, gave French Protestants (who were mostly*

Reformed and controlled much of south central France) certain religious privileges and brought France a measure of peace after its Wars of Religion. It granted the Reformed free exercise of their faith in their areas (approximately 200 towns and

---

** Henry IV, *Edict of Nantes;* Louis XIV, *Revocation of the Edict of Nantes* *cities), and state subsidy for their troops and pastors. The Edict was unique in its time, for unlike other religious settlements it established toleration for most Protestants and Catholics to live side by side. When Louis XIV revoked the Edict of Nantes in 1685, turmoil resulted. Some 50,000 Huguenots disobeyed the Revocation by fleeing France, many of them coming to America.*[34]

Henry, by the grace God King of France and of Navarre, greeting: . . .

We have, by this perpetual and irrevocable edict, established and proclaimed and do establish and proclaim:

First, that the recollection of everything done by one party or the other between March, 1585,[35] and our accession to the crown, and during all the preceding period of troubles, remain obliterated and forgotten, as if no such things had ever happened. . . .

We ordain that the Catholic Apostolic and Roman religion shall be restored and reestablished in all places and localities of this our kingdom and countries subject to our sway, where the exercise of the same has been interrupted, in order that it may be peaceably and freely exercised, without any trouble or hindrance. We forbid very expressly all persons of whatever estate, quality, or condition, from troubling, molesting, or disturbing ecclesiastics in the celebration of divine service, in the enjoyment or collection of tithes, fruits, or revenues of their benefices, and all other rights and dues belonging to them. . . .

In order to leave no occasion for troubles or differences between our subjects, we have permitted, and herewith permit, those of the religion called Reformed to live and abide in all the cities and places of this our kingdom and countries of our sway, without being annoyed, molested, or compelled to do anything in the matter of religion contrary to their consciences . . . upon condition that they comport themselves in other respects according to that which is contained in this our present edict. . . .

We also permit those of the said religion to make and continue the exercise of the same in all villages and places of our dominion where it was established by them and publicly enjoyed several and divers times in the year 1597, up to the end of the month of August, notwithstanding all decrees and judgments to the contrary. . . .

We very expressly forbid to all those of the said religion its exercise, either in respect to ministry, regulation, discipline, or the public instruction of children, or otherwise, in this our kingdom and lands of our dominion, otherwise than in the places permitted and granted by the present edict. It is forbidden as well to perform any function of the said religion in our court or retinue, or . . . in our city of Paris. . . .

We also forbid all our subjects, of whatever quality and condition, from carrying off by force or persuasion, against the will of their parents, the children of the said religion, in order to cause them to be baptized or confirmed in the Catholic Apostolic and Roman Church. The same is forbidden to those of the said religion called Reformed, upon penalty of being punished with special severity. . . .

Books concerning the said religion called Reformed may not be printed and publicly sold, except in cities and places where the public exercise of the said religion is permitted.

We ordain that there shall be no difference or distinction made in respect to the said religion, in receiving pupils to be instructed in universities, colleges, and schools; nor in receiving the sick and poor into hospitals, retreats, and public charities.

[*Revocation of the Edict of Nantes*] Louis, by the grace of God King of France and Navarre, to all present and to come, greeting:

King Henry the Great, our grandfather of glorious memory, desired that the peace which he had procured for his subjects after the grievous

---

[34] Both readings taken, with editing, from James Harvey Robinson, *Readings in European History,* vol. 2.

[35] *March, 1585:* near the beginning of the French Wars of Religion between Protestants and Catholics.

losses they had sustained in the course of domestic and foreign wars should not be troubled on account of the so-called Reformed religion, as had happened in the reigns of the kings, his predecessors. By his edict, granted at Nantes in the month of April, 1598, he regulated the procedure to be adopted with regard to those of the said religion, and the places in which they might meet for public worship, established extraordinary judges to administer justice to them, and provided in particular articles for whatever could be thought necessary for maintaining the tranquillity of his kingdom and for diminishing mutual aversion between the members of the two religions, so as to put himself in a better position to labor, as he had resolved to do, for the reunion to the Church of those who had so lightly withdrawn from it.

And now we perceive, with thankful acknowledgment of God's aid, that our endeavors have attained their proposed end. . . . [W]e have determined that we can do nothing better . . . than entirely to revoke the said Edict of Nantes, with the special articles granted as a sequel to it, as well as all that has since been done in favor of the said religion.

We now suppress and revoke the edict of our said grandfather, given at Nantes in April, 1598, in its whole extent. . . . In consequence we desire, and it is our pleasure, that all the churches of those of the so-called Reformed religion, situated in our kingdom, countries, territories, and the lordships under our crown, shall be demolished without delay. We forbid our subjects of the so-called Reformed religion to meet any more for the exercise of the said religion in any place or private house, under any pretext whatever. . . .

We command all ministers of the so-called Reformed religion, who do not choose to become converts and to embrace the Catholic, apostolic, and Roman religion, to leave our kingdom and the territories subject to us within a fortnight of the publication of our present edict . . . on pain of being sent to the galleys.

We forbid private schools for the instruction of children of the so-called Reformed religion, and in general all things, whatever which can be regarded as a concession of any kind in favor of the said religion. As for children who may be born of persons of the so-called Reformed religion, we desire that now the parish priests baptize them. . . . [T]hereafter the children shall be brought up in the Catholic, apostolic, and Roman religion, which we expressly enjoin the local magistrates to see done. . . .

We repeat our most express prohibition to all our subjects of the so-called Reformed religion, together with their wives and children, against leaving our kingdom, lands, and territories subject to us, or transporting their goods and effects therefrom under penalty of the men being sent to the galleys and the women being imprisoned.

Jesuit Missions in Asia*

Francis Xavier, a charter member of the Jesuits, was an ideal Jesuit missionary. Although he has been criticized for a lack of understanding of Asian religions and his use of the Inquisition, his effective missionary work aroused much interest in Europe. In 1541, he went to India, where he converted thousands and established schools and a *college. In 1549 he sailed to Japan to introduce Catholicism there, and in 1552 he died while taking Christianity to the Chinese. He was canonized as a saint in 1622. This 1543 letter reporting his progress in India shows Xavier's zealous labors and strategy.*[36]

---

* Francis Xavier, Letter to the Society at Rome

[36] From H. J. Coleridge, *The Life and Letters of St. Francis Xavier* (London: Burns & Oates, 1876).

It is now the third year since I left Portugal. . . . Francis Mancias and I are now living among the Christians of Comorin. They are very numerous, and increase greatly every day. When I first came I asked them if they knew anything about our Lord Jesus Christ. . . . I picked out the most intelligent and well read of them, and then sought out with the greatest diligence men who knew both languages. We held meetings for several days, and by our joint efforts and with infinite difficulty we translated the Catechism into the Malabar tongue. I learned it by heart, and then I began to go through all the villages of the coast, calling around me by the sound of a bell as many as I could, children and men. I assembled them twice a day and taught them the Christian doctrine. Thus, in the space of a month, the children had it well by heart. And all the time I kept telling them to go on teaching in their turn whatever they had learned to their parents, family, and neighbors.

Every Sunday I collected them all, men and women, boys and girls, in the church. They came with great readiness and with a great desire for instruction. Then, in the hearing of all, I began by calling on the name of the most holy Trinity, Father, Son, and Holy Ghost, and I recited aloud the Lord's Prayer, the Hail Mary, and the [Apostles'] Creed in the language of the country: they all followed me in the same words, and delighted in it wonderfully. . . . We teach them the Commandments in [a similar] way. . . . I make them all, and particularly those who are to be baptized, repeat the form of general confession. . . .

You may understand from this how many people I brought into Christianity: it often happens that I am hardly able to use my hands from the fatigue of baptizing. Often in a single day I have baptized whole villages. Sometimes I have lost my voice and strength altogether with repeating again and again the Creed and the other forms. The fruit that is reaped by the baptism of infants, as well as by the instruction of children and others, is quite incredible. These children, I

trust heartily, by the grace of God, will be much better than their fathers. They show an ardent love for the Divine law, and an extraordinary zeal for learning our holy religion and imparting it to others. Their hatred for idolatry is marvelous. They get into feuds with the heathen about it, and whenever their own parents practice it, they reproach them and come to tell me at once. Whenever I hear of any act of idolatrous worship, I go to the place with a large band of these children, who very soon load the devil with a greater amount of insult and abuse than he has lately received of honor and worship from their parents, relations, and acquaintances. The children run at the idols, upset them, dash them down, break them to pieces, spit on them, trample on them, kick them about, and in short heap on them every possible outrage.

A great number of natives came from all parts to entreat me to take the trouble to go to their houses and call on God by the bedsides of their sick relatives. . . . Then I hit on a way of serving all at once. As I could not go myself, I sent around children whom I could trust in my place. They went to the sick persons, assembled their families and neighbors, recited the Creed with them, and encouraged the sufferers to conceive a certain and well founded confidence of their restoration. Then after all this, they recited the prayers of the Church. To make my tale short, God was moved by the faith and piety of these children and of the others, and restored a great number of sick persons' health both of body and soul. How good He was to them! He made the very disease of their bodies the occasion of calling them to salvation, and drew them to the Christian faith almost by force! I have also charged these children to teach the rudiments of Christian doctrine to the ignorant in private houses, in the streets, and the crossways. As soon as I see that this has been well started in one village, I go on to another and give the same instructions and the same commission to the children, and so I go through the whole number of their villages in order.

INSTITUTION

Luther Reforms the Mass*

As this reading makes clear, Luther was conservative in adapting the Latin Mass for his Evangelical churches. He retained most of the structure (gathering, confession, scripture, sermon, communion, dismissal) and wording of the Latin Mass. He did, however, insist on an end to all practices that smacked of transubstantiation and required that the Bible be preached well at every service. The following is Luther's reform of the Sunday service for the laity.[37]

The Mass vestments, altars, and lights may be retained until they shall change by themselves, or it shall please us to change them. If any will take a different course in this matter, we shall not interfere. But in the true Mass, among sincere Christians, the altar should not be retained, and the priest should always turn himself towards the people as, without doubt, Christ did at the Last Supper. That, however, must bide its time.

At the beginning then we sing a spiritual song or a psalm in German in the first tone. Then the Kyrie Eleison,[38] to the same tone, but three times and not nine times. . . . Then the priest reads a Collect[39]. . . . The Epistle is sung in the eighth tone.[40] . . . After the Epistle is sung a German hymn, "Now we pray to the Holy Spirit," or some other hymn, by the whole choir. Then the Gospel is read in the fifth tone, also with the face turned towards the people. After the Gospel [reading] the whole congregation sings the Creed in German.

Then follows the sermon, on the Gospel of the Sunday or holy day. . . . After the sermon shall follow a public paraphrase of the Lord's Prayer, with an exhortation to those who are minded to come to the Sacrament. . . . Then the Office and Consecration proceeds, as follows: "Our Lord Jesus Christ, in the same night," etc. (I Cor. 11.23ff). I think that it would be in accordance with the Last Supper if the sacrament were distributed immediately after the consecration of the bread before the blessing of the cup. So say both Luke and Paul: "Likewise also the cup after supper." Meanwhile, there might be sung the Sanctus in German or the hymn "God be Praised," or the hymn of John Hus, "Jesus Christ our Savior." And after this should come the consecration of the chalice and its delivery, with the singing of whatever remains of the above-mentioned hymns, or of the *Agnus Dei* in German.

For the sake of good order and discipline in going up [to receive communion], men and women must not go up together but the women after the men. Men and women should have separate places in different parts of the church. . . .

The elevation [of the elements during the prayer of consecration] we desire not to abolish but to retain. It fits in well with the Sanctus in German, and means that Christ has commanded us to think of Him. Just as the sacrament is bodily elevated and yet Christ's body and blood therein are invisible, so through the word of the preacher He is commemorated and uplifted, and in the reception of the sacrament recognized and worshipped. Yet it is all a matter of faith and not of sight, how Christ gave His body and blood for us and still daily intercedes with God to bestow His grace upon us.

Then comes the Sanctus [hymn] in German, "Isaiah the Prophet Saw." Then follows the prayer: "We thank thee, Almighty Lord God. . . ."

---

* Martin Luther, *The German Mass and Order of Divine Service*, 3

[37] From Kidd, *Documents of the Continental Reformation*, 199–202.

[38] *Kyrie Eleison:* Greek name for the prayer of confession, "Lord have mercy [upon us], Christ have mercy, Lord have mercy."

[39] *collect:* short prayer at the beginning of worship.

[40] *tone:* one of the Gregorian chant melodies.

The Blessing concludes the service: "The Lord bless thee and keep thee. . . ."

So much for daily Divine Service and for teaching the Word of God, especially with a view to influencing the young and alluring the simple. Those who come out of curiosity and the desire to gape at something new will soon be sick and tired of the whole thing, as they were before of Divine Service in Latin. For that was sung and read in church daily, and yet the churches were deserted and empty. Already they are prepared to do the same with the German service. So it is best that Divine Service should be arranged with an eye to the young and to those simple folk that may perhaps come to it. As for the rest, no law nor order, exhortation nor driving, that one can devise is of any good to induce them to go willingly to Divine Service. . . .

Protestant Hymns*

The Protestant Reformers insisted that worship become, as the Greek root of liturgy *suggests, the work of the people and not just the clergy. To this end, they promoted hymns for the whole congregation. Martin Luther's 1527 hymn given here, one of dozens that he wrote, is widely regarded as the theme song of the Magisterial Reform; yet its language is so generally Christian that one can find it today in many Catholic hymnbooks.*[41] *The 1545 hymn attributed to John Calvin expresses the theme of his theology, the sovereignty of God and the confidence it gives the believer.*[42]

A mighty fortress is our God,
A bulwark never failing;
Our helper he amid the flood
Of mortal ills prevailing.
For still our ancient foe[43]
Doth seek to work us woe;
His craft and power are great,

And, armed with cruel hate,
On earth is not his equal.

Did we in our own strength confide,
Our striving would be losing;
Were not the right man on our side,
The man of God's own choosing.
Dost ask who that may be?
Christ Jesus, it is he,
Lord Sabaoth his name,
From age to age the same,
And He must win the battle.

And though this world, with devils filled,
Should threaten to undo us,
We will not fear, for God hath willed
His truth to triumph through us.
The prince of darkness grim,
We tremble not for him,
His rage we can endure,
For lo! his doom is sure,
One little word shall fell him.

That word above all earthly powers,
No thanks to them, abideth;
The Spirit and the gifts are ours
Through Him who with us sideth;
Let goods and kindred go,
This mortal life also;
The body they may kill,

---

* Martin Luther, "A Mighty Fortress Is Our God"; John Calvin, "I Greet Thee, Who My Sure Redeemer Art"
[41] Taken from *The Worshipbook* (Philadelphia: Westminster, 1970), 292; translated by F. H. Hedge, 1853.
[42] Taken from *The Presbyterian Hymnal* (Louisville: Westminster/John Knox Press, 1990); trans. F. H. Hedge, 1852.
[43] *ancient foe:* the devil.

God's truth abideth still,
His kingdom is forever.

[Calvin, "I Greet Thee, Who My Sure Re-
    deemer Art"]
I greet Thee, who my sure Redeemer art,
My only trust and Savior of my heart,
Who pain didst undergo for my poor sake;
I pray Thee from our hearts all cares to take.

Thou art the King of mercy and of grace,
Reigning omnipotent in every place:

So come, O King, and our whole being sway;
Shine on us with the light of Thy pure day.

Thou art the life, by which alone we live,
And all our substance and our strength receive;
Sustain us by Thy faith and by Thy power,
And give us strength in every trying hour.

Our hope is in no other save in Thee;
Our faith is built upon Thy promise free;
Lord, give us peace, and make us calm and sure,
That in Thy strength we evermore endure.

Reestablishment of the Roman Inquisition*

On July 21, 1542, Pope Paul III reconstituted the Roman Inquisition for the specific purpose of combating Protestantism and witchcraft. The Inquisition operated, of course, mostly in officially Catholic areas and nations, where it was successful in stamping out the growth of Protestantism.[44]

From the beginning of our assumption of the apostolic office we have been concerned for the flourishing of the Catholic faith and the purging of heresy. Those seduced by diabolical wiles should then return to the fold and unity of the Church, and those who persist in their damnable course should be removed and their punishment serve as an example to others. Nevertheless we hope that the mercy of God, the prayers of the faithful, and the preaching of the learned will cause them to recognize their errors and come back to the Holy Catholic Church. If any delay, they should be induced by the authority of the sacred, ecumenical and general council, which we hope speedily to convene. Therefore we deferred

the establishment of the Inquisition of Heretical Pravity. But now, for a variety of reasons, the council has not met and the enemy of the human race has disseminated even more heresy among the faithful and the robe of Christ is torn. . . .

Lest things grow worse while waiting for a council, we have appointed our beloved son, Giovanni Pietro Caraffa, as Inquisitor General with jurisdiction throughout Christendom including Italy and the Roman Curia.[45] . . . [He and his subordinates] are to investigate by way of inquisition all and single who wander from the way of the Lord and the Catholic faith, as well as those suspected of heresy, together with their followers and abettors, public or private, direct or indirect. The guilty and the suspects are to be imprisoned and proceeded against up to the final sentence. Those judged guilty are to be punished in accord with canonical penalties. After the infliction of death their property may be sold. The aid of the civil arm may be invoked to implement whatever measures are deemed necessary. Anyone who dares to impede this will incur the anger of Almighty God and of the blessed Apostles Peter and Paul.

---

* Pope Paul III, *It Is Allowed from the Beginning* (*Licet ab initio*) Introduction, 1–3, 13

[44] Translated by the author from *Magna bulla Romanarum*, vol. 1, 762–64, as found in Kidd, *Documents of the Continental Reformation*, 347–50.

---

[45] *Roman Curia:* the entire papal court, including its bureaucracy.

Establishment and Rules of the Jesuit Order*

In 1539 seven young Catholic priests formed a "Company [Order] of Jesus" in Rome, and in 1540 the Pope officially established it. It grew rapidly, spread by its appeal to activism and obedience. Becoming known for their effective educational methods and missionary activity in Asia and the New World, the Jesuits spearheaded the Catholic church's attack on Protestant theology.[46]

We have recently learned that our beloved sons Ignatius de Loyola, Pierre Lefevre, Jacob Laynez, Pasquier Brouet, Francis Xavier, Alfonzo Salmeron, Simon Rodriguez, John Codure, and Nicholas Bobadilla, priests, masters of arts, and graduates of the University of Paris, and students of some years' standing in theology coming from several parts of the world, inspired, as they piously believe, by the Holy Spirit, united themselves some time ago to dedicate their lives in a society to the perpetual service of our Lord Jesus Christ and ourselves and our successors in the Roman Pontificate.

For many years they have labored laudably in the vineyard of the Lord. They have publicly preached the Word of God according to a stated permission, privately admonished the faithful to a good and blessed life, stimulated them to pious meditation, ministered to the sick, and instructed the young and ignorant in the essential doctrines of the Christian faith. Indeed, they have fulfilled all the commandments of love for the consolation of souls in whatever lands they visited. Then they gathered in this beautiful city and remained within its confines in order to complete the union of their society in Christ. In accordance with the principles which they have learned by experience will further their ends, they have drawn up a rule

of life in conformity with evangelical precepts and the canonical sanctions of the Fathers. Their rule is the following:

Whoever desires to fight for God under the banner of the Cross in our society, which we want to be characterized by the name of Jesus, and who wishes to serve the Roman pontiff, his vicar on earth, shall take a solemn vow of perpetual chastity. He shall remind himself that he is a member of a society founded for the special purpose of providing spiritual consolation for the furtherance of souls in Christian living and doctrine, the propagation of faith by public preaching, and the ministry of the Word of God, spiritual exercises and deeds of mercy, and above all the instruction of the ignorant in the Christian religion and by hearing the confession of Christian believers. He shall take care that he constantly keep God and the purpose of this society, which is virtually a way to God, always before his eyes. . . . [6] All members should know that the entire society and its individual members are fighting for God in faithful obedience to our most holy lord, the Pope, and to the other Roman bishops who succeed him. Although the Gospel teaches, as we know and confess, that all Christian believers are subject to the Roman pontiff as their head and as vicar of Christ, yet . . . we pledge ourselves to a special vow, in addition to the general obligation. We pledge to fulfil whatever the present Roman pontiff, or any future one, may decree concerning the welfare of souls and the propagation of the faith. We are to fulfill within our ability any task assigned to us without excuse or pretense. We will obey even if he should send us to the Turks or any other infidels, even those living in the region called India, or to heretics, schismatics or unbelievers of any kind. . . .

None of us shall have any ambition or rivalry whatever for missions and provinces. . . . Both for the sake of the wide activities of the order and also for the assiduous practice of humility, we are

---

* Pope Paul III, *Rules of the Church Militant* (*Regimini militantis ecclesiae*) 1–16
[46] Translated by the author from *Magna bulla Romanarum* vol. 1, 743–45, as found in Kidd, *Documents of the Continental Reformation*.

bound always to obey the commander in every matter pertaining to the organization of the society. We shall recognize Christ as present in him, and shall do him reverence as far as is seemly. . . .

We have found that the happier, purer and more edifying life is that removed as far as possible from all contagion of avarice and patterned as much as possible after evangelical poverty. We know that our Lord Jesus Christ will furnish the necessities of food and clothing to his servants who seek only the kingdom of God; therefore, each and every member shall vow perpetual poverty.

Jesuit Rules for Thinking with the Church*

The rules for the Jesuits, published in 1548, stress absolute and unquestioning obedience to the pope, an emphasis probably drawn from Ignatius' military experience. Note their implicitly anti-Protestant character.[47]

In order to have the proper attitude of mind in the Church Militant we should observe the following rules:

1. Putting aside all private judgment, we should keep our minds prepared and ready to obey promptly and in all things the true spouse of Christ our Lord, our Holy Mother, the hierarchical Church.

2. To praise sacramental confession and the reception of the Most Holy Sacrament once a year, and much better once a month, and better still every week, with the requisite and proper dispositions.

3. To praise the frequent hearing of Mass, singing of hymns and psalms, and the recitation of long prayers, both in and out of church; also the hours arranged for fixed times for the whole Divine Office, for prayers of all kinds and for the canonical hours.

4. To praise highly religious life,[48] virginity, and continence; and also matrimony, but not as highly as any of the foregoing. . . .

6. To praise the relics of the saints by venerating them and by praying to these saints. Also to praise the stations, pilgrimages, indulgences, jubilees, Crusade indulgences, and the lighting of candles in the churches.

7. To praise the precepts concerning fasts and abstinences, such as those of Lent, Ember Days, Vigils, Fridays, and Saturdays; likewise to praise acts of penance, both interior and exterior. . . .

13. If we wish to be sure that we are right in all things, we should always be ready to accept this principle: I will believe that the white that I see is black, if the hierarchical Church so defines it. For I believe that between the Bridegroom, Christ our Lord, and the Bride, His Church, there is but one spirit, which governs and directs us for the salvation of our souls, for the same Spirit and Lord, who gave us the Ten Commandments, guides and governs our Holy Mother Church.

14. Although it is true that no one can be saved unless it be predestined and unless he have faith and grace, still we must be very careful of our manner of discussing and speaking of these matters.

15. We should not make predestination a habitual subject of conversation. If it is sometimes mentioned we must speak in such a way that no person will fall into error, as happens on occasion when one will say, "It has already been determined whether I will be saved or lost, and in spite of all the good or evil that I do, this will not be changed." As a result, they become apathetic and neglect the works that are conducive

---

* Ignatius Loyola, *Spiritual Exercises*
[47] Taken from W. H. Longridge, *The Spiritual Exercises of St. Ignatius of Loyola* (London: Mowbray, 1955).
[48] *the religious life:* as priest, monk or nun.

to their salvation and to the spiritual growth of their souls. . . .

17.   Also in our discourse we ought not to emphasize the doctrine that would destroy free will. We may therefore speak of faith and grace to the extent that God enables us to do so, for the greater praise of His Divine Majesty. But, in these dangerous times of ours, it must not be done in such a way that good works or free will suffer any detriment or be considered worthless.

18.   The generous service of God for motives of pure love should be most highly esteemed. However, we should praise highly the fear of His Divine Majesty, for filial fear and even servile fear are pious and most holy things. When one cannot attain anything better or more useful, this fear is of great help in rising from mortal sin. After this first step one easily advances to filial fear which is wholly acceptable and pleasing to God our Lord, since it is inseparable from Divine Love.

The Council of Trent Reforms the Mass*

By the fifth century, the term Mass *was applied to the service of the Eucharist. It does not denote the people "massed" together, but comes from the formula at the conclusion of the service, "Go, this is the dismissal [Latin* missa = *Mass]." When the doctrine of transubstantiation was developed, the idea prevailed that the Mass was not a corporate action of the church in making thanksgiving (Eucharist) to God, but rather the action of Christ who manifests himself at the moment of consecration of the elements and offers himself as an "unbloody sacrifice" to God. The Canon (unchanging portion of the long Eucharistic Prayer) of the Mass was spoken by the priest in a mostly quiet voice, who faced the altar with his back to the congregation during the Eucharist. Thus the people could not hear, and most of the service was in Latin anyway. While the different types of Latin Mass rituals were current during the Middle Ages, the Roman form of the Mass became compulsory for almost all Catholics in the world. This is the Mass that existed in Roman Catholic Christianity until the middle of the twentieth century and the reforms of the Second Vatican Council. The wording of the* Canon of the Mass *given here is largely the same today, but the italicized portions (instructions to the priest) were revised in the twentieth century.*[49]

CELEBRANT: Just it is, and fitting, right, and for our lasting good, that we should always and everywhere give thanks to thee, Lord, holy Father, almighty and eternal God, through Christ our Lord. It is through him that thy majesty is praised by Angels, adored by Dominations, feared by Powers; through him that the heavens and the celestial Virtues join with the blessed Seraphim in one glad hymn of praise. We pray thee let our voices blend with theirs as we humbly praise thee, singing: *Here the bell is rung three times.* Holy, holy, holy art thou, Lord God of hosts. Thy glory fills all heaven and earth. Hosanna in high heaven! Blessed be he who is coming in the name of the Lord. Hosanna in high heaven! *The celebrant, bowing low over the altar, says silently:* So, through Jesus Christ, thy Son, our Lord, we humbly pray and beseech thee, most gracious Father, to accept and bless these offerings, these oblations, these holy, unblemished sacrificial gifts. We offer them to thee in the first place for thy holy Catholic Church, praying that thou wilt be pleased to keep and guide her in peace and unity throughout the world; together with thy servant our Pope N., and N. our bishop, and all who believe and foster the true Catholic and Apostolic faith.

Remember, Lord, thy servants N. and N. (*here the celebrant makes silent mention of those for whom he wishes to pray*), and all here present. Their faith and devotion are known to thee. On their behalf we offer, and they too offer, this

---

* *Canon of the Order for Low Mass*
[49] From Hugo H. Hoever, ed. *Saint Joseph Daily Missal* (New York: Catholic Book Publishing Co., 1920), 673–697.

sacrifice in praise of thee, for themselves and for all who are theirs, for the redemption of their souls, for the hope of safety and salvation, paying homage to thee, their living, true, eternal God. United in the same holy fellowship we reverence the memory, first, of the glorious ever-virgin Mary, Mother of our God and Lord Jesus Christ, and likewise that of thy blessed apostles and martyrs Peter and Paul, Andrew, James, John, Thomas, James, Philip, Bartholomew, Matthew, Simon, and Jude; of Linus, Cletus, Clement, Sixtus, Cornelius, Cyprian, Laurence, Chrysogonus, John and Paul, Cosmas and Damian; and of all thy saints. Grant for the sake of their merits and prayers that in all things we may be guarded and helped by thy protection; through the same Christ our Lord. Amen. *The bell is rung once as the celebrant spreads his hands over the bread and wine. He continues:* And so, Lord, we thy servants, and with us thy whole household, make this peace offering which we entreat thee to accept. Order our days in thy peace, and command that we be rescued from eternal damnation and numbered with the flock of thy elect. We pray thee, God, be pleased to make this offering wholly blessed, a thing consecrated and approved, worthy of the human spirit and of thy acceptance, so that it may become for us the Body and Blood of thy dearly beloved Son, our Lord Jesus Christ.

He takes the host in his hands and consecrates it, saying: He, on the day before he suffered death, took bread into his holy and worshipful hands, and lifting up his eyes to thee, God, his almighty Father in heaven, and giving thanks to thee, he blessed it, broke it, and gave it to his disciples, saying: Take, all of you, and eat of this, FOR THIS IS MY BODY.[50] *The bell is rung three times as he genuflects,[51] shows the Sacred Host to the*

people,[52] *and genuflects again. He now consecrates the wine, saying:* In like manner, when he had eaten supper, taking also this goodly cup into his holy and worshipful hands, and again giving thanks to thee, he blessed it, and gave it to his disciples, saying: Take, all of you, and drink of this, FOR THIS IS THE CHALICE OF MY BLOOD, OF THE NEW AND EVERLASTING COVENANT, A MYSTERY OF FAITH. IT SHALL BE SHED FOR YOU AND MANY OTHERS, SO THAT SINS MAY BE FORGIVEN. *He genuflects, saying:* Whenever you shall do these things, do them in memory of me.

He then shows the chalice to the people, genuflecting after doing so. The bell is again rung three times. He continues: Calling therefore to mind the blessed Passion of this same Christ, thy Son, our Lord, and also his resurrection from the grave, and glorious ascension into heaven, we thy servants, Lord, and with us all thy holy people, offer to thy sovereign majesty, out of the gifts thou hast bestowed upon us, a sacrifice that is pure, holy, and unblemished, the sacred Bread of everlasting life, and the Cup of eternal salvation. Deign to regard them with a favorable and gracious countenance, and to accept them as it pleased thee to accept the offerings of thy servant Abel the Just, and the sacrifice of our father Abraham, and that which thy great priest Melchizedek sacrificed to thee, a holy offering, a victim without blemish. *Bowing low over the altar, he says:* Humbly we ask it of thee, God almighty: bid these things be carried by the hands of thy holy angel up to thy altar on high, into the presence of thy divine majesty. And may those of us who by taking part in the sacrifice of this altar shall have received the sacred Body and Blood of thy Son, be filled with every grace and heavenly blessing; through the same Christ our Lord, Amen.

Remember also, Lord, thy servants N. and N., who have gone before us with the sign of faith and sleep the sleep of peace. *Here the celebrant*

---

[50] *FOR THIS IS MY BODY:* these capitalized words, and those that follow in this prayer, are spoken slowly and emphatically as the moment in which the transformation takes place.

[51] *genuflects:* bends the (right) knee to the floor.

---

[52] *Shows the sacred host to the people:* the instructions in the missal (Mass book) for laity say at this point, "When he elevates the Sacred Host, look at it and say, 'My Lord and My God!'"

makes silent mention of those dead for whom he wishes to pray. To them, Lord, and to all who rest in Christ, grant, we entreat thee, a place of cool repose, of light and peace; through the same Christ our Lord, Amen. *Striking his breast and raising his voice as he says the first three words, he continues:* To us also, thy sinful servants, who put our trust in thy countless acts of mercy, deign to grant some share and fellowship with thy holy apostles and martyrs: with John, Stephen, Matthias, Barnabas, Ignatius, Alexander, Marcellinus, Peter, Felicity, Perpetua, Agatha, Lucy, Agnes, Cecily, Anastasia, and all thy saints. Into their company we pray thee to admit us, not weighing our deserts, but freely granting us forgiveness; through Christ our Lord. . . .

The celebrant makes the sign of the cross three times over the chalice with the Sacred Host, and twice between the chalice and himself. Then he raises the Host and chalice slightly, saying meanwhile: Through him, and with him, and in him, thou, God, almighty Father, in the unity of the Holy Spirit, hast all honor and glory. *Replacing the Host and chalice upon the altar, he then chants or says aloud:* World without end. Amen.

Let us pray. Urged by our Savior's bidding, and schooled by his divine ordinance, we make bold to say: Our Father, who art in heaven, hallowed be thy name. Thy kingdom come. Thy will be done, on earth as it is in heaven. Give us this day our daily bread. And forgive us our trespasses, as we forgive those who trespass against us. And lead us not into temptation: *Response by the assistant:* But deliver us from evil. *Celebrant (softly):* Amen.

Taking the paten in his right hand, he continues silently: Deliver us, we pray thee, Lord, from every evil, past, present, and to come, and at the intercession of the blessed and glorious evervirgin Mary, Mother of God, of thy blessed apostles Peter and Paul, of Andrew, and of all the saints (*he crosses himself with the paten and kisses it*), be pleased to grant peace in our time, so that with the help of thy compassion we may be ever free from sin and safe from all disquiet. *He then breaks the Sacred Host over the chalice, saying:* Through the same Jesus Christ, thy Son, our

Lord, who is God, living and reigning with thee in the unity of the Holy Spirit: *He concludes the prayer aloud:* World without end. Amen.

He makes the sign of the Cross thrice with a particle of the Sacred Host over the chalice, chanting or saying aloud: The peace of the Lord be always with you. *Response:* And with you. *Then he drops the particle into the chalice and continues silently:* May this sacramental mingling of the Body and Blood of our Lord Jesus Christ be for us who receive it a source of eternal life. Amen.

I will take the Bread of Heaven, and will call upon the name of the Lord. *He takes the two pieces of the Sacred Host in his left hand. Then, saying the opening words audibly each time and striking his breast with his right hand as he does so he says three times:* Lord, I am not worthy that thou shouldst come under my roof, but say only the word, and my soul will be healed. *The bell is rung as he says these words, and those of the congregation who are to communicate go to the altar rails. The celebrant crosses himself with the Sacred Host, saying:* The Body of our Lord Jesus Christ preserve my soul for everlasting life. Amen. *He then receives the Host. After a short pause the celebrant collects any fragments of the Host that may be on the corporal,*[53] *and puts them into the chalice saying:* What return shall I make to the Lord for all that he has given me? I will take the chalice of salvation and invoke the name of the Lord. Praised be the Lord! When I invoke his name I shall be secure from my enemies. *Crossing himself with the chalice, he says:* The Blood of our Lord Jesus Christ preserve my soul for everlasting life. Amen. *He drinks the contents of the chalice.* . . .

He then goes to the altar rails and gives Holy Communion, saying to each communicant: The Body of our Lord Jesus Christ preserve your soul for everlasting life. *When all have communicated he returns to the altar and replaces the ciborium in the tabernacle.*[54]

---

[53] *corporal:* linen cloth on the altar, on which the elements are consecrated.

[54] *ciborium:* a covered, goblet-shaped vessel holding the consecrated hosts; *tabernacle:* a locked receptacle on the wall or the altar holding the ciborium.

TEACHING

Breaking Down the Barriers to Reform*

Luther's Ninety-five Theses *immediately cut into the sales of indulgences. Church authorities responded to Luther, and a heated debate ensued that quickly broke beyond the topic of indulgences. By 1520, Luther had been excommunicated and was organizing a reformed, evangelical church in Germany. One of his early writings was an appeal to the religious and patriotic feelings of the German princes and people. This 1520 essay develops Luther's doctrine of vocation and the priesthood of all believers in the context of an attack on the "three walls" by which Rome defends itself from reform. It features, throughout and especially toward the end, an appeal to the patriotic sentiments of its readers.*[55]

Dr. Martin Luther, to his Most Serene and Mighty Imperial Majesty, and to the Christian Nobility of the German nation: The grace and strength of God be with you, Most Serene Majesty! And you, most gracious and well beloved lords!

The Romanists have, with great adroitness, drawn three walls round themselves, with which they have protected themselves, so that no one could reform them. All Christendom has suffered for this. First, if pressed by the temporal power, they have affirmed and maintained that the temporal power has no jurisdiction over them, but, on the contrary, that spiritual power is above the temporal. Second, when they are admonished with the Scriptures, they objected that no one may interpret the Scriptures but the Pope. Thirdly, if they are threatened with a council, they invented the notion that no one may call a council but the Pope. . . .

Let us attack the first wall. There has been a fiction by which the Pope, bishops, priests, and monks are called the "spiritual estate"; princes, lords, artisans, and peasants are the "temporal estate." This is an artful lie and hypocritical invention, but let no one be made afraid by it, for this reason: all Christians are truly of the spiritual estate, and there is no difference among them, except of office. As St. Paul says (I Cor. 12), we are all one body, though each member does its own work so as to serve the others. This is because we have one baptism, one Gospel, one faith, and are all Christians alike; baptism, Gospel, and faith alone make spiritual and Christian people. As for the unction by a pope or a bishop, tonsure, ordination, consecration, and clothes differing from those of the laity—all this may make a hypocrite or an anointed puppet, but never a Christian or a spiritual person. Thus we are all consecrated as priests by baptism. . . .

To put the matter more plainly, if a little company of pious Christian laymen were taken prisoners and carried away to a desert, and had not among them a priest consecrated by a bishop, and were there to agree to elect one of them . . . and were to order him to baptize, to celebrate the mass, to absolve and to preach, this man would as truly be a priest, as if all the bishops and all the popes had consecrated him. That is why, in cases of necessity, every man can baptize and absolve,[56] which would not be possible if we were not all priests. . . .

It must have been the archfiend himself[57] who said, as we read in the canon law, "If the pope were so perniciously wicked as to be dragging hosts of souls to the devil, yet he could not be deposed." This is the accursed, devilish foundation on which they build at Rome. They think the whole world may go to the devil rather than that they should be opposed in their trickery. If a man were to escape punishment simply because

* Martin Luther, *An Appeal to the Ruling Class*
[55] Taken, with editing, from C. M. Jacobs, *Works of Martin Luther*, vol. 2 (Philadelphia: Holman, 1915), 65–79.

[56] *every man . . . absolve:* according to Roman Catholic law.
[57] *archfiend himself:* the devil.

he was above his fellows, then no Christian might punish another, since Christ has commanded that each of us esteem himself the lowest and humblest of all.

The second wall is even more tottering and weak: namely their claim to be considered masters of the Scriptures. . . . If the article of our faith is right, "I believe in the holy Christian Church," the Pope cannot alone be right. Otherwise we must say, "I believe in the Pope of Rome," and reduce the Christian Church to one man, which is a devilish and damnable heresy. Besides that, we are all priests, as I have said, and have all one faith, one Gospel, one Sacrament. How then should we not have the power of discerning and judging what is right or wrong in matters of faith? . . .

The third wall falls by itself, as soon as the first two have fallen. If the Pope acts contrary to the Scriptures, we are bound to stand by the Scriptures to punish and to constrain him, according to Christ's commandment . . . "tell it unto the Church" (Matt. 18). . . . If then I am to accuse him before the Church, I must collect the Church together. . . . Therefore when need requires, and the Pope is a cause of offence to Christendom, in these cases whoever can best do so, as a faithful member of the whole body, must do what he can to procure a true free council. No one can do this as well as the temporal authorities, especially since they are fellow-Christians, fellow priests. . . .

What is the use in Christendom of those who are called "cardinals"? I will tell you. In Italy and Germany there are many rich convents, endowments, holdings, and benefices. As the best way of getting these into the hands of Rome, they created cardinals, and gave to them the bishoprics, convents, and prelacies, and thus destroyed the service of God. That is why Italy is almost a desert now. The convents are destroyed, the sees consumed, the revenues of the prelacies and of all the churches drawn to Rome. . . . Now that Italy is sucked dry, they come to Germany. They begin in a quiet way, but we shall soon see Germany brought into the same state as Italy. . . .

Poor Germans that we are—we have been deceived! We were born to be masters, and we have been compelled to bow the head beneath the yoke of our tyrants, and to become slaves. Name, title, outward signs of royalty, we possess all these; force, power, right, liberty, all these have gone over to the popes, who have robbed us of them. They get the kernel, we get the husk. . . . It is time the glorious Teutonic people should cease to be the puppet of the Roman pontiff. . . . Let the emperor then be a true emperor, and no longer allow himself to be stripped of his sword or his scepter!

Conflict over Justification*

The center of Luther's theology, and of the Protestant Reformation as a whole, is justification by faith alone. Salvation does not depend on human deeds, but on a living trust in Jesus Christ in whose death God has freely forgiven sin. In his early Lectures on Romans (not published until after his death), Luther states his teaching that a person can be justified but still a sinner.[58] *The second selection* is the Roman Catholic response as spelled out at the Council of Trent; it stresses the cooperation of divine grace and human effort.[59]

It is as with a sick man who believes his physician as he assures him that he will most certainly get well. In the meantime, he obeys his orders in the hope of recovery and abstains from whatever is

* Martin Luther, *Lectures on Romans;* Council of Trent, *Decree on Justification*

[58] From Wilhelm Pauck, ed., *Luther: Lectures on Romans,* Library of Christian Classics, vol. 15 (Philadelphia: Westmin-

ster, 1961), 127–37. Copyright 1961 Westminster Press. Used by permission.

[59] From Philip Schaff, *Creeds of Christendom,* vol. 2 (New York: Harper, 1919), 89–100.

forbidden to him, lest he slow up the promised cure and get worse again, until finally the physician accomplishes what he has so confidently predicted. Can one say that this sick man is healthy? No; but he is at the same time both sick and healthy. He is actually sick, but he is healthy by virtue of the sure prediction of the physician whom he believes. For he reckons him already healthy because he is certain that he can cure him, indeed, because he has begun to cure him and does not reckon him his sickness as death.

In the same way, Christ, our good Samaritan, brought the man who was half dead, his patient, to an inn and took care of him (Luke 10:30 ff.) and commenced to heal him, having first promised to him that he would give him absolutely perfect health unto eternal life. He does not reckon him his sin for death, but in the meantime holding up to him the hope that he will get well, he forbids him to do or not to do anything that might impede his recovery and make his sin worse. Now can we say that he is perfectly righteous? No; but he is at the same time both a sinner and righteous, a sinner in fact but righteous by virtue of the reckoning and the certain promise of God that he will redeem him from sin in order, in the end, to make him perfectly whole and sound. And, therefore, he is perfectly whole in hope, while he is in fact a sinner, but he has already begun to be actually righteous, and he always seeks to become more so, always knowing himself to be unrighteous. (But if now this patient should like his feebleness so much that he does not want to be entirely cured, will he then not die? Yes, he will. And so it is with people who follow their desires in the world. Or when someone imagines that he is not sick but healthy and spurns the physician, he is of this sort. This is wanting to be justified and to be whole by one's own works.) . . .

So then, this life is a life of cure from sin. It is not a life of sinlessness, as if the cure were finished and health had been recovered. The church is an inn and an infirmary for the sick and for convalescents. Heaven, however, is the palace where the whole and the righteous live. . . . Yet here on earth righteousness does not yet dwell, but by healing sins it meanwhile prepares for itself a dwelling place.

All the saints had this understanding of sin, as David prophesied in Ps. 32. And they all confessed themselves to be sinners, as the books of Blessed Augustine show. Our theologians, however, have neglected to consider the nature of sin and have concentrated their attention upon good works. They have been concerned to teach only how good works might be made secure, but not how with fervent prayers one must humbly seek the grace that heals and how one must acknowledge himself a sinner. . . . This is also the reason why there is, in the church today, such frequent relapse after confessions. The people do not know that they must still be justified, but they are confident that they are already justified; thus they come to ruin by their own sense of security, and the devil does not need to raise a finger. This certainly is nothing else than to establish righteousness by means of works. And even if they implore the grace of God, they do not do so rightly but only in order to get rid of the work of sin. But true Christians have the spirit of Christ and act rightly, even if they do not understand what we have just said. They act before they come to understand why they behave as they do. Indeed, they obtain more understanding from life than from doctrine.

[*Decree on Justification* by the Council of Trent] The Holy Synod declares first, that, for the correct and sound understanding of the doctrine of Justification, it is necessary that each one recognize and confess as follows. Whereas all men had lost their innocence in the prevarication of Adam . . . they were so far the servants of sin, and under the power of the devil and of death, that not the Gentiles only by the force of nature, but not even the Jews by the very letter itself of the law of Moses, were able to be liberated, or to arise, from it. But free will, attenuated as it was in its powers, and bent down, was by no means extinguished in them.

Whence it came to pass that the heavenly Father, the Father of mercies, and the God of all comfort, when that blessed fullness of the times was come, sent unto men, Jesus Christ, his own Son . . . that he might both redeem the Jews who were under the Law and that the Gentiles, who followed not after justice, might attain to justice, and that all men might receive the adoption of sons. God has put him forward as a propitiator, through faith in his blood, for our sins, and not for our sins only, but also for those of the whole world.

He died for all yet do not all receive the benefit of his death, but those only to whom the merit of his passion is communicated. If they were not born propagated of the seed of Adam, people would not be born unjust. By that propagation, they contract through him, when they are conceived, injustice as their own. So, if they were not born again in Christ, they never would be justified; in that new birth there is bestowed upon them, through the merit of passion, the grace whereby they are made just.

In these words, a description of the Justification of the impious is indicated. It is a change from that state wherein man is born a child of the first Adam, to the state of grace, and of the adoption of the sons of God, through the second Adam Jesus Christ, our Savior. This change, since the promulgation of the Gospel, cannot be effected without the laver of regeneration,[60] or the desire for it. . . .

---

[60] *the laver* [washing] *of regeneration:* baptism.

The Synod furthermore declares, that in adults, the beginning of Justification is to be derived from the prevenient grace of God, through Jesus Christ. That is to say, it comes from his calling, whereby, without any merits existing on their part, they are called. They who by sins were alienated from God are disposed through his quickening and assisting grace to convert themselves to their own justification, by freely assenting to and cooperating with grace. While God touches the heart of man by the illumination of the Holy Ghost, neither is man himself utterly inactive while he receives that inspiration, for he is also able to reject it. Yet is he not able, by his own free will, without the grace of God, to move himself unto justice in his sight. . . .

Having been thus justified, and made the friends and servants of God, advancing from virtue to virtue, they are renewed, as the Apostle says, day by day, that is, by mortifying the members of their own flesh, and by presenting them as instruments of justice unto sanctification. Through the observance of the commandments of God and of the Church, faith cooperating with good works, they increase in that righteousness which they have received through the grace of Christ, and are still further justified as it is written . . . "Do you see that by works a man is justified, and not by faith only."[61]

---

[61] James 2:14.

A Summary of Zwinglian Belief *

Berthold Haller and Francis Kolb, Protestant ministers in Berne, wrote this short statement of faith. It was revised, published, and publicly defended in debate by Zwingli in 1528.[62]

1. The Holy Christian Church, whose only Head is Christ, is born of the Word of God,

abides in it, and does not listen to the voice of a stranger.

2. The Church of Christ does not add to the laws and ordinances of the Word of God. Consequently, human traditions are not binding upon us except so far as they are grounded on and ordained by the Word of God.

3. Christ is the only wisdom, righteousness, redemption, and satisfaction for the sins of the whole world. To acknowledge any other salvation or satisfaction is to deny Christ.

---

* *The Ten Berne Theses*
[62] From Philip Schaff, *The Creeds of Christendom* (New York: Harper & Row, 1877).

4. That the body and blood of Christ are substantially and corporally received in the bread of the Eucharist cannot be proved from the Bible.

5. Current use of the Mass in which Christ is offered to God the Father for the sins of the living and the dead is contrary to Scripture, a blasphemy against the immortal sacrifice, passion and death of Christ, and in its abuse an abomination before God.

6. As Christ alone died for us, so he is also to be adored as the only Mediator and advocate between God the Father and believers. Therefore, it is contrary to the Word of God to propose and invoke other mediators.[63]

7. There is nothing in Scripture about a purgatory after this life. Consequently, all services for the dead, such as vigils, requiems . . . are vain.

8. Making pictures for worship is contrary to the Word of God in the New and Old Testaments. Hence, if appointed to be worshipped, they should be abolished.

9. Holy marriage is in the Scripture forbidden to no class,[64] but all are commanded to avoid harlotry and unchastity.

10. As an openly immoral woman is under a heavy ban according to the Scripture, it follows that unchastity and engaging prostitutes are in no class more shameful than in the priesthood.

---

[63] *invoke other mediators:* pray to the saints for their intercession.

[64] *Holy marriage . . . class:* this is directly against mandatory clerical celibacy.

The First Anabaptist Confession*

The first Anabaptist stirrings arose from Zwingli's reform, much to his consternation. When he attacked their call for adult-only baptism, their views on the civil government and their reputed social disorder, the Anabaptists responded in 1527 with a confession of faith written largely by Michael Sattler. Its formal name is A Brotherly Union of a Number of Children of God Concerning Seven Articles. *It does not summarize all the Anabaptist form of Christianity, but rather those points on which it disagreed with the magisterial reformers.*[65]

Dear brethren and sisters: we who have been assembled in the Lord at Schleitheim on the Border make known in points and articles to all who love God that as concerns us we are of one mind to abide in the Lord as God's obedient children, [His] sons and daughters, we who have been and

shall be separated from the world in everything, [and] completely at peace. To God alone be praise and glory without the contradiction of any brethren. In this we have perceived the oneness of the Spirit of our Father and of our common Christ with us. For the Lord is the Lord of peace and not of quarreling, as Paul points out. That you may understand in what articles this has been formulated you should observe and note [the following]. . . .

First, baptism shall be given to all those who have learned repentance and amendment of life and who believe truly that their sins are taken away by Christ; and to all those who walk in the resurrection of Jesus Christ and wish to be buried with Him in death, so that they may be resurrected with Him; and to all those who with this significance request it [baptism] of us and demand it for themselves. This excludes all infant baptism, the highest and chief abomination of the pope. In this you have the foundation and testimony of the apostles. Matt. 28, Mark 16, Acts 2, 8, 16, 19.

Second, the ban shall be employed with all those who have given themselves to the Lord, to

---

* *The Schleitheim Confession*
[65] From J. C. Wenger, "The Schleitheim Confession of Faith," *Mennonite Quarterly Review* 19 (October 1945): 247–52. Copyright © 1945 Mennonite Quarterly Review. Used by permission.

walk in His commandments, and with all those who are baptized into the one body of Christ and who are called brethren or sisters, and yet who slip sometimes and fall into error and sin, being inadvertently overtaken. The same shall be admonished twice in secret and the third time openly disciplined or banned according to the command of Christ. Matt. 18. . . .

Third, all those who wish to break one bread in remembrance of the broken body of Christ, and all who wish to drink of one drink as a re-membrance of the shed blood of Christ, shall be united beforehand by baptism in one body of Christ which is the church of God and whose Head is Christ. For as Paul points out we cannot at the same time be partakers of the Lord's table and the table of devils. . . .

Fourth, a separation shall be made from the evil and from the wickedness which the devil planted in the world, in this manner: simply that we shall not have fellowship with them [the wicked] and not run with them in the multi-tude of their abominations. . . . From all this we should learn that everything which is not united with our God and Christ cannot be other than an abomination which we should shun and flee from. By this is meant all popish and anti-popish[66] works and church services, meetings and Church attendance, drinking houses, civic affairs, the commitments [made in] unbelief and other things of that kind, which are highly re-garded by the world and yet are carried on in flat contradiction to the command of God, in accor-

dance with all the unrighteousness which is in the world. From all these things we shall be sep-arated and have no part with them for they are nothing but an abomination. . . .

Fifth, the pastor in the Church of God shall be one who out-and-out has a good report of those who are outside the faith. This office shall be to read, to admonish and teach, to warn, to discipline, to ban in the church, to lead out in prayer for the advancement of all the brethren and sisters, to lift up the bread when it is to be broken, and in all things to see to the care of the body of Christ, in order that it may be built up and developed, and the mouth of the slanderer be stopped. . . .

Sixth, God ordains the sword outside the per-fection of Christ. It punishes and puts to death the wicked, and guards and protects the good. In the law the sword was ordained for the pun-ishment of the wicked and for their death, and the same [sword] is [now] ordained to be used by the worldly magistrates. In the perfection of Christ, however, only the ban is used for a warn-ing and for the excommunication of the one who has sinned, without putting the flesh to death—simply the warning and the command to sin no more. . . . Finally it will be observed that it is not appropriate for a Christian to serve as a magistrate. . . .

Seventh, the oath is a confirmation among those who are quarreling or making promises. In the law it is commanded to be performed in God's Name, but only in truth, not falsely. Christ, who teaches the perfection of the law, prohibits all swearing to His [followers], whether true or false.

---

[66] *anti-popish:* Lutheran and Zwinglian.

The Voices of Protestant Women*

On September 20, 1523, the noblewoman Argula von Grumbach wrote a letter to the University of

---

*Argula von Grumbach, Letter to the University of Ingol-stadt; Lady Jane Grey, *A Certain Communication**

Ingolstadt denouncing its removal of a young pro-fessor of theology, Arsacius Seehofer, from his post for espousing Lutheran theology. Her letter, along with other writings, was widely published, and she became the first Protestant woman writer (and

*probably the first woman ever) to use the print-
ing press for her cause. Her writing is remarkable for its rhetorical power, its understanding
and use of scripture, and its incipiently "feminist"
approach.*[67]

*The second reading features another woman's
understanding of the Protestant version of Christianity. In literary form it is close to a catechism.
Four days before her execution in 1553 at the age
of sixteen, Jane Grey wrote out her dialogue with
a Master Feckenham. Grey, the daughter of
Henry VIII's niece, had participated in a plot to
deprive the staunchly Catholic Mary Tudor of her
rights to the English throne after the death of Ed-
ward VI, which failed when the English people supported Mary.*[68]

How in God's name can you and your university
expect to prevail, when you deploy such foolish
violence against the word of God; when you
force someone to hold the holy Gospel in their
hands for the very purpose of denying it, as you
did in the case of Arsacius Seehofer?[69] When
you confront him with an oath and declaration
such as this, and use imprisonment and even the
threat of the stake to force him to deny Christ
and his word?

Yes, when I reflect on this my heart and all my
limbs tremble. What does Luther or Melanchthon teach you but the word of God? You condemn them without having refuted them. Did
Christ teach you so, or his apostles, prophets, or
evangelists? Show me where this is written! You
lofty experts, nowhere in the Bible do I find that
Christ, or his apostles, or his prophets put people
in prison, burnt or murdered them, or sent them
into exile.... Don't you know what the Lord says
in Matthew 10? "Have no fear of him who can
take your body but then his power is at an end.

But fear him who has power to dispatch soul and
body into the depths of hell."

One knows very well the importance of one's
duty to obey the authorities. But where the word
of God is concerned neither Pope, Emperor nor
princes—as Acts 4 and 5 make so clear—have
any jurisdiction. For my part, I have to confess,
in the name of God and by my soul's salvation,
that if I were to deny Luther and Melanchthon's
writing I would be denying God and his word,
which may God forfend for ever. Amen....

My heart goes out to our princes, whom you
have seduced and betrayed so deplorably. For I
realize that they are ill informed about divine
Scripture. If they could spare the time from other
business, I believe they, too, would discover the
truth that no one has a right to exercise sovereignty over the word of God. Yes, no human being, whoever he is, can rule over it. For the word
of God alone—without which nothing was made
—should and must rule.

If one could enforce faith, why weren't all unbelievers given instructions to believe long ago?
The difficulty is that it is the word of God which
has to reach us, not flesh and blood. You won't
be able to gain any such fame with Arsacius Seehofer, prettying him up with his coerced and dic-
tated oath, calling him a Master of Arts. For you
have forgotten one thing: that he is only eighteen years old, and still a child. Others won't forget. From the way in which the news has come
to me from other places in such a short time, you
will surely be notorious throughout the entire
world....

Have no doubt about this: God looks merci-
fully on Arsacius, or will do so in the future, just
as he did on Peter, who tested the Lord three
times. For each day the just person falls seven
times and gets up on his feet again. God does
not want the death of the sinner, but his conversion and life. Christ the Lord himself feared
death; so much so that he sweated a bloody
sweat. I trust that God will yet see much good
from this young man. Just as Peter, too, did much
good work later, after his denial of the Lord.
And, unlike this man, he was still free, and did

[67] Taken from Peter Matheson, ed., *Argula von Grumbach: A
Woman's Voice in the Reformation* (Edinburgh: Clark, 1995).
Copyright © 1995 T. & T. Clark. Used by permission.
[68] From the *Harleian Miscellany,* vol. 1 (London: Dutton,
1808), 369–71.
[69] Seehofer had been forced to recant his teaching.

not suffer such lengthy imprisonment, or the threat of the stake.

A disputation is easily won when one argues with force, not Scripture. As far as I can see that means that the hangman is accounted the most learned. It's easy to see, though, that the devil has helped to arrange this fine hullabaloo. God will not put up with your ways much longer. In 2 Corinthians 1 Paul says: "the devil turns himself into an angel of light." So it is no wonder that confidence tricksters turn themselves into apostles of Christ. Remember Matthew 10: "There has to be conflict, the son against the father, the daughter against the mother, the bride against the mother in law, and one's servants will become one's enemies." And John 16: "The time will come when they will kill you and think that they do God a service. For they know neither the Father nor me." And Paul in 1 Corinthians 11: "Conflict must take place, so that those who are approved may be revealed." Also 2 Corinthians 4: "If the Gospel is hidden, it is to those who are perishing."

Are you not ashamed that [Seehofer] had to deny all the writings of Martin [Luther], who put the New Testament into German, simply following the text? That means that you dismiss all the holy Gospel and the Epistles and the story of the Apostles and so on as heresy. It seems there is no hope of a proper discussion with you. And then there are the five books of Moses, which are being printed too. Is that nothing? It would be easier, and more profitable, to engage in discussion with a Jew. I hear nothing about any of you refuting a single article [of Seehofer] from Scripture. What I do hear is that a learned lawyer came forward to him and asked: "Why was he crying? Wasn't he a heretic?" But jurisprudence has no value here.

I beseech you for the sake of God, and exhort you by God's judgement and righteousness, to tell me in writing which of the articles written by Martin [Luther] or Melanchthon you consider heretical. In German not a single one seems heretical to me. And the fact is that a great deal has been published in German, and I've read it all. . . .

I have no Latin; but you have German, being born and brought up in this tongue. What I have written to you is no woman's chitchat, but the word of God; and (I write) as a member of the Christian Church, against which the gates of Hell cannot prevail. Against the Roman, however, they do prevail. Just look at that church! How is it to prevail against the gates of Hell? God give us his grace, that we all may be saved, and may (God) rule us according to his will. Now may his grace carry the day. Amen.

[Lady Jane Grey, *A Certain Communication*]

FECKENHAM: Why is it necessary to salvation to do good work and it is not sufficient to believe?

JANE: I deny that and I affirm that faith alone saves. But it is meet for Christians, in token that they follow their master Christ, to do good works, yet may we not say that they profit to salvation. For, although we have all done all that we can, yet we are unprofitable servants, and faith only in Christ's blood saves.

F: How many sacraments are there?

J: Two: the one the sacrament of baptism, and the other the sacrament of our Lord's supper.

F: No, there are seven.

J: In what Scripture find you that?

F: Well, we will talk about it later. But what is signified by your two sacraments?

J: By the sacrament of baptism, I am washed with water and regenerated by the Spirit; and that washing is a token to me that I am the child of God. The sacrament of the Lord's Supper is offered unto me as a sure seal and testimony that I am by the blood of Christ, which He shed for me on the Cross, made partaker of the everlasting kingdom.

F: Why, what do you receive in that bread? Do you not receive the very body and blood of Christ?

J: No surely, I do not believe so. I think that at that supper I receive neither flesh nor blood, but only bread and wine. The bread that is broken, and the wine when it is drunk, put me in mind, how that for my sins the body of Christ was broken and His blood shed on the cross: and, with that bread and wine, I received the benefits that came by [the] breaking of His body and the shedding of His blood on the cross for my sins.

F: Why, doth not Christ speak these words: "Take, eat, this is my body?" Require we any plainer words? Doth not He say that it is His body?

J: I grant He says so, and so He says: "I am the vine, I am the door," but yet He is never the vine nor door. Doth not St. Paul say that He calls those things that are not as though they were? God forbid that I should say that I eat the very natural body and blood of Christ for then either I should pluck away my redemption or else there were two bodies, or two Christs. The one body was tormented on the Cross; . . . then if they did eat another body . . . either He had two bodies, [or] else, if his body [was] eaten, it was not broken upon the cross; . . . if it were broken upon the cross, his disciples did not eat it. . . .

F: You ground your faith upon such authors as say and unsay both with [one] breath, and not upon the church to whom you ought to give credit.

J: No, I ground my faith upon God's Word and not upon the church. For if the church be a good church, the faith of the church must be tried by God's Word, and not God's Word by the church neither yet my faith. Shall I believe the church because of its antiquity? Or shall I give credit to that church that taketh away from me that half part of the Lord's supper, and will let no one receive it in both hands but themselves? By denying it to us, they deny part of our salvation. I say that is an evil church, and not the spouse of Christ but the spouse of the devil, that alters the Lord's supper, and both takes from it and adds to it. To that church I say God will add plagues, and from that church will He take his part out of the Book of Life. Do you not learn that of St. Paul, when he ministered it to the Corinthians in both kinds? Shall I believe that church? God forbid.

F: That was done of a good intent of the church to avoid a heresy that sprang [within] it.

J: Why, shall the church alter God's will and ordinances for a good intent? . . .

With these and like persuasions, he [Feckenham] would have had me . . . lean to the [Roman] church, but it would not be. There were many more things about which we reasoned, but these were the chief.

Calvin on Predestination*

The doctrine of election or predestination, that God chooses some people to be redeemed and leaves others in their sin, goes back to the foundation of Christianity and was fully developed by Augustine (on whom Calvin increasingly drew in his treatment of predestination). Almost all Christians shared it in some way. Because the center of John Calvin's theology was the sovereignty of God, and because of controversy over predestination, he developed his statement of this doctrine more fully than other reformers. (The reader may want to begin with the final paragraph, designed as a summary of this doctrine.)[70]

The covenant of life is not preached equally to all people, and it does not gain the same acceptance among all. . . . This difference shows the wonderful depth of God's judgment. It certainly also serves the decision of God's eternal election. By

---

* John Calvin, *Institutes* 3.21.1–2, 7

[70] Translated by the author from P. Barth and W. Niesel, eds., *Johannis Calvini: Opera Selecta* (Munich: Kaiser, 1928).

God's desire salvation is freely offered to some while others are denied access to it.

But large and difficult questions spring up at once. . . . Election is a perplexing issue to many people. They suppose that nothing is more unreasonable than that out of the common multitude of humankind some people should be predestined to salvation, others to destruction. How mistakenly they entangle themselves will become clear in the following discussion. Moreover, in the very darkness that frightens them appears not only the usefulness of this teaching, but its very sweet fruit as well. We shall never be certainly convinced, as we need to be, that our salvation flows from the spring of God's free grace until we know his eternal election. It illumines God's grace by this contrast: God does not indiscriminately adopt all people into the hope of salvation, but gives to some what is denied to others. . . .

Those who shut the gates so that no one may dare enter into this doctrine wrong both humans and God. Nothing else will make us humble as we ought to be, nor shall we otherwise sincerely feel how much we owe to God. Christ teaches our only ground for firmness and confidence. It is this: in order to free us from all fear and make us victorious in so many dangers, traps and deadly struggles, Christ promises that whatever the Father has entrusted into his keeping will be safe.[71] We can conclude from this that all those who do not know that they belong to God will be miserable, because they are constantly afraid for their salvation. Those who are blind to the three benefits we have noted[72] would wish the foundation of our salvation to be moved from underneath us. They serve their own interests and the interests of other believers very badly. The Church becomes apparent to us, as Bernard rightly teaches, when "the church could not otherwise be found or recognized among humanity, since it lies marvelously hidden . . . within the bosom of a blessed predestination and within the mass of miserable condemnation."[73] . . .

"We have entered the path of faith," says Augustine. "Therefore, let us stay steadfastly on it. It leads us to the King's chamber, where all the treasures of knowledge and wisdom are hidden. The Lord Christ Himself . . . said: 'I have . . . many things to say to you, but you cannot bear them now'.[74] We must walk, we must advance, and we must grow, so that our hearts may comprehend those things, which we cannot yet understand. If the Last Day finds us still advancing, we shall learn then what we could not learn now."[75] . . . This point is most important to understand: seeking any other knowledge of predestination than what the Word of God reveals to us is no less mad than if one should try to walk in a pathless desert, or to see in darkness. We must not be ashamed to be ignorant of something in this matter, in which there is a certain learned ignorance. Rather, we must willingly refrain from seeking a kind of knowledge which is foolish, dangerous, and even deadly. If a perverse curiosity agitates us, we do well to oppose it with this restraining thought: just as too much honey is not good, so for the curious the investigation of glory is not turned into glory.[76] There is good reason for us to be deterred from this insolence, because it can only plunge us into ruin. . . .

Scripture clearly shows that God long ago established an eternal and unchangeable plan. By it he determined those who receive eternal salvation, and those whom, on the other hand, he devotes to destruction. We argue that, regarding the elect, this plan was founded upon God's free grace, not at all upon human merit. God's just but incomprehensible judgment has locked the door of life to those whom he has given over to damnation. We regard the call to salvation as a testimony that one is elected. We see the experi-

---

[71] John 10:28–29.

[72] *three benefits we have noted:* receiving God's free mercy, seeing God's glory, and becoming more humble.

[73] Bernard (of Clairveaux), *Sermons on the Song of Songs* 78.4.

[74] John 16:24.

[75] Augustine, *Commentary on John's Gospel* 53.7.

[76] An allusion to Proverbs 25:27.

ence of justification as another sign of its manifestation, until we come into the glory, which is the fulfillment of that election. The Lord seals his elect by call and justification; and by depriv-

ing those who are condemned of the knowledge of himself and the sanctification of his Spirit, he reveals the judgment that awaits them.

The Creed of Trent*

In 1564, the Council of Trent adopted a short official creed summarizing its actions in a more accessible format. The creed was to be recited in parish churches and made binding upon converts.[77]

With a firm faith I believe and profess all and every one of the things contained in that Creed which the holy Roman Church makes use of: "I believe in one God the Father Almighty," etc. [The Nicene Creed]

I most steadfastly admit and embrace apostolic and ecclesiastic traditions, and all other observances and constitutions of the same Church.

I also admit the Holy Scriptures, according to that sense which our holy mother Church has held and does hold, to which it belongs to judge the true sense and interpretation of the Scriptures. I will never take and interpret them otherwise than according to the unanimous consent of the Fathers.

I also profess that there are truly and properly seven sacraments of the new law instituted by Jesus Christ our Lord, and necessary for the salvation of mankind, although all are not for everyone: baptism, confirmation, the eucharist, penance, extreme unction, holy orders, and matrimony; and that they confer grace; and that baptism, confirmation, and ordination cannot be reiterated without sacrilege. I also receive and admit the received and approved ceremonies of the Catholic Church, used in the solemn administration of the aforesaid sacraments.

I embrace and receive all and every one of the things that have been defined and declared in the holy Council of Trent concerning original sin and justification.

I profess, likewise, that in the Mass there is offered to God a true, proper, and propitiatory sacrifice for the living and the dead; and that in the most holy sacrament of the eucharist there is truly, really and substantially, the body and blood, together with the soul and divinity of our Lord Jesus Christ; and that there is made a change of the whole essence of the bread into the body, and of the whole essence of the wine into the blood, a change the Catholic Church calls transubstantiation. I also confess that under either kind alone [78] Christ is received whole and entire, and a true sacrament.

I firmly hold that there is a purgatory, and that the souls therein detained are helped by the assistance of the faithful. Likewise, that the saints reigning with Christ are to be honored and invoked, and that they offer up prayers to God for us, and that their relics are to be venerated.

I most firmly assert that the images of Christ, and of the perpetual Virgin the Mother of God, and also of other saints, ought to be had and retained, and that due honor and veneration are to be given them. I also affirm that Christ left the power of indulgences in the Church, and that the use of them is most wholesome to Christian people.

I acknowledge the holy Catholic Apostolic Roman Church for the mother and mistress of all

---

* *Profession of Tridentine Faith*

[77] Philip Schaff, *Creeds of Christendom*, vol. 2 (New York: Harper, 1919), 207–10.

---

[78] *either kind alone:* i.e., either bread or wine. This is to affirm the withholding of the wine from laity.

churches; and I promise and swear true obedience to the Bishop of Rome, successor to St. Peter, Prince of the Apostles, and Vicar of Jesus Christ. I likewise receive with certainty and profess all other things delivered, defined, and declared by the Sacred Canons and General Councils, particularly by the holy Council of Trent. I condemn, reject, and anathematize all things contrary thereto, and all heresies that the Church has condemned, rejected, and anathematized. I do, at this present, freely profess and truly hold this true Catholic faith, without which no one can

be saved. I promise most constantly to retain and confess the same entire and inviolate, with God's assistance, to the end of my life. I will take care, as far as in me lies, that it shall be held, taught, and preached by my subjects, or by those whom I care for by virtue of my office. This I promise, vow, and swear; so help me God, and these holy Gospels of God.[79]

---

[79] *these holy Gospels of God:* the gospel book which the person taking the oath is touching.

Catholic Reform Mysticism*

Teresa of Avila, Spain (1515–1582), was a Carmelite nun and a reformer of the Carmelite order who was also a mystic and writer. Her main work is The Interior Castle, *a book of mystical piety written for her fellow nuns. Teresa's mysticism was to prove a leading element in the Catholic Reformation.*[80]

Today while beseeching our Lord to speak for me because I wasn't able to think of anything to say nor did I know how to begin to carry out this obedience, there came to my mind what I shall now speak about, that which will provide us with a basis to begin with. It is that we consider our soul to be like a castle made entirely out of a diamond or of very clear crystal, in which there are many rooms, just as in heaven there are many dwelling places. For in reflecting upon it carefully, Sisters, we realize that the soul of the just person is nothing else but a paradise where the Lord says He finds His delight. So then, what do you think that abode will be like where a King so powerful, so wise, so pure, so full of all good things takes His delight? I don't find anything

---

* Teresa of Avila, *The Interior Castle* 1, 5, 7–9, 15
[80] From Kieran Kavanaugh and Otilio Rodriguez, trans., *Teresa of Avila: The Interior Castle* (New York: Paulist, 1979). Copyright © 1979 by the Missionary Society of St. Paul the Apostle in the State of New York. Used by permission of Paulist Press.

comparable to the magnificent beauty of a soul and its marvelous capacity. Indeed, our intellects, however keen, can hardly comprehend it, just as they cannot comprehend God; but He Himself says that He created us in His own image and likeness.

Well, if this is true, as it is, there is no reason to tire ourselves in trying to comprehend the beauty of this castle. Since this castle is a creature and the difference, therefore, between it and God is the same as that between the Creator and His creature, His Majesty in saying that the soul is made in His own image makes it almost impossible for us to understand the sublime dignity and beauty of the soul. . . .

5.   Well, getting back to our beautiful and delightful castle we must see how we can enter it. It seems I'm saying something foolish. For if this castle is the soul, clearly one doesn't have to enter it since it is within oneself. How foolish it would seem were we to tell someone to enter a room he is already in. But you must understand that there is a great difference in the ways one may be inside the castle. For there are many souls who are in the outer courtyard—which is where the guards stay—and don't care at all about entering the castle, nor do they know what lies within that most precious place, nor who is within, nor even how many rooms it has. You

have already heard in some books on prayer that the soul is advised to enter within itself; well, that's the very thing I'm advising. . . .

7.   Insofar as I can understand, the gate of entry to this castle is prayer and reflection. I don't mean to refer to mental more than vocal prayer, for since vocal prayer is prayer it must be accompanied by reflection. A prayer in which a person is not aware of whom he is speaking to, what he is asking, who it is who is asking and of whom, I do not call prayer however much the lips may move. Sometimes it will be so without this reflection, provided that the soul has these reflections at other times. Nonetheless, anyone who has the habit of speaking before God's majesty as though he were speaking to a slave, without being careful to see how he is speaking, but saying whatever comes to his head and whatever he has learned from saying at other times, in my opinion is not praying. Please God, may no Christian pray in this way. Among yourselves, Sisters, I hope in His Majesty that you will not do so, for the custom you have of being occupied with interior things is quite a good safeguard against failing and carrying on in this way like brute beasts. . . .

8.   Well now, let's get back to our castle with its many dwelling places. You mustn't think of these dwelling places in such a way that each one would follow in file after the other; but turn your eyes toward the center, which is the room or royal chamber where the King stays, and think of how a palmetto has many leaves surrounding and covering the tasty part that can be eaten. So here, surrounding this center room are many other rooms; and the same holds true for those above. The things of the soul must always be considered as plentiful, spacious, and large; to do so is not an exaggeration. The soul is capable of much more than we can imagine, and the sun that is in this royal chamber shines in all parts. It is very important for any soul that practices prayer, whether little or much, not to hold itself back and stay in one corner. Let it walk through these dwelling places which are up above, down below, and to the sides, since God has given it such great dig-

nity. Don't force it to stay a long time in one room alone. Oh, but if it is in the room of self-knowledge! How necessary this room is—see that you understand me even for those whom the Lord has brought into the very dwelling place where He abides. For never, however exalted the soul may be, is anything else more fitting than self-knowledge; nor could it be even were the soul to so desire. For humility, like the bee making honey in the beehive, is always at work. Without it, everything goes wrong.

9.   I don't know if this has been explained well. Knowing ourselves is something so important that I wouldn't want any relaxation ever in this regard, however high you may have climbed into the heavens. While we are on this earth nothing is more important to us than humility. So I repeat that it is good, indeed very good, to try to enter first into the room where self-knowledge is dealt with rather than fly off to other rooms. This is the right road, and if we can journey along a safe and level path, why should we want wings to fly? Rather, let's strive to make more progress in self-knowledge, for in my opinion we shall never completely know ourselves if we don't strive to know God. By gazing at His grandeur, we get in touch with our own lowliness; by looking at His purity, we shall see our own filth; by pondering His humility, we shall see how far we are from being humble. . . .

15.   Now then, what would happen, daughters, if we who are already free from these snares, as we are, and have entered much further into the castle to other secret dwelling places should turn back through our own fault and go out to this tumult? There are, because of our sins, many persons to whom God has granted favors who through their own fault have fallen back into this misery. In the monastery we are free with respect to exterior matters; in interior matters may it please the Lord that we also be free, and may He free us. Guard yourselves, my daughters, from extraneous cares. Remember that there are few dwelling places in this castle in which the devils do not wage battle. True, in some rooms the

guards (which I believe I have said are the faculties) have the strength to fight; but it is very necessary that we don't grow careless in recognizing the wiles of the devil, and that we not be deceived by his changing himself into an angel of light. There's a host of things he can do to cause us harm; he enters little by little, and until he's done the harm we don't recognize him.

ETHICS

Christian Freedom*

Here Luther develops his teaching on moral freedom and obligation in the context of his leading teaching of justification by faith. Note Luther's contrast between the inner and outer man.[81]

To make the way smoother for the unlearned—for I serve only them—I shall set down the following two propositions concerning the freedom and the bondage of the spirit: A Christian is a perfectly free lord of all, subject to none. A Christian is a perfectly dutiful servant of all, subject to all.

These two theses seem to contradict each other. If, however, they should be found to fit together they would serve our purpose beautifully. Both are Paul's own statements, who says in 1 Cor. 9, "For though I am free from all men, I have made myself a slave to all," and in Rom. 13, "Owe no one anything, except to love one another." Love by its very nature is ready to serve and be subject to him who is loved. So Christ, although he was Lord of all, was "born of woman, born under the law" and therefore was at the same time a free man and a servant, "in the form of God" and "of a servant."

Let us start, however, with something more remote from our subject, but more obvious. Man has a twofold nature, a spiritual and a bodily one. According to the spiritual nature, which men refer to as the soul, he is called a spiritual, inner, or new man. According to the bodily nature, which men refer to as flesh, he is called a carnal, outward, or old man, of whom the Apostle writes in 2 Cor. 4, "Though our outer nature is wasting away, our inner nature is being renewed every day." Because of this diversity of nature the Scriptures assert contradictory things concerning the same man, since these two men in the same man contradict each other, "for the desires of the flesh are against the Spirit, and the desires of the Spirit are against the flesh," according to Gal. 5.

First, let us consider the inner man to see how a righteous, free, and pious Christian, that is, a spiritual, new, and inner man, becomes what he is. . . .

One thing, and only one thing, is necessary for Christian life, righteousness, and freedom. That one thing is the most holy Word of God, the gospel of Christ, as Christ says, John 11, "I am the resurrection and the life; he who believes in me, though he die, yet will be free indeed"; and Matt. 4, "Man shall not live by bread alone, but by every word that proceeds from the mouth of God." . . . From this you once more see that much is ascribed to faith, namely, that it alone can fulfill the law and justify without works. You see that the First Commandment, which says, "You shall worship one God," is fulfilled by faith alone. If you were nothing but good works from the soles of your feet to the crown of your head, you would still not be righteous or worship God or fulfill the First Commandment, since God cannot be worshiped unless you ascribe to him the glory of truthfulness and all goodness which is

---

* Martin Luther, *Treatise on Christian Liberty*
[81] Taken, with editing, from W. A. Lambert, *Works of Martin Luther,* vol. 2 (Philadelphia: Holman, 1915), 312–14, 323–25.

due him. This cannot be done by works but only by the faith of the heart. . . .

Now let us turn to the second part, the outer man. . . . Although, as I have said, a man is abundantly and sufficiently justified by faith inwardly, in his spirit, and so has all that he needs, except insofar as this faith and these riches must grow from day to day even to the future life; yet he remains in this mortal life on earth. In this life he must control his own body and have dealings with men. Here the works begin; here a man cannot enjoy leisure; here he must indeed take care to discipline his body by fasting, watchings, labors, and other reasonable discipline and to subject it to the Spirit so that it will obey and conform to the inner man and faith and not revolt against faith and hinder the inner man, as it is the nature of the body to do if it is not held in check. The inner man, who by faith is created in the image of God, is both joyful and happy because of Christ in whom so many benefits are conferred upon him. Therefore it is his one occupation to serve God joyfully and without thought of gain, in love that is not constrained.

While he is doing this, behold, he meets a contrary will in his own flesh which strives to serve the world and seeks its own advantage. This the spirit of faith cannot tolerate, but with joyful zeal it attempts to put the body under control and hold it in check.

In doing these works, however, we must not think that a man is justified before God by them, for faith, which alone is righteousness before God, cannot endure that erroneous opinion. We should think of the works of a Christian who is justified and saved by faith because of the pure and free mercy of God, just as we would think of the works which Adam and Eve did in Paradise, and all their children would have done if they had not sinned. We read in Genesis 2 that "The Lord God took the man and put him in the Garden of Eden to till it and keep it." Now Adam was created righteous and upright and without sin by God so that he had no need of being justified and made upright through his tilling and keeping the garden; but, that he might not be idle, the Lord gave him a task to do, to cultivate and protect the garden. This task would truly have been the freest of works, done only to please God and not to obtain righteousness, which Adam already had in full measure and which would have been the birthright of us all. . . .

We conclude, therefore, that a Christian lives not in himself, but in Christ and in his neighbor. Otherwise he is not a Christian. He lives in Christ through faith, in his neighbor through love. By faith he is caught up beyond himself into God. By love he descends beneath himself into his neighbor. Yet he always remains in God and in his love.

Luther and Calvin on the Role of Women in the Church*

Both Luther and Calvin, despite their rejection of clerical celibacy, did not give women a significantly fuller role in the church than did the Roman Catholic church. In the first reading, Luther argues that women only have the right to preach if men are unwilling to preach (i.e., rarely or never). In the sec- *ond reading, Calvin calls head covering and silencing of women a church law that can legitimately be made for order and decorum but alterable if conditions change.*

The papists quote to us the saying of Paul (1 Cor. 14): "The women should keep silence in the church; it is not becoming for a woman to preach. A woman is not permitted to preach, but she should be subordinate and obedient." They

---

* Martin Luther, *The Misuse of the Mass;* J. Calvin, *Institutes* 4.10.28–31

argue from this that preaching cannot be common to all Christians because women are excluded. My answer to this is that one also does not permit the mute to preach, or those who are otherwise handicapped or incompetent. Although everyone has the right to preach, one should not use any person for this task, nor should anyone undertake it, unless he is better fitted than the others. To him the rest should yield and give place, so that the proper respect, discipline, and order may be maintained. Thus Paul charges Timothy to entrust the preaching of the Word of God to those who are fitted for it and who will be able to teach and instruct others.[82] The person who wishes to preach needs to have a good voice, good eloquence, a good memory, and other natural gifts; whoever does not have these should properly keep still and let somebody else speak. Thus Paul forbids women to preach in the congregation where men are present who are skilled in speaking, so that respect and discipline may be maintained; because it is much more fitting and proper for a man to speak, a man is also more skilled at it.

Paul did not forbid this out of his own devices, but appealed to the [Old Testament] law, which says that women are to be subject. From the law Paul was certain that the Spirit was not contradicting Himself by now elevating the women above the men after He had formerly subjected them to the men; but rather, being mindful of His former institution, He was arousing the men to preach, as long as there is no lack of men. How could Paul otherwise have single-handedly resisted the Holy Spirit, who promised in Joel: "And your daughters shall prophesy"? Moreover, we read in Acts: "Philip had four unmarried daughters, who all prophesied." And Miriam the sister of Moses was also a prophetess. And Huldah the prophetess gave advice to pious King Josiah, and Deborah did the same to Duke Barak; and finally, the song of the Virgin Mary is praised throughout the world. Paul himself in

1 Corinthians 11 instructs the women to pray and prophesy with covered heads. Therefore order, discipline, and respect demand that women keep silent when men speak; but if no man were to preach, then it would be necessary for the women to preach.

[Calvin, *Institutes*] It is worthwhile to define more clearly what meant by that decorum which Paul commends, and also by order [1 Cor. 14:40].

The first purpose of decorum is that, when rites are used which promote reverence toward holy things, we become holier by such helps. The second purpose is that modesty and seriousness, which ought to characterize all honorable acts, may greatly shine there. The first purpose of having good order is that those in charge know the rule and law of good governing, and that the people who are governed become accustomed to obedience to God and proper discipline. Its second purpose is so that, when we have the church in good order, it has peace and quietness. . . .

As a consequence, decorum cannot exist where there is nothing but empty pleasure. We see such an example in the theatrical props that the papists use in their sacred rites. Nothing appears there except the mask of useless elegance and fruitless extravagance. For us, decorum is something so fitted to the reverence of the sacred mysteries that it may be a suitable exercise for devotion, or at least will serve as an appropriate adornment of the act. Even this adornment should not be fruitless, but should encourage believers to treat sacred rites with great modesty, piety, and reverence. Ceremonies, to be exercises of piety, must lead us straight to Christ. . . .

There are examples of [decorum] in Paul. Profane drinking should not be mingled with the Sacred Supper of the Lord [1 Cor. 11:21–22], and women should not go out in public with uncovered heads [1 Cor. 11:5]. We have many others in daily use, such as: we pray with knees bent and head bare; we administer the Lord's sacraments not carelessly, but with some dignity; in burying the dead we use decency. . . .

---

[82] II Timothy 2:2.

There are the hours set for public prayers, sermons, and sacraments. At sermons there are quiet and silence, appointed places, the singing together of hymns, fixed days for the celebration of the Lord's Supper, the fact that Paul forbids women to teach in the church [1 Cor. 14:34], and the like. Especially there are rules that maintain discipline, such as catechizing, church censures, excommunication, fasting, and whatever can be referred to the same list.

Thus all church regulations which we accept as holy and helpful should be classified in two ways: the first type pertains to rites and ceremonies; the second to discipline and peace. . . .

But there is danger here. On the one hand, false bishops seize from this the pretext to excuse their impious and tyrannous laws; and on the other, some are too scrupulous and, warned of the above evils, leave no place whatever for holy regulations. Consequently, I must declare that I approve only those human regulations that are founded upon God's authority, drawn from Scripture, and, therefore, wholly divine.

Let us take, for example, kneeling when solemn prayers are offered. Is it a human tradition, which anyone may rightly repudiate or neglect? I say that it is human, and it is also divine. . . .

What sort of freedom of conscience could there be in excessive attentiveness and caution [to regulations]? Indeed, it will be very clear when we realize that these are not fixed and permanent sanctions by which we are bound, but outward rudiments for human weakness. Although not all of us need them, we all use them, for we are mutually bound, one to another, to nourish mutual love. This may be recognized in the examples set forth above. What? Does religion consist in a woman's shawl, so that it is unlawful for her to go out with a bare head? Is that decree of Paul's concerning silence [of women] so holy that it cannot be broken without great offense? Is there in bending the knee or in burying a corpse any holy rite that cannot be neglected without offense? Not at all. For if a woman needs such haste to help a neighbor that she cannot stop to cover her head, she does not offend if she runs to her with head uncovered. And there is a place where it is no less proper for her to speak than to remain silent.

Calvin on the Calling of All Christians*

This chapter of the Institutes, *"How We Must Use the Present Life and Its Helps," is often cited as important in the Protestant Reformation's impact on culture and economics. The sociologist Max Weber, in his influential book* The Protestant Ethic and the Spirit of Capitalism *(1905), argued that Calvin's concept of calling, which states that Christians have a duty to work well in this life for the glory of God and the good of others, is linked to the assurance that one is predestined to eternal life. If one works well and prospers, the argument goes, it is a sign of divine approval. This, Weber claimed, led to a "Protestant work ethic" that still is present today in modern society, although in a more secularized form.*[83]

By elementary instruction, Scripture . . . informs us about the correct use of earthly benefits. This matter must not be neglected in the ordering of our life. If we are to live, we also must use those helps necessary for living. We also cannot avoid those things that seem to serve enjoyment more than necessity. Therefore we must hold to a rule so we can use them with a clear conscience, whether for necessity or for enjoyment. The

---

* John Calvin, *Institutes* 3.10

[83] Translated by the author from P. Barth and W. Niesel, eds., *Johannis Calvini: Opera Selecta* (Munich: Kaiser, 1928).

Lord lays down this rule in his word when he teaches that the present life is for his people like a pilgrimage, on which they are hastening toward the heavenly kingdom. If we must simply pass through this world, we certainly ought to use its good things insofar as they help rather than hinder our course. Paul rightly persuades us to use this world as if not using it, and to buy goods with the same attitude as one who sells them.[84]

But this topic is a slippery one and slopes on both sides into error. Let us try to place our feet where we may safely stand. Some otherwise good and holy men, when they saw intemperance and dissoluteness . . . desired to correct this dangerous evil. This plan occurred to them: they allowed people to use physical goods only as necessity required. A godly plan indeed, but they were far too severe. For they would bind people's consciences more tightly than the Word of the Lord does, which is a very dangerous thing. . . .

[2] Let this be our principle: the use of God's gifts is correct when it follows the purpose for which their Author created and destined them for us, since he created them for our good, not for our destruction. . . . If we ponder why God created food, we shall find that God meant not only to provide for necessity but also for our enjoyment and happiness. Thus the purpose of clothing, apart from necessity, is beauty and decency. Grasses, trees and fruits have a beauty of appearance and pleasantness of smell even apart from their human uses. If this were not true, the prophet would not have counted them among the blessings of God: "wine gladdens the heart of man, and oil makes his face shine."[85] Scripture would not remind us repeatedly, in commending God's kindness, that God gave all such things to us humans. The natural qualities of things demonstrate sufficiently why and how we may enjoy them. Has the Lord clothed the flowers with the great beauty that greets our eyes, the sweetness

of smell that comes into our nostrils, and yet forbid our eyes to be affected by that beauty, or our sense of smell by the sweetness of that odor? . . . In a word, did God not make many things attractive to us apart from their necessary use?

Away, then, with that inhuman philosophy which allows only a necessary use of the creation, malignantly deprives us of the correct fruit of God's goodness. It robs people of all their senses and degrades them to a block. On the other hand, we must diligently resist the lust of the flesh; unless it is kept in order, it overflows uncontrollably. It has, as I have said, its own advocates, who permit everything under the pretext of freedom. One way to restrain it to determine that all things were created for us to recognize the Author and give thanks for his kindness toward us. Where is your thanksgiving if you gorge yourself with so much fine dining and wine that you either become stupid or unfit for the duties of faith and your calling? . . . Many people so enslave all their senses to enjoyment that their mind is overwhelmed. Many are so delighted with marble, gold and pictures that they themselves become marble. They turn, so to speak, into metal and are like paintings. Others are so overcome by the sweet smell of the kitchen that they are unable to smell anything spiritual. . . .

The second rule is this. Those who have narrow and slim resources should know how to do without things patiently. They must not be troubled by an immoderate desire for them. If they keep this rule of moderation, they will make considerable progress in the Lord's school. . . . This is my point: those who are ashamed of inexpensive clothing will brag when they get costly clothing; those who are not content with a simple meal are troubled by their desire for a more elegant one, and they will intemperately abuse those elegances if they come their way. Those who bear their deprivation and humble condition with a reluctant and troubled mind often fall into arrogance when they are advanced to honors. To this reason, then, let all those for whom the pursuit of piety is not pretentious try to learn, by the apostle's example, how to be

---

[84] I Corinthians 7:30–31.
[85] Psalm 104:15.

filled and to be hungry, to be prosperous and needy.[86]

Scripture has a third rule that regulates the use of earthly things. We said something about this when we discussed the precepts of love. It decrees that all things are given to us by the kindness of God and destined for our benefit. Thus they are, as it were, entrusted to us; we must one day give an account of them. This saying must continually sound in our ears: "Render account of your stewardship" [Luke 16:2]. At the same time let us remember by whom such reckoning is required: God who has strongly commended abstinence, seriousness, frugality and moderation. God also hates excess, pride, ostentation and vanity. . . .

[6] Finally, this point should be emphasized. The Lord commands each one of us in all life's actions to look to God's calling. God knows human nature, its burning with great restlessness, its fickleness that carries here and there, its ambition that longs to embrace various things at once. So that our stupidity and rashness do not turn everything upside-down, God has appointed duties for every person in their particular way of life. No one may thoughtlessly transgress these limits. God has named these various ways of life "callings." Therefore each individual has a way of life assigned by the Lord as a sort of sentry post so that he may not wander about throughout life. . . .

It brings no small relief from cares, labors, troubles and other burdens for a person to know that God is our guide in all these things. The magistrate will discharge his functions more willingly. The head of the household will confine himself to his duty. All people will deal with the discomforts, vexations, weariness and anxieties in their way of life when they have been persuaded that the burden was laid upon them by God. From this arises a singular consolation: no task will be so sordid and lowly that it will not shine and be very precious in God's sight, provided you obey your calling in it.

---

[86] Philippians 4:12.

RELATIONS

An Early Appeal for Religious Toleration*

In 1524, the south German Anabaptist leader Balthasar Hubmaier wrote a tract arguing for complete religious toleration, in particular against the practice of executing heretics.[87]

Heretics are those who wickedly oppose the Holy Scriptures, the first of whom was the devil. . . . Also heretics are those who cast a veil over the Scriptures and interpret them other than the Holy Spirit directs. . . . One should overcome them with holy knowledge, not angrily but softly, although the Holy Scriptures contain angry things. . . . If they will not be taught by strong arguments or evangelical reasons, then let them be, and leave them to rage and be mad. . . .

The law that condemns heretics to the fire builds up Zion in blood and Jerusalem in wickedness. . . . The inquisitors are the greatest heretics of all, since they condemn heretics to the fire against the command of Christ, and root up the weeds before the time of harvest.[88] For Christ did not come to butcher, kill and burn, but that

---

* Balthasar Hubmaier, *On Heretics and Those Who Burn Them*
[87] Taken, with editing, from H. C. Vedder, *Balthasar Hubmaier* (New York: Putnam's Son, 1905).

---

[88] Matthew 13:28.

those who live might live more abundantly. We should pray and hope for repentance, as long as man lives. A Turk or a heretic is not convinced by either the sword or fire, but only with patience and prayer; and so we should wait for the judgment of God with patience.

It is no excuse, as they claim, that they give heretics over to the secular power [to be exe-cuted]. . . . The secular power rightly and properly puts to death those criminals who injure the bodies of the defenseless, but those who belong to God cannot injure anyone. . . . Hence to burn heretics is in appearance to profess Christ, but in reality to deny him. . . . It is clear to everyone, even the blind, that a law to burn heretics is an invention of the devil. The truth cannot be killed.

Ignatius on Combating Protestants*

Ignatius had a constant concern to check the growth of Protestantism. Here he freely admits to members of his order the failings of the Roman Catholic Church and urges drawing on the most effective Protestant methods to spread Roman Catholicism.[89]

Seeing the progress which the heretics have made in a short time, spreading the poison of their evil teaching throughout so many countries and peoples . . . it would seem that our society, having been accepted by Divine Providence among the efficacious means to repair such great damage, should be solicitous to prepare the proper steps, such as are quickly applied and can be widely adopted, thus exerting itself to the utmost of its powers to preserve what is still sound and to restore what has fallen sick of the plague of heresy, especially in the northern nations.

The heretics have made their false theology popular and presented it in a way that is within the capacity of the common people. They preach it to the people and teach it in the schools, and scatter booklets that can be bought and understood by many, and make their influence felt by means of their writings when they cannot do so by their preaching. Their success is largely due to the negligence of those who should have shown some interest; and the bad example and the ignorance of Catholics, especially the clergy, have made such ravages in the vineyard of the Lord.

Hence it would seem that our Society should make use of the following means to put a stop and apply a remedy to the evils that have come upon the Church through these heretics.

In the first place, the sound theology that is taught in the universities and seeks its foundation in philosophy, and therefore requires a long time to acquire is adapted only to good and alert minds. Because the weaker ones can be confused and, if they lack foundations, collapse, it would be good to make a summary of theology to deal with topics that are important but not controversial, with great brevity. There could be more detail in matters controversial, but it should be accommodated to the present needs of the people. It should solidly prove dogmas with good arguments from Scripture, tradition, the councils, and the doctors, and refute the contrary teaching. It would not require much time to teach such a theology, since it would not go very deeply into other matters. In this way theologians could be produced in a short time who could take care of the preaching and teaching in many places. The abler students could be given higher courses that include greater detail. Those who do not succeed in these higher courses should be removed from them and put in this shorter course of theology.

The principal conclusion of this theology, in the form of a short catechism,[90] could be taught to children, as the Christian doctrine is now

---

* Ignatius, Letter of August 13, 1554
[89] *Letters of St. Ignatius of Loyola,* 345–47 (MI XII, No. 27).

[90] *catechism:* an instructional manual laid out in question and answer form, very popular with the Protestant Reformers.

taught, and likewise to the common people who are not too infected or too capable of subtleties. This could also be done with the younger students in the lower classes, where they could learn it by heart. . . .

Another excellent means for helping the Church in this trial would be to multiply the colleges and schools of the society in many lands, especially where a good attendance could be expected. . . .

Not only in the places where we have a residence, but even in the neighborhood, the better among our students could be sent to teach the Christian doctrine on Sundays and feast days. Even the extern students, should there be suitable material among them, could be sent by the rector for the same service. Thus, besides the correct doctrine, they would be giving the example of a good life, and by removing every appearance of greed they will be able to refute the strongest argument of the heretics—the bad life and the ignorance of the Catholic clergy.

The heretics write a large number of booklets and pamphlets, by means of which they aim at taking away all authority from the Catholics, and especially from the society, and set up their false dogmas. It would seem expedient, therefore, that ours here also write answers in pamphlet form, short and well written, so that they can be produced without delay and bought by many. In this way the harm that is being done by the pamphlets of the heretics can be remedied and sound teaching spread. These works should be modest, but lively; they should point out the evil that is abroad and uncover the evil machinations and deceits of the adversaries. A large number of these pamphlets could be gathered into one volume. Care should be taken, however, that this be done by learned men well grounded in theology, who will adapt it to the capacity of the multitude.

With these measures it would seem that we could bring great relief to the Church, and in many places quickly apply a remedy to the beginnings of the evil before the poison has gone so deep that it will be very difficult to remove it from the heart. But we should use the same diligence in healing that the heretics are using in infecting the people. We will have the advantage over them in that we possess a solidly founded, and therefore an enduring, doctrine. . . .

Truce between Protestants and Catholics*

Warfare between Lutheran and Catholic states in Germany broke out in the year of Luther's death, 1546. In 1555, an agreement between the warring parties was signed in Augsburg. It established some freedom of religion for both parties and established the principle of "whose region, his religion": the official and dominant faith of each section of Germany was determined by the faith of its ruler. More a truce than a treaty, the Peace of Augsburg lasted until the Thirty Years' War in 1618.[91]

Peace between their Imperial and Royal Majesties, on the one hand, and the Electors and States of the realm, on the other. . . .

We wish to secure again peace and confidence, in the minds of the states and subjects toward each other, and to save the German nation, our beloved Fatherland, from final dissolution and ruin; we, on the one hand, have united and agreed with the Electors and States, that from henceforth no one of whatsoever honor, rank or character, for any cause, or upon any pretense whatsoever, shall engage in feuds, or make war upon, rob, seize, invest, or besiege another. . . . In order that such peace may be better established and made secure and enduring between his Roman Imperial Majesty[92] and us, on the one hand, and the electors, princes, and states of the Holy Empire of the German nation on the other,

* *The Peace of Augsburg*
[91] Taken, with editing, from J. H. Robinson, *Readings in European History*, vol. 2 (Boston: Ginn, 1906).

[92] *Roman Imperial Majesty:* Charles V, the Holy Roman Emperor.

we agree that no one shall make war upon any estate of the empire on account of the Augsburg Confession and the doctrine, religion, and faith of the same, nor injure nor do violence to those states that hold it, nor force them, against their conscience, knowledge, and will, to abandon the religion, faith, church usages, ordinances, and ceremonies of the Augsburg Confession, where these have been established, or may hereafter be established, in their principalities, lands, and dominions. Nor shall we, through mandate or in any other way, trouble or disparage them, but shall let them quietly and peacefully enjoy their religion, faith, church usages, ordinances, and ceremonies, as well as their possessions, real and personal property, lands, people, dominions, governments, honors, and rights. . . .

On the other hand, the states that have accepted the Augsburg Confession shall allow his Imperial Majesty, princes and states of the Holy Empire, who adhere to the old religion, to abide in like manner by their religion, faith, church usages, ordinances, and ceremonies. They shall also leave undisturbed their possessions, real and personal property, lands, people, dominions, government, honors, and rights, rents, interest, and tithes. . . .

All others who are not adherents of either of the above-mentioned religions are not included in this peace, but shall be altogether excluded. . . .

When our subjects and those of the electors, princes, and states, adhering to the old religion or to the Augsburg Confession, wish, for the sake of their religion, to go with wife and children to another place in the lands, principalities, and cities of the electors, princes, and states of the Holy Empire, and settle there, such going and coming, and the sale of property and goods, in return for reasonable compensation for serfdom and arrears of taxes . . . shall be everywhere unhindered, permitted, and granted. . . .

But since in many free and imperial cities both religions, namely, our old religion and that of the Augsburg Confession, have already come into existence and practice, the same shall remain hereafter and be held in the same cities. Citizens and inhabitants of the said free and imperial cities, whether spiritual or secular in rank, shall peacefully and quietly dwell with one another. No party shall venture to abolish the religion, church customs, or ceremonies of the other, or persecute them. . . .

The *Heidelberg Catechism* on the Roman Mass*

Olevianus and Ursinus, two Reformed German theologians, wrote the Heidelberg Catechism in 1563. Like all catechisms, it has an instructional use in the churches, especially in preparation for confirmation. Usually seen as one of the finest and most influential statements of Reformed theology, the catechism is generally positive, as seen in its Question 1. But hostility between Protestants and Catholics grew so sharp that even their most positive documents bore the scars of hatred. Question 80 was not a part of the original catechism, but was added in the second edition by order of Elector Fred-erick III in response to the anathemas of Protestantism at the Council of Trent. The parts in brackets were added in the third edition.[93]

Q. 1: What is your only comfort in life and in death?

A: That I, with body and soul, both in life and in death, am not my own, but belong to my faithful Savior Jesus Christ, who with his precious blood has fully satisfied for all my sins, and redeemed me from the power of the devil. He so

---

* *Heidelberg Catechism*, Q. 1, 80

[93] Taken, with editing, from Philip Schaff, *Creeds of Christendom*, vol. 3 (New York: Harper, 1919), 307–08, 335–36.

preserves me that without the will of my Father in heaven not a hair can fall from my head; yes, that all things must work together for my salvation. Therefore, by his Holy Spirit, he also assures me of eternal life, and makes me heartily willing and ready henceforth to live unto him.

Q. 80: What difference is there between the Lord's Supper and the Popish Mass?

A: The Lord's Supper testifies to us that we have full forgiveness of all our sins by the one sacrifice of Jesus Christ, which he himself has once accomplished on the cross [and that by the Holy

Ghost we are grafted into Christ, who with his true body is now in heaven at the right hand of the Father, and is to be there worshipped]. But the Mass teaches that the living and the dead have not forgiveness of sins through the suffering of Christ unless Christ is still daily offered for them by the priests [and that Christ is bodily under the form of bread and wine, and is therefore to be worshipped in them]. And the Mass at bottom is nothing else than a denial of the one sacrifice and passion of Jesus Christ [and an accursed idolatry.].

Reformed and Anglican Views of the Relation of Church and State*

The Magisterial Reformation encouraged a close relationship between the church and the state. In the first reading, John Calvin explains his view of this relationship, in which the state is subject to the laws of God. Unlike Anabaptists, Calvin did not advocate that the church should dictate to the state, or that the state should base its laws only and directly on Scripture.[94] In the second reading, Richard Hooker (1554–1600) argues that the church and state (here called the commonwealth*) are in essence one; the church is the state from a Christian viewpoint.[95] This position became the leading Anglican idea in relating church and state.*

The establishment of civil justice and outward morality seems alien to the spiritual doctrine of faith that I have been discussing, but what follows will show that I am right in joining them. In fact, necessity compels me to do so. This is especially true for two reasons. On the one hand, in-

sane and barbarous people furiously attempt to overturn this divinely established order. On the other hand, the flatterers of rulers do not hesitate to set them against the rule of God by unreasonably enlarging their powers. Unless both these evils are stopped, pure faith will perish. Moreover, if we know how lovingly God has provided in this matter for humankind, greater zeal for piety will flourish in us and show our gratefulness to God.

But before we enter into the matter itself, we must keep in mind the distinction which we previously made. We must not (as commonly happens) unwisely mingle these two types of government, which have a completely different nature. For certain people, when they hear that the gospel brings a freedom from kings and magistrates, but looks to Christ alone, think that they cannot benefit by their freedom as long as any human power is over them. . . .

Civil government has its purpose as long as we live among people. It is to respect and protect the worship of God, to defend sound doctrine and the position of the church, to adjust our life to the human society, to form our social behavior to civil righteousness, to reconcile us with one another and to promote general peace and tranquility. All of this is indeed unnecessary if

---

* John Calvin, *Institutes* 4.20.1–3, 31–32; R. Hooker, *Laws of Ecclesiastical Polity*

[94] Translated by the author from P. Barth and W. Niesel, eds., *Johannis Calvini: Opera Selecta,* vol. 5 (Munich: Kaiser, 1928), 471–74, 501–502.

[95] Taken, with editing, from J. Keble, *The Works of Richard Hooker* (London: Oxford University Press, 1841).

God's kingdom, as it is now among us, wipes out the present life. But God wants us to be pilgrims on the earth while we aspire to our true homeland, and if our pilgrimage requires such help, those who take these helps from us deprive us of our very humanity. Our opponents argue that the church of God ought to be so perfect that its government is the law. But they stupidly imagine a perfection that can never be found in a community of people. . . .

We must understand that doing away with government is outrageous barbarity. Its function among humans is no less than that of bread, water, sun and air; indeed, its place of honor is far more excellent. It does not merely see to it, as all these do, that men breathe, eat, drink and are kept warm, even though it encompasses all these activities when it provides for their living together. Government does not, I repeat, do only this. It also prevents idolatry, sacrilege against God's name, blasphemies against His truth and other public offenses against religion from arising and spreading among the people. It prevents the public peace from being disturbed; it provides that everyone may keep property safe and sound; that people may carry on blameless dealings among themselves; that honesty and modesty may be preserved. In sum, it provides that a public manifestation of religion may exist among Christians and that humanity be maintained among people. . . .

But in that obedience which we have shown to be due the authority of rulers, we must always make one exception. Indeed, it is most important that such obedience never lead us away from obedience to God to whose will the desires of all kings ought to be subject, to whose decrees all their commands ought to yield, to whose majesty their rule ought to be submitted. How absurd it would be if in satisfying humans you should incur the displeasure of God, for whose sake you obey humans themselves!

[Richard Hooker, *Laws of Ecclesiastical Polity*] A church is naturally different from a commonwealth, because a commonwealth is defined in one way and a church in another way. There are people who hold that the Church and the commonwealth are corporations that are distinct not only in nature and definition but also in substance. According to their theory the members of the Church cannot perform any of the duties of the state, and the members of the state cannot perform any of the duties of the Church. If they do so, they violate the law of God, who divided them and requires that Church and state should function as independent entities because they are so completely separated. Each of them depends upon God, but neither depends upon the other's approval for anything it has to do.

Our opinion is the opposite of this, for we say that the care of religion should be the common concern of every state. Those states that embrace the true religion have the name of the Church in distinction from those states that do not accept the true religion. Every state, therefore, has a religion, but every state does not have the true religion; and only those states that have the true religion have the Church. It is the truth of religion that distinguishes a church from states that do not have the Church.

When we speak of true religion we are using the term in the broad sense, and not in the sense of every detail of religious truth. There are states that deviate from the truth in particular points, but which, in comparison with states that hold a heathen religion, may be said to profess the true religion. Thus, although in antiquity there were many states throughout the world, it was only the commonwealth of Israel that had the true religion and was for that reason the Church of God. The Church of Jesus Christ is made up of all the states that hold the religious truth that is distinctive of Christianity. Therefore, we may say that, as a state, a commonwealth maintains religion, and as a Church that state maintains that religion which God has revealed by Jesus Christ.

We see, therefore, that according to our view the Church is a society of men organized first of all as a public or civil government, and second distinguished from other states by the exercise of the Christian religion. With those, however, who take the opposite view from ours,[96] the Church is a group of men united together and distinguished from other groups by the exercise of the Christian religion, and necessarily and perpetually divided from the body of the commonwealth. Even if we have a state made up exclusively of Christians, the Church of Christ and the commonwealth are two corporations each existing independently of each other.

Our view is different from that which holds that Church and state are two corporations. Here in England there is not a man who is a member of the Church of England who is not a member of the commonwealth; and there is not a man who is a member of the commonwealth who is not a member of the Church of England. . . . There is a distinction between Church and state, and yet the same group is both Church and state. Thus it is that no one who is a member of one can be denied to be a member of the other.

The church and commonwealth, therefore, are a single corporation, which is called a commonwealth in relation to its secular law and government, and is called a church in relation to its submission to the spiritual law of Jesus Christ. These two sets of laws make necessary two different sets of offices, and therefore there are officers in charge of one set of laws and not the other; yet, society as a whole is not divided, and is not cut into two separate societies.

---

[96] *the opposite view from ours:* those nonconformists, especially Baptists, who argue for separation of church and state.

GLOSSARY

Anabaptists "rebaptizers," the Radical Reformers who insisted on adult baptism only and other characteristic doctrines.

Calvinist see **Reformed Church.**

catechism a document in question-and-answer form for the instruction of the laity.

Catholic Reformation the changes in the Roman Catholic Church in the sixteenth and seventeenth centuries, especially as a result of the Council of Trent (1545). Also known as **Catholic Reform;** formerly known as the **Counter-Reformation.**

confession a full, definitive formulation of doctrine, especially of the various Protestant churches.

Evangelicals "those who follow the Gospel"; the first name of the sixteenth-century Christian reforming movement.

indulgence a writing certifying the remission of temporal punishment, especially in purgatory.

Magisterial Reformation the Lutheran and Reformed branches of the Reformation, which emphasized a role for government ("magistracy") in the life of the church.

Protestant a term used after 1529 to describe those who protested against the beliefs and practices of the Church of Rome by forming their own churches.

Protestant Reformation the sixteenth-century movement for reform of the church.

Radical Reformation the Anabaptist wing of the Reformation.

Reformation a series of changes in Christianity from the fourteenth through the seventeenth centuries, but especially in the sixteenth century, which is known as the **Reformation Era.**

Reformed Church the name of the churches of the Protestant branch founded by John Calvin; in the British Isles, the Reformed branch was known as **Presbyterian** for the system of government by elders (*presbyters*). Also known as **Calvinist** churches.

theses propositions for academic debate.

QUESTIONS FOR STUDY AND DISCUSSION

1.   Discuss the many meanings of the term *Reformation*.

2.   To what extent, in your opinion, was the Catholic Reformation a "Counter-Reformation," and to what extent a long overdue reform from within?

3.   How did Protestants and Catholics disagree over the basic doctrine of salvation?

4.   Discuss this statement: "In the sixteenth century, to reform the church meant changing the world."

5.   What was the role of women in the Protestant Reformation? In what sense was the Reformation a "mixed blessing" for women?

6.   What are the strengths and weaknesses of the Roman Catholic teaching, reasserted against Protestants in this era, that the Christian faith consists just as much of tradition as Scripture?

7.   Discuss the idea of the Protestant work ethic as found in the writings of Calvin and Luther. To what degree is a "work ethic" Protestant (or even Calvinist) rather than generally Christian?

8.   Compare the writings of the Magisterial Reformation with those of the Anabaptist wing of the Reformation on the differing doctrines of the church.

9.   Discuss the rising protests in this period against using execution as a method of keeping the Christian church "pure."

SUGGESTIONS FOR FURTHER READING

G. Bray, ed., *Documents of the English Reformation*. Minneapolis: Fortress, 1994. A full documentary source for the Reformation in England, with some small attention to Scotland; begins in 1526 and goes until 1700.

H. J. Hillerbrand, ed., *The Reformation: A Narrative History Related by Contemporary Observers and Participants*. Grand Rapids, MI: Baker, 1964. A rich, interesting source of primary Reformation documents and pictures, woven together in a simple narrative style. Covers both the Protestant and Catholic reforms.

Denis R. Janz, ed., *A Reformation Reader: Primary Texts with Introductions*. Minneapolis: Fortress, 1999. Covers the late medieval background and both Protestant and Catholic Reform.

M. D. W. Jones, *The Counter-Reformation*. Cambridge Topics in History Series. Cambridge, UK: Cambridge University Press, 1995. Uses a wide variety of primary sources, with good introductions and questions for study.

J. C. Olin, *Catholic Reform from Cardinal Ximenes to the Council of Trent, 1495–1563*. New York: Fordham University Press, 1990. Introduction and an excellent sampling of documents.

G. H. Williams, *Spiritual and Anabaptist Writers: Documents Illustrative of the Radical Reformation*. Library of Christian Classics, vol. 25. Philadelphia: Westminster, 1957. Translations with full introductions and annotations of such Anabaptists as Blaurock, Müntzer, Franck, and Menno Simon.

CHAPTER SIX

Early Modern Christianity (1600–1900)

❖ In a small apartment in Beijing, China, a group of Chinese Roman Catholics have met secretly for prayer and mutual encouragement. Because they have no priest, the Mass cannot be celebrated. They are a part of the Chinese Catholic church that keeps its primary allegiance to Rome and has refused to join the Catholic group that is regulated by the communist government. Their situation reminds them of the situation of early Christians in the Roman empire, who were also under the suspicion of their government and faced persecution.

❖ In New York City, a new translation of the New Testament published by Oxford University Press causes a stir. Billed as the first thoroughly inclusive Bible, it features "thoroughly nonsexist" wording. Some hostile critics deride it as the "politically correct version" and a dangerous innovation. However, students of Christianity recognize that this type of translation has a rich pedigree in America. It can trace its roots to the influential, and even more controversial, "Women's Bible" of 1898.

❖ In Los Angeles, filmmakers work on *Star Trek III,* a new science-fiction film set in the twenty-third century. They discuss the music to accompany a key event in the film, the funeral of the character known as Spock, an emotional scene filled with sorrow but with a hint of hope. The tune they select for inclusion in the film, "Amazing Grace," has an early modern Protestant origin. Now it belongs to the church throughout the world and potentially—as the film suggests—to the universe.

INTRODUCTION

The period between the Reformation of the sixteenth century and the twentieth century was a time of both consolidation and growth for Christianity. In Europe, and then in North America, Protestantism and Roman Catholicism settled into a long-term standoff, protecting their spheres of territorial strength and settling into predictable theological argument against each other. The Eastern Orthodox branch of Christianity, which did not feel the main effects of the Reformations, continued on its traditional course stressing ancient doctrine and liturgy. Confessionalism and orthodoxy ruled the day in the seventeenth century. But with the rise of the secular spirit of the Enlightenment in the eighteenth century, all Western Christianity found itself challenged. Devotional piety was strengthened as one response to secularism, and new churches such as the Methodist denomination arose. In the nineteenth century, the spirit of secular reason posed two other challenges to Christian tradition: a scientific, evolutionary understanding of human life and a historical understanding of the Bible. Also in the nineteenth century, a movement began that would profoundly alter the future of Christianity—vigorous foreign missions spreading Protestant (and, to a lesser degree, Roman Catholic) Christianity to the whole world and sparking an ecumenical movement among almost all parts of world Christianity.

Names

No widely accepted name for the years 1600–1900 has emerged in scholarship, even though this time frame is often employed in historical writing about Christianity. This lack probably results from the absence of one single defining event or group of events, such as the Reformation in the period that precedes it. Therefore, a few more generic, less than fully descriptive names have emerged.

Some scholars refer to this period as the Post-Reformation. This is a truism that says little to describe the period itself. *Post-Reformation* could just as well apply to the twentieth century and beyond, but no one uses that appellation. Sometimes this period is named after some of its main theological movements, such as Confessional Christianity, Scholastic Orthodoxy, the Age of Pietism or Christianity in the Enlightenment Era. But these terms are all too limited, and too theologically oriented, to serve as a comprehensive name for the entire period. Older scholarship has used the term *modern* on the assumption that the Reformation was a bridge between the medieval world and our own time. More recent scholarship seems to prefer the term *early modern* to distinguish this time from our own (modern) time. Like the terms *modern* and *Post-Reformation* above, *early modern* does not say much at all about the content of this period. But since scholars of the Christian tradition use this term most often and since historians generally recognize it as well, we will use *early modern* here to refer to the three centuries prior to the twentieth in Western history.

Historical Sketch

After the Reformation, Western Christianity was divided between a solidly Roman Catholic south and a predominantly (although mixed) Protestant north. Protestantism was in turn divided between the Lutheran, Reformed, Anglican and Baptist wings. The East was largely untouched by the Reformation and continued on its course set by the ancient church.

By the end of the sixteenth century, the trends of confessionalism and scholasticism had already set into Lutheran and Reformed (and to a lesser extent Anabaptist) churches. Because of the rather settled situation, with each Protestant church occupying its own parts of Europe, the only competition left between the churches was intellectual. **Confessionalism** brought a drive for doctrinal correctness and a narrowing focus of the literary genre of confessions written during the first generations of the Reformation. As the churches of the mainstream Reformation focused on their denominational distinctions and continued to do battle against the Roman church, they grew farther apart, even to the point of hostility.

Scholasticism grew along with confessionalism on the continent. It stressed rational explanation and defense of the various Protestant belief systems, especially with reasoning drawn from Aristotle. (The similarities with late medieval scholasticism in the Roman Catholic church are striking, and it is not accidental that the name for both movements is the same.) Human reason was given a large role in understanding and defending doctrine, and theology became more logical, philosophical, and speculative. As time went on, theologians dealt only with other theologians. Large systematic theologies, some on the order (but not quite the size) of a Protestant *Summa Theologiae,* were produced. The practical, biblical orientation of Luther and Calvin was lost, and theology became more academic and remote.

The reaction against confessionalism and scholasticism was not slow in coming. **Pietism** arose in the last half of the seventeenth century, born with Philip Jakob Spener's *Pia Desiderata* ("Pious Considerations," 1675). Spener rebelled against the confessionalism and scholastic orthodoxy of his day, which he viewed as sterile and lifeless. He proposed a continuing Reformation to bring the goals of Luther to fulfillment: personal Bible study, mutual correction and encouragement in Christian living, and spiritual growth for all laity. The leadership of the Lutheran churches tried to suppress Pietism, but it soon became a major movement. English Puritanism also had its Pietist aspects, and the Methodist movement in the Anglican Church was Pietist as well. Even in the Roman Catholic church, the Jansenist movement in France and then in North America, although not considered a part of Pietism, also promoted personal piety and holier living among the laity. Each of these manifestations of Pietism had a similar aim, to encourage a deeper seriousness for personal Christian faith and daily life.

In the eighteenth century, Pietism took on the major goal of counteracting the influence on Christianity of the **Enlightenment,** the period of secularization of culture led by the philosophical position that posited a reason cut off from faith. The Enlightenment's rationalism and "free thinking" was easier for the church to deal with when it took the more radical form of aggressive atheism and **secularism,** the idea that human life can be fully lived without reference to God or any religion, as it did in the French Revolution. But when the Enlightenment led to more subtle changes in the church itself, such as the introduction of modern historical sciences and their application to the Bible and theology, the affect on Christianity was more profound. Especially in Protestant faculties of German universities, the application of these new methods of scholarship led to a radical questioning of the historical and rational basis of the Christian faith. The discovery of other religions, especially the ancient religions of Asia, led to a questioning of the uniqueness and absoluteness of Christianity (a questioning, as we will see in the next chapter, that still continues today). As the effects of the Enlightenment worked their way into literature, politics, and ultimately everyday life in Europe and then America, the special privileges that Christianity had enjoyed in the Western world since Constantine began to erode. The Enlightenment's separation of church and state, and the ideas of religious toleration and freedom associated with it, came especially to America and then to Europe in a generally milder way. Another result of the Enlightenment was **Deism,** which adapted Christianity to reason by downplaying the supernatural.

The nineteenth century saw the challenge of secular reason continue. Historical scholarship continued to chip away at some of the old certainties of the Christian faith. Even more challenging to traditional belief were the discoveries in natural science. The work of Charles Darwin, especially his books *The Origin of Species* (1859) and *The Descent of Man* (1871), called into question the ancient Christian beliefs in the special creation of humanity in the image of God. As evolutionary theory became accepted in the natural sciences, Christianity had a hard time adapting. Although Protestant churches were more directly and immediately affected by the Enlightenment and its heirs, Roman Catholicism later saw its affects in Catholic **Modernism,** a liberal movement in the nineteenth century that denied the exclusive truth of Christianity. Not until the twentieth century would Catholic, Protestant, and (to lesser extent) Eastern Orthodox churches come to grips with the challenges of modern knowledge. The relation between faith and knowledge will no doubt continue to be, as it has in almost every era of Christianity, a lively and important issue.

Despite the challenge of secularism, nineteenth-century Christianity was broadly optimistic about the prospects of the faith in the twentieth century. One factor in this positive outlook was the powerful missionary movement. Most of the churches of the West, Protestant and Catholic, set out to evangelize the entire world, or at least the large parts of it not yet exposed to the gospel. Although the missionary and the colonial/ commercial conqueror marched together (as they had often done in the past, especially in the New World), the nineteenth century saw the beginning of their separation. The twentieth century would witness the independence of almost all the churches founded in this, "the great century" of Christian mission, in which Christianity finally became the global religion that the term *catholic* implies.

This mission movement led directly to the other great cause for Christian optimism, the ecumenical movement. **Ecumenism** is respect, cooperation, and even re-uniting of the badly fractured Christian church. As the Protestant (not Roman Catholic and Protestant) missionaries cooperated "on the ground" in foreign missions, their old attitudes to the differences between Protestants began to change. In the context of non-Western cultures and non-Christian religions, the similarities among all Christians appeared more numerous and powerful than their differences. Soon the new co-operation on the mission field began to travel back home to the missionaries' churches of origin in North America and Europe, and the ecumenical movement that would dominate twentieth-century Christianity was born.

Literary Genres of the Primary Sources

The early modern period saw a continued use of many of the older genres in the Christian tradition. This is especially true of Eastern Christianity; with its reverence for ancient Christian tradition, Orthodoxy was hesitant to develop new forms of literary expression. (The popular *Way of the Pilgrim* was one such new story.) The primary sources of Western Christianity reflected new situations and tasks, but many of the old literary forms were still employed. *Histories* continue to be written, and the apologetic aims of history-writing last seen in the ancient period of Christianity return as Protestants and Catholics both write (and sometimes rewrite) the story of the past to justify their own churches. *Apologetic* writings themselves continue from the Reformation in a strong way, as Protestants and Catholics directly attack each other and defend themselves from attack. In the later part of the modern period, both abolitionists and feminists would use the apologetic genre for their purposes. Some apologetic is doctrinal, and others more personal/emotional, such as abolitionist writings, and the anti-Catholic fabrications of Maria Monk. *Letters,* especially official letters, also remain important as a means of communication and publication. *Sermons* gain new importance in both Protestant and Catholic traditions as a result of the Reformation's emphasis on the indoctrination and moral formation of the laity. Finally, *academic writing,* such as the systematic and philosophical presentation of the faith, regains the importance it had in the high Middle Ages but lost in the Reformation. Roman Catholics turned to Aquinas, and mainstream Protestant groups also drew on reason and philosophy to defend their doctrines intellectually: first against Roman Catholics, then against each other, and finally against the rising power of secularism.

One new genre, the **journal,** or formal personal diary, comes into common use in this period. Although St. Augustine of Hippo's ancient *Confessions* is a chronologically ordered work about himself, it is really more of an autobiography than a journal. Journals were rare in the Middle Ages and in Reformation times. But in early modern times, many religious leaders wrote day-by-day reflections on their activities. George Fox and John Wesley are the two most prominent examples. These journals should be read not just as personal diaries, which in a sense they are, but as formal accounts of the founding of a movement.

EVENTS

The Rise of Puritanism*

William Law had a bright career ahead of him as a priest in the Church of England when, upon the coronation of George I, he refused the loyalty oath to the king as head of the church. Law then became a well-respected writer of devotional classics. In 1729, he wrote A Serious Call to a Devout and Holy Life, *which had a profound influence on most types of British Christianity, including the early Methodist movement. This reading expresses one of the key ideas of Reformed life and thought—that all of life should be made holy.*

As a good Christian should consider every place as holy because God is there, so he should look upon every part of his life as a matter of holiness because it is to be offered unto God. The profession of a clergyman is a holy profession because it is a ministration in holy things, an attendance at the altar. But worldly business is to be made holy unto the Lord by being done as a service to him and in conformity to his divine will. For as all men and all things in the world as truly belong unto God as any places, things, or persons that are devoted to divine service, so all things are to be used, and all persons are to act in their several states and employments, for the glory of God.

Men of worldly business therefore must not look upon themselves as at liberty to live to themselves, to sacrifice to their own humors[1] and tempers because their employment is of a worldly nature. But they must consider that as the world and all worldly professions as truly belong to God as persons and things that are devoted to the altar, so it is as much the duty of men in worldly business to live wholly unto God as it is the duty of those who are devoted to divine service.

---

* William Law, *A Serious Call to a Devout and Holy Life*

[1] *humors:* basic emotions.

As the whole world is God's, so the whole world is to act for God. As all men have the same relation to God, as all men have all their powers and faculties from God, so all men are obliged to act for God with all their powers and faculties. As all things are God's, so all things are to be used and regarded as the things of God. For men to abuse things on earth and live to themselves is the same rebellion against God as for angels to abuse things in heaven, because God is just the same Lord of all on earth as he is the Lord of all in heaven. . . .

Clergymen must live wholly unto God in one particular way, that is, in the exercise of holy office, in the ministration of prayers and sacraments, and a zealous distribution of spiritual goods. But men of other employments are in their particular ways as much obliged to act as the servants of God and live wholly unto him in their several callings. This is the only difference between clergymen and people of other callings. . . .

This is the common business of all persons in this world. It is not left to any women in the world to trifle away their time in the follies and impertinence of a fashionable life, nor to any men to resign themselves up to worldly cares and concerns. The rich must not gratify their passions in the indulgences and pride of life, nor the poor to vex and torment their hearts with the poverty of their state. But men and women, rich and poor, must with bishops and priests walk before God in the same wise and holy spirit, in the same denial of all vain tempers and in the same discipline and care of their souls. They must do this not only because they have all the same rational nature and are servants of the same God, but because they all want the same holiness to make them fit for the same happiness to which they are all called. It is therefore absolutely necessary for all Christians, whether men or women, to consider themselves as persons that are devoted to holiness, and so order their common ways of life by such rules of reason and piety as may turn it into continual service unto almighty God.

Reaction to Witchcraft Trials*

In the Salem, Massachusetts, witchcraft trials of 1692, the accused were found guilty on the basis of that person's "specter" appearing to someone in a dream and doing harm. Such "evidence" was impossible to refute. Cotton Mather (1663–1728), pastor of Boston's Second Congregational Church and the colony's leading theologian, began to doubt the validity of such evidence. Eventually he and his father, Increase Mather (1639–1723), led the way in the discrediting of spectral evidence (although they did believe in witches, as this reading shows). Once such evidence was no longer so readily believed, the accusations soon ceased. In all New England, about forty people were hanged. While the witchcraft hysteria was rightly seen as an evil by many people in New England, its duration and toll were remarkably small compared with Europe's extensive witchhunts.[2]

I must humbly beg you that in the management of the affair in your most worthy hands, you do not lay more stress upon pure specter testimony than it will bear. When you are satisfied or have good, plain, legal evidence that the demons which molest our poor neighbors do indeed represent such and such people to the sufferers, though this be a presumption, yet I suppose you will not reckon it a conviction that the people so represented are witches to be immediately exterminated. . . . I believe that the just God ordinar-

---

* Cotton Mather, *Tests for Witches*

[2] Kenneth Silverman, ed., *Selected Letters of Cotton Mather* (Baton Rouge: Louisiana State University Press, 1971), 36–37, 39–40. Used by permission.

ily provides a way for the speedy vindication of the persons thus abused. Moreover, I do suspect that persons who have too much indulged themselves in malignant, envious, and malicious ebullitions of their souls, may unhappily expose themselves to the judgment of being represented by devils, of whom they never had any vision, and with whom they have much less written any covenant. I would say this: upon the bare supposal of a poor creature's being represented by a specter, and great progress be made by the authority in ruining a poor neighbor so represented, it may be that a door may be thereby opened for the devils to obtain from the courts in the invisible world a license to proceed unto most hideous desolations upon the repute and repose of such as have yet been kept from the great transgression. If mankind has thus far consented to the credit of diabolical representations, the door is opened! Perhaps there are wise and good men that may be ready to style one who advances this caution an advocate of the witch. But in the winding up [of witchcraft trials], this caution will certainly be wished for. . . .

The business of this witchcraft is very much transacted upon the stage of imagination. Yet we know that, as in treason there is an imagining which is a capital crime, here also the business thus managed in imagination yet may not be called imaginary. The effects are dreadfully real. Our neighbors are most really tormented, really murdered, and really acquainted with hidden things, which are afterwards proved plainly to have been realities. . . . Our neighbors at Salem Village are blown up, after a sort, with an infernal gunpowder; the train [of gunpowder] is laid in the laws of the kingdom of darkness limited by God himself.

The Religious Experience of Jonathan Edwards*

The Puritan theologian Jonathan Edwards remains the greatest theological genius and religious leader America has produced. As a preacher he led a religious revival in the 1730s in Northampton, Massachusetts, that foreshadowed the Great Awakening, a series of national religious revivals from 1725–1760. As a philosophical theologian, he produced a synthesis of the new philosophy of Newton and Locke and Calvinism. This selection, written in the early 1740s, shows Edwards's characteristic care in analyzing religious experience and his Reformed commitment to the sovereignty of God.[3]

From my childhood up, my mind had been full of objections against the doctrine of God's sovereignty, in choosing whom he would to eternal life, and rejecting whom he pleased; leaving them eternally to perish, and be everlastingly tormented in hell. It used to appear like a horrible doctrine to me. But I remember the time very well, when I seemed to be convinced, and fully satisfied, as to this sovereignty of God and his justice in thus eternally disposing of men, according to his sovereign pleasure. . . . And there has been a wonderful alteration in my mind, with respect to the doctrine of God's sovereignty, from that day to this; so that I scarce ever have found so much as the rising of an objection against it, in the most absolute sense, in God's showing mercy to whom he will show mercy, and hardening whom he will. . . .

Not long after I first began to experience these things, I gave an account to my father of some things that had passed in my mind. I was pretty much affected by the conversation we had together. When the conversation was ended, I walked abroad alone, in a solitary place in my father's pasture, for contemplation. As I was walking there, and looking upon the sky and clouds, there came into my mind so sweet a sense of the glorious majesty and grace of God, as I know not how to express. I seemed to see them both in a

---

* Jonathan Edwards, *Personal Narrative*
[3] Jonathan Edwards, *The Works of President Edwards,* vol. 1 (New York: Leavett & Allen, 1852), 16–18, 23.

sweet conjunction; majesty and meekness joined together: it was a sweet, and gentle, and holy majesty; and also a majestic meekness; an awful sweetness; a high, and great, and holy gentleness.

After this my sense of divine things gradually increased, and became more and more lively, and had more of that inward sweetness. The appearance of every thing was altered; there seemed to be, as it were, a calm, sweet cast, or appearance of divine glory, in almost every thing. God's excellency, his wisdom, his purity and love, seemed to appear in every thing; in the sun, moon and stars; in the clouds and blue sky; in the grass, flowers, trees; in the water and all nature; which used greatly to fix my mind. I often used to sit and view the moon for a long time; and in the day, spent much time in viewing the clouds and sky, to behold the sweet glory of God in these things: in the meantime, singing forth, with a low voice, my contemplations of the Creator and Redeemer. . . .

I now sought an increase of grace and holiness, and a holy life, with much more earnestness, than ever I sought grace before I had it. I used to be continually examining myself, and studying and contriving for likely ways and means, how I should live in a holy manner, with far greater diligence and earnestness, than ever I pursued any thing in my life; but yet with too great a dependence on my own strength; which afterwards proved a great damage to me. My experience had not then taught me, as it has done since, my extreme feebleness and impotence, every manner of way; and the bottomless depths of secret corruption and deceit there was in my heart. . . .

I have a much greater sense of my universal, exceeding dependence on God's grace and strength, and mere good pleasure, of late, than I used formerly to have; and have experienced more of an abhorrence of my own righteousness. The very thought of any joy arising in me, on any consideration of my own amiableness, performances, or experiences, or any goodness of heart or life, is nauseous and detestable to me. And yet, I am greatly afflicted with a proud and self-righteous spirit, much more [obviously] than I used to be formerly. I see that serpent rising and putting forth its head continually, everywhere, all around me.

Though it seems to me, that in some respects, I was a far better Christian, for two or three years after my first conversion, than I am now. I lived in a more constant delight and pleasure; yet of late years, I have had a more full and constant sense of the absolute sovereignty of God, and a delight in that sovereignty; and have had more of a sense of the glory of Christ, as a Mediator revealed in the gospel.

The Origins of Pietism*

The Pietist movement began with the publication of Philip Spener's Pia Desiderata *("Pious Considerations") in 1675. Spener, a Lutheran pastor, complained about dry, dull orthodoxy in the Lutheran church in Germany and proposed ways for reform, most importantly regular and serious Bible study for all Christians. Pietism became a movement within Lutheranism but also deeply affected many parts of the Reformed churches, and in Anglicanism it helped to give birth to the Methodist move-ment. The influence of Pietism continues today in many branches of Protestantism.*[4]

Every careful reader of Luther's writings will have observed with what earnestness the sainted man stressed spiritual priesthood, by which not only ministers, but also all Christians have been made priests through their Redeemer, anointed with the Holy Spirit, and consecrated to spiritual

---

* Philip Spener, *Pious Considerations*

[4] Spener, *The Spiritual Priesthood* (Philadelphia: Fortress, 1917).

priestly functions. . . . [A]ll spiritual offices belong to all Christians without distinction, although their regular and public administration is committed to the ordained ministers. However, in a case of necessity they may also be performed by others, and especially those offices, which are not of a public character, shall always be exercised at home and in common life by all.

Indeed it has been one of the chief stratagems of the hateful devil that under the papacy all these spiritual offices were turned over to the clergy alone. For this reason they also haughtily appropriated to themselves alone the name of spiritual, which is really common to all Christians. Other Christians were excluded from these spiritual offices, as if it were not proper for them earnestly to study the Word of the Lord, much less to instruct, admonish, reprove and comfort others, and to do privately what the ministers of the Church have to do publicly, as though these were matters attached to their office alone. Hereby, on the one hand, the so-called laymen were made indolent in things which ought justly also to concern them, from which resulted frightful ignorance and thereby wild life. On the other hand, the so-called spirituals were able to do what they pleased, because nobody was permitted to look into their cards or make the least protest. This arrogated monopoly of the spiritual estate, together with the debarring of the laity from the Scriptures, was one of the chief means under the papacy by which papal Rome established, and where it still holds sway, maintains its power over poor Christians. Hence no severer blow could have been given to it than when Luther showed, on the contrary, that all Christians have been called to spiritual offices. They are not only authorized, but, if they wish to be real Christians, are in duty bound to fulfill them. They are not called to the public administration of them, for which, in view of the equal right of all, appointment by the congregation is required.

Accordingly the Christian is obligated to offer prayer, thanks, good works, alms, etc., for himself and what pertains to him. He is also obligated to study the Word of the Lord earnestly and to teach, reprove, exhort, convert and edify others, especially those of his own house, as grace is given to him, to observe their life, to pray for all, and as much as possible to have a care for their salvation. If people were shown this, everyone would give more heed to himself and become active in those things which pertain to his own and his neighbor's edification. . . .

For my part, I am quite confident that if in every congregation only a few could be led to do these two things, to make diligent use of the divine Word and to exercise their priestly functions, especially in fraternal admonition and correction, much would be gained. Then others would be gradually won, and finally the entire Church would be noticeably improved.

The Conversion of John Wesley*

The conversion of John Wesley marked the beginnings of the Methodist movement. Wesley had witnessed the Moravian Pietist movement onboard a ship bound for Georgia, and was deeply impressed. Upon his return, he sought like Luther to find "the faith whereby alone we are saved." In May 1738, he found his way to a meeting in Aldersgate Street in London, where he discovered this faith and, in his famous phrase, felt his heart to be "strangely warmed."[5]

What occurred on Wednesday, 24, I think best to relate at large,[6] after premising what may make it the better understood. Let him that cannot

---

[5] J. Emory, *The Works of the Reverend John Wesley, A.M.* (New York: Methodist Episcopal Church, 1831).
[6] *at large:* in a fuller way.

receive it, ask of the Father of lights, that he would give more light to him and me.

I believe, till I was about ten years old I had not sinned away that "washing of the Holy Ghost" which was given me in baptism; having been strictly educated and carefully taught, that I could only be saved "by universal obedience, by keeping all the commandments of God"; in the meaning of which I was diligently instructed. And those instructions, so far as they respected outward duties and sins, I gladly received, and often thought of. But all that was said to me of inward obedience, or holiness, I neither understood nor remembered. I was indeed as ignorant of the true meaning of the Law, as I was of the Gospel of Christ.

The next six or seven years were spent at school; where outward restraints being removed, I was much more negligent than before, even of outward duties, and almost continually guilty of outward sins, which I knew to be such, though they were not scandalous in the eye of the world. However, I still read the Scriptures, and said my prayers, morning and evening. And what I now hoped to be saved by was, (1) Not being so bad as other people; (2) Having still a kindness for religion; and (3) Reading the Bible, going to church, and saying my prayers.

Being removed to the University[7] for five years, I still said my prayers both in public and in private, and read, with the Scriptures, several other books of religion, especially comments on the New Testament. Yet I had not all this while so much as a notion of inward holiness. . . .

When I was about twenty-two, my father pressed me to enter into holy orders. At the same time, the providence of God directing me to Kempis's "Christian Pattern,"[8] I began to see that true religion was seated in the heart, and that God's Law extended to all our thoughts as well as words and actions. I was, however, very angry at Kempis for being too strict. Yet I had

frequently much sensible comfort in reading him, such as I was an utter stranger to before. Meeting likewise with a religious friend, which I never had till now, I began to alter the whole form of my conversation, and to set in earnest upon a new life. I set apart an hour or two a day for religious retirement. I communicated[9] every week. I watched against all sin, whether in word or deed. I began to aim at, and pray for, inward holiness. So that now, "doing so much, and living so good a life," I doubted not but that I was a good Christian.

Removing soon after to another college,[10] I executed a resolution which I was before convinced was of the utmost importance—shaking off at once all my trifling acquaintance. I began to see more and more the value of time. I applied myself closer to study. I watched more carefully against actual sins; I advised others to be religious, according to that scheme of religion by which I model led my own life. I read Mr. Law's "Christian Perfection" and "Serious Call," although I was much offended at many parts of both.[11] . . .

In this refined way of trusting to my own works and my own righteousness, (so zealously inculcated by the mystic writers), I dragged on heavily, finding no comfort or help therein, till the time of my leaving England. On shipboard, however, I was again active in outward works; where it pleased God of his free mercy to give me twenty-six of the Moravian brethren for companions, who endeavored to show me "a more excellent way." But I understood it not at first. I was too learned and too wise. So that it seemed foolishness unto me. I continued preaching, and following after, and trusting in, that righteousness whereby no flesh can be justified.

---

[7] *the University:* Wesley was a student in Christ Church College of Oxford University.

[8] *"Christian Pattern":* the *Imitation of Christ.*

[9] *communicated:* received Holy Communion.

[10] *another college:* Wesley was then a fellow of Lincoln College, Oxford.

[11] *Mr. Law . . . both:* Wesley refers to the Puritan author William Law; the parts with which he was "much offended" were probably the Reformed teachings of divine election to salvation, which Wesley opposed strongly throughout his life.

All the time I was at Savannah[12] I was thus beating the air. Being ignorant of the righteousness of Christ, which, by a living faith in him, bringeth salvation "to every one that believeth," I sought to establish my own righteousness; and so laboured in the fire all my days. . . . In this vile, abject state of bondage to sin, I was indeed fighting continually, but not conquering. Before, I had willingly served sin; now it was unwillingly; but still I served it. I fell, and rose, and fell again. . . .

In my return to England, January, 1738, being in imminent danger of death, and very uneasy on that account, I was strongly convinced that the cause of that uneasiness was unbelief; and that the gaining a true, living faith, was the "one thing needful" for me. . . .

---

[12] *Savannah:* in the colony of Georgia.

I continued thus to seek [assurance of salvation by faith], (though with strange indifference, dullness, and coldness, and unusually frequent relapses into sin) till Wednesday, May 24. I think it was about five this morning, that I opened my Testament on those words: "There are given unto us exceeding great and precious promises, even that ye should be partakers of the Divine nature," II Peter 1:4. Just as I went out, I opened it again on those words, "Thou art not far from the Kingdom of God." . . .

In the evening I went very unwillingly to a society in Aldersgate Street, where one was reading Luther's preface to his Epistle to the Romans. About a quarter before nine, while he was describing the change which God works in the heart through faith in Christ, I felt my heart strangely warmed. I felt I did trust in Christ, Christ alone for salvation. An assurance was given me, that he had taken away my sins, even mine, and saved me from the law of sin and death.

The Birth of Quakerism*

Even in childhood George Fox had visions he called "openings." He concluded that a building could not be the "church" but only a "steeple house," for the true church is located in people's hearts. (Today Quaker buildings for worship are called "meeting houses.") His vision of social equality, peace, and the inner light of Christ that could guide everyone inspired the readers of the journal he left at his death. The Society of Friends he founded in the 1650s soon became known as the "Quakers" because of their shaking in religious emotion. This reading narrates an incident in Fox's life and a portion of a letter related to it. The Elizabethan English (e.g., the use of thee *and* thou) *characteristic of Fox and later Quakers has been retained.*[13]

When I came to eleven years of age, I knew pureness and righteousness; for while I was a child I was taught how to walk so as to be kept pure. The Lord taught me to be faithful in all things, and to act faithfully two ways, namely, inwardly to God, and outwardly to man. . . .

At another time it was opened in me, "That God who made the world did not dwell in temples made with hands."[14] This at the first seemed strange, because both priests and people used to call their temples or churches, dreadful places, holy ground, and the temples of God. But the Lord showed me clearly that he did not dwell in these temples which men had commanded and set up, but in people's hearts. . . .

Then I heard of a great meeting to be at Leicester for a dispute, wherein Presbyterians, independents, Baptists, and common-prayermen[15]

---

* George Fox, *Journal*
[13] George Fox, *The Journal of George Fox* (Philadelphia: Friends' Book Store, 1850), pp. 55, 59–61, 73–74, 274.

[14] Acts 7:48.
[15] *common-prayermen:* i.e., Anglicans.

were said to be all concerned. The meeting was in a steeple house; to which I was moved by the Lord God to go, and be amongst them. I heard their discourse and reasoning, some being in pews, and the priest in the pulpit, an abundance of people being gathered together. At last one woman asked a question out of Peter,[16] What that birth was, a being born again of incorruptible seed, by the Word of God, that liveth and abideth for ever? The priest said to her, I permit not a woman to speak in the church; though he had before given liberty for any to speak. Whereupon I was wrapped up as in a rapture, in the Lord's power, and I stepped up, and asked the priest, Dost thou call this place [the steeplehouse] a church? or dost thou call this mixed multitude a church? . . . But, instead of answering me, he asked me what a church was. I told him, The church was the pillar and ground of truth, made up of living stones, living members, a spiritual household, which Christ was the head of: but he was not the head of a mixed multitude, or of an old house made up of lime, stones, and wood. This set them all on a fire. . . .

When the Lord God and his Son Jesus Christ sent me forth into the world to preach his everlasting gospel and kingdom, I was glad that I was

commanded to turn people to that inward light, spirit, and grace, by which all might know their salvation and their way to God; even that Divine Spirit which would lead them into all truth, and which I infallibly knew would never deceive any.

But with and by this divine power and spirit of God, and the light of Jesus, I was to bring people off from all their own ways, to Christ the new and living way; from their churches, which men had made and gathered, to the church in God, the general assembly written in heaven, which Christ is the head of. . . .

Having got a little respite from travel, I was moved to write an epistle to friends, as followeth: "All friends of the Lord everywhere, whose minds are turned in toward the Lord, take heed to the light within you, which is the light of Christ: which, as you love it, will call your minds inward, that are abroad in the creatures: so your minds may be renewed by it, and turned to God in this which is pure, to worship the living God, the Lord of hosts over all the creatures. That which calls your minds out of the lusts of the world, will call them out of the affections and desires, and turn you to set your affections above. The same that calls the mind out of the world, will give judgment upon the world's affections and lusts, that which calls out your minds from the world's teachers and the creatures, to have your minds renewed.

---

[16] *Peter:* the question refers to I Peter 1:23.

The Beginnings of the Protestant Missionary Movement*

William Carey, a British Baptist pastor, argued that the commission of Jesus to the apostles, "Go into all the world, and preach the gospel to every creature," was still binding on Christians. As a missionary to India, he laid the basis for Western-style education, opposed such typical practices of the time such as slavery and widow burning, and did agricultural research. Carey's 1792 pamphlet sparked perhaps the greatest period of missionary activity

since the early church. Within forty years every important Protestant church in Europe and North America had its own organized foreign mission society.[17]

We cannot allege a natural impossibility in [engaging in foreign missions]. It has been said that we ought not to force our way, but to wait for

---

* William Carey, *An Inquiry into the Obligation of Christians to Use Means for the Conversion of the Heathen*

[17] William Carey, *An Enquiry into the Obligation of Christians to Use Means for the Conversion of the Heathen* (Leicester: Ann Ireland, 1792).

the openings, and leadings of Providence. But it might with equal propriety be answered in this case, neither ought we to neglect embracing those openings in providence which daily present themselves to us. What openings of providence do we wait for? We can neither expect to be transported into the heathen world without ordinary means, nor to be endowed with the gift of tongues, &c. when we arrive there. . . . Natural impossibility can never be pleaded so long as facts exist to prove the contrary. Have not the popish missionaries surmounted all those difficulties which we have generally thought to be insuperable? Have not the missionaries of the Unitas Fratrum, or Moravian Brethren, encountered the scorching heat of Abyssinia, and the frozen climes of Greenland, and Labrador their difficult languages, and savage manners? Or have not English traders, for the sake of gain, surmounted all those things which have generally been counted insurmountable obstacles in the way of preaching the gospel? Witness the trade to Persia, the East-Indies, China, and Greenland, yea even the accursed slave-trade on the coasts of Africa. Men can insinuate themselves into the favor of the most barbarous clans, and uncultivated tribes, for the sake of gain; and how different so ever the circumstances of trading and preaching are, yet this will prove the possibility of ministers being introduced there. . . .

It has been objected that there are multitudes in our own nation, and within our immediate spheres of action, who are as ignorant as the South-Sea savages, and that therefore we have work enough at home, without going into other countries. That there are thousands in our own land as far from God as possible, I readily grant, and that this ought to excite us to ten-fold diligence in our work, and in attempts to spread divine knowledge amongst them is a certain fact. But that it ought to supersede all attempts to spread the gospel in foreign parts seems to [lack] proof. Our own countrymen have the means of grace, and may attend on the word preached if they choose it. They have the means of knowing the truth, and faithful ministers are placed in almost every part of the land, whose spheres of ac-

tion might be much extended if their congregations were but more hearty and active in the cause. But with them the case is widely different, who have no Bible, no written language (which many of them have not), no ministers, no good civil government, nor any of those advantages which we have. Pity, humanity, and much more Christianity, call loudly for every possible exertion to introduce the gospel amongst them. . . .

Secondly, as to their uncivilized, and barbarous way of living, this can be no objection to any, except those whose love of ease renders them unwilling to expose themselves to inconveniences for the good of others. It was no objection to the apostles and their successors, who went among the barbarous Germans and Gauls, and still more barbarous Britons! They did not wait for the ancient inhabitants of these countries to be civilized, before they could be Christianized, but went simply with the doctrine of the cross. Tertullian could boast that "those parts of Britain which were proof against the Roman armies, were conquered by the gospel of Christ." . . .

Can we as men, or as Christians, hear that a great part of our fellow creatures, whose souls are as immortal as ours, and who are as capable as ourselves of adorning the gospel, and contributing by their preaching, writings, or practices to the glory of our Redeemer's name, and the good of his church, are enveloped in ignorance and barbarism? Can we hear that they are without the gospel, without government, without laws, and without arts, and sciences; and not exert ourselves to introduce amongst them the sentiments of men, and of Christians? Would not the spread of the gospel be the most effectual means of their civilization? . . .

If congregations were to open subscriptions of one penny, or more per week, according to their circumstances, and deposit it as a fund for the propagation of the gospel, much might be raised in this way. . . . Many persons have of late left off the use of West-India sugar, on account of the iniquitous manner in which it is obtained. Those families who have done so, and have not substituted any thing else in its place, have not only cleansed their hands of blood, but have made a saving to their families, some of six pence, and some of a shilling a week. If this, or a part of this were appropriated to the uses before-mentioned, it would abundantly suffice. We have only to keep the end in view, and have our hearts thoroughly engaged in the pursuit of it, and means will not be very difficult.

The Founding of the African Methodist Episcopal Church*

Richard Allen was a slave who bought his freedom, grew prosperous, and became the first African American to be ordained in the Methodist Church. Because of racial animosity against African-American Methodists by white Methodists in Philadelphia, a separate African Methodist Episcopal Church was organized in 1816, largely along the lines of its predecessor church. Richard Allen was appointed its first bishop.[18]

I thought I would stop in Philadelphia a week or two. I preached at different places in the city. My labor was much blessed. I soon saw a large field open in seeking and instructing my African brethren, who had been a long forgotten people and few of them attended public worship. I preached in the commons, in Southwark, Northern Liberties, and wherever I could find an opening. I frequently preached twice a day, at 5 o'clock in the morning and in the evening, and it was not uncommon for me to preach from four to five times a day. I established prayer meetings; I raised a society in 1786 for forty-two members. I saw the necessity of erecting a place of worship for the colored people. I proposed it to the most respectable people of color in this city; but here I met with opposition. . . . We viewed the forlorn state of our colored brethren, and that they were destitute of a place of worship. They were considered as a nuisance.

A number of us usually attended St. George's church in Fourth street; and when the colored people began to get numerous in attending the church, they moved us from the seats we usually sat on, and placed us around the wall, and on Sabbath morning we went to church and the sexton stood at the door, and told us to go in the gallery. He told us to go, and we would see where to sit. We expected to take the seats over the ones we formerly occupied below, not knowing any better. We took those seats. Meeting had begun, and they were nearly done singing, and just as we got to the seats, the elder said, "Let us pray." We had not been long upon our knees before I heard considerable scuffling and low talking. I raised my head up and saw one of the trustees, having hold of the Rev. Absalom Jones, pulling him up off of his knees, and saying, "You must get up— you must not kneel here." . . . By this time prayer was over, and we all went out of the church in a body, and they were no more plagued with us in the church. This raised a great excitement and inquiry among the citizens, in so much that I believe they were ashamed of their conduct. But my dear Lord was with us, and we were filled with fresh vigor to get a house erected to worship God in. . . .

We then hired a store-room, and held worship by ourselves. Here we were pursued with threats of being disowned, and read publicly out of meeting if we did continue worship in the place we had hired; but we believed the Lord would be our friend. We got subscription papers out to raise money to build the house of the Lord. . . . We entered into articles of agreement for a lot.

We bore much persecution from many of the Methodist connection. But we have reason to be thankful to Almighty God, who was our deliverer. The day was appointed to go and dig the cellar. I arose early in the morning and addressed the throne of grace, praying that the Lord would

* Richard Allen, *Life Experience and Gospel Labors of the Rt. Rev. Richard Allen*

[18] Richard Allen, *The Life Experience and Gospel Labors of the Rt. Rev. Richard Allen* (Nashville: Abingdon, 1960), 24–35.

bless our endeavors. Having by this time two or three teams of my own—as I was the first pro-poser of the African church, I put the first spade in the ground to dig a cellar for the same. This was the first African Church or meeting house that was erected in the United States of America. . . .

Notwithstanding we had been so violently persecuted by the elders, we were in favor of being attached to the Methodist connection. I was confident that there was no religious sect or denomination would suit the capacity of the col-ored people as well as the Methodist; for the plain and simple gospel suits best for any people; for the unlearned can understand, and the learned are sure to understand; and the reason that the Methodist is so successful in the awakening and conversion of the colored people is the plain doc-trine and having a good discipline. . . .

I bought an old frame [building] that had been formerly occupied as a blacksmith shop, from Mr. Sims, and hauled it on the lot in Sixth near Lombard street, that had formerly been taken for the Church of England. I employed carpenters to repair the old frame, and fit it for a place of worship. In July 1794, Bishop As-bury[19] being in town I solicited him to open the church for us which he accepted. The Rev. John Dickins sung and prayed, and Bishop Asbury preached. . . .

Many of the colored people in other places were in a situation nearly like those of Phila-delphia and Baltimore, which induced us, in April 1816, to call a general meeting, by way of Conference. Delegates from Baltimore and other places which met those of Philadelphia, and taking into consideration their grievances, and in order to secure the privileges, promote union and harmony among themselves, it was re-solved: "That the people of Philadelphia, Balti-more, etc., etc., should become one body, under the name of the African Methodist Episcopal Church."

---

[19] *Bishop Asbury:* Francis Asbury, American Methodist bishop and the major force in the rise of Methodism in America.

The Birth of Mormon Christianity*

In this reading, Joseph Smith recounts his first vi-sion, received in 1820, in which he learned that the forms of Christianity known to him were false. He would go on to form the one true church, the Church of Jesus Christ of Latter-Day Saints, infor-mally known as the Mormons. This reading conveys the characteristic Latter-Day Saint attitude to-ward other Christian churches.[20]

My mind at times was greatly excited, the cry and tumult were so great and incessant. The Pres-byterians were most decided against the Baptists and Methodists, and used all the powers of both reason and sophistry to prove their errors, or, at least, to make the people think they were in error. On the other hand, the Baptists and Methodists in their turn were equally zealous in endeavor-ing to establish their own tenets and disprove all others.

In the midst of this war of words and tumult of opinions, I often said to myself, what is to be done? Who of all these parties are right; or, are they all wrong together? If any one of them be right, which is it, and how shall I know it? While I was laboring under the extreme difficulties caused by the contests of these parties of reli-gionists, I was one day reading the Epistle of James, first chapter and fifth verse, which reads, "If any of you lack wisdom, let him ask of God, that giveth to all men liberally, and upbraideth not; and it shall be given him."

---

* Joseph Smith.
[20] Taken from B. H. Roberts, *History of the Church of Jesus Christ of Latter-Day Saints,* 2d ed., vol. 1 (Salt Lake City: Deseret, 1964), 4–6. Copyright 1964 Deseret Press. Used by permission.

Never did any passage of Scripture come with more power to the heart of man than this did at this time to mine. It seemed to enter with great force into every feeling of my heart. I reflected on it again and again, knowing that if any person needed wisdom from God, I did. . . . So, in accordance with this determination to ask God, I retired to the woods to make the attempt. It was on the morning of a beautiful, clear day, early in the spring of eighteen hundred and twenty. It was the first time in my life that I had made such an attempt, for amidst all my anxieties I had never yet made the attempt to pray vocally.

After I had retired to the place where I had previously designed to go, having looked around me, and finding myself alone, I kneeled down and began to offer up the desires of my heart to God. I had scarcely done so, when immediately I was seized upon by some power which entirely overcame me, and had such an astonishing influence over me as to bind my tongue so that I could not speak. Thick darkness gathered around me, and it seemed to me for a time as if I were doomed to sudden destruction. But, exerting all my powers to call upon God to deliver me out of the power of this enemy which had seized upon me, and at the very moment when I was ready to sink into despair and abandon myself to destruction—not to an imaginary ruin, but to the power of some actual being from the unseen world, who had such marvelous power as I had never before felt in any being—just at this moment of great alarm, I saw a pillar of light exactly over my head, above the brightness of the sun, which descended gradually until it fell upon me.

It no sooner appeared than I found myself delivered from the enemy that held me bound. When the light rested upon me I saw two personages, whose brightness and glory defy all description, standing above me in the air. One of them spoke unto me, calling me by name, and said—pointing to the other—"THIS IS MY BELOVED SON, HEAR HIM."[21]

My object in going to inquire of the Lord was to know which of all the sects was right, that I might know which to join. No sooner, therefore, did I get possession of myself, so as to be able to speak, than I asked the personages who stood above me in the light, which of all the sects was right—and which I should join. I was answered that I must join none of them, for they were all wrong. The personage who addressed me said that all their creeds were an abomination in His sight: that those professors were all corrupt; that "they draw near to me with their lips, but their hearts are far from me; they teach for doctrines the commandments of men: having a form of godliness, but they deny the power thereof."[22] He again forbade me to join with any of them. . . . When the light had departed, I had no strength; but soon recovering in some degree, I went home. And as I leaned up to the fireplace, mother inquired what the matter was. I replied, "Never mind, all is well—I am well enough off." I then said to my mother, "I have learned for myself that Presbyterianism is not true."

---

[21] *This . . . Him:* Mark 9:7.
[22] *they draw near . . . thereof:* a quotation from Isaiah 29:13.

Phoebe Palmer and the Beginnings of the Holiness Movement*

Phoebe Palmer was a founder of the Holiness movement in nineteenth-century American Protestantism, which tried to preserve the original teachings of John Wesley on entire sanctification and Christian perfection. Entire sanctification *takes place in an emotional experience similar to (prior) conversion and enables one to live without conscious sin. The Holiness movement was important for American Evangelicalism and resulted in the founding*

---

* Phoebe Palmer, *Entire Devotion to God,* Introduction

of many denominations, camp meeting associations, and schools. It also was supportive of women's rights to ordination; ironically, the first women to gain a measure of equality in Christianity did so in one of the most doctrinally conservative churches. This excerpt from her 1845 book, fully titled Present to My Christian Friend on Entire Devotion to God, *shows Palmer's leading ideas and evangelistic fervor.*[23]

My beloved Christian friend,

Will you accept this little token of regard from one deeply interested in your welfare? I have received your friendship as a precious gift from God. . . . Then, beloved one, let us be faithful to each other; and may our communings during our short sojourn here be so directed as shall in the highest possible degree tell towards our well-being in eternity.

Permit me then, beloved one, to ask, Are you ready? Have you on the white robe? No longer think of holiness as a doctrine peculiar to a *sect,* but rather as a doctrine peculiar to the *Bible,* as the only fitness for admission to the society of the bloodwashed in Heaven.

If you are not holy as a Christian, you are not a Bible Christian. . . . Gospel holiness is that state which is attained by the believer when, through faith in the infinite merit of the Savior, body and soul, with every ransomed faculty, are ceaselessly presented as a living sacrifice to God. . . . Holiness implies salvation from sin, redemption from *all* iniquity. Though being saved from all sin at present, yet the soul that has been brought into the experience of this state well knows that it is not saved to the uttermost. It finds that, in the entire surrender of the world, it has but "laid aside every weight." And now, with undeviating purpose and unshackled feet, it runs with increasing rapidity and delight in the way of his commandments, gaining new accessions of wisdom, power, and love, every other grace, daily.

---

[23] Taken from Phoebe Palmer, *Entire Devotion to God* (New York: Privately published, 1845).

INSTITUTION

Rules for the Methodist Societies*

All who had a "desire to flee from the wrath to come, to be saved from their sins" were eligible to join John Wesley's society. Wesley boasted that his followers "do not impose, in order to their admission, any opinions whatsoever. . . . The Presbyterian may be a Presbyterian still, the Independent and Anabaptist use his own mode of worship. They think and let think." Wesley did insist that those who continued in the Society observe certain rules, which were adopted for his societies in 1743 and are still printed in Methodist books of church government. Many of the rules were typical of Pietist movements and are still followed in some way by many conservative Protestant churches throughout the world today.[24]

It is therefore expected of all who continue therein, that they should continue to evidence their desire of salvation, First; By doing no harm: by avoiding evil in every kind; especially that which is most generally practiced. Such as: the taking the name of God in vain; the profaning the day of the Lord, either by doing ordinary work thereon, or by buying or selling; drunkenness, buying or selling spirituous liquors, or drinking

---

* *Doctrines and Disciplines of the Methodist Church*

[24] *Doctrines and Disciplines of the Methodist Church* (New York: Methodist Publishing House, 1940), 31–34.

them (unless in cases of extreme necessity); fighting, quarrelling, brawling; going to law;[25] returning evil for evil or railing for railing; the using of many words in buying or selling; the buying or selling uncustomed goods; the giving or taking things on usury, that is, unlawful interest; uncharitable or unprofitable conversation, particularly speaking evil of magistrates or ministers; doing to others as we would not they should do unto us; doing what we know is not for the glory of God: as the putting on of gold, or costly apparel; the taking such diversions as cannot be used in the name of the Lord Jesus; the singing those songs, or reading those books, which do not tend to the knowledge or love of God; softness, and needless self-indulgence; laying up treasures upon earth; borrowing without a probability of paying; or taking up goods without a probability of paying for them.

Secondly, it is expected of all who continue in these societies that they should continue to evidence their desire for salvation by doing good; by being, in every kind, merciful after their power; as they have opportunity, doing good of every possible sort, and as far as possible, to all men. [They should do good] to their bodies, of the ability which God giveth, by giving food to the hungry, by clothing the naked, by visiting or helping them that are sick, or in prison. [They should do good] to their souls, by instructing, reproving, or exhorting all we have any intercourse[26] with; trampling underfoot that enthusiastic doctrine of devils, that "we are not to do good unless our heart is free to it." By doing good, especially, to them that are of the household of faith, or groaning so to be[27]; by employing them preferably to others, buying from each another, helping each other in business; and that so much the more because the world will love its own, and them only. By all possible diligence and frugality, that the gospel be not blamed. . . .

Thirdly, it is expected of all who desire to continue in these societies that they should continue to evidence their desire of salvation by attending upon all the ordinances of God. Such are: the public worship of God; the ministry of the word, either read or expounded; the supper of the Lord; family and private prayer; searching the Scriptures; and fasting, or abstinence.

---

[25] *going to law:* suing.

[26] *intercourse:* dealings.
[27] *groaning so to be:* on the verge of conversion.

Hymns of Pietism and Rationalism*

All types of Christians further enriched the hymnody of the church in this period, especially in Protestant Christianity influenced by Pietism. (The emotional power of music has always lent itself to expressing the emotional in religion.) Charles Wesley, John's brother, was a prolific hymn writer, and Methodism soon became known for its vigorous hymn singing. His "Come, Sinners" is given here.

John Newton's "Amazing Grace" conveys a strongly evangelical tone and has become one of the most famous of Christian hymns. Finally, Joseph Addison's poem set to music, "The Spacious Firmament on High," is a good example of Christian hymnody as influenced by Enlightenment rationalism. It focuses on the natural world's testimony to the existence and goodness of God.

---

* Charles Wesley, "Come, Sinners, to the Gospel Feast"; John Newton, "Amazing Grace"; Joseph Addison, "The Spacious Firmament on High"

["Come, Sinners, to the Gospel Feast"]
Come sinners, to the gospel feast;
Let every soul be Jesus' guest:

Ye need not one be left behind,
For God hath bidden all mankind.

Sent by my Lord, on you I call;
The invitation is to all:
Come all the world! come, sinner, thou!
All things in Christ are ready now.

Come, all ye souls by sin oppressed,
Ye restless wanderers after rest;
Ye poor, and maimed, and halt, and blind,
In Christ a hearty welcome find.

My message as from God receive;
Ye all may come to Christ and live:
O let his love your hearts constrain,
Nor suffer him to die in vain.

See him set forth before your eyes,
That precious, bleeding sacrifice:
His offered benefits embrace,
And freely now be saved by grace.

["Amazing Grace"]
Amazing grace—how sweet the sound—
That saved a wretch like me!
I once was lost, but now am found,
Was blind, but now I see.

'Twas grace that taught my heart to fear,
And grace my fears relieved;
How precious did that grace appear
The hour I first believed!

Through many dangers, toils and snares,
I have already come;

'Tis grace has brought me safe thus far,
And grace will lead me home.

The Lord has promised good to me,
His word my hope secures;
He will my shield and portion be
As long as life endures.

["The Spacious Firmament on High"]
The spacious firmament on high,
With all the blue ethereal sky,
And spangled heaven, a shining frame,
Their great Original proclaim;
The unwearied sun, from day to day,
Does his Creator's power display,
And publish to every land
The work of an almighty hand.

Soon as the evening shades prevail,
The moon takes up the wondrous tale,
And nightly to the listening earth
Repeats the story of her birth;
While all the stars that round her burn,
And all the planets in their turn,
Confirm the tidings as they roll,
And spread the truth from pole to pole.

What though in solemn silence all
Move round this dark terrestrial ball?
What though no real voice nor sound
Amid the radiant orbs be found?
In reason's ear they all rejoice,
And utter forth a glorious voice;
Forever singing, as they shine,
"The hand that made us is divine."

Papal Infallibility Decreed*

In 1870, the First Vatican Council decreed papal infallibility as a binding doctrine. It teaches that the bishop of Rome in his official character, when he speaks officially on matters of faith and morals, is entirely free from error and needs no confirmation from a general council or other parts of the church. This decree caused a stir in some parts of Catholicism and widened the split between Protestants and Roman Catholics.[28]

---

* *The Dogmatic Decree of the Vatican Council*

[28] Philip Schaff, *Creeds of Christendom*, vol. 2 (New York: Harper, 1919), 262–63, 270–71.

Wherefore, resting on plain testimonies of the Sacred Writings, and adhering to the plain and express decrees both of our predecessors, the Roman Pontiffs, and of the General Councils, we renew the definition of the ecumenical Council of Florence,[29] in virtue of which all the faithful of Christ must believe that the holy Apostolic See and the Roman Pontiff possesses the primacy over the whole world, and that the Roman Pontiff is the successor of blessed Peter, Prince of the Apostles, and is the true vicar of Christ, and head of the whole Church, and father and teacher of all Christians; and that full power was given to him in blessed Peter to rule, feed, and govern the universal Church by Jesus Christ our Lord; as is also contained in the acts of the General Councils and in the sacred Canons.

Hence we teach and declare that by the appointment of our Lord the Roman Church possesses a superiority of ordinary power over all other churches, and that this power of jurisdiction of the Roman Pontiff, which is truly episcopal, is immediate.[30] To this power all of whatever rite and dignity, both individually and collectively, are bound, by their duty of hierarchical subordination and true obedience, to submit not only in matters which belong to faith and morals, but also in those that appertain to the discipline and government of the Church throughout the world, so that the Church of Christ may be one flock under one supreme pastor through preservation of unity both of communion and of profession of the same faith with the Roman Pontiff. This is the teaching of Catholic truth, from which no one can deviate without loss of faith and of salvation. . . .

Therefore faithfully adhering to the tradition received from the beginning of the Christian faith, for the glory of God our Savior, the exaltation of the Catholic religion, and the salvation of Christian people, the sacred Council approving, we teach and define that it is a dogma divinely revealed: the Roman Pontiff, when he speaks *ex cathedra*,[31] that is, when in discharge of the office of pastor and teacher of all Christians by virtue of his supreme Apostolic authority, he defines a doctrine regarding faith or morals to be held by the universal Church, by the divine assistance promised to him in blessed Peter, is possessed of that infallibility with which the divine Redeemer willed that his Church should be endowed for defining doctrine regarding faith or morals; and that therefore such definitions of the Roman Pontiff are irreformable of themselves, and not from the consent of the Church.

---

[29] *Council of Florence:* held from 1438 to 1445, this conference of Greek and Latin Christians sought unsuccessfully to mend the breach between Eastern and Western Christianity. It affirmed, at least in the Roman understanding, the primacy of the pope over all Christianity.

[30] *immediate:* the pope has direct authority over all the church, not dependent on councils, local bishops or abbots, etc.

[31] *ex cathedra:* Latin, "from the [bishop's] chair."

Russian Orthodoxy in America*

Because of trade and some settlement, the Russian Orthodox church had a strong presence in Alaska and along the Pacific coast all the way to northern California in the eighteenth and nineteenth centuries. This survey of Russian Orthodox life reports the condition of the Orthodox Church in Alaska, especially among Native Americans, at the beginning of the century.[32]

---

* "Description of Orthodoxy in America"

[32] From *Overland Monthly* magazine, 2d series, no. 155 (November 1895): 478–79.

In 1861 there were in the Russian American colonies seven churches and thirty-five chapels, several of them, including the cathedral, having been built at the cost of the Russian American Company, which also kept them in repair. The cost of maintenance was defrayed by voluntary contributions, and by the profits realized from the sale of candles. At about this time the total capital of the churches amounted to more than 255,000 rubles, and was kept by the treasurer of the Company, interest at five per cent being allowed upon it. The contributions to the Church were made partly in money and partly in furs, the Company allowing the Church from seven to fourteen rubles for the skin of a sea otter. The Company expended on behalf of the Church nearly 40,000 rubles per annum, and built a residence for the Bishop at a cost of 30,000 rubles.

At the time of the transfer of Russian America to the United States, the Greek Church maintained a considerable establishment, consisting of a Bishop, three priests, two deacons, and numerous acolytes, at Sitka. Then the Bishop made Oonalashka[33] his headquarters, and now San Francisco is his seat, from which place as a center he administers the whole of his vast diocese, apportioning the funds at his disposal according to the needs of the various parishes. . . .

When a community is too poor to maintain a priest or reader, the Bishop, with money supplied to him from Russia, defrays the cost of maintaining a chapel there. Where there is no resident priest, the higher rites of the church, such as baptism, marriage, etc., are performed by a regularly ordained clergyman from Oonalashka, Belkovsky, Sitka, or even from San Francisco, who makes the entire round of the religious establishments in Alaska about once in two years.

Outwardly the Aleuts are intensely pious, greeting you with a prayer, and bidding you farewell with a blessing. Before a meal they always ask the blessing of God; when they enter a neighbor's house, they cross themselves, and in most of their dwellings there is a picture of a patron saint, towards which the members of the household turn on rising in the morning and retiring at night. They will assemble for prayer whenever a priest's services can be obtained; and no matter how long the service may be, they give it their whole attention without manifesting any signs of weariness or impatience. They listen with the greatest interest to the reading of the Bible, and keep all fast-days and other religious observances strictly. In every village there is a church or chapel; the churches being erected and kept in repair, and the chapels supported, by the natives. No other religious denominations have succeeded among the Aleuts except the Greek Church, the ornate services and frequent festivals of which appeal strongly to their taste. They willingly contribute towards the maintenance of a Reader or Deacon, who performs the daily services, and teaches the young people to read, first in the Aleut dialect, and then in Russian.

The best specimen of a Greek church and one of the most interesting structures in the United States is the cathedral at Sitka, whose dome and graceful spires are the most striking objects of that town, the peculiar green hue of their roofs catching the tourist's eye ere the steamer has yet touched the wharf. The church is a cruciform wooden building, consisting of a nearly square hall, with a sanctuary to the east, and chapels on its north and south sides. It is well lighted by windows in and below the dome, which is supported by columns of the Byzantine order and has suspended from its center a heavy silver candelabrum. The church also contains eight fine silver candlesticks more than four feet in height. The belfry has a fine peal of bells, the original cost of which was 8,700 rubles in silver. On the altar used to rest a representation in miniature of the Holy Sepulcher wrought in silver and gold, and the communion cup was of gold set with diamonds. But many of the books and vestments that were formerly at Sitka are now in San Francisco, brought by Bishop Vladimir.

---

[33] *Oonalashka:* the easternmost island of the Aleutian Islands.

TEACHING

Two Samples of Missionary Preaching*

Francisco Davila was a Spanish priest who served as a missionary to Peru. He preached this sermon in Fraechua, an Incan language, to Peruvian natives in 1646, attempting to persuade them to practice a purer form of Christianity. Davila shows a great understanding of his flock, but also a readiness to justify the sufferings of the Incas at the hands of the Spanish in terms of divine providence and punishment for sin.[34]

The author of the second selection, Jonathan Edwards, was a master of rhetoric and of shaping the emotional response of his audience. "Sinners in the Hand of an Angry God" is the most famous "hell-fire and brimstone" sermon ever preached, but it is not representative of either the tone or content of Edwards's preaching as a whole. The aim of this sermon is to reach members of Edwards's parish whom he considered unconverted; it is missionary preaching within the church.[35]

I am the good shepherd of the llamas, the shepherd with a great heart. For his llamas he has no fear of death. The shepherd who receives wages, and whose animals, his llamas, do not belong to him, when he sees a puma leaping, flees and runs away as fast as he can. The puma seizes a llama and scatters the others. And that is because the shepherd receives wages, because the animals are not his. I am the good shepherd who knows his animals, and the animals also know me.

But if he is the shepherd, who and what are his llamas, his animals? We are, and we alone. All human beings, men and women, are the llamas of Jesus Christ.

Perhaps one of you may now say in your heart: "Father, we others, we Indians, are not as the whites, we have a different origin, a different form, and so we are not the llamas of God, and the God of the whites is not the God of the Indians. Since the time of our ancestors we have had our huacca, our idols, and our umu, our priests.

"Moreover, before the whites came here the runas [the Indians] multiplied prodigiously in the wild sierra, on the heathland. The maize, the sweet potato, the quinua, the occa, the llama, the animals that provide wool, all this food were ours.

"At that time there were no thieves . . . But since the white men have come, all the runas have become thieves. If that is the case, then we Indians are different from the whites, we are not the same thing. Consequently, we cannot see how we can be the llamas, the animals of Jesus Christ. Because of that, we others, we Indians, are only Christians outwardly, in appearance; we feign the mass, the sermon, the confession, because we are afraid of the padre and the corregidor.[36]

"Our hearts think only of our huacca, because with them things went well with us. And now, see that we have suffering and the villages that once became Christian have disappeared. Even their names have gone and we do not know them. The whites have taken all our fields. And spinning, weaving, making rugs, is something reserved for the corregidor."

My son, I am glad that you have said all that, and glad to have heard it. Glad in one part of my mind, but in another I am pained and sad-

---

* Francisco Davila, "The Good Shepherd"; Jonathan Edwards, "Sinners in the Hand of an Angry God"

[34] Jean Comby and Diarmaid MacCulloch, *How to Read Church History*, vol. 2 (New York: Crossroad, 1993), translated by John Bowden and Margaret Lydamore from the French *Pour lire l'histoire de l'Eglise*, tome 2 published in 1986 by les Editions du Cerf, 29 bd. Latour-Maubourg, Paris. Copyright les Editions du Cerf 1986 with additional material by Diarmaid MacCulloch. English edition copyright SCM Press, Ltd., 1989. Used with permission of the Crossroad Publishing Company, New York, and SCM Press, Ltd., London, 73.

[35] "Sinners in the Hand of an Angry God"; from C. H. Faust and T. H. Johnson, *Jonathan Edwards* (New York: Hill & Wang, 1935), 160–72.

[36] *padre:* priest; *corregidor:* military official.

dened. Why am I glad? Because I know your heart, what you think, and that I can care for you as though you were sick. And why am I saddened? It is because up to now the Indians have not believed have not accepted the word of God, though they have heard so many sermons, so much teaching. . . .

Hear me and take heed. All that happens, life and death, multiplication and disappearance, health and disease, everything in this world and the other is solely in accordance with the will of God. Consequently, when it is his will, the people of one nation conquer another nation and dominate it; and another day, the conquerors become the conquered. But many times, if he annihilates a province with many towns and many people, we can see that it is because they had sinned.

It is because of their prior faults that God has begun to chastise the Incas, making them die. . . . God has not done that simply by chance; he has done it with his very great, unsurpassable knowledge. The whites have been the alguazils[37] of God. They have come for that purpose. . . . Otherwise, for not having worshipped the true God, and also for other faults, the souls of all the Indians would go to hell. . . .

We are all created by God; we are the animals of Jesus Christ. He is our true shepherd, who has given us his word to eat so that we might be saved thanks to it and he might lead us on high, into the golden enclosure, the country in which one does not have to die. Whereas in the life that you lead it is the accursed devil, the liar, who is your shepherd, to lead you with his lies to the torments of hell. . . . Spit on the devil, the sorcerer, the witch, and follow God alone, Jesus Christ.

[Edwards, "Sinners in the Hand of an Angry God"] Thus it is that natural men[38] are held in the hand of God, over the pit of hell; they have deserved the fiery pit, and are already sentenced to it. God is dreadfully provoked, his anger is as great towards them as to those that are actually suffering the executions of the fierceness of his

wrath in hell, and they have done nothing in the least to appease or abate that anger. Neither is God in the least bound by any promise to hold them up one moment. The devil is waiting for them, hell is gaping for them, the flames gather and flash about them, and would fain[39] lay hold on them, and swallow them up; the fire pent up in their own hearts is struggling to break out: and they have no interest in any Mediator, there are no means within reach that can be any security to them. In short, they have no refuge, nothing to take hold of; all that preserves them every moment is the mere arbitrary will, and uncovenanted, unobliged forbearance of an incensed God.

This awful subject may awaken unconverted persons in this congregation. What you have heard is the case of every one of you that are out of Christ. That world of misery, that lake of burning brimstone, is extended abroad under you. There is the dreadful pit of the glowing flames of the wrath of God; there is hell's wide gaping mouth open; and you have nothing to stand upon, nor any thing to take hold of; there is nothing between you and hell but the air; it is only the power and mere pleasure of God that holds you up. . . .

Your wickedness makes you as it were heavy as lead, and to tend downwards with great weight and pressure towards hell; and if God should let you go, you would immediately sink and swiftly descend and plunge into the bottomless gulf, and your healthy constitution, and your own care and prudence, and best contrivance, and all your righteousness, would have no more influence to uphold you and keep you out of hell, than a spider's web would have to stop a falling rock. . . .

The God that holds you over the pit of hell, much as one holds a spider, or some loathsome insect over the fire, abhors you, and is dreadfully provoked: his wrath towards you burns like fire; he looks upon you as worthy of nothing else, but to be cast into the fire; he is of purer eyes than to

---

[37] *alguazils:* divinely appointed agents.
[38] *natural men:* persons prior to conversion.

[39] *fain:* gladly.

bear to have you in his sight; you are ten thousand times more abominable in his eyes, than the most hateful venomous serpent is in ours. You have offended him infinitely more than ever a stubborn rebel did his prince; and yet it is nothing but his hand that holds you from falling into the fire every moment. . . .

How dreadful is the state of those that are daily and hourly in the danger of this great wrath and infinite misery! But this is the dismal case of every soul in this congregation that has not been born again, however moral and strict, sober and religious, they may otherwise be. Oh that you would consider it, whether you be young or old! There is reason to think that there are many in this congregation now hearing this discourse that will actually be the subjects of this very misery to all eternity. We know not who they are, or in what seats they sit, or what thoughts they now have. It may be they are now at ease, and hear all these things without much disturbance, and are now flattering themselves that they are not the persons, promising themselves that they shall escape. . . .

It is doubtless the case of some whom you have seen and known, who deserved hell no more than you, and who heretofore appeared as likely to have been now alive as you. Their case is past all hope; they are crying in extreme misery and perfect despair; but here you are in the land of the living and in the house of God, and have an opportunity to obtain salvation. What would not those poor damned hopeless souls give for one day's opportunity such as you now enjoy!

And now you have an extraordinary opportunity, a day wherein Christ has thrown the door of mercy wide open, and stands calling and crying with a loud voice to poor sinners; a day wherein many are flocking to him and pressing into the kingdom of Christ. . . . How awful is it to be left behind at such a day. Therefore, let every one that is out of Christ, now awake and fly from the wrath to come. The wrath of almighty God is now undoubtedly hanging over a great part of this congregation: "Let every one fly out of Sodom. Haste and escape for your lives, look not behind you, escape to the mountain lest you be consumed." [40]

_____

[40] Genesis 19:17.

The Immaculate Conception of Mary*

In 1854, Pope Pius IX decreed that the mother of Jesus is absolutely free from all implication in the fall of Adam and its sinful consequences for the rest of humanity. Like most Christian doctrines, it was the result of a long development, even struggle. Pius acted after he was assured that he needed neither scriptural evidence or a chain of tradition to the apostles to define this dogma. The culmination of the increasing veneration of Mary since the high Middle Ages, this decree has served to widen the gap between Roman Catholicism and both Protestantism and Eastern Orthodoxy. [41]

_____

* Pope Pius IX, *Ineffabilis Deus*
[41] Taken from Philip Schaff, *Creeds of Christendom*, vol. 2 (New York: Harper, 1919), 211–12.

Since we have never ceased in humility and fasting to offer up our prayers and those of the Church to God the Father through his Son, that he might deign to direct and confirm our mind by the power of the Holy Ghost, after imploring the protection of the whole celestial court, and after invoking on our knees the Holy Ghost the Paraclete, under his inspiration we pronounce, declare, and define, unto the glory of the Holy and Indivisible Trinity, the honor and ornament of the holy Virgin the Mother of God, for the exaltation of the Catholic faith and the increase of the Christian religion, by the authority of our Lord Jesus Christ and the blessed Apostles Peter and Paul, and in our own authority, that the doctrine which holds the Blessed Virgin Mary to have been, from the first instant of her conception, by a singular grace and privilege of almighty God, in view of the merits of Jesus Christ the Savior of Mankind, preserved free from all stain of original sin, has been revealed by God, and is, therefore, to be firmly and constantly believed by all the faithful. Therefore, if some should presume to think in their hearts otherwise than we have defined (which God forbid),

they shall know and thoroughly understand that they are by their own judgment condemned, have made shipwreck concerning the faith, and fallen away from the unity of the Church; and, moreover, that they, by this very act, subject themselves to the penalties ordained by law, if, by work or writing, or any other external means, they dare to signify what they think in their hearts.

The High-Water Mark of Protestant Liberalism*

Friedrich Schleiermacher's On Religion: Speeches to Its Cultured Despisers, *written in 1799, sought to make a place for religion among the cultured intellectuals of Germany, most of whom were turning away from any formal faith. Schleiermacher emphasized the role of emotion in religion, hoping to appeal to the current interest in emotion in the Romantic movement.*[42]

In the second reading, Adolf von Harnack, often called the "father of church history" for his influence in the academic study of early Christianity, summarizes many of the themes of liberal theology. Harnack speaks here of "God the Father and the infinite value of the human soul," into which "the brotherhood of man" was later inserted to form the most characteristic slogan of Protestant liberalism at its heyday.[43]

It may be an unexpected and even a marvelous undertaking, that any one should still venture to demand from the very class that have raised themselves above the vulgar, and are saturated with the wisdom of the centuries, attention for a subject so entirely neglected by them. I confess that I am aware of nothing that promises any easy success,

whether it be in winning for my efforts your approval, or in the more difficult and more desirable task of instilling into you my thought and inspiring you for my subject. Faith has never been every man's affair. At all times but few have discerned religion itself, while millions, in various ways, have been satisfied to juggle with its trappings. Now especially the life of cultivated people is far from anything that might have even a resemblance to religion. Just as little, I know, do you worship the Deity in sacred retirement, as you visit the forsaken temples. In your ornamented dwellings, the only sacred things to be met with are the sage maxims of our wise men, and the splendid compositions of our poets. Suavity and sociability, art and science have so fully taken possession of your minds, that no room remains for the eternal and holy Being that lies beyond the world. I know how well you have succeeded in making your earthly life so rich and varied, that you no longer stand in need of an eternity. Having made a universe for yourselves, you are above the need of thinking of the Universe that made you. You are agreed, I know, that nothing new, nothing convincing can any more be said on this matter, which on every side by sages and seers, and I might add by scoffers and priests, has been abundantly discussed. To priests, least of all, are you inclined to listen. . . . All this I know, and yet, divinely swayed by an irresistible necessity within me, I feel myself compelled to speak, and cannot take back my invitation that you and none else should listen to me. . . .

---

* Friedrich Schleiermacher, *On Religion: Speeches to Its Cultured Despisers;* A. von Harnack, *What Is Christianity?*

[42] Friedrich Schleiermacher, *On Religion: Speeches to Its Cultured Despisers* (London: Paul, Trench, Trubner & Co., 1893), 1–2, 12–13, 14–16, 18–19, 21.

[43] Adolf Harnack, *What Is Christianity?* (New York: G. P. Putnam's Sons, 1901), 51–52, 61–63, 70–72.

Let us then, I ask you, examine whence exactly religion has its rise. Is it from some clear intuition, or from some vague thought? Is it from the different kinds and sects of religion found in history, or from some general idea that you have perhaps conceived arbitrarily? . . .

You are doubtless acquainted with the histories of human follies, and have reviewed the various structures of religious doctrine from the senseless fables of wanton peoples to the most refined Deism, from the rude superstition of human sacrifice to the ill-put together fragments of metaphysics and ethics now called purified Christianity, and you have found them all without rhyme or reason. I am far from wishing to contradict you. Rather, if you really mean that the most cultured religious system is no better than the rudest, if you only perceive that the divine cannot lie in a series that ends on both sides in something ordinary and despicable, I will gladly spare you the trouble of estimating further all that lies between. Possibly they may all appear to you transitions and stages towards the final form. Out of the hand of its age each comes better polished and carved, till at length art has grown equal to that perfect plaything with which our century has presented history. . . . What are all these [theological] systems, considered in themselves, but the handiwork of the calculating understanding, wherein only by mutual limitation each part holds its place? What else can they be, these systems of theology, these theories of the origin and the end of the world, these analyses of the nature of an incomprehensible Being, wherein everything runs to cold arguing, and the highest can be treated in the tone of a common controversy? And this is certainly—let me appeal to your own feeling—not the character of religion.

[Harnack, *What Is Christianity?*] If, however, we take a general view of Jesus' teaching, we shall see that it may be grouped under three heads. They are each of such a nature as to contain the whole, and hence it can be exhibited in its entirety under any one of them: Firstly, the kingdom of God and its coming; Secondly, God the Father and the infinite value of the human soul; Thirdly, the higher righteousness and the commandment of love. . . .

First, the kingdom of God and its coming. Jesus' message of the kingdom of God runs through all the forms and statements of the prophecy which, taking its color from the Old Testament, announces the day of judgment and the visible government of God in the future, up to the idea of an inward coming of the kingdom, starting with Jesus' message and then beginning. . . .

The kingdom has a triple meaning. Firstly, it is something supernatural, a gift from above, and not a product of ordinary life. Secondly, it is a purely religious blessing, the inner link with the living God; thirdly, it is the most important experience that a man can have, that on which everything else depends; it permeates and dominates his whole existence, because sin is forgiven and misery banished. . . .

Second, God the Father and the infinite value of the human soul. To our modern way of thinking and feeling, Christ's message appears in the clearest and most direct light when grasped in connection with the idea of God the Father and the infinite value of the human soul. Here the elements which I would describe as the restful and rest giving in Jesus' message, and which are comprehended in the idea of our being children of God, find expression. I call them restful in contrast with the impulsive and stirring elements; although it is just they that are informed with a special strength. But the fact that the whole of Jesus' message may be reduced to these two heads—God as the Father, and the human soul so ennobled that it can and does unite with him—shows us that the Gospel is in no wise a positive religion like the rest; that it contains no statutory or particularistic elements; that it is, therefore, religion itself. . . .

Third, the higher righteousness and the commandment of love. This is the third head, and the whole of the Gospel is embraced under it. To represent the Gospel as an ethical message is no depreciation of its value. . . .

Firstly: Jesus severed the connection existing

in his day between ethics and the external forms of religious worship. He would have absolutely nothing to do with the self-seeking pursuit of "good works" in combination with the ritual of worship. He exhibited an indignant contempt for those who allow their neighbors, nay, even their parents, to starve, and on the other hand send gifts to the temple. He will have no compromise in the matter. Love and mercy are ends in themselves; they lose all value and are put to shame by having to be anything else than the service of one's neighbor.

Secondly: in all questions of morality he goes straight to the root, that is, to the disposition and the intention. It is only thus that what he calls the "higher righteousness" can be understood. The "higher righteousness" is the righteousness that will stand when the depths of the heart are probed. Here, again, we have something that is seemingly very simple and self-evident. Yet the truth, as he uttered it, took the severe form: "It was said of old . . . but I say unto you." After all, then, the truth was something new; he was aware that it had never yet been expressed in such a consistent form and with such claims to supremacy. . . .

Thirdly: what he freed from its connection with self-seeking and ritual elements, and recognized as the moral principle, he reduces to one root and to one motive—love. He knows of no other, and love itself, whether it takes the form of love of one's neighbor or of one's enemy, or the love of the Samaritan, is of one kind only. It must completely fill the soul; it is what remains when the soul dies to itself. In this sense love is the new life already begun. But it is always the love which serves, and only in this function does it exist and live.

Attack on Dead Orthodoxy*

Søren Kierkegaard (1813–1855), a brilliant and enigmatic philosopher-theologian, is widely regarded today as the forerunner of the existentialist school of philosophy. His varied theological writings, which like his philosophical works attacked German idealism and particularly the philosophy of Hegel, stressed the total otherness of God and the necessity for total personal commitment in faith. In this reading, he bitterly and sarcastically attacks the formal, conformist Christianity into which he claimed Protestantism had fallen.[44]

We are what is called a "Christian" nation—but in such a sense, that not a single one of us is in the character of the Christianity of the New Testament, any more than I am, who again and again have repeated, and do now repeat, that I am only a poet. The illusion of a Christian nation is due doubtless to the power which number exercises over the imagination. I have not the least doubt that every single individual in the nation will be honest enough with God and with himself to say in solitary conversation, "If I must be candid, I do not deny that I am not a Christian in the New Testament sense; if I must be honest, I do not deny that my life cannot be called an effort in the direction of what the New Testament calls Christianity, in the direction of denying myself, renouncing the world, dying from it, etc.; rather the earthly and the temporal become more and more important to me with every year I live." . . . But when there are 100,000 [saying this], one becomes confused.

People tell a ludicrous story about an innkeeper. . . . It is said that he sold his beer by the bottle for a cent less than he paid for it. When a certain man said to him, "How does that balance

* Søren Kierkegaard, *Attack upon "Christendom"*

[44] Søren Kierkegaard, *Attack upon "Christendom,"* trans. W. Lowrie (Princeton: Princeton University Press, 1944), 30–31, 34–35, 38, 181. Used by permission of Princeton University Press.

the account? That will lose money," he replied, "No, my friend, it's the big number that does it"—big number, that also in our time is the almighty power. When one has laughed at this story, one would do well to take to heart the lesson that warns against the power which number exercises over the imagination. For there can be no doubt that this innkeeper knew very well that one bottle of beer that he sold for 3 cents meant a loss of 1 cent when it cost him 4 cents. Also with regard to ten bottles the innkeeper will be able to hold fast that it is a loss. But 100,000 bottles! Here the big number stirs the imagination, the round number runs away with it, and the innkeeper becomes dazed—it is a profit, says he, for the big number does it. So also with the calculation which arrives at a Christian nation by adding up units which are not Christian, getting the result by means of the notion that the big number does it. . . .

Christ required "followers" and defined precisely what he meant: that they should be salt, willing to be sacrificed, and that a Christian means to be salt and to be willing to be sacrificed. But to be salt and to be sacrificed is not something to which thousands naturally lend themselves, still less millions, or (still less!) countries, kingdoms, states, and (absolutely not!) the whole world. On the other hand, if it is a question of gain and of mediocrity and of twaddle (which is the opposite of being salt), then the possibility of the thing begins already with the 100,000, increases with every million, reaching its highest point when the whole world has become Christian. For this reason "man" is interested and employed in winning whole nations of Christians, kingdoms, lands, a whole world of Christians—for thus the thing of being a Christian becomes

something different from what it is in the New Testament.

And this end has been attained, has been best attained, indeed completely, in Protestantism, especially in Denmark, in the Danish eventempered, jovial mediocrity. When one sees what it is to be a Christian in Denmark, how could it occur to anyone that this is what Jesus Christ talks about: cross and agony and suffering, crucifying the flesh, suffering for the doctrine, being salt, being sacrificed, etc.? No, in Protestantism, especially in Denmark, Christianity marches to a different melody, to the tune of "Merrily we roll along, roll along, roll along"—Christianity is enjoyment of life, tranquilized, as neither the Jew nor the pagan was, by the assurance that the thing about eternity is settled, settled precisely in order that we might find pleasure in enjoying this life.

And this in my opinion is the falsification of which official Christianity is guilty: it does not frankly and unreservedly make known the Christian requirement. Perhaps because it is afraid people would shudder to see at what a distance from it we are living, without being able to claim that in the remotest way our life might be called an effort in the direction of fulfilling the requirement. . . .

In the magnificent cathedral the Honorable and Right Reverend Geheime-General-Ober-Hof-Predikant,[45] the elect favorite of the fashionable world, appears before an elect company and preaches *with emotion* upon the text he himself elected: "God has elected the base things of the world, and the things that are despised"— and nobody laughs.

---

[45] *Geheime . . . Predikant:* literally, "Church-General-High-Court-Preacher."

The Oxford Movement and Doctrinal Development*

The Oxford scholar John Henry Newman (1801– 1890) was the moving spirit behind the Oxford (or

---

* John Henry Newman, *An Essay on the Development of Christian Doctrine*

Tractarian) movement in the Church of England, which sought to draw the church closer to its Catholic roots. While writing his Essay on the Development of Christian Doctrine *in 1845, Newman decided to become a Roman Catholic. Despite this defection, or perhaps because of it, the Oxford move-ment continued (and still continues) to exert great influence on Anglican thinking about the na-ture of the church. In this reading, Newman re-lates historical concerns to the issue of the devel-opment of Christian doctrine. His key idea is that the development of dogma was not innovation, but rather the outer unfolding of inner, implicit potentials.*

The development of dogmatic theology . . . was a silent and spontaneous process. It was wrought out and carried through under the fiercest con-troversies, and amid the most fearful risks. The Catholic faith was placed in a succession of per-ils. . . . Large portions of Christendom were, one after another, in heresy or schism. . . . But these disorders were no interruption to the sustained and steady march of the sacred science from im-plicit belief to formal statement. . . .

That in the long course of centuries, and in spite of the failure, in points of detail, of the most gifted Fathers and Saints, the Church thus wrought out the one and only consistent theory which can be taken . . . proves how clear, simple, and exact her vision of doctrine was. . . .

The integrity of the Catholic developments is still more evident when they are viewed in con-trast with the history of other doctrinal systems. Philosophies and religions of the world have each its day, and are parts of a succession. They sup-plant and in turn are supplanted. But the Catho-lic religion alone has had no limits. . . . If it were a falsehood, or a corruption, like the systems of men, it would be weak as they are. . . .

Catholicism has borne, and can bear, prin-ciples or doctrines that in other systems of reli-gion quickly degenerate into fanaticism or infi-delity. This might be shown at great length in the history of the Aristotelic philosophy within and without the church; or in the history of Monachism,[46] or of Mysticism. . . . The theology of St. Thomas, nay of the Church of his period, is built on that very Aristotelianism, which the early Fathers denounce as the source of all un-belief. The exercises of asceticism, which are so graceful in St. Anthony, so touching in St. Basil, and so awful in St. Germanus, do but become a melancholy and gloomy superstition even in the most pious persons who are cut off from the Catholic communion.

It is true, there have been seasons when, from the operation of external or internal causes, the Church has been thrown into what was almost a state of dissolution; but her wonderful revivals, while the world was triumphing over her, is a fur-ther evidence of the absence of corruption in the system of doctrine and worship into which she has developed. . . . She pauses in her course, and almost suspends her functions; she rises again, and she is herself once more. Doctrine is where it was, and usage, and precedence, and principle, and policy; there may be changes, but they are consolidations or adaptations.

---

[46] *Monachism:* monasticism.

ETHICS

The Struggle over Slavery*

The most difficult moral issue in nineteenth-century British and American Christianity, and in other parts of the world as well, was the issue of

* Bishop John England, *On the Subject of Domestic Slavery;* H. Jacobs, *Incidents in the Life of a Slave Girl, Written by Herself*

slavery. Most defenders of slavery pointed to the Bible, which seemed to permit it. Opponents of slavery pointed to an interpretation of the Bible as well, but they also powerfully appealed to evils in the experience of slavery. The first reading, from John England, the Roman Catholic bishop of

Charleston, South Carolina, sums up the argu-ment most Christians who favored slavery used to support it.[47] The second reading is from the life story of Harriet Jacobs, a North Carolina slave.[48]

In the New Testament we find instances of pious and good men having slaves, and in no case do we find the Savior imputing it to them as a crime, or requiring their servants' emancipation. . . . In many of his parables, the Savior describes the master and his servants in a variety of ways, with-out any condemnation or censure of slavery. In Luke xvii, he describes the usual mode of acting towards slaves as the very basis upon which he teaches one of the most useful lessons of Chris-tian virtue. . . .

Nor did the apostles consider the Christian master obliged to liberate his Christian servant. St. Paul in his epistle to Philemon acknowledges the right of the master to the services of his slave for whom however he asks, as a special favor, pardon for having deserted his owner. . . . Thus a runaway slave still belonged to his master, and though having become a Christian, so far from being thereby liberated from service, he was bound to return thereto and submit himself to his owner. . . .

It will now fully establish what will be neces-sary to perfect the view which I desire to give, if I can show that masters who were Christians were not required to emancipate their slaves, but had pointed out the duties which they were bound as masters to perform, because this will show under the Christian dispensation the legal, moral and religious existence of slave and master.

The apostle [Paul] . . . wrote of slaves who had believing or Christian masters. The inspired penman did not address his instructions and ex-hortations to masters who were not of the house-hold of the Faith. . . . Thus when he addresses masters, they are Christian masters. Ephes. vi, 9. "And you, masters, do the same things to them (servants) forbearing threatenings, knowing that the Lord both of them and you is in heaven: and there is no respect of persons with him,"—and again, Colos. iv, i, "Masters do to your servants that which is just and equal: knowing that you also have a master in heaven."

We have then in the teaching of the apostles nothing which contradicts the law of Moses, but we have much which corrects the cruelty of the Pagan practice. The exhibition that is presented to us is one of a cheering and of an elevated char-acter. It is true that the state of slavery is con-tinued under the legal sanction, but the slave is taught from the most powerful motives to be faithful, patient, obedient and contented, and the master is taught that though despotism may pass unpunished on earth it will be examined into at the bar of heaven. Though the slave owes him bodily service, yet the soul of this drudge, hav-ing been purchased at the same price as his own, and sanctified by the same law of regeneration, he who is his slave according to the flesh, is his brother according to the spirit. His humanity, his charity, his affection are enlisted and interested, and he feels that his own father is also the father of his slave, hence though the servant must read-ily and cheerfully pay him homage and perform his behests on earth, yet they may be on an equality in heaven. . . .

To the Christian slave was exhibited the hu-miliation of an incarnate God, the suffering of an unoffending victim, the invitation of this model of perfection to that meekness, that humility, that peaceful spirit, that charity and forgiveness of in-juries which constitute the glorious beatitudes. He was shown the advantage of suffering, the reward of patience, and the narrow road along whose rugged ascents he was to bear the cross, walking in the footsteps of his Savior. The cur-tains which divide both worlds were raised as he advanced, and he beheld Lazarus in the bosom of Abraham, whilst the rich man vainly cried to have this once miserable beggar allowed to dip

---

[47] John England, *Letters of the Late Bishop England to the Hon. John Forsyth, on the Subject of Domestic Slavery* (Balti-more: J. Murphy, 1844), 34–39.

[48] Harriet Jacobs, *Incidents in the Life of a Slave-Girl, Written by Herself,* ed. L. Maria Child (Boston, privately printed, 1861).

the tip of his finger in water and touch it to his tongue, for he was tormented in that flame.[49]

Thus did the legislator of Christianity, while he admitted the legality of slavery, render the master merciful, and the slave faithful, obedient and religious, looking for his freedom in that region where alone true and lasting enjoyment can be found.

[*Incidents in the Life of a Slave Girl, Written by Herself*] After the alarm caused by Nat Turner's insurrection had subsided,[50] the slave holders came to the conclusion that it would be well to give the slaves enough of religious instruction to keep them from murdering their masters. The Episcopal clergyman offered to hold a separate service on Sundays for their benefit. His colored members were very few, and also very respectable—a fact, which I presume, had some weight with him. The difficulty was to decide on a suitable place for them to worship. The Methodist and Baptist churches admitted them in the afternoon; but their carpets and cushions were not so costly as those at the Episcopal church. It was at last decided that they should meet at the house of a free colored man, who was a member.

I was invited to attend, because I could read. Sunday evening came, and, trusting to the cover of night, I ventured out. I rarely ventured out by daylight, for I always went with fear, expecting at every turn to encounter Dr. Flint, who was sure to turn me back, or order me to his office to inquire where I got my bonnet, or some other article of dress. When the Rev. Mr. Pike came, there were some twenty persons present. The reverend gentleman knelt in prayer, then seated himself, and requested all present, who could read, to open their books, while he gave out the portions he wished them to repeat or respond

to. His text was, "Servants, be obedient to them that are your masters according to the flesh, with fear and trembling, in singleness of your heart, as unto Christ."

Pious Mr. Pike brushed up his hair till it stood upright, and, in deep, solemn tones, began: "Hearken, you servants! Give strict heed unto my words. You are rebellious sinners. Your hearts are filled with all manner of evil. 'Tis the devil who tempts you. God is angry with you, and will surely punish you, if you don't forsake your wicked ways. You that live in town are eye-servants behind your master's back. Instead of serving your master faithfully, which is pleasing in the sight of your heavenly Master, you are idle, and shirk your work. God sees you. You tell lies. God hears you. Instead of being engaged in worshipping him, you are hidden away somewhere, feasting on your master's substance; tossing coffee-grounds with some wicked fortune-teller, or cutting cards with another old hag. Your masters may not find you out, but God sees you, and will punish you. O, the depravity of your hearts! When your master's work is done, are you quietly together, thinking of the goodness of God to such sinful creatures? No; you are quarrelling, and tying up little bags of roots to bury under the doorsteps to poison each other with. God sees you. You men steal away to every grog shop to sell your master's corn, so that you may buy rum to drink. God sees you. You sneak into the back streets, or among the bushes, to pitch coppers. Although your masters may not find you out, God sees you; and he will punish you. You must forsake your sinful ways, and be faithful servants. Obey your old master and your young master—your old mistress and your young mistress. If you disobey your earthly master, you offend your heavenly Master. You must obey God's commandments. When you go from here, don't stop at the corners of the streets to talk, but go directly home, and let your master and mistress see that you have come." . . .

I went home with the feeling that I had heard the Reverend Mr. Pike for the last time. Some of his members repaired to his house, and found

---

[49] *Lazarus . . . flame:* Luke 16:19–31.

[50] *After . . . had subsided:* In August of 1831, Nat Turner and his followers killed fifty-five whites in the largest slave uprising in American history. This occurred about forty miles from Jacob's home. A wave of terror swept the South as hundreds of slaves were killed in fear and reprisal.

that the kitchen sported two tallow candles; the first time, I am sure, since its present occupant owned it, for the servants never had any thing but pine knots. It was so long before the reverend gentleman descended from his comfortable parlor that the slaves left, and went to enjoy a Methodist shout. They never seem so happy as when shouting and singing at religious meetings. Many of them are sincere, and nearer to the gate of heaven than sanctimonious Mr. Pike, and other long-faced Christians, who see wounded Samaritans, and pass by on the other side.

The slaves generally compose their own songs and hymns; and they do not trouble their heads much about the measure. They often sing the following verses:

"Old Satan is one busy ole man;
He rolls dem blocks all in my way;
But Jesus is my bosom friend;
He rolls dem blocks away.

"If I had died when I was young,
Den how my stam'ring tongue would have
    sung;
But I am ole, and now I stand
A narrow chance for to tread dat heavenly
    land." . . .

Precious are such moments [of worship] to the poor slaves. If you were to hear them at such times, you might think they were happy. But can that hour of singing and shouting sustain them through the dreary week, toiling without wages, under constant dread of the lash? . . .

Are doctors of divinity blind, or are they hypocrites? I suppose some are the one, and some the other; but I think if they felt the interest in the poor and the lowly, that they ought to feel, they would not be so easily blinded. A clergyman who goes to the south, for the first time, has usually some feeling, however vague, that slavery is wrong. The slave holder suspects this, and plays his game accordingly. He makes himself as agreeable as possible; talks on theology, and other kindred topics. The reverend gentleman is asked to invoke a blessing on a table loaded with luxuries. After dinner he walks round the premises, and sees the beautiful groves and flowering vines, and the comfortable huts of favored household slaves. The southerner invites him to talk with these slaves. He asks them if they want to be free, and they say, "O, no, massa." This is sufficient to satisfy him. He comes home to publish a "South Side View of Slavery," and to complain of the exaggerations of abolitionists. He assures people that he has been to the south, and seen slavery for himself; that it is a beautiful "patriarchal institution"; that the slaves don't want their freedom; that they have hallelujah meetings, and other religious privileges.

What does he know of the half-starved wretches toiling from dawn till dark on the plantations? Of mothers shrieking for their children, torn from their arms by slave traders? Of young girls dragged down into moral filth? Of pools of blood around the whipping post? Of hounds trained to tear human flesh? Of men screwed into cotton gins to die? The slave holder showed him none of these things, and the slaves dared not tell of them if he had asked them.

There is a great difference between Christianity and religion at the south. If a man goes to the communion table, and pays money into the treasury of the church, no matter if it be the price of blood, he is called religious. If a pastor has offspring by a woman not his wife, the church dismisses him, if she is a white woman; but if she is colored, it does not hinder his continuing to be their good shepherd. . . .

No wonder the slaves sing, "Ole Satan's church is here below; Up to God's free church I hope to go."

The Birth of the Feminist Movement*

In 1837, Sara Grimké and her sister Angelina gave a popular series of lectures in New England against slavery. The Congregational General Association of Massachusetts attacked them for speaking out as women, and Sara wrote a pointed response in a series of letters to her friend Mary Parker, a prominent abolitionist. These letters were eventually published in book form. She argues primarily from the New Testament that women are equal to men. In the second reading, Elizabeth Cady Stanton, the famous campaigner for women's rights, introduces The Woman's Bible *(1898), the first and most influential feminist reading of the Bible.*

Dear Friend,

When I last addressed thee, I had not seen the Pastoral Letter of the General Association. It has since fallen into my hands, and I must digress from my intention of exhibiting the condition of women in different parts of the world, in order to make some remarks on this extraordinary document. I am persuaded that when the minds of men and women become emancipated from the thraldom of superstition and "traditions of men," the sentiments contained in the Pastoral Letter will be recurred to with as much astonishment as the opinions of Cotton Mather and other distinguished men of his day, on the subject of witchcraft. Nor will it be deemed less wonderful, that a body of divines should gravely assemble and endeavor to prove that woman has no right to "open her mouth for the dumb," than it now is that judges should have sat on the trials of witches, and solemnly condemned nineteen persons and one dog to death for witchcraft.

But to the letter. It says, "We invite your attention to the dangers which at present seem to threaten the FEMALE CHARACTER with wide-spread and permanent injury." I rejoice that they have called the attention of my sex to this subject, because I believe if woman investigates it, she will soon discover that danger is impending, though from a totally different source from that which the Association apprehends— danger from those who, having long held the reins of usurped authority, are unwilling to permit us to fill that sphere which God created us to move in, and who have entered into league to crush the immortal mind of woman. I rejoice, because I am persuaded that the rights of woman, like the rights of slaves, need only be examined to be understood and asserted, even by some of those, who are now endeavoring to smother the irrepressible desire for mental and spiritual freedom which glows in the breast of many, who hardly dare to speak their sentiments.

"The appropriate duties and influence of women are clearly stated in the New Testament. Those duties are unobtrusive and private, but the sources of mighty power. When the mild, dependent, softening influence of woman upon the sternness of man's opinions is fully exercised, society feels the effects of it in a thousand ways." No one can desire more earnestly than I do, that woman may move exactly in the sphere which her Creator has assigned her; and I believe her having been displaced from that sphere has introduced confusion into the world. It is, therefore, of vast importance to herself and to all the rational creation, that she should ascertain what are her duties and her privileges as a responsible and immortal being. The New Testament has been referred to, and I am willing to abide by its decisions, but must enter my protest against the false translation of some passages by the MEN who did that work, and against the perverted interpretation by the MEN who undertook to write commentaries thereon. (I am inclined to think, when we are admitted to the honor of studying Greek and Hebrew, we shall produce some

* Sara Grimké, *Letters on the Equality of the Sexes and the Condition of Woman;* Elizabeth Cady Stanton, ed., *The Woman's Bible,* Introduction

various readings of the Bible a little different from those we now have.)

The Lord Jesus defines the duties of his followers in his Sermon on the Mount. He lays down grand principles by which they should be governed, without any reference to sex or condition. . . . I follow him through all his precepts, and find him giving the same directions to women as to men, never even referring to the distinction now so strenuously insisted upon between masculine and feminine virtues: this is one of the anti-Christian "traditions of men" which are taught instead of the "commandments of God." Men and women were CREATED EQUAL; they are both moral and accountable beings, and whatever is right for man to do, is right for woman.

But the influence of woman, says the Association, is to be private and unobtrusive; her light is not to shine before man like that of her brethren; but she is passively to let the lords of the creation, as they call themselves, put the bushel over it, lest peradventure it might appear that the world has been benefitted by the rays of her candle. So that her quenched light, according to their judgment, will be of more use than if it were set on the candlestick. "Her influence is the source of mighty power." This has ever been the flattering language of man since he laid aside the whip as a means to keep woman in subjection. He spares her body; but the war he has waged against her mind, her heart, and her soul, has been no less destructive to her as a moral being. How monstrous, how anti-Christian, is the doctrine that woman is to be dependent on man! Where, in all the sacred Scriptures, is this taught? Alas! She has too well learned the lesson, which MAN has labored to teach her. She has surrendered her dearest RIGHTS, and been satisfied with the privileges which man has assumed to grant her; she has been amused with the show of power, whilst man has absorbed all the reality into himself. He has adorned the creature whom God gave him as a companion, with baubles and gewgaws, turned her attention to personal attrac-

tions, offered incense to her vanity, and made her the instrument of his selfish gratification, a plaything to please his eye and amuse his hours of leisure. . . . This doctrine of dependence upon man is utterly at variance with the doctrine of the Bible. In that book I find nothing like the softness of woman, nor the sternness of man: both are equally commanded to bring forth the fruits of the Spirit, love, meekness, gentleness, etc.

[Introduction to *The Woman's Bible*] From the inauguration of the movement for woman's emancipation, the Bible has been used to hold her in the "divinely ordained sphere" prescribed in the Old and New Testaments.

The canon and civil law; church and state; priests and legislators; all political parties and religious denominations have alike taught that woman was made after man, of man, and for man, an inferior being, subject to man. Creeds, codes, Scriptures and statutes, are all based on this idea. The fashions, forms, ceremonies and customs of society, church ordinances and discipline all grow out of this idea. . . .

The Bible teaches that woman brought sin and death into the world, that she precipitated the fall of the race, that she was arraigned before the judgment seat of Heaven, tried, condemned and sentenced. Marriage for her was to be a condition of bondage, maternity a period of suffering and anguish, and in silence and subjection, she was to play the role of a dependent on man's bounty for all her material wants, and for all the information she might desire on the vital questions of the hour, she was commanded to ask her husband at home. Here is the Bible position of woman briefly summed up.

Those who have the divine insight to translate, transpose and transfigure this mournful object of pity into an exalted, dignified personage, worthy our worship as the mother of the race, are to be congratulated as having a share of the occult mystic power of the eastern Mahatmas.[51]

---

[51] *Mahatmas:* Hindu gurus.

The plain English to the ordinary mind admits of no such liberal interpretation. The unvarnished texts speak for themselves. The canon law, church ordinances and Scriptures, are homogeneous, and all reflect the same spirit and sentiments.

These familiar texts are quoted by clergymen in their pulpits, by statesmen in the halls of legislation, by lawyers in the courts, and are echoed by the press of all civilized nations, and accepted by woman herself as "The Word of God." So perverted is the religious element in her nature, that with faith and works she is the chief support of the church and clergy; the very powers that make her emancipation impossible. When, in the early part of the Nineteenth Century, women began to protest against their civil and political degradation, they were referred to the Bible for an answer. When they protested against their unequal position in the church, they were referred to the Bible for an answer. . . .

Listening to the varied opinions of women, I have long thought it would be interesting and profitable to get them clearly stated in book form. To this end six years ago I proposed to a committee of women to issue a Woman's Bible. . . .

[T]here are some who write us that our work is a useless expenditure of force over a book that has lost its hold on the human mind. Most intelligent women, they say, regard it simply as the history of a rude people in a barbarous age, and have no more reverence for the Scriptures than any other work. So long as tens of thousands of Bibles are printed every year, and circulated over the whole habitable globe, and the masses in all English-speaking nations revere it as the word of God, it is vain to belittle its Influence. The sentimental feeling we all have for those things we were educated to believe sacred, do not readily yield to pure reason. I distinctly remember the shudder that passed over me on seeing a mother take our family Bible to make a high seat for her child at table. It seemed such a desecration. I was tempted to protest against its use for such a purpose, and this, too, long after my reason had repudiated its divine authority.

To women still believing in the plenary[52] inspiration of the Scriptures, we say give us by all means your exegesis in the light of the higher criticism learned men are now making, and illumine the Woman's Bible, with your inspiration. . . .

But the verbal criticism in regard to woman's position amounts to little. The spirit is the same in all periods and languages, hostile to her as an equal.

There are some general principles in the holy books of all religions that teach love, charity, liberty, justice and equality for all the human family, there are many grand and beautiful passages, the golden rule has been echoed and re-echoed around the world. There are lofty examples of good and true men and women, all worthy our acceptance and example whose luster cannot be dimmed by the false sentiments and vicious characters bound up in the same volume. The Bible cannot be accepted or rejected as a whole, its teachings are varied and its lessons differ widely from each other. . . .

The canon law, the Scriptures, the creeds and codes and church discipline of the leading religions bear the impress of fallible man, and not of our ideal great first cause, "the Spirit of all Good," that set the universe of matter and mind in motion, and by immutable law holds the land, the sea, the planets, revolving round the great center of light and heat, each in its own elliptic, with millions of stars in harmony all singing together, the glory of creation forever and ever.

---

[52] *plenary:* full.

Roman Catholicism on Social Change*

In 1891, Pope Leo XIII spoke out on the condition of the working classes. Without giving up any traditional claims of the church to a privileged social place, he urged an improvement in the social conditions of the working class for the good of society. This was to be the first in a series of important papal encyclicals on social justice, stretching to our time.[53]

It is clear that the main tenet of Socialism, community of goods, must be utterly rejected, since it only injures those whom it would seem to benefit. . . . The first and most fundamental principle, if one undertakes to alleviate the condition of the masses, must be the inviolability of private property. . . . Let it be taken for granted that workman and employer should, as a rule, make free agreements, and in particular would agree freely as to wages. There underlies a dictate of natural justice more imperious and ancient than any bargain between man and man, namely, that remuneration ought to be sufficient to support a frugal and well-behaved wage earner. If through necessity or fear of a worse evil the workman accepts harder conditions because an employer or contractor will afford him no better, he is made the victim of force and injustice. Those Catholics are worthy of all praise—and they are not a few—who, understanding what the times require, have striven . . . to better the condition of the working class without any sacrifice of the principles involved.

---

* Pope Leo XIII, *Rerum novarum*
[53] Taken, with editing, from J. J. Wynne, *The Great Encyclical Letters of Pope Leo XIII* (New York: Benziger, 1903).

RELATIONS

William Penn and Liberty of Conscience**

The Quaker William Penn believed that men and women were not to be coerced in matters of religion, for true Christianity flourished best where force was found least. Philadelphia, literally "brotherly love," was so named because on that principle, extended to all persons, a noble society can be built.[54]

Moderation, the subject of this discourse, is, in plainer English, liberty of conscience to church-dissenters: a cause I have, with all humility, undertaken to plead, against the prejudices of the times.

That there is such a thing as conscience, and the liberty of it, in reference to faith and worship towards God, must not be denied, even by those that are most scandalized at the ill use some seem to have made of such pretenses. But to settle the terms: by conscience, I understand, the apprehension and persuasion a man has of his duty to God: by liberty of conscience, I mean a free and open profession and exercise of that duty; especially in worship. But I always premise this conscience to keep within the bounds of morality, and that it be neither frantic or mischievous, but a good subject, a good child, a good servant, in all the affairs of life; as exact to yield to Caesar the things that are Caesar's, as jealous of withholding from God the thing that is God's. In brief, he must acknowledge the civil government under which he lives, and that maintains no principle hurtful to his neighbor in his civil property.

For he that in any thing violates his duty to these relations cannot be said to observe it to

---

** William Penn, "A Persuasive to Moderation to[ward] Church Dissenters"
[54] *The Select Works of William Penn*, 4th ed. (London: Phillips, 1825), vol. 2.

God, who ought to have his tribute out of it. Such do not reject their prince, parent, master, or neighbor, but God, who enjoins that duty to them. Those pathetic words of Christ will naturally enough reach the case, "In that ye did it not to them, ye did it not to me": for duty to such relations hath a divine stamp. Divine right runs through more things of our lives than we are aware of; and sacrilege may be committed against more than the church. Nor will a dedication to God, of the robbery from man, expiate the guilt of disobedience: for though zeal could turn gossip to theft, his altars would renounce the sacrifice.

The conscience then that I state, and the liberty I pray, carrying so great a salvo and deference to public and private relations, no ill design can, with any justice, be fixed upon the author,

or reflection upon the subject, which by this time, I think, I may venture to call a toleration.

But to this so much craved, as well as needed, toleration, I meet with two objections of weight, the solving of which will make way for it in this kingdom. And the first is a disbelief of the possibility of the thing. "Toleration of dissenting worships from that established, is not practicable," say some, "without danger to the state, with which it is interwoven." This is political. The other objection is, "That admitting dissenters to be in the wrong, (which is always premised by the national church) such latitude were the way to keep up the disunion, and instead of compelling them into a better way, leave them in the possession and pursuit of their old errors." This is religious. I think I have given the objections fairly; it will be my next business to answer them as fully.

Christianity Encounters Enlightenment Reason*

John Locke was an important empiricist philosopher in his time. In The Reasonableness of Christianity, *published in 1699, he set out a "reasonable Christianity" based solely on what he claimed to be an "attentive and unbiased" reading of the Bible. It features a Protestant understanding of Christianity.*[55]

In the second reading, Matthew Tindal sets forth his basic thesis: unlike Locke, who left a place for a special revelation and saving work in Christ, Tindal held that all the important elements of Christianity could be known by anyone at any time through the use of human reason, making a special revelation unnecessary. Tindal's work was so influential that it became known as the "Deist's Bible." Tindal writes in the form of a dialogue between A (himself) and B (his conversation partner).[56]

It is obvious to anyone who reads the New Testament that the doctrine of redemption, and consequently of the Gospel, is founded upon the supposition of Adam's fall. To understand, therefore, what we are restored to by Jesus Christ, we must consider what the Scriptures show we lost by Adam. . . .

To one that, thus unbiased, reads the Scriptures, what Adam fell from was the state of perfect obedience, which is called justice in the New Testament, though the word, which in the original signifies justice, be translated righteousness: and by this fall, he lost paradise, wherein was tranquillity and the tree of life; i. e. he lost bliss and immortality. . . .

If any of the posterity of Adam were just, they shall not lose the reward of it, eternal life and bliss, by being his mortal issue[57]: Christ will bring them all to life again; and then they shall be put every one upon his own trial, and receive judgment, as he is found to be righteous or not.

---

* John Locke, *The Reasonableness of Christianity;* Matthew Tindal, *Christianity as Old as Creation*

[55] *The Works of John Locke,* vol. 7 (London: W. Sharpe and Son, 1823), 5, 9–11, 14, 17–18, 123, 128–29, 132–33.

[56] From Matthew Tindal, *Christianity as Old as Creation,* 2d ed. (London: Williams, 1732), 11–15, 17.

---

[57] *issue:* descendant.

And the righteous, as our Saviour says, Matt. 25:46, shall go into eternal life. . . .

But yet, "all having sinned," Rom. 3:23, "and come short of the glory of God", i.e. the kingdom of God in heaven, which is often called his glory, both Jews and Gentiles, ver. 22, so that, by the deeds of the law, no one could be justified, ver. 20, it follows, that no one could then have eternal life and bliss. . . .

This then being the case, that whoever is guilty of any sin, should certainly die and cease to be, the benefit of life, restored by Christ at the resurrection, would have been no great advantage . . . if God had not found out a way to justify some, i.e. so many as obeyed another law, which God gave, which in the New Testament is called the "law of faith," Rom. 3:27, and is opposed to the "law of works." . . .

The difference between the law of works, and the law of faith, is only this: that the law of works makes no allowance for failing on any occasion. Those that obey are righteous. Those that in any part disobey are unrighteous, and must not expect life, the reward of righteousness. But by the law of faith, faith is allowed to supply the defect of full obedience; and so the believers are admitted to life and immortality, as if they were righteous. . . .

What we are now required to believe to obtain eternal life, is plainly set down in the Gospel. St. John tells us, John 3:36, "He that believeth on the Son, hath eternal life; and he that believeth not the Son, shall not see life." What this believing on him is, we are also told in the next chapter. "The woman saith unto him, I know that the Messiah cometh: when he is come, he will tell us all things. Jesus said unto her, I that speak unto thee am he. The woman then went into the city, and saith to the men, Come see a man that hath told me all things that ever I did. Is not this the Messiah? And many of the Samaritans believed on him for the saying of the woman, who testified that he told me all that she ever did. So when the Samaritans were come unto him, many more believed because of his words, and said to the woman, We believe not any longer, because of thy saying; for we have heard ourselves, and we know, that this man is truly the Saviour of the world, the Messiah," John 4:25–26, 28–29, 39–42. . . .

To convince men of this, he did his miracles: and their assent to, or not assenting to this, made them to be, or not to be of his church; believers, or not believers. . . .

The common objection [about the final judgment] is . . . "What shall become of all mankind, who lived before our Saviour's time, who never heard of his name, and consequently could not believe in him?" To this the answer is so obvious and natural, that one would wonder how any reasonable man should think it worth the urging. Nobody was, or can be, required to believe, what was never proposed to him to believe. . . . All then that was required, before his appearing in the world, was to believe what God had revealed, and to rely with a full assurance on God, for the performance of his promise; and to believe that in due time he would send them the Messiah, this anointed King, this promised Saviour and Deliverer, according to his word. . . .

There is another difficulty often met with, which seems to have something of more weight in it. That is. . . . what shall become of all the rest of mankind, who, having never heard of the promise or news of a Saviour, not a word of a Messiah to be sent, or that was come, have had no thought or belief concerning him?"

To this I answer, that God will require of every man, "according to what a man hath, and not according to what he hath not." . . . There were many, who being strangers to the commonwealth of Israel, were also strangers to the oracles of God, committed to that people. There were many to whom the promise of the Messiah never came. And so they were never in a capacity to believe or reject that revelation. Yet God had, by the light of reason, revealed to all mankind, who would make use of that light, that he was good and merciful. The same spark of the divine nature and knowledge in man, which, making him a man, showed him the law he was under as a man, showed him also the way of atoning the merciful, kind, compassionate Author and Father of him and his being, when he had transgressed that law. He that made use of this candle of the Lord, so far as to find what was his duty, could not miss to find also the way to reconciliation and forgiveness, when he had failed in his duty.

[Matthew Tindal, *Christianity as Old as the Creation*]

A: By Natural Religion, I understand the Belief of the Existence of a God, and the Sense and Practice of those Duties which result from the Knowledge we, by our Reason, have of him and his Perfections; and of ourselves, and our own Imperfections; and of the relation we stand in to him and our Fellow-Creatures; so that the Religion of Nature takes in every thing that is founded on the Reason and Nature of things. . . . I suppose you will allow, that 'tis evident by the Light of Nature, that there is a God; or in other words, a Being absolutely perfect, and infinitely happy in himself, who is the Source of all other Beings; and that whatever perfections the Creatures have, they are wholly derived from him.

B: This, no doubt, has been demonstrated over and over; and I must own, that I can't be more certain of my own Existence, than of the Existence of such a Being.

A: Since then it is demonstrable there is such a Being, it is equally demonstrable, that the Creatures can neither add to, or take from the Happiness of that Being; and that he could have no Motive in framing his Creatures, or in giving Laws to such of them as he made capable of knowing his Will, but their own Good.

To imagine he created them at first for his own sake, and has since required things of them for that Reason, is to suppose he was not perfectly happy in himself before the Creation; and that the Creatures, by either observing, or not observing the Rules prescribed them, could add to, or take from his Happiness.

If then a Being infinitely happy in himself, could not command his Creatures any thing for his own Good; nor an all-wise Being things to no

end or purpose; nor an all-good Being any thing but for their good: It unavoidably follows, nothing can be a part of the divine Law, but what tends to promote the common Interest, and mutual Happiness of his rational Creatures; and every thing that does so, must be a part of it.

As God can require nothing of us, but what makes for our Happiness; so he, who can't envy us any Happiness our Nature is capable of, can forbid us those Things only, which tend to our Hurt; and this we are as certain of, as that there is a God infinitely happy in himself, infinitely good and wise; and as God can design nothing by his Laws but our Good, so by being infinitely powerful, he can bring every thing to pass which he designs for that End. . . .

Our Reason, which gives us a Demonstration of the divine Perfections, affords us the same concerning the Nature of those Duties God requires; not only with relation to himself, but to ourselves, and to one another. These we can't but see, if we look into ourselves, consider our own Natures, and the Circumstances God has placed us in with relation to our Fellow-Creatures, and what conduces to our mutual Happiness: Our Senses, our Reason, the Experience of others as well as our own, can't fail to give us sufficient Information.

With relation to ourselves, we can't but know how we are to act; if we consider, that God has endowed Man with such a Nature, as makes him necessarily desire his own Good; and, therefore, he may be sure, that God, who has bestowed this Nature on him, could not require any thing of him in prejudice of it; but, on the contrary, that he should do every thing which tends to promote the Good of it. The Health of the Body, and the Vigor of the Mind, being highly conducing to our Good, we must be sensible we offend our Maker, if we indulge our Senses to the prejudice of these. . . .

As to what God expects from Man with relation to each other; every one must know his Duty, who considers that the common Parent of Mankind has the whole Species alike under his Protection, and will equally punish him for injuring others, as he would others for injuring him; and consequently, that it is his Duty to deal with them, as he expects they should deal with him in the like Circumstances. . . .

Having thus discovered our Duty, we may be sure it will always be the same; since Inconstancy, as it argues a Defect either of Wisdom or Power, can't belong to a Being infinitely wise and powerful: What unerring Wisdom has once instituted, can have no Defects; and as God is entirely free from all Partiality, his Laws must alike extend to all Times and Places.

From these premises, I think, we may boldly draw this conclusion, that if religion consists in the practice of those duties, that result from the relation we stand in to God and Man, our religion must always be the same. If God is unchangeable, our duty to him must be so too; if Human Nature continues the same, and men at all times stand in the same relation to one another, the duties which result from thence too, must always be the same. Consequently our Duty both to God and Man must, from the beginning of the world to the end, remain unalterable;

be always alike plain and perspicuous; neither changed in whole, or part: which demonstrates that no person, if he comes from God, can teach us any other Religion, or give us any Precepts, but what are founded on those Relations. . . .

B: In my Opinion you lay too great a Stress on fallible Reason, and too little on infallible Revelation; and therefore I must needs say, your arguing wholly from Reason would make some of less Candour than myself, take you for an errant Free-thinker.

A: Whatever is true by Reason, can never be false by Revelation; and if God can't be deceived himself, or be willing to deceive men, the light he hath given to distinguish between religious truth and falsehood, cannot, if duly attended to, deceive them in things of so great Moment. . . .

In a word, to suppose any thing in Revelation inconsistent with Reason, and at the same time, pretend it to be the will of God, is not only to destroy that proof, on which we conclude it to be the will of God, but even the proof of the Being of a God.

John Rolfe Explains His Marriage to Pocahantas*

Not all relations between Europeans and Native Americans led to tragic conflict. In 1614, John Rolfe, who introduced tobacco cultivation to European Americans, married the young Powhattan woman Pocahantas. The marriage itself helped to maintain peace with the Powhattans for some years. In his letter to Virginia's governor excerpted below, Rolfe explains his motives for marrying Pocahantas.[58]

But to avoid tedious preambles, and to come nearer the matter: first suffer me with your pa-

tience, to sweep and make clean the way wherein I walk, from all suspicions and doubts, which may be covered therein, and faithfully to reveal unto you, what should move me hereunto.

Let therefore this my well advised protestation, which here I make between God and my own conscience, be a sufficient witness, at the dread full day of judgement (when the secret of all men's hearts shall be opened) to condemn me herein, if my chief intent and purpose be not, to strive with all my power of body and mind, in the undertaking of so mighty a matter, no way led (so far as man's weakness may permit) with the unbridled desire of carnal affection. [Rather, I have acted] for the good of this plantation, for the honor of our country, for the glory of God, for my own salvation, and for the converting

---

* John Rolfe, Letter to the Virginia Company
[58] Leon G. Tyler, *Narratives of Early Virginia, 1606–1625* (New York: Charles Scribner's Sons, 1907), 240–42, 243–44.

to the true knowledge of God and Jesus Christ, an unbelieving creature, namely Pokahuntas. To whom my heart and best thoughts are, and have a long time been so in tangled, and enthralled in so intricate a labyrinth, that I was even wearied to unwind myself there out. But almighty God, who never fails his [own], that truly invoke his holy name hath opened the gate, and led me by the hand that I might plainly see and discern the safe paths wherein to tread. . . .

I never failed to offer my daily and faith full prayers to God, for his sacred and holy assistance. I forgot not to set before mine eyes the frailty of mankind, his [proneness] to evil, his indulgence of wicked thoughts, with many other imperfections wherein man is daily in snared, and oftentimes overthrown, and them compared to my present estate. Nor was I ignorant of the heavy displeasure which almighty God conceived against the sons of Levi and Israel for marrying strange wives,[59] nor of the inconveniences which may thereby arise, with other the like good motions which made me look about warily and with good circumspection, into the grounds and principal agitations, which thus should provoke me to be in love with one whose education hath been rude, her manners barbarous, her generation accursed, and so discrepant in all nutriture from myself, that oftentimes with fear and trembling, I have ended my private controversies with this: surely these are wicked instigations, hatched by him who seeks and delights in man's destruction.[60] So with fervent prayers to be ever preserved from such diabolical assaults (as I took those to be) I have taken some rest.

Thus when I had thought I had obtained my peace and quietness, behold another, but more gracious temptation hath made breaches into my holiest and strongest meditations; with which I have been put to a new trial, in a straighter manner then the former: for besides the many passions and sufferings which I have daily, hourly, yea and in my sleep endured, even awaking me to astonishment, taxing me with remissness, and carelessness, refusing and neglecting to perform the duty of a good Christian, pulling me by the ear, and crying: why dost not thou endeavour to make her a Christian? And these have happened to my greater wonder, even when she hath been furthest separated from me, which in common reason (were it not an undoubted work of God) might breed forgetfulness of a far more worthy creature. Besides, I say the holy spirit of God hath often demanded of me, why I was created? If not for transitory pleasures and worldly vanities, but to labour in the Lord's vineyard, there to sow and plant, to nourish and increase the fruits thereof, daily adding with the good husband in the Gospel, somewhat to the talent, that in the end the fruits may be reaped, to the comfort of the laborer in this life, and his salvation in the world to come? And if this be, as undoubtedly this is, the service Jesus Christ requires of his best servant: woe unto him that hath these instruments of piety put into his hands, and willfully despises to work with them. Likewise, adding hereunto her great appearance of love to me, her desire to be taught and instructed in the knowledge of God, her capableness of understanding, her aptness and willingness to receive . . . besides her own incitements stirring me up hereunto.

What should I do? Shall I be of so untoward a disposition, as to refuse to lead the blind into the right way? Shall I be so unnatural, as not to give bread to the hungry? or uncharitable, as not to cover the naked? Shall I despise to actuate these pious duties of a Christian? Shall the base fear of displeasing the world, overpower and with hold me from revealing unto man these spiritual works of the Lord, which in my meditations and prayers, I have daily made known unto him? God forbid. . . .

Now if the vulgar sort, who square all men's actions by the base rule of their own filthiness, shall tax or taunt me in this my godly labour: let them know, it is not any hungry appetite, to gorge myself with incontinency. If I would,

---

[59] *displeasure . . . strange wives:* a reference to Ezra 9–10, where Ezra forces Jewish men to give up their non-Jewish wives.

[60] *him . . . destruction:* the devil.

and were so sensually inclined, I might satisfy such desire, though not without a seared conscience, yet with Christians more pleasing to the eye, and less fearful in the offence unlawfully committed. . . .

But shall it please God thus to dispose of me (which I earnestly desire to fulfill my ends before set down) I will heartily accept of it as a godly tax appointed me, and I will never cease, (God assist-ing me) until I have accomplished, and brought to perfection so holy a work, in which I will daily pray God to bless me, to mine, and her eternal happiness. And thus desiring no longer to live, to enjoy the blessings of God, then [than] this my resolution doth tend to such godly ends, as are by me before declared: not doubting of your favorable acceptance, I take my leave. . . .

American Protestant Anti-Catholicism*

Hostility between Protestants and Catholics came to the New World. Probably no other literature from this time testifies as strongly to American Protestant anti-Catholic feeling as The Awful Disclosures of Maria Monk, *first published in 1836. This piece of anti-Catholic propaganda tells the supposed story of a young Canadian girl, Maria Monk, who witnessed secret crimes and immoralities in a Montreal, Canada, nunnery and escaped to tell about them. After some years Monk's story was proven to be a fraud, but not before her book became the number two bestselling novel of nineteenth-century America. This chapter tells the story of murder in the convent.*[61]

But I must now come to one deed, in which I had some part, and which I look back upon with greater horror and pain, than any occurrences in the Convent in which I was not the principal sufferer. It is not necessary for me to attempt to excuse myself in this or any other case. Those who have any disposition to judge fairly will exercise their own judgement in making allowances for me, under the fear and force, the commands and examples, around me. . . .

The time was about five months after I took the veil; the weather was cool, perhaps in September or October. One day, the [Mother] Su-perior sent for me and several other nuns, to receive her commands. We found the Bishop and some priests with her; and speaking in an unusual tone of fierceness and authority, she said, "Go to the room for the Examination of Conscience, and drag Saint Francis[62] upstairs.". . . When we reached the room where we had been bidden to seek her, I entered the door, my companions standing behind me. The young nun was standing alone, near the middle of the room; she was probably about twenty, with light hair, blue eyes, and a very fair complexion. I spoke to her in a compassionate voice, but at the same time with such a decided manner, that she comprehended my full meaning: "Saint Francis, we are sent for you.". . . The tears came to my eyes. I had not a moment's doubt that she considered her fate as sealed, and was already beyond the fear of death. She was conducted, or rather hurried, to the staircase, which was nearby, and then seized by her limbs and clothes, and in fact almost dragged upstairs. I laid my own hands upon her—I took hold of her too—more gently than some of the rest; yet I encouraged and assisted them in carrying her. I could not avoid it. My refusal would not have saved her, nor prevented her being carried up. . . .

When we entered with her the room to which she was ordered, my heart sunk within me. The Bishop, the Lady Superior, and five priests, namely Bonin, Richards, Savage and two others

---

* Maria Monk, *The Awful Disclosures of the Hotel Dieu Nunnery of Montreal*
[61] Maria Monk, *Awful Disclosures of the Hotel Dieu Nunnery of Montreal* (New York: Hoisington and Trow, 1836), 97–105.

---

[62] *Saint Francis:* a nun in residence.

were assembled for her trial, on some charge of great importance.

Father Richards began to question her, and she made ready but calm replies. . . . He asked her, among other things, if she was not sorry for what she had been overheard to say (for she had been betrayed by one of the nuns), and if she would not prefer confinement in the cells to the punishment which was threatened her. But the Bishop soon interrupted him, and it was easy to perceive that he considered her fate as sealed. In reply to some of the questions put to her, she was silent; to others I heard her voice reply that she did not repent of the words she had uttered . . . that she still wished to escape from the convent; and that she had firmly resolved to resist every attempt to compel her to the commission of crimes she detested. She added that she would rather die than cause the murder of harmless babies.[63]

"That is enough, finish her!" said the Bishop.

Two nuns instantly fell upon the young woman. . . . On the bed [in the room] the prisoner was laid with her face upward, and then bound with cords so that she could not move. In an instant another feather bed [mattress] was thrown upon her. One of the priests, named Bonin, sprung like a fury upon it first, and stamped on it with all his force. The nuns speedily followed him, until there were as many upon the bed as could find room, all did what they could not only to smother but to bruise her. During this time my feelings were almost too strong to be endured.

After the lapse of twenty minutes . . . Father Bonin and the nuns ceased to trample upon her, and stepped from the bed. All was motionless and silent beneath it.

They then began to laugh at such inhuman thoughts as occurred to some of them. . . . They alluded to the resignation of our murdered companion, and one of them tauntingly said, "She would have made a good Catholic martyr!" . . . After waiting a short time, the feather bed was taken off her, the cords unloosed, and the body taken by the nuns and dragged downstairs. I was informed that it was taken into the cellar, and thrown unceremoniously into a hole . . . covered with a great quantity of lime, and then sprinkled with a liquid. . . .

Some time afterward, some of St. Francis' friends called to inquire about her, and they were told that she had died a glorious death; and further told, that she made some heavenly expressions, which were repeated, in order to satisfy her friends.

---

[63] *the murder of harmless babies:* Monk had charged that babies born to nuns in the convent were baptized and immediately strangled to death, "to secure their everlasting happiness."

The Roman Catholic Church Confronts Secular Thought*

The Syllabus of Errors *is a list of eighty heretical opinions condemned by Pius IX in 1864. Its most controversial section proved to be the one that condemned the separation of (the Roman Catholic) church and state and asserted the power of the church over all society. The document itself is purely negative, condemning each proposition it lists, but it implies that the Catholic truth is to be found in the opposite of each condemned proposition. Despite these condemnations, the power of these ideas grew in the church until the last half of the twentieth century, when some of them were formally recognized as proper by the Church: freedom of religion, historical-critical study of the Bible, recognition of Protestants as Christians, and recognition of the (at least partial) validity of other religions.[64]*

---

* Pope Pius IX, *Syllabus of Errors*

[64] Philip Schaff, *The Creeds of Christendom,* vol. 2 (New York: Harper, 1919), 213–33.

The Syllabus of the principal errors of our time, which are stigmatized in the Consistorial Allocutions, Encyclicals, and other Apostolical letters[65] of our Most Holy Lord, Pope Pius IX.

On Pantheism, Naturalism, and Absolute Rationalism: 1. There exists no supreme, most wise, and most provident divine being distinct from the universe, and God is none other than nature, and is therefore subject to change. In effect, God is produced in man and in the world, and all things are God, and have the very substance of God. God is therefore one and the same thing with the world, and thence spirit is the same thing with matter, necessity with liberty, true with false, good with evil, justice with injustice. 2. All action of God upon man and the world is to be denied. 3. Human reason, without any regard to God, is the sole arbiter of truth and falsehood, of good and evil; it is its own law to itself, and suffices by its natural force to secure the welfare of men and or nations . . . . 5. Divine revelation is imperfect, and, therefore, subject to a continual and indefinite progress, which corresponds with the progress of human reason. . . .

On Indifferentism, Latitudinarianism: 15. Every man is free to embrace and profess the religion he shall believe true, guided by the light of reason. 16. Men may in any religion find the way of eternal salvation, and obtain eternal salvation. 17. We may entertain at least a well-founded hope for the eternal salvation of all those who are in no manner in the true Church of Christ. 18. Protestantism is nothing more than another form of the same true Christian religion, in which it is possible to be equally pleasing to God as in the Catholic Church.

Errors Concerning the Church and Her Rights: 19. The Church[66] is not a true, and perfect, and entirely free society, nor does she enjoy peculiar and perpetual rights conferred upon her by her Divine Founder, but it appertains to the civil power to define what are the rights and limits with which the Church may exercise authority. . . .

Errors about Civil Society: 39. The commonwealth is the origin and source of all rights, and possesses rights that are not circumscribed by any limits. 40. The teaching of the Catholic Church is opposed to the well-being and interests of society. . . . 42. In the case of conflicting laws between the two powers, the civil law ought to prevail. . . . 47. The best theory of civil society requires that popular schools open to the children of all classes, and, generally, all public institutes intended for instruction in letters and philosophy, and for conducting the education of the young, should be freed from all ecclesiastical authority, government, and interference. They should be fully subject to the civil and political power, in conformity with the will of rulers and the prevalent opinions of the age. 48. This system of instructing youth, which consists in separating it from the Catholic faith and from the power of the Church, and in teaching exclusively, or at least primarily, the knowledge of natural things and the earthly ends of social life alone, may be approved by Catholics. . . . 55. The Church ought to be separated from the State, and the State from the Church. . . .

Errors Concerning Christian Marriage: 65. It cannot be by any means tolerated, to maintain that Christ has raised marriage to the dignity of a sacrament. 67. By the law of nature, the marriage tie is not indissoluble, and in many cases divorce, properly so called, may be pronounced by the civil authority. . . . 73. A merely civil contract may, among Christians, constitute a true marriage. . . .

Errors Having Reference to Modern Liberalism: 77. In the present day, it is no longer expedient that the Catholic religion shall be held as the only religion of the State, to the exclusion of all other modes of worship. 78. Whence it has been wisely provided by law, in some countries called Catholic, that persons coming to reside therein shall enjoy the public exercise of their own worship. . . . 80. The Roman Pontiff can and ought to reconcile himself to, and agree with, progress, liberalism, and modern civilization.

---

[65] *consistorial allocutions . . . letters:* previous statements by Pius IX.

[66] *the Church:* refers throughout only to the Roman Catholic church.

The Debate over Evolution*

The relationship between Christianity and natural science, especially since the Renaissance, has not been an easy one. In the seventeenth century, the two clashed over astronomy; in the eighteenth, geology; in the nineteenth and through the twentieth, geology, then biology and psychology. Probably the greatest conflict between science and Christianity has been over evolution, and the readings here show how sharp and polarized Christianity was over it. In the first selection from 1874, the conservative Princeton theologian Charles Hodge attacks Darwinism, especially as popularized by Thomas Huxley, as undermining the whole of the Christian faith.[67] In the second selection from 1915, the Boston Congregationalist pastor Lyman Abbott makes room for both evolution and Christianity in a thorough revision of traditional Protestant teachings. He summarizes a position he held since the publication of his The Evolution of Christianity *in 1892.[68]*

Professor [Thomas] Huxley's advice to metaphysicians and theologians is, to let science alone. But do he and his associates let metaphysics and religion alone? . . . Professor Huxley tells the religious world that there is overwhelming evidence (scientific evidence, of course) that no event has ever occurred on this earth which was not the effect of natural causes. Hence there have been no miracles, and Christ is not risen. He says that the doctrine that belief in a personal God is necessary to any religion worthy of the name is a mere matter of opinion. . . .

What is to be thought of the special relation of Mr. Darwin's theory to the truths of natural and revealed religion? . . . We cannot see how the theory of evolution can be reconciled with the declarations of the Scriptures. Others may see it, and be able to reconcile their allegiance to science with their allegiance to the Bible. Professor Huxley, as we have seen, pronounces the thing impossible. . . . Mr. [John] Henslow, indeed, says Science and Religion are not antagonistic because they are different spheres of thought. This is often said by men who do not admit that there is any thought at all in religion; that it is merely a matter of feeling. The fact, however, is that religion is a system of knowledge, as well as a state of feeling. . . . Religion has to fight for its life against a large class of scientific men. . . .

The first objection to the theory [of Darwinism] is its *prima facie* incredibility. . . . Who can believe that all the plants and animals which have ever existed upon the face of the earth have been evolved from one germ? This is Darwin's doctrine. . . .

[Second,] [t]here is no pretense that the theory can be proved. Mr. Darwin does not pretend to prove it. . . . All that he claims for his theory is that it is possible. His mode of arguing is that if we suppose this and that, then it may have happened thus and so. Amiable and attractive as the man presents himself in his writings, it rouses indignation, in one class at least of his readers, to see him by such a mode of arguing reaching conclusions which are subversive of the fundamental truths of religion. . . .

[Third,] [a]ll the evidence we have in favor of the fixedness of the species is, of course, evidence not only against Darwinism but also against evolution in all its forms. . . . The conclusion of the whole matter is, that the denial of design in nature is virtually the denial of God.

[Abbott, *Reminiscences*] I was not long in coming to the conclusion that animal man was developed from a lower order of creation. . . . The objection that evolution could not be reconciled with Genesis gave me no concern, for I had long before decided that the Bible is no authority on scientific matters. To the sneer, "So you think your ancestor was a monkey, do you!" I replied, "I would as soon have a monkey as mud for an ancestor." . . . The question whether God made the

---

*Charles Hodge, *What Is Darwinism?;* Lyman Abbott, *Reminiscences*
[67] Taken, with editing, from Charles Hodge, *What Is Darwinism?* (New York: Scribner & Armstrong, 1874), 141–52.
[68] Taken, with editing, from L. Abbott, *Reminiscences* (Boston: Houghton Mifflin, 1915), 458–62, 485–86.

animal man by a mechanical process in an hour or by a process of growth continuing through the centuries is quite immaterial to one who believes that into man God breathes a divine life. . . . Without being dogmatic on that point, I became a radical evolutionist; by which I mean I accepted to the full John Fiske's aphorism: "Evolution is God's way of doing things."

The doctrine that growth, not manufacture, is God's way of doing things changed also my conception of God, of creation, of Jesus Christ, and of the Gospel. . . . The picture of a King on a great white throne, into whose presence I should come by and by when this earthly life is over, disappeared, and in its place came the realization of a Universal Presence, animating all nature as my spirit animates my body, and inspiring all life as a father inspires his children or a teacher his pupils. . . .

As I no longer looked up to an imaginary heaven for an imaginary God, so I no longer looked back to a creation completed in six days or six geological epochs. I saw in creation . . . "a process, not a product." Every day is a creative day. Nor did I any longer look back over an intervening epoch of eighteen centuries for a revelation of God either in history or human experience. I saw him in modern as truly as in ancient history, in the life of America as truly as in the life of Israel.

GLOSSARY

confessionalism a concern in the mainstream churches of the Protestant Reformation for correctness of doctrine based upon the Reformation confessions, such as the *Augsburg Confession*.

Deism emphasis upon God as a remote creator, but not redeemer; the belief in particular of a group of English and a few American thinkers during the Enlightenment who saw reason, not revelation, as the basis of Christianity.

ecumenism cooperation and closer relations between churches.

Enlightenment a broad movement of science and philosophy in the eighteenth century characterized by a belief in natural law, the power of human reason to guide life, and a rational approach to religion.

journal a formal personal diary; it came to use in this period and sometimes was published.

liberalism a broad movement from about 1850 to the present to free ("liberalize") Christianity from the conservative strictures of its past, accepting the truth of modern knowledge and trying to bridge the growing gap between Christianity and secular culture.

Modernism a form of Roman Catholic liberalism that denied the exclusive truth of Christianity, maintaining that the essence of Catholicism was its ability to convey the truth of a universal religious experience; condemned generally by Pope Pius IX in 1864 and specifically by Pius X in 1907.

Pietism a movement within Protestantism stressing the devotion (piety) of the common Christian; usually had an emotional, and sometimes anti-intellectual, thrust.

scholasticism A seventeenth-century Protestant application of reason, especially Aristotelianism, to theology.

secularism the idea that human life can be fully lived without reference to God.

QUESTIONS FOR STUDY AND DISCUSSION

1.   Why did Protestantism turn so quickly from the dynamism of the early Reformation to confessionalism and scholasticism?

2.   Explain the rise of Pietism. To what extent, in your knowledge, does the Pietist impulse still influence Protestant Christianity?

3.   What are the basic tenets of the Christian opposition to slavery? Why did it take so long for this opposition to arise?

4.   Explain the essence of Protestant liberalism. Why was Christian liberalism so slow in coming to the Roman Catholic Church?

5.   To what extent is religious liberty and toleration a product of the Enlightenment, and to what extent might it be an outworking of Christian ethical ideals of freedom of conscience?

6.   Why was America such a fertile soil for the growth of new forms of Christianity such as Mormonism?

7.   Explain why you agree or disagree with this statement: "It was in the nineteenth century that Christian women first found their true voice."

SUGGESTIONS FOR FURTHER READING

E. Gaustad, *A Documentary History of Religion in America,* 2d ed. Grand Rapids, MI: Eerdmans, 1993. The first volume covers most of early modern times in America, with some good attention to European antecedents.

P. Gay, *Deism.* New York: Van Nostrand, 1968. A full anthology, with introductions to each reading.

K. J. Hardman, *Issues in American Christianity: Primary Sources with Introductions.* Grand Rapids, MI: Baker, 1993. Coverage of nineteenth-century Protestant issues are especially good.

R. S. Keller and R. R. Ruether, *In Our Own Voices: Four Centuries of American Women's Religious Writing.* San Francisco: HarperSanFrancisco, 1995. A rich collection of women's writings from the main religious traditions of the United States.

C. L. Manschreck, *A History of Christianity: Readings in the History of the Church from the Reformation to the Present.* Englewood Cliffs, NJ: Prentice-Hall, 1964. The fullest documentary source book for early modern times in Christianity. Despite the title, this book also anthologizes theology.

CHAPTER SEVEN

Christianity in Modern Times (1900–Present)

❖ In Seoul, South Korea, worshippers gather at the largest single congregation in world Christianity. This church, which belongs to a Pentecostalist denomination, the Assemblies of God, counts more than 60,000 people as its members, and on a typical Sunday back-to-back services are held from dawn to dusk to accommodate them. Protestant Christianity—both mainstream and independent—has grown so strong in South Korea that it has begun to send Korean missionaries to other parts of the world. If its growth continues, shortly after the turn of the millenium South Korea will become the first predominantly Christian nation on the Asian mainland.

❖ In Moscow, Russia, workers finish rebuilding the Christ the Savior Cathedral near the Kremlin. This church was built in 1820 as a national thanksgiving for Russia's victory over the invading Napoleon Bonaparte, but it was secularized by the communist government during the twentieth century. At one point the church was used as a warehouse, and then an ice-skating rink, until finally Joseph Stalin ordered it destroyed in 1931. Despite the desperate financial condition of the Russian church and people, funds were raised to bring the church back to its former glory. At its rededication in 1997, Prime Minister Boris Yeltsin sat next to the Patriarch of Moscow. The Christ the Savior Cathedral has become a symbol of the rebirth of religious faith and national pride in a land until recently officially atheist.

INTRODUCTION

Christianity in the twentieth century experienced more growth and change than in any century since the sixteenth. It started on a note of optimism, but with the events of World War I and the rise of totalitarianism, theology and then the church took a more unoptimistic turn. Protestant theology throughout the world became more conservative in the middle third of the century but then was shaken by secularity (the "Death of God" movement, for example) and social challenges (the international student revolt, the civil rights struggle, the Vietnam War) in the 1960s. At the same time, however, the Roman Catholic church reformed itself in a massive way at the Second Vatican Council: updating theology and worship, affirming a more democratic structure in the church, and reaching out to other Christians and even non-Christians with a new openness. At the beginning of the twenty-first century, new challenges have arisen for world Christianity. With the fall of communism in Europe, Eastern Christianity took the lead in helping to rebuild the spirit of eastern European nations. In Western Christianity, the churches have been challenged by liberation movements, religious relativism and pluralism, and the growing diversity of believers. As the new millenium begins, Christianity is faced as never before with the opportunities and challenges of being a global religion in a rapidly changing world.

Names

Scholars of Christianity, like historians, generally refer to the last hundred years or so as the Modern period. In this usage, *modern* has the connotation of "recent, contemporary." In this sense, it is a not very illuminating label—every period is contemporary to the people living in it!

But *Modern Age* has other connotative meanings that give it a more illuminating content. *Modern* generally connotes a liberalizing of culture from the heavy hand of past tradition, reliance upon the certainties of scientific knowledge, and an optimistic belief in human progress. At its root, it is a belief in human reason to guide human life. The modern spirit, in the process of being born since the Enlightenment, came to the full light of day near the turn of the twentieth century in both Europe and North America. This spirit has suffused much of the last one hundred years; even those who argue against the spirit of modern times accept it to some extent.

In the last decade or so, **postmodernism** has arisen as an intellectual construct as the assumptions of the modern world have been questioned. On first look, this is an inherently vague term—how can our own time be "post-contemporary"? *Postmodernism* connotes the flip side of the modern outlook: life without the inherent optimism, scientific certainty, and cultural liberalism of modernism. Notions of cultural relativism and pluralism have thrived in the climate of postmodernism.

To illustrate the difference between modernism and postmodernism, one can point to scholarly interpretation and use of the Bible in the early modern and modern periods. (Documents from any period can be read in a postmodern way; we choose the Bible as an example.) The modern spirit is expressed in the historical-critical method: reasoned; objective; scientific; given to construction of holistic, even universal meaning from the Bible. This form of biblical interpretation was initiated in the Renaissance, carried out in the Protestant Reformation, but came to its fullness in early modern times. It has dominated most branches of Christianity in the twentieth century, except in those churches adhering strongly to fundamentalism. But at the last quarter of the twentieth century, the postmodern spirit has worked its way into the presuppositions and methods of biblical study. Subjectivity, especially the subjectivity of the contemporary reader(s), is given play. It no longer stresses a holistic reading acceptable to everyone, the assumption that the Bible has a single meaning. Rather, in this view, it has a plurality of specialized readings—feminist, narrative, liberationist, and others. Postmodernism has arrived in biblical study, but its spirit and methods can be found in almost every other approach to the study of Christianity past and present.

Historical Sketch

When the nineteenth century ended, the world experienced widespread optimism that the twentieth century would see significant improvements in all human life, and this expansive outlook was shared in the church. It was especially widespread in Protestantism, both liberal and conservative, and shared as well in parts of Catholicism and Orthodoxy. Many thought that the next era would be "*the* Christian century."

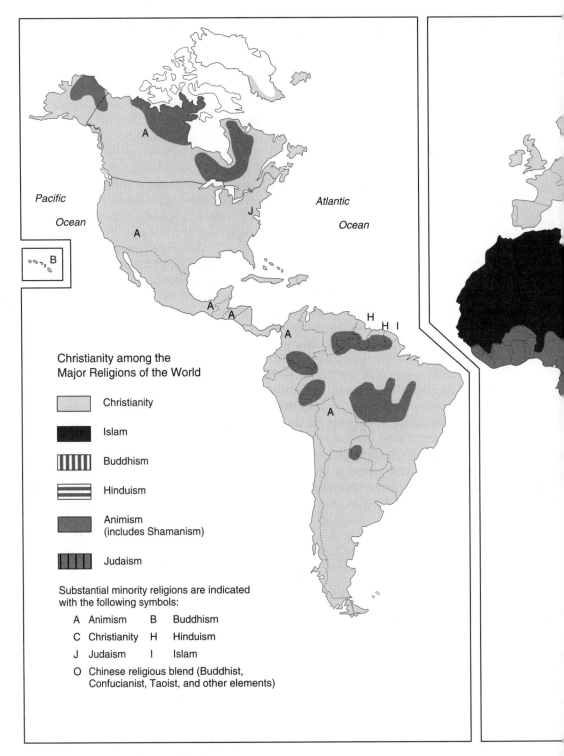

Christianity among the
Major Religions of the World

Christianity

Islam

Buddhism

Hinduism

Animism
(includes Shamanism)

Judaism

Substantial minority religions are indicated
with the following symbols:

A Animism   B Buddhism
C Christianity H Hinduism
J Judaism   I Islam
O Chinese religious blend (Buddhist,
   Confucianist, Taoist, and other elements)

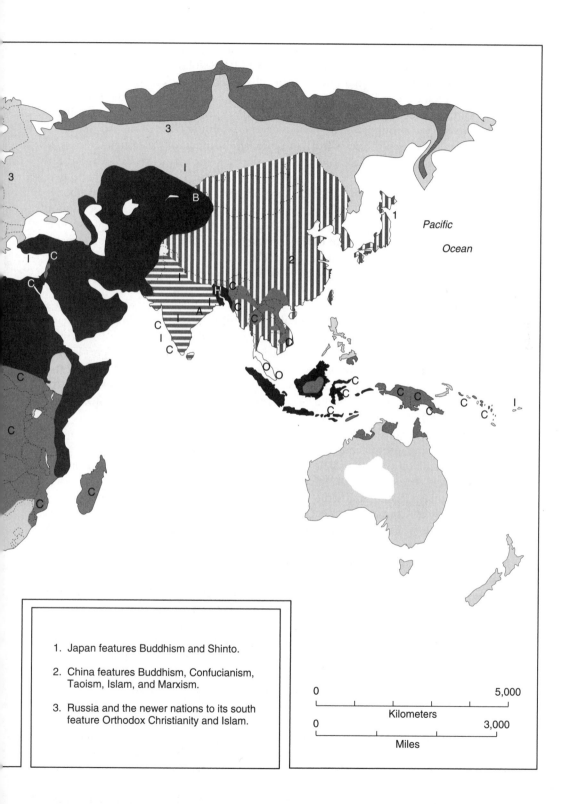

Pacific

Ocean

1. Japan features Buddhism and Shinto.

2. China features Buddhism, Confucianism, Taoism, Islam, and Marxism.

3. Russia and the newer nations to its south feature Orthodox Christianity and Islam.

0	5,000

Kilometers

0	3,000

Miles

The new era, however, was not to be one of untrammeled progress, but severe crisis and challenge. The carnage of World War I (1914–1918) followed by global economic depression began the movement away from cultural optimism. The rise of aggressive, totalitarian regimes first in Russia and then Italy and Germany led to the horrors of World War II (1939–1945), with its massive civilian casualties and Holocaust. Even the end of the war brought with it new uncertainties in the birth of the Atomic Age. All these events were to shake Christian optimism in much of Protestantism and in more liberal Catholicism to the roots. The result for some was a loss of faith, but for most a rethinking of the essence of Christianity. Karl Barth (1886–1968), who was to become the most influential theologian of the century, turned away from liberal, optimistic Protestantism to reassert the transcendent power of a gospel that cannot be synthesized with human culture. Barth stressed that Christianity is not a response to the human situation; it lives out of the self-revelation of God through the scriptures. The movement that he sparked came to be called **neo-Orthodoxy,** a new assertion in modern times of traditional, orthodox Christian theology, especially in its Reformed Protestant form.

After World War II, this movement came to the English-speaking world and had a direct effect on its theology and life for the next thirty years. Even those Protestant theologians who opposed the conservatism of neo-Orthodoxy also took a turn to more traditional themes of faith. The philosophical theologian Paul Tillich (1886–1965) stressed the ultimate importance of personal faith even as he addressed cultural concerns; the influential biblical scholar Rudolf Bultmann (1884–1976) linked a deep, existential faith to the essence of the Gospels as he reconstructed it in his historical research into the New Testament.

While this theological reassessment occurred, a movement for greater unity among the churches came into prominence. **Ecumenism** had been planted and nurtured in the mission fields of the various Protestant churches, where missionaries learned to minimize their denominational differences and cooperate together in the face of a non-Christian environment. In the twentieth century, the National (initially "Federal") Council of Churches in the United States and a World Council of Churches would be the institutional bearers of this movement. Individual denominations in North America, Europe and Asia would put aside their hostilities and merge into united denominations: Presbyterians, Lutherans, Methodists and others in the United States; several Protestant churches in Canada to form the United Church; three British Calvinist churches to form the United Reformed Church; and so on. Ecumenism has changed how theologians conceptualize the faith, how the different Christian churches relate to each other, and how grassroots Christians live out their faith in worship and daily life. This spirit of ecumenism also affected the Eastern Orthodox churches throughout the world; they have participated fully in the ecumenical movement from the start.

At the same time, a new movement for reform was gathering in the Roman Catholic church that would prove to be the most important Christian event of the twentieth century. During most of early modern times and the first half of the twentieth century, Catholicism had been insulated from dealing with the modern challenges of science, secularism, and religious toleration by the strength of its church structure. When a response to these challenges was deemed necessary, as in Vatican I, it usually took the form of a reassertion of the power and prerogatives of the Catholic church, especially its hierarchy.

When Pope John XXIII convened the **Second Vatican Council** in 1962, however, winds of reform pent up for seemingly hundreds of years blew through the church. In Vatican II, the Catholic Church recognized the status and role of the laity as essential to the church, reformed worship by putting masses in the vernacular language and increasing lay participation, opened ecumenical dialogue with Protestants and the Orthodox, affirmed for the first time religious liberty and toleration for all people, and took a new look at non-Christian faiths. The change was sudden and sweeping, and it soon impacted, at least indirectly, all types of Christianity in the world. But it seems to be a truism that periods of swift change are followed by times of consolidation. In the last two decades of the twentieth century, the Catholic Church seemed to pause from the swift changes while it wrestled with the implications of these reforms. At times, the wrestling—over issues like artificial birth control and the church's attitude to women—was and continues to be intense.

Four movements in Christianity have become increasingly important in the modern period. First, **feminism** (or its alternative term, "Women's Liberation") has stressed the full emancipation of women. It recognizes that the church by its teaching and practice has held women down and tried to make second-class Christians of them. Some feminists (Mary Daly, for example) have urged rejection of Christianity, arguing that it is irreformably patriarchal. Others take a more moderate approach, trying to recover the biblical roots of feminism, stressing the (admittedly few) women in Christian tradition who have played significant roles, and working toward full liberation of women within the various Christian churches. This latter approach still constitutes the mainstream of Christian feminism, and it will continue to be a potent force for years to come, in culture in general and in the church specifically. As the movement progresses, it is losing its European–North American orientation and will make more of an impact in the churches of Asia, Africa, and Latin America.

A second current is the **charismatic movement.** Stressing the supernatural *charismata*, "gifts of the Holy Spirit," this movement began near the turn of the century in conservative American Protestantism, but it has moved into mainstream Protestantism and Roman Catholicism as well. It is also found in charismatic or Pentecostal denominations, such as the Assemblies of God. Today the charismatic movement has spread almost throughout the Christian world. "Speaking in tongues" is its primary charism, or "spiritual gift," but other abilities, such as prophecy and healing, are often seen as well. The charismatic movement has often been divisive and controversial when it appears in other denominations, but it has brought new life as well. Some observers have estimated that Pentecostalists now make up between one-fourth and one-third of world Christians.

A third current movement is widely called **Liberation theology.** This is a misnomer, for the heart of "Liberation theology" is not theology so much as praxis. This movement stresses the active Christian mission of delivering the oppressed from evil social structures and situations. Using a combination of Marxist social analysis and the Christian Gospels, this movement was born in Roman Catholic theological circles in Latin America, which is still its center. But it has spread widely and been applied to several other movements: Women's Liberation, Black Liberation, and now Gay/Lesbian

Liberation. (The African-American civil rights movement in the 1950s and 1960s came before Black Liberation, but much of the Christian aspect of this continuing movement is now related to Liberation theology.) These new applications of Liberation Theology are still powerful influences in much of world Christianity, but the original form of political-social Liberation Theology in South America is waning.

The last movement to be considered here is **pluralism.** Throughout its long history, Christianity has been challenged by other religions, but the Enlightenment exacerbated this challenge. In recent times, with the rise of notions of the "shrinking world" and its "global village" along with postmodernism, pluralism has become a popular frame for reconceiving this relationship. It is especially strong among some academic theologians (John Hick, for example) and denominational leaders. Pluralism sees the claims of these religions as representing a truth that must be recognized seriously by Christians. No longer can Christianity claim to be *the* truth, the pluralist argues; it now is *a* truth among many. Pluralism's claims have not gone unchallenged among Christians who hold to the traditionally more exclusive views of the faith. The debate over pluralism is one of the hottest theological issues at the beginning of the third millennium.

Literary Genres of the Primary Sources

For the most part, the modern period has seen the continuation of the older genres of primary literary expression. Histories, letters, liturgies, creeds and confessions, sermons, academic treatises, and other forms have been updated for use in the new situations of modern times. All these types are represented in the readings in this chapter.

Two new literary genres arose in this period. One is, for lack of a better term, the *ecumenical agreement.* Usually constitutional or otherwise official in form, it spells out newfound agreements and ways of cooperation between previously divided churches. The second new type took its shape from the rise of modern mass media: the *press release.* As Christians have sought to influence the thought and life of the wider culture, they have adopted the press statement as a way of "getting the word out" and influencing public policy. This communication genre became especially common in the last half of the modern period.

EVENTS

The Height of Protestant Missions*

Robert E. Speer was a leading Presbyterian mission administrator. Like many missionaries, Speer saw denominational division as a great liability in the missionary effort and labored to transcend those divisions. Speer was especially farsighted in his advocating in 1919 that the newly created churches train their own native clergy and not continue as merely "colonial" extensions of American denominations.[1]

---

* Robert E. Speer, *The New Opportunity of the Church*

---

[1] From Robert E. Speer, *The New Opportunity of the Church* (New York: Macmillan, 1919), 94–95, 97–98.

[The "missionary enterprise"] has been in the world as an instrumentality of peace and international good will. Wherever it has gone, it has erased racial prejudice and bitterness, the great root of international conflict and struggle. It has helped men to understand one another. It has rubbed off the frictions. . . .

It has been an agency of righteousness. As the years have gone by, it alone has represented in many non-Christian lands the inner moral character of the Western world. By our political agencies and activities we have forced great wrongs upon the non-Christian peoples—commercial exploitation, the liquor traffic, and the slave trade upon Africa and the South Sea Islands, the opium traffic upon China. Against these things the one element of the West that has made protest has been the missionary enterprise. Year after year in those lands it has joined with what wholesome moral sentiment existed among the people in a death struggle against the great iniquities that Western civilization had encountered in the world. It has been an instrumentality of international righteousness.

It has been and is a great instrumentality of human service. It has scattered tens of thousands of men and women over many lands, teaching school in city and country, in town and village. It has built its hospitals by the thousand. It has sent its medical missionaries to deal every year with millions of sick and diseased peoples in Asia and Africa. It has been the one great, continuing, unselfish agency of unquestioning, loving, human service throughout the world, dealing not with emergency needs of famine and flood and pestilence alone, but, year in and year out, serving all human need and seeking to introduce into human society the creative and healing influences of Christ. . . .

Foreign missions have been a great agency of human unity and concord. They, at least, have believed and acted upon the belief that all men belong to one family. They have laughed at racial discords and prejudices. They have made themselves unpopular with many representatives of the Western nations who have gone into the non-Christian world, because they have not been willing to foster racial distrust, because they have insisted on bridging the divisions which separated men of different bloods and different nationalities. We are talking now about building the new world after the war. But it would be hopeless if we had not already begun it. We are talking about some form of international organization.[2] It may need to be very simple, with few and primitive functions, but it must come. And it can come only as first, we sustain in men's hearts a faith in its possibility; as second, we devise the instrumentalities necessary to it and make them effective; as third, we build up a spirit that will support it. Across the world for a hundred years the missionary enterprise has been the proclamation that this day must come, and that some such international body of relationships as this, based on right principles, must be set up among the nations of the world.

---

[2] *international organization:* the League of Nations.

The Birth of Pentecostalism*

The largest African-American Pentecostal group is the Church of God in Christ. Founded in 1895 by C. H. Mason, it has in its official history this explanation of glossolalia *(speaking in tongues). The charismatic movement has spread widely in the twentieth century through Roman Catholic and* *Protestant Christianity. This reading shows the biblical and experiential basis of glossolalia and the characteristic Pentecostalist insistence that every believer should speak in tongues.[3]*

---

[3] *History and Formative Years of the Church of God in Christ* (Memphis: Church of God in Christ Publishing House, 1969), 37–39. Copyright © 1969 Church of God in Christ Publishing House. Used by permission.

---

* *History and Formative Years of the Church of God in Christ*

And these signs shall follow those that believe: In my name shall they cast out devils; they shall speak with new tongues. Our Lord Jesus did not say that some of those that believe should speak with new tongues, but those that believe shall speak with new tongues. This promise is to those that believe; it is not to the unbeliever. When did this great work begin? On the day of Pentecost (Acts 2:1–5). . . .

This promise is to all that believe. Acts 2:38–39. They spake with tongues at Caesarea, when the Holy Ghost fell upon them which heard the word. Acts 10:1–5. . . .

Did God intend the speaking in tongues to be in the Church? [Yes, because] God hath set some in the Church, First Apostles; secondly, prophets; thirdly, teachers. After that, miracles; then gifts of healing—and helps, governments, diversities of tongues. I Cor. 12:28. For he that speaketh in an unknown tongue, speaketh not to men, but unto God, for no man understandeth him; howbeit in the spirit he speaketh mysteries. I Cor. 14:2. No man understands him, but the spirit is speaking the mysteries of God, through us. Is it wrong for one to pray in tongues? No, for if I prayed in an unknown tongue, my spirit prayeth but my understanding is unfruitful. I Cor. 14:14. Should we let the spirit pray in us if we do not know what he is saying? Yes, what is it then, I will pray with the spirit and with the understanding

also. I Cor. 14:15. We do not understand what to pray for as we ought to. Rom. 8:26. . . . Should we forbid to speak with tongues? No. Therefore, brethren, covet to prophesy and forbid not to speak with tongues. I Cor. 14:39.

Are we helped in any way to speak in tongues? Yes. He that speaketh in an unknown tongue edifieth himself. I Cor. 14:4. Would the Holy Ghost have all to speak with tongues? Yes. I would that ye all speak with tongues, but rather that ye prophesy. . . .

Speaking in tongues is the wonderful work of God. All that did not have this work in them on that day were amazed and in doubt about the wonderful work of God, and so it is today with all that have not this blessed work going on in them—they cannot understand it; they will say everything about it. Sinners, converted ones and sanctified ones and all wonder and will wonder when they hear or see this movement of the Holy Ghost going on in the saints of God. If the Holy Ghost does not speak in them, they can't understand His speaking the wonderful works of God in other tongues. Oh, dear ones, the word of every promise of God must enter into us before we can understand the wonderful works of the promise in others. The word giveth light and understanding that all may be baptized with this one baptism of the Holy Ghost.

Resistance to the Nazi Regime*

In 1934, German Protestants who opposed the Third Reich wrote a religious platform expressing their common concerns. It particularly opposed the "German Christians," a movement that had been created by and supported the Nazi regime. Largely written by the theologian Karl Barth, The Barmen Declaration has continued to exert a significant influence in German theology since World War II, and it has served since as a model statement of Christian resistance to totalitarian power. Note that each article begins with a quote from the

Bible, states the main point of belief, and then on the basis of both repudiates a key idea of Nazified Christianity.[4]

The assembled representatives of Lutheran, Reformed and United churches . . . hereby declare that we stand together on the foundation of the German Evangelical[5] Church as a federal union

---

* *The Barmen Declaration*

[4] Translated by the author from J. Beckman, *Kirchliches Jahrbuch, 1933–34* (Gütersloh, Ger.: Bertlesmann, 1948), 63–65.

[5] *Evangelical:* Protestant.

of German confessional churches. We are held together by confession of the one Lord of the one, holy, universal and apostolic church.

We declare, before the public view of all the Evangelical Churches of Germany, that the unity of this confession and thereby also the unity of the German Evangelical Church is severely threatened. In this year of the existence of the German Evangelical Church it is endangered by the more and more clearly evident style of teaching and action of the ruling ecclesiastical party of the German Christians and the church government which they run. This threat comes from the fact that the theological premise in which the German Evangelical Church is united is constantly and basically contradicted and rendered invalid, both by the leaders and spokesmen of the German Christians and also by the church government, by means of strange propositions. If they prevail, the church—according to all the creeds which are authoritative among us—ceases to be the church. If they prevail, moreover, the German Evangelical Church will become impossible as a federal union of confessional churches. . . .

In view of the destructive errors of the Christians and the present national church government, we pledge ourselves to the following evangelical truths:

1. "I am the way and the truth and the life: no man cometh unto the Father, but by me" (John 14:6). "Verily, verily, I say unto you, He that enters not by the door into the sheepfold, but climbs up some other way, the same is a thief and a robber." . . (John 10:1). Jesus Christ, as he is testified to us in the Holy Scripture, is the one Word of God, whom we are to hear, whom we are to trust and obey in life and in death. We repudiate the false teaching that the church can and must recognize yet other happenings and powers, images and truths as divine revelation alongside this one Word of God, as a source of her preaching.

2. "But of him are you in Christ Jesus, who of God is made unto us wisdom, and righteousness, and sanctification, and redemption" (I Cor.

1:30). Just as Jesus Christ is the pledge of the forgiveness of all our sins, just so—and with the same earnestness—is he also God's mighty claim on our whole life; in him we encounter a joyous liberation from the godless claims of this world to free and thankful service to his creatures. We repudiate the false teaching that there are areas of our life in which we belong not to Jesus Christ but another lord, areas in which we do not need justification and sanctification through him.

3. "But speaking the truth in love, may grow up into him in all things, which is the head, even Christ: from whom the whole body (is) fitly joined together and compacted . . ." (Eph. 4:15–16). The Christian church is the community of brethren, in which Jesus Christ presently works in the word and sacraments through the Holy Spirit. With her faith as well as her obedience, with her message as well as her ordinances, she has to witness in the midst of the world of sin as the church of forgiven sinners that she is his alone, that she lives and wishes to live only by his comfort and his counsel in expectation of his appearance. We repudiate the false teaching that the church can turn over the form of her message and ordinances at will or according to some dominant ideological and political convictions.

4. "You know that the princes of the Gentiles exercise dominion over them, and they that are great exercise authority upon them. But it shall not be so among you: but whosoever will be great among you, let him be your minister" (Matt. 20:25–26). The various offices in the church establish no rule of one over the other but the exercise of the service entrusted and commanded to the whole congregation. We repudiate the false teaching that the church can and may, apart from this ministry, set up special leaders[6] equipped with powers to rule.

5. "Fear God, honor the king!" (I Peter 2:17). The Bible tells us that according to divine arrangement the state has the responsibility to provide for justice and peace in the yet unredeemed

---

[6] *leaders:* the German original is Führer, Adolf Hitler's informal title.

world, in which the church also stands, according to the measure of human insight and human possibility, by the threat and use of force. The church recognizes with thanks and reverence toward God the benevolence of this, his provision. She reminds men of God's Kingdom, God's commandment and righteousness, and thereby the responsibility of rulers and ruled. She trusts and obeys the power of the word, through which God maintains all things. We repudiate the false teaching that the state can and should expand beyond its special responsibility to become the single and total order of human life, and also thereby fulfill the commission of the church. . . .

6. "Lo, I am with you always, even unto the end of the world" (Matt. 28:20). "The word of God is not bound" (II Tim. 2:9). The commission of the church, in which her freedom is founded, consists in this: in place of Christ and thus in the service of his own word and work, to extend through word and sacrament the message of the free grace of God to all people. We repudiate the false teaching that the church, in human self-esteem, can put the word and work of the Lord in the service of some wishes, purposes and plans or other, chosen according to desire.

The confessing synod of the German Evangelical Church declares that she sees in the acknowledgment of these truths and in the repudiation of these errors the not-to-be-circumvented theological foundation of the German Evangelical Church as a federal union of confessional churches. [The synod] calls upon all who can join in its declaration to be aware of these theological lessons in their ecclesiastical decisions. It begs all concerned to turn again in the unity of faith, of love, and of hope.

Verbum Dei manet in aeternam.[7]

---

[7] *Verbum Dei manet in aeternam:* Latin, "the Word of God remains forever."

Christians Struggle for Civil Rights*

On April 16, 1963, the Baptist minister and civil rights leader Martin Luther King, Jr., wrote this letter to Christian and Jewish clergy who had questioned his tactics. King had been jailed after one demonstration in Birmingham, Alabama. As this eloquent letter shows, although Christianity has been implicated in social evils, it has also pointed the way out of them.[8]

My Dear Fellow Clergymen:

While confined here in the Birmingham city jail, I came across your recent statement calling

my present activities "unwise and untimely." Seldom do I pause to answer criticism of my work and ideas. If I sought to answer all the criticisms that cross my desk, my secretaries would have little time for anything other than such correspondence in the course of the day, and I would have no time for constructive work. But since I feel that you are men of genuine good will and that your criticisms are sincerely set forth, I want to try to answer your statement in what I hope will be patient and reasonable terms. . . .

You deplore the demonstration taking place in Birmingham. But your statement, I am sorry to say, fails to express a similar concern for the conditions that brought about the demonstrations. I am sure that none of you would want to rest content with the superficial kind of social analysis that deals merely with effects and does not grapple with underlying causes. It is unfortunate that demonstrations are taking place in Birming-

---

* Martin Luther King, Jr., Letter from Birmingham Jail
[8] From Martin Luther King, Jr., *Why We Can't Wait* (New York: Harper & Row, 1963). Reprinted by arrangement with the Heirs to the Estate of Martin Luther King, Jr., c/o Writers House, Inc. as agent for the proprietor. Copyright 1963 by Martin Luther King, Jr., copyright renewed 1991 by Coretta Scott King.

ham, but it is even more unfortunate that the city's white power structure left the Negro community with no alternative. . . .

We know through painful experience that freedom is never voluntarily given by the oppressor; it must be demanded by the oppressed. Frankly, I have yet to engage in a direct-action campaign that was "well timed" in the view of those who have not suffered unduly from the disease of segregation. For years now I have heard the word "Wait!" It rings in the ear of every Negro with piercing familiarity. This "Wait" has almost always meant "Never." We must come to see, with one of our distinguished jurists, that "justice too long delayed is justice denied."

We have waited for more than 340 years for our constitutional and God-given rights. . . . Perhaps it is easy for those who have never felt the stinging darts of segregation to say, "Wait.". . . There comes a time when the cup of endurance runs over, and men are no longer willing to be plunged into the abyss of despair. I hope, sirs, you can understand our legitimate and unavoidable impatience.

You express a great deal of anxiety over our willingness to break laws. This is certainly a legitimate concern. Since we so diligently urge people to obey the Supreme Court's decision of 1954 outlawing segregation in the public schools, at first glance it may seem rather paradoxical for us consciously to break laws. One may well ask: "How can you advocate breaking some laws and obeying others?" The answer lies in the fact that there are two types of laws: just and unjust. I would be the first to advocate obeying just laws. One has not only a legal but a moral responsibility to obey just laws. Conversely, one has a moral responsibility to disobey unjust laws. I would agree with St. Augustine that "an unjust law is no law at all." . . .

I hope you are able to see the distinction I am trying to point out. In no sense do I advocate evading or defying the law, as would the rabid segregationist. That would lead to anarchy. One who breaks an unjust law must do so openly, lovingly, and with a willingness to accept the penalty. I submit that an individual who breaks a law that conscience tells him is unjust, and who willingly accepts the penalty of imprisonment in order to arouse the conscience of the community over its injustice, is in reality expressing the highest respect for law.

Of course, there is nothing new about this kind of civil disobedience. It was experienced sublimely in the refusal of Shadrach, Meshach and Abednego to obey the laws of Nebuchadnezzar, on the ground that higher moral law was at stake. It was practiced superbly by the early Christians, who were willing to face hungry lions and the excruciating pain of chopping blocks rather than submit to certain unjust laws of the Roman Empire. To a degree, academic freedom is a reality today because Socrates practiced civil disobedience. In our nation, the Boston Tea Party represented a massive act of civil disobedience.

We should never forget that everything that Adolf Hitler did in Germany was "legal" and everything the Hungarian freedom fighters did in Hungary was "illegal." It was "illegal" to aid and comfort a Jew in Hitler's Germany. Even so, I am sure that, had I lived in Germany at the time, I would have aided and comforted my Jewish brothers. If today I lived in a Communist country where certain principles dear to the Christian faith are suppressed I would openly advocate disobeying that country's anti-religious laws. . . .

You speak of our activity in Birmingham as extreme. At first I was rather disappointed that fellow clergymen would see my nonviolent efforts as those of an extremist. I began thinking about the fact that I stand in the middle of two opposing forces in the Negro community. One is a force of complacency, made up in part of Negroes who, as a result of long years of oppression, are so drained of self-respect and a sense of "somebodiness" that they have adjusted to segregation; and in part of a few middle-class Negroes who, because of a degree of academic and economic security and because in some ways they profit by segregation, have become insensitive to the problems of the masses. The other force is one of bitterness and hatred, and it comes perilously close to advocating violence. It is expressed in the various black nationalist groups that are springing up across the nation, the largest and best-known being Elijah Muhammad's Muslim movement.[9] Nourished by the Negro's frustration over the continued existence of racial discrimination, this movement is made up of people who have lost faith in America, who have absolutely repudiated Christianity, and who have concluded that the white man is an incorrigible "devil."

I have tried to stand between these two forces, saying that we need emulate neither the "do-nothingism" of the complacent nor the hatred and despair of the black nationalist. For there is the more excellent way of love and nonviolent protest. I am grateful to God, that, through the influence of the Negro church, the way of nonviolence became an integral part of our struggle. . . .

I have been so greatly disappointed with the white church and its leadership. Of course, there are some notable exceptions. I am not unmindful of the fact that each of you has taken some significant stands on this issue. . . . But despite notable exceptions, I must honestly reiterate that I have been disappointed with the church. I do not say this as one of those negative critics who can always find something wrong with the church. I say this as a minister of the gospel, who loves the church; who was nurtured in its bosom; who has been sustained by its spiritual blessings and who will remain true to it as long as the cord of life shall lengthen. . . .

There was a time when the church was very powerful—in the time when the early Christians rejoiced at being deemed worthy to suffer for what they believed. In those days the church was not merely a thermometer that recorded the ideas and principles of popular opinion; it was a thermometer that was a thermostat that transformed the mores of society. Whenever the early Christians entered a town, the people in power became disturbed and immediately sought to convict the Christians for being "disturbers of the peace" and "outside agitators." But the Christians pressed on, in the conviction that they were a "colony of heaven," called to obey God rather than man. Small in number, they were big in commitment. They were too God-intoxicated to be "astronomically intimidated." By their effort and example they brought an end to such ancient evils as infanticide and gladiatorial contest. . . .

Perhaps I have once again been too optimistic. Is organized religion too inextricably bound to the status quo to save our nation and the world? Perhaps I must turn my faith to the inner spiritual church, the church within the church, as the true church and the hope of the world. But again I am thankful to God that some noble souls from the ranks of organized religion have broken loose from the paralyzing chains of conformity and joined us as active partners in the struggle for freedom. They have left their secure congregations and walked in the streets of Albany, Georgia, with us. They have gone down the highways of the South on tortuous rides for freedom. Yes, they have gone to jail with us. Some have been dismissed from their churches, have lost the support of their bishops and fellow ministers. But they have acted in the faith that right defeated is stronger than evil triumphant. Their witness has been the spiritual salt that has preserved the true meaning of the gospel in these troubled times. They have carved a tunnel of hope through the dark mountain of disappointment.

I hope the church as a whole will meet the challenge of this decisive hour. But even if the church does not come to the aid of justice, I have no despair about the future. I have no fear about the outcome of our struggle in Birmingham even if our motives are at present misunderstood. We will reach the goal of freedom in Birmingham and all over the nation, because the goal of America is freedom. Abused and scorned though we may be our destiny is tied up with America's destiny. . . . We will win our freedom because the sacred heritage of our nation and the eternal will of God are embodied in our echoing demands. . . .

---

[9] *Elijah Muhammad's Muslim movement:* the Nation of Islam, now led by Louis Farakhan.

The Beginnings of Women's Liberation in Christianity*

In this sermon delivered in 1971 at the Memorial Church of Harvard University, the feminist theologian Mary Daly powerfully lays out some ideas that would become important in the church's experience of women's liberation. (Daly would later say that Christianity was essentially irreformable.) At the end of the reading, Daly led her listeners out of the chapel in an "exodus" to discover their new community in sisterhood, and the modern movement for liberation of women in Christianity was born.[10]

Sisters and other esteemed members of the congregation: There are many ways of refusing to see a problem—such as problem of the oppression of women by society in general and religion in particular. One way is to make it appear trivial. For example, one hears: "Are you on that subject of women again when there are so many important problems—like war, racism, pollution of the environment." One would think, to hear this, that there is no connection between sexism and the rape of the Third World, the rape of the Blacks, or the rape of land and water. Another way of refusing to see the problem of the oppression of men is to particularize it. For instance, one hears: "Oh, that's a Catholic problem. The Catholic church is so medieval." One would imagine, to listen to this, that there is no patriarchy around *here*. . . . Theology which is overtly and explicitly oppressive to women is by no means a thing of the past. Exclusively masculine symbolism for God, for the notion of divine "incarnation" in human nature, and for the human relationship to God reinforces sexual hierarchy. Tremendous damage is done, particularly in ethics, when theologians construct one-

dimensional arguments that fail to take women's experience into account. . . .

The courage to be and to see that is emerging in the women's revolution expresses itself in sisterhood—an event which is new under the sun. The so-called "sisterhoods" of patriarchy were and are in fact mini-brotherhoods, serving male interests and ideals. The ladies' auxiliaries of political parties, college sororities, religious orders of nuns—all have served the purposes of sexist society. In contrast to these, the new sisterhood is the bonding of women for liberation from sex role socialization. The very word itself says liberation and revolution.

There is no reason to think that sisterhood is easy. Women suffer from a duality of consciousness, as do the members of all oppressed groups. That is, we have internalized the image that males have created of "the woman," and this is in constant conflict with our authentically striving selves. One of the side effects of this duality is a kind of paralysis of the will. This is sometimes experienced as fear of ridicule, or of being considered abnormal, or—more basically—simply of being rejected, unwanted, unloved. Other effects of this dual consciousness are self-depreciation and emotional dependence. All of this is expressed in feminine anti-feminism—the direction by women of our self-hatred toward each other. Each of us has internalized the "male chauvinist pig." It exists inside our heads and it is a devil that must be exorcised and exterminated.

How can we do this? For women, the first salvific moment comes when we realize the fact of our exploitation and oppression. But—and this is an important "but"—unless the insight gives birth to externalized action it will die. This externalized action, or praxis, authenticates insight and creates situations out of which new knowledge can grow. It must relate to the building of a new community, to the bonding of women in sisterhood. . . .

Sisterhood, then, is in a very real sense an anti-church. In creating a counter-world to the soci-

---

* Mary Daly, "The Women's Movement: An Exodus Community"

[10] Mary Daly, "The Women's Movement: An Exodus Community," *Religious Education* 67 (September/October 1972): 327–33. Copyright © 1972 by Religious Education. Used by permission from the publisher, the Religious Education Association, 409 Prospect Street, New Haven, CT 06511-2177. All rights reserved.

ety endorsed by patriarchal religion women are at war with sexist religion as sexist. This is true whether we concern ourselves directly with religion or not. Women whose consciousness has been raised are spiritual exiles whose sense of transcendence is seeking alternative expressions to those available in institutional religion. Sisterhood is also functioning as church, proclaiming dimensions of truth which organized religion fails to proclaim. . . . Sisters: The sisterhood of man cannot happen without a real exodus. We have to go out from the land of our fathers into an unknown place. We can this morning demonstrate our exodus from sexist religion—a break which for many of us has already taken place spiritually. We can give physical expression to our exodus community, to the fact that we must go away.

We cannot really belong to institutional religion as it exists. It isn't good enough to be token preachers. It isn't good enough to have our ener-gies drained and co-opted. Singing sexist hymns, praying to a male god breaks our spirit, makes us less than human. The crushing weight of this tradition, of this power structure, tells us that we do not even exist.

The women's movement is an exodus community. Its basis is not merely in the promise given to our fathers thousands of years ago. Rather its source is in the unfulfilled promise of our mothers' lives, whose history was never recorded. Its source is in the promise of our sisters whose voices have been robbed from them, and in our own promise, our latent creativity. We can affirm now our promise and our exodus as we walk into a future that will be our own future.

Sisters—and brothers, if there are any here: Our time has come. We will take our own place in the sun. We will leave behind the centuries of silence and darkness. Let us affirm our faith in ourselves and our will to transcendence by rising and walking out together.

The Aftermath of Apartheid in South Africa*

One of the most notable changes in social and political affairs at the end of the twentieth century was the fall of apartheid, or racial separation and discrimination, in South Africa. Here a South African churchman and scholar puts these changes in global perspective.

South Africa recently experienced the single biggest transition in its history without excessive violence or war. Those present in 1994 will never forget the long lines of people waiting to cast their votes. Christians prayed and pleaded to God that South Africa be granted a peaceful transition. The miracle did happen.

Anyone who wants to understand something of South Africa's transition needs to see and un-derstand the bigger global picture. Global megatrends ultimately affect everyone. Without going into detail, a few contours of the global social changes which are taking place must be sketched.

First, the urbanization of Africa, still in process, implies cultural disruption of enormous proportion because the industrialized cities are basically Western in infrastructure and ethos. Poverty and cultural disorientation are playing havoc with the lives of millions of people. African cities have two faces: the Western side with offices, hotels, suburbs, and malls, while on the other side are the "shantytowns," or squatter settlements, where water, sanitation, transport, health care, and schools are lacking or absent.

Second, the Christendom era ended in South Africa in 1994 when the new secular dispensation came about. Religious freedom and human rights ushered in a new era in which the state no longer controls moral and religious values by law.

---

* H. Jurgen Hendriks, "The Religious Landscape in Post-Apartheid South Africa"

Individuals now have to make their own choices. The AIDS dilemma in Africa is directly related to this phenomenon. The decline in Christianity in South Africa is a first sign of the impact of this transition.

Third, a generational gap is causing tension in families and every sphere of society. The younger generation (with good school education) look down on the older people (who had no or poor education), reject their authority and forego their wisdom. Basically there are three groups. The traditionalists hold to the old values of either the apartheid era or traditional African cultural values. The second group is the struggle generation which fought on different sides of the apartheid divide and now have to face one another and reconcile. The white section of this group have educational and economical power; the predominantly black section has political and numerical power. A third and barely emerging group is the post-apartheid youth that is still wavering between being resolute fighters for a new non-racial South Africa with equal opportunities, or a group disillusioned because of broken promises.

Fourth, the effect of a globalized economy and competition is causing severe hardship all over Africa because Africa's infrastructure and culture is not geared to compete on that level. The massive debt problem of underdeveloped countries illustrate the point. In South Africa the new dispensation inherited a first world economy with a fairly good infrastructure. The new government opted for a capitalistic-oriented economic policy but is fighting a rearguard action with labour unions and the communist party in their own ranks.

Major challenges face South Africa, but also Africa at large. An African renaissance is needed: a new vision, resolve and leadership to address the challenges with which it is confronted. Political stability is needed: good government, administration and putting an end to corruption within the government. Only then can the high crime rate and general influence of corruption be addressed successfully. Also needed is a balance between sustainable development and sustainable community. Africa can teach the world about the value of "ubuntu," humanness and community, but it has to address the appalling influence of American imperialism (economically and through the media) on its traditional cultures, values, and family life. Poverty and unemployment must be eased, and curbing the population explosion is necessary. . . . Ecological issues are of grave concern. Africa's natural beauty and wildlife resources are a gift to the world and need better protection and care.

In all of this the church has a crucial role and challenge:

❖ The church must through its members permeate society with basic values so that the chronic sickness of crime, corruption and sexual misconduct, as well as the injustices of society, can be addressed.

❖ Many mainline churches are still stuck in a clerical paradigm. They need a contextualized, transformational theology approach that will empower the laity to address the most urgent needs of society.

❖ The spirituality of many Pentecostal/charismatic churches is a "made in America, health and wealth, signs and wonders" gospel. Indigenous Pentecostal churches with their liturgical emphasis on song, dance, rhythm and healing have an important contribution to make in Africa.

❖ The influential indigenous churches need theological training for their leadership in order to be able to be in a better position with regard to the inculturisation of the gospel.

❖ The church lacks a public character to speak out fearlessly against injustice and to play a prophetic role in the development of a multi-party democracy. Many churches tend to associate with a specific tribe and party; or, in order to prevent internal strife, they favor a one-party system.

❖ Ecumenical cooperation and religious tolerance is still a big challenge in Africa, especially in the local societies where the religions and churches have to work together.

❖ The church is growing in Africa because of sociological reasons. It is the one more-or-less dependable institution where people can meet, socialize, be encouraged, receive help with so many dire needs, and receive dignity and self-esteem through responsibility and work. However, many denominations are on a "church growth" spree in order to grow numerically without enough attention to the other dimensions of growth.

❖ Reconciliation. South Africa's Truth and Reconciliation Commission is an example of a reconciliation process, something that is needed in every region of Africa. The church has an enormous responsibility in this regard. Everywhere in Africa the church should adapt to a post-Constantinian era and play a prophetic and critical role in a secular political situation.

INSTITUTION

The World Council of Churches*

The World Council of Churches was founded in 1948 with an ecumenical assembly in Amsterdam. Many Protestant and Eastern Orthodox churches from around the world participated, although European and American churches took the lead. The Roman Catholic Church was not present but now holds observer status.[11]

I. [Basis] The World Council of Churches is a fellowship of churches which accept our Lord Jesus Christ as God and Savior. It is constituted for the discharge of the functions set out below.

II. [Membership] Those churches shall be eligible for membership . . . which express their agreement with the basis upon which the Council is founded and satisfy such criteria as the Assembly or the Central Committee may prescribe. Election to membership shall be by a two-thirds vote of the member churches represented at the Assembly, each member church having one vote. . . .

III. [Functions] The functions of the World Council shall be: (i) To carry on the work of the two world movements for Faith and Order and for Life and Work. (ii) To facilitate common action by the churches. (iii) To promote cooperation in study. (iv) To promote the growth of ecumenical consciousness in the members of all churches. (v) To establish relations with denominational federations of world-wide scope and with other ecumenical movements. (vi) To call world conferences on specific subjects. . . . (vii) To support the churches in their task of evangelism.

IV. [Organization] The World Council shall discharge its functions through the following bodies: (i) An Assembly which shall be the principal authority in the Council, and shall ordinarily meet every five years. . . . The members of the assembly shall be both clerical and lay persons—men and women. (ii) A central Committee which shall be a Committee of the Assembly and which shall consist of the President of the World Council, together with not more than ninety members chosen by the Assembly.

---

* Constitution of the World Council of Churches
[11] From G. K. A. Bell, *Documents on Christian Unity,* 1948–57, Fourth Series, no. 276 (London: Oxford University Press, 1958). Copyright © 1958 Oxford University Press. Used by permission.

A Second Vatican Council Sampler*

The Second Vatican Council, which met from 1962 until 1965, is a landmark in the history of the Roman church. Called by Pope John XXIII, it sought to explain the traditional faith of the Catholic church to modern people both inside and outside the church. Here are readings from three key documents to illustrate the changes that Vatican II brought and is still bringing.[12]

The Vatican Council declares that the human person has a right to religious freedom. Freedom of this kind means that all men should be immune from coercion on the part of individuals, social groups and every human power so that, within due limits, nobody is forced to act against his convictions nor is anyone to be restrained from acting in accordance with his convictions in religious matters in private or public, alone or in association with others. The Council further declares that the right to religious freedom is based on the very dignity of the human person as known through the revealed word of God and by reason itself. This right of the human person to religious freedom must be given such recognition in the constitutional order of society as will make it a civil right.

[Declaration on the Relation of the Church to non-Christian Religions] All men form but one community. This is so because all stem from the one stock which God created all people from the entire earth; and also because all share a common destiny, namely God. His providence, evident goodness and saving designs extend to all men against the day when the elect are gathered together in the holy city which is illuminated by the glory of God and in whose splendour all peoples will walk.

Men look to their different religions for an answer to the unsolved riddles of human existence. The problems that weigh heavily on the hearts of men are the same today as in ages past. What is man? What is the meaning and purpose of life? . . . How can genuine happiness be found? What happens at death? . . . The Catholic Church rejects nothing of what is true and holy in these religions. She has a high regard for the manner of life and conduct, the precepts and the doctrines which, although differing in many ways from her own teaching, nevertheless often reflect a ray of that truth which enlightens all men. Yet she proclaims, and is in duty bound to proclaim without fail, Christ who is the way, the truth and the life (John 14:6).

The Church also has a high regard for Muslims. They worship God, who is one. . . . They strive to submit themselves without reserve to the hidden decrees of God. . . . Although not acknowledging him as God, they worship Jesus as a Prophet,[13] his virgin Mother they also honor, and even at times devoutly invoke. . . . Over the centuries many quarrels and dissensions have arisen between Christians and Muslims. The sacred Council now pleads with all to forget the past, and urges that a sincere effort be made to achieve mutual understanding. . . .

Since Jews and Christians have a common spiritual heritage, this sacred council wishes to encourage and further mutual understanding and appreciation. . . . Even though the Jewish authorities and those who followed their lead pressed for the death of Christ, neither all Jews indiscriminately at that time, nor Jews today, can be charged with the crimes committed during his passion. It is true that the Church is the new people of God, yet the Jews should not be spoken of as rejected or accursed, as if this followed from Holy Scripture. . . . The Church reproves every form of persecution against whomsoever it

---

* Declaration on Religious Liberty, 2; Declaration on the Relation of the Church to Non-Christian Religions, 1–3; Pastoral Constitution on the Church in the Modern World

[12] From A. P. Flannery, *Documents of Vatican II* (North Port, NY: Costello Publishing, 1975). Copyright © 1975 Costello Publishing Company and A. P. Flannery. Used by permission.

---

[13] *they worship Jesus as a prophet:* most Muslims would emphatically disagree with this description of their religion.

may be directed. Remembering, then, her common heritage with the Jews and moved not by any political consideration, but solely by the religious motivation of Christian charity, she deplores all hatreds, persecutions, displays of antisemitism leveled at any time or from any source against the Jews.

[Pastoral Constitution on the Church in the Modern World] The joys and the hopes, the griefs and the anxieties of the men of this ages, especially those who are poor or in any way afflicted, these too are the joys and hopes, the griefs and the anxieties of the followers of Christ. Indeed, nothing genuinely human fails to raise an echo in their hearts. For theirs is a community composed of men. United in Christ, they are led by the Holy Spirit in their journey to the kingdom of their Father and they have welcomed the news of salvation which is meant for everyone. That is why this community realizes that it is

truly and intimately linked with mankind and its history. . . .

Unlike former days, the denial of God or of religion, or the abandonment of them, are no longer unusual and individual occurrences. . . . Modern atheism often takes on a systematic expression, which, in addition to other arguments against God, stretches the desire for human independence to such a point that it finds difficulties with any kind of dependence on God. . . .

The remedy to be applied to atheism, however, is to be sought in a proper presentation of the Church's teaching as well as in the integral life of the Church and her members. . . While rejecting atheism, root and branch, the Church sincerely professes that all men, believers and unbelievers alike, ought to work for the rightful betterment of this world in which we all live. Such an ideal cannot be realized, however, apart from sincere and prudent dialogue.

The Question of Women Priests in the Roman Catholic Church*

The feminist movement has impacted the church most sharply in its demands for the right for women to be ordained into all the offices of the churches. Published in 1977, this Vatican declaration was a response to ferment within the Catholic Church over the role of women. The Second Vatican Council had defined the church as the people of God and called for lay involvement in all aspects of church life, resulting in many public calls for the ordination of women to the priesthood. The declaration restates traditional arguments, most of which have also been used in the last 100 years by Protestants and the Eastern Orthodox Church. In 1995, the Vatican declared this position infallible and forbade all further discussion.[14]

The Catholic Church has never felt that priestly or episcopal ordination can be validly conferred on women. A few heretical sects in the first centuries, especially Gnostic ones, entrusted the exercise of the priestly ministry to women; this innovation was immediately noted and condemned by the Fathers, who considered it as unacceptable in the Church. It is true that in the writings of the Fathers one will find the undeniable influence of prejudices unfavorable to women, but nevertheless, it should be noted that these prejudices had hardly any influence on their pastoral activity, and still less on their spiritual direction. But over and above considerations inspired by the spirit of the times, one finds expressed—especially in the canonical documents[15] of the Antiochian and Egyptian traditions—this essential reason, namely, that by calling only men to the

---

* Joseph Cardinal Ratzinger. "Declaration on the Question of the Admission of Women to the Ministerial Priesthood"

[14] "Declaration on the Question of the Admission of Women to the Ministerial Priesthood," from Leonard Swidler and Arlene Swidler, eds., *Women Priests: A Catholic Commentary on the Vatican Declaration* (New York: Paulist Press, 1977), 38–40. Copyright © 1977 Paulist Press. Used by permission.

---

[15] *canonical documents:* not Scripture, but later authoritative writings.

priestly Order and ministry in its true sense, the Church intends to remain faithful to the type of ordained ministry willed by the Lord Jesus Christ and carefully maintained by the Apostles.

The same conviction animates medieval theology, even if the Scholastic doctors, in their desire to clarify by reason the data of faith, often present arguments on this point that modern thought would have difficulty in admitting or would even rightly reject. Since that period and up to our own time, it can be said that the question has not been raised again, for the practice has enjoyed peaceful and universal acceptance.

The Church's tradition in the matter has thus been so firm in the course of the centuries that the Magisterium[16] has not felt the need to intervene in order to formulate a principle which was not attacked, or to defend a law which was not challenged. But each time that this tradition had the occasion to manifest itself, it witnessed to the Church's desire to conform to the model left to her by the Lord.

The same tradition has been faithfully safeguarded by the Churches of the East. Their unanimity on this point is all the more remarkable since in many other questions their discipline admits of a great diversity. At the present time these same Churches refuse to associate themselves with requests directed towards securing the accession of women to priestly ordination.

Jesus did not call any woman to become part of the Twelve. If he acted in this way, it was not in order to conform to the customs of his time, for his attitude towards women was quite different from that of his milieu, and he deliberately and courageously broke with it. . . . Contrary to the Jewish mentality, which did not accord great value to the testimony of women, as Jewish law attests, it was nevertheless women who were the first to have the privilege of seeing the risen Lord, and it was they who were charged by Jesus to take the first paschal message to the Apostles themselves . . . in order to prepare the latter to become the official witnesses to the resurrection.

It is true that these facts do not make the matter immediately obvious. This is no surprise, for the questions that the Word of God brings before us go beyond the obvious. In order to reach the ultimate meaning of the mission of Jesus and the ultimate meaning of Scripture, a purely historical exegesis of the texts cannot suffice. But it must be recognized that we have here a number of convergent indications that make all the more remarkable the fact that Jesus did not entrust the apostolic charge to women. Even his Mother, who has so closely associated with the mystery of her Son, and whose incomparable role is emphasized by the Gospels of Luke and John, was not invested with the apostolic ministry.

---

[16] *Magisterium:* the teaching authority of the church.

Hymns of the Twentieth Century*

Christian hymns from more recent times often emphasize the social aspects of human life and the Christian faith more so than hymns from earlier periods. In the first reading, the lyrics of Harry Emerson Fosdick's famous hymn from 1930 expresses modern dimensions of conflict for the faith.[17] In the second, a Latin American hymn from 1971 expresses Christian faithfulness in the social context of poverty and class conflict.[18]

---

* H. E. Fosdick, "God of Grace and God of Glory"; J. A. Olivar and M. Manzano, "When the Poor Ones" ("Cuando el pobre")

[17] From *Lutheran Book of Worship* (Minneapolis: Augsburg, 1978), 415.

[18] From *The United Methodist Hymnal* (Nashville: United Methodist Publishing House, 1989), hymn 434. Copyright © 1980 The United Methodist Publishing House. Used by permission.

God of grace and God of glory,
On thy people pour thy power;
Crown thine ancient Church's story;
Bring her Bud to glorious flower.
Grant us wisdom, grant us courage,
For the facing of this hour.

Lo! the hosts of evil round us
Scorn thy Christ, assail his ways!
From the fears that long have bound us
Free our hearts to faith and praise.
Grant us wisdom, grant us courage,
For the living of these days.

Cure thy children's warring madness,
Bend our pride to thy control;
Shame our wanton, selfish gladness,
Rich in things and poor in soul.
Grant us wisdom, grant us courage,
Lest we miss thy kingdom's goal.

Save us from weak resignation
To the evils we deplore.
Let the search for thy salvation
Be our glory evermore.
Grant us wisdom, grant us courage,
Serving thee whom we adore.

["When the Poor Ones"]
When the poor ones who have nothing share
    with strangers,
When the thirsty water give unto us all,

When the crippled in their weakness strengthen
    others,
Then we know that God still goes that road
    with us.

When at last all those who suffer find their
    comfort,
When they hope though even hope seems
    hopelessness,
When we love though hate at times seems all
    around us,
Then we know that God still goes that road
    with us.

When our joy fills up our cup to overflowing,
When our lips can speak not words other than
    true,
When we know that love for simple things is
    better,
Then we know that God still goes that road
    with us.

When our homes are filled with goodness in
    abundance,
When we learn how to make peace instead of
    war,
When each stranger that we meet is called a
    neighbor,
Then we know that God still goes that road
    with us.

Christian Experience in Base Communities*

Christian "base communities," small groups of Christians in Central and Latin America organized for spiritual growth and social change, sprang up in the 1960's with the rise of liberation theology, and they have persisted despite its decline. The following essay by Adela Jiménez, a Mexican Roman Catholic lay leader, illustrates many important dimensions of Christian life in Latin America today.[19]

I am a Catholic, and the church has always asked of me the commitment to serve as the church.

---

* Adela Jiménez, "The Word of God is Teaching Us How to Speak"

[19] From the *Proceedings from the Dialogue on Investment in North and Latin America in Light of the International Debt Crisis,* sponsored by the American Lutheran Church at the Lutheran Center, Mexico City, February 26–March 1, 1987. Reprinted with permission.

This is my goal. After working with the church, I wanted to work outside—because I realized that the people who go to mass and religious functions are people who, more or less, know how to talk. But the poor didn't go. I think that it was desirable for the Word of God to reach the people who had never listened to this message.

I didn't go to school. I didn't even have one year of schooling. I was a girl raised in poverty. My parents had many children. And I was one of those who wasn't healthy enough to study. That's why I didn't study. But little by little, after I married, I began to hear the Word of God in the church. And that's where I began to find my way opening for me.

My husband helped me quite a bit in getting to know the Bible. We would listen to a text, and I would write it down. Very late at night, my husband would wake me and say, "Read what we heard today." I would read and I wouldn't understand anything, my friends. He would ask me, "What do you understand?" I would say, "I don't understand anything." "Read it again." And so I would read the text up to three or four times. Then I would say, "God is saying this to us." And he would say to me, "Yes, that's what God is saying." And that's how, little by little, I started to understand the Word of the Lord.

I don't understand the men who went to universities. They speak too high up. On one occasion, a theologian was giving us some very good lessons. But he spoke with very, very big words that we poor people don't understand. I told this theologian, after he had been speaking for quite a while, "Just a minute, please. If you want to speak to us poor people, you have to step down, and speak like poor people do, or you have to teach all of us to speak like you do, because I can't understand your words." Everyone behind me was poor like me. He said, "How about all of you? What do you say about it?" And everyone said, "It's true, we can't understand you." Now the man was very concerned and said, "We better make a handbook for poor people." I said, "It would be better if you study and walk with the poor in order for you to understand us, before we'll be able to understand you."

I meet with 18 small groups. I go each day to two or three communities. I come home late at night and my unrest is, "Why don't the men have work? How does the man with pay, even so little, earn for his family?" But the one without pay turns to drinking because this man has no courage to go home—because he has no money. It's true, people. When the children come home they ask for something to eat. How can one say to the child, "I don't have anything"? It's the mother who faces the situation, while the man goes crazy after alcohol. He says obscene words to his wife and children or hits them saying, "Leave me alone." These are the cases we find.

Friends, the situation that the people are living in is terrible. There is no bread. And we, the poor, are very, very sure, although we don't know much of the political situation, we are very sure about what we are living. We read the lessons from the Bible. We read them two or three times until we understand it, then we relate it to what's happening. And what is happening to us is not good. Wages are low. The poor man isn't earning anything.

Once I was invited to the Cathedral to tell these experiences to all the people who go there. It was a terrible beginning, because when the Father brought me to the microphone and said, "You have to talk," I said to the priest, "Hold me, please. I'm going to faint." And he said, "What do you mean, faint? It's only your nerves. Talk!" And I was filled with courage because I said, "I have to speak out what others do not say," because my brothers and sisters don't speak out.

And that's what we are doing in the small communities, trying to make the government hear us. We have achieved some things for some neighborhoods that didn't have water, that didn't have electricity, that didn't have streets. We started, as a little group, to get restless. How can we talk to the people? If they never paid attention to us in church (and when I speak of church I am speaking of the church hierarchy). Really, and unfortunately, our church hasn't served as it ought to. We go along with this great pain, this complex, this unease that we cannot express. The church has always made us keep quiet. When the priest spoke he always, always he spoke. And we, always, always nodding off in the pews, because he talked so much it made us sleepy. And we would leave at the end of the mass. We left half asleep. And once outside we wouldn't remember anything that he had said about the Word of God. This was confusing us more and more everyday making us feel so small.

This hasn't really gotten through to our communities. "Why don't we have water?" We all wonder why, why, why, until at last somebody says something. And this is what we are doing with the Word of God. The Word of God is teaching us how to speak, showing us how to ask for what we need, how to ask each other, "What is it that we need?"

TEACHING

The Rise of Biblical Criticism*

In this 1906 book, the great biblical scholar and medical humanitarian Albert Schweitzer reviewed and critiqued many nineteenth-century efforts to find "the real, historical Jesus." He concluded that they all created a Jesus in their own image. Schweitzer's own reconstruction was that an apocalyptic eschatology stood at the center of Jesus' ministry, an eschatology, Schweitzer says, we cannot adopt today. Yet the famous, moving conclusion to this book points to trust in a heroically dedicated Jesus. The conservative turn in theology after World War I would not look quite so negatively on the modern relevance of Jesus' eschatological vision.[20]

The study of the Life of Jesus has had a curious history. It set out in quest of the historical Jesus, believing that when it had found Him it could bring Him straight into our time as a Teacher and Savior. It loosed the bands by which He had been riveted for centuries to the stony rocks of ecclesiastical doctrine, and rejoiced to see life and movement coming into the figure once more, and the historical Jesus advancing, as it seemed, to meet it. But He does not stay; He passes by our time and returns to His own. What surprised and dismayed the theology of the last forty years was that, despite all forced and arbitrary interpretations, it could not keep Him in our time, but had to let Him go. He returned to His own time, not owing to the application of any historical ingenuity, but by the same inevitable necessity by which the liberated pendulum returns to its original position. . . .

Jesus means something to our world because a mighty spiritual force streams forth from Him and flows through our time also. This fact can neither be shaken nor confirmed by any historical discovery. It is the solid foundation of Christianity.

The mistake was to suppose that Jesus could come to mean more to our time by entering into it as a man like ourselves. That is not possible. First, because such a Jesus never existed. Secondly, because although historical knowledge can no doubt introduce greater clearness into an existing spiritual life, it cannot call spiritual life into existence. History can destroy the present; it can reconcile the present with the past; can even to a certain extent transport the present into the past; but to contribute to the making of the present is not given unto it. . . .

But the truth is, it is not Jesus as historically known, but Jesus as spiritually arisen within men, who is significant for our time and can help it.

---

* Albert Schweitzer, *The Quest of the Historical Jesus*
[20] Translated by the author from Albert Schweitzer, *Von Reimarus zu Wrede: Geschichte Der Leben-Jesu-Forchung* (Berlin, 1910).

Not the historical Jesus, but the spirit which goes forth from Him and in the spirits of men strives for new influence and rule, is that which overcomes the world.

It is not given to history to disengage that which is abiding and eternal in the being of Jesus from the historical forms in which it worked itself out, and to introduce it into our world as a living influence. It has toiled in vain at this undertaking. As a water-plant is beautiful so long as it is growing in the water, but once torn from its roots, withers and becomes unrecognizable, so it is with the historical Jesus when he is wrenched loose from the soil of eschatology, and the attempt is made to conceive Him "historically" as a Being not subject to temporal conditions. The abiding and eternal in Jesus is absolutely independent of historical knowledge and can only be understood by contact with His spirit which is still at work in the world. In proportion as we have the Spirit of Jesus we have the true knowledge of Jesus.

Jesus as a concrete historical personality remains a stranger to our time, but His spirit, which lies hidden in His words, is known in simplic-

ity, and its influence is direct. Every saying contains in its own way the whole Jesus. The very strangeness and unconditionedness in which He stands before us makes it easier for individuals to find their own personal standpoint in regard to Him. . . .

The historical Jesus, as He is depicted in the Gospels, influenced individuals by the individual word. They understood Him so far as it was necessary for them to understand, without forming any conception of His life as a whole, since this in its ultimate aims remained a mystery even for the disciples. . . .

He comes to us as One unknown, without a name, as of old, by the lakeside, He came to those men who knew Him not. He speaks to us the same word: "Follow thou me!" and sets us to the tasks which He has to fulfil for our time. He commands. And to those who obey Him, whether they be wise or simple, He will reveal Himself in the toils, the conflicts, the sufferings which they shall pass through in His fellowship, and, as an ineffable mystery, they shall learn in their own experience Who He is.

The Visions of Fundamentalism and Modernism*

Differences in doctrine had simmered between conservative and liberal Protestants since before 1800. But near the turn of the twentieth century, and especially in its early decades, these differences boiled over. In the nineteenth century, liberals had come to accept evolutionary theory, higher criticism of the Bible, and belief in social progress. Then conservatives fought back, insisting that certain "fundamental" teachings be preserved: scriptural inerrancy, the Virgin Birth, the divinity of Jesus Christ, Christ's substitutionary atonement on the cross, the bodily resurrection of Jesus, and his bodily

return at the end of time. In the first reading from 1925, J. Gresham Machen of Princeton Seminary published an article in the New York Times stating the essence of fundamentalist doctrine.[21] In the second reading from 1924, Shailer Matthews of the University of Chicago Divinity School explains the "faith of Modernism."[22] The names have been changed, but the struggle between liberal and conservative Christians continues.

---

[21] J. G. Machen, "What Fundamentalism Stands for Now," *New York Times,* 21 June 1925. Copyright © 1925 by The New York Times, June 21, 1925. Reprinted by permission.
[22] From Shailer Matthews, *The Faith of Modernism* (New York: Macmillan, 1924). Copyright © 1924 Macmillan Publishing Company.

The term fundamentalism is distasteful to the present writer and to many persons who hold views similar to his. It seems to suggest some strange new sect; whereas in point of fact we are conscious simply of maintaining the historic Christian faith and of moving in the great central current of Christian life. . . . Despite changes in the environment, there is something in Christianity which from the very beginning has remained the same. . . .

The basis of the Christian view of God—by no means all of it, but the basis of it—is simply theism: the belief, namely, that the universe was created, and is now upheld by a personal Being upon whom it is dependent but who is not dependent upon it. . . . The transcendence of God—what the Bible calls the holiness of God—is at the very root of the Christian religion. God is indeed, according to the Christian view, immanent in the world; but he is also personally distinct from the world. . . .

According to historic Christianity, all mankind are under the just condemnation of God, and are utterly helpless because of the guilt and power of sin. According to another very widespread type of belief, human resources are sufficient for human needs, and self-development, especially the development of the religious nature, is the Christian ideal. This type of belief is optimistic about human nature . . . while historic Christianity regards all mankind as being in itself hopelessly lost. . . .

We deserved eternal death, but the Son of God, who was Himself God, came into this world for our redemption, took upon himself the just punishment for our sins, died in our stead upon the cross, and finally completed His redeeming work by rising from the tomb in a glorious resurrection. There and there alone is found the Christian gospel; the piece of "good news" upon which all our hope is based. . . .

Acceptance of this New Testament account of Jesus involves a certain attitude toward Him that is widely different from the attitude assumed by many persons of the Church today. Jesus . . . was not the first Christian, the initiator of a new type of religious life, but stood in a far more fundamental and far more intimate relationship to Christianity than that, because He was the one who made Christianity possible by his redeeming work. At no point does our attitude appear in more characteristic fashion than just here.

[Matthews, *The Faith of Modernism*] The religious affirmations of the Modernist are not identical with any theology. They represent an attitude rather than doctrine, they involve creative living under the inspiration of Christian connections rather than a new orthodoxy. The Modernist knows that . . . the church cannot simply reaffirm the past.

In developing an intellectual apparatus for justifying the Christian life, we shall not feel the need of stressing certain doctrinal patterns which expressed the Christian convictions and attitudes of men in different circumstances and controlled by different social practices. We shall shape new patterns whenever they are needed, from life itself. . . .

The Modernist will cherish faith in Jesus Christ as the revealer of the saving God, but . . . he will not base that faith upon the virgin birth as the one and only means by which God can enter into human experience.

The Modernist will not insist upon miracles, but he believes that God is active and mysteriously present in the ordered course of nature and social evolution.

Because the Modernist thinks of God as immanent within His world, he counts upon divine help in every struggle for larger freedom and justice. The death of Christ, therefore, gets far richer significance for him as a revelation of such participation than is possible from analogies drawn from the sacrifices of the ancient world. . . .

Because he thus sees the character of God in Jesus, and therefore believes in the possibilities of a life like that of Jesus, the Modernist will practice good will himself and urge it as the only safe and promising motive for social, economic and national life. And he will never doubt that God's good will shall some day reign on earth.

The Heart of Neo-Orthodox Theology*

The greatest work of the Swiss theologian Karl Barth, and one that will ensure his continuing influence, is his twelve-volume Church Dogmatics. *The founder and leader of neo-Orthodoxy, Barth called for Christians to turn away from an easy identification of God and humanity, of church and culture. This reading, written in Barth's typically ponderous and demanding style, expresses well the center of his theology, reliance upon the Bible as the medium of God's revelation and Jesus Christ as the center of that revelation.*[23]

The Bible is the concrete medium by which the Church recalls God's revelation in the past, is called to expect revelation in the future, and is thereby challenged, empowered, and guided to proclaim. The Bible is, therefore, not itself and in itself God's past revelation, just as Church proclamation also is not itself and in itself the expected future revelation. But the Bible speaking to us and heard by us as God's Word attests the past revelation. The proclamation that speaks to us and is heard by us as God's Word promises the future revelation. By really attesting revelation, the Bible is the Word of God, and by really promising revelation proclamation is the Word of God. But the promise in proclamation rests upon the attestation in the Bible, the hope of future revelation upon faith in that which happened once for all. Therefore the decisive relation between the Church and revelation is the attestation of it by the Bible. The Bible, further, is not itself and in itself God's past revelation, but by becoming God's Word it attests God's past revelation and is God's past revelation in the form of attestation. . . .

Engaged in this service, the Biblical witnesses point beyond themselves. If we regard them as witnesses—and only as witnesses do we regard them genuinely, i.e. in the way in which they themselves wished to be regarded—then their self, which in its inward and outward restrictedness and emotion constitutes, so to speak, the matter of their service, must decidedly be regarded by us from the point of view of its form, as pointing away from themselves. They speak and write not for their own sakes, nor for the sake of their deepest inner possession or even need, but under the orders of that something else. Not to assert themselves, nor yet as the heroes or advocates of the cause they plead, but away beyond any immanent teleology, for the reason that they must speak and write about that something else. It is not themselves, and not, emphatically not, their own special experience of and relationship to God, that they wish to present to and urge upon the Church, but that something else by their own agency. But "by their own agency" not in the sense in which the man himself must be a more or less perfect organ for the manifestation of objective facts and values or subjective excitations (as is the case with the productions of science, politics, and art), but by their own agency in such a way that it is solely and exclusively the something else which compels and limits the perfect or imperfect human organ from without, the thing attested itself, which is what makes man a witness. . . .

Why and in what respect does the Biblical witness possess authority? In that it claims no authority whatsoever for itself, that its witness amounts to letting the Something else be the authority, itself and by its own agency. Therefore we do the Bible a poor honour, and one unwelcome to itself, when we directly identify it with this something else, with revelation itself. . . . Such direct identification of revelation and the Bible, which is the practical issue, is not one to be presupposed or anticipated by us. It takes place as an event, when and where the word of the Bible becomes God's Word, i.e. when and where the word of the Bible functions as the word of a witness, when and where John's finger points not

* Karl Barth, *Church Dogmatics* 1.1
[23] From Karl Barth, *Church Dogmatics* 1.1 (Edinburgh: Clark, 1936), 124–26. Copyright © 1936 T. & T. Clark, Ltd. Used by permission.

in vain but really pointedly, when and where by means of its word we also succeed in seeing and hearing what he saw and heard. Therefore, where the Word of God is an event, revelation and the Bible are one in fact, and word for word one at that. . . .

But for that very reason we should realize that and how far they are also always not one, how far their unity is really an event. The revelation upon which the Biblical witnesses gaze, looking and witnessing away from themselves, is, purely formally, different from the word of the witnesses just in the way in which an event itself is different from the best and most faithful narrative about it. But this difference is inconsiderable compared with the one which beggars all analogy, that in revelation we are concerned with Jesus Christ to come, who ultimately in the fullness of time did come. Literally we are, therefore, concerned with the singular Word spoken, and this time really directly, by God Himself. But in the Bible we are invariably concerned with human attempts to repeat and reproduce, in human thoughts and expressions, this Word of God in definite human situations, e.g. in respect of the complications of Israel's political position midway between Egypt and Babylon, or of the errors and confusions in the Christian Church at Corinth between A.D. 50–60.

Faith as Ultimate Concern*

When the Nazis came to power, Paul Tillich fled his native Germany and held teaching positions at a number of major American universities. Influenced by existentialist philosophy, he played a particularly important role in connecting Christian theology with the concerns of contemporary psychology, literature, and the arts. Although he is sometimes classified as a neo-Orthodox theologian, Tillich's leading ideas about the correlation of Christ and human culture are not at all neo-Orthodox. In this reading, Tillich develops the existential nature of faith.[24]

Ultimate concern is the abstract translation of the great commandment: "The Lord, our God, the Lord is one; and you shall love the Lord your God with all your heart, and with all your soul, and with all your mind, and with all your strength" [Mark 12:29]. The religious concern is ultimate; it excludes all other concerns from ultimate significance; it makes them preliminary. The ultimate concern is unconditional, independent of any conditions of character, desire, or circumstance. The unconditional concern is total: no part of ourselves or of our world is excluded from it; there is no "place" to flee from it [Ps. 139]. The total concern is infinite: no moment of relaxation and rest is possible in the face of a religious concern which is ultimate, unconditional, total, and infinite. . . .

The question now arises: What is the content of our ultimate concern? What does concern us unconditionally? The answer, obviously, cannot be a special object, not even God, for the first criterion of theology must remain formal and general. If more is to be said about the nature of our ultimate concern, it must be derived from an analysis of the concept "ultimate concern." Our ultimate concern is that which determines our being or not-being. Only those statements are theological which deal with their object in so far as it can become a matter of being or not-being for us. This is the second formal criterion of theology.

Nothing can be of ultimate concern for us which does not have the power of threatening and saving our being. The term "being" in this context does not designate existence in time and space. Existence is continuously threatened and saved by things and events which have no ultimate concern for us. But the term "being"

* Paul Tillich, *Systematic Theology*
[24] Paul Tillich, *Systematic Theology*, vol. 1 (Chicago: University of Chicago Press, 1951), 11–14, 49–50. Copyright © 1951 The University of Chicago Press. Used by permission.

means the whole of human reality, the structure, the meaning, and the aim of existence. All this is threatened; it can be lost or saved. Man is ultimately concerned about his being and meaning. "To be or not to be" in this sense is a matter of ultimate, unconditioned, total, and infinite concern. . . .

It is not an exaggeration to say that today man experiences his present situation in terms of disruption, conflict, self-destruction, meaninglessness, and despair in all realms of life. This experience is expressed in the arts and in literature, conceptualized in existential philosophy, actualized in political cleavages of all kinds, and analyzed in the psychology of the unconscious. It has given theology a new understanding of the demonic-tragic structures of individual and social life. The question arising out of this experience is not, as in the Reformation, the question of a merciful God and the forgiveness of sins; nor is it, as in the early Greek church, the question of finitude, of death and error; nor is it the question

of the personal religious life or of the Christianization of culture and society. It is the question of a reality in which the self-estrangement of our existence is overcome, a reality of reconciliation and reunion, of creativity, meaning and hope. We shall call such a reality the "New Being." . . .

But this answer is not sufficient. It leads immediately to the further question, "Where is this New Being manifest?" Systematic theology answers this question by saying: "In Jesus the Christ." This answer also has presuppositions and implications which it is the main purpose of the whole system to develop. Only this must be said here—that this formula accepts the ancient Christian baptismal confession of Jesus as the Christ. He who is the Christ is he who brings the new eon, the new reality. And it is the man Jesus who in a paradoxical assertion is called the Christ. Without this paradox the New Being would be an ideal, not a reality, and consequently not an answer to the question implied in our human situation.

"Religionless Christianity" *

Dietrich Bonhoeffer, a young Lutheran theologian and a leading influence on the Barmen Declaration, was imprisoned in 1943 for taking part in the resistance movement. While in prison Bonhoeffer carried out a remarkable correspondence with family and friends on personal and theological subjects. Toward the end of his confinement he began to speak of "religionless/worldly Christianity." Although Bonhoeffer was not permitted to work out these bold proposals before he was hanged in April 1945 on the charge of treason, his questions just prior to his death struck creative sparks in the minds of many. Bonhoeffer wrestles here with the role of Christianity as a religion in a secular age. His thoughts have a continuing effect on world Christianity.[25]

What is bothering me incessantly is the question what Christianity really is, or indeed who Christ really is, for us today. The time when people could be told everything by means of words, whether theological or pious, is over, and so is the time of inwardness and conscience and that means the time of religion in general. We are moving towards a completely religionless time; people as they are now simply cannot be religious any more. Even those who honestly describe themselves as "religious" do not in the least act up to it, and so they presumably mean something quite different by "religious."

Our whole nineteen-hundred-year-old Christian preaching and theology rest on the "religious a priori[26]" of mankind. "Christianity" has always

* Dietrich Bonhoeffer, *Letters and Papers from Prison*
[25] Reprinted with permission of Scribner, a division of Simon & Schuster from *Letters and Papers from Prison,* by Dietrich Bonhoeffer, revised, enlarged edition, translated by Reginald

Fuller, Frank Clark, et al. Copyright © 1953, 1967, 1971, by SCM Press, Ltd.
[26] *a priori:* assumption.

been a form—perhaps the true form—of "religion." But if one day it becomes clear that this a priori does not exist at all, but was a historically conditioned and transient form of human self-expression, and if therefore man becomes radically religionless—and I think that that is already more or less the case (how else is it, for example, that this war, in contrast to all previous ones, is not calling forth any "religious" reaction? What does that mean for "Christianity"?) . . .

How can Christ become the Lord of the religionless as well? Are there religionless Christians? If religion is only a garment of Christianity—and even this garment has looked very different at different times—then what is a religionless Christianity? . . .

The questions to be answered would surely be: What do a church, a community, a sermon, a liturgy, a Christian life mean in a religionless world? How do we speak of God—without religion, i.e., without the temporally conditioned presuppositions of metaphysics, inwardness, and so on? How do we speak (or perhaps we cannot now even "speak" as we used to) in a "secular" way about "God"? . . .

Religious people speak of God when human knowledge (perhaps simply because they are too lazy to think) has come to an end, or when human resources fail. . . . I've come to be doubtful of talking about any human boundaries (is even death, which people now hardly fear, and is sin, which they now hardly understand, still a genuine boundary today?). It always seems to me that we are trying anxiously in this way to reserve some space for God; I should like to speak of God not only on the boundaries but at the center, not in weaknesses but in strength; and therefore not in death and guilt but in man's life and goodness. As to the boundaries, it seems to me better to be silent and leave the insoluble unsolved. Belief in the resurrection is not the "solution" of the problem of death. God's "beyond" is not the beyond of our cognitive faculties. . . . God is beyond in the midst of our life. The church stands, not at the boundaries where human powers give out, but in the middle of the village. That is how it is in the Old Testament, and in this sense we still read the New Testament far too little in the light of the Old. How this religionless Christianity looks, what form it takes, is something that I am thinking about a great deal.

Rethinking the Relationship between God and the World*

In her writings, the contemporary theologian Sallie McFague develops the metaphorical (symbolic) character of Christian speaking about God. In this selection, she explains that the models for our speaking about God, especially the relationship between God and the world, should be expanded by the addition of new metaphors, particularly "God as Mother."[27]

We are letting the metaphor of the world as God's body try its chance. We are experimenting with a bit of nonsense to see if it can make a claim to truth. What if, we are asking, the "resurrection of the body" were not seen as the resurrection of particular bodies that ascend, beginning with Jesus of Nazareth, into another world, but as God's promise to be with us always in God's body, our world? What if God's promise of permanent presence to all space and time were imagined as a worldly reality, a palpable, bodily presence? What if, then, we did not have to go somewhere special (church) or somewhere else (another world) to be in the presence of God but

---

* Sallie McFague, *The World as God's Body*
[27] From Sallie McFague, *Models of God* (Minneapolis, MN: Fortress, 1987), 69–78, 84. Copyright © 1987 Fortress Press. Used by permission of Augsburg Fortress.

could feel ourselves in that presence at all times and in all places? What if we imagined God's presence as in us and in all others, including the last and the least?

As we begin this experiment we must once again recall that a metaphor or model is not a description. We are trying to think in an as-if fashion about the God-world relationship, because we have no other way of thinking about it. No metaphor fits in all ways, and some are more nonsense than sense. The king-realm kind of thinking about the God-world relationship sounds like sense because we are used to it, but reflection shows that in our world it is nonsense. For a metaphor to be acceptable, it need not, cannot, apply in all ways; if it did, it would be a description. One has to realize how not to apply a metaphor (to say God is the Father does not mean that God has a beard!) and also where it fails or treads on shaky ground. The metaphor of the world as God's body has the opposite problem to the metaphor of the world as the king's realm: if the latter puts too great a distance between God and the world, the former verges on too great a proximity. Since both metaphors are inadequate, we have to ask which one is better in our time, and to qualify it with other metaphors and models. . . .

A central issue is whether the metaphor of the world as God's body is pantheistic or, to put it another way, reduces God to the world. The metaphor does come far closer to pantheism than the king-realm model, which verges on deism, but it does not totally identify God with the world any more than we totally identify ourselves with our bodies. . . . The very fact that we can speak about our bodies is evidence that we are not totally one with them. On this model, God is not reduced to the world if the world is God's body. Without the use of personal agential metaphors, however, including among others God as mother, lover, and friend, the metaphor of the world as God's body would be pantheistic, for the body would be all there were. . . .

Furthermore, the model of the world as God's body suggests that God loves bodies: in loving the world, God loves a body. Such a notion is a sharp challenge to the long antibody, antiphysical, antimatter tradition within Christianity. This tradition has repressed healthy sexuality, oppressed women as sexual tempters, and defined Christian redemption in spiritualistic ways, thus denying that basic social and economic needs of embodied beings are relevant to salvation. To say that God loves bodies is to redress the balance toward a more holistic understanding of fulfillment. . . .

What this experiment with the world as God's body comes to, finally, is an awareness, both chilling and breathtaking, that we as worldly, bodily beings are in God's presence. It is the basis for a revived sacramentalism, that is, a perception of the divine as visible, as present, palpably present in our world. But it is a kind of sacramentalism that is painfully conscious of the world's vulnerability, its preciousness, its uniqueness. The beauty of the world and its ability to sustain the vast multitude of species it supports is not there for the taking. The world is a body that must be carefully tended, that must be nurtured, protected, guided, loved, and befriended both as valuable in itself—for like us, it is an expression of God—and as necessary to the continuation of life. We meet the world as a Thou, as the body of God where God is present to us always in all times and in all places. In the metaphor of the world as the body of God, the resurrection becomes a worldly, present, inclusive reality, for this body is offered to all: "This is my body." As is true of all bodies, however, this body, in its beauty and preciousness, is vulnerable and at risk: it will delight the eye only if we care for it; it will nourish us only if we nurture it. Needless to say, then, were this metaphor to enter our consciousness as thoroughly as the royal, triumphalist one has entered, it would result in a different way of being in the world. There would be no way that we could any longer see God as worldless or the world as Godless. Nor could we expect God to take care of everything, either through domination or through benevolence. . . .

Our profound need for a powerful, attractive imaginative picture of the way God is related to our world demands that we not only deconstruct but reconstruct our metaphors, letting the ones that seem promising try their chance. In particular I would make a case for experimenting in our time with mother, lover, and friend as three models that have been strangely neglected in the Judeo-Christian tradition. All three models represent basic human relationships. . . . Hence, if one is going to employ a personal model for God it makes sense to consider these three seriously.

A Protestant Creed from the Third World*

Third World churches have inherited the characteristic beliefs of their "mother churches," but in the process of indigenization they have had to relate these beliefs to local beliefs and conditions. Here we reproduce those parts in which one of the main Indonesian Protestant churches, formed in 1930, deals explicitly with its culture.[28]

Preamble 1. This Confession of Faith of the Huria Kristen Batak Protestant [H. K. B. P.] is the continuation of existing confessions of faith, namely the three confessions of faith which were acknowledged by the Fathers of the Church: (a) the Apostles' Creed, (b) the Nicene Creed, (c) the Athanasian Creed. 2. This Confession of Faith is the summary of what we believe and hope in this life and the life to come. 3. This Confession of Faith is the basis of the H. K. B. P. which must be preached, taught, and lived. 4. This Confession of Faith is the basis of the H. K. B. P. by which all false doctrine and heresy, contrary to God's Word, is rejected and opposed.

I. The Doctrine of God. We believe and we confess: God is one, without beginning and without end, almighty, unchangeable, trustworthy, omniscient, inscrutable, a righteous Judge, gracious, all bountiful. He fills heaven and earth. He is true, perfect in Holiness, full of love.

We reject and refute with this doctrine: the custom of calling God "grandfather," and the idea that God is only a good God contained in the conviction that "blessing may also be expected from the spirits of the grandfathers," as the heathen maintains. We also reject lucky days, fortune-telling, and reading fate in the lines of one's hands. We also reject with this doctrine the teaching that God's power is greater than his holiness and his love.

II. The Trinity of God. We believe and we confess: God is one and at the same time a Triune God, namely God the Father, God the Son, and God the Holy Spirit. The Father has begotten his Son of his own being from all eternity, that is, just as the Father is without beginning and without end, so also is the Son. Likewise the Holy Spirit, proceeding from God the Father and the Son, is without beginning and end.

We refute and reject with this doctrine the interpretation of the Trinity which speaks about the one God, the only God, with the understanding that it means that the Son and the Spirit are subordinated to the Father. We refute at the same time the doctrine which teaches that the essence of the Trinity is as follows: God the Father, his Son, the Lord Jesus Christ and the Mother, the Holy Spirit.

III. The Special Acts of the Triune God. We believe and confess: A. God, the Father, created, preserves, and governs all things visible and invisible. With this doctrine we reject and refute the doctrine of Fatalism (*Takdir* = determinism, *sibaran* = fate, *bagian* = predestined lot).[29]

---

* Huria Kristen Batak Protestant, *Confession of Faith*
[28] Translated by the author from H. F. deKleine, *Das Bekentnis der Huria Kritsa Batak Protestant (Batak-Kirche) auf Sumatra/Indonesia* (Sumatra: Rheinischen Missions-Gesellschaft, 1952).

[29] These items regarding a teaching of fate are related to Indonesia's Muslim majority.

B. God, the Son, who became man, born of the Virgin Mary, conceived by the Holy Spirit, called the Lord Jesus. Two natures are found in him, God and man inseparable in one Person; Christ is true God but at the same time true man. He has suffered under Pilate, who judged him. He was crucified on the cross in order to deliver us from our sins, from death, and from the rule of the Devil. He became the perfect sacrifice for reconciliation with God because of all the sin of mankind. He descended into hell after being buried and rose again the third day, ascended into heaven to sit on the right hand of God Jehovah, his Father, who is glorious forever. He is our intercessor in heaven. He rules all things until he will come again to this earth to judge the quick and the dead. . . .

C. God, the Holy Spirit, calls and teaches the congregation (Church) and preserves it in faith and in holiness through the Gospel to the honor of God. With this doctrine we refute and reject the doctrine which teaches that the Holy Spirit can descend upon man through his own power without the Gospel. In the same way we refute and reject the doctrine which teaches that the Holy Spirit only descends in times of ecstasy and speaking in tongues. Likewise we reject and refute the doctrine which teaches that the use of medicine is unnecessary and that it is sufficient to pray to the Holy Spirit. We reject and refute also the false prophecies made in the name of the Holy Spirit; also the dissolute life of people who teach that they are filled by the Holy Spirit. What we refute and reject here are the doctrines that falsely call upon the name of the Holy Spirit. . . .

VIII. The Church. A. We believe and confess: The Church is the assembly of believers in Jesus Christ, who are called, gathered, sanctified, and preserved by God through the Holy Spirit. With this doctrine we refute and reject . . . the interpretation which teaches that the Church is an assembly which is based upon and associated with the ancestral customs (*adat*) and the false thought that expects organization alone to impart life to the Church. . . .

XVI. With Regard to the Remembering of the Dead. We believe and confess: Men are destined to die, but after that there will be the Judgment. Then they rest from their work. Jesus Christ is the Lord of the living and the dead. When we remember the dead, then we remind ourselves of our own death and put our hope on the communion of believers with God and thus strengthen our heart in our struggle in this life.

With this doctrine we refute and reject the heathenish concept which teaches that the souls of the dead have influence on the living, as well as the doctrine which teaches that the soul of a dead person remains in the grave. We refute and reject also the doctrine of the Roman Catholics which teaches that there is a purgatory which must be experienced in order to purify the souls of the dead and to win eternal life, and that man may conduct a mass to intercede for the dead so that they come out of the purifying life earlier. We refute and reject the practice of praying to the souls of the saints and the hope that power or holiness may come from the dead (from their graves, from their clothes, their bones, mementos, relics).

Eastern Orthodoxy as Expressed in Its Eucharist*

Alexander Schmemann, the leading Russian Orthodox theologian of the twentieth century, interpreted Eastern Orthodoxy to the West from 1960 onward. His work shows the influence of exposure

to the liturgical movement and also knowledge of Roman Catholic–Protestant controversy on the Eucharist. He develops here the basic thought that the eucharistic sacrament is not a specialized act performed by the community or by the aesthetically and liturgically minded, but the activity by which the church is constituted. The Eastern church has

* Alexander Schmemann, *The World as Sacrament*

always centered itself in worship rather than in organization or doctrine; orthodoxy *means as much "right worship" as "right doctrine." Schmemann's exposition follows the order of the orthodox Eucharist, which in its essentials had reached its present form by the ninth century.*[30]

The Orthodox liturgy begins with the solemn doxology: "Blessed is the Kingdom of the Father, the Son and the Holy Spirit, now and ever, and unto ages of ages." From the beginning the destination is announced: the journey is to the Kingdom. This is where we are going—and not symbolically, but really. In the language of the Bible, which is the language of the Church, to bless the Kingdom is not simply to acclaim it. It is to declare it to be the goal, the end of all our desires and interests, of our whole life, the supreme and ultimate value of all that exists. To bless is to accept in love, and to move towards what is loved and accepted. The Church thus is the assembly, the gathering of those to whom the ultimate destination of all life has been revealed and who have accepted it. . . .

The next act of the liturgy is the entrance: the coming of the celebrant to the altar. It has been given all possible symbolical explanations, but it is not a "symbol." It is the very movement of the Church as passage from the old into the new, from "this world" into the "world to come" and, as such, it is the essential movement of the liturgical "journey." In "this world" there is no altar and the temple has been destroyed. For the only altar is Christ himself, his humanity—which he has assumed and deified and made the temple of God, the altar of his presence. And Christ has ascended into heaven. The altar, thus, is the sign that in Christ we have been given access to heaven, that the Church is the "passage" to heaven, the entrance into the heavenly sanctuary, and that only by "entering," by ascending to heaven does the Church fulfill itself, become what it is. . . .

Now, for the first time since the eucharistic journey began, the celebrant turns back and faces the people. Up to this moment he was the one who led the Church in its ascension, but now the movement has reached its goal. And the priest whose liturgy, whose unique function and obedience in the Church is to re-present, to make present the priesthood of Christ himself, says to the people: "Peace be with you." . . .

It is within this peace—"which passes all understanding"—that now begins the liturgy of the Word. Western Christians are so accustomed to distinguishing the Word from the sacrament that it may be difficult for them to understand that in the Orthodox perspective the liturgy of the Word is as sacramental as the sacrament is "evangelical." The sacrament is a manifestation of the Word. And unless the false dichotomy between Word and sacrament is overcome, the true meaning of both Word and sacrament, and especially the true meaning of Christian "sacramentalism" cannot be grasped in all their wonderful implications. The proclamation of the Word is a sacramental act par excellence because it is a transforming act. It transforms the human words of the Gospel into the Word of God and the manifestation of the Kingdom. And it transforms the man who hears the Word into a receptacle of the Word and a temple of the Spirit. . . .

As we proceed further in the eucharistic liturgy, the time has come now to offer to God the totality of all our lives, of ourselves, of the world in which we live. This is the first meaning of our bringing to the altar the elements of our food, the bread and wine. For we already know that food is life, that it is the very principle of life and that the whole world has been created as food for men. We all know that to offer this food, this world, this life to God is the initial "eucharistic" function of man, his very fulfilment as man. We know that we were created as celebrants of the sacrament of life, of its transformation into life in God, communion with God. We know that real life is "eucharist," a movement of love and adoration towards God, the movement in which alone the meaning and the value of all that exists can be revealed and fulfilled. We know that we

---

[30] Alexander Schmemann, *The World as Sacrament* (Syosset, NY: St. Vladimir's Seminary Press, 1973), 29–46. Copyright 1973 St. Vladimir's Seminary Press. Used by permission.

have lost this eucharistic life and, finally, we know that in Christ, the new Adam, the perfect man, this eucharistic life was restored to man. For he himself was the perfect Eucharist; he offered himself in total obedience, love and thanksgiving to God. God was his very life. And he gave this perfect and eucharistic life to us. In him God became our life. . . .

The Eucharist has so often been explained with reference to the gifts alone: What "happens" to bread and wine, and why, and when does it happen? But we must understand that what "happens" to bread and wine, happens because something has, first of all, happened to us, to the Church. It is because we have "constituted" the Church, and this means we have followed Christ in his ascension; because he has accepted us at his table in his Kingdom; because, in terms of theology, we have entered the eschaton, and are now standing beyond time and space; it is because all this has first happened to us that something will happen to bread and wine. . . .

This beginning of eucharistic prayer is usually termed the "Preface." And although this preface belongs to all known eucharistic rites, not much attention was given to it in the development of eucharistic theology. A "preface" is something that does not really belong to the body of a book. And theologians neglected it because they were anxious to come to the real "problems": those of consecration, the change of the elements, sacrifice, and other matters. It is here that we find the main "defect" of Christian theology; the theology of the Eucharist ceased to be eucharistic and thus took away the eucharistic spirit from the whole understanding of sacrament, from the very life of the Church. The long controversy about the words of institution[31] and the invocation of the Holy Spirit (*epiclesis*) that went on for centuries between the East and the West is a very good example of this "non-eucharistic" stage in the history of sacramental theology. . . .

And thus the preface fulfills itself in the Sanctus—the Holy, Holy, Holy of the eternal doxology, which is the secret essence of all that exists: "Heaven and earth are full of thy glory." We had to ascend to heaven in Christ to see and to understand the creation in its real being as glorification of God, as that response to divine love in which alone creation becomes what God wants it to be: thanksgiving, Eucharist, adoration. . . .

Up to this point the Eucharist was our ascension in Christ, our entrance in him into the "world to come." And now, in this eucharistic offering in Christ of all things to the One to whom they belong and in whom alone they really exist—now this movement of ascension has reached its end. We are at the paschal table of the Kingdom. What we have offered—our food, our life, ourselves, and the whole world—we offered in Christ and as Christ because he himself has assumed our life and is our life. And now all this is given back to us as the gift of new life and therefore—necessarily—as food.

"This is my body, this is my blood. Take, eat, drink." And generations upon generations of theologians ask the same questions. How is this possible? How does this happen? And what exactly does happen in this transformation? And when exactly? And what is the cause? No answer seems to be satisfactory. Symbol? But what is a symbol? Substance, accidents? Yet one immediately feels that something is lacking in all these theories, in which the Sacrament is reduced to the categories of time, substance, and causality, the very categories of "this world."

Something is lacking because the theologian thinks of the sacrament and forgets the liturgy. As a good scientist he first isolates the object of his study, reduces it to one moment, to one "phenomenon"—and then, proceeding from the general to the particular, from the known to the unknown, he gives a definition, which in fact raises more questions than it answers. But throughout our study the main point has been that the whole liturgy is sacramental, that is, one transforming act and one ascending movement. And the very goal of this movement of ascension

---

[31] *words of institution:* the words of Jesus establishing the sacrament, quoted from the gospels, especially "This is my body/blood."

is to take us out of "this world" and to make us partakers of the world to come. . . .

It is the Holy Spirit who manifests the bread as the body and the wine as the blood of Christ. The Orthodox Church has always insisted that the transformation of the eucharistic elements is performed by the epiclesis—the invocation of the Holy Spirit—and not by the words of institution. This doctrine, however, was often misunderstood by the Orthodox themselves. Its point is not to replace one "causality"—the words of institution—by another, a different "formula." It is to reveal the eschatological character of the sacrament. The Holy Spirit comes on the "last and great day" of Pentecost. He manifests the world to come. He inaugurates the Kingdom. He always takes us beyond. To be in the Spirit means to be in heaven, for the Kingdom of God is "joy and peace in the Holy Spirit." And thus in the Eucharist it is he who seals and confirms our ascension into heaven, who transforms the Church into the body of Christ and—therefore—manifests the elements of our offering as communion in the Holy Spirit. This is the consecration.

But before we can partake of the heavenly food there remains one last, essential and necessary act: the intercession. To be in Christ means to be like him, to make ours the very movement of his life. And as he "ever liveth to make intercession" for all "that come unto God by him" (Heb. 7:25), so we cannot help accepting his intercession as our own. The Church is not a society for escape—corporately or individually—from this world to taste of the mystical bliss of eternity. Communion is not a "mystical experience": we drink of the chalice of Christ, and he gave himself for the life of the world. The bread on the paten and the wine in the chalice are to remind us of the incarnation of the Son of God, of the cross and death. And thus it is the very joy of the Kingdom that makes us remember the world and pray for it. . . .

And now the time has come for us to return into the world. "Let us depart in peace," says the celebrant as he leaves the altar, and this is the last commandment of the liturgy. . . . And it is as witnesses of this Light, as witnesses of the Spirit, that we must "go forth" and begin the never-ending mission of the Church. Eucharist was the end of the journey, the end of time. And now it is again the beginning, and things that were impossible are again revealed to us as possible. The time of the world has become the time of the Church, the time of salvation and redemption.

The Theology of Liberation*

Gustavo Gutiérrez, a Catholic priest from Peru, is a pioneer of Liberation theology. This movement, which is especially strong in Latin America but has had a global impact, combines Marxist social analysis (on class conflict, the importance of economic realities, and other social issues) with the Christian message of salvation. This reading outlines the basic shape of the movement.[32]

---

* Gustavo Gutiérrez, *A Theology of Liberation*
[32] Gustavo Gutiérrez, "Liberation Praxis and Christian Faith," in R. Gibellini, ed., *Frontiers of Theology in Latin America* (New York: Orbis, 1979), 1–4, 8–9, 16. Copyright © 1979 Orbis Press. Used by permission.

The most recent years of Latin American history have been characterized by the discovery of the real-life world of "the other," of the poor and exploited and their compelling needs. In a social order fashioned economically, politically, and ideologically by a few for their own benefit, the "other" side has begun to make its voice heard. The lower classes of the populace, forced to live on the margins of society and oppressed since time immemorial, are beginning to speak for themselves more and more rather than relying on intermediaries. They have discovered themselves once again, and they now want the existing system to take note of their disturbing presence. They are less and less willing to be the passive objects of demagogic manipulation and social or charitable welfare in varied disguises. They want to be the active subjects of their own history and to forge a radically different society.

This discovery is made, however, only within the context of a revolutionary struggle. That struggle is calling the existing social order into question from the roots up. It insists that the people must come to power if society is to be truly free and egalitarian. In such a society private ownership of the means of production will be eliminated because it enables a few to expropriate the fruits of labor performed by the many, generates class divisions in society, and permits one class to be exploited by another. In such a reordered society the social takeover of the means of production will be accompanied by a social takeover of the reins of political power that will ensure people's liberty. Thus the way will be open to a new social awareness. . . .

For a long time, and still today in the case of many people, Latin American Christians displayed an almost total lack of concern for temporal tasks. They were subjected to a type of religious upbringing that viewed the "hereafter" as the locale of authentic life. The present life was seen as a stage-setting where people were put to the test so that their eternal destiny might be decided. . . . Eternal life was considered to be wholly a future life. It was not thought to be actively and creatively present in our present involvement in human history as well.

Such was the restricted vision of human life that prevailed. On the surface it seemed to bear the hallmark of spiritual and religious traits, but in reality it stemmed from a seriously reductionist view of the gospel message. The good will of some of those who sought to salvage the absolute character of God's kingdom in this defective way had no impact whatsoever on objective results. The gospel message was thus rendered as innocuous as a lap dog. From such a gospel the

great and powerful of this world had little to fear and much to gain. Their support and backing of it were quickly forthcoming. . . . The new turn of events began modestly enough. . . . Social injustice began to surface as the fundamental cause of the general situation. How could one claim to be a Christian if one did not commit oneself to remedying that situation? . . .

But the existence of the poor is not fated fact; it is not neutral on the political level or innocent of ethical implications. Poor people are byproducts of the system under which we live and for which we are responsible. Poor people are ones who have been shunted to the sidelines of our socio-cultural world. Poor people are those who are oppressed and exploited, who are deprived of the fruits of their labor and stripped of their life and reality as human beings. Poor people are members of the proletarian class. That is why the poverty of the poor is not a summons to alleviate their plight with acts of generosity but rather a compelling obligation to fashion an entirely different social order.

But we must consider this option carefully and notice its precise nature. When we opt for the poor in a commitment to liberation, we are forced to realize that we cannot isolate oppressed people from the social class to which they belong. If we were to do that, we would simply be sympathizing with their own individual situations. Poor and oppressed people are members of a social class which is overtly or covertly exploited by another social class. The proletariat is simply the most belligerent and clearcut segment of this exploited social class. To opt for the poor is to opt for one social class over against another; to take cognizance of the fact of class confrontation and side with the oppressed; to enter into the milieu of the exploited social class and its associated cultural categories and values; to unite in fellowship with its interests, concerns, and struggles.

ETHICS

The Social Gospel*

The Social Gospel movement in America at the turn of the twentieth century was led by its foremost prophet, Walter Rauschenbusch, who argued that only a socially oriented Christianity could be relevant for modern people. The strong note of optimism at the end of this reading is very expressive of American liberal Christianity one hundred years ago.[33]

The industrial and commercial life today is dominated by principles antagonistic to the fundamental principles of Christianity, and it is so difficult to live a Christian life in the midst of it that few men even try. If production could be organized on a basis of cooperative fraternity; if distribution could at least approximately be determined by justice; if all men could be conscious that their labor contributed to the welfare of all and that their personal well-being was dependent on the prosperity of the Commonwealth; if predatory business and parasitic wealth ceased and all men lived only by their labor; if the luxury of unearned wealth no longer made us all feverish with covetousness and a simpler life became the fashion; if our time and strength were not used up either in getting a bare living or in amassing unusable wealth and we had more leisure for the higher pursuits of the mind and the soul—then there might be a chance to live such a life of gentleness and brotherly kindness and tranquillity of heart as Jesus desired for men. It may be that the cooperative Commonwealth would give us the first chance in history to live a really Christian life without retiring from the world, and would make the Sermon on the Mount a philosophy of life feasible for all who care to try. . . .

In asking for faith in the possibility of a new social order, we ask for no Utopian delusion. We know well that there is no perfection for man in this life: there is only growth toward perfection. In personal religion we look with seasoned suspicion at any one who claims to be holy and perfect, yet we always tell men to become holy and to seek perfection. We make it a duty to seek what is unattainable. We have the same paradox in the perfectibility of society. We shall never have a perfect social life, yet we must seek it with faith. . . . At best there is always but an approximation to a perfect social order. The kingdom of God is always but coming.

But every approximation to it is worthwhile. Every step toward personal purity and peace, though it only makes the consciousness of imperfection more poignant, carries its own exceeding great reward, and everlasting pilgrimage toward the kingdom of God is better than contented stability in the tents of wickedness.

And sometimes the hot hope surges up that perhaps the long and slow climb may be ending. In the past the steps of our race toward progress have been short and feeble, and succeeded by long intervals of sloth and apathy. But is that necessarily to remain the rate of advance? In the intellectual life there has been an unprecedented leap forward during the last hundred years. Individually we are not more gifted than our grandfathers, but collectively we have wrought out more epoch-making discoveries and inventions in one century than the whole race in the untold centuries that have gone before. If the twentieth century could do for us in the control of social forces what the nineteenth did for us in the control of natural forces, our grandchildren would live in a society that would be justified in regarding our present social life as semi-barbarous. Since the Reformation began to free the mind and to direct the force of religion toward morality, there has been a perceptible increase of speed.

---

* Walter Rauschenbusch, *Christianity and the Social Crisis*
[33] Walter Rauschenbusch, *Christianity and the Social Crisis* (New York: Macmillan, 1907), 339–42, 419–22.

Humanity is gaining in elasticity and capacity for change, and every gain in general intelligence, in organizing capacity, in physical and moral soundness, and especially in responsiveness to ideal motives, again increases the ability to advance without disastrous reactions. The swiftness of evolution in our own country proves the immense latent perfectibility in human nature.

"Cheap Grace" and the Christian Life*

Like many Christian writers before him, the Lutheran pastor-theologian Dietrich Bonhoeffer found true eloquence in a prison cell. One of his books, The Cost of Discipleship, *spoke a powerful message by relating the costly demands of Christianity with the seeming ease with which the church assures people of their salvation. Bonhoeffer's death at the hand of the Nazi regime made his ideas about "costly grace" even more influential.*[34]

Cheap grace is the deadly enemy of our Church. We are fighting today for costly grace.

Cheap grace means grace sold on the market like cheapjacks' wares. The sacraments, the forgiveness of sin, and the consolations of religion are thrown away at cut prices. Grace is represented as the Church's inexhaustible treasury, from which she showers blessings with generous hands, without asking questions or fixing limits. Grace without price; grace without cost! The essence of grace, we suppose, is that the account has been paid in advance; and, because it has been paid, everything can be had for nothing. Since the cost was infinite, the possibilities of using and spending it are infinite. What would grace be if it were not cheap?

Cheap grace means grace as a doctrine, a principle, a system. It means forgiveness of sins proclaimed as a general truth, the love of God taught as the Christian 'conception' of God. An intellectual assent to that idea is held to be of itself sufficient to secure remission of sins. The Church which holds the correct doctrine of grace has, it is supposed, ipso facto a part in that grace. In such a Church the world finds a cheap covering for its sins; no contrition is required, still less any real desire to be delivered from sin. Cheap grace therefore amounts to a denial of the living Word of God, in fact, a denial of the Incarnation of the Word of God.

Cheap grace means the justification of sin without the justification of the sinner. Grace alone does everything, they say, and so everything can remain as it was before. "All for sin could not atone."[35] The world goes on in the same old way, and we are still sinners "even in the best life" as Luther said. Well, then, let the Christian live like the rest of the world, let him model himself on the world's standards in every sphere of life, and not presumptuously aspire to live a different life under grace from his old life under sin. That was the heresy of the enthusiasts, the Anabaptists and their kind. Let the Christian beware of rebelling against the free and boundless grace of God and desecrating it. Let him not attempt to erect a new religion of the letter by endeavoring to live a life of obedience to the commandments of Jesus Christ! The world has been justified by grace. The Christian knows that, and takes it seriously. He knows he must not strive against this indispensable grace. Therefore let him live like the rest of the world! Of course he would like to go and do something extraordinary, and it does demand a good deal of self-restraint to refrain from the attempt and content himself with living as the world lives. Yet it is

---

* Dietrich Bonhoeffer, *The Cost of Discipleship*

[34] Reprinted with the permission of Scribner, a division of Simon & Shuster from *The Cost of Discipleship* by Dietrich Bonhoeffer, translated from German by R. H. Fuller with some revision by Irmgard Booth. Copyright © 1959 by SCM Press, Ltd.

[35] *All for sin could not atone:* a quotation from the hymn, "Rock of Ages, Cleft for Me," by Augustus Toplady.

imperative for the Christian to achieve renunciation, to practice self-effacement, to distinguish his life from the life of the world. He must let grace be grace indeed, otherwise he will destroy the world's faith in the free gift of grace. . . . Cheap grace is not the kind of forgiveness of sin which frees us from the toils of sin. Cheap grace is the grace we bestow on ourselves.

Cheap grace is the preaching of forgiveness without requiring repentance, baptism without church discipline, Communion without confession, absolution without personal confession. Cheap grace is grace without discipleship, grace without the cross, grace without Jesus Christ, living and incarnate.

Costly grace is the treasure hidden in the field; for the sake of it a man will gladly go and sell all that he has. It is the pearl of great price to buy which the merchant will sell all his goods. It is the

kingly rule of Christ, for whose sake a man will pluck out the eye which causes him to stumble; it is the call of Jesus Christ at which the disciple leaves his nets and follows him.

Costly grace is the gospel which must be sought again and again, the gift which must be asked for, the door at which a man must knock. Such grace is costly because it calls us to follow, and it is grace because it calls us to follow Jesus Christ. It is costly because it costs a man his life, and it is grace because it gives a man the only true life. It is costly because it condemns sin, and grace because it justifies the sinner. Above all, it is costly because it cost God the life of his Son: "you were bought at a price," and what has cost God much cannot be cheap for us. Above all, it is grace because God did not reckon his Son too dear a price to pay for our life, but delivered him up for us. Costly grace is the Incarnation of God.

Catholic Controversy over Artificial Contraception*

Pope Paul VI's 1968 encyclical reaffirmed the opposition of the Roman Catholic church to any form of artificial birth control. The content of the encyclical was a shock to many Catholics around the world, as the special study commission appointed by Paul VI was correctly rumored to have reached a conclusion to permit artificial birth control. Before this commission issued its report, Paul VI acted on his own. On Human Life *has been the most controversial papal ruling of the twentieth century, not just for its impact on the lives of individuals and married couples but also for its impact on efforts for world population control. In the second reading, Roman Catholic theologians at the Catholic University of America in Washington, D.C., criticize the encyclical on several grounds and urge that, in conscience, it be disobeyed.*[36]

To the venerable Patriarchs, Archbishops and Bishops, and other local ordinaries in peace and communion with the Apostolic See, to priests, the faithful, and to all men of good will. Venerable brothers and beloved sons: . . .

The most serious duty of transmitting human life, for which married persons are the free and responsible collaborators of God the Creator, has always been a source of great joys to them, even if sometimes accompanied by not a few difficulties and by distress. At all times the fulfillment of this duty has posed grave problems to the conscience of married persons, but, with the recent evolution of society, changes have taken place that give rise to new questions which the Church could not ignore, having to do with a matter which so closely touches upon the life and happiness of men. . . .

The problem of birth, like every other problem regarding human life, is to be considered, beyond partial perspectives—whether of the biological or psychological, demographic or sociological orders—in the light of an integral vision of man and of his vocation, not only his natural

---

* Pope Paul VI, *On Human Life* (*Humanae vitae*); Theologians of the Catholic University of America, "Response to *Humanae vitae*"

[36] C. E. Curran and R. E. Hunt, *Dissent In and For the Church: Theologians and Humanae Vitae* (New York: Sheed & Ward, 1969), 24–26. Copyright © 1969 Sheed & Ward. Used by permission.

and earthly, but also his supernatural and eternal vocation. And since, in the attempt to justify artificial methods of birth control, many have appealed to the demands both of conjugal love and of "responsible parenthood" it is good to state very precisely the true concept of these two great realities of married life. . . .

Responsible parenthood . . . above all implies a more profound relationship to the objective moral order established by God, of which a right conscience is the faithful interpreter. The responsible exercise of parenthood implies, therefore, that husband and wife recognize fully their own duties towards God, towards themselves, towards the family and towards society, in a correct hierarchy of values.

In the task of transmitting life, therefore, they are not free to proceed completely at will, as if they could determine in a wholly autonomous way the honest path to follow; but they must conform their activity to the creative intention of God, expressed in the very nature of marriage and of its acts, and manifested by the constant teaching of the Church. . . . The Church, calling men back to the observance of the norms of the natural law, as interpreted by its constant doctrine, teaches that each and every marriage act must remain open to the transmission of life. . . .

[W]e must once again declare that the direct interruption of the generative process already begun, and, above all, directly willed and procured abortion, even if for therapeutic reasons, are to be absolutely excluded as licit means of regulating birth. Equally to be excluded, as the teaching authority of the Church has frequently declared, is direct sterilization, whether perpetual or temporary, whether of the man or of the woman. Similarly excluded is every action which, either in anticipation of the conjugal act, or in its accomplishment, or in the development of its natural consequences, proposes, whether as an end or as a means, to render procreation impossible.

To justify conjugal acts made intentionally infecund, one cannot invoke as valid reasons the lesser evil, or the fact that such acts would constitute a whole together with the fecund acts already performed or to follow later, and hence

would share in one and the same moral goodness. In truth, if it is sometimes licit to tolerate a lesser evil in order to avoid a greater evil or to promote a greater good, it is not licit, even for the gravest reasons, to do evil so that good may follow therefrom . . . . Consequently it is an error to think that a conjugal act which is deliberately made infecund and so is intrinsically dishonest could be made honest and right by the ensemble of a fecund conjugal life.

The Church, on the contrary, does not at all consider illicit the use of those therapeutic means truly necessary to cure diseases of the organism, even if an impediment to procreation, which may be foreseen, should result therefrom, provided such impediment is not, for whatever motive, directly willed.

If there are serious motives to space out births, which derive from the physical or psychological conditions of husband and wife, or from external conditions, the Church teaches that it is then licit to take into account the natural rhythms immanent in the generative functions, for the use of marriage[37] in the infecund periods only, and in this way to regulate birth without offending the moral principles which have been recalled earlier.

The Church is coherent with herself when she considers recourse to the infecund periods to be licit, while at the same time condemning, as being always illicit, the use of means directly contrary to fecundation, even if such use is inspired by reasons which may appear honest and serious. In reality, there are essential differences between the two cases; in the former, the married couple make legitimate use of a natural disposition; in the latter, they impede the development of natural processes. . . .

Upright men can even better convince themselves of the solid grounds on which the teaching of the Church in this field is based, if they care to reflect upon the consequences of methods of artificial birth control. Let them consider, first of all, how wide and easy a road would thus

---

[37] *the use of marriage:* sexual intercourse. The type of birth control advocated here is commonly called the "rhythm method."

be opened up towards conjugal infidelity and the general lowering of morality. Not much experience is needed in order to know human weakness, and to understand that men—especially the young, who are so vulnerable on this point—have need of encouragement to be faithful to the moral law, so that they must not be offered some easy means of eluding its observance. It is also to be feared that the man, growing used to the employment of anticonceptive practices, may finally lose respect for the woman and, no longer caring for her physical and psychological equilibrium, may come to the point of considering her as a mere instrument of selfish enjoyment, and no longer as his respected and beloved companion.

Let it be considered also that a dangerous weapon would thus be placed in the hands of those public authorities who take no heed of moral exigencies. Who could blame a government for applying to the solution of the problems of the community those means acknowledged to be licit for married couples in the solution of a family problem? Who will stop rulers from favoring, from even imposing upon their peoples, if they were to consider it necessary, the method of contraception which they judge to be most efficacious? . . .

It can be foreseen that this teaching will perhaps not be easily received by all: Too numerous are those voices—amplified by the modern means of propaganda—which are contrary to the voice of the Church. To tell the truth, the Church is not surprised to be made, like her divine founder, a "sign of contradiction," yet she does not because of this cease to proclaim with humble firmness the entire moral law, both natural and evangelical. Of such laws the Church was not the author, nor consequently can she be their arbiter; she is only their depositary and their interpreter, without ever being able to declare to be licit that which is not so by reason of its intimate and unchangeable opposition to the true good of man.

[Statement on *Humanae vitae*] As Roman Catholic theologians we respectfully acknowledge a distinct role of hierarchical *magisterium* (teach-

ing authority) in the Church of Christ. At the same time, Christian tradition assigns theologians the special responsibility of evaluating and interpreting pronouncements of the magisterium in the light of the total theological data operative in each question or statement. We offer these initial comments on Pope Paul VI's Encyclical on the Regulation of Birth.

The Encyclical is not an infallible teaching. History shows that a number of statements of similar or ever greater authoritative weight have subsequently been proved inadequate or even erroneous. . . .

Many positive values concerning marriage are expressed in Paul VI's Encyclical. However, we must take exception to the ecclesiology implied and the methodology used by Paul VI in the writing and promulgation of the document: they are incompatible with the Church's authentic self-awareness as expressed in and suggested by the acts of the Second Vatican Council itself. The Encyclical consistently assumes that the Church is identical with the hierarchical office. . . .

Furthermore, the Encyclical betrays a narrow and positivistic notion of papal authority, as illustrated by the rejection of the majority view presented by the Commission established to consider the question, as well as by the rejection of the conclusion of a large part of the international Catholic theological community.

Likewise, we take exception to some of the specific ethical conclusions contained in the Encyclical. They are based on an inadequate conception of natural law. . . . Even the minority report of the papal commission noted grave difficulty in attempting to present conclusive proof of the immorality of artificial contraception based on natural law.

Other defects include: overemphasis on the biological aspects of conjugal relations as ethically normative; undue stress on sexual acts and on the faculty of sex viewed in itself, apart from the person and the couple . . . unfounded assumptions about "the evil consequences of methods of artificial birth control"; indifference to Vatican II's assertion that prolonged sexual abstinence may cause "faithfulness to be imperiled and its quality of fruitfulness to be ruined"; an almost total disregard for the dignity of millions of human beings brought into the world without the slightest possibility of being fed and educated decently. . . .

It is common teaching in the Church that Catholics may dissent from authoritative, noninfallible teachings of the magisterium when suffi-cient reasons for doing so exist. Therefore, as Roman Catholic theologians, conscious of our duty and our limitations, we conclude that spouses may responsibly decide according to their conscience that artificial contraception in some circumstances is permissible and indeed necessary to preserve and foster the values and sacredness of marriage.

Christianity and the Natural Environment*

In 1967, the historian Lynn White published an address to the American Association for the Advancement of Science in which he blamed Christianity for the environmental crisis. This essay is the most influential statement in modern times about the relationship of Christianity and the natural environment. Few realize that White also proposed a way out of the crisis by way of Christianity, via the vision of St. Francis.[38]

What people do about their ecology depends on what they think about themselves in relation to things around them. Human ecology is deeply conditioned by beliefs about our nature and destiny—that is, by religion. To Western eyes this is very evident in, say, India or Ceylon. It is equally true of ourselves and of our medieval ancestors.

The victory of Christianity over paganism was the greatest psychic revolution in the history of our culture. It has become fashionable today to say that for better or worse we live in "the post-Christian age." Certainly the forms of our thinking and language have largely ceased to be Christian, but to my eye the substance often remains amazingly akin to that of the past. Our daily habits of action, for example, are dominated by an implicit faith in perpetual progress which was unknown either to Greco-Roman Antiquity or to the Orient. . . .

What did Christianity tell people about their relations with the environment? . . . Christianity inherited from Judaism not only a concept of time as nonrepetitive and linear but also a striking story of creation. By gradual stages a loving and all-powerful God had created light and darkness, the heavenly bodies, the earth and all its plants, animals, birds, and fishes. Finally, God had created Adam and, as an afterthought, Eve to keep man from being lonely. Man named all the animals, thus establishing his dominance over them. God planned all of this explicitly for man's benefit and rule: no item in the physical creation had any purpose save to serve man's purposes. And, although man's body is made of clay, he is not simply part of nature: he is made in God's image.

Especially in its Western form, Christianity is the most anthropocentric religion the world has seen. As early as the second century both Tertullian and St. Irenaeus of Lyons were insisting that when God shaped Adam he was foreshadowing the image of the incarnate Christ, the Second Adam. Man shares, in great measure, God's transcendence of nature. Christianity, in absolute contrast to ancient paganism and Asia's religions (except, perhaps, Zoroastrianism), not only established a dualism of man and nature but also insisted that it is God's will that man exploit nature for his proper ends. . . .

When one speaks in such sweeping terms, a note of caution is in order. Christianity is a complex faith, and its consequences differ in differing contexts. What I have said may well apply to the medieval West, where in fact technology made

---

* Lynn White, "The Historical Roots of Our Ecologic Crisis"
[38] From Lynn H. White, "The Historical Roots of Our Ecologic Crisis," *Science* 155, n. 3767 (March 10, 1967). Copyright © 1967 by the American Association for the Advancement of Science. Used by permission.

spectacular advances. But the Greek East, a highly civilized realm of equal Christian devotion, seems to have produced no marked technological innovation after the late seventh century, when Greek fire[39] was invented. The key to the contrast may perhaps be found in a difference in the tonality of piety and thought which students of comparative theology find between the Greek and the Latin Churches. . . . The Greek saint contemplates; the Western saint acts. The implications of Christianity for the conquest of nature would emerge more easily in the Western atmosphere.

The Christian dogma of creation, which is found in the first clause of the Creeds, has another meaning for our comprehension of today's ecologic crisis. By revelation, God had given man the Bible, the Book of Scripture. But since God had made nature, nature also must reveal the divine mentality. The religious study of nature for the better understanding of God was known as natural theology. In the early Church, and always in the Greek East, nature was conceived primarily as a symbolic system through which God speaks to men: the ant is a sermon to sluggards; rising flames are the symbol of the soul's aspiration. This view of nature was essentially artistic rather than scientific. While Byzantium preserved and copied great numbers of ancient Greek scientific texts, science as we conceive it could scarcely flourish in such an ambience.

However, in the Latin West by the early thirteenth century natural theology was following a very different bent. It was ceasing to be the decoding of the physical symbols of God's communication with man and was becoming the effort to understand God's mind by discovering how his creation operates. The rainbow was no longer simply a symbol of hope first sent to Noah after the Deluge: Robert Grosseteste, Friar Roger Bacon, and Theodoric of Freiberg produced startlingly sophisticated work on the optics of the rainbow, but they did it as a venture in religious understanding. From the thirteenth

century onward into the eighteenth, every major scientist, in effect, explained his motivations in religious terms. Indeed, if Galileo had not been so expert an amateur theologian he would have got into far less trouble: the professionals resented his intrusion. It was not until the late eighteenth century that the hypothesis of God became unnecessary to many scientists. . . .

We would seem to be headed toward conclusions unpalatable to many Christians. Since both science and technology are blessed words in our contemporary vocabulary, some may be happy at the notions, first, that, viewed historically, modern science is an extrapolation of natural theology and, second, that modern technology is at least partly to be explained as an Occidental,[40] voluntarist realization of the Christian dogma of man's transcendence of, and rightful mastery over, nature. But, as we now recognize, somewhat over a century ago science and technology, hitherto quite separate activities, joined to give mankind powers which, to judge by many of the ecologic effects, are out of control. If so, Christianity bears a huge burden of guilt.

I personally doubt that disastrous ecologic backlash can be avoided simply by applying to our problems more science and more technology. Our science and technology have grown out of Christian attitudes toward man's relation to nature which are almost universally held not only by Christians and neo-Christians but also by those who fondly regard themselves as post-Christians. Despite Copernicus, all the cosmos rotates around our little globe. Despite Darwin, we are not, in our hearts, part of the natural process. We are superior to nature, contemptuous of it, willing to use it for our slightest whim. A governor of California, like myself a churchman but less troubled than I, spoke for the Christian tradition when he said (as is alleged), "When you've seen one redwood tree, you've seen them all."[41] To a Christian a tree can be no more than a physi-

---

[39] *Greek fire:* a flammable mixture used in warfare.

[40] *Occidental:* one from the West, as opposed to Asia.

[41] "*When you've seen . . . all*": the governor in question is Ronald Reagan.

cal fact. The whole concept of the sacred grove is alien to Christianity and to the ethos of the West. For nearly two millennia Christian missionaries have been chopping down sacred groves, which are idolatrous because they assume spirit in nature.

What we do about ecology depends on our ideas of the man-nature relationship. More science and more technology are not going to get us out of the present ecologic crisis until we find a new religion, or rethink our old one. The beatniks and hippies, who are the basic revolutionaries of our time, show a sound instinct in their affinity for Zen Buddhism and Hinduism, which conceive of the man-nature relationship as very nearly the mirror image of the Christian view. These faiths, however, are as deeply conditioned by Asian history as Christianity is by the experience of the West, and I am dubious of their viability among us.

Possibly we should ponder the greatest radical in Christian history since Christ: St. Francis of Assisi. . . . The key to an understanding of Francis is his belief in the virtue of humility, not merely for the individual but for man as a species. Francis tried to depose man from his monar-

chy over creation and set up a democracy of all God's creatures. With him the ant is no longer simply a homily for the lazy, flames a sign of the thrust of the soul toward union with God; now they are Brother Ant and Sister Fire, praising the Creator in their own ways as Brother Man does in his. . . .

The greatest spiritual revolutionary in Western history, St. Francis, proposed what he thought was an alternative Christian view of nature and man's relation to it: he tried to substitute the idea of the equality of all creatures, including man, for the idea of man's limitless rule of creation. He failed. Both our present science and our present technology are so tinctured with orthodox Christian arrogance toward nature that no solution for our ecologic crisis can be expected from them alone. Since the roots of our trouble are so largely religious, the remedy must also be essentially religious, whether we call it that or not. We must rethink and refeel our nature and destiny. The profoundly religious, but heretical, sense of the primitive Franciscans for the spiritual autonomy of all parts of nature may point a direction. I propose Francis as the patron saint of ecologists.

The Debate over Homosexuality*

The relation of lesbians and gay men to Christian faith and church is the most divisive issue facing the Western church today. (African and Asian Christians are typically adamant against legitimizing same-sex practice.) Two of the best and fullest statements are reproduced here. James Nelson develops his argument with the Methodist quadrilateral: scripture, tradition, reason, experience.[42] In the second reading, Cardinal Joseph Ratzinger's

reinforcement of the traditional position against arguments like Nelson's is typical of Protestant opposition as well.[43] The debate over this issue rages in many North American and European churches, but only one mainline American church, the United Church of Christ, officially ordains self-affirming homosexuals as clergy.

Not many texts in Scripture—perhaps seven at most—speak directly about homosexual behavior. We have no evidence of Jesus' teachings on or concern with the issue. The subject, obviously,

---

* James Nelson, *Body Theology;* Joseph Cardinal Ratzinger, Letter to the Bishops of the Catholic Church on the Pastoral Care of Homosexual Persons

[42] From James Nelson, *Body Theology.* Copyright © 1992 Westminster Press. Used by permission of Westminster/John Knox Press.

[43] From Joseph Ratzinger, Letter to the Bishops of the Catholic Church on the Pastoral Care of Homosexual Persons, 1968.

is not a major scriptural preoccupation. In any event, what conclusions can we reach from careful assessment of the few texts in question?

My own conclusions, relying on the work of a number of contemporary biblical scholars, are several:

We receive no guidance whatsoever about the issue of sexual orientation. The issue of "homosexuality"—a psychosexual orientation—simply was not a biblical issue. Indeed, the concept of sexual orientation did not arise until the mid-nineteenth century. Certainly, biblical writers knew of homosexual acts, but they apparently understood those acts as being done by heterosexual people (they assumed everyone was heterosexual). Thus, when persons engaged in same-sex genital behavior, they were departing from their natural and given orientation. Regardless of our beliefs about the morality of same-sex expression, it is clear that our understanding of sexual orientation is vastly different from that of the biblical writers.

It is true, we do find condemnation of homosexual acts when they violate ancient Hebrew purity and holiness codes. We do find scriptural condemnation of homosexual prostitution. We do find condemnation of those homosexual acts which appear to be expressions of idolatry. We do find condemnation of pederasty, the sexual use of a boy by an adult male for the latter's gratification.

Note several things at this point. First, scriptural condemnation is also evident for similar heterosexual acts—for example, those that violate holiness codes (intercourse during menstruation), commercial sex, idolatrous heterosexual acts (temple prostitution), and the sexual misuse of minors. Further, the major questions that concern us in the present debate simply are not directly addressed in Scripture. Those unaddressed issues are the theological and ethical appraisal of homosexual orientation and the question of homosexual relations between adults committed to each other in mutuality and love. . . .

This is by no means to suggest that these sources have little to say to us. Consider Scrip-

ture. As L. William Countryman reminds us,[44] the New Testament frames its particular sexual ethic in terms of purity and property systems that no longer prevail among us. Thus, we cannot simply take numerous New Testament injunctions and assume that they apply literally to significantly different contexts. . . . Even if many specific scriptural prescriptions and proscriptions regarding sex are not the gospel's word for today, there are still more basic and utterly crucial scriptural foundations for our sexual ethic.

What are some of those foundations? Surely, they include such affirmations as these: the created goodness of our sexuality and bodily life; the inclusiveness of Christian community, unlimited by purity codes; the equality of women and men; and the service of our sexuality to the reign of God. That incorporation of our sexuality into God's reign means expression in acts shaped by love, justice, equality, fidelity, mutual respect, compassion, and grateful joy. These are criteria that apply regardless of one's orientation. Scripture also offers ample testimony that sexual acts that degrade, demean, and harm others and ourselves are contrary to God's intent and reign. . . .

The postbiblical tradition provides no more unambiguous guidance on specific sexual expressions than does Scripture. Selective literalism in use of the tradition is almost as common as it is in the use of Scripture itself. Most of us would fully endorse the tradition's movement toward monogamy and fidelity. Many of us would endorse the tradition's growth toward the centrality of love as the governing sexual norm. Many of us would celebrate those parts of the tradition that not only tolerate but positively affirm gays and lesbians, including lesbian and gay clergy. But few of us would endorse those elements of tradition that baptize patriarchal oppression, endorse violence against women, oppress lesbians and gays, exalt perpetual virginity as the superior state, or declare that heterosexual rape is a lesser

---

[44] *L. William Countryman:* A New Testament scholar who has written on New Testament views of sexuality.

sin than masturbation (since the latter is a sin against nature while the former, while also sinful, is an act in accordance with nature). As with Scripture, it is impossible to find one consistent, coherent sexual ethic in the postbiblical tradition.

Of what use, then, is the long sweep of Christian tradition regarding homosexual orientation and expression? On this subject, I believe that tradition most helpfully poses a series of questions—challenges to much of our conventional Christian wisdom.

One question is this: Has the church's condemnation of gay and lesbian people been consistent throughout its history? As Yale historian John Boswell has demonstrated, a careful examination of tradition yields a negative answer. . . .

The tradition suggests a[nother] question: Is it true that procreation has always been deemed primary to the meaning and expression of Christian sexuality? That is, if we do not use our sexuality with the intent to procreate or at least with the possibility of doing so, is there something deficient about it? It is an important question, for the procreative norm has often been used to judge lesbians and gays adversely: "Your sexuality is unfit to bless because your acts are inherently nonprocreative." . . .

Still the answer is no. In the seventeenth century, a number of Christians—especially among the Puritans, Anglicans, and Quakers—began to teach, preach, and write about a new understanding. It appeared to them that God's fundamental purpose in creating us as sexual beings was not that we might make babies, but that we might make love. It was love, intimacy, mutuality, not procreation, that were central to the divine intention for sexuality. Some Puritans, for example, declared that if children were born to a marriage, that was "an added blessing," but not the central purpose of the marriage.

The centrality of love, companionship, and mutual pleasure in the meaning of sexuality has been embraced by most Protestants during the last three hundred years and, in practice, by numerous Catholics, even if not with Vatican approval. The proof in heterosexual relations is the use of contraception as a decision of conscience. Most of us do not believe we must be open to procreation each time we make love—in fact, we believe strongly to the contrary. The curious double standard still exists, however; the procreative norm has been smuggled in the back door and applied negatively to lesbians and gay men.

One of the ways we honor our God-given reason [the third element in the quadrilateral] is in striving for consistency and adequacy in our theological judgments. These two age old tests of the philosophers are perennially relevant. Consistency eschews the use of double standards. Adequacy prods us to judgments that do justice to the widest range of data. Reason is also expressed in the various sciences, our disciplined human attempts to understand creation. Biological, psychological, and social sciences can shed significant light on questions of sexual orientation. What, for example, might we learn?

In 1948 Alfred Kinsey and his associates jarred America with the first major study of the sexual behaviors of persons in this society. In his volume on the male, he presented two things that particularly caught the public eye regarding sexual orientation. One was the continuum on which orientations might be represented. Challenging either-or assumptions (one is either homosexual or heterosexual), Kinsey introduced evidence suggesting that we might be "both/and." The other finding, widely reported in the press, was Kinsey's discovery that at least 50 percent of the male population had experienced homosexual genital relations at some time in their lives, and for 37 percent of them it was orgasmic behavior after puberty. This alone startled many, simply because it appeared to be evidence that same-sex attraction and expression were not just the province of a tiny minority.

Though most of us tend toward one or the other side, it is probable that the vast majority of us are not exclusively either heterosexual or homosexual. . . . Most of us have more bisexual capacities than we have realized or than we have been taught in a bifurcating society. This recognition is of particular importance when we come to try to understand some of the dynamics of homophobia.

Another question on which the sciences shed some light is the origin of sexual orientation. While there is still much debate, at least two things seem clear. One is that our orientations are given, not freely chosen. The likelihood is that they arise from a combination of genetic and hormonal factors, together with environmental and learning factors—both nature and nurture. The other general agreement is that our sexuality is established rather early in life, most likely somewhere between the ages of two and five, and thereafter are largely resistant to any dramatic changes. "Therapies" that attempt to change persons from homosexual to heterosexual are now discredited by reputable scientists. Such procedures may change certain behaviors, they may make some people celibate, but they will not change deep feelings and most likely will produce great psychic and emotional confusion. These facts, too, are relevant to the theological-ethical questions. . . .

These issues do not exhaust, but simply illustrate, the ways in which the uses of human reason, including the human sciences, provide important insights for our theological reflection and understanding of Scripture.

The fourth and last area of insight comes from experience. . . . Our experience of homophobia, in careful examination, provides one key example. The term refers to deep and irrational fears of same-sex attraction and expression or, in the case of lesbians and gay men, internalized self-rejection. Though the word was coined only within recent decades, the reality has long been with us. Another term, heterosexism, more recently has come into use. It too is helpful, for it reminds us that prejudice against gays and lesbians is not simply a private psychological dynamic but, like racism and sexism, is also structured deeply into our institutions and cultural patterns. . . .

Further, confronting my own fears meant confronting my fears of sexuality as such—my erotophobia. Though I had long enjoyed the sexual experience, I came to realize that, reared in a du-

alistic culture, I was more distanced from my sexuality than I cared to admit. Reared as a male and conditioned to repress most bodily feelings, reared as "a good soldier" and taught to armor myself against any emotional or physical vulnerability, I discovered I was more alienated from my body than I had acknowledged. Gay males and lesbians brought into some kind of dim awareness my own erotophobia because they represented sexuality in a fuller way. . . .

Homophobia thrives on dualisms of disincarnation and abstraction that divide people from their bodily feelings and divide reality into two opposing camps. As never before we need gracious theologies. Homophobia thrives on theologies of works justification, wherein all persons must prove their worth and all males must prove their manhood. As never before we need erotic theologies. Homophobia thrives on erotophobia, the deep fear of sexuality and pleasure. Homophobia thrives in eros-deprived people because it grows in the resentments, projections, and anger of those whose own hungers are not met. . . . Though its varied dynamics are complex, the root cause of homophobia is always fear, and the gospel has resources for dealing with fear. . . .

["Letter to the Bishops of the Catholic Church on the Pastoral Care of Homosexual Persons"]

1.   The issue of homosexuality and the moral evaluation of homosexual acts have increasingly become a matter of public debate, even in Catholic circles. Since this debate often advances arguments and makes assertions inconsistent with the teaching of the Catholic Church, it is quite rightly a cause for concern to all engaged in the pastoral ministry. . . .

The Catholic moral viewpoint is founded on human reason illumined by faith and is consciously motivated by the desire to do the will of God our Father. The Church is thus in a position to learn from scientific discovery but also to transcend the horizons of science and to be confident that her more global vision does greater justice to the rich reality of the human person in his spiritual and physical dimensions, created by God and heir, by grace, to eternal life. . . .

3. Explicit treatment of the problem was given in this Congregation's "Declaration on Certain Questions Concerning Sexual Ethics" of December 29, 1975. That document stressed the duty of trying to understand the homosexual condition and noted that culpability for homosexual acts should only be judged with prudence. At the same time the Congregation took note of the distinction commonly drawn between the homosexual condition or tendency and individual homosexual actions. These (actions) were described as deprived of their essential and indispensable finality, as being "intrinsically disordered," and able in no case to be approved of (cf. n. 8, 4). . . . Special concern and pastoral attention should be directed toward those who have this condition, lest they be led to believe that the living out of this orientation in homosexual activity is a morally acceptable option. It is not.

4. An essential dimension of authentic pastoral care is the identification of causes of confusion regarding the Church's teaching. One is a new exegesis of Sacred Scripture which claims variously that Scripture has nothing to say on the subject of homosexuality, or that it somehow tacitly approves of it, or that all of its moral injunctions are so culture-bound that they are no longer applicable to contemporary life. These views are gravely erroneous and call for particular attention here.

5. It is quite true that the Biblical literature owes to the different epochs in which it was written a good deal of its varied patterns of thought and expression. The Church today addresses the Gospel to a world which differs in many ways from ancient days. But the world in which the New Testament was written was already quite diverse from the situation in which the Sacred Scriptures of the Hebrew People had been written or compiled, for example.

What should be noticed is that, in the presence of such remarkable diversity, there is nevertheless a clear consistency within the Scriptures themselves on the moral issue of homosexual behav-

ior. The Church's doctrine regarding this issue is thus based not on isolated phrases for facile theological argument but on the solid foundation of a constant Biblical testimony. The community of faith today, in unbroken continuity with the Jewish and Christian communities within which the ancient Scriptures were written, continues to be nourished by those same Scriptures and by the Spirit of Truth whose Word they are. . . .

6. Providing a basic plan for understanding this entire discussion of homosexuality is the theology of creation we find in Genesis. God, by his infinite wisdom and love, brings into existence all of reality as a reflection of his goodness. He fashions mankind, male and female, in his own image and likeness. Human beings, therefore, are nothing less than the work of God himself; and in the complementarity of the sexes, they are called to reflect the inner unity of the Creator. They do this in a striking way in their cooperation with him in the transmission of life by a mutual donation of the self to the other.

In Genesis 3, we find that this truth about persons being an image of God has been obscured by original sin. There inevitably follows a loss of awareness of the covenantal character of the union these persons had with God and with each other. The human body retains its "spousal significance," but this is now clouded by sin. Thus, in Genesis 19:1–11, the deterioration due to sin continues in the story of the men of Sodom. There can be no doubt of the moral judgment made there against homosexual relations. In Leviticus 18:22 and 20:13, in the course of describing the conditions necessary for belonging to the Chosen People, the author excludes from the People of God those who behave in a homosexual fashion.

Against the background of this exposition of theocratic law, an eschatological perspective is developed by St. Paul when, in I Cor. 6:9, he proposes the same doctrine and lists those who behave in a homosexual fashion among those who shall not enter the Kingdom of God. In Rom. 1:18–32, still building on the moral traditions of his forebears but in the new context of the confrontation between Christianity and the pagan society of his day, Paul uses homosexual behavior as an example of the blindness which has overcome humankind. Instead of the original harmony between Creator and creatures, the acute distortion of idolatry has led to all kinds of moral excess. Paul is at a loss to find a clearer example of this disharmony than homosexual relations. Finally, I Timothy 1, in full continuity with the biblical position, singles out those who spread wrong doctrine and in v. 10 explicitly names as sinners those who engage in homosexual acts.

7. The Church, obedient to the Lord who founded her and gave to her the sacramental life, celebrates the divine plan of the loving and life-giving union of men and women in the sacrament of marriage. . . .

To choose someone of the same sex for one's sexual activity is to annul the rich symbolism and meaning, not to mention the goals, of the Creator's sexual design. Homosexual activity is not a complementary union, able to transmit life; and so it thwarts the call to a life of that form of self-giving which the Gospel says is the essence of Christian living. This does not mean that homosexual persons are not often generous and giving of themselves; but when they engage in homosexual activity they confirm within themselves a disordered sexual inclination which is essentially self-indulgent. . . .

8. Thus, the Church's teaching today is in organic continuity with the Scriptural perspective and with her own constant Tradition. Though today's world is in many ways quite new, the Christian community senses the profound and lasting bonds which join us to those generations who have gone before us, "marked with the sign of faith." Nevertheless, increasing numbers of people today, even within the Church, are bringing enormous pressure to bear on the Church to accept the homosexual condition as though it were not disordered and to condone homosexual activity. . . .

9. The movement within the Church, which takes the form of pressure groups of various names and sizes, attempts to give the impression that it represents all homosexual persons who are Catholics. As a matter of fact, its membership is by and large restricted to those who either ignore the teaching of the Church or seek somehow to undermine it. It brings together under the aegis of Catholicism homosexual persons who have no intention of abandoning their homosexual behavior. One tactic used is to protest that any and all criticism of or reservations about homosexual people, their activity and lifestyle, are simply diverse forms of unjust discrimination.

There is an effort in some countries to manipulate the Church by gaining the often well-intentioned support of her pastors with a view to changing civil statutes and laws. This is done in order to conform to these pressure groups' concept that homosexuality is at least a completely harmless, if not an entirely good, thing. Even when the practice of homosexuality may seriously threaten the lives and health of a large number of people, its advocates remain undeterred and refuse to consider the magnitude of the risks involved.

The Church can never be so callous. It is true that her clear position cannot be revised by pressure from civil legislation or the trend of the moment. But she is really concerned about the many who are not represented by the pro-homosexual movement and about those who may have been tempted to believe its deceitful propaganda. She is also aware that the view that homosexual activity is equivalent to, or as acceptable as, the sexual expression of conjugal love has a direct impact on society's understanding of the nature and rights of the family and puts them in jeopardy.

10. It is deplorable that homosexual persons have been and are the object of violent malice in speech or in action. Such treatment deserves condemnation from the Church's pastors wherever it occurs. It reveals a kind of disregard for others which endangers the most fundamental principles of a healthy society. The intrinsic dignity of each person must always be respected in word, in action, and in law. But the proper reaction to crimes committed against homosexual

persons should not be to claim that the homosexual condition is not disordered. . . .

It has been argued that the homosexual orientation in certain cases is not the result of deliberate choice; and so the homosexual person would then have no choice but to behave in a homosexual fashion. Lacking freedom, such a person, even if engaged in homosexual activity, would not be culpable. Here, the Churches wise moral tradition is necessary since it warns against generalizations in judging individual cases. In fact, circumstances may exist, or may have existed in the past, which would reduce or remove the culpability of the individual in a given instance; or other circumstances may increase it. What is at all costs to be avoided is the unfounded and demeaning assumption that the sexual behavior of homosexual persons is always and totally compulsive and therefore inculpable. What is essential is that the fundamental liberty which characterizes the human person and gives him his dignity be recognized as belonging to the homosexual person as well. As in every conversion from evil, the abandonment of homosexual activity will require a profound collaboration of the individual with God's liberating grace.

12. What, then, are homosexual persons to do who seek to follow the Lord? Fundamentally, they are called to enact the will of God in their life by joining whatever sufferings and difficulties they experience in virtue of their condition to the sacrifice of the Lord's Cross. That Cross, for the believer, is a fruitful sacrifice since from that death come life and redemption. While any call to carry the cross or to understand a Christian's suffering in this way will predictably be met with bitter ridicule by some, it should be remembered

that this is the way to eternal life for all who follow Christ. . . . Christians who are homosexual are called, as all of us are, to a chaste life. As they dedicate their lives to understanding the nature of God's personal call to them, they will be able to celebrate the Sacrament of Penance more faithfully and receive the Lord's grace so freely offered there in order to convert their lives more fully to his Way. . . .

15. We encourage the Bishops, then, to provide pastoral care in full accord with the teaching of the Church for homosexual persons of their dioceses. No authentic pastoral program will include organizations in which homosexual persons associate with each other without clearly stating that homosexual activity is immoral. . . . An authentic pastoral program will assist homosexual persons at all levels of the spiritual life. . . .

16. From this multi-faceted approach there are numerous advantages to be gained, not the least of which is the realization that a homosexual person, as every human being, deeply needs to be nourished at many different levels simultaneously.

The human person, made in the image and likeness of God, can hardly be adequately described by a reductionist reference to his or her sexual orientation. Everyone living on the face of the earth has personal problems and difficulties, but challenges to growth, strengths, talents and gifts as well. Today, the Church provides a badly needed context for the care of the human person when she refuses to consider the person as a "heterosexual" or a "homosexual" and insists that every person has a fundamental identity: the creature of God, and by grace, his child and heir to eternal life.

Some Ethical Issues Surrounding Genetic Engineering*

A group of Christian and other religious leaders held a conference in May 1995 in Washington, D.C., to discuss ethical issues surrounding current

progress in genetic engineering. More than 185 religious leaders, from eighty denominations and other religions as well, announced their opposition to the patenting of genetically engineered animals and human genes, cell lines, tissues, organs, and

---

* "Joint Appeal against Human and Animal Patenting"

embryos. Today a growing controversy surrounds the safety of genetically engineered foods.[45]

1.   The participants do not oppose the effort to use genetic engineering to create new drugs and cure diseases. They argue however, that the genetic blueprints of life are the province of God and cannot be owned as "patented inventions" by any human being or institution.

2.   The very idea that the genetic blueprints of all of life are human inventions simply because scientists discover them is like asserting that chlorine and the other chemical elements found in nature also should have been patentable by the scientists who first isolated their properties.

3.   By turning life into a patented invention, the government drains life of its intrinsic nature and sacred value. Inventions are merely instrumental and driven by the logic of engineering values —including efficiency, utility, profitability and quantifiability. There is no place in the world of machines for love, empathy, stewardship, reverence, and awe.

4.   By redefining God's Creations as "inventions," the government lays the legal and philosophical foundation for scientists and companies to assume the role of God. Inventions are made to be upgraded, streamlined and perfected— raising the prospect of potential abuse and misuse of human and animal genetic material.

---

[45] Press release, Conference on Genetic Patenting, May, 1995.

5.   The biotechnology companies protest that their only interest is to cure diseases, develop lifesaving drugs and create more efficient farm products, and that patents are needed to insure an adequate return on their research and development. What they don't mention is that much of the money that has gone into their research and development has come not from investors, but from American taxpayers in the form of government subsidies for the basic research. Now these same companies want to benefit a second time by being given an exclusive monopoly to commercially exploit genetically engineered animals and human genes and cells as patented inventions. Companies with patent monopolies will charge needy patients exorbitant fees for many life saving drugs.

6.   Some of the religious leaders attending the press conference pointed out that there are many successful products on the market today, including drugs, medical procedures and farm products which are not "protected" by patents. A patent is simply the guarantee of an exclusive government "monopoly" to an individual or company to market an "invention" for a given number of years without having to fear competition by other companies. While the biotechnology companies might consider it heresy, said one of the participants, the fact is that some things in life are more important than "monopolizing" profits. Life is more than a commodity. The blueprints of God's Creation should not be handed over to scientists and corporations just to insure greater profits.

RELATIONS

Orthodoxy and Roman Catholicism Move Closer*

Eastern Christendom has opened doors long shut (for nearly a thousand years) toward its Western counterpart. In 1979, Pope John Paul II journeyed

---

* Joint Statement of Pope John Paul II and Patriarch Demetrios I

to Constantinople to meet with Patriarch Demetrios I of the Greek Orthodox Church. One of their accomplishments was to remove the mutual anathemas from the eleventh century. As their "Joint Statement" indicates, both looked toward that day "when we will finally be able to concelebrate the

Divine Eucharist." However, no more significant progress toward the reuniting of East and West has been made since this statement, and lately some tensions have been reemerging.[46]

We, Pope John Paul II and Ecumenical Patriarch Demetrios I, thank God who has granted that we meet to celebrate together the feast of the apostle Andrew, the first called and the brother of the apostle Peter. "Praised be the God and Father of our Lord Jesus Christ, who has bestowed on us in Christ every spiritual blessing in the heavens" (Eph. 1:3).

It is in seeking the sole glory of God through the accomplishment of his will that we affirm anew our firm will to do all that is possible to hasten the day when full communion between the Catholic Church and the Orthodox Church will be reestablished and when we will finally be able to concelebrate the Divine Eucharist.

We are grateful to our predecessors, Pope Paul VI and Patriarch Athenagoras I, for all they have done to reconcile our churches and to make them progress in unity. The progress made in the preparatory stage permits us to announce that the theological dialogue is going to begin and to make public the list of members of the mixed

Orthodox-Catholic commission which will be entrusted with it.

This theological dialogue has as its goal not only to progress toward the reestablishment of full communion between the Orthodox and Catholic sister Churches, but further to contribute to the many dialogues which are going on in the Christian world in quest of its unity.

The dialogue of charity (cf. Jn. 13:34; Eph. 4:1–7), rooted in a complete fidelity to the one Lord Jesus Christ and to his church (cf. Jn. 17:21), has opened the way to a better understanding of mutual theological positions and, from there, to new approaches to theological work and to a new attitude toward the common past of our churches. This purification of the collective memory of our churches is an important fruit of the dialogue of charity and an indispensable condition of future progress. This dialogue of charity must continue and be intensified in the complex situation which we have inherited from the past and which constitutes the reality in which our effort must go on today.

We desire that progress in unity may open new possibilities for dialogue and collaboration with believers of other religions and with all men of good will, so that love and brotherhood may win over hatred and opposition between men. We hope thus to contribute to the coming of a true peace in the world. We implore this gift from him who was, who is and who is to come, our only Lord and our true peace.

---

[46] From *Greek Orthodox Theological Review* 25 (Summer, 1980): 129–30. Copyright © 1980 the Greek Orthodox Theological Review. Used by permission.

The Search for Unity among Diverse Orthodox Americans*

Like most other branches of Christianity in America, Eastern Orthodoxy has existed in the national/ethnic forms that immigrants brought to America: Russian, Greek, Ukrainian, Serbian, and others. In 1970, under the leadership of Metropolitan Ireney of the (Russian) Orthodox Church in America, the following statement was made in an effort to

overcome these divisions. The full realization of this unity, however, has proven elusive. Note how the language of Western ecumenism has reemerged in the Eastern churches.[47]

---

[47] From C. J. Terasu, *Orthodox America 1794–1976* (Syosset, NY: Orthodox Church in America, 1975), 277. Copyright © 1975 by the Orthodox Church in America. Used by permission.

---

* "Message to All Orthodox Christians in America"

In the Name of the Father and of the Son and of the Holy Spirit. Amen.

We the Bishops, clergy and laity of the Orthodox Church in America, united in Our Lord and Savior Jesus Christ at our All-American Church Council, address this message to all our brothers in the Orthodox Faith in America.

The grace and the mercy of God be with you. Time has come for us to fulfill Christ's prayer, "that all may be one . . . that the world may believe that Thou has sent me" (John 17:21). Our witness to the truth of our Orthodox Faith on this continent, where we Orthodox are a minority, lies in our perfect and total unity. How can the world accept and believe our claim to be the One, Holy, Catholic and Apostolic Church, of having kept in its fullness the Orthodox faith, if we ourselves are divided? We have the same Faith, the same Tradition, the same hope, the same mission. We should then constitute one Church, visibly, organically, fully. Such is the requirement of our Orthodox Faith and we know that always and everywhere the Orthodox Church has existed and exists as one Church. There can, therefore, be no excuse for our jurisdictional divisions, alienation from one another, and parochialism. The removal of such divisions and the organic unity of all Orthodox in America is the goal of our Church and we invite you to become a part of the unity. But we also know and fully acknowledge that we have come from different backgrounds and have been nourished by various traditions within the same and unique Orthodox Tradition. We firmly believe that this variety constitutes the richness of American Orthodoxy and that whatever is true, noble, inspiring and Christian in our various customs and practices ought to be fully preserved and, if possible, shared. Therefore, although we insist that the One Orthodox Church here must be the home of all, we equally stress that there must be no loss of our respective national and cultural heritages and certainly no domination of any group by any other but a full equality, total trust and truly Christian brotherhood. As we send you the peace and love of our First Council as the Orthodox Church in America, we assure you that we understand ourselves first and foremost as the servants of the full unity of the Church in the freedom, love and mutual respect of all churches and dioceses of our Orthodox Church in the World and in this blessed land of America.

Glory to our Lord Jesus Christ, with the Father and the Holy Spirit, unto ages of ages. Amen.

The Debate over Christianity and Religious Pluralism*

Both modernism and postmodernism have posed a critical question: In the light of so many religions, each claiming to be true, how can Christianity claim exclusive truth and finality? Put another way, Is Jesus the savior or just a savior? Christians have always lived in relation to people of different religions, but in recent times this question seems more pressing. In the first reading, John Hick, the foremost pluralist, argues that all religious faith is essentially the same and that Christianity must give up its claims to exclusive religious truth.[48] In the second reading, the leading Canadian Evangelical, Clark H. Pinnock, defends traditional notions of the uniqueness of Jesus against pluralist attack.[49]

[48] From John Hick, *God Has Many Names* (Philadelphia: Westminster, 1982) 48, 66–67, 74–75. Copyright © 1992 Westminster Press. Used by permission of Westminster/John Knox Press.

[49] Clark H. Pinnock, *A Wideness in God's Mercy* (Grand Rapids, MI: Zondervan, 1992), 64–69. Copyright © 1992 by Clark H. Pinnock. Used by permission of Zondervan Publishing House.

* John Hick, *God Has Many Names;* Clark H. Pinnock, *A Wideness in God's Mercy*

Why should religious faith take a number of such different forms? Because, I would suggest, religious faith is not an isolated aspect of our lives but is closely bound up with human culture and human history, which are in turn bound up with basic geographical, climatic, and economic circumstances. Now one could, as I mentioned earlier, conclud[e] that the belief in God is entirely a human projection, guided by cultural influences. But the alternative interpretation is that there is some genuine awareness of the divine, but that the concrete form which it takes is provided by cultural factors. On this view these different human awareness of the Eternal One represent different culturally conditioned perceptions of the same infinite divine reality. . . .

In the light of the phenomenological similarity of worship in these different traditions we have to ask whether people in church, synagogue, mosque, gurdwara,[50] and temple are worshiping different Gods or are worshiping the same God? Are Adonai and God, Allah and Ekoamkar, Rama and Krishna different gods, or are these different names for the same ultimate Being? There would seem to be three possibilities. One is that there exist, ontologically, many gods. But this conflicts with the belief concerning each that he is the creator source of the world. A second possibility is that one faith-community, let us say our own, worships God while the others vainly worship images which exist only in their imaginations. But even within Christianity itself, is there not a variety of overlapping mental images of God—for example, as stern judge and predestinating power, and as gracious and loving heavenly Father—so that different Christian groups, and even different Christian individuals, are worshiping the divine Being through their different images of him? And do not the glimpses which I have just offered of worship within the various religious traditions suggest that our Christian images overlap with many non-Christian images of God? If so, a third possibility must seem the most probable, namely, that there is but one

God, who is maker and lord of all; that in his infinite fullness and richness of being he exceeds all our human attempts to grasp him in thought; and that the devout in the various great religions are in fact worshiping that one God, but through different, overlapping concepts or mental icons of him. . . .

But let me now turn to the effects which a pluralist view of religion has upon one's understanding of and relationship to one's own tradition. However imperfectly (and in fact very imperfectly) this is reflected in my own life, I feel irrevocably challenged and claimed by the impact of the life and teaching of Jesus; and to be thus decisively influenced by him is, I suppose, the basic definition of a Christian. How then is my Christian faith changed by acceptance of the salvific character of the other world religions?

The older theological tradition of Christianity does not readily permit religious pluralism. For at its center is the conviction that Jesus of Nazareth was God—the second Person of a divine Trinity living a human life. It follows from this that Christianity, and Christianity alone, was founded by God in person on the only occasion on which he has ever become incarnate in this world, so that Christianity has a unique status as the way of salvation provided and appointed by God himself. If this claim is to have real substance and effect, it follows that the salvation thus made possible within Christianity cannot also be possible outside it. This conclusion was drawn with impeccable logic in the Roman dogma *Extra ecclesiam nulla salus* (Outside the church, no salvation), with its nineteenth-century Protestant missionary equivalent (Outside Christianity, no salvation). But in the light of our accumulated knowledge of the other great world faiths this conclusion has become unacceptable to all except a minority of dogmatic diehards. For it conflicts with our concept of God, which we have received from Jesus, as the loving heavenly Father of all mankind; could such a Being have restricted the possibility of salvation to those who happen to have been born in certain countries in certain periods of history?

---

[50]*gurdwara:* Sikh house of worship.

But perhaps salvation is not the issue. Perhaps salvation is taking place, not only within Christianity but also outside it, while the unique Christian gospel is that God became man in Jesus to make this possible. The doctrine of atonement thus becomes central. This suggestion appeals to some as a means of acknowledging God's saving work throughout mankind while retaining the dogma of the unique centrality of Christ as the only savior of the world. But in doing so it sacrifices the substance of the older position. For the nerve of the old dogma was the imperative which it generated to convert all people to faith in Jesus as their lord and savior: "No one comes to the Father, but by me" and "There is salvation in no one else, for there is no other name under heaven given among men by which we must be saved." That nerve is cut when we acknowledge the other great world religions as also areas of divine salvation. The other kind of attempt to have it both ways, exemplified by Karl Rahner's picture of devout persons of other faiths as "anonymous Christians,"[51] is too manifestly an ad hoc contrivance to satisfy many. For it is as easy, and as arbitrary, to label devout Christians as anonymous Muslims, or anonymous Hindus, as to label devout Hindus or Muslims as anonymous Christians.

Because such responses are inadequate, it seems to me necessary to look again at the traditional interpretation of Jesus as God incarnate. Such a reconsideration is in any case required today by the realization that the historical Jesus almost certainly did not in fact teach that he was in any sense God; and also by the fact that Christian thought has not yet, despite centuries of learned attempts, been able to give any intelligible content to the idea that a finite human being, genuinely a part of our human race, was also the infinite, eternal, omnipotent, omniscient creator of everything other than himself. The proper conclusion to draw, as it seems to me, is that the idea of divine incarnation is a metaphorical (or, in technical theological language, a mythological) idea. When a truth or a value is lived out in a human life, it is a natural metaphor to speak of its being incarnated in that life. Jesus lived in full openness to God, responsive to the divine will, transparent to the divine purpose, so that he lived out the divine agape[52] within human history. This was not a matter of his being of the same substance as God the Father, or of his having two complete natures, one human and the other divine. Agape is incarnated in human life whenever someone acts in selfless love; and this occurred in the life of Jesus to a startling and epoch-making degree. Whether he incarnated self-giving love more than anyone else who has ever lived, we cannot know. But we do know that his actual historical influence has been unique in its extent. . . .

When we see the incarnation as a mythological idea applied to Jesus to express the experienced fact that he is our sufficient, effective, and saving point of contact with God, we no longer have to draw the negative conclusion that he is man's one and only effective point of contact with God. We can revere Christ as the one through whom we have found salvation, without having to deny other points of reported saving contact between God and man. We can commend the way of Christian faith without having to discommend other ways of faith. We can say that there is salvation in Christ without having to say that there is no salvation other than in Christ.

[Pinnock, *A Wideness in God's Mercy*] Theological pluralists have a problem with Christology. Were Jesus to be decisive for all nations, that would be unconducive to dialogue and cooperation among the religions. Therefore, ways must be found to reinterpret historical data so as to eliminate finality claims from Christology. They must be diminished so they do not constitute a

---

[51] *Karl Rahner's . . . anonymous Christians:* The twentieth-century Roman Catholic theologian argued that those who are basically life compatible with Christianity can be considered Christians.

[52] *agape* (ah-GAH-pay): love.

barrier to interreligious peace. . . . [Pluralists] need a way for Jesus to be unique for his followers, but not necessarily for others. . . . Pluralists think that belief in the finality of Jesus Christ stands in the way of our appreciating other religions and getting along smoothly with them.

A radical approach to the problem of high Christology in the New Testament is adopted by John Hick. First, he outright denies any uniqueness claims on the part of Jesus. . . . Second . . . he transposes all the uniqueness claims made on behalf of Jesus by the New Testament witness onto the level of noncognitive love language. Third, he attempts to locate the Christology of the Incarnation in a hypothetical context of the development of traditions. Fourth, he adds that there are various insuperable logical problems with belief in Incarnation. This supplies a philosophical backup objection should all else fail.

Unfortunately, none of his points sticks firmly. First, one cannot deny Jesus' claim to uniqueness on the basis of critical exegesis. While granting his point about Jesus not making explicit

claims to Incarnation, the implicit claims Jesus does make solidly ground the more-developed views of his person after the Resurrection. . . . Second, transposing claims for Jesus' uniqueness made by the biblical witnesses onto the level of noncognitive love language is an unacceptable put-down of their sincerely held beliefs. . . . Third, there is Christological development in early doctrine, and the Incarnation is noticeable in that development. But the Christology being developed there is already very high, with the event of Jesus' Resurrection, and constitutes an unpacking of what is implicit from the beginning. . . . Fourth, as to whether belief in the Incarnation is rational or not, two things can be said. First, the problem of finality is much larger than belief in the Incarnation. In many other ways the biblical witnesses lift up Jesus as Lord of the universe. Second, not everyone is as impressed as Hick by the logical problems of believing in the Incarnation. A large number of thoughtful Christians find the belief coherent, even true and magnificent.

Martyrdom in Guatemala*

The end of the twentieth century witnessed an increase in persecution of Christians in the developing world. From the 1970s through most of the 1990s, Guatemala was wracked by a brutal war waged by its military government against its own people, especially Mayan Indians. In 1998, a report was released that documented firsthand the sufferings of the people. Two days later, Bishop Juan Gerardi, coordinator of the Human Rights Office that issued the report, was murdered by unknown assailants. Here are a few excerpts from the section of the report on violence against Christian believers.[53]

---

* Human Rights Office of the Archdiocese of Guatemala, *Guatemala: Never Again!*
[53] From REMHI: Recovery of Historical Memory Project, *Guatemala: Never Again!* (New York: Orbis, 1999), 48–49. Used by permission.

We had to leave behind the ancestors and the dead. They separated us from sacred sites and, also, you couldn't practice anymore, you couldn't be religious. There was military control; we had to ask permission to go out to work. (1981)

They sent a letter to the house saying that we shouldn't go to the chapel anymore, that we shouldn't pray. I didn't stop praying; what I did was pray at home, with my father, every Saturday and Sunday, because we could no longer go to the chapel. (1982)

The patrollers and the army arrived at Chisis village, in the Cotzal municipality. They entered each house and took the men from their homes. . . . They rounded up a total of about one hundred people. They took some of them into the church, already beaten up. And then they set the house of God on fire, with all the people inside. (1980)

The town was abandoned in 1982, and so the church property was deserted. When we returned on August 15, 1982, I realized that the army was using the temple [church] as a barracks. Inside there were three rows of beds for all the troops, and they also had a huge pile of fertilizer that the captain told me was from the El Aguacate farm.

A Dissent on Contemporary Ecumenism*

Not all the voices of the last hundred years have approved of the ecumenical movement. However, voices of opposition rarely come today from within the mainline Protestant traditions. Here Randall Balmer, an Episcopal layperson and a leading historian of American religion, presents a strong dissent.[54]

Last week's vote by the Evangelical Lutheran Church in America to move toward closer cooperation with the Episcopalians represents another unfortunate step down the blind alley of ecumenism. If these denominations hoped that such actions can stanch the hemorrhaging of their members, I can't imagine a less productive strategy.

The ecumenical movement—the impulse to unite all followers of Christ—takes its cue from Jesus' wish, recorded in John 17, that his followers "may all be one." Not long after the Reformation led to the splintering of Christianity into countless denominations, ecumenical sentiment began asserting itself in earnest.

The drive toward Christian unity, especially among Protestants, intensified during the cold war. American Protestants, who in the 1950's considered themselves the guardians of middle-class respectability, wanted to adopt a more corporate management style, to avoid a duplication of efforts and to present a united front against the perils of Communism. (My wife, for example, was told as a child that she must attend church to help keep the Soviets at bay.)

The ecumenical movement led to the formation of the National Council of Churches in 1950 and to the construction of the Interchurch Center in Manhattan, a place where different denominations could house their offices next to one another. The idea was to promote understanding and cooperation among believers who shared basic Protestant beliefs, even though they differed in particular doctrines.

Aside from the suspect theology underpinning the movement—I believe that Jesus was pointing toward unity in some future age, not in the present world—ecumenism has been a largely unmitigated failure. Yes, it has taught us the importance of mutual respect and communication across religious traditions, but it has also led to a diminution of theological distinctiveness.

Mainline Protestant denominations in America have suffered appallingly from a lack of definition, doctrinal or otherwise. It's no longer easy to distinguish readily between, say, a Presbyterian and a Congregationalist, or a Methodist and a Lutheran.

To a degree, ecumenism has collapsed beneath the weight of its own pretensions. Turning from the fight against Communism, ecumenism preached cooperation, even with political radicals. It aspired to unite all Protestants, but in so doing it ratcheted its doctrines down to the lowest common denominators of agreement: peace, justice and inclusiveness. These are noble principles, but they are unlikely to inspire popular allegiance. History demonstrates, moreover, that the most durable religions in America have been exclusive, not inclusive, with very carefully delimited theological distinctions.

The effect of ecumenism on mainline denominations has been devastating. According to every

---

* Randall Balmer, "United We Fall"

[54] From *The New York Times,* 28 August 1999. Copyright © 1999 by The New York Times Company. Reprinted by permission.

empirical index—attendance, membership, giving—mainline Protestants have declined since the mid-1960s, while more conservative, evangelical groups have grown. Evangelicals, by contrast, are theologically well defined, often to a fault. You may not like their doctrines, but they have little trouble articulating what they believe and what distinguishes them from other groups.

Although denominational leaders resolutely deny any connection between ecumenism and decline, many Americans have opted for the clarion call of evangelicalism and other clearly defined groups rather than the uncertain sounds emanating from mainline Protestantism. Tragically, in an increasingly pluralistic society, mainline Protestants are the only religious group lacking a voice. Mainline Protestants have exchanged their theological and historical heritage for a mess of pottage, an ideology so calculated not to give offense that its very blandness is offensive.

These Protestants—Lutherans, Presbyterians, Episcopalians, Congregationalists, Methodists—must regain the courage of their convictions. Their salvation lies in a recovery of their own traditions rather than in the chimera of unity.

Lutheran-Catholic Agreement on Justification*

In 1999 the Roman Catholic Church and the Lutheran World Federation, which represents most Lutherans, reached a historic agreement on the doctrine of justification by faith alone. This doctrine has been the main theological division between Protestants and Catholics since the Reformation, and the new agreement on it has given rise to the hope of further ecumenical progress.[55]

Opposing interpretations and applications of the biblical message of justification were in the sixteenth century a principal cause of the division of the Western church and led as well to doctrinal condemnations. A common understanding of justification is therefore fundamental and indispensable to overcoming that division. By appropriating insights of recent biblical studies and drawing on modern investigations of the history of theology and dogma, the post-Vatican II ecumenical dialogue has led to a notable convergence concerning justification, with the result that this Joint Declaration is able to formulate a consensus on basic truths concerning the doctrine of justification. In light of this consensus, the corresponding doctrinal condemnations of the sixteenth century do not apply to today's partner.

The Lutheran churches and the Roman Catholic Church have together listened to the good news proclaimed in Holy Scripture. This common listening, together with the theological conversations of recent years, has led to a shared understanding of justification. This encompasses a consensus in the basic truths; the differing explications in particular statements are compatible with it.

In faith we together hold the conviction that justification is the work of the triune God. The Father sent his Son into the world to save sinners. The foundation and presupposition of justification is the incarnation, death, and resurrection of Christ. Justification thus means that Christ himself is our righteousness, in which we share through the Holy Spirit in accord with the will of the Father. Together we confess: By grace alone, in faith in Christ's saving work and not because of any merit on our part, we are accepted by God and receive the Holy Spirit, who renews our hearts while equipping and calling us to good works.

All people are called by God to salvation in Christ. Through Christ alone are we justified,

---

* The Vatican and the Lutheran World Federation, "Joint Declaration on Justification"

[55] From the *1997 Pre-Assembly Report to Congregations* of the Evangelical Lutheran Church in America, Section 1, pp. 67–69. Used by permission.

when we receive this salvation in faith. Faith is itself God's gift through the Holy Spirit who works through Word and Sacrament in the community of believers and who, at the same time, leads believers into that renewal of life which God will bring to completion in eternal life. We also share the conviction that the message of justification directs us in a special way towards the heart of the New Testament witness to God's saving action in Christ: it tells us that as sinners our new life is solely due to the forgiving and renewing mercy that God imparts as a gift and we receive in faith, and never can merit in any way.

The doctrine of justification, which takes up this message and explicates it, is more than just one part of Christian doctrine. It stands in an essential relation to all truths of faith, which are to be seen as internally related to each other. It is an indispensable criterion, which constantly serves to orient all the teaching and practice of our churches to Christ. When Lutherans emphasize the unique significance of this criterion, they do not deny the interrelation and significance of all truths of faith. When Catholics see themselves as bound by several criteria, they do not deny the special function of the message of justification. Lutherans and Catholics share the goal of confessing Christ, who is to be trusted above all things as the one Mediator (1 Timothy 2:5–6) through whom God in the Holy Spirit gives himself and pours out his renewing gifts.

[The Good Works of the Justified] We confess together that good works—a Christian life lived in faith, hope, and love—follow justification and are its fruits. When the justified live in Christ and act in the grace they receive, they bring forth, in biblical terms, good fruit. Since Christians struggle against sin their entire lives, this consequence of justification is also for them an obligation they must fulfill. Thus both Jesus and the apostolic Scriptures admonish Christians to bring forth the works of love.

According to Catholic understanding, good works, made possible by grace and the working of the Holy Spirit, contribute to growth in grace, so that the righteousness that comes from God is preserved and communion with Christ is deepened. When Catholics affirm the "meritorious" character of good works, they wish to say that, according to the biblical witness, a reward in heaven is promised to these works. Their intention is to emphasize the responsibility of persons for their actions, not to contest the character of those works as gifts, or far less to deny that justification always remains the unmerited gift of grace.

The concept of a preservation of grace and a growth in grace and faith is also held by Lutherans. They do emphasize that righteousness as acceptance by God and sharing in the righteousness of Christ is always complete. At the same time, they state that there can be growth in its effects in Christian living. When they view the good works of Christians as the fruits and signs of justification and not as one's own "merits," they nevertheless also understand eternal life in accord with the New Testament as unmerited "reward" in the sense of the fulfillment of God's promise to the believer.

[The Significance and Scope of the Consensus Reached] The understanding of the doctrine of justification set forth in this Declaration shows that a consensus in basic truths of the doctrine of justification exists between Lutherans and Catholics. In light of this consensus the remaining differences of language, theological elaboration, and emphasis in the understanding of justification described [earlier] are acceptable. Therefore the Lutheran and the Catholic explications of justification are in their difference open to one another and do not destroy the consensus regarding basic truths.

Thus the doctrinal condemnations of the sixteenth century, in so far as they relate to the doctrine of justification, appear in a new light: The teaching of the Lutheran churches presented in this Declaration does not fall under the condemnations from the Council of Trent. The condemnations in the Lutheran Confessions do not apply to the teaching of the Roman Catholic

Church presented in this Declaration. Nothing is thereby taken away from the seriousness of the condemnations related to the doctrine of justification. Some were not simply pointless. They remain for us "salutary warnings" to which we must attend in our teaching and practice.

Our consensus in basic truths of the doctrine of justification must come to influence the life and teachings of our churches. Here it must prove itself. In this respect, there are still questions of varying importance which need further clarification. These include, among other topics,

the relationship between the Word of God and church doctrine, as well as ecclesiology, authority in the church, ministry, the sacraments, and the relation between justification and social ethics. We are convinced that the consensus we have reached offers a solid basis for this clarification. The Lutheran churches and the Roman Catholic Church will continue to strive together to deepen this common understanding of justification and to make it bear fruit in the life and teaching of the churches.

APPENDIX: A LOOK INTO CHRISTIANITY'S POSSIBLE FUTURE*

The end of the twentieth century has seen a good deal of analysis of the Christian past and speculation about its future. Here is a thoughtful analysis of the possible future of world Christianity based on the direction of recent trends.[56]

Looking backward is my usual business as a historian. . . . My characteristic gaze is in the rearview mirror, not up the road. Still, the recent past gives some clues for what lies ahead, even though no one can say with any precision what is up there.

1. THE END OF CHRISTENDOM

For years social scientists have viewed the United States as an anomaly because it is a highly modernized society with a secular civic polity that is still very religious. Religious adherence and practice—still overwhelmingly Christian—are much more prevalent here than in Europe, Canada, and the British Isles. Yet the popular culture of the United States . . . is becoming more crude and

vulgar, more openly pagan, and more tolerant of anti-Christian expression. The United States is still a long way from the advanced state of post-Christian secularity and neo-paganism that now prevails in Western Europe, but the trend is in a similar direction.

The sector of North American Christianity that shows this decline most dramatically is the cluster of older denominations known as mainline Protestantism. These churches were for nearly two centuries the chaplains to the nation's civic soul and the dominant cultural expressions of faith. Over the past century, however, their cultural hegemony has been challenged repeatedly, first by the Roman Catholics, then by American Jewry, then by upstart Protestant evangelical movements, and most recently by the combination of an even greater religious pluralism and public secularity. The mainline denominations have suffered a continuing decline of members as well as diminished influence. Membership in the Presbyterian Church (U.S.A.), for example, has over the past three decades declined by a third. For many years, the more conservative, evangelical Protestant churches boasted that they were growing rapidly, picking up the slack in Protestant adherence. Today their growth rates too are

* Joel Carpenter, "Christianity in the New Millenium"
[56] From *Perspectives: A Journal of Reformed Thought*, December 1999. Reprinted by permission.

slackening, and some of them have experienced a numerical decline.

Those Protestant evangelical churches that are still vigorously growing, and the mainline denominations that have staved off decline, benefit from increasing numbers of people of color in their ranks: African-Americans, U.S. Hispanics, and large cohorts of recent immigrants from Latin America, Asia, and Africa. Whole new denominations are springing up from these sources as well. Latino evangelicos in particular are experiencing explosive growth; now fully a quarter of their population in the United States is evangelical/pentecostal.

The Roman Catholic Church continues to grow numerically and to gain influence in American life. Catholics have done a better job of enlisting their offspring than have the mainline Protestants, and Catholicism has been a haven for millions of traditionally Catholic new immigrants, especially from Southeast Asia and Latin America. The American Catholic Church has some serious problems to address, most notably a crisis of vocations to replenish the rapidly thinning ranks of priests and sisters. A full solution is not yet in sight, but the church is at present making do with more lay ministry and with imported priests and sisters. An outspoken, evangelistic, and activist pope has increased the Roman church's salience in the United States, as have a series of carefully wrought pastoral letters by the American bishops on matters of public concern, such as war and peace and the economy. . . . Around the world the Roman communion has become an outspoken champion of democracy, human rights, and economic justice. . . . The overall direction and reputation of the Church in public affairs has shifted dramatically in a pro-democratic direction. . . .

Still, if there is perhaps as much grassroots religious vitality in some sectors as there is decline in others, how can one say that the United States is becoming more secular and even pagan? What has changed most dramatically is not the level of religiosity so much as the implicit social contract concerning religion's public role and its power to shape public morality. Forty-five years ago, grand national religious institutions such as the National Council of Churches and the National Catholic Welfare Conference spoke with collective authority to other grand national institutions, such as the "big three" broadcasting networks. Today, both religion and communications are much more segmented, and the main driver on both fronts, it seems, is whether one can find a particular niche in the market. Christianity and other religions increasingly occupy lifestyle niches, and they have decreasing opportunities to stake out a larger presence in public arenas. That is the current trend, and in the new century it will continue. . . .

In the United States, consumerist capitalism and the Internet-and-cable TV-driven culture of illusion and amusement will continue to vitiate Christianity. Virtual reality will continue to compete with face-to-face community, sound bites will chase away real dialogue, opinion polling will erode deliberative decision-making, and interest-driven politics will militate against legislators acting on behalf of some notion of the common good. One of our age's cultural critics and prophets, Neil Postman, sees popular Christianity in America emulating this culture more than challenging it. Instead of offering people a counter-cultural alternative to these patterns, Christian ministries follow them, making it possible for people to feel good at a seeker service or a stadium event without joining a real community of faith in worship and godly work.

Questions of public morality and justice in this emerging culture will continue to dissolve into questions of feasibility and marketability. Geneticists map pieces of the human genetic code and copyright their findings as commercial patents. Human cloning soon will become a reality, and people of faith will face the challenge of defining what constitutes humanity and basic human rights. The market will not make such distinctions. Neither will it help with the environmental questions that will not go away, regardless of how much we ignore them: questions of energy consumption, waste, pollution, and depletion of resources. Will the churches of the West have the spiritual and moral resolve to address these problems and stand against these threatening trends? Most American believers remain blissfully ignorant of such matters, and leaders in these communions face a massive task of moral and ethical education. When what we need is a more critical spiritual and intellectual edge, "feel-good Christianity" persists as the dominant trend in consumerist America.

Looking only at ourselves in the North Atlantic world, it is easy to slip into an elegiac, even apocalyptic mood concerning the role of Christianity in the coming century. . . . When we look elsewhere, however, the picture changes considerably. If anything, the material conditions and future prospects for them look even more daunting. The spiritual and religious prospect, however, is deeply hopeful.

2. LATIN AMERICAN REVIVALS

In Latin America, where for centuries the Roman Catholic faith has been dominant, evangelical Protestantism has been growing rapidly for thirty years. In Brazil, where nearly 90 percent of the nation is Catholic but less than 10 percent of Catholics regularly attend church, the Protestant minority, with very strong patterns of religious commitment, probably is the majority in church on Sunday morning. In Guatemala, fully a third of the nation is now Protestant. One should use "Protestant" advisedly, because the vast majority of the emerging non-Catholic Christians are in the Pentecostal Movement, not the older Protestant traditions.

What will become of Latin American society and culture as a result of this momentous religious change? We can only speculate, of course, but what one sees in many places where Protestantism grows is social fragmentation and civil strife. Traditional leaders resent the rift in community solidarity when evangelicals do not participate in the revelry of religious festivals or enter the emerging business class. Violence breaks out, evangelical churches are burned, and people

get hurt. As the Protestant movement gains some social footing, however, we might expect to see challenges to the age-old patterns of class, property ownership, and politics in Latin America, especially as the middle class grows and gains more power. Great Britain and the United States provide historical precedents for this pattern, but it is not certain that the Latin American evangelicos will develop the drive for democracy and social reform that transformed British and American society and politics 150 years ago.

3. AFRICA: THE NEXT CHRISTIAN HEARTLAND?

At the beginning of the twentieth century, there were fewer than nine million Christians in all of Africa. At the beginning of the twenty-first century, there are a third of a billion. Over the next quarter-century, that number may well double. The African continent, especially its regions south of the Sahara, is now home to the world's fastest-growing concentration of Christian movements and traditions, Orthodox, Catholic, Protestant, and other varieties as well, both mission-founded and African-instituted. Waves of disease, violence, and famine make the African scene resemble crisis-laden late medieval Europe, or perhaps the Book of Revelation. These tragedies will continue in the years to come, and among the professional Africa watchers, opinion is deeply divided as to whether the continent will ever climb out of the crisis mode and find its own way forward.

There is a source of hope for Africa, however, that even the most sanguine secular pundits often ignore: a rising generation of post-colonial Christian leaders in the church itself but also in government and civil society. In some African countries that have found their way back from the abyss, Uganda being a notable example, this new generation of Christian leadership is forming the backbone for civic peace, economic growth, and democratic polity. One of the most strategic works for the international Christian mission today is the development of African

Christian leaders. Some of the most strategic agencies for these nations' future, it then follows, are the student Christian movements that presently nurture those potential leaders. Likewise, a growing number of Christian groups in Africa are developing their own faith-centered colleges and universities. These incubators of devoted and visionary leaders are critical to the continent's future.

In the coming century, while the cycles of poverty, disease, civic meltdown, and civil war will continue in parts of Africa, might it be possible that one by one, new and more stable nations will rise from the ashes? We have seen this positive trend happen in several places recently, like Uganda and Mozambique, and in its peaceful transition to democracy, South Africa avoided a great tragedy and gave fresh hope to other African democrats. Given the restoration of elected government in Nigeria, might we have hope for that great nation too?

4. CHRISTIANITY IN ASIA: THE GREAT CHALLENGE

Christianity was born in Western Asia and has been present in points further east since ancient times. The modern missions movement, signified by William Carey's mission to India in 1792, looked first and most intently toward the East. Asia's advanced civilizations and ancient traditions of theological, philosophical, and ethical thought, Western missionary theorists assumed, would make that continent the most congenial receiver of the Christian message. Christianity has grown in Asia, nearly fifteen-fold over the past century, from 20 million adherents in 1900 to some 300 million today. In this, the most populous region of the world, however, Christians remain a tiny minority, both in Asia's largest nations and its smallest. . . .

The vast stretches of Western Asia, from India to the Mediterranean and Red Seas, where once Christian churches had extensive influence, are now the heartlands of Islam. Christian communities exist in nearly all of these countries; some are the protectors of ancient tradition, and some are the result of missionary efforts over the past 150 years. The rise of militant Islamic traditionalist movements over the past twenty-five years has in many places coincided with a quickening of Christian evangelistic effort. The result has been persecution, especially in places that have reinstated Islamic law or have strong movements for its institution, such as Iran and Pakistan. Christians across the region, from Egypt to Pakistan, are emigrating to the West in large numbers, and in some places the long-term viability of the churches is in jeopardy.

In both India and China, however, Christianity continues to grow. As it does, it challenges the cultural and political powers. Indian nationalism is resurgent just now, and Hindu nationalist organizations have been emboldened in their denunciations of Christian evangelism and philanthropy. In this permissive climate, nationalist agitators have incited riots against churches. Last year, Indian nuns were beaten and raped, and an Australian missionary and his sons were trapped in their car and burned. Indian Christians seem bolder these days in reaching beyond their traditional strongholds, but as they enter areas of Hindu strength, they experience increased resentment and persecution.

Christianity in China challenges the powers as well. Catholicism in particular is viewed as a threat to the state's authority. The current Polish pope instigated the fall of Communism in Eastern Europe, Chinese rulers believe, and they are determined not to let this foreign-led religion have its way in their land. The Catholic Church in China is split between those congregants who have accepted state-appointed bishops and those unauthorized Catholics who look to Rome. In like fashion the Protestant wing of the faith is divided into registered and unregistered religious bodies. Leaders of unauthorized Christian groups, Catholic and Protestant, are regularly harassed and jailed, and their congregations closed. Nevertheless, Christianity remains strong and vibrant in China; having multiplied in number at least twenty-fold since the missionaries were expelled a half-century ago. The Chinese government is allowing increasing privileges for registered groups, including theological seminaries and publishing services. Foreign Christians who bring valued skills in languages and business, or who can stimulate university intellectual life, are welcome in China so long as they do not proselytize. For the past decade since the Tienanmen Square debacle, intellectuals' interest in Christianity has been growing, but it is not yet apparent how many intellectuals will convert their interest in Christianity into institutional commitments.

Such a quick and very broad-brushed tour of global Christianity hardly suffices to explain the faith's dynamism and the challenges it encounters in diverse settings, but it does give some concreteness to one of the most stunning trends of the twentieth century. Christianity has experienced a major shift in its demographic base. Whereas in 1900 only 18 percent of the world's church members lived outside of Europe and Northern America, now 60 percent of all Christians live outside of the North Atlantic quadrant. Christianity is truly a global religion, predominantly non-Western, and its patterns of thought, worship and witness, even in the West, are bound to reflect this new reality in the coming century.

GLOSSARY

charismatic movement in modern times, a type of worship and church life that emphasizes the immediate presence and power of the Holy Spirit, especially in speaking in tongues.

ecumenism the movement to heal the historic divisions between the various Christian churches.

feminism the movement in society, the church, and religious studies to bring about the equality of women and men.

historical Jesus a term used in early modern and modern times to refer to the "real" Jesus of history as he actually lived, taught, and died, especially as opposed to the interpretation of Jesus in the later church.

Liberation theology a theological and practical movement emphasizing the deliverance in the present of the oppressed from their sinful oppressors; it began with liberation theology of the poor in Latin America, but now refers to liberation of other groups as well.

neo-Orthodoxy a movement begun by Karl Barth and others marking a return to a more conservative, Reformational Protestant theology.

pluralism the affirmation of the distinct values of different groups within a nation or culture; also, the notion that truth itself is diverse.

postmodernism an intellectual movement, gradually establishing itself now in the academy and "trickling down" into other aspects of culture, that celebrates pluralism, diversity, and particular truths, as opposed to the broad rational, universal truths of early modern and modern times.

Second Vatican Council the 1960s Roman Catholic council that introduced several major reforms into the practice of the church.

QUESTIONS FOR STUDY AND DISCUSSION

1. In what ways are the twentieth-century and the nineteenth-century movements in Christianity for the liberation of women similar and dissimilar?

2.   Explain how Nelson and Ratzinger both use scripture, reason, and tradition but reach such different results.

3.   In what direction will Sallie McFague take the three metaphors (God as mother, lover, and friend) with which the selection from her *Body Theology* closes?

4.   Explain the tensions in the Roman Catholic church over movement for reform (e.g., Vatican II) with restatement of tradition (e.g., on women as priests). How would a Catholic traditionalist explain this? a Catholic liberal?

5.   Critique this statement by Herbert J. Muller: "Christianity does not constitute our best hope, at least for our earthly future. An established religion remains by nature a deeply conservative force, not a creative one. The churches have long brought up the intellectual rear of our civilization, and despite their social conscience their claims to spiritual leadership are still weakened by their engrained tendency to resist new knowledge and aspiration."

6.   What, in your opinion, are the most important issues facing Christianity in the near future?

SUGGESTIONS FOR FURTHER READING

C. E. Braaten and R. W. Jenson, *A Map of Twentieth-Century Theology.* Philadelphia: Fortress, 1995. Thirty-seven readings from key theologians in the twentieth century, but with no treatment of liberation theologies.

D. B. Clendenin, *Eastern Orthodox Theology: A Contemporary Reader.* Grand Rapids: Baker, 1995. An anthology of contemporary Orthodox analysis of its traditions.

E. Gaustad, *A Documentary History of Religion in America Since 1865,* 2d ed. Grand Rapids, Mich.: Eerdmans, 1993. A rich source of primary readings for this period.

M. Kinnamon and B. Cope, *The Ecumenical Movement: An Anthology of Key Texts and Voices.* Grand Rapids: Eerdmans, 1996. An excellent anthology of the primary documents of ecumenism.

A. P. Flannery, *Documents of Vatican II.* Grand Rapids, MI: Eerdmans, 1975. A new, fluent translation of all the documents of Vatican II.

U. King, *Feminist Theology from the Third World: A Reader.* London: S.P.C.K., 1994. 38 key texts representing the voices of Asian, African and Latin American women, and those working among minorities in the developed world.

Index

(Note: Boldface entries indicate glossary pages where items are defined.)